# Gower Handbook
# of Project
# Management

# GOWER HANDBOOK OF PROJECT MANAGEMENT

Edited by
J. Rodney Turner
and
Stephen J. Simister

Previous editions edited by Dennis Lock

Gower

First edition published 1987
Second edition published 1994

This edition published by
Gower Publishing Limited
Gower House
Croft Road
Aldershot
Hampshire GU11 3HR
England

Gower
131 Main Street
Burlington
Vermont 05401
USA


British Library Cataloguing in Publication Data
Gower handbook of project management. – 3rd ed.
  1. Industrial project management
  I. Turner, J. Rodney II. Simister, Stephen J. III. Handbook of
project management
  658.4'04


ISBN 0 566 08138 5


Library of Congress Cataloging-in-Publication Data
Gower handbook of project management / edited by J. Rodney Turner, Stephen J. Simister.—3rd ed.
    p. cm.
  "Previous editions edited by Dennis Lock."
  Includes index.
  ISBN 0-566-08138-5
  1. Industrial project management—Handbooks, manuals, etc. I. Turner, J. Rodney
(John Rodney), 1953– II. Simister, Stephen J.

  T56.8 G69 2000
  658.4'04—dc21
                                         99-057562


Typeset in Century Old Style by Bournemouth Colour Press, Parkstone and printed in Great Britain by MPG Books Ltd, Bodmin.

# Contents

**Part II    Context**

# List of figures

# Notes on contributors

## THE EDITORS

**Rodney Turner** is Professor of Project Management in the Department of Business and Organization of the Faculty of Economic Sciences, Erasmus University, Rotterdam, and a founding director of EuroProjex, the European Centre for Project Excellence. He is also a member of the associate faculty at Henley Management College.

After leaving Oxford University, where he undertook work leading to a doctorate and was a post-doctoral research fellow at Brasenose College, he spent several years with ICI working on engineering design, construction and maintenance projects in the petrochemical industry. He also worked as a consultant in project management with Coopers and Lybrand before joining Henley Management College. He has been with Erasmus University since 1997.

Professor Turner works as a project management consultant, lectures worldwide and has published several books and papers on project management, including the best-selling *Handbook of Project-based Management*. He edits the *International Journal of Project Management*, is Vice-President and immediate past Chairman of the Association for Project Management and President of the International Project Management Association.
rodneyturner@europrojex.com

**Stephen Simister** is a director of EuroProjex, the European Centre for Project Excellence. He is a consultant and lecturer in project management, specializing in assisting clients to scope and define project requirements to meet their business needs. He has experience of most business sectors and has been involved in all stages of project life cycles.

Previously, Stephen worked for Bovis Program Management, an international construction consultancy, in its London European headquarters, where he provided consultancy project management services and support to project managers working on Bovis projects worldwide.

A member of the Association for Project Management, Stephen is chairman of the Contracts & Procurement Specific Interest Group, which provides the focal point for all contract and procurement issues in relation to project management. He is also a chartered building surveyor with the Royal Institution of Chartered Surveyors and sits on the construction procurement panel, which provides advice to surveyors on all matters relating to procurement, especially during the initial phases of a construction project.

Stephen has a doctorate in project management from the University of Reading where he maintains close links. He lectures and undertakes research contracts at a number of academic institutions including Oxford University, London School of Economics, UMIST, Henley Management College and the Stockholm Institute of Technology. He has published widely in the field of project management, risk and value management. He is the joint editor of a new publication entitled *Construction Project Management* which draws on current best practice from over twenty contributing authors in construction and engineering project management.
stevesimister@europrojex.com

**Dennis Lock** is a freelance writer. His early career began as an electronics engineer with the General Electric Company. His subsequent management experience has been successful, and exceptionally wide, in industries ranging from electronics to heavy machine tools and mining engineering. He is a Fellow of the Institute of Management Services, Fellow of the Association for Project Management and a Member of the Institute of Management. Mr Lock carries out lecturing and consultancy assignments in the UK and overseas, lecturing on masters' programmes at Southampton and Surrey Universities, and has written or edited many successful management books.

## THE AUTHORS

**Erling S. Andersen** is Professor of Information Systems and Project Management at the Norwegian School of Management BI. He holds a Master in Economics from the University of Oslo. Before joining NSM BI he was Associate Professor in economics at the University of Oslo, Dean of NKI College of Computer Science and Professor of Information Science at the University of Bergen. He has published several books and articles on information technology, systems development, project management and management in general. His

book *Goal Directed Project Management* (written with Kristoffer Grude and Tor Haug) is translated into several languages.
erling.s.andersen@bi.no

**Peter Baily** is a Fellow of the CIPS. He has been a consultant and a contributor to courses and conferences in several European countries, in Singapore and in the USA. He became the first full-time lecturer in purchasing in Britain at about the time his book *Purchasing and Supply Management* was first published. This was the first comprehensive treatment of the subject to appear in this country, or in fact anywhere outside the USA. Many lecturers and professors have followed his lead. He is also co-author of the standard textbook for students of the subject, *Purchasing Principles and Management*.

**Denise Bower** is a lecturer in the Centre for Research in the Management of Projects at UMIST. She is also a consultant to Oriel Group Practice and Indeco, internationally recognized project management consultancies. Her recent work includes the evaluation of procurement strategies, assessment of corporate strategy, the development of organizational partnering guidelines, the evaluation of the success criteria for a number of partnering arrangements and recommendations of contract strategies for overseas projects. Denise is directing doctoral studies in the area of procurement and contracts, her particular area of research interest being in the optimization of the procurement of contracted services. In recognition of her work she is a member of post-Latham Working Group 12, which produced the guide *Partnering in the Team*. Denise is the Director of continuing education courses in project and contract management for UMIST and EPCI, an international consortium of predominantly oil and gas companies. She is the author and joint author of many books and publications, including *Engineering Project Management, Dispute Resolution for Infra-structure Projects* and *Managing Risk in Construction*.
denise.bower@umist.ac.uk

**Chris Chapman** is Professor of Management Science in the School of Management, Southampton University. He is a past Director of the School, a past President of the Operational Research Society and founding chair of the Specific Interest Group on Project Risk Management of the Association for Project Management. Project risk management has been the focus of his research and consultancy for about twenty-five years. He has published two books and a number of papers on this subject. Past clients included BP International, Gulf, IBM UK, MOD, AEA Technology, Sir William Halcrow and Partners, UK Nirex, NatWest Bank, Ontario Hydro, Alaska Power Authority and the US Department of Energy.
cbc@soton.ac.uk

**Christian Dawson** is currently employed as a full-time lecturer in the Department of Computer Science at Loughborough University. He obtained his Ph.D. in 1994 in software development management from Loughborough University. Since that time he has become an active researcher in project management and is often employed in project management and risk management consultancy work. He has had numerous project management papers published and has secured external funding for a number of research projects. He is also on the refereeing panel for two international journals and is often called upon to present at local seminars.
c.w.dawson1@lboro.ac.uk

**Roland Gareis** is Professor and head of the Projektmanagement Group at the University of Economics and Business Administration, Vienna. He is also head of Project Management Austria Consulting, Austria's project management national association, and of Roland Gareis Consulting.
roland.gareis@wu-wien.ac.at

**Alistair Godbold** is Business Systems Manager with the Finance Division National Air Traffic Services Ltd. He is a chartered engineer, a member of the Association for Project Management and he holds a B.Sc. (Hons) in computing science and an MBA in project management. He has been a project manager for ten years, managing high technology safety-related air traffic control systems projects and latterly the implementation of finance systems and business process change. He is a member of the IEE professional group looking at engineering and society. His interests include ethics and engineering on which he has written and lectured.
apgodbold@iee.org

**Bob Graham** is an independent management consultant and educator in project management organizational creativity and the implementation of change. He is also a Senior Associate at Primavera Systems in Bala Cynwyd, Pennsylvania, and the Strategic Management Group in Philadelphia. At the Wharton School of the University of Pennsylvania, Dr Graham taught project management in the Wharton Executive Education Programme. His work there stressed the importance of people in project management. He was also a Research Associate with the Management and Behavioural Science Centre. Dr Graham holds a BS in systems analysis from Miami University, an MBA and Ph.D. in business administration from the University of Cincinnati and an MS in cultural anthropology from the University of Pennsylvania.
bobg@smginc.com

**Geoff Haley** was admitted as a solicitor in 1979 and holds a Masters Degree in Business Administration and a Diploma in Marketing. He is a partner at Arnold & Porter, a law firm headquartered in Washington DC. Geoff is based in its London office and undertakes construction and project finance activities. Geoff lectures extensively on public–private partnership and privatization issues, both in the UK and overseas. He has had articles published and has contributed to several books on project finance, and is the author of *A to Z of BOOT – How to Create Successful Structures for BOOT Projects* and *Negotiating International Infrastructure Projects*. He is Chairman of the International Project Finance Association and Honorary Professor of Law at the University of Keele.

**Alan Harpham** is a director of P⁵ the Power of Projects, a management consultancy focused on programme management, project management and executive coaching. Alan is also part-time Chairman of the APM Group, established in 1993 as the trading arm of the Association for Project Management. (He chairs the APM Group's Benchmarking Forum and is Project Director for the IPMA – 15th World Congress in Project Management to be held in London in May 2000.) He is a former Managing Director and senior consultant of Nichols Associates (now part of the Nichols Group), one of the UK's leading consultancies in project and change management. Before this Alan was an early Director of Cranfield University's M.Sc. in Project Management and started his own project management consultancy. Alan's early career was as an engineer and line manager with John Laing, where he rose to become Overseas Contracts Manager for its M & E activities. His M & E experience included construction of the UK's first major North Sea oil rig and a large contract for a PVC plant in Poland where he took a significant proportion of the workforce (over a thousand men) from the UK. Alan describes himself as what Charles Handy calls 'a portfolio manager'.
alan@harpham.com

**Martina Huemann** is a lecturer and doctoral researcher at the Projekt-management Group at the University of Economics and Business Administration, Vienna. She has a masters degree from the university. Her research interests are project management competencies.
martina.huemann@wu-wien.ac.at

**Anne Keegan** is a Post-Doctoral Researcher at RIBES (the Rotterdam Institute of Business Economic Studies) and lecturer in the Department of Business and Organization in the Faculty of Economics of Erasmus University, Rotterdam. She undertakes research in the fields of human resource management and

organization theory, concentrating on project-based organizations and knowledge intensive and professional firms. She regularly presents at conferences on HRM, knowledge intensive firms and project management, and has experience teaching in management, industrial relations, innovation and international business at Trinity College, Dublin. Dr Keegan studied management and business at Trinity College Dublin and did her doctorate there on the topic of 'Management Practices in Knowledge Intensive Firms'. She has also worked as a consultant in the area of human resource management and organizational change to firms in the computer, food, export and voluntary sectors in Ireland.
keegan@few.eur.nl

**Bill McElroy** is an Executive Director with the Nichols Group, a leading UK management consultancy specializing in project management and change management. He is a certificated member of the Association for Project Management reflecting his hands-on experience in managing projects. He has also led training and consultancy assignments in a wide variety of sectors. Bill has twice won the APM's Sir Monty Finneston Award for his work in developing the management of strategic change.
bill.mcelroy@nichols.uk.com

**David Marsh** is a consultant, lecturer and author who has particular expertise in the introduction and implementation of structured methods for project and programme management. From an early career in industrial and civil engineering he moved into computing in 1974 to design and build a national computerized database for the water industry. After seven years of running this database he joined the UK Government's Cabinet Office as a consultant and trainer in structured project management and system development methods. He then joined an international computer services company for five years as a Managing Consultant. He now runs his own consultancy and training organization providing services to support structured programme and project management methods and their supporting infrastructures. He is a regular presenter at international seminars, national events and conferences. David has written many articles and books on PRINCE and programme management. He is Chairman of the PRINCE User Group Executive Committee, a Director of PRINCE User Group Ltd and was a member of the PRINCE Design Authority Board and the PRINCE Technical Committee. He was a founder member of the Association for Project Management Special Interest Group for Programme Management. David also designed the new ISEB courses for the Certificates in Programme and Project Support.
david.marsh@m-m-p.co.uk

**Peter Marsh** is principal of Peter Marsh Associates (contract consultants). He qualified as a solicitor but is now retired, and has an honours degree in management sciences. He was chief contracts officer of the National Coal Board before becoming central contracts manager for AEI (and then GEC). He later joined STC as manager, contract administration, subsequently becoming projects manager for its Submarine Cable Division. Mr Marsh then held a number of senior appointments with companies in the George Wimpey Group, which included commercial director of British Smelter Construction, director of business development for George Wimpey International and a director of Wimpey Major Projects. He is the author of *Contract Negotiation Handbook* (2nd edition, 1984) and *Contracting for Engineering and Construction Projects* (3rd edition, 1988), both published by Gower.

**Tony Merna** is the senior partner of the Oriel Group Practice, a multidisciplinary consultancy organization based in Manchester, and a part-time lecturer in the Centre for the Research in the Management of Projects, UMIST where he lectures and supervises M.Sc. and Ph.D. research projects. During the last ten years Tony has been involved in advising both UK and international organizations on methods of implementing and financing turnkey/concession/franchise/ BOOT contracts for process, water, transportation and infrastructure facilities. Tony is also author and co-author of a number of books covering topics such as project finance, dispute resolution, concession contracts, tender evaluation, BOOT projects and the Private Finance Initiative.
tony@orielgroup.freeserve.co.uk

**Chris Mills** is a senior consultant with the Nichols Group and has provided expertise and advice on managing programmes and projects for clients in the utilities and transportation sectors in the UK and overseas. He holds an honours degree in civil engineering from Imperial College, London, and an MBA from Cranfield University and is a member of the Association for Project Management.
chris.mills@nichols.uk.com

**Ruth Murray-Webster**, MAPM, is a managing consultant with PMP Services Ltd. Her background and experience has combined roles as a trainer and training manager, quality manager, project and programme manager. Ruth is an experienced assessor of business performance in line with the Business Excellence Model promoted by the European Foundation for Quality Management (EFQM) and the British Quality Foundation (BQF). Ruth's experience is supported by membership of the Institutes of Quality Assurance, Personnel & Development and Management Consultancy, and of the Association for Project Management. She has

recently completed the research stage for a Master of Business Administration from Henley Management College, studying the effect of cultural differences on business success within international joint ventures.
rmurraywebster@pmp.uk.com

**David Partington** is a chartered engineer whose career spans more than twenty years as a practitioner, consultant and lecturer in project management. He has experience of managing many types of projects for a variety of organizations in the UK, South America and the Middle East. He has an M.Sc. in project management and a Ph.D. in organizational behaviour. David is currently a lecturer in project management at Cranfield School of Management, where his research interests include project team behaviour, knowledge management and the implementation of planned organizational change. He is co-author of the Proaction project and programme management simulations.
d.partington@cranfield.ac.uk

**Jim Pearce**, after completing an honours degree in applied chemistry, worked as a plant manager in a heavy chemical plant and with a major pharmaceutical organization as a shift chemist. Prior to joining RoSPA Jim worked for an international research and development centre as Safety and Fire Officer. During his employment with the Society he has been responsible for the development and delivery of courses including the NEBOSH National Diploma. He also assists organizations to develop their health and safety management systems via both auditing and advisory activities. Jim was a training provider representative on the Executive Committee of NEBOSH from 1991 to 1997. He drafted several questions that were used in Diploma examinations and is also author of the 'Passwords' series of possible NEBOSH Diploma questions and answers featured in RoSPA's journal *OS&H*.

**Richard Pharro** is managing director of the APM Group, founded in 1993 as the operating company of the Association for Project Management, the UK's national project management association. He is a qualified civil engineer and had 20 years' experience in construction project management before founding the APM Group. He is a former council member of the APM.
richard.pharro@apmgroup.co.uk

**David Rees**, professionally trained with UK Post Office Telecoms as a management services and works study analyst, left industry to pursue a lecturing career at Guildford College of Technology, where his attention turned towards the human aspects of communication. As a result of this interest, David launched

an enterprise, Cultural Fluency, providing clients with language, culture and management training services. Currently his areas of activity focus on cultural consultancy and training for large transnational companies, and the strategic management of his enterprise. He is an associate faculty member of Henley Management College, a visiting lecturer at many overseas institutions and a member of the Institute of Personnel & Development and Institute of Management.
enquire@cultural-fluency.com

**Tony Reid** is chairman of the Special Interest Group on Project Organization for the Association for Project Management. He is a consultant in the areas of project organization and teamworking, and runs his own consulting, coaching and partner facilitation company.
tony@manach.clara.co.uk

**Geoff Reiss** is managing director of Hydra Development Corporation Ltd, a company he co-founded to develop information systems for programme management. He is also Chairman of the Specific Interest Group on Programme Management, a joint SIG of the Association for Project Management and the British Computer Society. He is author of *Project Management Demystified* and *Programme Management Demystified*.
geoff.reiss@hydradev.com

**Fotis Skountzos** graduated from the National Technical University of Athens in 1992 with an M.Eng. in mining and metallurgical engineering and then worked on the Athens Olympic Metro, being responsible for the construction of a large diameter tunnel. He then took an M.Sc. in engineering project management at UMIST and graduated in 1998 after completing his dissertation on partnering. Since then he has worked as a project manager for A.D.K. SA, consulting engineers in Athens.
fotchrys@otenet.gr

**Nigel Smith** is Head of Construction Project Management Group in the School of Civil Engineering, University of Leeds. Professor Smith has obtained external funding for research projects valued at over £750 000, undertaken in collaboration with industrial partners. As a Project Director of the European Construction Institute, he is currently heading a DETR-funded research project regarding the use of incentive contracts. He has been organizer, chair or co-chair of international conferences in Florence, Budapest, Trondheim, Moscow and Bonn. Professor Smith has published widely with 14 books and over eighty refereed publications to his credit.
n.j.smith@leeds.ac.uk

**Michel Thiry**, MAPM, PMP, CVS, CVM, is a managing consultant with PMP Services Ltd. Michel is certified in both project management and value management in the USA and the UK. He is presently pursuing an M.Sc. in organizational behaviour at Birkbeck College (University of London). He regularly speaks and publishes on project and value management at an international level and is author of the book *Value Management Practice*. He has delivered numerous training sessions in project and value management, both in Canada and in Europe. Michel has more than twenty-five years' professional experience in projects, gained in North America and Europe. Following a fruitful career in construction, Michel has now focused on strategic management consultancy, specifically change, value and programme management, as well as the management of strategic training programmes. In addition to his professional experience, Michel has participated in the translation of the PMI-PMBoK in French. He was also professional coordinator for the development of the 'Project Management Step-by-Step'© CD-Rom.
mthiry@pmp.uk.com

**Stephen Ward** is Senior Lecturer in the School of Management of the University of Southampton. He combines his academic role with numerous consultancy projects based on project risk management, and has published widely.
scwams@socsci.soton.ac.uk

**John Wateridge** is a senior lecturer at Bournemouth University. He has been lecturing in information systems, systems analysis and IS/IT project management for ten years. He received his Ph.D. in 1997. Before joining Bournemouth University, he worked for ten years in industry as a computer programmer, systems analyst and project manager.
jwaterid@bmth.ac.uk

# Preface

The *Gower Handbook of Project Management* is written as an encyclopaedia for the profession of project management. It is intended as a reference book for practising managers and students and trainees in project management. In particular it is a useful text for people studying for professional exams in project management and for people seeking certification all around the world.

The first and second editions, edited by Dennis Lock, were very successful. Our aim has been to build on the excellent pedigree of the previous editions. We have used as a structure a version of the Project Management Body of Knowledge (PMBoK), developed by Rodney Turner and published in an editorial in the *International Journal of Project Management* in February 1996, and updated in February 2000. This is not too dissimilar to the approach used previously by Dennis Lock. Rodney Turner has also tried to relate his PMBoK to others published in Europe and North America, so that people studying for certification as project management professionals can use this book as a reference source.

A small number of chapters have been retained from the second edition, and these have been brought up to date. Most chapters have been written from scratch, usually using new authors. This is in no way meant to be disrespectful to the previous authors. We have our own network, different from Dennis Lock's (and some of the previous authors turned down our request to update their chapters). Dennis Lock has remained a significant contributor to this third edition and we are grateful for his support.

We do not necessarily share the views of all the authors, although, as editors, we have not published anything with which we violently disagree. However, we believe it is healthy for the reader to be given a number of different perspectives, so the ideas published are not necessarily all consistent.

We hope that this book will run to further editions. Like Microsoft's products, we expect there to be a *Gower Handbook of Project Management* published at regular intervals. And like Microsoft's products we will start the development of the next release straight away. We would therefore be grateful for feedback from our readers as to how they think the book can be improved. What chapters worked for you? Which ones could be improved? Which should be dropped, and what new chapters would you like to see? We would also welcome offers from people who feel able to contribute chapters in areas that are missing, or believe that they could do a better job than the published chapter. You can tell what has not been covered from the Body of Knowledge as shown in Figure 1.1, and as described in Chapter 1.

Please contact us by e-mail at the addresses given below or visit our web page, http://www.europrojex.com

| | |
|---|---|
| Rodney Turner | Stephen Simister |
| East Horsley | Oxford |
| rodneyturner@europrojex.com | stevesimister@europrojex.com |
| turner@few.eur.nl | s.j.simister@omr.co.uk |

# 1

# An encyclopaedia for the profession of project management

## Rodney Turner

I was pleased when Gower asked me to edit the third edition of its *Handbook of Project Management*. I had been saying for some time that project management as a profession needed an encyclopaedia to capture the Body of Knowledge. If project management is an accidental profession, then my deliberate profession is as a mechanical engineer (though those who know my career will know that for me becoming a mechanical engineer was almost as accidental as becoming a project manager). However, in the mechanical engineering profession there is a yearbook which provides a record of the current state of the art of mechanical engineering. The book is substantial. Every year new chapters are added, some are removed and many are revised. I would very much like this handbook eventually to achieve the same status for project management. That, of course, depends on the success of the current edition.

In this chapter I consider what we think we understand by project management as a profession and the scope of the Project Management Body of Knowledge, and thereby set out the strategy behind the contents and structure of this handbook.

## PROJECT MANAGEMENT AS A PROFESSION

The Oxford Dictionary gives several meanings for the word 'profession', including:

a vocation requiring higher learning;
an avowal (of faith)

The first is given as the main definition. The second derives from the word to profess, meaning to avow one's faith. I think the first is what most of us think we mean when we talk of project management being a profession. Indeed, many people may be somewhat surprised that I have even bothered to include the

1

second definition. However, those readers of a philosophical bent may realize that the question 'Is project management a profession?' could be either an ontological question or an epistemological question. In layman's terms that means that it may simply be a question of the nature of being of project panagement. Or, more subtly, that project management is open to understanding through knowledge. If it is merely a question of the nature of being of project management, then our belief that project management works and delivers beneficial results to its advocates is an avowal of faith. We use project management because we have faith that it works. If, on the other hand, project management is demonstrably open to examination and understanding through knowledge, then it can be said to be a vocation requiring higher learning. The knowledge enables professionals to improve their performance and thereby deliver additional benefit through the better management of their projects.

Thus the seeking of a Project Management Body of Knowledge and its capture in an encyclopaedia, handbook or yearbook is not some idle pastime, but an essential element of achieving full professional status for project managers and project management. Therefore, let us now consider the scope of the Project Management Body of Knowledge.

## THE BODY OF KNOWLEDGE

Up to 1998 the development of the Project Management Body of Knowledge suffered from the not-invented-here syndrome. Versions and variants were produced by:

- the Project Management Institute (PMI) in the USA;
- the Association for Project Management (APM) in the United Kingdom, and adopted by the Netherlands and Scandinavian countries;
- national associations in Switzerland, Germany and France, as adaptations of the UK one, but reflecting local culture;
- the International Project Management Association (IPMA);
- the Australian Institute of Project Management (AIPM) as Australian National Competency Standards;
- by me as editor of the *International Journal of Project Management*.

The *Guide to the Project Management Body of Knowledge* (Duncan 1996) was produced by PMI and has received wide recognition. (This was the third edition, the first and second editions appearing in 1984 and 1987.) Some would say it has become a *de facto* global standard. It is under constant review and a new edition is expected shortly.

APM developed a Body of Knowledge in 1992, re-issued several times since. After six years, APM believed a major revision was due and in 1998 commissioned the Centre for Research in the Management of Projects (CRMP) at UMIST to undertake research into the Body of Knowledge (Morris 1999). CRMP interviewed 127 people from 105 organizations. It redesigned the Body of Knowledge from first principles, leading to a substantially different structure, but covering substantially the same areas. It produced two different groupings of the knowledge areas. One is the version derived from first principles, called Guide to the PMBoK. However, it was decided that it might be confusing to the marketplace if a substantially different Body of Knowledge was launched. After all, many organizations had put substantial effort into developing training and development programmes around the existing BoK. Hence a second grouping of the knowledge areas has been produced, which is an adaptation of APM's existing BoK. This increases the number of knowledge areas from 40 to 44.

For most of the 1990s attempts to develop a European Body of Knowledge proved to be a triumph of nationalism over globalization. However, in 1999, IPMA issued the *IPMA Competence Baseline* (ICB) (Caupin *et al.* 1999). This represents the core elements of the BoKs from Britain, France, Germany and Switzerland. It is presented in three columns, English, German and French. The three columns are not a direct translation of each other, but represent the same sense. As a competence baseline, it focuses on the skills required to manage a project, whereas PMI's PMBoK focuses on the knowledge used by project managers and their teams. The ICB has greater claim to the status of global standard than PMI's PMBoK, since IPMA has over thirty member national associations from America, Europe, Africa and Asia.

The Australian National Competency Standards produced by AIPM predated most European BoKs, but are limited in their application to Australia. They are also very definitely definitions of competence rather than knowledge and are written as such.

## A COMPARISON OF THE COVERAGE

Figure 1.1 gives a comparison of the coverage of:

- the BoK as proposed by me in editorials in the *International Journal of Project Management* in 1996 and 2000;
- IPMA's ICB;
- APM's previous 40-element version of the BoK;
- UMIST's Guide to the BoK;
- UMIST's strawman proposal for a 44-element APM BoK;
- PMI's Guide to the PMBoK®.

| LJPM BoK | Ch | IPMA ICB | APM BoK | UMIST Guide | UMIST strawman | PMI Guide |
| --- | --- | --- | --- | --- | --- | --- |
| D3 Proposal and feasibility | 25 | 31 Problem solving | | 5 Strategy<br>21 Modelling | 4 Strategic plan | 5.1 Initiation |
| D4 Design and appraisal | 26 | 4 Systems & integration | 3.2 Planning | 5 Project plan | 15 Management plan | 4.1 Plan development |
| D5 Implementation | 26 | 19 Performance | 1.9 Integration | 17 Production | 11 Integrative management | 4.2 Execution |
| D6 Progress | | 20 Control | 3.6 Performance<br>2.2 Control, coordination | 14 Change control<br>15 Performance management<br>20 Value engineering | 27 Monitoring, control<br>28 Performance management<br>29 Change control | 4.3 Overall control<br>10.3 Progress reporting |
| D7 Commissioning & close-out | | 11 Close-out | 3.9 Change control<br>1.11 Close-out | 17 Handover<br>43 Close-out | 42 Handover | 10.4 Admin. closure |
| **E Commercial** | PV | | | | | |
| E1 Value and benefit | 27, 28 | 7 Appraisal | 1.7 Project appraisal | | 5 Project appraisal | |
| E2 Finance | 29 | 16 Cost and finance | 4.3 Finance | 25 Financial management | 6 Financial management | |
| E3 Cash flow management | | 42 Finance & accounting | | | | |
| E4 Taxation | | | | | | |
| E5 Insurance | | | | | | |
| **F Contractual** | PVI | | | | | |
| F1 Organization design | 30 | | 2.1 Organization design | | | |
| F2 Partnerships, alliances | 31 | | | | | |
| F3 Procurement | 35, 34 | 27 Procurement | 4.6 Procurement | 26 Procurement | 31 Procurement | 12 Procurement |
| F4 Bidding | 36 | | | | | |
| F5 Contract administration | 33 | | | | 34 Contract admin. | |
| F6 Materials, purchasing & supply | 35 | 27 Procurement | | | 33 Purchasing | |
| F7 Contract law | 32 | 27 Procurement | 4.5 Law | | | |
| F8 Claims | 37 | | | | | |
| F9 International projects | | | | | | |
| **G People** | PVII | | | | | |
| G1 Management structure | 38 | 22 Project organization | | 29 Organization | 26 Project organization | 9.1 Organization plan |
| G2 Teams | 40 | 23 Teamwork | 2.6 Team building | 31 Teamwork | 36 Teamwork | 9.2 Team development |
| G3 Individuals | | | 2.5 Delegation | | 39 Stress | |
| G4 Managing and leading | 41 | 24 Leadership | 2.4 Leadership | 32 Leadership | 37 Leadership | |
| G5 Stakeholders | 42, 43 | 25 Communication<br>26 Conflicts & crises | 2.3 Communication<br>2.7 Conflict | 16 Information<br>33 Conflict | 30 Information management<br>38 Conflict | 10 Communications<br>2.2 Stakeholders |
| G6 Competence | 39 | 32 Negotiation, meetings | 2.8 Negotiation | 34 Negotiation | | |
| G7 Culture | 44 | 36 Organizational learning | 2.9 Personnel development | 35 Personnel management | 40 Personnel management | |

**Figure 1.1** The Project Management Body of Knowledge – topic areas and coverage of several versions *continued*

| IJPM BoK | Ch | IPMA ICB | APM BoK | UMIST Guide | UMIST strawman | PMI Guide |
|---|---|---|---|---|---|---|
| G8 Ethics | | | | | | |
| G9 Change | 45 | 37 Managing change | | | | |
| **H  General management** | | | | | | |
| H1 Human resource management | | 35 Personnel development | 4.9 Industrial relations | 35 Personnel management | 40 Personnel management<br>41 Industrial relations | 1.4 Other disciplines |
| H2 Marketing | | 33 Permanent organization | 4.2 Marketing & sales | 24 Marketing & Sales | 2 Marketing & Sales | 2.3 Organizational influences |
| H3 Operations | | 34 Business processes | 4.1 Operations & technical | | | |
| H4 Information technology | | 29 Informatics | | | | 2.4 General management skills |
| H5 Finance & accounting | | 42 Finance & accounting | | | | |
| H6 Technology, innovation | | | | 19 Technology management | | |
| H7 Strategy | | | | | | 2.4 General management skills |
| H8 Governance | | | | | | |

**Figure 1.1  *Concluded***

My version has the greatest coverage. I seem to give much greater emphasis to financial and contractual issues than anyone else. The versions produced by IPMA, APM and UMIST have substantially similar coverage. PMI has the lowest coverage. But two points are relevant:

- PMI states quite clearly that its Guide applies to the core elements used by *all* project managers, whereas the others are guides to the totality of project management.
- PMI uses much larger groupings and I may not have always split them appropriately, especially in the areas of the management of functionality, requirements and configuration.

Figure 1.1 shows that there is substantial agreement about the Project Management Body of Knowledge. The process of trying to agree the BoK is likened to the drawing of a map of a continent. It is easy to draw the outline of the continent; more difficult to agree and draw the political map. Indeed, different maps may be useful for different purposes – a political map, a geographic map, a demographic map, an agricultural map. Figure 1.1 shows that there is substantial agreement about the shoreline of the continent. I seem to think that there are two substantial offshore islands, which others think are only weakly linked. But we do seem to have substantially different views about how the continent is divided.

My version of the BoK (the first column in Figure 1.1) is the basis for the structure and content of this book. The chapters covering the various topics are shown in the second column. Figure 1.1 should help readers find chapters relevant to topic areas in the other BoKs, particularly useful if they are studying for professional exams based on those BoKs.

## A FINAL PUSH FOR A GLOBAL VERSION

Since 1999 there have been further attempts to achieve global agreement on the PMBoK. Initially, a glossary of terms was developed to define the extent of the PMBoK, the size and shape of the continent. There is a comparative glossary of project management terms posted on the web (Wideman 1999). Further work is continuing to compile a more extensive list from the index entries in a range of highly regarded books on project management. The intention is then to agree the extent of project management and the division of the knowledge into topic areas. One or more breakdowns of the topic areas may be produced. This work requires the substantial cooperation of people from five continents (Africa, Asia, Australasia, Europe and North America) and is more difficult than it might appear. The International Project Management Association has now sponsored a Global Working Party on Standards to take this work forward.

## THE KNOWLEDGE AREAS

Figure 1.1 defines the intended scope and structure of this book. To complete this introductory chapter, I will outline the scope of each one of the knowledge areas to give the reader a complete picture of the full scope of project management. It is inevitable that in trying to group the knowledge topics into related areas there is some overlap between topics and a topic in one area may be closely related to a topic in another. This particularly true of the organization of the project and its benefit to the parent organization.

### A  GENERAL

There are issues that relate to why projects exist, their nature and the nature of project management. These also describe how an organization adopts a strategy for project and programme management.

#### A1: Implementing strategy through projects

Organizations undertake projects to achieve development objectives, (see Figure 1.2). They need to do something differently from the way it has been done in the past, and they need to undertake a project to implement the new way of working. They may do the projects for themselves or for client organizations.

#### A2: Managing programmes of projects

The majority of projects (90 per cent) take place as part of a portfolio of several projects. Programme management is the way of coordinating projects in a portfolio and prioritizing the sharing of resources between them to deliver additional benefit. The additional benefit may be the achievement of higher level objectives than could be achieved by each project alone (Figure 1.2) or the reduction of risk or disruption.

#### A3: Managing projects

Projects are unique, novel and transient endeavours undertaken to achieve novel development objectives (Figure 1.2). They involve considerable risk and uncertainty. Project management is the process of reducing that risk and uncertainty to achieve the development objectives.

#### A4: Success and strategy

Figure 1.2 shows that to achieve the development objectives at every level

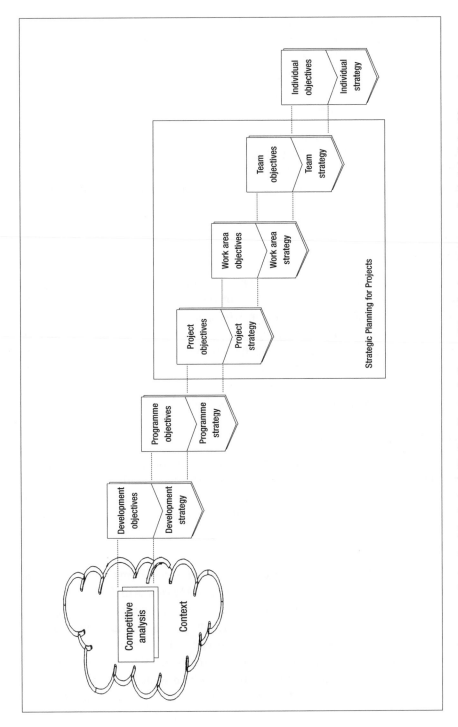

**Figure 1.2  A cascade of development objectives for organizations, and the role of programmes and projects in their achievement**

requires the formulation of a strategy. First, the manager needs to identify how the stakeholders will judge the successful achievement of the objective, and what key success factors will help to deliver those criteria. This will then form the basis of a strategy. This applies equally for programme and project objectives.

## A5: Processes and procedures

Standards have been developed which give guidance about previously proven successful methods of delivering programme and project objectives (based on standard success criteria and success factors). Organizations should maintain standard procedures and guidelines based on international standards and their previous experience, and should develop individual project procedures manuals for the projects they undertake.

## A6: Systems and the project office

As part of implementing procedures, and managing the successful delivery of projects, an organization needs a system for monitoring and reporting progress so that corrective action can be taken where necessary. The systems will be based on standard and individual project procedures. They may be computer- or paper-based. Many organizations will have a project or programme office to administer the systems either for individual large projects or for all the projects in the programmes they undertake. Organizations may need different systems for programmes and individual large projects.

## A7: Audits and health checks

Audits and health checks are undertaken for two reasons. The first is to ensure that a project is progressing satisfactorily, in accordance with the systems and procedures. The second is to learn from the success and failures of a completed project to improve the organization's standard procedures for future projects.

## A8: The systems approach

There are those who think that project management is a systems science and that systems theory can contribute to its understanding. My view is that systems science has much to offer, but project management is more social science than systems science. The systems approach therefore warrants one chapter in a book like this (alongside the nine or more for the social science), but not in this edition. My concern is that systems science is like sirens on the rocks, singing a sweet melody and attracting unwary sailors to their doom. Like Odysseus, the project manager should deafen his or her team to the sirens' song and be lashed to the mast.

## B   EXTERNAL CONTEXT

Projects and programmes take place in an external context, which creates the need for the project, influences people's perceptions of its success and can enhance or impede the successful delivery of the objectives. The analysis of these issues is sometimes called PESTLE analysis (political, economic, social, technical, legal and environmental).

### B1: Political, economic, social and technical

These issues are the PEST of PESTLE. A project is influenced by Politics, that is the policies of national and local government, and by politics, the policies of managers, staff and the trade unions that represent them. The project is influenced by national macroeconomic issues, inflation and interest rates, and by the microeconomic performance of the parent organization. It is influenced by social issues, the lives of the managers, staff and the local community, and by the technology of the industry and the technical capability of the parent organization.

### B2: Legal

The project is influenced by the laws of the land, consisting of Acts of Parliament, regulations and local by-laws. It will also be influenced by the policies and procedures of the parent organization, some of them backed up or required by national or local law.

### B3: Environmental

The project will have an impact on the environment, both in a social sense (B1) and in a physical sense. Morally, that impact should be managed, but the management of the impact may also be controlled by national or local law and regulation.

### B4: Value, benefit and finance

The parent organization undertakes the project to achieve its development objectives, to achieve some business need. It is expected that the project will deliver benefit and to that end the parent organization makes finance available to pay for the work. The cost of the finance and the capital will be repaid out of the benefit delivered by the project. In order to repay the finance, the project's objectives must be delivered in a timely fashion or the interest charged will exceed the project's ability to generate revenues.

## C  INTERNAL IMPLEMENTATION

To deliver the objectives successfully, the manager must manage the project's internal workings. This has three dimensions: various functions, the life cycle and different levels of strategic implementation (Figure 1.2). This first area of the internal implementation deals with the functions. The life cycle and the levels are linked, and are dealt with in the next sector.

### C1: Functionality and value

The first three functions deal with what conventionally comes under the management of 'scope'. First, to generate the revenue just identified, the project's product (objectives) must meet certain requirements or perform certain functions, generically known as *functionality*. The functionality will generate revenue, or make savings, which will repay the finance. The value of the functionality (value for money) is measured by the ratio of the cost of achieving the functionality (or parts of it) to the benefit it delivers. The management of this ratio is known as *value management*.

### C2: Configuration and product breakdown

The project's product, or objectives, consists of components, at several levels of breakdown, each of which deliver parts of the functionality. Those components usually need to be individually designed and made and then assembled (or configured) to produce the whole product and hence provide the total functionality. The process of designing, making and assembling the components to achieve the required functionality is known as *configuration management*. To realize a consistent, coherent end product may require several versions of the design and even some false starts in the delivery of components, and so configuration management is closely related to change control. The value of each component also needs managing through value management (C1).

### C3: Scope of work

The design, fabrication and assembly of the components into a working product requires the doing of work. The management of this work is what some people in a very narrow sense think of as project management, and so this can almost be thought of as the core function, the core knowledge topic. However, from this chapter you can see that it is just one of about fifty knowledge topics. My own view, developed recently, is that nobody manages work on a project; they manage the input of resources and the delivery of results. In this book, work management is treated as part of configuration management, and the management of resources is considered separately.

### C4: Organization and resources

Organization appears for the first time here. In order to be able to do the work, it is necessary to determine what skills are required, the roles and responsibilities of people with those skills and the numbers required. The involvement of those people must be managed and their activities coordinated.

### C5: Quality

To perform effectively, the project's products must be delivered to certain standards and criteria. First, the product must perform to provide the functionality expected, and to solve the problem and deliver the benefit and value expected of it. It must also meet other performance requirements or service levels, such as availability, reliability and maintainability, and have acceptable finish or polish.

### C6: Cost

To be of value, the functionality must not cost more than a certain amount. Clearly the more benefit it delivers, the more can be spent on its delivery. The cost of the product, and the value it gives, must be estimated and the cost controlled within those limits while the work is done.

### C7: Time

Likewise, to provide benefit, the project's products must be obtained within a certain time to satisfy the need and to cover both interest and capital payments on the finance. Hence, the timing of the work must be managed. Sometimes very tight time constraints must be met, but normally they are more flexible. Also, on many projects the work of different resources must be carefully coordinated, and that will also be achieved through the management of the timing of the work.

### C8: Risk

Projects being unique, novel and transient are inherently risky; more so than the routine work of organizations. This is what differentiates project management from the management of normal operations. Risk management is therefore an essential part of project management.

## C9: Safety and health

In all working environments, the safety and health of people doing the work must be of paramount concern to managers, mainly for moral reasons. However, since some managers do not seem to behave ethically towards their employees, this area is now also tightly controlled by law. Some people sweep managing the environment (B3) in with safety and health. However, my view is that safety and health are internal issues, whereas the environment is an external one.

## D  LIFE CYCLE

Because projects are transient, their delivery goes through a cycle of development, from germination of the idea through initiation, design and delivery to commissioning and handover to the client and close-out of the work. This cycle is known as the life cycle. It was once said to me that it should be called the 'life', since 'cycle' implies a return to the start. However, I think life cycle is a good biological metaphor, as the project goes from germination through growth and maturity and eventual metamorphosis into a butterfly, a new and successful operation. As we progress through the life cycle, the plans and design of the product or objectives are developed in increasing detail. We gain greater understanding of the objectives and how they will be delivered, and that feeds into increasing detail in the plans. This is linked to the breakdown of the product into components at lower levels and the definition of the configuration at those levels. Because we develop the lower level definition at successive stages of the life cycle, the levels are essentially linked to the stages.

## D1: The life cycle

There are many different versions of the life cycle, but they all essentially contain the steps of germination of the idea, proposal and initiation, design and appraisal, mobilization of the team, execution and control, integration of the team and their work, testing, commissioning and handover of the project's product and close-out of the work.

## D2: Start-up

The difference between project start and start-up has been likened to the difference between starting the engine in a private car to the complex sequence of activities required to start the diesel engine of a ship or high-speed locomotive. A complex sequence of activities are required to start the project, to mobilize the team, to initiate the project definition process, to obtain agreement to the project objectives and plan to deliver them.

### D3: Proposal, initiation and feasibility

At this stage, the problem the project is to solve (or the opportunity it is to exploit) is identified. Several options for solving the problem are developed, functional designs produced, and their respective costs and benefits are estimated to the current level of accuracy. The best solution, if any, is chosen for further definition. A high level, strategic plan for the design and execution of the project is developed. The information generated so far is incorporated into a Project Definition Report.

### D4: Design and appraisal

The chosen solution is developed further. As systems design is produced, and the costs and benefits estimated at this level of accuracy, the project is appraised using formal investment appraisal techniques and, if found acceptable, finance is sought. A more detailed plan for implementation is developed. The information generated at this stage is incorporated into a Project Manual.

### D5: Implementation

Work is undertaken to deliver the project's products. The first step in this process may be to produce the detailed designs and control plans needed for execution, as opposed to the systems design and plans required for appraisal. A key feature of project management, which sets it apart from normal operations, is the integrative function. Operations management emphasizes discrete functions, project management integrated teams. This is in evidence throughout the life cycle, but particularly at this stage. The work of the project members must be integrated, the work of the design, execution and commissioning teams must be integrated, the work of project team and client must be integrated.

### D6: Progress control

Throughout all stages, progress must be controlled, but particularly during implementation. The timing of the work must be controlled to coordinate the input of project team members and to ensure that the product is delivered at a time which will provide benefit and repay the finance. The cost must be controlled to ensure that the work is done for the estimated costs, within the approved budget, to enable revenues to repay the finance. Cash flow must also be controlled so that money is spent as it becomes available, as the loan is drawn or money is released by the client. A technique called *earned value analysis* (related to normal management cost accounting) can be used to control cost and time. The quality of the product must be delivered in accordance with the specification, in such a way that the product performs its required duty. The configuration of the product must be controlled so as to deliver the required functionality.

### D7: Commissioning and close-out

The work of the project is brought to a timely and efficient conclusion. The product is tested and commissioned, and handed over to the operations team. They must be trained in the use of the product, and operational and logistical procedures must be put in place. The client ensures that it is receiving the benefit required to repay the project finance, and the contractor obtains sign-off from the client and receives final payment. The project team is disbanded and debriefed. The project performance is audited and lessons learnt for future projects.

## E   COMMERCIAL

There are several commercial and financial issues relating to the way the project is financed.

### E1: Value and benefit

The value for the project must be appraised by comparing projected cash inflows (revenues and savings) to expected cash outflows (costs) using standard investment appraisal techniques.

### E2: Finance

Finance must be raised from any one of a number of sources. The simplest is to obtain money from the parent organization. Alternatively, money can be secured from other equity shareholders or as loans from banks. There are also a number of specialist sources of finance. The costs and benefits of different sources of finance must be compared and a financial package produced for the project.

### E3: Cash flow management

As the work on the project progresses, the rate of expenditure must be controlled: too fast a rate can drive the parent organization into liquidation as money is spent faster than it becomes available; too slow a rate is expensive since money is being spent on interest for borrowed finance, but it is not yet working to produce income.

### E4: Taxation

Even rich people have to pay taxes. It is important to understand the tax laws of the country. What counts as capital expenditure and what as revenue? What tax exemptions and grants are available? How can capital exemptions be worked to the best advantage? How can expenditure be phased to best tax advantage? In ten years of searching this is one area that I have not been able to find anyone working in the field of project management to write about. Nobody seems to want to know.

### E5: Insurance

The sponsor's investment and the financiers' money need to be protected against unexpected loss. Some risks are insurable, such as fire, civil strife and transport losses. Severe weather can be insured, but not inclement weather. Trading losses cannot be insured. There are ways of insuring the project without involving insurance companies: money can be set aside in the budget, currency can be bought forward, other futures and all manner of risky financial instruments can be used to hedge other swings in the financial markets. Again, in ten years of searching, I have not been able to find anyone to write about the insurance of projects.

## F  CONTRACTUAL

On anything but the smallest projects, the sponsor will not have the necessary resources in-house to undertake the project. Hence, it is almost always necessary to buy in external goods and services. This requires organizations to develop and use a range of commercial skills.

### F1: Organization design

As part of the process of developing the project organization and identifying the roles and responsibilities (C4), the sponsor needs to identify what skills exist internally within the organization, and which do not. The latter will need to be procured externally. It will also be necessary to procure most of the materials to be consumed on the project and much of the supporting plant and equipment. Furthermore, on large projects, many of the management roles will be taken by external contractors. These may include project director, design manager, construction manager and site supervisor. These roles need to be defined. Again, it is part of the integrative role of project management to coordinate all of these management and work-related activities.

### F2: Partnerships and alliances

One way of obtaining necessary skills is to form a partnership or alliance. The essential feature of a partnership as opposed to the more normal contractual relationship is that the parties share the risk of the project as equals. They are jointly and severally responsible for the performance of the project.

### F3: Procurement

Most skills will be obtained through traditional contracts. Under procurement, I place the more strategic issues of developing a contract strategy and placing contracts, especially for the supply of skills and services. The more detailed matter of actually issuing purchase orders, especially for the supply of materials, I place under purchasing below. Having identified what skills and management roles need to be bought in, the promoter or sponsor needs to develop a contract strategy. A common approach for naive promoters of large projects is to appoint a managing contractor (who may also be the design consultant), and leave it to him or her to manage all other contracts on their behalf. The contract strategy will identify the scope of supply of the contracts and the payment methods. This will depend on the nature of the work to be done and the risk. Invitations to tender will then be issued, bids appraised, successful bidders short-listed and final negotiations undertaken, leading to the signing of the contracts.

### F4: Bidding

On the other side of the relationship, potential contractors receive notification of the potential opportunity and then receive the invitations to tender. They will decide whether or not they want to bid and, if so, they will draw up a bid strategy, prepare their bids, and if successfully shortlisted enter the final negotiations leading to signing of the contracts.

### F5: Contract administration

Once under way, the contract needs to be administered from both sides. The parties must agree control meetings, payment and completion terms, processes for dealing with variations and other issues.

### F6: Materials, purchasing and supply

Materials, plant and equipment used on the project will need to be sourced externally. The materials required will be identified through the design process, and the plant and equipment through the planning process. Potential suppliers will be identified, competitive quotes obtained and orders placed. The materials, plant and equipment need to be transported to the project site and stored before they are used. An initial set of spares may be bought as part of the project and included in the capital cost. Sometimes the supply of maintenance spares for the life of the project's product may also be negotiated as part of the initial order. This is called *integrated logistics support.*

### F7: Contract law and standard forms

As well as understanding how the law influences the project as part of its context (B2), the team involved in the procurement of goods and services need to have a detailed knowledge of the law of contract. In most countries the law of contract involves the concepts of offer, acceptance, consideration, functions, validity, mistakes, terms and conditions, termination and remedies. It is necessary in signing a contract to say under which country's law the contract applies, as that is where any claim will be made. This may be the home country of the client or supplier, the country where the supply is made or the country where the project is undertaken. Within Europe, it is also necessary to understand the impact of European directives. There are many standard forms of contract which help organizations in their arrangement. Standard forms are usually published by professional institutions from engineering or building. The UK's Association for Project Management has published a standard form for project management consultancy services.

### F8: Claims

On a contract, minor claims may arise through variations in the scope of work. The extent to which these cause disruption or excessive cost depends on the working arrangement between the client and contractor, and the methods they have agreed for dealing with variation. Major claims arise where one party to the contract has defaulted, or where the other party feels significantly aggrieved. Unfortunately, where a sensible claims procedure does not exist for dealing with minor variations, these can escalate into major claims.

### F9: International projects

International projects arise where a client doing work in their own country uses a contractor from another, or where a client doing work in a foreign country uses a contractor from the host country, or where both client and contractor are working in a foreign country. The first two scenarios are the more common. The firm working in what is for it a foreign country needs to take a number of precautions and may even seek a local firm to represent its interests. Both parties need to understand the culture, customs and language of the other. The foreign firm also needs to understand the local legal systems and government regulations, and through a PESTLE analysis to be aware of any increased risk, especially from the political situation in the host country.

## G  PEOPLE

I said earlier (A8) that project management may be viewed as a systems science or a social science. I said I believe it is more social science than systems science, but in most of what has gone between you may have gained the impression that it is systems not social. Some of the areas, such as the PESTLE analysis (Area B), contract law (F7) and international projects (F9), were quite definitely social sience. But most of the rest was more about systems. This area of the Project Management Body of Knowledge is about the social science, managing the needs of all the people involved in the project. A balanced approach to management requires the integrated management of the task, the team and the individual. Knowledge areas A to F dealt with the management of the task. Topics G2 and G3 deal with the teams and the individuals. (I might be open to the charge that this is not very balanced, but this book is mainly about project management. Although we need to consider the special nature of project teams, and the working of individuals on projects, volumes are devoted to those subjects.) The whole of this knowledge area is devoted to the management of the wider project team.

### G1: Managing people

Projects are unique, novel and transient, and hence standard Human Resource Management concepts do not apply to the project-based firm. Every project requires a new structure and so some of the core concepts such as job design need rethinking. There are three core concepts of HRM theory in particular which need novel approaches in a project organization. These are the selection of people to work for the organization, the management of their careers and their and the organization's learning and development.

### G2: Teams

Project teams are formed to undertake a unique and novel task and are transient in their existence. The team needs to be formed and raised to peak performance. This will be part of the mobilization process (D2). Achieving peak team performance is critical to project success. The team should be composed of a balanced set of individuals with complimentary strengths and weaknesses. The team also needs to be properly disbanded at the end of the project so that its members can look forward to their future work, and they need to be properly debriefed so that the organization can learn from their experiences.

## G3: Individuals

Many people view individuals merely as members of the team. That is incorrect. The people who make up the team have needs as individuals. They must be briefed and motivated, and their concerns must be taken into account. They have families, social lives and needs, which must be regarded in planning the project work. The members of the team need to be developed, empowered, motivated, rewarded, counselled and disciplined, and this must be done in a way that melds the needs of the individuals with the needs of the team.

## G4: Managing and leading

Volumes have been written on the elusive quality of leadership, and volumes have been devoted to the question of whether leaders are born or made. My view is that some people are born bad leaders and no amount of training or development will overcome that. But the majority of people are born with inherent leadership skills and they can learn to develop these. Understanding the skills and styles of good leadership can improve the performance of a project manager in leading the team and motivating the individuals in the team to great things. One of the most important skills of a good leader is to be able to communicate the vision for the project, and the process of achieving that vision.

## G5: Stakeholders

The wider project team encompasses people beyond those people doing the work of the project. There are many people whose lives are affected by the project and its outcomes, and most of these have a view on the project. Some people view it positively, some negatively. Some can influence the outcome, some cannot. Where they view the project negatively, and can influence the outcome, they will work to undermine the project and that can lead to conflict. The project manager needs to communicate the vision, communicate the process, to win everybody over to the sense of the project. He or she also needs to negotiate everybody's involvement in the project, making them aware of how it can lead to positive outcomes for them and what contribution is expected from them.

## G6: Competence development

Organizational and individual learning is problematic in the project-based firm. The functional structures which traditionally own knowledge are absent. It is difficult for unique, novel and transient projects to retain knowledge. New ways must be found for storing and distributing knowledge. Similarly, individual development does not follow the traditional path, up the ladder, up the silo of the

21

function. However, projects offer an opportunity to provide people with a richer development path where they gather a wider range of experiences. The organization needs to find a way of managing that process, without constraining it, to develop individuals to meet the needs of future projects and to ensure that the knowledge and experiences of the organization are widely distributed. Developing people by 'sitting next to Nellie' seems to be important in project organizations, since individuals' experiences make up more than half of their competence development.

## G7: Culture

The team is composed of many individuals, with different backgrounds. As we saw earlier (F9), international teams are now common and the project manager and team members need to be aware of cultural differences. However, there is a view that the cultural differences between different professions can be greater than those between nations. Hence even people working within a single country need to be aware of difference that can arise from a person's professional, religious, class, educational, gender, age and other backgrounds.

## G8: Ethics

Several times, especially under the headings of environment (B3) and safety and health (C9), I have said that people should behave morally. Often the law has to intervene. Experience shows that even though many people think the moral road is the more expensive road, it can lead to greater rewards, and on earth, not just in heaven. The ethical approach usually produces the greater good for everyone, and people respect that and respond in like fashion.

## G9: Change

Project management is about the management of change, so understanding the concepts of change management can be critical to project success. It will impact on the team (G2), the individuals in the team (G3) and the stakeholders (G5). It will also impact on the success and strategy of the project (A4) and the project definition (C1 and D3). It pervades the whole project.

## H  GENERAL MANAGEMENT

Most versions of the BoK also deal with some of the general management skills required by project managers. Some of these are directly related to knowledge topics above, these just being their interpretation in the unique, novel and transient context of projects or project-based organizations.

### H1: Human resource management

There are many elements of human resource management: terms and conditions of employment, industrial relations, career development, work and organizational design, organizational learning, leadership, team development and individual empowerment and motivation. You will recognize many of these topics above.

### H2: Marketing and customers

Marketing is the process by which an organization identifies its customers and the products they want to buy and tries to influence their buying habits. There are ways of identifying the marketing mix (the four P's: product, price, promotion and place of sale) and the product portfolio and making improvements to both. Marketing is significant to projects in two ways. The project-based firm, selling bespoke products and services, obviously needs to identify its customers and the products and services they want to buy. In routine organizations, the marketing process will lead to the identification of new products, technologies or organizational structures needed to service the market, and the implementation of those changes will be undertaken through projects (or at least it ought to be).

### H3: Operations

Above I have identified the processes required to manage projects. Organizations also need to define the processes required to manage their routine operations.

### H4: Information technology

I talked earlier about identifying the information management needs of projects (A6). Organizations need to identify the information needs of all their business processes across all areas of management and all functions.

### H5: Finance and accounting

Organizations must manage the cash. Firms in the private sector need to generate cash to operate and to grow, and they need to make profits to provide returns to shareholders. Organizations in the public and voluntary sectors need to ensure that they do not overspend their budgets, and that they get value for money. That will not happen by accident, it must be planned and controlled.

### H6: Technology and innovation

Technology may be viewed as part of operations and innovation as part of marketing. I have included this separate category, because I see operations as being about defining the business processes. The knowledge of the technology that adds value for the organization is a key part of its competitive advantage, and so that knowledge, that technology, should be managed carefully and separately from routine operations. Innovation is essential to maintain competitive advantage.

### H7: Strategy

At the end we are back where we started. Projects are undertaken to help organizations deliver their strategic plans. The strategic planning process is essential for the survival of organizations, and it is the strategic planning process that generates projects. There is not one without the other, and there is no organization without either.

### H8: Governance

And absolutely nothing happens without governance. In a narrow sense governance (in the private sector) is the legally defined roles of directors and the company secretary. In a slightly wider sense governance is the planning, influencing and conducting of the policy and affairs of an organization. It is the role of the directors and company secretary (or equivalent roles in the public sector), it is strategic planning and implementation through projects, and it is leadership (communicating the vision, communicating the process).

There are chapters in this book on most of the knowledge topics listed above in sectors A to G, and for some there are two chapters. There are a few knowledge areas for which I was not able to source material or for which understanding is not yet well enough advanced for a suitable chapter to be written. It was not intended to include anything on general management skills, sector H.

## REFERENCES AND FURTHER READING

Caupin, G., Knöpfel, H., Morris, P. W. G., Motzel, E. and Pannebäcker, O. (eds) (1999), *ICB: IPMA Competence Baseline*, International Project Management Association Zurich.

Duncan, W. R. (ed.) (1996), *The Guide to the Project Management Body of Knowledge*, Project Management Institute, Sylva, NC.

Morris, P. W. G. (1999), *Association for Project Management Body of Knowledge Review*, Centre for Research in the Management of Projects, UMIST, Manchester.

Thermistocleous, G. and Wearne, S. H. (2000), 'Project management topic coverage in journals', *International Journal of Project Management*, **18**(1).

Turner, J. R. (1996), 'International Project Management Association global qualification, certification and accreditation', Editorial, *International Journal of Project Management*, **14**(1).

Turner, J. R. (2000), 'The global body of knowledge, and its coverage by the referees and members of the International Editorial Board of this journal', Editorial, *International Journal of Project Management*, **18**(1).

Wideman, R. M (1999), 'A comparative glossary of project management terms', http://www.pmforum.org/warindex.htm.

# Part I
# Projects

# INTRODUCTION TO PART I

In Part I we consider the *raison d'être* of project management, as a tool to help organizations achieve their corporate strategy. We also explore the strategy of undertaking a project or programme of projects, how an organization approaches the need to deliver a project successfully.

## Chapter 2: Implementing strategy through programmes of projects

David Partington sets the scene for the book in Chapter 2. He describes the relationship between project management and corporate strategy, and shows that they are mutually dependent disciplines: without project management, strategists cannot implement their plans; without strategic management, project managers will implement the wrong things. He discusses several issues arising from this synergy. He then describes some of the pitfalls encountered in adopting the programme approach. Many of the issues he introduces are addressed in subsequent chapters.

## Chapter 3: Managing programmes of projects

In Chapter 3 Ruth Murray-Webster and Michel Thiry examine the management of a portfolio of projects, managed together for added advantage. They consider a definition of programme management, and show how it covers several different types of programmes. They explain how programmes and projects are different, and how programmes link projects to corporate strategy. They also give a brief overview of the programme management processes as an introduction to Chapter 7.

### Chapter 4: Projects and project management

Rodney Turner describes projects and their management in Chapter 4. This is, of course, the core topic of this book, but the two previous chapters should have set projects in the context of the parent organization and the programme of which they are a part. In this chapter Rodney Turner describes the three dimensions of project management. The first is the nature of projects and the features which make their management different from the management of routine operations. The second is the management of the projects and the life cycle approach required to address their transience. Finally there are the levels, which integrate work of projects with the strategy of the programme and parent organization. He also considers three additional issues, the cultural element of projects, coping with projects with uncertain goals and work methods, and project management as sailing a yacht.

### Chapter 5: Project success and strategy

In Chapter 5 Rodney Turner considers how we judge projects to be successful and how a knowledge of the success criteria can be used to derive a strategy for the successful implementation of projects. He introduces the seven forces model and links this to the Body of Knowledge.

### Chapter 6: Processes and procedures

In Chapter 6 Richard Pharro considers the use of project processes and procedures. Rodney Turner showed in Chapter 4 that the transience of projects implies their management is more process-based than functionally based and the life cycle represents that process. Several standard procedures have been developed to represent the process, including BS6079, PRINCE 2 and ISO 10,006. Many organizations develop their own standard procedures and these will be tailored to an individual procedures manual for each project.

### Chapter 7: Information systems for programme management

Geoff Reiss describes the use of information systems in the management of programmes of projects in Chapter 7. He assesses the different types of systems available, showing how these systems fall short of the needs of programme management. He then presents several models of the need for programme management systems and gives a vision of the future. He also describes four essential roles of programme management.

## Chapter 8: The programme and project support office

David Marsh describes the programme and project support office in Chapter 8. He explains how to implement them, and outlines the functions of each. He also describes the elements of a cost–benefit analysis of adopting a project support office, showing the costs, but also the expected savings.

## Chapter 9: Project health checks

In Chapter 9 John Wateridge describes health checks and audits. He discusses the use of post-implementation reviews to learn from the successes and failures of completed projects, and health checks to review progress in a project underway. He also introduces audits as a tool to prevent undersirable outcomes, especially those arising from illegal behaviour.

# 2 Implementing strategy through programmes of projects

*David Partington*

In the last few decades, and in particular since the early 1980s, the increasingly complex commercial environment has focused the attention of business leaders on achieving and sustaining the economic performance of their organizations. The resulting emphasis on the determinants of success and failure of firms has led to a sharp growth in interest in the formulation and implementation of corporate strategy. The discipline of strategic management has thus become significant, both as a field of academic study and as an essential senior management activity.

Strategic management, like the modern forms of project management (which are the subject of this handbook), has had a short and dramatic rise to prominence. It is no coincidence that the two disciplines have grown in parallel, since they are closely related. They share a central concern for change in the world of organizations, a world which is changing faster than ever before. In the last few decades of the twentieth century businesses were faced with unprecedented social and technological developments, accompanied by wide-reaching shifts in the global competitive and legislative environment. Individuals, firms and sectors were bombarded with a quickening succession of sudden threats and extraordinary opportunities.

This powerful cocktail of change has led to growing economic volatility, causing profound and irreversible changes in the nature of managerial work. Many established managers, whose competence was previously based on a highly developed ability to operate in a command-and-control hierarchy, are seeing a relentless erosion of the value and relevance of their skills. In the new world, members of an emerging breed of effective managers know that an instinct for striking a balance between defining and planning the unknowable, while moving forward with purposeful action, has become an essential 'sixth sense'.

The stark challenge facing corporate leaders today is to bring about perpetual change in a desired direction, both *on* and *within* an increasingly unstable world.

Firms must find ways of blending agility with direction, creativity with control and flexibility with structure. In an attempt to cope with paradoxes such as these, corporate and business strategies are increasingly designated and managed as internal programmes of change, each with defined business aims and implementation plans. Further, mirroring the different levels of strategy in an organization, strategic programmes are broken down into discrete interrelated projects with cost, schedule and quality objectives.

This chapter reviews the attractions and challenges of implementing strategy through programmes of projects. The chapter has two principal themes. First, it examines the underlying reasons for the rapid growth in the programme and project approach, which has arisen from the match between the fundamental principles of project management and current ideas about strategic management. Second, it describes the challenges and pitfalls inherent in adopting project and programme management for implementing strategy.

## STRATEGY AND PROJECTS

The developing integration of the disciplines of strategic management and project management is an important part of the current transformation of organizational life. Several important environmental trends have been accompanied by developments in understanding about the ways organizations work. Together these factors have tended to attract strategic leaders to a structured programme and project management approach to the implementation of strategic change. These factors are discussed below.

### INTEGRATING STRATEGIC PLANNING AND IMPLEMENTATION

In the early years of strategic management, analysts sought to determine management best practice by identifying the strategies that led to superior financial performance. The focus was on *what* strategies led to success, rather than *how* they should be implemented. As a result, in the 1960s and 1970s, early studies of corporate strategy in practice, under labels such as 'business policy' and 'general management', emphasized the formative, planning stages of strategy. Subsequently, demands for greater analytical and theoretical sophistication in formulating strategy were met by writers such as Michael Porter (1980, 1985). His ideas about competitive strategy provided a framework for executives to analyse their industrial environment. Managers could identify which generic strategies would help to maximize their firm's performance by using models introduced by Porter and other writers, including the five forces model, the value chain, Ansoff's matrix, the product portfolio matrix and others.

However, these early developments under-emphasized the process of putting plans into practice. In the 1980s, as more and more seemingly rational strategies were seen to fail, ideas about the role of top management in the execution of strategy changed. Foreign competition and industrial decline, especially in the USA, led to an intensification of interest in Japanese-influenced work practices and in overcoming resistance to change in implementing them. It was becoming apparent not only that implementing strategy was at least as challenging as planning it, but also that the pace of change in the commercial environment meant it was no longer possible to separate planning from implementation. Strategic managers needed processes that could integrate the two stages.

Coincidentally, many organizations were gaining experience in the use of formalized project management processes. Many of these early project management 'methodologies' were designed for use on internal information systems/information technology (IS/IT) development projects. They were based on practices developed in the mature project industries such as aerospace, defence and petrochemicals. Partly because of their conceptual origins in 'external', client–contractor endeavours, these early IS/IT-oriented project management procedures tended to emphasize delivery of the systems' technical functionality rather than the implementation problems commonly associated with their adoption.

Studies increasingly showed that IS/IT project failures were more commonly attributable to management's failure to address 'people issues' than to technical challenges (Wateridge 1995; Pinto and Millet 1999). Awareness of the need for 'soft' project management skills was growing, and project managers with talent in integrating technical and behavioural aspects were in demand.

For many organizations, it was a logical step to capitalize on their IS/IT project management know-how, and to extend existing project management processes to the integration and implementation of all aspects of strategy and organizational development, not just those parts that were directly associated with IS/IT. By focusing on the delivery of business benefits, using an integrative, disciplined approach which paid attention to soft as well as hard aspects, the ultimate likelihood of success in implementing strategic plans was enhanced. Thus modern ideas about project management have evolved from their traditional origins in large engineering projects in the post-Second World War era, through their later appearance in systems development projects, to their present role embracing the implementation of all forms of strategic organizational change.

## USING SEPARATE PROCESSES TO BRING ABOUT CHANGE

The implementation choice facing strategic leaders may be simplified and expressed as two extreme alternatives. At one end of the spectrum, broad corporate missions and strategic objectives may be set by senior managers as the basis for detailed planning and implementation by divisional, regional and departmental managers, using existing organizational processes within the existing structure. The danger of this approach comes from the assumption that existing cultures and business processes can change themselves, or that systems designed for managing the routine can be used to manage change. In reality, ideas can easily become diffused, diluted, compromised or postponed as managers and staff resist what they see as wave after wave of undesirable or contradictory directives. At best, intended benefits remain only partially realized. The alternative is to implement corporate change initiatives separately, using temporary processes and structures, through integrated programmes of projects. A properly coordinated programme approach has the clear, well-established advantage that it enables change to be managed outside the constraining norms and processes of the existing culture.

## INTEGRATION ACROSS STRATEGIC LEVELS

Three different levels of strategy are commonly distinguished:

1. At the *corporate* level, strategy is concerned with what businesses the company as a whole should be in, and with justifying why – in terms of added value – those business units should be grouped together corporately.
2. At the *business* level, strategy involves determining what markets a business unit is competing in, how it should compete, where it wants to go and how it should get there. The answer to the last question will result in the creation of programmes of projects to enable business units to achieve their strategies.
3. *Operational* level strategies focus on the role of individual departments and functions (marketing, human resources, manufacturing, finance, etc.), and on individual programmes or projects, in delivering the business level strategy.

The hierarchical relationship between strategies at different levels finds full resonance with the fundamental premise of work breakdown underlying the programme and project approach. Corporate level strategies represent the highest level of programmes. These are subdivided into a linked hierarchy of lower-level programmes and projects at the business and operational levels. In this way organization-wide goals and missions may be translated into systematically coordinated action without losing sight of overarching objectives. At each level the full benefits of effective project management may be obtained, with each programme or project having its own objectives, scope, resources, schedule and designated leader.

## THE NEED FOR CONTROLLED FLEXIBILITY

In addition to the increasing focus on strategic implementation, there has been a growing acceptance that it is impossible to separate the processes of strategic choice from implementation as a deterministic sequence of activities. The reason is clear. The business blueprint on which a chosen strategy has been based will almost certainly undergo continual change over the implementation life cycle. Unless the organization is able to remain focused on the alignment between business activities, capabilities and environment, and to make timely adjustments to its strategic direction, it will always be pursuing the wrong strategy. Concern for formulating effective, agile business strategy has therefore been accompanied by a growing realization of the benefits of implementing that strategy as a series of flexible, integrated programmes and projects of change.

In this context flexibility does not mean that managers should be constantly reacting in an uncontrolled way to every event or environmental shift which might be impacting on their organization's portfolio of change programmes. On the contrary, once an organization has embarked on a defined strategic programme the process by which it deviates from that programme should be as carefully managed as the process by which the programme was initiated. Programme and project management offer controlled flexibility in two ways. First, by applying the discipline of formalized change control, the full implications of a defined change in a project's scope can be assessed before the change is formally approved. Second, having agreed and approved a change of objectives and scope, the full effects of changes, even those with organization-wide impact, can be cascaded and controlled through the hierarchy of corporate, business and operational programmes and projects.

## THE EFFECTIVENESS OF TEAM-BASED STRUCTURES

One of the most important and pervasive changes in the recent history of organizations has been the move towards the arrangement of non-routine tasks as project work in temporary team-based structures, each with a designated leader. The logic behind this trend is based on two simple features of organizational life.

The first is concerned with the problems inherent in multiple accountability for defining and executing project tasks. In an organization which is structured as a pure functional hierarchy, projects will almost certainly suffer problems of definition of responsibility between departments such as marketing, finance and production. Some project activities will overlap more than one department, possibly leading to duplication, misunderstanding and unproductive conflict. Other activities will 'fall between the cracks', with no department assuming responsibility for their execution.

The problems associated with departmental responsibility may be addressed through the use of matrix organization structures. Within such an arrangement, individuals are partly or fully seconded from their functional department to one or more projects, with their contribution to each project controlled by a project leader. The matrix approach supposedly combines the benefits of a task-focused, integrated project team with the stability and continuity of expertise offered by a departmental hierarchy. Sometimes a purer form of project organization is preferred, in which individuals are brought together solely for the execution of a single project. Whether a pure project structure or a matrix compromise is adopted for the implementation of a change initiative, the project team approach is likely to offer significant advantages of improved definition and control over the purely functional alternative.

The second reason for the rise of the project team is the speed of execution which results from the team's focus on the project task and objectives. On strategic projects where speed is important, such as the acquisition and integration of another firm or the development of a new product, a project team is more likely to provide the flexibility needed to enable the organization to beat the competition to successfully exploit a strategic opportunity.

## THE RISE OF COOPERATIVE STRATEGIES

Increasingly, strategies involve the planning, development and dissolution of alliances between organizations. Frequently these are global, although it is not just international alliances that are associated with competitive strength. Domestic alliances are common. When firms do not have the time to develop essential new skills to meet a new market, they are increasingly likely to try to acquire those skills through an alliance. As well as such horizontal alliances, vertical links are widespread. Firms are urged to improve performance by moving work between their organization and its customers and suppliers. In the new spirit of cooperation distributors and retailers may become surrogate employees.

As team-based and cooperative strategies for coping with the pace of change become the norm, boundaries within and between organizations are becoming increasingly blurred. This trend places a premium on integrating mechanisms which minimize those aspects of the cooperative venture which may be left to chance. The effective management of alliances has become an important and specialized integrating role, calling for the kinds of skills inherent in the project approach. State-of-the-art methodologies for the effective management of the cooperative process emphasize systematic identification of the objectives and scope of an alliance. They direct managers towards formal analysis of the roles and responsibilities of its partners over a calculable, finite life cycle.

## THE CENTRALITY OF ORGANIZATIONAL LEARNING

The notion of organizational knowledge as a resource has gathered momentum. The growing popularity of the 'resource-based' view of the firm among strategic leaders reflects this. The resource-based view holds that firms achieve competitive advantage through the development and application of idiosyncratic firm resources. In order to achieve sustainable advantage, these resources must be valuable, rare, costly to imitate and non-substitutable. They might include tangible and intangible resources, including employee skills and capabilities, firm reputation, patents, brands, unique locations or technologies, unique routines, and organizational capabilities such as manufacturing or product development methodologies.

The premium value attached to knowledge-intensive capabilities is further enhanced by the constant need for firms to experiment, to envisage the future and to test their ideas about the way they should be changing. As a result, strategies are increasingly concerned with the acquisition, internal development, accumulation, exploitation and diffusion of knowledge. This trend has great significance for the programme and project approach to the implementation of change at all levels. If change is allowed to happen in an ad hoc fashion, significant opportunities for organizational learning will be missed. It is widely acknowledged that if an organization is able to learn by means of a formalized, organization-wide process of programme and project review it will have a significant competitive advantage.

## CHALLENGES OF THE PROGRAMME APPROACH

The experience of many firms has shown that a simple, structured, realistic, well-communicated programme approach to planning and implementing change enhances the likelihood of success in delivering planned benefits. The approach does, however, present several fundamental management challenges. These are discussed below.

## MISUNDERSTANDING THE ROLES OF MANAGERS AND SPONSORS

One of the more widespread problems for firms which are new to the project approach is failure to understand the respective roles of the project manager and the project sponsor. The project manager's task is often defined in relation to the achievement of the traditional project objectives: cost, schedule and quality. The sponsor's two basic duties are 1) to ensure that projects align with strategy, and remain so throughout their life cycle, and 2) to take primary responsibility for the delivery of the projects' quantified business benefits. Frequently, even when the project manager's task is well understood, the sponsor's is not. Two problems commonly arise:

1. The wrong individual assumes the sponsorship role. This may be because he or she has no direct, overriding stake in the project, in the sense of being the senior manager with the 'most to lose' if the project fails. Alternatively, it may be because the prevailing organizational culture allows – or even encourages – the sponsor to delegate the role to someone lower down the organization.
2. The sponsor can become over-involved in the detail, undermining the essential autonomy and responsibility of the project manager.

Two documents, the Business Requirements Definition (BRD) and Project Requirements Definition (PRD), are commonly used to help overcome these problems by defining and separating the two roles at the outset of a project. These two definition documents are used to provide as precise a mandate as possible for the project manager. It is in the interests of both parties to take the opportunity at the outset of the project to define *why* the project is being done (the sponsor's responsibility), and *what* it entails (the project manager's responsibility). The typical content of the documents is as follows.

1. *Business Requirements Definition (BRD)*
   1.1 Business aims
   1.2 Summary project description
   1.3 Indication of project's priority within business
   1.4 Performance requirements (musts and wants)
   1.5 Project objectives (cost, time, quality and relative priorities)
   1.6 Constraints
   1.7 Success criteria (quantify measurable business aims)

2. *Project Requirements Definition (PRD)*
   2.1 Refinements of all BRD elements
   2.2 Project scope
   2.3 Deliverables
   2.4 Functional requirements, to meet performance requirements

2.5 Acceptance criteria

2.6 Risk analysis

2.7 Assumptions

A project is more likely to succeed with the benefit of a thoroughly developed BRD and PRD, which should also be simple and precise.

## BARRIERS TO ORGANIZATIONAL LEARNING

It is widely accepted that the only successful competitive business organizations in the future will be those that exploit their intellectual capital – building, maintaining and using an effective knowledge base. For strategic implementers this means learning lessons from the success and failure of every product market innovation, every corporate alliance, every IS/IT initiative and every internal restructuring. Projects provide opportunities for formalized learning through an effective project review system. However, as experienced project managers know, two factors mitigate against project reviews achieving their full potential:

1. It is a fact of project life that at the end of any project, when significant opportunities exist for consolidating learning, key people will simply no longer be there to contribute. The most effective review processes are often those which take opportunities for consolidating learning not just at the end of the project, but at key points and at regular intervals in the project's life cycle.

2. Many organizations admit the existence of a 'blame culture', which proves to be a highly effective deterrent to learning from past mistakes. In addition, psychologists tell us that it is human nature to take credit for good performance but to blame the environment for poor performance. It is therefore doubly important for senior managers to deal with those aspects of an organization's culture which discourage openness to learning. Even without such constraints the pace of change will ensure that the appropriate dissemination and organization-wide use of learning will remain a challenge.

A further strategic issue relating to organizational learning is the growing need for strategists to focus on cross-sector activity, not just firms operating in their own sector. Unless an organization is consistently the first among its competitors to exploit each new technological development, to surmount each successive socio-organizational problem, to anticipate the full effects of each new legislative change, it will have to wait for a competitor to get there first. Those who are unable to learn across sectors will always be running to catch up. Fear of sharing knowledge is increasingly becoming a dinosaur trait. Those who are able to learn from organizations outside their own industry sector will stand to win.

## CONFLICTS OF PRIORITIZATION AND RESOURCE ALLOCATION

Inevitably, projects in organizations compete for resources. In organizations where strategic initiatives are allowed to devolve in an uncontrolled way, the prioritization issues become localized, with different line managers in different parts of the organization taking their own priority decisions, based on their own views about the order of importance of different project and non-project responsibilities. The resulting lack of direction is one of the strongest arguments for a centralized, project-based approach to corporate-wide change. In a structure where projects are separated and coordinated by senior sponsors, the resource issue is naturally more manageable, but two potential problems remain:

1. There is a danger of over-simplification. If project X is declared to have higher priority than project Y, this can easily be interpreted as a requirement to satisfy *all* of project X's resource requirements ahead of project Y's. In such circumstances project Y might be stifled completely, despite any claims to merit. This problem can be reinforced by the unthinking use of computer-based planning and scheduling tools for multiproject resourcing which work on the basis of this blunt, absolute approach. Often a more balanced view is appropriate, using a flexible resource plan which may be less than ideal but which nevertheless allows both projects to proceed.
2. Resource prioritization problems can occur when staff are seconded from their functional department to work on a project and their departmental managers are expected to operate just the same without them. Where departmental managers' performance criteria relate to their dealings with customers, their reaction when asked to lose their scarce operational staff to projects is predictably reticent. This problem is common in process intensive organizations, for example financial services and retail, which may for good reasons be relative newcomers to the project environment. The clear implication, which is sometimes difficult for cost-conscious senior managers to accept, is that every change agenda has a cost over and above the operational needs of the company. Businesses must be adequately resourced for change, not just staffed at the minimum level for dealing with operational needs.

## REWARDING A PROJECT CULTURE

Many organizations adopting project-based management approaches to change experience problems arising from the fundamentally different nature of projects from their day-to-day operational routines. Two issues relating to the reward of project performance in such organizations may need to be addressed:

1. Staff who are asked to move temporarily from their departmental 'home' to work on a project can feel they are being punished, sidelined away from the real business into something which will end, possibly signalling the termination of their employment with the company. In these circumstances, the company needs to work towards establishing a culture in which project work is seen as highly valued. Managers should find ways of rewarding project secondees and fostering a positive attitude towards projects. Some organizations address this issue by making project work an important component of the staff appraisal process and an essential prerequisite for promotion at all levels.

2. Hourly paid overtime is often the norm in companies which deal with a fluctuating, deadline-sensitive workload. In the project environment, however, it is rarely an effective way of increasing productivity, except in the very short term when an extra push may be needed to meet a particular project deadline. Companies developing a project culture often find that allowing project managers to reward staff effort through bonuses for meeting project targets is more cost-effective, more productive and ultimately more popular with project staff than overtime.

## RESISTING OVER-BUREAUCRATIC PROJECT MANAGEMENT PROCESSES

Project management has become a burgeoning profession in which many people make a living from selling project management training programmes and packaged project management systems, processes and methodologies. Firms lacking project management experience are sometimes encouraged to embark on initiatives to procure and introduce over-complex project management processes and to train staff in their use. An unfortunate consequence in some cases is that 'project management' is seen as inherently complex and bureaucratic, and is abandoned. Two implications need to be borne in mind:

1. Modern project management has evolved from the need to bring integration and control to technically complex, multi-organization engineering and systems projects. Some of the discipline's most fundamental principles are universally relevant, whatever the project. These include the concept of the project having a finite life cycle and that of the project manager being the single point of integrative responsibility. The appropriateness and applicability of other aspects of project management are strongly dependent on the characteristics of the particular project and its context. It should not be assumed that the degree of planning and control formality and the applicability of tools and techniques

should be consistent across projects. Project management's full-blown bureaucratic weaponry may be entirely appropriate on large capital-intensive projects. On many classes of project, however, it is possible to achieve the benefits of project management by paying attention to the basics, but using a process that is simple and flexible.

2. A common objective of strategic initiatives is to encourage participation, abandon hierarchy, foster team work and empower individuals. Introducing project management is itself an example of such an initiative. If project management is introduced in a heavy-handed, top-down, expert-led way, this sends the wrong message. If procedures have not been developed with appropriate input from users, the users inevitably view them with lack of ownership, even alienation, especially if they are based on an imported generic package. The most successful project management methodologies are based on the kinds of projects typically undertaken by the firm. They are developed with managed input from users, taking into account key aspects of corporate and national culture.

## ACCEPTING PARADOX AND UNCERTAINTY

Along with growing uncertainty about the future, both for individuals and organizations, there has been a move away from management approaches which over-emphasize rationality and predictability towards those which embrace paradox and uncertainty. The decline of the stable organizational hierarchy has been accompanied by a decline in certain values which used to be prized, such as technical perfection, compliance and respect for tradition. Such values have been displaced by more outward-looking, customer-focused ideals, as well as concerns for creativity, resourcefulness and solutions to new problems which are practical, if imperfect. In the new regime, what people have done in the past is increasingly unimportant compared with what they are doing now. Employees need to seek new projects as a learning vehicle, relying less on paternalistic notions of continuity and career progression.

Essential aspects of project life, such as the need to tolerate uncertainty, perpetual change and transience, create a match between the project and programme approach and the new management paradigm. As a result, project management and team-working skills are at a premium and in some industries in short supply. Many organizations introducing project-based approaches are faced with the problem that not everybody has either the inclination or the aptitude for working in this uncertain world. Such skill shortfall may be addressed partly through training and team-building activities and partly through recruitment, although some firms find that recruiting staff with the right skills and attitudes can be difficult, especially when staff selection processes have no effective way of appraising project team skills.

## CONCLUSIONS

This chapter has shown why, for many organizations, project management's time has come. Across the range of commercial sectors a new alignment is arising between the principles of project management and the needs of strategic management. The chapter has also pointed out some of the pitfalls in implementing and maintaining a culture of project and programme management. There is no doubt that the implementation of planned strategic change is difficult. It challenges the skills of managers at all organizational levels to the limit and beyond. It demands a highly professional approach. A mark of experienced professionals in any sphere of endeavour is that when asked to do a job they will first demand that they have at least the minimum necessary raw materials and tools. Those who are charged with introducing or applying the project approach should think carefully before attempting such an undertaking. Their tool kit is the autonomy and opportunity to do the job, the necessary financial and human resources and the self-belief – that comes from education and experience – in their competence to overcome resistance and to build the necessary support.

## REFERENCES AND FURTHER READING

Buchanan, D. A. and Boddy, D. (1992), *The Expertise of the Change Agent*, Prentice-Hall, New York.

Cleland, D. I. and Gareis, R. (eds) (1994), *Global Project Management Handbook*, McGraw-Hill, London.

Felkins, P. K., Chakiris, B. J. and Chakiris, K. N. (1993), *Change Management: A Model for Effective Organizational Performance*, Quality Resources, New York.

Hatch, M. J. (1997), *Organization Theory: Modern, Symbolic-Interpretive and Postmodern Perspectives*, Oxford University Press, Oxford.

Johnson, G. and Scholes, K. (1997), *Exploring Corporate Strategy: Text and Cases*, Prentice-Hall, London.

Pinto, J. K. and Millet, I. (1999), *Successful Information Systems Implementation: The Human Side*, 2nd edition, Project Management Institute, Sylva, NC.

Porter, M. E. (1980), *Competitive Strategy*, Free Press, New York.

Porter, M. E. (1985), *Competitive Advantage*, Free Press, New York.

Turner, J. R., Grude, K. V. and Thurloway, L. (1996), *The Project Manager as Change Agent*, McGraw-Hill, London.

Wateridge, J. F. (1995), 'IT projects: a basis for success', *International Journal of Project Management*, **13**(3).

## RELATED TOPICS

| | |
|---|---|
| Tools for strategic analysis | Porter 1980, 1985; Johnson and Scholes 1997 |
| Business case for the project | Chapter 13 |
| Functionality and value | Chapter 14 |
| Proposal and feasibility | Chapter 25 |
| Project appraisal | Chapter 27 |

# 3 Managing programmes of projects

## Ruth Murray-Webster and Michel Thiry

This chapter considers the management of programmes of projects, that is the actual management of a portfolio of projects to achieve additional benefit. Chapter 2 described how organizations achieve their corporate strategy through programmes of projects. This chapter describes a strategy for undertaking those programmes. The chapter starts by defining programme management and describing various configurations of programmes. It then shows how programmes help link projects and strategy and gives an overview of the methods and techniques used. Chapter 7 describes systems for implementing those tools and techniques.

## WHAT IS PROGRAMME MANAGEMENT?

The discipline of programme management (or program management) is emerging as a fundamental method of ensuring that an organization gains maximum benefit from the integration of project management activities. As with any emergent discipline, there are variations in the interpretation and implementation of programme principles, methods and techniques used by different organizations and practitioners. Significant work on programme management was carried out in 1994 by the Central Computer and Telecommunications Agency (CCTA) looking at the management of information systems (IS) related programmes in governmental organizations. This work was revised in 1999. The CCTA's definition of programme management is:

> Programme management is the co-ordinated management of a portfolio of projects that change organisations to achieve benefits that are of strategic importance.
>
> (CCTA 1999)

The discipline is clearly significant in sectors other than those associated with information systems, and other definitions have emerged since 1994.

Organizations have used the term 'programme' or 'program' to define a number of things, from a collection of projects with something in common to very large projects! Our own experience with a number of organizations has led us to define programmes as follows. The concept of purposefulness is central to this definition.

> A programme is a collection of change actions (projects and operational activities) purposefully grouped together to realize strategic and/or tactical benefits.

Increasingly there is a recognition that programmes should be the means of ensuring that an organization's strategy and initiatives are efficiently and coherently implemented, a way of dealing with emergent change in the business environment and a way of gaining optimal use of resources:

> Unaligned organization is a waste of energy, whereas commonality of direction develops resonance and synergy.
>
> (Tsuchiya 1997)

Project management has wide-ranging and proven benefits – including an ability to implement change effectively within an organization. The emergence of programme management as a discipline should not be seen as a devaluation of project management; on the contrary, the effective implementation of programme management enables project managers and projects to achieve their objectives even more effectively.

A key question, therefore, is 'Why is effective project management not enough?' At the heart of the answer are issues relating to change in the business environment. Change is accelerating and some aspects of the nature of the change are mutually exclusive to project management, like emergent (unplanned) change for example. The pressure to change can come from both external and internal sources to the organization, therefore falling outside the scope of project management. Externally, it is triggered by customers, competition, shareholders and other stakeholders; internally, by personnel driven by changing needs for systems, structures, culture and management styles. Additionally, the incremental nature of change often results in what is called a 'change deficit', where the rate of externally driven change is faster than the internal response to that change. The implications of this for business success are obvious.

Accordingly, strategic processes must take into account both deliberate and emergent change. A deliberate change is usually part of a strategy; most projects and project outcomes can be considered as a 'deliberate change'. Deliberate change is submitted to a formal process of analysis, design and planning; its implementation is subjected to a formal control process, which is usually initiated from the top down. An emergent change is caused by an unpredictable input that triggers a change in an ongoing process, it being a strategy, a project or ongoing operations. A mechanism for identifying and managing emergent change needs to be put in place in strategic and operational plans. Emergent change requires a reactive, adaptive strategy and is often initiated from the bottom up. David Hurst (1995) developed what he named an 'ecocycle' to describe change in organizations (Figure 3.1). In this figure, the solid line represents the 'performance loop' or 'conventional life cycle', triggered by choice; the dotted line represents the 'learning loop', triggered by crisis. Projects should have a sound mainstream management process and, at the same time, maintain the capability to deal with emergent changes at different stages of development.

Project management is effective when the aims and business case for the project can be stated as clear and measurable objectives of time, cost and performance (or quality). Once these objectives are established, the project manager needs to focus and lead the team towards their achievement. Changes to project objectives must be managed in a formal and structured way and are seen as a risk (see Chapter 15). Frequent changes, or changes that affect the fundamental aims of the project, deflect focus from the project team and can cause confusion at best and serious demotivation at worst. Thus, projects are the most effective vehicle for delivering deliberate or planned change in an organization, once a choice has been made, and are not meant to address frequent or fundamental changes in objectives, more associated with crisis.

The nature of emergent change is such that rapid responses are often required to maintain the organization's competitive position or compliance with market

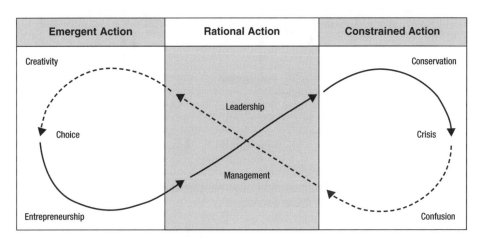

**Figure 3.1 The change eco-cycle**
*Source*: Adapted from Hurst (1995: 103)

and/or regulatory expectations. Such responses may mean modifying or replacing existing project objectives with more appropriate solutions, altering the relative priority between projects, utilizing key staff in different areas of the business or any other such actions. Best practice project management is difficult to achieve when the scope and/or deliverables are wide-ranging or unclear. It is not reasonable to expect project managers and project teams to:

- focus on delivering specific project objectives; *and*
- develop effective responses to emergent change.

The capabilities and competencies required to deal with these issues differ widely; the latter requires a broad organizational perspective, the former a focused view of the deliverables. Organizations must recognize this fact and develop effective structural responses to address it. Additionally, the claim of some organizations that 'all work is a project' often goes too far; an integrative framework for projects *and* 'business as usual' is needed, rather than a forced fit of all work into projects. Figure 3.2 shows programme management as 'the missing link' – the means of effectively bridging the gap between a strategy, subjected to emergent change, and projects. Crucially, programme management can be the vehicle in the organization for ensuring that strategic needs are actually implemented and planned benefits delivered.

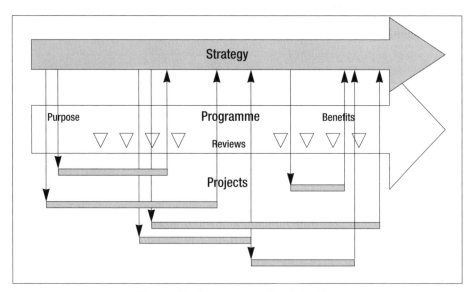

Figure 3.2 Programmes as the missing link

## PROJECTS AND PROGRAMMES: KEY DIFFERENCES

Within projects, business objectives are translated into finite time, cost and performance (quality) objectives. In programmes, business needs and expectations, derived from broad stakeholder analysis, are translated into benefits through more fluid objectives. One could say that projects are aimed at achieving set deliverables with the least possible resources, whereas programmes are aimed at making best use of resources to achieve the most benefits. Whereas projects require a more 'efficient' approach, programmes will strive for a more 'effective' perspective, very much based on the principles of value management.

Within projects, benefits are delivered through a single undertaking and relatively short life cycle. In programmes, benefits are delivered incrementally by each project and action undertaken during the life cycle of the programme; they can correspond to a product, a strategy, a market opportunity, a change process or even the organization's survival. Subprojects, within a project, represent distinct work packages derived through breakdown of the project's outcome and, as such, their own outcome is directly related to the project deliverable. Projects and other work within programmes are not defined through task decomposition, it is more the grouping, or combining of those, which contributes to the programme's outcome (organizational benefits).

In terms of leadership skills, the project manager needs to be proactive and task focused to deliver specific outcomes; it is a directive role. A programme is an organizing framework that requires prioritization, management of interfaces, communication skills at a high organizational level and improved resource utilization across the organization. The programme manager needs to be aware of strategic objectives and wide business benefits; it is a facilitative, enabling role.

## PROGRAMME CONFIGURATIONS

As with all emergent disciplines, several perspectives exist on the optimal ways to configure programmes to achieve strategic objectives and deal with change. As previously stated, in all cases programmes require some purposeful grouping of work focused on achieving business objectives. Three configurations have emerged from research into how organizations actually manage programmes (Pellegrinelli 1997). Different practitioners may use different descriptors for each configuration but the underlying principles remain the same.

## PORTFOLIO OR CHUNKED CONFIGURATION

Perhaps the most obvious configuration is where projects and other associated work are grouped around a common *theme*. This common theme may be a business unit, knowledge area and/or group of resources. Primary advantages of portfolio programmes are related to organizational efficiency. Benefits are that they:

- facilitate project prioritization where necessary;
- provide a mechanism for focusing scarce resources;
- enable better resource allocation and utilization;
- identify and manage dependencies;
- leverage existing knowledge and skills;
- highlight weaknesses in capabilities and development needs;
- ease control over multiple projects.

## STRATEGIC OR GOAL-ORIENTED CONFIGURATION

In this configuration, projects and other work are grouped around a common *aim* or *purpose*. This common aim is most often a strategic objective where there can be some uncertainty of the specific final outcomes. Projects and other work will not all be defined at the start of the programme – work can be added or taken away in a coordinated and consolidated way, focused on the primary business aims and benefits. The advantages of strategic programmes are related to organizational effectiveness. Benefits are that they:

- translate business needs into tangible actions;
- foster learning loop and creativity;
- reduce uncertainty and ambiguity through iterative development;
- support integrated review and approval processes;
- allow integration of emergent inputs;
- recognize chaos theories (see Planning phase, pp. 58–9).

## INCREMENTAL OR HEARTBEAT CONFIGURATION

In this configuration, projects and other work are grouped around a common *platform*. This platform may be a process, business system or infrastructure. Primary advantage of incremental programmes are related to effectively coordinating and integrating business-wide continuous improvement initiatives. Benefits are that they:

- provide an integrative framework for continuous improvement;
- group initiatives into coherent and efficient actions;

- release changes in controlled 'heartbeats';
- enable continuous reassessment within holistic perspective;
- support short-term requests with long-term strategy;
- capture bottom-up innovation initiatives.

None of these configurations needs to be used alone. Every situation or organization requires one or more of these programme configurations. Whether an organization uses these terms and groupings or others, the ultimate objective is to find ways to manage work in a way that:

- uses limited resources to maximize results;
- achieves business and stakeholder benefits;
- optimizes emergent change and captures bottom-up initiatives;
- avoids delivery of solutions no longer needed by the customers ('white elephants').

Whatever the configuration, programmes should provide a framework where:

- changes can easily be identified;
- causes and effects should be clear;
- benefits and risks are clearly outlined;

so that the organization can swiftly:

- interpret emergent inputs;
- adapt to correct mismatches;
- innovate to support opportunities.

## HOW PROGRAMMES LINK STRATEGY WITH PROJECTS

Organizational maturity is important to ensure the success of a programme culture. An organization must be ready to:

- acknowledge its own cultural perspective – shared interpretative framework;
- match the programme configuration to this perspective to create a strong foundation;
- develop a programme culture through a mix of structuring, training and doing;
- achieve a balance between firm central direction and maximum individual autonomy.

The strategic process within an organization analyses the cultural and political framework of the business – stakeholder expectations, business needs, market trends, environmental issues, human resources, knowledge management and business processes – and translates these into a set of strategic objectives and/or key performance indicators (KPI). Organizations require a method of translating these KPIs into clear, quantifiable goals for staff working in operations or projects, and of continuously assessing their suitability. Programmes can be the framework to achieve this. The programme life cycle can ensure that emergent change will be analysed and managed through a 'learning loop' of 'sensemaking' (Weick 1995), creativity and evaluation based on *value management* (see Chapter 14). Decisions made in response to change in the business environment can then be implemented through a 'performance loop' of planning, execution and control based on *project management*, as demonstrated in the Figure 3.3.

These 'learning loops' are repeated at each review/approval stage of a project to reassess deliverables against business objectives, using value management methodology. Different labels are attached to each stage of the programme life cycle by different practitioners. We have chosen to use familiar project management stages to label programme phases. Our experience has demonstrated that, in most cases, the programme life cycle needs to incorporate the key stages and actions shown in Figure 3.4. There are significant organizational implications linked to the implementation of programme management, in terms of structures, culture, management styles and working

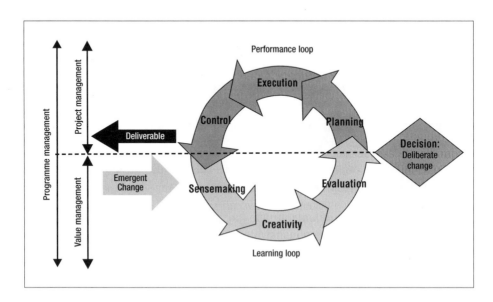

**Figure 3.3 The programme eco-cycle**
*Source*: Thiry 1999

practices, as well as the role and competency requirements of programme and project managers. All need to encourage free flow of information across projects and throughout the programme management organization – from contributors in the strategic process to staff and other key players in the value chain. Open sharing of issues and risks is required with well-defined procedures for change control, conflict escalation and resolution, often caused by prioritization of projects and allocation of resources. Both risks and opportunities need to be managed during the learning loop in order to achieve optimum benefits (Drucker 1989).

| Life cycle stage | Key actions |
|---|---|
| Definition | Identify purpose of programme |
| | Develop strategy (deliberate, emergent or combined) |
| | Analyse 'fit' of new requirements with other programmes and redefine as required |
| | Create organization for the programme |
| | Develop critical success factors (CSFs) and their relative priority |
| Planning | Establish creative process for optimal selection and grouping of projects and other work into the programme – best fit to deliver benefits |
| | Define project briefs/business case and get funding/approval for the first group of projects and other work |
| | Allocate responsibilities |
| | Develop review/approval system for projects and change management process |
| | Establish communication system within and outside the programme. |
| Implementation | Proactively assess and manage programme environment |
| | Reassess validity of plan on a continuous basis |
| | Analyse project and other work performance against CSFs |
| | Ensure planned processes and procedures are operational, including change and configuration management |
| | Manage stakeholder expectations against results |
| Appraisal | Assess performance against CSFs as well as emerging benefits |
| | Identify potential risks and opportunities – stop or modify projects if needed |
| | Analyse any emergent change from business environment |
| | Ensure that lessons are learned and registered for future feedback |
| | Loop back to programme definition to re-confirm or change elements therein |

Figure 3.4   Actions through the programme life cycle stages

# PROGRAMME METHODS AND TECHNIQUES

Several organizational and project management methods and techniques are useful for programme management.

## DEFINITION PHASE

The definition phase of the programme is the sensemaking step of the learning loop, where actors are making sense of the required response to a pressure to change. The first step is to analyse stakeholders' needs and expectations. Needs analysis is triggered by the stakeholders' expectations. Stakeholders can be defined as:

> Individuals or organizations positively or negatively affected by the outcomes of the programme and which may have an influence on it.

The programme management team needs to:

- identify the stakeholders;
- determine their needs and expectations;
- manage and influence those expectations.

The first step is to do a *stakeholder analysis* (see Chapters 42 and 43), a process to identify all the stakeholders and their potential influence on the programme. Usually the identification is performed through a brainstorming session. Stakeholders are then classified and categorized. We suggest five areas of classification, of which the team should use two:

1. Sector of activity (organization, supplier, customer, user, regulatory body, pressure group)
2. Decision-making level (policy-maker to implementation/operations)
3. Type of need:
    - hard benefits (economic, technical, operational)
    - soft benefits (power, politics, communications)
4. Structural layer (senior, middle or line management; team participant)
5. Influence of the project (rainmaker to affected party)

Once the stakeholders and their influence on the programme have been identified, the programme team and key stakeholders need to perform a *functional analysis* (see Chapter 14). The functional analysis consists of identifying the needs and expectations of each stakeholder to build them into a model called a function breakdown structure (FBS) (Thiry 1997) (Figure 3.5). The FBS represents the needs and expectations of the stakeholders, classified in order of importance from the 'purpose' of the programme to the actions required to accomplish it (soft to hard; intangible to tangible; abstract to concrete); it also identifies the critical success factors (CSFs). Figure 3.5 shows a partial FBS from an organizational change programme. It demonstrates the use of the 'how-why' logic to classify functions/objectives and uses the same rules as the work breakdown structure (WBS) to ensure proper scope coverage.

Once the team have identified the purpose of the programme through the FBS, they need to assess the measure of success of the programme by:

- verifying intent versus capability;
- setting scope and configuration;
- identifying 'performance targets';
- establishing 'criteria level tolerance'.

Financial criteria are not sufficient any more to ensure the success of a programme. Organizations must look at the whole picture of organizational effectiveness.

The EFQM Excellence Model® (Business Excellence Model) is an effective

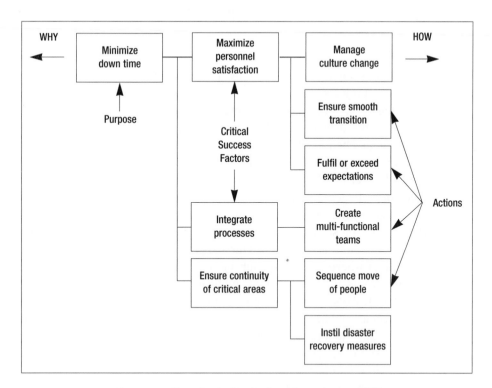

Figure 3.5   Example of a function breakdown structure (FBS)

tool for an organization to conduct self-assessment of all aspects of its operations from leadership and strategy formulation, through management of its people, customers and partners to business results measured in financial and non-financial terms. The model provides a framework which clearly demonstrates the linkages between business results and the approaches taken (cause and effect), and provides a simple methodology for organizational learning and continual improvement. The EFQM Excellence Model® is a proven tool for internal performance measurement and external benchmarking. Often linked to this, the balanced scorecard technique is increasingly used by leading organizations as a means of policy and strategy deployment. These techniques ensure the communication of clear, quantifiable goals through the organization. As such, the EFQM Excellence Model® and the balanced scorecard are a good framework for programmes, particularly as they promote the discipline of balance across financial, customer and internal business processes and learning and growth business elements, and require quantifiable goals for non-financial parameters.

This process constitutes the end of the definition phase. The programme management team is now ready to tackle the planning phase by choosing projects/actions that will constitute the programme.

## PLANNING PHASE

The planning phase consists of strategy planning and selection of actions (projects). As in projects, the strategy consists of integrating the activities required to deliver the expected benefits. The main difference is that the programme strategy will be of a much higher level than a project strategy and will allow for emergent change. It is labelled an 'umbrella' (only boundaries and guidelines set) or 'process' (influence through control points) strategy (Mintzberg and Waters 1985) and is akin to the chaos theory of management. The chaos theory of management states that it is not possible to predict any events and therefore plan with accuracy in the long term (Stacey 1993; Levy 1994).

The first step for the selection of actions is to generate alternatives; this is the creativity phase of the learning loop. Our experience recommends the use of creativity sessions where a cross-section of stakeholders is invited. The group must focus on benefits, defer judgement and be innovative (use cross-fertilization and piggybacking). We strongly recommend the use of an external facilitator for these sessions. One could ask: 'Why use creativity sessions?' Our answer is: to overcome resistance to change; structure the creative process; avoid early rejection of ideas; control overpowering individuals; encourage shy individuals; and generate a large number of ideas.

The evaluation phase consists of evaluating the options generated in the creativity phase. The first step is to establish the selection criteria. These will be based on the CSFs established earlier, but should be at a more tangible and measurable level. Ideas are categorized and prioritized using a number of methods, depending on the time available and the complexity of the problem. A number of ideas are then selected to be developed. The evaluation process comprises the following steps:

1. Eliminating unfeasible or impractical alternatives.
2. Classifying alternatives in terms of the selection criteria.
3. Identifying risks and opportunities (advantages and disadvantages) for each.
4. Balancing between intuitive (qualitative) and rational (quantitative) assessment.
5. Developing a choice matrix based on achievability/benefits or probability/impact.

The benefits of the implementation of risk management at a project level are undisputed. Risk management supports decision-making in uncertain circumstances, enables the adjustment of strategy to counter threats and exploit opportunities, and can maximize advantages through a proactive approach. At a programme level, risk management is focused on strategic and programme specific aspects including inter-project issues and is predominantly associated with wide-ranging stakeholders and business uncertainties. The tools and techniques of risk management in programmes are similar to those in projects but with a wider perspective. But, especially with programmes, effective strategies should be focused on maximizing opportunities, and action should not be based solely on risk avoidance, which is merely a limitation to action.

## IMPLEMENTATION PHASE

The implementation phase of programmes mainly consists of the review, alignment and approval process and change/configuration management, which are the link between the organizational strategy and the projects. The review process is usually linked to the project gateways and many organizations have developed extensive procedures for this process. Figure 3.6 shows how the review process could be implemented for a project.

The objectives of the change management process are to influence the factors that create change, determine that a change has occurred, identify the scope of changes and manage the actual changes. The methods used to achieve these objectives are value management and risk management; the tools consist of change requests (if needed), corrective measures and a change control system. The change control system requires the programme manager to take the following action:

1. Define a value-based process for change-related decision-making.
2. Define responsibilities for change decisions.
3. Include all critical success factors.
4. Develop a procedure to update project documents.
5. Review the risk management plan.
6. Gain the buy-in and commitment of teams.
7. Review the change control system with the team, project sponsor and key stakeholders.

One important point in change management is to control the effects of the change to make sure it is achieving the expected benefits. The programme manager should keep a change register for each project, stating the change, expected benefits and constraints, as well as the responsible party. Configuration management is the control of the outcome of a project. It should be based on quality assurance and control principles.

Efficient and effective use of an organization's human resources is an obvious feature and benefit of programme management. Knowledge resource planning (KRP) (O'Neil 1999) consists of making the best use of scarce resources of highly skilled knowledge. Often plagued by imbalance between project demands and resource shortages, programme managers need a robust plan to manage

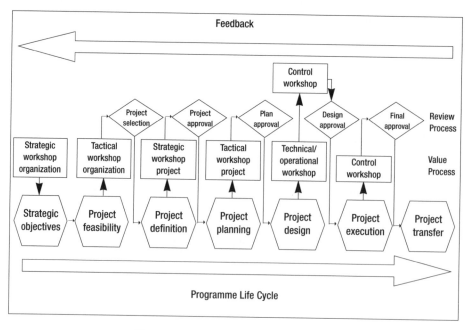

**Figure 3.6 The programme review process**

common resource pools. There is a need to align key resources with strategic objectives and use the best resources available on the most sensitive or significant projects. As more and more organizations are moving towards ERP (enterprise resource planning) tools and real-time budgeting and performance measurement, it becomes necessary to manage resources with a systemic and holistic view. KRP is a series of processes that balances the demand and supply of knowledge resources across the organization. It is based on three simple steps:

1. Demand planning – model of the organization's workload.
2. Supply planning – model of the entire capacity/availability of resources.
3. Assignment and allocation planning – prioritization/alignment of resources with corporate goals.

Assignment is based on allocating resources in priority to the key/strategic projects. The 'best' people are placed on the most significant jobs.

Following these steps, the most important point is to 'negotiate' resources allocation between projects and between projects and functional areas. Once accepted, commitments must be held on the basis of the plans developed. The programme manager may be required to facilitate the process.

## APPRAISAL PHASE

The appraisal phase is based on the assessment of benefits and the feedback of the lessons learned into the organization. To be effective, it requires formal procedures like project reviews with stakeholders, maintenance of a database on past projects, peer reviews and presentation of completed projects. One of the most useful tools for feedback is the establishment of project/programme management knowledge forums or centres of excellence where project and programme managers can share information and experiences.

Many writers have recognized in recent times that the implementation of an effective support office for programmes and projects is increasingly a significant contributor to the achievement of business objectives and programme benefits. At its most basic, the support office can provide efficient and effective monitoring and reporting for programmes – freeing up programme managers to concentrate on communications and stakeholder management and to address emergent change. Many other benefits can be achieved through the support office if it is established as a 'centre of excellence' or 'knowledge forum' for programme and project management; many organizations do not have the extensive expertise provided by a group of professional programme and project managers. Services can then include mentoring, coaching, review activities and training, and provide a focus for the assimilation and implementation of organizational learning.

## CONCLUSIONS

Contrary to what some have argued, projects and programmes are not a matter of 'either-or', but rather complementary elements contributing to total organizational effectiveness. An organization that undertakes a series of projects without a proper programme structure cannot expect to reap all the benefits of project management, which are directly related to delivering outcomes with limited resources (Hobbs *et al.* 1999). Much time, monies and energy are lost in coordination and interface between competing projects if there is not an overarching programme to integrate the organization's strategy and its effective delivery.

## REFERENCES AND FURTHER READING

CCTA (1994a), *An Introduction to Programme Management*, Stationery Office, London.

CCTA (1994b), *Programme Management Case Studies: Volume 1*, Stationery Office, London.

CCTA (1999), *Managing Successful Programmes*, Stationery Office, London.

Drucker, P. (1989), *Managing for Results*, Heinemann Professional, London.

Grundy, T. (1997), 'Strategy implementation and project management', *International Journal of Project Management*, **16**(1).

Hobbs, B., Ménard, P., Laliberté, M. and Coulombe, R. (1999), 'A project office maturity model', *Project Management Institute 30th Annual Seminars & Symposium Proceedings*, PMI Communications, Drexel Hill, PA.

Hurst, D. K. (1995), *Crisis and Renewal: Meeting the Challenge of Organizational Change*, Harvard Business School Press, Boston, MA.

Johnson, G. and Scholes, K. (1997), *Exploring Corporate Strategy: Text and Cases*, Prentice-Hall, London.

Levy, D., (1994), 'Chaos theory and strategy: theory, management and managerial implications', *Strategic Management Journal*, **15**: 167–78.

Mintzberg, H., Ahlstrand, B. and Lampel, J. (1998), *Strategy Safari*, Prentice-Hall, London.

Mintzberg, H. and Waters, J. A. (1985), 'Of strategies, deliberate and emergent', *Strategic Management Journal*, **6**(3).

O'Neil, J. (1999), 'Short-staffed? Maximise scarce resources with knowledge resource planning', *PM Network*, February.

Pellegrinelli, S. (1997), 'Programme management: organising project-based change', *International Journal of Project Management*, **15**(3).

Rea, P. J. and Kerzner, H. (1998), *Strategic Planning: A Practical Guide*, Van Nostrand Reinhold, New York.

Stacey, R. D. (1993), *Strategic Management and Organizational Dynamics*, Pitman, London.

Thiry, M. (1997), *Value Management Practice*, Project Management Institute, Sylva, NC.

Thiry, M. (1999), 'Would you tell me please which way I ought to go from here? Is change a threat or an opportunity?' *Proceedings of the 30th PMI Annual Symposium, Philadelphia*, Project Management Institute, Sylva, NC.

Tsuchiya, S. (1997), 'Simulation/gaming, an effective tool for project management', *Proceedings of the 28th PMI Annual Symposium, Chicago*, Project Management Institute, Sylva, NC.

Turner, J. R. (1999), *The Handbook of Project-based Management*, 2nd edition, McGraw-Hill, London.

Weick, K. E. (1995), *Sensemaking in Organizations*, Sage Publications, London.

## RELATED TOPICS

# 4 Projects and project management

*Rodney Turner*

To achieve the new business development objectives identified through its strategic planning process (Chapter 2), an organization needs to undertake projects or programmes of projects (Chapter 3). These it will manage for itself, or commission another organization (a contractor) to manage on its behalf. (To achieve its existing performance objectives, the organization will continue to run its existing, routine operations.) Thus projects are novel endeavours, undertaken to deliver new development objectives. They are necessarily transient, since if they become established they become part of the routine operations of the organization. Indeed, many projects will end with the creation of a new routine operation. Projects will also be unique. Although the development objective may be very similar to one delivered in the past, the very fact that the project is being undertaken later, under a different macro- and micro-economic environment, with new technology, means it can never be identical to the previous project. (We shall see later that the more a project can be made a repeat of a similar project in the past, the lower the inherent risk and uncertainty. Reducing the uniqueness of a project is an ideal aim.) Hence a project is a unique, novel and transient endeavour, undertaken to achieve a new development objective. Project management is the process by which that endeavour is planned, monitored and controlled to successfully achieve the development objective.

That very simple statement begs a lot of questions, particularly (as we shall see in the next chapter) as to what we mean by 'successfully'. But that does not matter, it gives a simple understanding of what we are trying to achieve, subject to clarification of the definitions.

The management of this unique, novel and transient endeavour is very different from the management of the routine operation. In the former, the problem is coping with the inherent risk and uncertainty, and that requires the use of flexible and thus essentially inefficient yet effective management approaches. In the latter, the emphasis is on maintaining the status quo, which is known to work and hence involves little uncertainty, and making the management approaches which are known to be effective, ever more efficient.

In this chapter I introduce projects and project management. I consider the three dimensions of project management: the project, the management process and the levels. In describing the project, I introduce the management functions and in describing the management process, I introduce the life cycle and the concept of the process approach. I also consider three additional issues: PSO projects, that is projects involving both technical and cultural objectives; the goals and methods matrix, that is the idea that projects may not have well defined goals, nor well defined methods of delivering those goals; and the concept of project management being like sailing a yacht.

## PROJECTS: THE ENDEAVOUR

### FEATURES OF PROJECTS

Projects are unique, novel and transient endeavours undertaken to deliver novel business development objectives. These features of projects create stresses which make their management requirements different from the management of routine operations.

### 1. The transience creates urgency

To be worthwhile and to repay the investment, the development objectives must be achieved by a certain time. Sometimes those time constraints are very tight, there is a very narrow market window for the output from the project. If the market window is missed, the project has no value. However, more often, the market window is broader and though the project will be worth less if it is late, the loss in value from later delivery has to be balanced against a potential greater value if more time is spent developing the project's output. Unfortunately, the timescale often receives undue emphasis. There are time pressures in routine operations. However, because they are routine, it is known how much can be done in a given time, and so there is less likelihood of committing to impossibly tight timescales.

### 2. The novelty creates the need for integration

There are interfaces between the different organizational units working on the project, interfaces between the different areas of work on the project, interfaces between the different levels of the project. Because the project is novel, these interfaces cannot be precisely defined. They need to be defined and managed as the project progresses. Interfaces exist in routine operations, especially between the functions of the organization. However, because the work is routine, the interfaces are unchanging. One function can do the work it is responsible for, and pass the intermediate product through the interface, knowing it will meet the needs of the function on the other side. That will not happen on a project because neither the nature of the intermediate product nor the needs of the next step in the process can be precisely prescribed in advance. They need to be approached in an almost ad hoc way, with the project team members responding to the nature of the interface as it is actually experienced.

## 3. The uniqueness creates risk and uncertainty

As we have just seen, it is not possible to predict precisely the nature of the intermediate products developed at successive stages of the project, and even less well defined is the work required to deliver the intermediate products. In a routine operation, the work has been done many times before, and so it is known precisely what work will deliver what intermediate products. Furthermore, because the work will be done many times, it can be of value putting a large amount of planning effort into the production engineering, to hone the definition of the production processes. That is just not the case on a project. As the work is unique, it will only be done once; the planning effort will only be recovered once. The project must have a plan. It is essential to coordinate the input of resources and ensure that the product is delivered at such a time and cost as to make a profit. However, the plan needs to be more strategic, focusing on the coordination and integration. The detail levels of the plan need to be almost flexibly defined as the project progresses. And necessarily, the uncertainty and the risk must be overtly managed as part of the complete project management process.

These three features of transience, novelty and uniqueness, and the stresses they create, urgency, integration and uncertainty, define projects and project management. Projects and project management are not defined by the so called 'triple constraint' of time, cost and functionality; all managers have to mange those, from both projects and operations. Projects and project management are defined by the triplex of transience, novelty and uniqueness, and the related triplex of urgency, integration and uncertainty. In order to address these dual triplexes, the project plans need to be phased, flexible and goal-directed.

They need to be phased, because more information about the project, its products and the work required to deliver them will become available as the project progresses. Hence, the plan needs to be developed to the current level of available detail at each stage of the project. Phasing the plans also helps to manage the urgency. The phased plans give a clear indication of the progress to the eventual product. Furthermore, the returns can be better managed. More time can be spent in the low-cost, development phase of the project, to enable the delivery phase, when real money is spent, to be undertaken quickly and efficiently.

The plans need to be flexible to cope with the uncertainty. We cannot predict the future, we cannot say how things will turn out. We can only do that in a production environment because of the wealth of previous experience. Hence we must build flexibility into the project plans to be able to respond to the unknowns. As I said above, in a production environment, large amounts of effort will be put into developing the plans, to make the process as efficient as possible, and the efficiency improvements will continue throughout the production phase. Not only does the information not exist to create the efficient plans for the project, efficiency is positively detrimental as there is no flexibility to respond to the unknowns as they arise. It is a cliché, but the plans must be effective, not efficient.

The plans also need to be goal-directed to cope with the uncertainty. As I said above, there is uncertainty both in the goals (intermediate products) and in the method of delivering them. However, there is usually less uncertainty about the goals. There are several reasons for this. First, it is often known what components comprise the eventual product, even if their precise specification is not known. Hence the goals can be identified, even if not precisely described. I said above we want the project to be successful, even if we don't know what we mean by successful. We can define what we mean as the project progresses. Second, it is often not possible to define the work until the goals are identified. Hence we can define the goals independently of the work, but not the work independently of the goals. Research has shown that we are more likely to be successful if we know the goals and not the work, rather than vice versa.

## FUNCTIONS THAT NEED MANAGING

I have previously identified five functions that need to be managed on a project to deliver the project's product (Turner 1999). These are scope, organization (skills), quality, cost and time. In reality there are more like eight. Scope can be broken into three, functionality, configuration and work, and quality can be broken into quality (finish) and safety and health. Hence, in order to deliver the project's products, the manager needs to manage the following:

1. *Functionality*  To provide value, the project's products must perform certain functions, either to generate revenue or to make savings.

2. *Configuration* The project's product will have several components, which individually will provide some of the functionality and together will provide it all.

3. *Work* Work needs to be done to build the components of the product, to configure them into the complete product and to commission the product to deliver the functionality.

4. *Organization* Skills are required to do the work. These skills need to be identified and their roles and responsibilities defined. The amount of work of each skill type needs to be estimated and their input coordinated (integrated) during the work of the project.

5. *Quality* To perform properly, and generate value, the project's product must be designed to certain specifications and delivered to a given 'finish'.

6. *Cost* To be worthwhile, the project's product must cost less than the value it will generate. The cost must be managed. Furthermore, all the resources, including the cost, must not be consumed faster than the rate which they become available.

7. *Time* Again, to be worthwhile, the project's product must be obtained by a certain time, so that the value generated covers the cost of financing the expenditure and repays the outlay. Also, managing time is essential to coordinate the consumption of all the resources including the cost.

8. *Safety and health* People deserve to be able to work and earn a living without risk of injury or death. Unfortunately people are sometimes their own worst enemies here, driving without wearing seat belts, visiting the construction site without a hard hat, taking part in risky sports. Sometimes this is caused by thoughtlessness as to the risks, sometimes it is done in full knowledge of the risks because of the thrill involved.

## PROJECT MANAGEMENT: THE PROCESS

Project management has been described as:

The process of converting vision into reality.

(Adesh Jain)

This captures the essential nature of project management as a process with a beginning and an end. The process starts with a vision that it is possible to obtain value in some way. That vision is then converted into a mission, a concept that there is a journey we can undertake to achieve our vision. We then define the journey. We identify the end point, and the route to be followed from start to finish. We develop a strategy for the journey, including intermediate staging posts

**69**

that will be visited on the way. We then head off. Along the route, we need to identify the actual roads to be followed between the staging posts, perhaps work out the actual timing of the steps, and monitor and control our progress along the way. Then, as we reach the end, we need to home in on our destination, make sure we reach the right spot and that we gain the value for which the journey was undertaken. This metaphor of a journey defines four essential stages or phases of a project:

1. *Proposal, initiation and feasibility* The vision is seen. It is described and it is determined that it is valuable to achieve it. Several potential routes for reaching the vision are identified and the relative advantages of these are compared both to each other and to the value of achieving the vision. One option is chosen for further analysis (assuming that the cost is justified by the benefit).

2. *Definition, appraisal and strategic planning* A strategic plan for the project is developed. The end product of the project is described and intermediate products or milestones for its delivery identified. These too are described. The cost of the project and the value of the end product are determined to a greater level of accuracy, and it is determined whether the project is worthwhile. If it is, finance is sought.

3. *Implementation and control* The work of the project is planned in greater detail. (Detail design and planning cannot be done until finance is obtained.) The work is undertaken. Progress is monitored and if performance is diverging from plan, corrective action is taken. (I have not said it under the two earlier stages, but the plans and progress reports must cover all eight functions of management above.)

4. *Finalization and close-out, testing, commissioning and handover* The work of the project is completed. The project's product is tested against the performance requirements, commissioned and handed over to the operators, together with operating and maintenance procedures. The final control loop ensures that the benefit is obtained. The team is disbanded and debriefed, and the organization attempts to learn the lessons of this project and capture them for future projects.

There are many definitions of the life cycle with more or less numbers of stages. As I have said above, because the work of the project cannot be precisely defined, what will be handed over from one stage to the next cannot be precisely defined. An essential part of project management is the integrative function of making certain that the people working on two successive stages work together to ensure that the product that is handed over meets the needs of the next stage, of all subsequent stages and of the eventual customer. This is an essential feature of both PRINCE 2, produced by the CCTA, and ISO 10,006.

## THE LEVELS

Figure 1.2, and the above discussion, illustrate that the project's product and the work of the project are defined over several levels. There are three essential levels which are developed at successive stages of the project.

1. *The integrative level*   The project is integrated into the parent organization. The vision and mission are determined by defining the organization's development objectives, the programme and project objectives. This is done in the feasibility stage.
2. *The strategic level*   A strategic plan for implementing the project is developed. In particular this consists of the intermediate staging posts or milestones, the main components of the project's product. A strategy for delivering these is developed. This is done in the definition stage.
3. *The detail or tactical level*   Team and individual objectives and work plans are derived. Detail work methods are planned, monitored and controlled. This is done in the implementation stage.

Not only successive stages must be integrated, but also successive levels. The top level is called the integrative level because that is where the project is integrated into the business, but at all levels, one level must be integrated into the higher level.

## ADDITIONAL ISSUES

There are three further issues which I feel are important to consider while describing projects and their management.

### PSO PROJECTS: TECHNICAL AND CULTURAL OBJECTIVES

During the late 1980s and early 1990s, there was a development of understanding of the role of cultural issues in projects. From the genesis of project management in the 1940s until the mid-1980s, projects were viewed in terms of technology. Whether it was an engineering project, a building project, a product development project or an information technology (IT) project, a project was viewed almost totally as a technical endeavour. In all four types there was hardware to be built, and in the last case software to be written. In the mid-1980s people began to realize that in order to make the hardware work it was necessary to undertake certain 'cultural' activities, that is:

- the writing of management procedures;
- the redeployment of staff to obtain new skills and dispose of old;
- the creation of new organization structures.

This cultural work also had to be managed as part of the project and it was more difficult than the technical work. The most significant proponents of this approach were Andersen, Grude and Haug (1984). (Their book has now been translated into Danish, Swedish, English, Dutch, Italian and German.) But then in the late 1980s the consultants took this a stage further. They pointed out that, since the cultural changes were more difficult to achieve, there was only so far the organization could be changed in one step. Almost anything was possible with the technical activities, but the cultural activities were a limiting factor. Since the cultural activities were a necessary step to make the new technology work, they limited the potential technical activities. The cultural work was not an add-on to the technical work; it was the main determinant of project success. In the early 1990s business process re-engineering (BPR) was very popular, and it was said that in fact the cultural activities were the main purpose of the project and the technology merely a facilitator of cultural change. We have moved back from that position, but it is now widely accepted that the cultural work:

- is a significant part of every project, at least of equal, if not more, significance that the technical work;
- has to be managed as an essential part of the project;
- influences the extent of the technical work that can be achieved;
- is a significant part of the development objectives of the parent organization;
- is both a key criterion and a key determinant of project success.

## THE GOALS AND METHODS MATRIX

I spoke extensively above of coping with uncertainty of the goals and uncertainty of the methods of achieving the goals. It was widely thought up to the mid-1990s that every project has well-defined goals. Indeed some people said you did not have a project until the goals were well defined. The Association for Project Management, in its Body of Knowledge (Morris 1992), defined a project in terms of well-defined goals.

My own view is that you do not have a project until you have a vision, that is an organizational development objective. But even as a vision that may be fairly ill-defined in terms of exactly what is to be achieved. Figure 4.1 illustrates the goals and methods matrix (developed by Turner and Cochrane 1993). It identifies four types of projects:

1. Those with well-defined goals and well-defined methods of achieving the

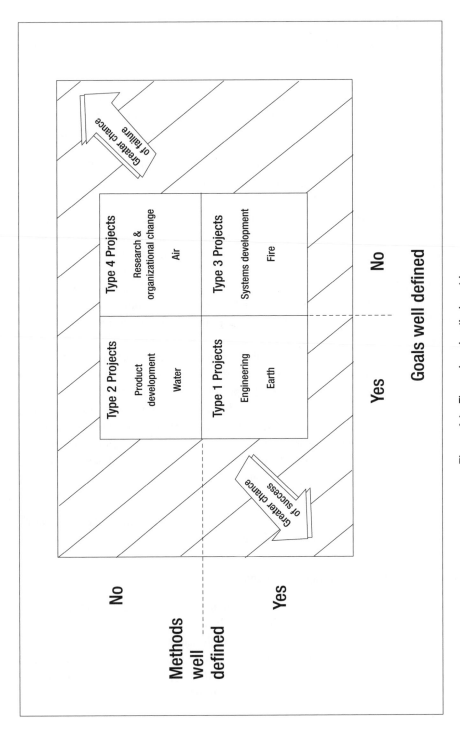

**Figure 4.1 The goals and methods matrix**

goals. These are typified by engineering projects. They tend to be planned in terms of well-defined and understood activities. The role of the project manager is a conductor, leading the team through a well-known score, just imposing his or her own interpretation and tempo.

2. Those with well-defined goals, but poorly defined activities. These are typified by product development projects. They tend to be planned in terms of the known deliverables, with the method of achieving those deliverables planned on a rolling wave basis, as information becomes available as to how best to achieve the goals. The role of the project manager is coach, training the team in standard plays, but leaving them to play the game as it evolves.

3. Those with poorly defined goals, but well defined methods. These are typified by information systems projects. They are planned in terms of life cycle stages. The goals are defined in conceptual terms, but their specification is refined through the stages of the project. The role of the project manager is that of master craftsman. He or she has a team knowledgeable in the techniques and able to copy the master's style. But when they are painting their portion of the Sistine Chapel ceiling, they will have to paint around the unknown flaws they encounter.

4. The final type has both poorly defined objectives and work methods. These are typified by research and organizational change projects. They are planned in terms of gateways or hurdles. If a project is to be successful, it must pass through a gateway on a certain day. If it does not, the gateway closes forever. The role of project manager is that of an eagle. He or she must hover above the project and see it in the context of the parent organization, and then be able to dive down to deal with an issue, before rising up above the project again. These projects are more likely to be successful if the goals are defined first, followed by the work methods.

Configuration management, by which the definition of the goals and work methods are refined is described in Chapter 15.

## PROJECT MANAGEMENT AS SAILING A YACHT

I have developed an analogy of project management being like sailing a yacht. The analogy works on two levels, the micro-level and the macro-level.

If you are sailing in a yacht race, you usually sail around a triangular course, the longest leg of which is arranged to be directly into the wind. If while sailing that leg, you aim your yacht directly at the next buoy, you get blown backwards. You need to sail across wind to achieve something you can achieve. Then you tack in the opposite direction and sail a bit further up wind. You tack back and forth, slowly moving upwind at each tack, until you reach a point where you can shoot for the buoy. Life is like this. You cannot always achieve your desired objective in one go. You need to tack towards your objective, a step at a time. We met this concept in the cultural objectives. You cannot change the organization fully in one step but must tailor your ambitions to what you can achieve, to achieve your objective in several steps.

As you are tacking along one leg, you don't set your sail and tiller rigidly and say 'My plan is to sail exactly 100 yards at this setting, and good project management is sticking rigidly to my plan.' No! You constantly monitor the direction of the wind and adjust your sail and tiller setting accordingly. And if the wind comes around far enough, you may be better tacking in the opposite direction; that may take you closer to the buoy, your next objective. You constantly monitor your performance and your key success factors and adjust your plan accordingly to achieve your objective in the best way possible.

At the macro-level, I use the example of the Whitbread Round the World Yacht Race. Before the yachts head off, the skippers spend months studying weather maps to determine their strategy for the race based on average and likely conditions. But when they are bobbing around in the ocean, they don't set their sails for the average or likely conditions. They set them for the actual conditions. But in spite of the fact that the yachts can only start with a strategic plan and have to tailor their detail plan, there are three outcomes:

- They can predict the duration of the race (nine months) to a high degree of accuracy, to within 5 per cent.
- The boats that come first and second are very close to each other; after nine months of responding to uncertainty, the best and second best boats, which have encountered the same conditions, are very close.
- There is a large degree of luck involved – life's like that!

## REFERENCES AND FURTHER READING

Andersen, E. S., Grude, K. V. and Haug, T. (1984), *Målrettet Projektstyring*, NKI Forlaget, Rud (published in English as *Goal Directed Project Management*, 2nd edition, Kogan Page, London, 1995).

CCTA (1996), *Prince 2: Project Management for Business*, Stationery Office, London.

ISO (1998) *ISO 10,006, Quality Management – Guidelines to Quality in Project Management*, International Standards Organization, Geneva.

Morris, P. G. W. (1992), *The APM Project Management Body of Knowledge*, Association for Project Management, High Wycombe.

Turner, J. R. (1999), *The Handbook of Project-based Management*, 2nd edition, McGraw-Hill, London.

Turner, J. R. and Cochrane, R. A. (1993), 'The goals and methods matrix: coping with projects for which the goals and/or methods of achieving them are ill-defined', *International Journal of Project Management*, **11**(2).

## RELATED TOPICS

| | |
|---|---|
| Strategic planning and implementation | Chapter 2 |
| Programme management | Chapter 3 |
| Success criteria and strategy | Chapter 5 |
| The management process | Chapter 6 and Part IV |
| Project management functions | Part III |
| Configuration management | Chapter 15 |

# 5 Project success and strategy

## Rodney Turner

I said in the introduction to the last chapter that project management is the process by which the project is successfully delivered. I said then that the statement begs the question of what we mean by 'successfully', but said in the subsequent discussion that we could define (or refine) what we mean by success as the project progresses. Having identified success criteria, we need to determine a project strategy to achieve those criteria. We need to identify the key success factors and develop a project management approach based around those factors which will deliver the success criteria. Traditional project managers focus on cost and time and develop intricate planning and control systems to manage those criteria. At least their second step is correct; having identified what they consider to be important, they focus their attention on that (although I do feel at times that the plans are overly sophisticated – in the true meaning of the word). Where they fail is at the first step. They do not think about whether cost and time are truly the most important success criteria for their project.

Research now shows that the most important determinant of project success is agreeing the success criteria with all the stakeholders before you start. You might challenge me that this is inconsistent with what I said above about defining the success criteria as you go along. What I am saying is that before you start you need to identify who all the stakeholders are, and you need to agree with them the nature of the success criteria. As the project progresses, you may well need to refine your understanding of the success criteria, with the identified stakeholders, using a process of configuration management (see Chapter 15).

In this chapter, I consider the issue of project success. I describe the recent research into project success and suggest possible success criteria for projects. I then show how this information can be used to develop a strategy for the management of a project. I introduce the seven forces model of project strategy, and show how the seven forces are related to the Body of Knowledge as outlined in Chapter 1, and hence to the structure of this book.

## JUDGING PROJECT SUCCESS

You will often hear project managers repeating the mantra that their objective is to finish their projects 'on time, within budget, to quality'. Although these are not formally stated as the success criteria, that is implied by this statement. When you ask a project manager what he or she means by 'to quality', the response is sometimes, 'in accordance with the specification', and when you ask what if the specification is wrong, he or she will imply that it is never wrong or say that the specification will be put right. And when you ask by what criteria it will be put right, you are back at the beginning, like the famous campfire song. Of course, this just shows that the mantra of 'on time, within budget, to quality' is as meaningless as it is glib.

So how do you judge the successful outcome for a project? The simple truth is that you cannot determine your implementation strategy until you know how success is to be judged. Until you know your final destination, you cannot know which road to take. And if all the members of the team are not clear about what the final destination is, they will be trying to travel down different roads, sometimes with their own objectives in mind.

Wateridge (1995) investigated the question of project success. He asked people to recall two projects they had worked on, to say what their role was (sponsor, user, designer or project manager), to say whether each project was successful or not, and against what criteria they made their judgement. On successful projects, they all agreed that the criteria was to provide value for the sponsor, and on unsuccessful projects:

- the sponsor wanted value;
- the users wanted good functionality;
- the designers wanted best design;
- the managers wanted to finish on cost and time.

What a surprise! If everyone is pulling in the same direction, the project is successful. If they are all pulling in different directions, the project is unsuccessful. But the really sad thing is that what people are focusing on in unsuccessful projects is important. To provide value for the sponsor:

- you need good functionality;
- you need a well-designed system;
- you need to finish at or near cost and time.

However, there seems to be a way of trying to optimize what is important to you, but damaging the whole system. Or you can achieve a near optimum of what is important to you, but within the constraint that you have to optimize the whole system. You can pull the team apart or push it together. Figure 5.1 gives a longer list of success criteria for a project. But the overriding criterion is that the project should provide value for the sponsor.

Some project managers have said, on hearing me say this, that in their annual appraisal they are judged by how many of their projects are finished on cost and time, not how many provide value for the sponsor. They ask whether that means their appraisal system is not oriented to successful projects. I have to say, unfortunately not. However, this does raise another issue. On the last day of the project you can determine whether the project finished on cost and time, even to quality as set out in the specification. You may not be able to tell whether it provided value for the sponsor; you may not determine that until several years after the project has finished. As I have said, cost and time are key determinants of providing value for the sponsor. Finishing at or near time and cost are necessary conditions for value, just not sufficient conditions, nor even the main conditions in many cases. But sometimes they are the only conditions you can determine on the last day of the project. What is needed is a way of determining the project's potential for providing value to judge the project manager against. But such tools are only just being developed (see Chapter 13).

Figure 5.1 gives a list of potential success criteria for a project. In reality the actual success criteria for a given project will be an amalgam of some or all of these. Furthermore, different stakeholders on a project will be focusing on different criteria. Hence the need to identify who all the potential stakeholders are before you start, and to agree with them some balanced basket of success criteria. John Wateridge, in Chapter 9, gives a project health check, or questionnaire, that can help you to agree the success criteria with the stakeholders. Then as the project progresses, you need to use configuration management to refine the understanding of the different criteria and the balance between them. In this way you increase the chance that at the end of the project most of the stakeholders if not delighted with the project will at least be satisfied

---

- The product delivered by the project achieves its stated business purpose.
- It makes a profit for the owner, sponsor or promoter.
- It meets the needs of the owner, the operators or users, the consumers and the community.
- The project delivers the prestated objectives.
- They are delivered with the required functionality and with the required quality.
- They are delivered at an appropriate time and for an appropriate cost.
- The project meets the needs of the project team.
- The work makes a profit for the project team.

---

**Figure 5.1   Project success criteria**

with the outcome, increasing the chance that the project will be viewed as successful. Also, by understanding the success criteria at the start, you can choose a strategy for project implementation that addresses those criteria, which takes us into the next section.

## A STRATEGY FOR PROJECT IMPLEMENTATION

Having determined the objectives of the project and the success criteria, it is then necessary to determine a strategy for the implementation of the project which will deliver those objectives and criteria. Figure 1.2 shows that we need a strategy to implement objectives at every level of management. We need a strategy for implementing our business objectives, (described by David Partington in Chapter 2), we need a strategy for implementing our programme objectives (see Chapter 3), and likewise we need a strategy for implementing our project objectives. Project teams and team members will also need a strategy for implementing their team and individual objectives respectively.

### THE SEVEN FORCES MODEL

Based on the work of Morris (1987, 1997), I developed the seven forces model for the strategic implementation of projects (Figure 5.2). This model shows seven forces acting on a project, for which you need policies to manage all seven. The seven forces are as follows.

#### Two forces external to the parent organization

1. The drivers arising from the sponsorship of the organization's financiers, the benefit they expect and the urgency that creates.
2. The resistance arising from political, economic, social, technical, legal and environmental influences in the project's context.

#### Two forces internal to the parent organization, but external to the project

3. The drivers arising from the definition of the project required to deliver the returns to the financiers.
4. The resistance arising from the attitudes of people within the organization.

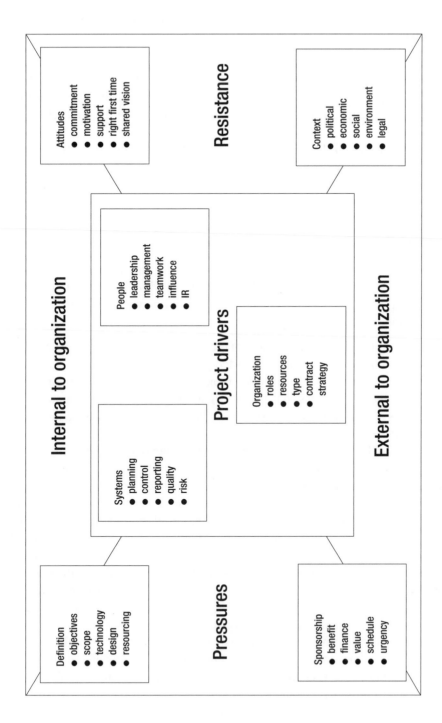

Figure 5.2 The seven forces model of project management

**Three drivers from within the project, the people, systems and organization of project management**

5. The people working on the project, their knowledge and skills, needs for careers, team working, leadership and industrial relations.
6. The management systems to be used to manage functionality, configuration, work, organization, quality, cost, time, risk and safety, and the life cycle to be followed.
7. The organization of the project, the roles and responsibilities of the people working on the project, the numbers required and the need to procure additional skills from outside the parent organization where they don't exist internally.

## THE SEVEN FORCES AND THE BODY OF KNOWLEDGE

There is a simple relationship between the seven forces and the areas of the Body of Knowledge as outlined in Chapter 1. In accordance with what I said at the time, the seven forces model does not change the Body of Knowledge, it is just another way of mapping it.

1. Forces 1 and 2 make up the context of the project (knowledge area B) and the need to finance the project (knowledge area E). We need policies for managing all the influences from the project's context. These are the returns expected by the project's and parent organization's sponsors, promoters or financiers and the influences arising from the project's environment, including stakeholders in the community.
2. Forces 3 and 6 make up the systems for implementation of the project. We need policies for how we will manage functionality, configuration, project organization, quality, cost, time, risk and safety (knowledge area C), and the life cycle (knowledge area D). Force 3 addresses policies on how the project will be defined to meet the needs of the parent organization. This includes objectives, functionality and configuration. Figure 5.2 also shows that Force 3 includes policies on the technology to be used in the development of the project's product. I did not address this overtly in the definition of the Body of Knowledge in Chapter 1. However, reference to Figure 1.1 shows it figures heavily in the UMIST Body of Knowledge (Morris 1999), as it does in Figure 5.1 (also developed originally by Morris).
3. Forces 4 and 5 represent the people on the project and in the parent organization (knowledge area G). We need policies for leadership and team building, industrial relations and stakeholder management. We also need policies for ethical behaviour.

4. Finally, Force 7 represents the resourcing of the project and the need to procure goods and service externally (knowledge area F).

## DETERMINING A STRATEGY FOR PROJECT IMPLEMENTATION

To determine your strategy for project implementation, you need to use a model of the Body of Knowledge to help you identify those factors which will contribute to the achievement of your objectives and success criteria, and then develop a policy for how those factors will be managed. To help identify the relevant factors you can use:

- a model like that in Figure 5.2;
- one of the versions of the Body of Knowledge (Figure 1.1); or
- the table in Figure 9.2 developed by John Wateridge from his research into the success of projects.

Whatever you do, remember to focus on those issues that will deliver your objectives and your criteria for success. Do not focus on issues because they are conventionally thought to be important to project success. The conventional issues may be important to you, or others may be. Once you have determined your strategy for project implementation, then that should be recorded in your Project Definition Report and Project Manual (see Chapter 24).

## REFERENCES AND FURTHER READING

Morris, P. W. G. (1997), *The Management of Projects*, 2nd edition, Thomas Telford, London.

Morris, P. W. G. (1999), *Association for Project Management Body of Knowledge Review*, Centre for Research in the Management of Projects, UMIST, Manchester.

Morris, P. W. G. and Hough, G. (1987), *The Anatomy of Major Projects: A Study of the Reality of Project Management*, Wiley, Chichester.

Turner, J. R. (1999), *The Handbook of Project-based Management*, 2nd edition, McGraw-Hill, London.

Wateridge, J. H. (1995), 'IT projects: a basis for success', *International Journal of Project Management*, **13**(3).

## RELATED TOPICS

# 6 Processes and procedures

## Richard Pharro

Is it a process, is it a methodology, is it a method, is it a framework or is it a standard? Whatever it is called, its purpose is to aid management of the process to successfully deliver a project. Projects are always undertaken within an enterprise culture. An enterprise can be either for profit or not for profit. Projects require the complete involvement of a project team, a consistent vocabulary, appropriate tools, a framework within which they are managed, a process by and a standard to which they are delivered. The culture and focus of the project team and the critical success factors will vary significantly but all projects need to be managed in a way that engenders confidence in the project sponsor. During the delivery process, the project sponsor requires interim milestones or checkpoints to be met and the final project, rather than the original idea, to be right for its needs, thereby giving it maximum opportunity to obtain the business benefits from the project.

The rationale for a project stems from the corporate objectives and its part in the programme to deliver them (see Chapters 2 and 3). In Chapter 4, four different types of project are defined in Figure 4.1. They are classified in terms of clarity of *what* is required and *how* to do it. A good process should be capable of dealing with all four types of projects, with:

- clear requirements: clear delivery process (solution);
- clear requirements: unclear delivery process;
- unclear requirements: clear delivery process;
- unclear requirements: unclear delivery process.

In this chapter we consider standard methods of project management, that is standard processes and procedures. We start by considering what is understood by a method (framework, methodology, standard) and then describe the three commonly used in Europe, BS6079, PRINCE and ISO 10,006.

## METHOD

A method, or methodology, is a structured approach for delivering a project. It should be derived from a defined project process and be capable of accommodating all four types of projects. Its purpose is to provide clarity in the following areas:

1. The project's objectives.
2. Roles and responsibilities of the key project participants.
3. A series of checkpoints at which progress and relevance can be reviewed and checked.
4. A set of procedures for the day-to-day management of the project team.
5. Control metrics for work between stages to provide early warnings of potential problems.

The project's deliverables are developed as part of the corporate management or strategic planning process (see Chapter 2) used to establish the business case for the project. There are various techniques by which the project's objectives can be established which will vary depending on the type of project. Developing the business case is usually omitted from the project management method but is an essential part of the process of project management. This is not a semantic differentiation but is important in understanding the benefits of both a process and a method. The method is therefore a part of the process.

### WHAT IS THE PROJECT MANAGEMENT PROCESS?

The process must include all stages of the project management life cycle to define how inputs are to be converted into desired customer outputs (see Chapter 23). Within this life cycle two stages are usually outside the responsibility of the project team (Figure 6.1):

1. *Strategic planning* Developing the business case.
2. *Review* Ensuring that the lessons learned are used to update the organization's corporate and project management procedures.

Once approved by the sponsoring organization, the business case or rationale for the project will define in high-level terms the reason for the project and what outcome is sought. This will determine the type of project. For example, if the business case identifies a requirement for a new production line to increase capacity by 30 per cent, both the requirements and the solution should be capable of being developed in detail by the project team. If the business case identifies an opportunity to launch an entirely new product the project team would want to

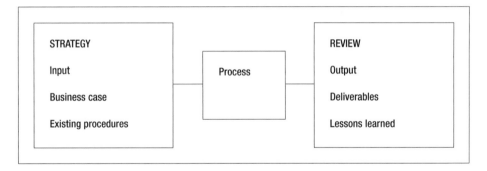

Figure 6.1    The project management process, from inputs to outputs

undertake a series of feasibility studies before selecting a single option for detailed development. In this case both the 'what' and the 'how' for providing maximum benefit are unclear. Regardless of the type of project, the project management method must be capable of delivering the project to achieve the objectives defined in the business case.

## WHAT IS A METHOD?

The method is a set of management processes each with clearly defined resources and activities, which transform inputs into the outputs defined in the business case. This encompasses all the traditional project management activities essential to planning, doing, managing, reviewing and controlling the work required to deliver the project. Many methods are available; most are either proprietary or based on specific planning techniques, but there are only three which are clearly in the public domain and are non-proprietary:

1. BS6079 A Guide to Project Management
2. PRINCE 2 Managing Successful Projects
3. ISO 10,006 Quality Management – Guidelines to Quality in Project Management

They vary in approach and depth of content due to the different objectives of the sponsoring organizations and background and make-up of the authoring panels. The benefit of this is that one of these 'standard' processes should be suitable for your project. None should be used blindly and probably none is the perfect solution, but any of them should help you establish an environment in which to increase the chance of project success.

This chapter covers the content of these three processes in depth and does not attempt to compare or recommend, as to do this in isolation would be meaningless.

## BS6079 A GUIDE TO PROJECT MANAGEMENT

The guide identifies ten stages in a project:

1. *Concept, basic ideas* Consideration of technical feasibility, commercial acceptability and a balance between costs and benefits (see Chapters 2, 13, 14, 25 and 27).
2. *Feasibility* Identify those ideas worth developing further and find a senior manager to champion the project. Collect information throughout the organization and appoint the project manager (see Chapters 14, 25 and 27).
3. *Authorization* Obtained at the appropriate level within the organization (see Chapter 27).
4. *Implementation including design* Doing of the work of the project (see Chapter 26).
5. *Procurement, fabrication and installation* Buying in of goods and services, making of components and configuration of the deliverables (see Part VI and Chapter 15).
6. *Control/accountability, periodic reviews and updates* Ensuring that the project is completed in accordance with its success criteria (see Chapters 5 and 26).
7. *Completion and handover* (The absence of a chapter on completion and commissioning is explained in the introduction to Part IV.)
8. *Operation* Running of the facility to deliver the expected benefit and pay for the cost of doing the project and for decommissioning.
9. *Close-down and cease operations* Shut-down of the facility.
10. *Termination and disposal of residual assets* Clear-up.

Senior management is responsible for establishing the objectives and constraints of the project. It must also ensure that proper operational procedures and controls are in place and subsequently used and must delegate the appropriate level of authority to the project manager to ensure its delivery.

### THE PROJECT MANAGEMENT PROCESS IN BS6079

The project management process in BS6079 is divided into two parts:

1. Project planning
2. Project control

Project planning is the development of a workable project plan that describes tasks in terms of who does what, when, at what cost and to what specification. This needs to be at a level of detail the project manager considers necessary and sufficient for effective and efficient project control. The second part of the process is to use the plan to control and coordinate the progress of the project. A basic project plan should contain the following sections:

1. Introduction and summary
2. Commitment acceptance
3. Project work breakdown structure
4. Schedule
5. Statement of work

The suggested process within BS6079 is shown in Figure 6.2.

## PROJECT PLANNING

The steps of project planning are listed below:

1. Authorization can be for the whole project or up to a specified milestone at which point further authorization will be dependent upon satisfactory progress:
   - Authorization starts the project management process.
2. Establishing the project team includes the establishment of accountability and authority levels for the project manager, setting up a communication framework for the project team and developing incentive mechanisms to be used where necessary.
3. Development of a project work breakdown structure (WBS). The product-based WBS is the commonest and most useful form but the project could be broken down by activity or cost elements.
4. Assigning a single accountable task owner to project tasks is essential for the successful delivery of the task but at the same time it is important to avoid having too many task owners as that could lead to an unmanageable number of tasks and owners.
5. Develop a statement of work (SOW) for project tasks. The statement of work provides the requirements for each task and should contain:
   - a task reference code;
   - a summary description of the requirement;
   - the accountable task owner;
   - a list of key deliverables;
   - timescales for the deliverables;
   - a schedule of task dependencies and subsidiary tasks;
   - a schedule of costs by cost element;
   - an assessment of risks associated with the task;

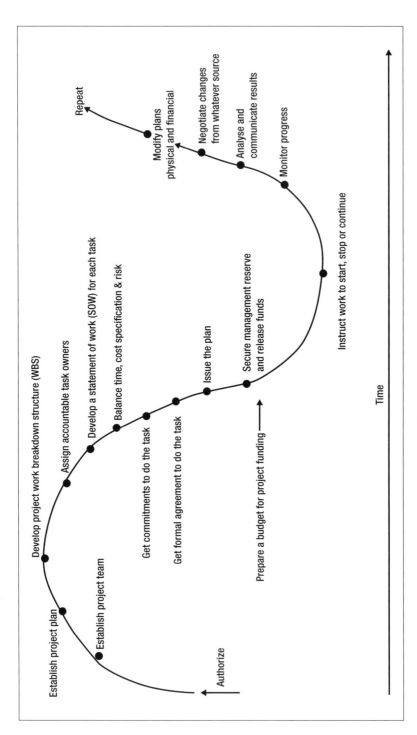

**Figure 6.2  The BS6079 project management process flow**

*Source*: This extract from BS6079:1996 is reproduced with the permission of BSI under licence number 2000SK/0109.The complete standard can be obtained by post from BSI Customer Services, 389 Chiswick High Road, London W4 4AL.

- performance measurement and task completion criteria;
- a description of the work content of the task;
- reporting requirements.

6. Balance time, cost integrity of specification and risk to achieve the optimum solution for carrying out the project.
7. Obtain commitments to do project tasks. It is recommended that task owners be asked to agree formally to their obligation to deliver the task within its stated parameters and that the resources needed for the task are available.
8. Issue the project plan.

## PROJECT CONTROL

Once the plan has been issued, the following guidelines should be used for its control:

- The project manager should be responsible for the control of the project plan and needs to authorize any changes. BS6079 clearly assumes that the project manager has authority for approving changes and revisions to plan.
- Issue of a revised agreed project plan should automatically cancel all previous issues.
- Each issue of the project plan should have a unique reference number.
- The reasons for the changes should be fully documented.
- Work should not be released from a draft project plan.
- No item of work should be included in more than one project plan.
- The plan does not need to be re-issued if the change is minor provided all project plan holders are notified of the change.
- The project manager should confirm that the revised plan does not jeopardize any contractual obligations.

The following are the suggested elements of project control.

### Manage the project budget

The project manager is responsible for ensuring that sufficient funds are available for the project, and for releasing funds to the task owners in accordance with the budget while retaining a management reserve to cover unexpected problems or small changes. The task owner is responsible for ensuring that the costs incurred in carrying out the work are allocated to the correct code in the project WBS.

### Instruct work to begin, continue and stop

The project manager requests goods or services to be provided in accordance with the plan and the formal termination of the project following formal acceptance of the final project deliverables by the sponsor.

### Monitor progress

Progress is monitored through regular reports from the task owners to the project manager and the following are considered essential elements of the progress reports:

- Actual costs reported against planned cost and variances
- Time and cost at completion for each task
- Earned value

### Manage the project

The project manager is responsible for coordinating the reports submitted by the task owners and keeping them and the sponsor informed of any potential difficulties.

### Assess and manage risks

The risk of success or failure should be assessed continuously by means of the cost and time estimates, and alternative courses of action agreed with the task owner to mitigate the risk.

### Motivate task owners

The project manager is responsible for motivating the task owners through good communication and performance incentives.

### Negotiate

The project manager succeeds or fails on an ability to negotiate effectively, in particular in convincing the task owners of their role as stakeholders in the project.

### SUMMARY OF BS6079

BS6079 assumes a full product life cycle from inception through to decommissioning of the completed project at the end of its useful life. It is most suitable for large engineering projects and once the project is underway expects the project manager to have full control with only limited recourse to the sponsor or owner. It is not prescriptive regarding project management techniques but does recommend that a product breakdown structure is used and highlights the benefits of using earned value for measuring progress.

## PRINCE 2

PRINCE (**Pr**ojects **in** **C**ontrolled **E**nvironments) is a method covering the organization, management and control of projects. PRINCE was first developed in 1989 as a UK government standard for IT project management. The latest version of PRINCE 2, first published in 1996, is a generic approach for the management of all types of projects. PRINCE is far more detailed than BS6079 and provides greater detail on what should be done within the process.

The following sections contain text and diagrams from *Managing Successful Programmes with PRINCE 2* (CCTA 1996) which have been included with kind permission from the CCTA and the Controller of HMSO.

### THE PROJECT MANAGEMENT PROCESS IN PRINCE 2

The process model in PRINCE 2 is shown in Figure 6.3. PRINCE uses the following eight processes to manage the project.

#### Directing a project (DP)

Directing a project runs from the start-up of the project until its closure. This process is the responsibility of the project board that represents the business, user and supplier interests in the project. The high level representation of these three parties ensures that timely decisions can be made by informed people representing all the interests associated with the project.

Some people are concerned by the supplier's involvement but providing appropriate commercial safeguards are agreed PRINCE does encourage a partnership approach in delivering projects. The project board manages by exception and through pre-agreed decision points. Its key responsibilities are:

- starting the project off on the right foot (project initiation);
- committing resources for the next stage (managing stage boundaries);
- monitoring progress, providing advice and guidance, reacting to exception situations (ad hoc management);
- confirming the project outcome and bringing the project to a controlled close (project closure).

This process does not cover the day-to-day activities of the project manager.

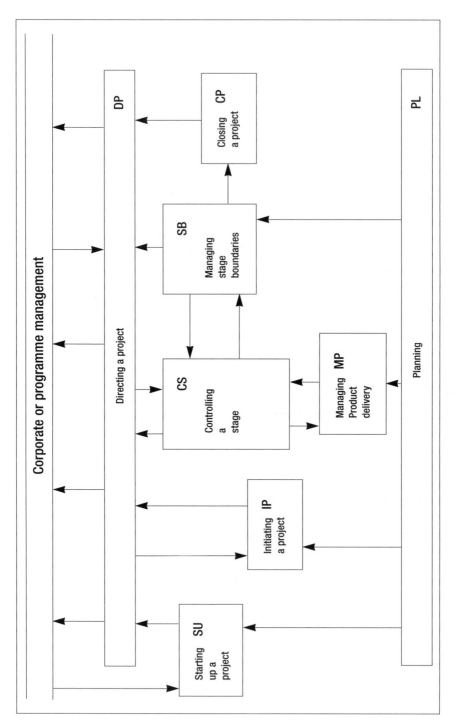

**Figure 6.3   The PRINCE 2 process model**

### Starting up a project (SU)

This is the first process in PRINCE 2. This stage is driven by the project mandate, which defines in high level terms the reason for the project and the required outcome. The amount of detail and clarity of the defined outcome depend on the type of project. It often takes far more time and effort than originally envisaged by the project sponsor to complete this stage, which involves developing and agreeing the following project management documents (called products in PRINCE terminology):

- A risk log
- The project approach (in general terms how a solution will be provided)
- The project brief
- Designing and as far as possible appointing the project management team
- The initiation stage plan

### Initiating a project (IP)

This process develops the project plans in more detail and records them in the project initiation document, which forms the baseline for the project. Its objectives are to:

- document and confirm that an acceptable business case exists for the project and that there is sufficient justification to proceed;
- enable and encourage the project board to take ownership of the project;
- ensure a firm and accepted foundation to the project prior to commencement of the work by establishing a stable management basis on which to proceed;
- agree to the commitment of resources for the first stage of the project;
- provide the baseline for the decision-making processes required during the project's life;
- ensure that the investment of time and effort required by the project is made wisely, taking account of the risks to the project.

### Managing stage boundaries (SB)

This process provides the project board with key decision points to enable it to decide whether to:

- continue with the project as planned;
- make minor or major changes dictated by factors external to the project;
- revise the expected outcome of the project in line with a changed business case;
- terminate the project as its deliverables are no longer viable.

For projects of the Type 3 or Type 4 categories in Figure 4.1 (p. 73) the stage boundary is the point at which the project board agrees the details for the next stage. The benefits of this process are:

● assuring the project board that all deliverables planned in the current stage plan have been completed as defined;
● providing the information needed for the project board to assess the continuing viability of the project;
● providing the project board with information needed to approve completion of the current stage and to authorize the start of the next stage, together with its delegated tolerance level;
● recording any measurements or lessons which can help later stages of this project and/or other projects.

The products of this process are:

● the status of the current plan showing performance against the original stage plan;
● the next stage plan, for which approval is sought;
● a revised project plan;
● the updated risk log;
● a revised business case;
● an updated lessons learned report;
● changes to the structure or staffing of the project management team;
● an end stage report to the board prepared by the project manager detailing the stage achievements.

### Controlling a stage (CS)

This process describes monitoring and control activities of the project manager involved in ensuring that a stage stays on course and reacts to unexpected events. The process forms the core of the project manager's work on the project. Throughout a stage there will be a cycle of:

● authorizing work to be done;
● gathering progress information about that work;
● reviewing the situation;
● reporting;
● taking any necessary corrective action;
● risk management;
● change control.

Products produced during this stage, on a cyclical basis are:

- new work packages;
- highlight reports;
- project issues (suggestions, change requests, reports of items outside of specification);
- an updated risk log;
- a regularly updated stage plan.

There may also be the need for:

- an exception report/exception plan (notification when the project is expected to exceed its agreed tolerances).

## Managing product delivery (MP)

The objective of this process is to ensure that whatever is to be created or supplied through work packages to create the project is delivered by:

- negotiating details of work packages with the project manager;
- making certain that work on products contained in the work packages is effectively authorized and agreed;
- ensuring that work conforms to the requirements of interfaces identified in the work package;
- ensuring that the work is done;
- assessing work progress and forecasts regularly;
- ensuring that completed products meet quality criteria;
- obtaining approval for the completed products.

Products created or updated during this process are:

- team plans;
- quality log updates, giving the project manager a view of quality work being done;
- new project issues;
- risk log updates;
- checkpoint reports, regular progress reports from a team to a project manager.

## Closing a project (CP)

The purpose of this process is to execute a controlled close to the project. The process covers the project manager's work to wrap up the project either at its end or at premature close. Most of the work is to prepare input to the project board to obtain its confirmation that the project may close. And the outcome of the project is handed over to the customer. The objectives of closing a project are, therefore, to:

- check the extent to which the objectives set out in the project initiation document have been met;
- confirm the customer's acceptance of the deliverables;
- verify to what extent all expected products have been handed over and accepted by the customer;
- confirm that maintenance and operation arrangements are in place (where appropriate);
- make any recommendations for follow-on actions (follow-on action recommendations);
- capture lessons resulting from the project and complete the lessons learned report;
- prepare an end-project report;
- archive the project files;
- produce a post-project review plan;
- notify the host organization of the intention to disband the project organization and resources (end-project notification).

### Planning (PL)

Planning is a repeatable process and plays an important role in other processes. It is covered in detail in Part III. PRINCE 2 uses a product-based approach which involves:

- establishing what products are needed;
- determining the sequence in which each product should be produced;
- defining the form and content of each product;
- resolving what activities are necessary for their creation and delivery.

In addition, the process produces:

- a product checklist, which is a table of the products to be produced by the work planned;
- the risk log, updated with any risk changes brought about by the plan.

### PRINCE COMPONENTS

The above processes drive the project management activities and use eight components to produce the management documents (Figure 6.4).

### Organizational structure

The PRINCE project management structure is based on a customer/supplier environment. The structure assumes that there will be a customer who will

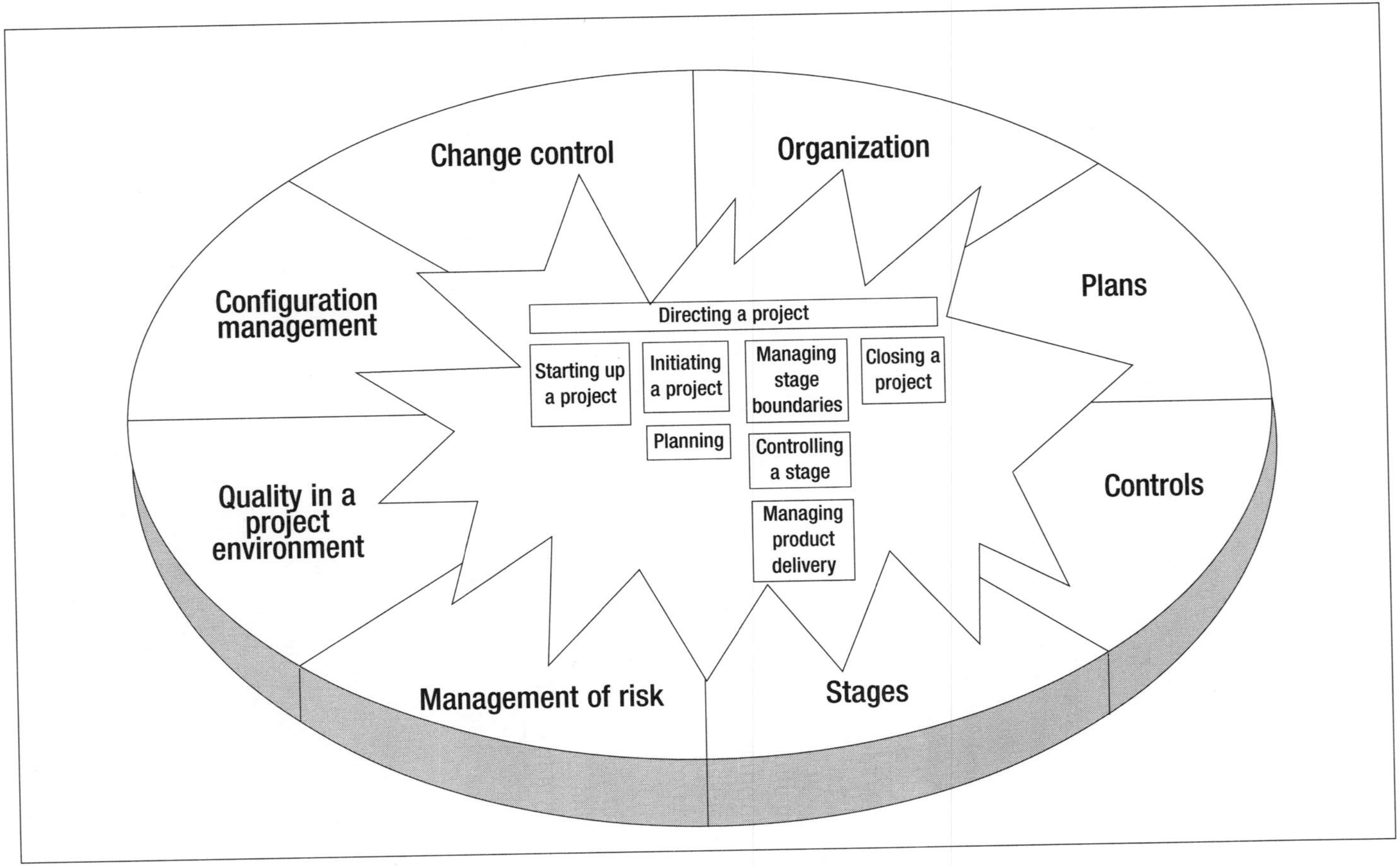

Figure 6.4 The PRINCE 2 components

The diagram shows an oval containing:

Plans
Controls
Organization
Change control
Stages
Configuration management
Quality in a project environment
Management of risk

Central star contains:
Directing a project
Starting up a project
Initiating a project
Planning
Managing stage boundaries
Controlling a stage
Managing product delivery
Closing a project

specify the desired outcome, make use of the outcome and probably pay for the project, and a (prime) supplier who will provide the resources and skills to create that outcome. The customer and supplier may be part of the same corporate body or may be independent of one another.

To be flexible and meet the needs of different environments and different project sizes, PRINCE defines roles which might be allocated, shared, divided or combined according to the project's needs. Associated with this is the concept that responsibilities for a role can be moved to another role or delegated, but should not be dropped. Some of the PRINCE roles cannot be shared, or delegated if they are to be undertaken effectively. The project manager role cannot be shared, nor can the project manager or project board roles be delegated. Corporate cultures differ, but PRINCE can be used no matter what corporate organization structure exists. PRINCE separates the management of the project from the work required to develop the products and concentrates on the former. A fundamental principle is that the project organization structure has four layers responsible for:

- direction of the project;
- day-to-day management of the project;
- team management;
- the work to create the products, that is the team members.

The first three are known as the PRINCE project management team.

## Planning

When asked to describe a plan, many people think only of some sort of bar chart showing timescales. A PRINCE plan is more comprehensive. It should contain the following elements (making maximum use of charts, tables and diagrams for clarity):

- The products to be produced.
- The activities needed to create those deliverables.
- The activities needed to validate the quality of deliverables.
- The resources and time needed for all activities (including quality control).
- The need for people with specific skills.
- The dependencies between activities.
- External dependencies for the delivery of information, products or services.
- When activities will occur.
- The points at which progress will be monitored and controlled.

PRINCE proposes two basic levels of planning, the project plan and the stage plan, to reflect the needs of the different levels of management involved in the project. A stage plan may be broken down into a number of team plans (where, for example, a number of teams may be contributing to the work). Where a stage or project plan is forecast to exceed its tolerances, an exception plan is put forward which will replace a stage plan or lead to a revised project plan. The principal idea behind the levels is that the lower the level, the shorter the plan's time frame and the more detail it contains. The project chooses the levels and, therefore, the number of plans it needs according to its size and extent of risk exposure.

## Controls

There are various levels of control in the project. Most controls in PRINCE are event-driven, including all the decision-making ones. There are some time-driven controls such as regular progress feedback. At the project level there is overall control by the project board, which receives information from the project manager (and any assurance roles appointed) and has control over whether the project continues, stops or changes direction or scope. PRINCE applies the concept of 'management by exception' where the project board is concerned. Once a stage plan has been approved the project board is kept informed by reports during the stage. The project manager informs the project board immediately if any exception situation is forecast. The major controls for the project board are as follows:

1. Project initiation
   ● Should the project be undertaken?
2. End stage assessment
   ● Has the stage been successful?
   ● Is the project still on course?
   ● Is the business case still viable? Are the risks still under control?
   ● Should the next stage be undertaken?
3. Highlight reports
   ● Regular progress reports during a stage.
4. Exception reports
   ● Early warning of any forecast deviation beyond tolerance levels.
5. Mid-stage assessment
   ● The project board jointly considers what action to take in response to a forecast deviation.
6. Project closure
   ● Has the project delivered everything expected?
   ● Are any follow-on actions necessary?
   ● What lessons have been learned?

Work package authorization is a control which the project manager uses to allocate work to individuals or teams. It includes controls on quality, time and cost and identifies reporting and handover requirements. The individuals or teams monitor progress through the work package and report back to the project manager via checkpoints or other identified means (such as risk 'triggers'). There is a controlled close to ensure that the project does not drift on for ever, but does not finish until the project manager can satisfy the project board that the objectives specified in the project initiation document have been achieved.

### Stages

In some methods the word 'phase' is used as an equivalent to the PRINCE stage. Most of what in PRINCE terms will be stages will be divisions of 'implementation' in the product life cycle. Product life cycle phases are not the same as PRINCE stages. Stages are partitions of the project with decision points. A stage is a collection of activities and products whose delivery is managed as a unit. As such it is a subset of the project, and in PRINCE terms it is the element of work which the project manager is managing on behalf of the project board at any one time.

The use of stages in a PRINCE project is mandatory; the number of stages is flexible and depends on the needs of the project. A small project may need only two stages: an initiation stage with the remainder of the project as the second stage. The initiation stage may last only a matter of hours, but is essential to ensure that there is a firm basis for the project, understood by all parties. Most projects need to be broken down into more manageable stages to enable the correct level of planning and control to be exercised. PRINCE uses stages to deal with management decision points. The decisions form the basis of the end-stage assessments carried out in authorizing a stage or exception plan. The benefits of these end-stage assessments are that they:

- provide a 'fire break' for the project by encouraging the project board to assess the project viability at regular intervals;
- ensure that key decisions are made prior to the detailed work needed to implement them;
- clarify previously unknown or ill-defined parts of the project's direction or products;
- clarify the impact of an identified external influence such as the corporate budget round or the finalization of legislation.

Uncertainty can often mean that it is only possible to plan in detail the activities and products of a limited amount of the work of the project. The rest of the project's work can only be planned in broad outline. The adoption of stages deals with this problem by having two different but related levels of plan, that is a detailed stage plan and an outline project plan.

### Management versus technical stages

Technical stages cover elements such as design, build and implementation and are a separate concept from the management stages used in PRINCE. Technical stages are typified by the use of a particular set of specialist skills. Management stages equate to commitment of resources and authority to spend. Often the two types of stages will coincide, for instance where the management decision is based on the output from the technical stage. However, on other occasions the stages will not coincide. There might be more than one technical stage within a management stage. For example, the project board might decide to combine all the technical stages that investigate a need and produce a specification into one management stage. One plan would be approved to cover all the work, with project board commitment before the work started and a review at the end. In a project which is (technically) innovative, a technical stage might be divided into more than one management stage.

The PRINCE approach is to concentrate the management of the project on the management stages since these will form the basis of the planning and control processes. This ensures that the customer's management rather than the technical team's drives the project. Where the desired management stages do not coincide with the technical stages, technical work can be broken down so that its activities are divided over two management stages. This can be problematic where the management stage ends part way through one or more elements of specialist work, since it can be difficult to establish whether the specialist work is under control. Product-based planning is invaluable here since by using it the project manager can identify the detailed products involved in any element of specialist work and all the products which are due to be produced within the confines of any given management stage. This information can then be used to assess completion or otherwise of the stage.

The process of defining stages is fundamentally a process of balancing how far ahead in the project it is sensible to plan and where the key decision points need to be on the project. This makes it flexible enough to cater for any type of project.

### Risk

Risk is a major factor to be considered during the management of a project. Project management must control and contain risks if a project is to stand a chance of being successful. The management of risk is covered in Chapter 21.

### Quality

Within projects, quality is a question of identifying what it is about the project's products or services that makes them fit for their purpose of satisfying stated needs. Projects should not rely on implied needs. These lead to uncertainty and, as such, are of little use. The product description may need to be updated if a change to the product is agreed. A product description should not be changed, once approved, without passing through change control.

The quality review is the primary technique in making quality work for PRINCE. A quality review is a procedure undertaken by all those with a vested interest in the product to ensure a product's completeness and adherence to standards. It is a team review of a product with the emphasis on checking the product for errors (as opposed to, say, improved design). The deliverable, in the context of a quality review, is any product which has been evaluated against mostly subjective criteria involving elements of judgement or opinion. This will typically be a document, such as a plan, a report or a drawing, but could be other products such as models, mock-ups or prototypes. The objectives of a quality review are to:

- produce a product which meets business, user and specialist requirements;
- assess the conformity of a product against set criteria;
- provide a platform for product improvement;
- involve all those who have a vested interest in the product;
- spread ownership of the product;
- obtain commitment from all vested interests in the product;
- provide a mechanism for management control.

Quality reviews must be properly planned with input from the assurance function to:

- identify the products which will be subject to quality review;
- plan the timescale for each quality review;
- identify the reviewers and add them to resource plans.

Quality management is dealt with in more detail in Chapter 16.

### Configuration management

No organization can be fully efficient or effective unless it manages its assets, particularly if the assets are vital to the running of the organization's business. The project's assets likewise have to be managed. The assets of the project are the products that it develops. Within the context of project management the purpose of configuration management is to identify, track and protect the project's products. Configuration management is part of the quality control of a project. Without it, managers have little or no control over the products being produced, what their status is, where they are, whether they can be changed, what the latest version is. If more than one version of a product has been created, then configuration management is required. Configuration management for documentation products (both management and specialist) is of equal importance to configuration management for deliverables.

Configuration management is dealt with in detail in Chapter 15.

## Change

Changes can potentially ruin any project unless they are carefully controlled. Change is, however, highly likely. In PRINCE all potential changes are dealt with as project issues. One consideration at project initiation should be who can authorize changes to what the project is to produce. In a project where few changes are envisaged, it may be reasonable to leave this authority in the hands of the project board. But projects may be in a dynamic environment where there are likely to be many requests to change the initial agreed scope of the project:

- Is the project board prepared to make the time available to review all change requests?
- Does it wish to consider only the top priority changes and delegate decisions on minor changes to another body?
- How will changes be funded?
- Will the project board go back to corporate or programme management to vary funding, timetable or scope each time a change is desired?

In some projects the project board may choose to delegate consideration of changes to a group called a 'change authority'. A budget to pay for changes is normally given to this change authority. This arrangement can avoid a number of mid-stage assessments in projects where the frequency of project issues is forecast to be high. The project board needs to decide before the project moves out of initiation where the authority for making changes lies, and these responsibilities must be written into the appropriate job definitions.

Change is dealt with as part of configuration management in Chapter 15.

## SUMMARY OF PRINCE

PRINCE assumes that a project mandate is given and explicitly recognizes the role of the project's owner and users in the decision-making process. It also differentiates between management, technical and life cycle stages, which makes it easier to link into a business management system. It requires the development of a product-based plan but is non-prescriptive regarding the management tools and techniques used on the project.

## ISO 10,006: GUIDELINES TO QUALITY IN PROJECT MANAGEMENT

ISO 10,006 Quality Management – Guidelines to Quality in Project Management recognizes that successful projects demand appropriate quality of both the project processes and the project product. Detailed consideration of the quality of the project product is outside the scope of the guide, which focuses on the quality of the project management process. The guide does not identify specific techniques or develop much detail on how these areas should be managed and controlled. Ten project management processes are identified. These are related to the elements of the *Guide to the Project Management Body of Knowledge* published by the North American Project Management Institute, the right-hand column in Figure 1.1.

### 1.  STRATEGIC (CHAPTERS 2 AND 5)

These processes organize and manage realization of other processes, with focus on satisfying the stakeholder's requirements through a combination of processes and products to meet the project's objectives.

● Strategic Process: setting the direction for the project and managing realization of the other project processes

### 2.  INTERDEPENDENCY MANAGEMENT (CHAPTERS 3 AND 10)

These processes recognize that an action in one area of the project will usually affect other areas. This is a wider concept than configuration management and involves balancing all decisions with the project's objectives. It covers the following areas:

● *Project initiation and project plan development* Evaluating customer and other stakeholder requirements, preparing a project plan and initiating other processes.
● *Interaction management* Managing interactions between the project processes.
● *Change management* Anticipating change and managing it across all processes.
● *Closure* Closing processes and obtaining feedback.

**106**

### 3.  SCOPE-RELATED (CHAPTERS 14, 15, 20 AND 26)

Scope includes defining the high level concepts and a broad description of the project's product, its characteristics and how they are to be measured and assessed together with its breakdown into manageable activities and the control of those activities. This includes the following activities:

- *Concept development*  Defining in broad outline what the project product will do.
- *Scope development and control*  Documenting the product's characteristics in measurable terms, and controlling them.
- *Activity definition*  Identifying and documenting activities and the steps required to achieve the project objectives.
- *Activity control*  Controlling the actual work carried out in the project.

### 4.  TIME-RELATED (CHAPTERS 19 AND 26)

These processes include establishing dependencies and duration of all activities leading to developing the schedule, and controlling activities to achieve the completion date:

- *Activity dependency planning*  Identifying interrelationships and the logical interactions and dependencies among project activities.
- *Estimation of duration*  Estimating the duration of each activity in connection with the specific conditions and the required resources.
- *Schedule development*  Interrelating the project time objectives, activity dependencies and their durations as the framework for developing general and detailed schedules.
- *Schedule control*  Controlling the realization of the project activities, to confirm the proposed schedule or to take adequate actions for recovering from delays.

### 5.  COST-RELATED (CHAPTERS 18 AND 26)

These processes aim to forecast and manage costs to ensure completion within budget by appropriate estimating, budgeting and cost control:

- *Cost estimation*  Developing cost estimates for the project.
- *Budgeting*  Using results from the estimates to produce the project budget.
- *Cost control*  Controlling costs and deviations from the budget.

## 6. RESOURCE RELATED (CHAPTER 20)

The purpose of these processes is to plan and control resources. They help to identify what is required, for how long, and where they fit within the project schedule. Actual use compared against planned use is a significant part of project control.

- *Resource planning* Identifying, estimating, scheduling and allocating all resources.
- *Resource control* Comparing actual usage against resource plans and taking action if needed.

## 7. PERSONNEL-RELATED (CHAPTERS 17 AND 40)

People determine the quality and success of the project. These processes aim to create an environment in which people contribute effectively and efficiently to the project through appropriate organizational structures, staff allocation and team development.

- *Organizational structure definition* Defining a project organizational structure tailored to suit the project needs, including identifying roles in the project and defining authority and responsibility.
- *Staff allocation* Selecting and assigning sufficient personnel with appropriate competence to suit the project needs.
- *Team development* Developing individual and team skills and ability to enhance project performance.

## 8. COMMUNICATION-RELATED (CHAPTERS 42 AND 43)

These processes aim to facilitate the exchange of all project information, covering its generation, collection, dissemination, and storage and ultimate disposition.

- *Communication planning* Planning the information and communication systems of the project.
- *Information management* Making necessary information available to project organization members and other stakeholders.
- *Communication control* Controlling communication in accordance with the planned communication system.

## 9. RISK-RELATED (CHAPTER 21)

Risks are related to uncertainties throughout the project and may affect the project processes or the project product. These processes aim to minimize the impact of potential negative events and take full advantage of any opportunities for improvement. Processes should exist to identify, assess, develop responses and control all risks.

- *Risk identification*   Determining risks in the project.
- *Risk estimation*   Evaluating the probability of occurrence of risk events and the impact of risk events on the project.
- *Risk response development*   Developing plans for responding to risks.
- *Risk control*   Implementing and updating the risk plans.

## 10.  PURCHASING-RELATED (PART VI)

These processes deal with the purchase, acquisition or procurement of products obtained for the project. They include definition of requirements, contractor analysis, tendering procedures and contract control.

- *Purchasing planning and control*   Identifying and controlling what is to be purchased and when.
- *Documentation of requirements*   Compiling commercial conditions and technical requirements.
- *Evaluation of subcontractors*   Evaluating and determining which subcontractors should be invited to supply products.
- *Subcontracting*   Issuing invitations to tender, tender evaluation, negotiation, preparation and placing of the subcontract.
- *Contract control*   Ensuring that subcontractors' performance meets contractual requirements.

### SUMMARY OF ISO 10,006

The guide is explicit on what should be considered in ensuring that the project management process covers the appropriate issues. It is not comparable to either BS6079 or PRINCE 2 but provides an excellent checklist. It does not differentiate between simple and complex projects but anyone using the guide would be left in no doubt regarding what should be considered to achieve the required quality of the process. The guide focuses on the standard of management of the project and does not cover the 'doing' of the activities necessary to complete the project.

## CONCLUSIONS

Probably the biggest difficulty facing the authors of any process is drafting a document suitable for a wide variety of users. None of these processes can be used in isolation and assure project success. They all need to be applied by someone who understands what is required and can tailor the processes to their particular project, in short a project manager!

As can be seen from each model, the project process is initiated by a defined business need. Without this mandate the project manager cannot establish his or her personal terms of reference and the rest of the project plan. The strategic planning and decision-making tools used to identify what should be undertaken rightly lie in the corporate, rather than the project tool kit. Consequently there can be no project without this stage and no project can deliver any business benefit if this stage is done badly. Without a clear recognition of need, no project management process can economically deliver a project of benefit to the business.

On completion the lessons learned from the project need to be incorporated into the corporate and project procedures if they are to be of any real benefit. For this simple, but often overlooked reason, the process must be flexible and adaptable. Without this continuous improvement and development of the processes they soon fall into disrepute and are shortly thereafter ignored.

To obtain maximum benefit projects must be seen to make a significant contribution to the introduction of new ways of working or new products to the organization. A project aware organization should establish a corporate framework (BS6079) as one way of including the corporate needs.

Within this framework projects should be managed in a structured and controlled way to ensure timely and accurate delivery of the project deliverables and clear reporting procedures to senior corporate management. PRINCE provides a method suitable for any project type and tailorable to suit the scale and importance of the project and the skill level of the project manager.

ISO 10,006 provides a comprehensive checklist to ensure all elements of the project are managed in a way that is compatible with the corporate quality management systems and at the appropriate level of detail for the specific project.

Project management processes have a reputation of being strait-jackets rather than flexible management guidelines. It is not the methods that are at fault but the way they are used by the project management team.

Good luck with your process.

## REFERENCES AND FURTHER READING

BS6079, *A Guide to Project Management*, British Standards Institute, London.

CCTA (1996), *Managing Successful Projects with PRINCE 2*, The Stationery Office, London.

Duncan, W. R. (ed.) (1996), *The Guide to the Project Management Body of Knowledge*, Project Management Institute, Sylva, NC.

ISO (1998), *ISO 10,006, Quality Management – Guidelines to Quality in Project Management*, International Standards Organization, Geneva.

## RELATED TOPICS

# 7 Information systems for programme management

*Geoff Reiss*

This chapter describes the information systems available for programme planning and management. The current breed of software tools, which were developed in the context of project management, are not adequate for the needs of programme management. Existing tools were developed in the single project arena and have been modified to extend their applicability into the multiproject situation with varying degrees of success.

In Chapter 3, programme management is defined and the difference between programme and project management explained. A brief description of the programme management process was then given. In this chapter, the information system tools to support programme management are described. Rather than providing a detailed description of the information systems and their use, a more practical description is given of how they support and faciltitate the programme management process.

To ensure an understanding of the arguments the current breed of project planning systems are briefly examined and categorized and their applicability to the programme management environment commented upon. This may help an organization searching for a software system suitable for its needs. Feedback from a number of companies using current commercial tools in a programme management environment is distilled into a model of the programme planning process and some examples of the use of tools are outlined. This model may help an organization considering how to plan its programme workload with current commercially available tools. Having established a framework the chapter goes on to discuss the shortfall in functionality between the needs of the programme management team and that provided by the current products. Finally, a view of an environment in which imaginary tools are employed to suit the multiproject environment is outlined.

# PROJECT PLANNING AND CONTROL TOOLS

There is a very wide range of project planning and control tools commercially available. Most are called project *management* tools, but I suggest that is inappropriate as there is a great deal more to project management than is offered in a software package. There are a very large number of systems available, and to help to understand the different types and how they may apply to programme management, I think it is worthwhile categorizing the systems. I propose three categories: heavyweight, stand-alone and introductory.

### HEAVYWEIGHT

This class of project planning software centres on a multi-user project or programme planning system. Typically these systems were designed to run in a distributed environment like UNIX or VMS, where a central processor is operated by many people at terminals connected to a main computer. Increasingly these systems are being modified to run on PC LAN systems and they can be operated on a single powerful PC. Their nature normally assumes a multiple user environment. They are typically found in the planning office of a large project or programme management environment. They are usually unlimited in terms of maximum number of tasks, resources and other elements.

These systems tend to be expensive and usually require professional consultancy input at the implementation stage. Implementation tends to be a significant commitment as the hardware and software require considerable investment and installation. The purchasing organization often requires the support of professional consultancy to tailor the system to its requirements, and is immediately faced with training and implementation costs. It may establish a full-time team (project office) to support the many users of the system.

Such systems tend to have an open database. The database will normally be a proprietary tool and task data will be held in fields within it. This means that the data can be accessed to create links with other management systems, for example job costing, executive information systems and accounts software. The links necessary are normally forged by a bespoke piece of software with the associated costs of such development.

Heavyweight systems are very powerful and not easy to use. They are aimed at a full time planner – someone who will spend much of his or her working day producing and modifying project plans. These systems, and the companies which supply them, include:

- Artemis from Lucas Management Systems;

- Cascade from Mantix;
- Openplan from Welcome Software Technology;
- Planview from Planview Inc.;
- Primavera from Primavera Inc.;
- PX from PSDI Ltd.

Costs are in the range of £2000 to £10 000 per user.

## STAND-ALONE SYSTEMS

This class covers the majority of 'project management' software packages. Stand-alone systems are sold widely. At the simpler end of the range, they can be purchased by mail order from vendors who sell a range of software applications. You can even buy Microsoft Project in the departure lounge of an airport. For the more professional purchase one is likely to obtain several copies from a specialist project management software house. These tools are dominated by the Windows operating system, and are mostly based on the following basic processes:

- Create a critical path model of the project.
- Analyse that plan.
- Produce bar charts and other scheduling reports.
- Add resources to the tasks and produce resource histograms.
- Add costs to the tasks and produce cost forecasts.
- Set a baseline and monitor actual progress against that baseline.

The analysis phase, which used to take a few minutes, has become on modern fast computers virtually instantaneous for small plans. For large plans a discernible wait is apparent. With small plans it is possible to switch between PERT chart and bar chart views instantaneously. PERT chart views show the tasks that make up the plan in a network with their logical links, demonstrating how they depend on each other. Bar charts show the timing of the tasks as calculated from the PERT diagram by the time analysis algorithm. Some systems merge these two views by adding links to the bar chart display. Such systems allow most of the manipulation of the plan to be done whilst viewing the bar chart, which is very convenient. On large plans with complex logic, these displays tend to become very confusing.

These systems are produced by a range of organizations, some big and some small, including:

- Project from Microsoft;
- Project Workbench from ABT International;
- Hydra from Hydra Development Corporation Limited;

- Superproject from Computer Associates;
- Timeline from Symantec Corporation.

These tools offer a user interface familiar to Windows users and so are easily handled by a part-time project planner. Typically the operative will not be a full-time planner but will use the system once or twice a week as a part of a more general project management role.

These tools offer some programme management features. They permit the creation of one large plan from a number of small plans. This merging of plans allows many plans to be brought together in an attempt to foresee multiproject resource demands and logical conflicts.

Some systems offer a navigation facility so the user can find his or her way through the many plans on the system to locate a specific project, phase or task. Considerable management guidance is required to ensure that the many project plans are consistent in terms of conventions for task- and resource-naming as this is essential for multiproject management. Some systems offer electronic mail facilities within or associated with the project management software so that messages about the workload and actual achievement can be sent and received.

Stand-alone systems tend to use their own internal database, which is not accessible by the user. To exchange data between the system and other software applications the user must use one of the following:

1. *OLE2 (Object Linking and Embedding version 2) and DDE (Dynamic Data Exchange)* When mastered these allow data transfer between software packages that support the appropriate protocols.
2. *File export* Most systems offer a file export command which copies the data into a file format that can be accessed by another software package or transferred into a database.
3. *Cut and paste* Most Windows systems support the concept of cutting data out of one software package for pasting into another.
4. *ODBC* Some systems support Open Database Connectivity, which is a standard language for reading and writing files. Selecting the ODBC option normally saves the file in a common format. This is a version of the file export method.

Costs are generally in the £300 to £1200 range.

### INTRODUCTORY

This covers a class of project management tools aimed at the beginner – the planner who will be using the software on an irregular basis and whose needs are simple. Such systems tend be purchased by mail order and based around the

Windows environment on the PC platform. Interchange of data with other systems may be impossible or more complex, but the systems are very easy to operate and often lean towards presentation as much as planning. These tools are strong in their ability to turn out quick, neat, presentable bar charts for communication purposes. Systems and their vendors include:

- Charts Now from Deepak Sareen Associates;
- Instaplan from Deepak Sareen Associates;
- Suretrak from Primavera Systems Inc.

## THE DIFFERENCES BETWEEN PROGRAMME AND PROJECT PLANNING

There are some clear differences between programme planning and project planning. I am here using these terms as follows:

- Programme planning is the planning, monitoring and control of a portfolio of projects.
- Project planning is the same activities applied to a single project.

Some of the differences in planning between the two environments are discussed below.

### PROJECT PLANNING

Traditional planning tends to be executed on one project at a time. The project is usually independent of other projects within the company but dependent on its context. Projects may be physically or geographically distant from the office. Resources are less important than in the programme management sphere. It is often considered normal to recruit and hire resources for the life of the single project. Resources do not expect to be retained within the project team beyond the life of the project. Projects tend to be dissimilar to each other. The nature of the one-off project tends to make such projects greatly different to previous projects. Their plans may be complex. The planning team may use critical path techniques to establish the most efficient process for project achievement. Bridge and power station builders spend much of their time investigating alternative methods of construction before selecting one. Planning is concerned with the 'how' issues as well as the 'when' issues. There is a need to minimize demand for resources, to reduce the number of people and other resources hired in for the project and therefore to minimize costs. There is a definite start and end to the project and there is usually one single objective with which nearly everyone can identify.

## PROGRAMME PLANNING

Programme planning involves many simultaneous projects which conflict with each other, interact with each other and depend upon each other. The planning tends to concentrate on resources as these are the key cash flow within the company. The projects are likely to be similar to each other and the plans tend to be straightforward so simple bar charts are often adequate. There is little time spent on evaluating and selecting a method for executing each project as the methods are normally well established. Planning is mainly concerned with the 'when' issues. There is a need to maximize the utilization of resources so that maximum effort is derived from a relatively fixed resource pool. While additional team members can be recruited to join the staff on a long-term basis and while it is often possible to contract some work out, the fundamental resource pool is either fixed or slow to change. There is no definite start and end to the programme as a whole. New projects are constantly being added to the work plan and old projects are discarded as they are delivered. There are many different objectives within the programme management environment – some people are motivated by their own projects, others are motivated to run an efficient functional department, others are trying to keep costs down over the whole project portfolio.

# A MODEL OF THE PROGRAMME PLANNING PROCESS

There are many models of the project planning process but relatively few of the programme planning process. I hope that the model outlined below and the following discussion of various applications of this model will assist in the search for an appropriate approach within any organization. The range of programme management and organizational models dictates that there must be a range of approaches appropriate to those environments. For that reason I have attempted to outline the common factors I have noticed within a number of organizations. This is not a truly scientific or rigorous set of models but is the result of my visits to a wide range of programme management organizations to examine their ways of working. There are five stages in the planning of a portfolio of projects:

1. *Planning* Each project is planned in terms of time and resource requirements. This is similar to the planning of a single project as each project tends to be planned in a normal, one-off project style. Frequently, as projects tend to be similar or based on a familiar pattern, the initial planning is achieved by reference to a standard plan or even based on a standard or previous plan.

2. *Transmission*   Once the individual project plans have been produced, and as new plans are created, the next stage is the transmission of the individual plans to a central location.

3. *Consolidation*   This part of the process begins with the combining of the many individual project plans into one programme plan. In many organizations this consolidation stage needs to be carried out frequently, as new project plans are added to the total workload and existing plans are updated.

4. *Resolution*   Once the plans have been consolidated the examination of cross-project conflicts and the decision-making processes to improve that plan can begin. The demand for resources across the whole organization's workload can be seen and conflicts predicted. Problems connected with the interdependence of one project on another can be inspected and evaluated. When these problems have been established and measured, the programme management team can take decisions to resolve the conflicts.

5. *Reporting*   Decisions taken by the programme management team frequently affect the individual project teams. A reporting mechanism often exists so that these decisions can be communicated back to the individual project teams. Decisions usually involve the delaying of a project to improve the efficiency of the programme as a whole or the lengthening of a project's duration to reduce demand for precious resources. It may mean the cancellation of a project.

Having established this simple model of the process we can examine different approaches for dealing with these stages. Each approach I have observed in practice.

## THE STAND-ALONE MODEL

Planners work with their own copy of a popular, low cost, PC-based project planning system to plan their individual projects. Such systems are cheap and easy to use and suit admirably the planning of single projects. These plans get transmitted regularly (perhaps weekly or fortnightly) via floppy disk or over a local area network (LAN) to a project or programme office where they are consolidated into a complete plan using another installation of the same software. The project office may need special expertise in the intricacy of the software and a powerful, fast PC to manage the large amounts of data. The project office staff can inspect histograms and summary bar charts and, especially important, bar charts of like work, for example all the design office work. The programme planning team can experiment with alternative strategies and schedules in an effort to locate a more efficient programme plan.

This approach has the advantage of allowing each project team to plan their own work so that they 'own' their plans. The project office takes a supporting role advising the programme management team of conflicts which are generally in terms of resource over-demands. A high degree of consistency amongst the many project plans is essential. If the many project planners do not use the same terminology for resource names, task numbering and naming conventions the consolidation process will be unsuccessful. Project teams may be unwilling or unable to plan their projects in appropriate detail and may not envisage a benefit to doing so. If the project teams are not encouraged to submit their plans on a regular basis the process will not be successful.

Decisions taken from the multiproject perspective are communicated by meetings, reports and other verbal means. Individual planners must alter their plans to bring them in line with the programme's requirements. An advantage of this stand-alone approach is the potential for a step-by-step installation of such a system. The consolidation facility can be implemented separately at a later date.

## THE INTEGRATED MODEL

In this case, the organization purchases multiple site licences of a heavyweight programme or multiproject planning system. Planners have access to the tool through a local terminal, which might be a PC or a terminal on a UNIX or VMS system. Each project is planned locally and the design of the system makes transmission and consolidation completely automatic. Once again, a small team in a project office examine the cross-project demands and report problems. The programme planning team can experiment with alternative strategies and schedules in an effort to locate a more efficient programme plan.

These systems are expensive and complex to use. A high level of expertise is required from individual project planners. The tendency is for a small number of enthusiasts to enter data on behalf of themselves and other less computer literate users. Once again consistency of naming conventions and regular updating are essential if the programme management is to have a useable model of the workload. The heavyweight system can be used to enforce planning standards on the planning teams. Decisions taken in light of the cross-project workload can be entered into the system within the project office as well as being communicated verbally and on paper. This means that feedback on the implications of conflicts can be directly entered in terms of modified plans.

Such systems involve a 'big bang' approach and implementation is a major exercise. Access must be controlled so that authority to alter the parts of the model rests with appropriate people. Typically, these systems are supported by a project office staffed by full-time employees.

## THE COMBINATION MODEL

To get the best of both worlds, some organizations create a combination system. Each project team uses a simple stand-alone PC-based planning system and the project office uses a more powerful system to integrate the individual project plans. The individual plans are created and kept up to date on the PC-based single project system and the files are transferred to the heavyweight system for consolidation. It is likely that such an organization would have a LAN. The project office team manipulate the data within the heavyweight system and report on conflicts across the projects. The data flow is normally one-way so that decisions are communicated from the programme management team to the individual project managers by meetings, phone or verbally. Some 'consolidation' tools are beginning to appear in an effort to ease this approach. If the consolidation tool permits, the programme planning team can experiment with alternative schedules in an effort to locate a more efficient programme plan.

There are problems of data compatibility that must be resolved before such a system can work. There will be regular transfer of data from the single project plans into the multiproject tool and file compatibility has to be simple and reliable. The problems of consistency of data described above exist. It is possible for a file transfer program to be written that converts and validates the data from each single system. There is an implementation advantage as it is possible for an organization to establish an ethos where projects are individually planned long before implementing the consolidation tool.

## THE CUSTOM MODEL

This is similar to the stand-alone approach but differs in that a purpose-built piece of software is created to manage consolidation. The specific advantage is that the purpose-built software can be automated in its efforts to consolidate the data and generate reports based on that data. Once again, a high degree of consistency is required across the projects in task numbering and resource names, but the purpose built software can check for consistency as a part of the consolidation process. The purpose built software might be used to report specific problems and could search for problems that are likely to exist. As the purpose-built software will probably not be as powerful as a traditional planning system it is unlikely that the programme planning team will have the ability to experiment with the programme plan to seek efficient schedules. Reports of the decision would almost certainly be verbal.

# A VISION OF THE FUTURE

I have a vision of the future of programme management tools which comes from my contacts and observations of people who are trying to plan their programmes with existing tools.

## ROLE-ORIENTED PLANNING TOOLS

Traditional project management systems assume that their users will be project managers or, more precisely, project planners. The user interface and emphasis of the software stems from the genesis of such systems, which dates back to large projects where it was the project planners who produced project plans for the single project under consideration. In the programme management environment, tools designed in this way tend to be used by a breed of planners in much the same way. However, it should now be possible to provide one tool with a number of different role-related user interfaces. Such a tool would be designed to offer facilities to the project planners, and to all the people fulfilling the other roles identified in Figure 7.1.

## AN ACTIVE ROLE FOR THE SOFTWARE

Traditionally the output of project management software has been a model of the project, just as a budget is a model of a department's finances. The plan models what the project team aim to do, and the team use the model to test ideas, communicate their plans and monitor progress. Compare this with an accounts system which models the organization's financial affairs, but also directly produces cheques, invoices, salary payments and bank statements. Here the system is also playing a vital role in the management of the organization. Role-related software can likewise move into the centre of programme management activity to play an active role much more like an accounts system. I do not mean to suggest that the software should make decisions about which department should perform a task or which resource is best suited to a type of work. I do mean that a large number of such decisions could be taken by individuals based on an understanding of their sphere of influence over the corporate plan, and that those decisions could be transmitted via the programme management software. In other words the software could provide each member of the programme management team with appropriate data and communicate the decisions that individuals make. A programme management software package might pass on instructions to resources, relay information on work done and handle requests from project managers for work to be done.

## GOOD PRACTICE

Such a system would allow those in control of the organization to encourage or enforce the organizational standards on the project and resource managers. A methodology could be reinforced as the system might be used by the organization to prevent certain actions being taken without certain other approvals. Also the organization could insist through the software that only given managers have authority over the plan – project managers could perhaps only work with tasks within their own sphere of influence. Functional managers might be barred from changing any tasks but would have sole authority over the allocation of resources within their department.

## TECHNOLOGY

The technology that makes new solutions possible includes LANs, WANs and client/server architecture. The increasingly popular connectivity of systems means that many people involved in a programme can have access via a simple Windows PC to a powerful system that plays a central role in planning and managing the workflow. Also the technology means that the 'big bang' approach of the multi-user system and the associated degree of commitment and risk can be avoided. With a LAN-based system it should be possible to test the software with a few users in one department and allow the use of the software to spread slowly through the organization.

## A HYPOTHETICAL PROGRAMME PLANNING ENVIRONMENT

Here is a hypothetical example of the programme planning system of the future in use within a typical programme management organization. The programme management role uses the organizational breakdown structure to decide which project managers should be given responsibility for each project or package of work. At this stage each project might only be defined by a single bar and a single sum of money. As a project manager accepts a project from the programme manager, he or she can expand its detail by working with the work breakdown structure as it affects the relevant project. Alternatively, the project manager might work with a bar chart to develop the plan into appropriate detail. The project manager might calculate the skill requirements of the tasks within the project in terms of programmer/days or engineer/hours. The project plan joins many other project plans in a central database. Essentially these tasks are requests for work to be done.

Each resource manager views only the tasks from the many projects that demand the skills of the department. Perhaps all of the design-related tasks are extracted and displayed for the Design Department Manager. This functional or resource manager allocates real resources to these tasks, hence satisfying the demand for skills. The resource manager only requires a display dealing with resource allocation plus a display that allows the maintenance of records about the team members and their skills. The allocation information from the many functional managers is again stored centrally. Each human resource can therefore get a simple display showing what work he or she has in the next few days or weeks. Resources can record actual achievement and later submit a time sheet recording actual achievement. This time sheet data from the many resources feeds back into the tasks in the many project plans and updates them accordingly.

## THE IMPORTANCE OF FEEDBACK

I believe that there is an especially important role of the feedback loop within this environment. Ideally the system should loop back with feedback so that people are advised what has been actually happening. Time sheet input is very common in some environments particularly those where most work is done by highly paid professionals – areas like software development and R&D. Update information is created as everyone enters data into time sheets which are fed back into and update the project plans. I believe strongly that there must be some human intervention in this process.

## THE SOFTWARE NEED

Therefore I think we need software systems that:

- put software on centre stage – not just as an external modelling process, but as an internal, central modelling process that everyone can use in the way that suits them;
- model the organizational methodology and management style;
- support decisions and communicate them;
- can be used to encourage people to talk together and think ahead together;
- have clear benefits for everyone;
- can be installed without a 'big bang' commitment;
- are easy to use; and
- incorporate a time sheet.

Perhaps in the next few years the field of project management will expand to provide true programme management software tools. I do not think there are many systems today that truly meet the need.

## PROGRAMME MANAGEMENT ROLES

To conclude this chapter, we consider four essential roles in the programme management context. In any discussion of programme management, four roles are repeatedly mentioned. Three are shown in Figure 7.1, and the aims and responsibilities of each of the four roles are shown in Figure 7.2 (a–d). The four roles are as follows:

1. Senior or programme managers (who act as referees or umpires)
2. Project managers (product champions, project leaders)
3. Functional managers (resource managers, departmental heads)
4. Resources (operatives, workers)

These four roles do not here always refer to individuals but to functions performed by individuals. For example, planning may be undertaken by a manager on a part-time basis. One day per week, this manager takes on the role of project planner, and for the other four days acts as project manager or runs a functional department. Similarly the planning role might absorb the efforts of ten people on a full-time basis. The relationship between people and roles depends on the organization, its workload and the people within it.

Project managers may have no resources of their own but they do have projects to get done. They get these projects done by getting the functional or departmental managers to allocate or loan resources to their projects. Across the top of the matrix are the functional managers and they have teams of people who provide specialist services.

The senior management function sits above and around both axes of the matrix. The senior management hires, directs and fires the functional managers and the project managers. These people understand the priorities of the organization and have authority over the project managers and functional managers. Therefore the senior management will act as umpire or referee to settle priority issues when the demands of many projects overload a functional department's ability to provide resources for a period of time.

The resources or operatives work within a functional department and do work on the projects that pass through their hands. Projects are pulled across the matrix, spending time in each department as they are progressed towards completion. These resources are allocated to work on the projects in a variety of ways. Sometimes resources are seconded to the project on a full-time or part-time basis, sometimes the department contracts to do the work. Most organizations do not have a 100 per cent project workload. Any programme management organization is likely to have a continuing background workload of non-project work. The resources will be involved in project work and a raft of other work that

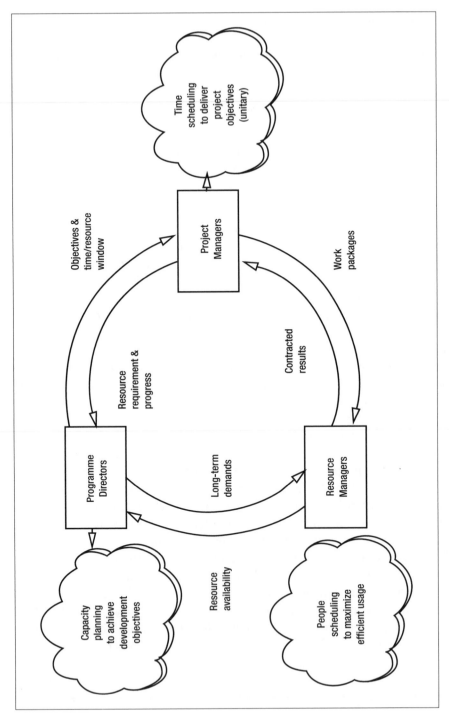

Figure 7.1   Three (of four) roles of programme management

---

## Programme management

**Aims**   Programme managers are concerned with the management of the enterprise's workload, which is made up of a number of projects and continuing work. They must deliver a cohesive set of projects which collectively meet the organization's needs or its customers' needs. They will also have responsibility for maintaining appropriate pools of specialist resources in functional groups.

**Responsibilities**   To achieve these aims programme managers will:

- define programme goals based on the organization's strategy or competitive position;
- continually evaluate potential enterprise-wide benefits of internal projects to justify the programme in terms of the changing corporate objectives;
- evaluate risks and benefits from external projects;
- describe the scope and boundaries of the programme;
- maintain the work breakdown structure to fragment the workload amongst the project management team;
- maintain the organizational breakdown structure to manage the resource teams;
- control the content and membership of the programme, project management and functional teams;
- establish and operate an approval procedure by which projects can be checked and approved;
- initiate the programme infrastructure by gaining approval at board level to embark on a feasibility study for the programme;
- approve project budgets and timescales in appropriate detail;
- assign projects to project managers;
- manage conflicts between projects and between functions;
- monitor progress against project milestones or in appropriate detail;
- experiment, model and make decisions about future workload and opportunities. Work with potential projects and workload;
- consider the strategic implications of each project;
- understand the impact of one project on another;
- administer links between projects (between different project managers);
- approve changes in project status, e.g. give permission to start a project or a phase;
- maintain a library of standard projects and resource outputs;
- ensure that projects are formally closed;
- inspect forecast assignment of resources and demands for skills;
- deal with enterprise-wide calendars, indicate plans, down time, etc.;
- administer standard projects in an organization's library;
- analyse past project performance and monitor feedback systems;
- examine past projects for trends.

**Figure 7.2a   Aims and responsibilities of programme directors**

does not conveniently break down into projects. The background workload might include maintenance of equipment, looking after users of old projects and marketing activities on new projects. They all involve doing work and take time but are not connected with the project workload.

---

## Project management

**Aims**   The management and successful delivery of specific, named projects.

**Responsibilities**   To achieve these aims project managers will:

- drive projects through the enterprise;
- plan what tasks are required for a project;
- estimate and enter task durations;
- estimate work content and skill requirements for tasks;
- establish and agree milestones;
- administer tasks, dependencies and skills required for each task;
- negotiate timescales with resource managers;
- agree resource allocation with resource management;
- deduce the project's structure through work breakdown structures and PERT models;
- receive and utilize resources seconded by the resources managers;
- subcontract packages of work to the resource management;
- monitor progress and adjust timescales of key points in the project if necessary;
- define deliverables of tasks and projects;
- estimate budgets and timescales for projects;
- gain approval for budgets and plans;
- set project time targets based on proposed plan and inspect and modify targets;
- set project status, i.e. proposed, committed, complete;
- deal with project calendars, indicate plans, down time, etc.;
- produce and distribute project plans and budgets;
- update project plans to reflect actual progress;
- compare actual and planned progress;
- understand the impact of one project on another;
- build projects from elements held in a corporate library of standard projects or parts of projects;
- make and modify notes either verbal or written relating to each task;
- delegate to resource managers the responsibility for completing tasks.

---

Figure 7.2b   Aims and responsibilities of project managers

## Resource management

**Aims**    The management of a number of specific, named resources and their prioritization across projects to deliver the projects successfully, within the requirement of efficient utilization of the resources

**Responsibilities**    To achieve these aims resource managers will:

- record expected availability of individual resources (holidays, overtime, etc.);
- allocate or estimate skill levels (capabilities) to resources;
- allocate specific resources within a department and/or enterprise to satisfy the requirements made for certain skills by project managers;
- second resources to a project manager for a period of time;
- perform tasks as requested by the project managers;
- predict, communicate and resolve resource shortfalls;
- bear responsibility for maintenance of specific areas of OBS;
- negotiate timescales with project managers;
- optimize resource utilization;
- maintain resource output tables and database of production outputs;
- instruct resources on their next work;
- ensure that time sheets are completed on time;
- work within departmental budgets.

Figure 7.2c   Aims and responsibilities of resource managers

## Operations/operatives/resources

**Aims**    Performing work directly towards the project's goals.

**Responsibilities**    To achieve these aims resources will:

- perform work on the tasks within the projects;
- measure and report on actual achievement, work done;
- update estimates of work remaining;
- compare remaining work with work planned;
- compare work done with work planned;
- receive instructions on future work;
- enquire on the history of work completed;
- understand how their own work fits into the total plan.

Figure 7.2d   Aims and responsibilities of operatives

## RELATED TOPICS

# 8 The programme and project support office

*David Marsh*

All programmes and projects are by nature transient. They are defined, commissioned, executed and closed. They are not a continuous process in their own right. Unless a programme or project support office is implemented then the organization will be forced to develop a supporting infrastructure for each new programme and project and the lessons learnt from one cannot be passed onto the next. In addition, without some central focus point for programmes and projects, monitoring and control can become a logistical and actual nightmare. Thus unless the organization only ever executes one programme or a very small number of projects there is a vital need to establish some form of programme and/or project support office (PSO).

Having implemented a programme and/or project support office the functionality and support provided can be extended into assisting the programme and project management processes. In some organizations this extension has meant that they become an essential part of the process itself, for example organizing contracts or purchases. In extreme situations they have moved into creating and managing the programme or project themselves. The extension of the functionality of the programme and project support office into these added-value areas is largely dependent on the environment in which the organization operates. In relatively stable environments they are likely to assume the more traditional role of support to the programme and project management process. However, in a more volatile environment they are likely to be seen as the agent of change.

In this chapter we describe the establishment of a programme or project support office. We consider the functions of each, and their costs and benefits.

## IMPLEMENTING A PROGRAMME OR PROJECT SUPPORT OFFICE

A programme or project support office can be implemented as a physical entity, as a logical entity or as a combination of the two. In the physical entity form, a team of staff are established and allocated to the office. In the logical implementation, no staff are allocated to carry out the functions, but they are generally executed by the systems, procedures and processes of the organization. Such logical implementations do have to have a custodian and be supervised. It is essential therefore to establish a process or a person to take responsibility to ensure that this monitoring and control takes place and to be the focus for the definition and implementation of any updating that is required.

### Why are programme and project support offices required?

The answer to this question is, in essence, to provide the organization with a focus and the means of addressing the need to:

- maintain, update and extend the scope of the programme and project support infrastructure;
- support the planning of the programme and projects;
- support the monitoring and control of the programmes and projects;
- ensure that the programme and projects have the required technical and business integrity;
- provide a repository for the experience and knowledge gained;
- audit the use of the programme and project support infrastructure.

### What should a programme or project support office provide?

This question is rather like asking 'What is the length of a piece of string?' – it depends on the organization and the scope of the programmes and/or projects it undertakes. However, there does appear to be a fairly common set of functions carried out by the PSO across many organizations, although the processes they operate and the amount or level of support they provide varies considerably. The common functions are outlined in the following sections for both the programme support office and the project support office.

## THE PROGRAMME SUPPORT OFFICE

The typical functions that a programme support office either provides or supports are as follows:

1. Defining the contents of the programme.
2. Quantifying the programme's benefits and costs.
3. Assessment and management of risk.
4. Identification of the component projects.
5. Monitoring and control of processes.
6. Capturing experience and knowledge.
7. Providing specialist skills.
8. Maintaining the programme support infrastructure.

## DEFINING THE CONTENTS OF THE PROGRAMME

The responsibility for identifying the need for, and content of, the programme rests with the organization's strategic and business planning function. It is initially assisted in this by the programme director(s) and then latterly by the remainder of the individual programme executive or board (the business change, technical or design manager and the programme manager). The PSO can support this process in a number of ways, for example by gathering, analysing and presenting information to assist in identifying what business areas the programme is to address and its likely goals. This support role can be purely administrative or it can extend to include the gathering and analysis of inter-organization or departmental information to provide benchmarks and targets or goals for the programme. Such support is vital to ensure that any decisions made and targets set are based on fact rather than supposition.

## QUANTIFYING THE BENEFITS AND COSTS OF THE PROGRAMME

Once the direction and content of the business strategy and the supporting programmes has been decided, it is vital to quantify their benefits and costs. A number of such quantifications are required, including:

- the benefits planned to be realized;
- the resources required to implement the programme(s); and
- the availability of resources, at the right time and in the required quantity/quality.

To provide support to these processes the PSO will require access to data held by a number of the organization's departments. Obtaining access to the appropriate level of accurate and up-to-date information to support this process can involve considerable changes in working practices and procedures. Experience has shown that a failure to appreciate this and to first model the information requirements before installing an information gathering process and support system can result in either an over-bureaucratic system or one that operates with inaccurate information.

## ASSESSING AND MANAGING RISK IN THE PROGRAMME

In all undertakings there is an element of risk and when embarking on a deliberate programme(s) of change that involves doing something new, the number of and level of risks can increase dramatically. There is a wide range of approaches to identifying and managing such risks. The PSO can help ensure that this process is:

- carried out;
- consistent;
- regularly updated;
- reflective of experience gained and/or lessons learnt; and
- facilitated.

As with the quantification process, the PSO must ensure that it has the information required to support this process and the skills to see that it has been correctly applied.

## IDENTIFYING AND INITIATING THE COMPONENT PROJECTS

The PSO may provide a range of support services to the programme manager(s) in the identification and initiation of the constituent programmes and projects. The services and information systems which are needed to enable it to perform these functions can be free-standing or interlinked with those used for project support. This information may include:

- project or system development methods and metrics;
- resource and asset availability;
- planning and control standards and systems;
- project risk assessment information.

The principal support provided by the PSO is that of the research and production of 'position' and other papers, and the initiation of the constituent projects.

## PROGRAMME MONITORING AND CONTROL PROCESS

Once the programme(s) have been established, the organization must ensure that it regularly monitors progress and, if necessary, instigates control action. The PSO can serve both the programme(s) and individual projects by carrying

134

out this function. It can also help to identify where any actual or potential bottlenecks may occur. In order that this support is provided in the most efficient and effective manner it is essential that this function is also planned and modelled before installing an information gathering process, so that the collection and collation of the progress reports can be made with ease and accuracy.

## CAPTURING EXPERIENCE AND KNOWLEDGE GAINED

It is very likely that having carried out one programme the organization will commission others. It is important that the lessons learnt and the experience gained is captured for use on these subsequent programme(s). The information collected may be about the opportunities and/or problems encountered in executing the programme and the constituent projects. Other information that is vital for the PSO to collect and analyse is the difference between what was planned to happen and what actually did happen, so that allowances can be made for this in future, or countermeasures employed to contain it.

## PROVIDING SPECIALIST SKILLS

The PSO can be operated on a logical basis rather than a physical one. In the logical PSO, the programme support infrastructure holds all the information and support tools required to assist the programme manager(s). The skills and experience needed to carry out the maintenance and updating of this logical PSO infrastructure may be located in a number of places. If it is decided to establish a physical PSO then the organization will need to allocate staff to it, on either a full- or a part-time basis, who have the following skills and experience:

- business analysis;
- financial analysis;
- information technology and other technology specialisms;
- planning and control;
- strategic and business risk analysis and management;
- programme and project management; and
- information administration and management.

## THE PROGRAMME SUPPORT INFRASTRUCTURE

One of the key roles of the PSO will be to build, maintain and update the programme support infrastructure. Typically this infrastructure comprises the following:

- The agreed procedures and standards to be used by the programme manager.
- Example documents from previous projects and programmes.
- Metrics and other resource usage information from previous projects.
- The resource and other asset registers for the organization.
- Software and other tools to assist with all the programme management processes.

## THE PROJECT SUPPORT OFFICE

The typical functions that a project support office provides are as follows:

1. Defining and planning the project.
2. Quantification of the project's costs and benefits.
3. Risk management.
4. Monitoring and control.
5. Supply of experience and knowledge.
6. Supporting project management process.
7. Capturing experience and knowledge.
8. Providing specialist skills.
9. Maintaining the project support infrastructure.

### DEFINITION AND PLANNING OF A PROJECT

Most projects do not exist in isolation and are likely to be part of a programme or portfolio of projects. The PSO can assist the organization in defining each of the component projects. In particular it can assist in the identification and establishment of any links that exist between the projects and the nature and content of such interfaces. The support provided by the PSO to the project planning process often overlaps with that of programme support, as they are both involved in the development of plans for the projects though from different perspectives. These overlaps are usually addressed by the organization using the same basic information but applying it in two ways. For example, organizations will use an extremely 'broad-brush' approach to programme planning, whilst the project planning tends to be more detailed. What is important is that these processes interlink and use a consistent approach.

### QUANTIFYING THE COSTS AND BENEFITS OF THE PROJECT

The initial quantification of the costs and benefits of an individual project may well have been carried out as part of the definition of the programme that contains it. This high level analysis produces a degree of accuracy suitable for the programme definition process but will not be precise enough for individual projects. Therefore it is common practice to update and refine the initial coarse analysis into a detailed and more accurate assessment. This process can be carried out by the project's development team. However, it is unusual for such a team to possess all the skills needed to prepare the analysis. In addition, the need for a consistent approach and the use of standard accounting and other conventions (including impartiality) may indicate to the organization that this analysis is better prepared by the PSO or another independent team.

## RISK MANAGEMENT PROCESS

As at the programme level, there is an element of risk in all projects. When executing a project, the organization will encounter various types and levels of risks. There is a wide range of approaches available for identifying and managing such risks. The PSO can ensure that this process is:

- carried out;
- consistent;
- regularly updated;
- reflective of experience gained and/or lessons learnt; and
- facilitated.

As with the support provided to the quantification process the PSO must ensure that it has the information required for this process and the skills to see that it has been correctly applied. The unique position of the PSO in being able to see across all the projects also ensures that any new risks, avoidance and containment strategies that are developed can be applied to other projects as appropriate.

## MONITORING AND CONTROL PROCESS

Once the project has been initiated the relevant project board must regularly monitor the progress made and, if necessary, instigate control action. The PSO can serve both the individual projects and the programme by carrying out this function. It can also help to identify where any actual or potential bottlenecks occur. To ensure that this support is provided in an efficient and effective manner it is essential that this function is integrated with the planning process and the collection of 'actuals', so that the collection of information and its collation into progress reports can be made with ease and accuracy. The monitoring and control process can be further supported by the production of 'what-if?' analysis of the eventual outcomes of the project. To provide such monitoring in the most efficient and effective manner it is essential that this function is planned and modelled before the systems that are to provide the information are developed and implemented.

## SUPPLY OF EXPERIENCE AND KNOWLEDGE

Typically the PSO supplies the organization with information about relevant experiences and knowledge gained from previous projects for the project managers of today's projects. This can be, at its most simplest manifestation, oral advice and, at the other extreme, coaching or counselling. The PSO may well have staff or other resources that it supplies to projects to form either the project management team and/or specialists to assist the project's work. The adoption of this type of PSO enables a level of consistency to be achieved across projects that is otherwise difficult to attain. Indeed if such a centralized function is supported by an effective and efficient infrastructure of procedures, systems and standards it is possible to have a project manager and other members of the project management team involved in a number of projects simultaneously. This strategy has enabled some organizations to dramatically reduce the number of project managers they require.

## SUPPORTING THE PROJECT MANAGEMENT PROCESS AND PROCEDURES

Under this heading can be found a wide variety of activities. Rather than list them all it is better to consider what support the project management processes and procedures may require. Typically these are:

- updating and maintaining project management documents;
- project accounting;
- resource contract administration;
- capital goods acquisition;
- liaison with external suppliers;
- contract and other negotiations;
- work plans and time sheets;
- progress reports;
- standards definition;
- quality control review administration and organization;
- filing and administration;
- configuration management.

Which of these are delegated to the PSO and which should be carried out by specialist departments, the project manager or the project development team must be decided in advance of the project being commissioned. The need to plan and coordinate the development of a supporting infrastructure for projects is often overlooked. Indeed most PSOs end up with a disjointed collection of functions rather than an integrated infrastructure. This occurs because the functions were not developed and implemented as part of a plan but simply because it seemed a logical thing to do at the time!

## CAPTURING EXPERIENCE AND KNOWLEDGE GAINED

The final function and, perhaps for most organizations the main reason why they implement a PSO, is the capturing of information about the experiences and knowledge gained from previous projects. The widespread use of structured approaches to project management and system development has assisted this by providing a framework for the collection of experience and knowledge. The PSO can add to this the collection of information on:

- skills used on previous projects;
- skills available in the organization;
- project or system development methods that work and those that do not;
- development metrics;
- common faults found at quality control reviews;
- example products.

This information must be collected and collated so that it can be used by the PSO and 'recycled' for the good of future programmes and projects.

## PROVIDING SPECIALIST SKILLS

The staffing of the PSO can also be on a logical basis rather than a physical one. The logical basis is where the project support infrastructure holds all the information and support tools required to assist the project manager to complete his or her tasks. However, that infrastructure will need to be maintained and updated. The skills and experience needed to carry out this maintenance and updating may be located in a number of places in the organization – including the project managers who use the infrastructure. If it is decided to establish a physical PSO, the organization needs to allocate staff who have the following skills and experience:

- project management;
- quality management;
- configuration management;

- planning and control;
- risk analysis;
- consultancy support; and
- information administration and management.

## PROJECT SUPPORT INFRASTRUCTURE

A key role of the PSO is to maintain and update the project support infrastructure (and perhaps even to build it). Typically this infrastructure comprises the following:

- the agreed procedures and standards to be used by the project manager;
- example documents from previous projects;
- metrics and other resource usage information from previous projects;
- the resource and other asset registers for the organization; and
- software and other tools to assist with all the project management processes.

# COSTS AND BENEFITS OF THE PSO

It is vital that the organization has an accurate and agreed definition of the PSO's terms of reference and also the business case for its establishment and operation. Without this the true purpose of the PSO will not be understood and the organization will not obtain the added-value benefits that it should provide. Also without these definitions it is likely that there will be confusion about the role of the PSO and often it declines into just an administration support unit. This section examines how the organization should define the reasons for the PSO and its business case.

## ESTABLISHING THE REASON FOR THE PSO

It is vital to first establish why the organization needs such an investment, and then to define terms of reference for it before starting to construct a business case to justify the investment. This definition must identify the functions that the PSO is to supply or support and the scope (extent or use) of the services to be provided. The reasons for establishing a PSO can be classified into two categories:

- Direct financial
- Qualitative and indirect financial

### Direct financial

The direct financial benefits are those that typically reduce the effort needed by the programme and project manager (an expensive resource) to carry out the programme and project management processes. Ideally the person who prepared the business case would carry out a quantification or work measurement survey to identify how much effort is spent at present on such activities, then determine/estimate what reduction in effort and cost could be achieved by the use of a PSO.

Experience has shown that without a PSO the programme and project manager will expend between 7 and 17 per cent of his or her total availability on the operation of project and programme management processes. This percentage can be reduced by over 50 per cent if the PSO is tasked with providing support to all the major infrastructure functions such as planning, monitoring and control.

### Qualitative and indirect financial

In this category are those PSOs that are installed primarily to achieve better control of programme and project management processes and to ensure that the organization benefits from the experience or knowledge gained from other programmes and projects. There are some quantifiable benefits but they tend to be intangible or indirect. In such circumstances the business case is based on cost avoidance rather than direct savings. Examples of such cost avoidance are:

- reduction in effort putting right repeated mistakes;
- reduction in effort in developing standards.

### DEVELOPING THE BUSINESS CASE – COSTS

A common mistake made in developing an analysis of the costs is not to look widely enough into the organization to identify and assess all of them. The following checklist has been used to avoid this happening and to provide a start point for the analyst.

### What will it cost for the PSO to provide the services?

The costs associated with the activities of the PSO can be calculated as follows:

1. The collection of the data/information to be provided
   - Define the data/information that will be required.
   - Calculate the cost of the collection and cleaning of the data.
   - Estimate/calculate the cost of the storage of the data.

2. The cost of the PSO infrastructure
   - Define the contents of the programme or project support infrastructure to be provided.
   - Estimate/calculate the cost of the development and installation of that infrastructure.
   - Identify and define the cost of maintaining the infrastructure.
3. The cost of non-use: define the costs that organization will incur in:
   - Having the PSO staff research and identify the support needed for the programmes and projects of the future.
   - Preparing the infrastructure to support the programmes and projects of the future.

## DEVELOPING THE BUSINESS CASE – BENEFITS

Similarly it is all too easy not to look widely enough into the organization when assessing the benefits. The following checklist has been used to provide a start point for the benefits calculation.

### The benefits of using a PSO

The benefits associated with the activities of the PSO can be calculated as follows:

1. Knowledge capture
   - What will be the reduction in effort required by programme and project managers to develop programme and project management process documents (plans and reports)?
2. Central focus
   - What will be the benefits from having either a central audit or a policing function?
   - What will be the benefits of having spare resources to assist with programmes or projects if required (e.g. in the event of absence due to unforeseen circumstances etc.)?
3. Added value
   - What is the worth to the organization of having the experience of one programme or project being available to others?
4. Centre of excellence
   - What is the benefit to the organization of not repeating previous errors and mistakes?
   - What is the benefit of shortening the learning curve of new programme and project managers?

## OTHER CONSIDERATIONS

The PSO can also assume the role of the auditor of, or consultant to, the individual programme and project managers. If this role is incorporated into the PSO business case then a benefit equal to the cost of providing this service from other sources should be included. In developing the business case it is also worth considering whether the PSO should operate a recharge mechanism to those parts of the organization that are using its services. If it is decided to operate on a recharge basis then the justification of the PSO can become either simpler or more complicated. It becomes simpler in that essentially the justification for its existence is made by the people who use it, that is they will not use it if it does not provide value for money. It becomes more complicated when such a scenario leads to problems in selling the idea to the organization and the programme and project managers who will use its services. Also the cost–benefit analysis can become more complex.

## SUMMARY

The need for an organization to implement and install a PSO largely depends on its own environment, as do the functions to be provided. It is critical that:

- the needs of the organization for these services are defined;
- they are implemented in an integrated framework to obtain the maximum benefit from the investment in programmes and projects;
- the PSO captures and retains, for the future of the organization, the experience and knowledge acquired as a consequence of current projects and programmes.

## REFERENCES AND FURTHER READING

Bartlett, J. (1998), *Managing Programmes of Business Change*, Project Manager Today Publications, Bradford.

Marsh, D. (2000), *The Programme and Project Support Handbooks*, Project Manager Today Publications, Bradford.

## RELATED TOPICS

# 9 Project health checks

## John Wateridge

Project management is a difficult task. Project managers have to coordinate a number of complex issues, including the human, technical and financial inputs to their projects. Projects are notorious for being seen as failures, whether they be engineering (such as the Channel Tunnel) or information systems/information technology (IS/IT) development (such as TAURUS, London Ambulance Service Computer-Aided Despatch) or whatever. They often exceed the budget constraints and if the facility is ever delivered, it is often late. Stakeholders (clients, sponsors, project managers, the general public) are not satisfied with the process and the outcome. What often happens, however, is that these various stakeholders have identified their own success criteria and they have not appreciated other views on how success is to be measured. Each stakeholder has not known what the others are aiming at. They have not agreed on how success was to be measured in the first place.

Project managers have several tools which enable them to meet the criteria identified by the stakeholders and ensure that the project runs smoothly. First, they can examine archive files for reviews of previous projects to ascertain lessons learnt and apply them in their current project. Unfortunately, post-implementation reviews are often not completed as part of the system life cycle or are carried out superficially. Second, project managers can conduct project audits to detect and prevent any possible fraud, malfunction or other threat to the smooth running of the project. Project audits are usually detailed checks of the project and its control processes, which ought to be conducted by external, independent consultants. Third, and perhaps most importantly, what project managers can do simply and easily is to carry out health checks on the project. These can be used to confirm that everybody is pulling in the same direction, that the success criteria have been agreed by the stakeholders, that appropriate factors, tools and techniques are being applied and that the right team skills are available to the team.

Achieving time, cost and specification are commonly accepted measures of success. However, this does not go far enough in defining the success criteria (see Chapter 5). Performance of the actual product produced and the revenue stream it generates can be equally, if not more, important. It would seem that very few projects assess the effectiveness of the product and whether the project delivered what was needed and the benefits realized. This is seldom done after the handover of the project and seemingly never during the project. If any review is held to understand the project lessons, it is usually a post-implementation review which does nothing for the success of the project in hand. Yet simple diagnostic techniques can be used during the project to assess whether all stakeholders are pulling in the same direction.

Organizations implement projects as a mechanism for change (such as increasing effectiveness, competitiveness and profitability). If they do not develop and change in response to the changing environment, they are likely to cease to exist. Having undertaken a project, organizations need to make efforts to ensure that the project achieves its purpose. When undertaking a project, stakeholders need to be aware of how the project is to be perceived as a success. More importantly, the different stakeholders must be aware of the different viewpoints and agree on the criteria as the foundation for the project to succeed. Health checks address this issue and help to identify any misunderstandings or differences of opinion. Organizations can then take action to overcome those problems that are fundamental to project success. Health checks also help project mangers and other stakeholders focus on the problems and misunderstandings and identify improvements in the way the project is progressing. Project managers must continually ask themselves questions such as:

- Does everybody understand and agree the direction of the project?
- Are we all moving in the direction to succeed?
- Are we employing the necessary factors to deliver the success criteria?
- Are we using appropriate tools and techniques?
- Do we have the right skills?

A project health check is a simple project management tool which gives project managers answers to these questions. Project managers receive a multitude of reports and statistics (such as Gantt charts and network diagrams) to assess the status of the project. However, these tools tell project managers where they are on the project and whether the project is falling behind the schedule; they do not give answers to the questions above.

This chapter describes post-implementation reviews, health checks and audits. Post-implementation reviews and health checks can be conducted by all project managers and can give substantial benefits – health checks to the project in hand, post-implementation reviews to future projects. Detailed audits are substantial endeavours, conducted by external consultants, and so are only briefly described.

## POST-IMPLEMENTATION REVIEW

Post-implementation reviews are an essential tool to learn the lessons of one project for the benefit of future projects to be undertaken by the organization. They will assess how well the project was managed, whether it achieved its success criteria, whether it achieved the expected benefit, and what led to any shortfall. This may not be easy. There may be resistance from project stakeholders, even senior managers, who lack commitment. A project review, if conducted at all, is usually held soon after implementation and examines only the readily apparent lessons, without looking deep within the project to extract the real lessons. This is equally true of both public and private sector projects. Furthermore, very often it is only high profile projects that have an in-depth review or inquiry. People are prone to conceal errors and oversights rather than attempt to report and analyse them. This situation has been one of the major barriers to success for projects in the past. It may be that many companies do not want the bad publicity that public reporting brings. It is seen as preferable to sweep the results 'under the carpet'.

A post-implementation review needs to look at two different aspects of the project:

- A management analysis of the lessons to be learned for the benefit of future projects.
- A post-implementation audit of the actual working of the delivered product.

The management analysis can be conducted immediately after the handover of the facility. It needs to be carried out with input from all members of the team – technicians, users, quality assurance. It needs to address the successes and the failures of the project. It must not be seen as a witch-hunt. It must be a constructive review of what was good about the project and what was bad. It should address a number of issues, including:

- the estimates of manpower compared with actual effort;
- the total costs of the project compared to estimates;
- the reasons for the variances between the plan and the actual spend;
- the improvements in the conduct of the project (what would have been done differently with the benefit of hindsight).

Improvements in the conduct of the project will include many aspects and factors that impacted on the project such as communication and consultation, project mission, risk management, planning and control, tools and techniques, capability of the project team, education and training. This review should be conducted against the project procedures manual. It should be a review of all aspects of the procedures manual, and improvements should be made to the standard manual for incorporation into the company standard. The company standard should not be viewed as being fixed for all time, but should be improved project by project, benefiting from the lessons learnt.

The post-implementation audit of the working of the product can only take place some time after handover. It is best carried out by an independent body so that the audit itself looks objectively at the delivered product, how it met the requirements and objectives and any weaknesses in the product. When auditing an information system project, for example, the audit should examine areas such as:

- the reliability of the system;
- the adequacy of the documentation (particularly user training documentation);
- the responsiveness of the system;
- the objectives of the system as against the delivered product.

As user needs tend to develop over time in response to the changing business environment, the post-implementation audit needs to assess the real objectives as opposed to those that may have been defined at the outset of the project.

## PROJECT HEALTH CHECK

The reluctance to learn from past failures is only part of the problem. A post-implementation review is always retrospective. It can only examine the project and indicate lessons for future projects. Every project needs to discover, as part of the project start-up process, the issues dealt with in reviews from other projects. All stakeholders will need to discuss the outcome and decide whether the procedures can be adapted for the benefit of the project.

A post-implementation review does not help the project under review. There will be little or no effect on the perception of success or failure amongst the stakeholders of the project. If the project is perceived to have failed, a post-implementation review will not turn it into a success. However, if a project is subject to a continuous review process throughout its life cycle, the project manager would be able to identify areas of concern within the project team. These areas of concern will involve the critical success factors, the tools and techniques used, the skills required by the team for completing the tasks, the communication and interpersonal aspects. Most importantly, different stakeholders will have different perceptions of the success criteria and how they will measure the success of the project. The project manager may view short-term objective criteria (such as time and cost) as the important criteria; users may be looking into the long-term, more subjective, criteria (such as achieving purpose, meeting quality constraints). It is exactly this lack of understanding of the aspirations of the different stakeholders which has often led to the perception of failure, particularly in the eyes of the business community. A health check is a way of overcoming these problems.

There have been a number of attempts (Pinto and Slevin 1989; O'Connell 1993) to provide a diagnostic tool for project managers to assess the relative success of projects. These attempts are fairly crude and they are mainly retrospective, thereby only helping future projects to learn from failure. Pinto and Slevin recommend periodic review but their project implementation profile concentrates on their ten critical success factors, not on any success criteria to measure success. They provide little or no assistance to achieve a successful outcome for the project subject to the diagnostic process. They do highlight, however, the importance of reviewing projects and learning from the project experiences.

An example of a health check is given in Figure 9.1, which appears at the end of the chapter (pp. 154–8). This is the result of extensive research examining the reasons for the failure of IS/IT projects. A number of projects were assessed to identify whether each one was deemed a success or not. Each of the projects was examined from different viewpoints (for example project managers, sponsors, users, systems analysts). These stakeholders gave their views on project success and failure.

Research has shown that there is little agreement on success criteria. This clearly shows, as has been suggested earlier, different stakeholders pulling in different directions and aiming at different targets. Project managers consider time and cost constraints as important success criteria, whereas users wish to be satisfied with the product. Sponsors want the project to achieve its purpose and provide value. There are also wide differences in the perception of the factors that contribute to success. Project managers use the wrong factors to develop their success criteria. It is of paramount importance when attempting to deliver a project on time and within budget (whether it be an IS/IT, engineering, construction or whatever project) to plan and monitor the project and secure senior management support. However, these factors are less important if the project's main criteria for success is achieving its purpose. In this case user involvement and the establishment of clear objectives are paramount. With this apparent difference of opinion on how projects are measured for success and the fact that many IS/IT projects are perceived to have failed, there is a need for a diagnostic tool that:

- provides feedback during the project on its current state;
- allows the project team to identify their important (and not so important) success criteria;
- provides feedback to the project manager on project issues and direction;
- gives an assessment of the team's views on the progress of the project;
- identifies the areas where improvements could be made before the project proceeds too far.

It is necessary for the project manager to review the project regularly. The management and development process is dynamic and requires regular review so that any change is recognized and accommodated at the earliest opportunity. The project health check addresses these key issues. The project health check given here is based on the project diagnostic developed by Grude, which aims to discover whether organizations are ready to achieve their objectives through projects. The health check in Figure 9.1 specifically examines individual projects and assesses the effectiveness of the project to achieve success. It provides the project manager with the ability:

- to monitor the projects in the early stages;
- to understand in outline what skills are needed on the project;
- to focus on the problem areas in the project;
- to anticipate problems;
- to rectify any problems that may have already occurred on the project.

It is a series of questions for all participants on the project to answer. It enables the project manager and the team to identify the successful aspects of the project and recognize the areas which need improvement and change. It addresses the fundamental aspects of:

- success criteria;
- success factors;
- methodologies, tools and techniques;
- skills required;
- project execution.

As we have seen earlier, stakeholders often pull in different directions and do not appreciate the ambitions of others. Consequently, the start point of any health check should be defining the criteria to enable the project manager to check that everybody agrees with them. Then, and only then, can the project manager define the factors and tools and techniques to deliver success.

The health check allows the project manager to evaluate and appraise the project, thereby understanding the strengths and weaknesses of the project. It needs to be completed at the start of the project and at regular intervals throughout. The project manager will examine the variances in scores – where one person marks a statement as 5 or 6 and another marks it as 1 or 2 – and assess whether these variances are affecting the project. These differences of opinion must be discussed and opinions brought closer together so that all stakeholders are moving in the same direction.

## PROJECT HEALTH CHECK STRUCTURE

The main emphasis of the health check is on ensuring that all stakeholders agree on the success criteria and are, therefore, pulling in the same direction. It is divided into five parts, examining the five key elements. Part 1 is used to identify the important project success criteria and the understanding of the general goals and objectives of the project – the project mission – and how the project fits into the overall strategy. All project stakeholders need to define the important (and less important) success criteria as they perceive them.

Part 2 examines the factors that are being used on the project to deliver the success criteria. The factors identified need to be used with the main success criteria from Part 1 to analyse whether the appropriate factors are being employed to deliver the success criteria. The matrix in Figure 9.2 (p. 159) can be used in the analysis. It shows the success criteria and the factors on which project managers need to concentrate to deliver the main success criteria identified in Part 1 of the health check. Part 3 assesses whether appropriate tools, techniques and methodologies are available, are being used by the project team and are being applied well. This part also examines the use of computer-based tools on the project and whether they are being used effectively. Part 4 identifies the requirement for additional skills (for organizing, planning and controlling the project) which need to be acquired by the project manager and other members of the team. Part 5 examines the execution of the project and whether appropriate methods (for example the project life cycle or risk management) are being used. It examines the resources of the project and asks whether they are appropriate. It also examines the problems with the project and whether they are being addressed.

Respondents are asked to rate the 85 statements on scale of 1 to 6; 1 strongly disagreeing with the statement, 6 strongly agreeing with the statement. As many as possible of the project team and stakeholders need to complete the health check so that the project manager can get a full picture of the project's status. Most importantly, it should be completed as part of a regular review process. The project manager needs to assess the answers in three ways:

1. Investigate when the answer should be a high mark (5 or 6) but the team mark it low (1 or 2) or vice versa. This would indicate that something is seriously wrong with the project. There is a potential problem if statements are marked moderately (3 or 4). Why are some of the team not agreeing strongly with the statement?
2. Investigate when an answer shows significant variation between respondents – one respondent marks the statement as 1 but another marks it as 6. This might indicate that communication within the project is poor.
3. Check the success criteria highlighted in Part 1 with the factors shown in Part 2. Where there is a difference of opinion on success criteria, this needs to be addressed before any assessment of the appropriate factors is made.

Spreads and averages are important. The average indicates how well the problem area is being addressed; the spread will indicate how the team understand the project performance. The health check is a set of statements which can be used as a diagnostic tool to assess the success of the project at times during its execution. It will help to highlight problem areas. However, the results must be discussed with the project team in order to overcome these problem areas.

Having used the health check now several times, I can say that, almost always, for every question the spread, variance and difference from the 'right' answer are correlated. That is some members of the team always mark the right answer. Where the difference between the average answer and the right answer is small, so too is the spread ($s$) and variance ($v$). Where it is large, then again so too is the spread and variance. Thus if $X$ is the average response for a question, $P$ is the right answer and $D$, the difference, is $P - X$, then,

- $D$ of less than 1.5 shows strong agreement of the team on that issue;
- $D$ of between 1.5 and 2.5 shows weak disagreement of the team on that issue;
- $D$ greater than 2.5 shows strong disagreement of the team on that issue.

Only twice in several tests has $D$ been greater than 3.0.

## PROJECT AUDITS

Throughout the project there must be a system of controls over the whole project. Each control has a specific goal to prevent an undesired outcome from occurring or to prevent some loss from happening. The controls are as follows:

1. *Deterrence and prevention* To deter possible fraudulent activity (for example financial loss) and prevent erroneous processing (for example hardware and

software errors) in project computer systems, particularly those dealing with project accounting.

2. *Detection*    Any fraud must be detected early in order to rectify the situation as early as possible. Very often the existence of controls simply acts as a deterrent;

3. *Investigation*    Through either internal or external audits.

These controls are directed at a number of issues. Computer systems, both hardware and software, sometimes fail but, more importantly, the weakest links in any system are the people who interface with the system. This is often apparent with intentional fraud by inaccurate data processing to gain some financial advantage. Data processing is now much faster and complex which gives workers an opportunity for embezzlement. Another fraudulent activity is the copying of data, programs or software (for example copying company data to leak to a competitor, taking copies of word processing or accounting packages for one's own use).

Companies' computers are prone to sabotage or vandalism from disgruntled or disaffected employees or external pressure groups (such as animal rights groups). Added to this threat of sabotage is the problem of unauthorized access to computer systems usually by 'hackers' gaining access via modern telecommunications. In other cases employees may gain access to parts of the system to which they are not entitled. Unauthorized access has the added problem of the potential introduction of viruses. However, viruses can be introduced unintentionally by illegal copies of software being copied by employees onto company computers.

These threats should be controlled by system audits, both internal and external. Both types are required to control and deter potential fraudulent activity. Auditors must understand system functions, document, evaluate and test the internal controls and finally report on the systems. They must be able to report on the accuracy of financial statements, the reliability of the systems that provide the information and provide advice on potential fraud and errors.

| Part 1: Success criteria | | | | | | | |
|---|---|---|---|---|---|---|---|
| No. | Statement | Score | X | S | V | P | D |
| 1.1 | The success criteria for the project are defined. | 1 2 3 4 5 6 | | | | 6 | |
| 1.2 | The success criteria for the project are agreed. | 1 2 3 4 5 6 | | | | 6 | |
| 1.3 | I believe the success criteria are appropriate. | 1 2 3 4 5 6 | | | | 6 | |
| 1.4 | The project should achieve quality constraints. | 1 2 3 4 5 6 | | | | 6 | |
| 1.5 | The project should be a commercial success. | 1 2 3 4 5 6 | | | | 6 | |
| 1.6 | The users should be happy. | 1 2 3 4 5 6 | | | | 6 | |
| 1.7 | The sponsors should be happy. | 1 2 3 4 5 6 | | | | 6 | |
| 1.8 | The project team should be happy. | 1 2 3 4 5 6 | | | | 6 | |
| 1.9 | The project meets its stated objectives. | 1 2 3 4 5 6 | | | | 6 | |
| 1.10 | The system should achieve its purpose. | 1 2 3 4 5 6 | | | | 6 | |
| 1.11 | The project should be delivered on time. | 1 2 3 4 5 6 | | | | 6 | |
| 1.12 | The project should be delivered within budget. | 1 2 3 4 5 6 | | | | 6 | |
| 1.13 | The project should contribute to the organization's overall business strategy. | 1 2 3 4 5 6 | | | | 6 | |
| 1.14 | There is a clear relationship between the project and business plans and strategies. | 1 2 3 4 5 6 | | | | 6 | |
| 1.15 | The project team do not appreciate the important success criteria. | 1 2 3 4 5 6 | | | | 1 | |
| 1.16 | I am confident the project will be a success. | 1 2 3 4 5 6 | | | | 6 | |
| 1.17 | The project goals are clear to me. | 1 2 3 4 5 6 | | | | 6 | |
| 1.18 | The goals have been explained to the team. | 1 2 3 4 5 6 | | | | 6 | |
| 1.19 | I can explain the benefits of the project. | 1 2 3 4 5 6 | | | | 6 | |
| 1.20 | The project has unrealistic completion date. | 1 2 3 4 5 6 | | | | 1 | |
| | Sum | | | | | | |
| | Average | | | | | | |

Key: X = average response; S = spread; V = variation; P = 'right' answer; D = difference between X and P

**Figure 9.1  Project health check** *continued*

| Part 2: Success factors | | | | | | | |
|------|------|------|------|------|------|------|------|
| No. | Statement | Score | X | S | V | P | D |
| 2.1 | The estimates for the project are realistic. | 1 2 3 4 5 6 | | | | 6 | |
| 2.2 | Project estimates are generally over-optimistic. | 1 2 3 4 5 6 | | | | 1 | |
| 2.3 | Estimates were developed in consultation with the person allocated to the task. | 1 2 3 4 5 6 | | | | 6 | |
| 2.4 | The project has been planned strategically. | 1 2 3 4 5 6 | | | | 6 | |
| 2.5 | The project plans are understandable to all. | 1 2 3 4 5 6 | | | | 6 | |
| 2.6 | The project plans are often changed. | 1 2 3 4 5 6 | | | | 1 | |
| 2.7 | Our plans focus too much on the completion date and not an intermediate results/dates. | 1 2 3 4 5 6 | | | | 1 | |
| 2.8 | The project plan effectively utilizes resources. | 1 2 3 4 5 6 | | | | 6 | |
| 2.9 | I am happy with the plans and estimates. | 1 2 3 4 5 6 | | | | 6 | |
| 2.10 | The project participants are motivated well to achieve the project objectives. | 1 2 3 4 5 6 | | | | 6 | |
| 2.11 | Responsibilities are not well delegated. | 1 2 3 4 5 6 | | | | 1 | |
| 2.12 | The clients and users know their roles and responsibilities. | 1 2 3 4 5 6 | | | | 6 | |
| 2.13 | I am happy with the leadership shown by senior management. | 1 2 3 4 5 6 | | | | 6 | |
| 2.14 | I am happy with the leadership shown by project management. | 1 2 3 4 5 6 | | | | 6 | |
| 2.15 | Communication and consultation channels have been effectively set up. | 1 2 3 4 5 6 | | | | 6 | |
| 2.16 | There is poor communication between the project participants. | 1 2 3 4 5 6 | | | | 1 | |
| 2.17 | The users are involved effectively. | 1 2 3 4 5 6 | | | | 6 | |
| 2.18 | Communication channels are poor. | 1 2 3 4 5 6 | | | | 1 | |
| 2.19 | The project managers do not fully report project status to sponsors/users' project teams. | 1 2 3 4 5 6 | | | | 1 | |
| 2.20 | Corrective measures are always taken in time when the project encounters problems. | 1 2 3 4 5 6 | | | | 6 | |
| 2.21 | All roles and responsibilities are well defined. | 1 2 3 4 5 6 | | | | 6 | |
| 2.22 | All parties are fully committed to the plan. | 1 2 3 4 5 6 | | | | 6 | |
| 2.23 | Resources are available at the right time. | 1 2 3 4 5 6 | | | | 6 | |
| 2.24 | Procedures for handling priorities are adequate. | 1 2 3 4 5 6 | | | | 6 | |
| 2.25 | Quality assurance is not a major aspect of the projects. | 1 2 3 4 5 6 | | | | 1 | |
| | Sum | | | | | | |
| | Average | | | | | | |

Figure 9.1   Project health check *continued*

| No. | Statement | Score | X | S | V | P | D |
|-----|-----------|-------|---|---|---|---|---|
| | *Part 3: Tools, techniques and methodologies* | | | | | | |
| 3.1 | The tools, techniques and methods available for planning the project are adequate. | 1 2 3 4 5 6 | | | | 6 | |
| 3.2 | The tools, techniques and methods available for controlling the project are adequate. | 1 2 3 4 5 6 | | | | 6 | |
| 3.3 | The tools, techniques and methods available for organizing the project are adequate. | 1 2 3 4 5 6 | | | | 6 | |
| 3.4 | I agree that the tools, techniques and methods used are appropriate. | 1 2 3 4 5 6 | | | | 6 | |
| 3.5 | The development tools and methods are sufficient for the project. | 1 2 3 4 5 6 | | | | 6 | |
| 3.6 | The management tools and methods are sufficient for the project. | 1 2 3 4 5 6 | | | | 6 | |
| 3.7 | The development tools and methods are poorly applied on the project. | 1 2 3 4 5 6 | | | | 1 | |
| 3.8 | The management tools and methods are poorly applied on the project. | 1 2 3 4 5 6 | | | | 1 | |
| 3.9 | The chosen methodologies stifle creativity during the project. | 1 2 3 4 5 6 | | | | 1 | |
| 3.10 | There are established methods which are to be used. | 1 2 3 4 5 6 | | | | 6 | |
| 3.11 | These established methods are being used on this project. | 1 2 3 4 5 6 | | | | 6 | |
| 3.12 | I believe these methods are appropriate for the project. | 1 2 3 4 5 6 | | | | 6 | |
| 3.13 | There are computer-based tools available for this project. | 1 2 3 4 5 6 | | | | 6 | |
| 3.14 | Computer-based tools are being used effectively. | 1 2 3 4 5 6 | | | | 6 | |
| 3.15 | The project uses methods for assessing and managing risks. | 1 2 3 4 5 6 | | | | 6 | |
| | Sum | | | | | | |
| | Average | | | | | | |

**Figure 9.1  Project health check** *continued*

| Part 4: Skills | | | | | | | |
|---|---|---|---|---|---|---|---|
| No. | Statement | Score | X | S | V | P | D |
| 4.1 | There are the necessary skills available to plan the project. | 1 2 3 4 5 6 | | | | 6 | |
| 4.2 | There are the necessary skills available to organize the project. | 1 2 3 4 5 6 | | | | 6 | |
| 4.3 | There are the necessary skills available to control the project. | 1 2 3 4 5 6 | | | | 6 | |
| 4.4 | There are the necessary skills available to develop the system. | 1 2 3 4 5 6 | | | | 6 | |
| 4.5 | Project management is unable to handle fully the human relations aspects. | 1 2 3 4 5 6 | | | | 1 | |
| 4.6 | Conflicts are resolved easily and satisfactorily. | 1 2 3 4 5 6 | | | | 6 | |
| 4.7 | The project plan overestimates the skills and competences of the team. | 1 2 3 4 5 6 | | | | 1 | |
| 4.8 | Project management is astute in dealing with the politics of the project. | 1 2 3 4 5 6 | | | | 6 | |
| 4.9 | Project management is unable to inspire others. | 1 2 3 4 5 6 | | | | 1 | |
| 4.10 | Project management is good at getting the project team working together. | 1 2 3 4 5 6 | | | | 6 | |
| | Sum | | | | | | |
| | Average | | | | | | |

**Figure 9.1  Project health check** *continued*

| No. | Statement | Score | X | S | V | P | D |
|---|---|---|---|---|---|---|---|
| Part 5: Execution | | | | | | | |
| 5.1 | A life cycle approach is being applied. | 1 2 3 4 5 6 | | | | 6 | |
| 5.2 | I agree with the life cycle used. | 1 2 3 4 5 6 | | | | 6 | |
| 5.3 | An effective start-up meeting was held for this project. | 1 2 3 4 5 6 | | | | 6 | |
| 5.4 | The right people are allocated to the project. | 1 2 3 4 5 6 | | | | 6 | |
| 5.5 | Project team members are carrying out appropriate activities. | 1 2 3 4 5 6 | | | | 6 | |
| 5.6 | Resources for the project are well selected. | 1 2 3 4 5 6 | | | | 6 | |
| 5.7 | There are no problem areas during the project. | 1 2 3 4 5 6 | | | | 6 | |
| 5.8 | I do not foresee any problem areas on the project. | 1 2 3 4 5 6 | | | | 6 | |
| 5.9 | The management of the project is excellent. | 1 2 3 4 5 6 | | | | 6 | |
| 5.10 | The project team has appropriate members at appropriate times. | 1 2 3 4 5 6 | | | | 6 | |
| 5.11 | The project risks were assessed at the outset of the project. | 1 2 3 4 5 6 | | | | 6 | |
| 5.12 | I believe that the assessments of risks are appropriate. | 1 2 3 4 5 6 | | | | 6 | |
| 5.13 | The project risks are not being well managed. | 1 2 3 4 5 6 | | | | 1 | |
| 5.14 | The deliverables are fully identified. | 1 2 3 4 5 6 | | | | 6 | |
| 5.15 | The deliverables are quality assured constantly. | 1 2 3 4 5 6 | | | | 6 | |
| | Sum | | | | | | |
| | Average | | | | | | |

Figure 9.1   Project health check *concluded*

| Factors | Criteria | | | | | | | | |
|---|---|---|---|---|---|---|---|---|---|
| | Commercial success | Meets user requirement | Meets budget | Happy users | Achieves purpose | Meets timescales | Happy sponsor | Meets quality | Happy team |
| Leadership | P | | | S | | | S | | P |
| Motivation | P | | | S | | | | | P |
| Planning | P | S | P | S | | | | S | S |
| Development method | | S | | S | S | P | S | P | |
| Monitoring | | | P | | | | | P | |
| Management method | | | | | | P | | | S |
| Delegation | | | | S | | | | | P |
| Communication | | P | | P | | | P | | P |
| Clear objectives | S | P | | | P | | | | |
| User involvement | S | P | | P | P | | P | S | |
| Management support | P | | P | P | | P | P | P | |

**Figure 9.2   Linking success criteria and success factors**

Key: P = primary success factor
S = secondary success factor

159

## REFERENCES AND FURTHER READING

Abdel-Hamid, T. K. and Madnick, S. E. (1990), 'The elusive silver lining: how we fail to learn from software development failures', *Sloan Management Review*, Fall, 39–48.

DeMarco, T. (1982), *Controlling Software Projects*, Yourdon, New York.

Hougham, M. (1996), 'London Ambulance Service computer-aided despatch system', *International Journal of Project Management*, **14**(2): 103–10.

Morris, P. W. G. and Hough, G. H. (1987), *The Anatomy of Major Projects*, Wiley, Chichester.

O'Connell, F. (1993), *How To Run Successful Projects*, Prentice-Hall, London.

Pinto, J. K. and Slevin D. P. (1989), 'The Project Implementation Profile', *Proceedings of the 20th Project Management Institute Annual Symposium, Atlanta, Georgia, Oct 7–11*, Project Management Institute, Sylva, NC.

Turner, J. R. (1999), *The Handbook of Project-based Management*, 2nd edition, McGraw-Hill, London.

Turner, J. R., Grude, K. V. and Thurloway, L. (1997), *The Project Manager as Change Agent*, McGraw-Hill, London.

Wateridge, J. (1995), 'IT projects: a basis for success', *International Journal of Project Management*, **13**(3): 169–72.

## RELATED TOPICS

Projects success and strategy          Chapter 5

Managing value, benefit and finance    Chapter 13

Managing function and value            Chapter 14

# Part II
# Context

# INTRODUCTION TO PART II

In Part II we consider the interrelationship of the project with its context. The context consists of the political, economic, social, technical, legal and environmental influences of the project on its surroundings and vice versa. The analysis of these influences is called PESTLE analysis. Some people call the surroundings the environment. We can use whatever vocabulary we want. However, to retain precision here we refer to the project's total surroundings as its context, and reserve the word environment to describe its physical surroundings, that proportion of the biosphere it has an impact on.

### Chapter 10: Political, economic, social and technical, influences – PEST

In Chapter 10 Alan Harpham considers the PEST of PESTLE. He defines each of these influences and considers each in turn.

### Chapter 11: The legal context

Geoff Haley considers the impact of the law on projects in Chapter 11. He describes procurement, planning and inquiry and environmental legislation, and the law of tort, that is the duty of reasonable care we all have to our fellow citizens.

### Chapter 12: Managing the environment

In Chapter 12 Rodney Turner considers the impact of the project on its environment and how that can be managed. He describes how to develop an environmental strategy for both the parent organization and the project. He examines key environmental principles and methods for accounting for the impact of a project on the environment. He describes how to conduct an environmental impact assessment and how to obtain planning consent.

### Chapter 13: Projects for shareholder value

Projects are undertaken to add value to the sponsoring organization and in the private sector that ultimately means adding shareholder value. In Chapter 13 Rodney Turner explains shareholder value analysis, a way of calculating the worth of a company. He shows how to use this model to analyse the impact of projects on shareholder value and illustrates how this impact is critically dependent on the financial ratios of the company. He gives some examples from the UK's top 100 companies and makes a direct comparison of two that demerged during the 1990s.

# 10 Political, economic, social and technical influences – PEST

*Alan Harpham*

To coin a phrase, 'few projects are islands'. Very few projects are totally unaffected by their surroundings of one form or another. They are usually set in a number of contexts, and each context will be likely to affect the outcome of the project and will have an effect on the way the project needs to be managed. There are several possible contexts, the more obvious being:

- political
- economic
- social
- technical
- legal, and
- environmental.

This is easily remembered as the mnemonic PESTLE, or for the French speaking 'Le Pest'! The rest of this chapter will concentrate on the first four – PEST – with legal and environmental contexts being dealt with in the following two chapters.

Depending on the nature of the project, its location, purpose and objectives, and its owner and the project strategy selected, the impact of each of these project contexts will vary. For example, not all projects will have a political context. Some clearly will, such as those involving public funding or having an impact on the local society or ecology, for example a new road or railway. The political context will be much less apparent for those projects involving private funding and having no impact on local society, such as a new piece of computer software for an industrial organization.

It is generally accepted that there are three essential players in the project organization – the sponsor, the project manager and the user or operator of the delivered asset. Each of them has a different set of success criteria for the project (see Chapter 5) and will therefore take a different view of the impact of these different project contexts.

Ultimately the responsibility for monitoring the different project contexts and their likely impact on the project outcome, and its success or otherwise, rests with the project sponsor. The sponsor is the individual accountable to the project-owning organization for the investment in the project. Clearly the other two important players – the project manager and the user/operator – have a duty of care for the project to support the sponsor in this role.

The impact of the project context may far outweigh other project considerations and have a significant impact on the project outcome and its success or otherwise. For example, the Alaska oil pipeline was eight years late and some ten times over budget, but was a great commercial success (not to be confused with successful project management). The project had suffered many problems from its context, not least the demands of the environmentalists for crossing points for migrating elk. The reason for its overall success was a six-day war in the Middle East, which had the immediate effect of increasing the price of oil fortyfold. This totally altered the dynamics of the business case for the project and the increased revenue stream swamped the delays and cost overruns.

## TERMINOLOGY AND DEFINITIONS

The following definitions are taken from the *Concise Oxford Dictionary* (COD) and The *American Heritage Dictionary of the English Language* (AHD).

### POLITICAL

Politics is defined as:

> The science and art of government, political affairs or life. [COD]

> or

> The art or science of government or governing, especially the governing of a political entity, such as a nation, and the administration and control of its internal and external affairs. [AHD]

Political as an adjective applies to the state or its government, public affairs or politics.

Government is further defined as:

> The system of governing, or ruling with authority, conducting the policy actions and affairs of the State. [COD]

## ECONOMIC

Economics is defined as:

The practical science of the production and distribution of wealth, and also as the condition of a country as to material prosperity. [COD]

or

The social science that deals with the production, distribution, and consumption of goods and services and with the theory and management of economies or economic systems. [AHD]

## SOCIAL

Social is defined as:

Living in companies, gregarious, not fitted for or not practising solitary life, interdependent, co-operative, practising division of labour, concerned with the mutual relations of men, of society. [COD]

or

living together in communities, of or relating to communal living, of or relating to society. [AHD]

Society is defined as:

The social mode of life, the customs and organisation of a civilised nation, or a social community, or an association of persons united by a common aim, interest, or principle. [COD]

We more commonly use culture as a word to describe the customs and organization of a society. Society can be local, national or international

## TECHNICAL

Technology is defined as:

The science of the industrial arts. [COD]

or

The application of science, especially to industrial or commercial objectives, or the scientific method and material used to achieve a commercial or industrial objective. [AHD]

## POLITICAL

The political context covers two areas:

- *Politics* (capital P) surrounding the project from the outside including the impact on the project of all the major external stakeholders, including national and international ones.
- *politics* (little p) within the project, created by 'local' stakeholders not acting in concert.

### INTERNATIONAL

As we can see in the above definitions, Politics is the context created by the government of the nation in which the project is being executed, but may also be influenced by the politics and government of a foreign supplying or client organization. For example, for defence projects it is invariably necessary to obtain permission of the exporting government for the export. This will be given, or withheld, based on the exporting government's view of the 'political' state of the recipient government, and not always disclosed to the public of the exporting nation. As we often see, these opinions can change over time, frequently at changes of government.

This and the law of the host nation are two major project risks to be managed. Most contracts relate the contract law to the law of the project host nation. Most contracts endeavour to exclude the risk of changes to the law that take place after award of contract, although this is not always possible and may form a significant part of the commercial risk of the contract.

Another major risk of international trade has been the unfair calling of performance bonds. A bond is a guarantee, usually financial, underwritten by a bank or insurance company. Bonds relate to the performance of the delivered item, the performance during its delivery, assembly and erection, the guarantee that having submitted an offer the supplier will deliver at the price offered or performance to time. Most western countries offer their exporting industries some protection for unfair calling of performance bonds and unfair changes to contract terms and conditions through 'political risk' cover. The private insurance industry is also increasingly offering this type of insurance. The premiums relate to the previous and current experience of the host government's behaviour with very high premiums being offered for perceived high-risk countries and in some cases no insurance being offered at all. The most famous incidence of unfair calling of bonds relates to Colonel Gaddafi of Libya who, when he first came to power in the 1960s, ordered the calling of all the bonds relating to projects going on in Libya at the time. He did this to improve Libya's finances and this was the first international unfair calling of bonds. As banks, whose word is their bond, underwrite most bonds, they tend to pay up 'on demand', even for bonds that are conditional. The terms of the bond are generally that the bank pays on demand and the purchaser of the bond is then liable for the repayment of the monies paid by the bank. The risk in other words is generally with the supplier.

The final and most difficult risk is the one of personal safety of staff sent to deliver the 'project' in the overseas location, particularly where there is political instability. Hostage taking has recently been on the increase and indeed some companies will not put their staff, or themselves, at such risk. In the late 1990s, we saw terrible examples of this in Eastern Europe with four telecommunications workers consequently losing their lives.

Each exporting company has to weigh up these political risks, their own culture and likely response if such situations occur, and the protection, both financial and political, that would be available. They then have to look at this against the commercial considerations and the attitudes and beliefs of their own staff. Most senior managers find this one of the hardest areas in which to make judgement.

## NATIONAL

In the early 1970s, I was involved in the construction of one of the first North Sea oil rigs in North East England. This was during the era of the 'three-day week', when most of industry was compelled to work a three-day week by the then government. This was in response to the situation in the Middle East and the lack of international oil and its consequent high price. We were right in the public eye as one of the projects to turn the country's fortunes around. Indeed, we had the authority from government to put suppliers back on a full week. The media were all over the project for the latest news, creating news where it did not exist, and political visits by members of government and Westminster politicians were the order of the day. Politics often seemed more important than the progress of the job and certainly needed careful management. We even had to create a project public relations (PR) office on-site, an almost unheard of event in the early 1970s. Before that, my experience of PR in a contracting company was restricted to a head-office function that organized 'topping out' ceremonies and handled the media and press releases. Later in my career, the Nimrod Airborne Early Warning project was under extreme pressure, and as we now know was ultimately cancelled after an expenditure in excess of £1bn. This may well have been more to do with public perception of progress on the project, as a result of a BBC Panorama programme reviewing it, than the actual state of the project.

The lesson from these two and many more examples is that for projects in the public domain – those funded by government, those that affect society and our environment – the proactive management of the project public relations is essential. The project team needs to drive the media programme rather than constantly having to react to the media and its inquisitions.

The Political scene is a volatile one. We live with changing governmental attitudes and cycles of change that react to economic cycles. Privatize–nationalize–privatize – the latest fashion! Governments often know best, or think they do. They often become dogmatic about the solutions; for example Tony Blair's 'New Labour' government's desire for more PPP (Public Private Partnership) projects, a variant on the previous government's PFI (Private Finance Initiative) as *the* way to fund public projects. They should remember there is a right strategy for *each* project; not a universal strategy right for all projects. The Central Electricity Generating Board nearly discovered this back in the 1970s and 1980s, according to a NEDO report of the early 1980s. Governments should also remember that we originally created them and the taxes they levy to pay for social projects that the private sector could neither afford nor bear the associated risks of. Now, at times, we seem to be going backwards with governments attempting to get the private sector to undertake levels of risk that are too great. Governments have often failed to realize that they can create partnerships with the private sector for public projects but need to set the right risks and rewards to maximize the 'value for money' of the project for society. Some PFI schemes have just been a way of paying contractors more to build the project than might have been achieved with a different project strategy. Governments until recently also failed to realize that their funding is often best suited to priming the front end of a project. They should focus on the definition of requirements, the design of a project strategy effective for its realization and the development of the best 'value for money' case for the scheme. The UK Government appears to be responding to this idea as a result of the Bates and Gershon reports. Sir Malcolm Bates is Chairman of Pearl, and his report focused on improving the PFI; Peter Gershon is Managing Director of Marconi Electronic Systems Ltd, and his report focused on improving Whitehall procurement processes. As a direct result of these reports, the Government announced in mid-1999 that it was planning

> to create a new private sector led body to help increase and improve investment in the UK's public services from private sources. Partnerships UK, the new body, will employ City experts to help the public sector get the best deal from the PFI and other forms of public–private partnerships. A new Office of Government Commerce is also being set up as part of a shake up in how Whitehall goes about managing its £13 billion a year procurement budget. In announcing Partnerships UK [PUK for short and already being referred to as PUKE] the Government says it will not operate as a bank, instead it will be able to provide development funding to get PFI deals off the ground, where

existing forms of private finance are not available. In these cases it will, where necessary, provide a range of financial products, tailored to the needs of the public sector bodies in the early stages of the procurement process, which enhance, rather than undermine, existing flows of private finance. PUK will act as a project manager for PFI deals, providing public sector organisations with expert advisory and implementation skills.

Amen to all that. However, we should remember that at the same time the Water Regulator is determined to adjust the equation for that industry, political commentators are critical of the level of rewards being achieved in the privatized rail industry, and the right way to involve the private sector in the London Underground is proving elusive.

It is likely to take some time to get the right balance in each and every public–private partnership project. Some may have noticed that when water was re-privatized the Regulator called for a five-year fixed investment plan based on cost – AMP 1. (It sounded to me exactly like the Eastern European rigid economic planning system that I had witnessed when working in Poland in the late 1970s and which had become so discredited in the East and West.)

The world of media has also been transformed in recent years. It is less restrained and colludes less with the Establishment to keep stories under wraps. It is also not averse to making the news rather than reporting it. There are better physical communications; we all know more and, increasingly, quicker than before. The media is a fantastic agent of change, but it can also destroy projects and project teams very quickly. Effective management of the media is a critical success factor for today's projects in the political and social arena. (Ways of managing the media, another stakeholder of the project, are given towards the end of the section on social influences.) Shell discovered this to its cost when outmanoeuvred by Greenpeace on the destruction of the Brent Spar Rig. Shell had come up with the best technical solution, but lost the 'war of words' against a better media campaign organizer. As we all now know, Greenpeace admitted afterwards that the outcome was not in fact the 'best' solution, and it conceded in the end that Shell's original plan was a better one.

The level of government and European regulations is on the increase, partially caused by the growth of privatized utilities. These have often had to create spurious competition and have also increased more regulations as our knowledge of the impact of projects on the environment has increased. Gaining planning consent for new projects is often the most critical stage. Consents for major projects are becoming more complex, not simpler, and possibly rightly so. Public Enquiries are becoming more common place, have better organized objectors, take longer and are very difficult to estimate time-wise for project planning purposes. They are often dependent on the actions of those with no interest or stake in the project outcome.

171

Obtaining planning permission to build is just the beginning, as BNFL discovered on its Thorp project. The environmentalists challenged BNFL's right to operate the plant (as opposed to build it) right through to its opening. The problems are not necessarily over once permission to build has been obtained, as more extreme lobbyists will continue to protest and stage sit-ins and similar publicity-seeking protests, as the projects building the M3 extension over Twyford Down and Manchester Airport's second runway discovered.

We live in changing times. As the public becomes increasingly disillusioned with politicians so politicians change policy or *in extremis* are voted out and a new party takes power with the desire to change or to be seen to provide new policies. Government-financed projects can change midstream, particularly while governments are still wedded to annualized budgeting and payment for everything out of revenue. Governments do not operate a balance sheet and notions of investing for future wealth creation are not measured.

## INTERNAL

Almost as important as the national Politics surrounding projects are the internal politics, within both the team and the surrounding local stakeholders. A stakeholder is defined as anybody having an interest in the outcome of the project and is not constrained to those having a financial interest (typically called the shareholders). Internal politics includes the effects of the attitudes, behaviour and interactions between team members, such as:

- the project sponsor or client, and any support team;
- the project manager and his or her project management team;
- the various teams and individuals provided by project suppliers, including PM consultants, designers, QSs, main contractors, contractors, subcontractors and suppliers;
- subgroups or individuals, often having conflicting aims and objectives and who can play 'politics' in order to achieve their objectives at the expense of others.

Another complication is that subgroups may play 'politics' amongst themselves with their own, different goals. Sir Michael Latham's report (1994) on the construction industry concluded, like many reports before it, that all those engaged on a project need to agree a common set of goals and take cognizance of each other's objectives, especially where they appear to be in conflict. He called it 'partnering' (see Chapter 31). However, partnering requires changes in behaviour, attitudes and values by all the parties involved. The construction industry is discovering that this requires leadership from the top and hard work to bring about the necessary changes, including briefings, joint workshops and teambuilding initiatives.

In addition to managing the politics in the team, the project management team also need to manage the expectations of those not directly in the team – other stakeholders. This involves proper communications with them, listening to their concerns, being open about the project plans and seeking to accommodate changes within the plan to reduce their concerns to an acceptable level. Thus the 'interpersonal skills' of the sponsor and project manager and their ability to manage the 'softer' tasks within the project are of increasing importance. Communications by the sponsor, his or her project manager and the project management team with the world of politics (P and p) are also increasingly important. They need to manage the 'messages' about the project by directing a proactive PR approach, rather than a reactive one, 'always on the back foot', defensively answering questions and criticisms about the project.

Of course, the team cannot always avoid having to react to media or lobby group attacks on the project. However, if they have in place a proactive PR strategy there are likely to be less things to react to and the team will be better prepared to react to those that do occur. The team must identify all the stakeholders and their groupings and actively listen to them to hear their concerns and issues. Ideally, these concerns and issues need to be dealt with before the project is fully defined. The team need to run 'message' campaigns to explain the risks of the project in ways to which people can easily relate. For example, a new management science is developing called 'risk communications'. This attempts to compare risks to other human risks we face. National Grid, for example, has compared the risk of getting leukaemia while living near overhead power lines with other illness statistics to show it is a very low risk. The team need to 'sell' the idea of the project and its benefits as widely as possible. They must identify local champions and support them, giving them information and materials to enhance their communications. Increasingly recognized in social projects is the need for 'social entrepreneurs' who live and work in a local community and want to transform it. One of the examples in Charles Handy's book *The Alchemist* (1999), is Andrew Mawson and the Bromley-by-Bow community centre. Andrew is now working with others on a national scheme (the Community Action Network) to identify and support social entrepreneurs in their communities. The project team needs to plan the project PR strategy like the project – identifying issues and events, risks and stakeholders, and a plan to manage them. This includes planning a programme of PR activities and events, a budget and developing contingency plans for the risks identified.

In the past most large infrastructure projects were managed on the 'we know best' autocratic style, with little information given to stakeholders. 'Consultation' is now the order of the day. We have to demonstrate that we have consulted widely, considered the impact on the environment through environmental impact studies and taken 'reasonable' steps to overcome the concerns and issues raised. It looks increasingly likely from events unfolding in North America with the indigenous population, that we will soon be facing the idea of projects only proceeding under 'consensus'. Obtaining agreement from everyone may seem to be nearly impossible and is likely to increase the timescale and expense of future projects significantly, and it will require even more management effort – a sign of changing attitudes of society. It will certainly require even greater skills from project managers and sponsors, especially in handling people and the soft project issues and tasks.

## ECONOMIC

I once asked a foreign politician what the economics of a particular project were and he replied 'What has economics got to do with it?' He was reflecting the reality of some political projects where the economics is not the most important thing, but the winning of marginal votes and political prestige is. At the time of its construction, the Humber Bridge was perceived as a political project with little economic justification, as are any number of overseas projects built at the political whim of a national leader with a big ego. However, in reality, the economic climate of a project is important at two levels – the macro and the micro.

By macro, I mean those factors that influence the economic or profitable outcome of the project. These include capital and operational cost estimates; delivery times; increase in revenue through sales or cost savings; performance of the project deliverables – ultimately the delivery of the benefits forecast at the outset (see Chapter 27). The sponsor is responsible for monitoring forecasts for each of these costs during execution to determine if and when the project will deliver the forecast benefits. If forecasts are threatening the economics of the project, it is the sponsor's task to determine changes and in the worst case to stop the project. Most projects in the private sector are based on the microeconomic model (the business case) and it is this that is generally used to obtain sanction to proceed. There are exceptions where the project justification is 'regulatory', that is what is necessary for the organization to do to remain compliant with regulations. The threat to such an organization is ultimately economic as failure to meet regulations may cause it to lose its operating licence and thus the opportunity to generate revenue. Since government sets most regulations, either directly or indirectly, Politics plays a part here. At the micro level, the organization should have processes to appraise and approve both the definition (feasibility) and implementation stages (see Chapters 25, 26 and 27). This appraisal ensures that there is a proper definition of the project (or of the definition stage), why the project is being done (its purpose), what is to be delivered and when and for how much. It also includes a feasible plan to show how project delivery will be achieved. Approval will typically focus on return and risks and will seek to ensure that there is a match with the risk/return profile of the organization. The measure of return is a variable, but most organizations today take account of the value of money over time (it can be invested) and use discounted cash flow as well as methods such as payback and return on capital.

Macroeconomics also affect project outcome. Macroeconomics covers interest rates, inflation, exchange risks, political economic risks and factors that may affect the microeconomics of the project, but are outside the control of the project sponsor or manager. As for political risk, some of these risks are insurable. Most private companies, unless they manage a large portfolio of projects and can share the risk or stand it themselves, will lay off risk by insurance or some alternative means, such as buying foreign currency forward and so on.

On government projects, other economic modelling techniques are sometimes used, such as cost–benefit analysis (see Chapters 14 and 27), where all costs and benefits are identified, including social ones. For example, on a motorway project benefits might include saving on lost time for motorists and fewer accidents, and costs might include loss of land use, noise pollution for adjacent houses and so on. Each social cost and benefit is converted into a monetary value and taken into account in the microeconomic appraisal. More recently, governments have used PFI and PPP to bring private finance into public projects. The economics, and in particular the risk sharing of these schemes, is complex and often questionable. At the creation stage, we need to understand why the project is being done. Is there an owner? Without a robust owner and user the project is unlikely to get off the ground. How will it work? How will it fulfil its purpose? How will the revenue flows get back to the owner of the asset? Recent privatized rail and other projects have made funding and operation ever more complex. As private funding has become a global trend, so supplier companies are sharing the risk of the project costs and revenues. This increases the risks and means the supplier only gets a return if the asset continues to operate and deliver revenue. This is a positive step as it focuses economic decisions on the 'whole asset life', rather than on short-term delivery decisions. Build, own, operate and transfer (BOOT) projects are on the increase globally. However, we have yet to see many reach the 'transfer' state. This will become a problem if we are trying to 'transfer' a liability, for example an old, worn-out plant. Local law may force us to keep operating the plant at our cost, or even to leave the responsibility for decommissioning with the provider!

## SOCIAL

The greatest social influences on a project are those deriving from the local culture. All societies face the same broad issues. With time, a society or community develops a common set of answers to these questions, which form the 'culture' of the society or community (see Chapter 44). Culture can be considered at macro and micro levels. Macro culture is that stereotyping we give to different nationalities and races. Micro cultures are those relating to a local community, a professional community or some other membership grouping such as a church community. We can analyse the culture of communities affected by a project and plan our particular project management strategies to take account of the particular culture. We in turn need to guard against being ethnocentric, believing our way of doing things to be the best way, and seek to be cosmopolitans, belonging to the world and free from local, provincial or national ideas, prejudices or attachments. Sadly, historically, most cultures have set out to dominate others – the 'we know best' syndrome – and have underrated other cultures and their achievements. Listen to what one Wintu holy woman said of the white people:

> The White People never cared for land or deer or bear ... We don't chop down the trees. We only use the dead wood. But the white people plow up the ground, pull down the trees, kill everything. The tree says, 'Don't. I am sore. Don't hurt me.' ... How can the spirit of the earth like the White Man? Everywhere the White Man has touched it, it is sore.

'Stand over there while we build this plant, road, railway, information system. It may be for you, but we won't need your help', was the way many large international project teams used to work. Given the extraordinary achievements of other cultures – the pyramids in Egypt and South America, the Great Wall of China, the Roman Empire and its utilities, the Alhambra Palace in Spain – and their work and social organization, how did we become so arrogant? There is no such thing as a 'good' or 'bad' culture; only the way it is in another culture. From their perspective what they do, what they believe and how they behave is the 'norm'. It is we who are 'odd'. A cosmopolitan project sponsor or manager is capable of taking a holistic view. Each of the following areas plays a part in project success:

- Understanding the costs and benefits to a particular community – cost, time and quality are insufficient measures of success for the local community.
- The suitability of the project for its environment.
- The success of 'technology transfer'.
- Meeting the desires of the local community and its culture.
- The commercial viability of the project.

We are rapidly becoming more aware of the needs of our environment and how we should protect it, and we are being forced to treat our international clients as partners in projects and to recognize that we are doing the project to meet their needs, not ours. However, much improvement is still required. First and foremost, the project creation stage of the life cycle is critically important to the outcome of the project. It is a very delicate stage in the life cycle where the project team has to balance the creativity of definition against the discipline of getting things properly defined and fixed. Freeze it too early and many potential project benefits will be lost. Fail to freeze it at an appropriate time for the project and the rate of change will be greater than the rate of progress.

To understand another culture we need to analyse it. According to Harris and Moran (1996), there are three ways to analyse a culture, either by its components (Figure 10.1), by its characteristics or by its systems (Figure 10.2). I personally find the latter two easier methods for the analysis. At Cranfield University, we referred to the course covering this area as 'managing cultural differences' or the 'course of lists'. It entails asking lots of questions about the culture, generating the answers and examining our understanding of the answers. This will make the team better prepared to work in the new culture and better able to manage the project in context. Particular issues that are likely to require managerial sensitivity are authority, communications, 'face' or loss of it, motivation, risk taking, pace of work, politics, ethical understandings and religion. We should also be aware that not only are there cultural differences between nations, there is even greater cultural difference between professions. We noted in the section on the political context that there are many stakeholders to a project (some are listed in Figure 10.3), and these all have their own culture. However, the greatest danger of cultural analysis is stereotyping – assuming that everyone from that culture will behave the same way. They will not. We must not stereotype!

An important area of cultural difference is ethics, and this is a new and growing management science (see Chapter 45). Many business schools include it in their syllabus and the UK's Institute of Business Ethics is now 10 years old and can provide helpful material on establishing a company code of ethics. Of course, the ethics practised vary between different cultures and again we have to be careful not to judge another culture's ethics from our own beliefs. 'If no one

| | |
|---|---|
| ● Human nature | ● Relationship to nature |
| ● Relationship to others | ● Human action |
| ● Temporal focus | ● Spatial conception |

**Figure 10.1 Components of culture**

177

---

*Characteristics*

- Communications and language
- Beliefs and attitudes
- Sense of self and space
- Food and feeding habits
- Rewards and recognition

- Mental process and learning
- Relationships
- Dress and appearance
- Time and time consciousness

Systems

- Kinship
- Political
- Association
- Recreational

- Educational
- Religious
- Health

---

**Figure 10.2   Characteristics and systems of culture**

---

- Bankers and funders
- Influential figures
- Media
- Local government
- Contractors

- Shareholders
- Members of Parliament
- Users/customers
- Local authorities
- Suppliers

- Landowners
- Pressure/lobby groups
- Opinion formers
- Regulatory bodies
- Employees

---

**Figure 10.3   Stakeholders to a project**

has paid the police in Azalea for over four years, is it surprising that they demand "on-the-spot" fines and accept bribes in lieu of the fine?'

Furthermore, there is a growth in business studies of the 'spiritual' dimension of work and management. MODEM, an ecumenical church group encouraging dialogue between those interested in leadership and management and those interested in faith, published in 1999 a handbook, *Leading Managing Ministering – Challenging Questions for Church and Society*, which has begun to establish an agenda in this area. My own chapter in the book, 'Why would a businessman study theology?', looks to theology and spirituality as possible informers of leadership and management. After all, management studies have looked to a number of other 'ologies such as sociology and psychology, why not theology? It is certainly true that religion is one of the main shapers of a society's culture. Indeed, in the United Kingdom, recent surveys show that 70 per cent of the nation profess to be Christians and 70 per cent of these believe in the resurrection, but less than 14 per cent attend a church, however infrequently, and less than 2 per cent regularly attend the established church. None the less, the impact and influence of Christianity on the culture of the UK and its values is still very high.

Many factors that shape a project are external to it. Failure to manage them can cause failure, for example CrossRail, Brent Spar and London Ambulance System projects and the First Stock Exchange share transfer system, and (if surveys are to be believed) over 50 per cent of IT projects. Many project resources are within the control or influence of stakeholders, for example finance, 'political will' and staff attitudes. Lobby groups or action groups that are determined to 'stop' a project are becoming increasingly well organized, have greater access to the media and can create real problems for projects. It is important to work with such groups and try to remove their 'heat' as early as possible, in particular, finding champions amongst their number who can be 'converted' to the project and the safeguards the project team have put in place. Therefore maintaining a continuous (not one-off) development of relationships with stakeholders (two-way process of listening and negotiating) is significant for achieving the successful outcome of the project. The process of stakeholder management has seven steps:

1. Identify all the project success criteria and the resource needs.
2. Identify and critically analyse all the stakeholder groups and their likely levels of interest.
3. Link the stakeholder analysis to the project risk analysis.
4. Identify strategies for each stage of the project, for each stakeholder group – the communication plan. These strategies should focus on the desired stakeholder response. For example, if you need the full support of a group, don't just write a letter, go and see them, talk to them, listen and respond.
5. Monitor external and internal influences on the project and particularly any changes.
6. Monitor the factors that affect the stakeholder disposition towards the project and their levels of satisfaction with it.
7. Repeat this process formally and informally throughout the life of the project.

It is important to be prepared to alter the strategy in response to changes to the project or its environment. Examples of the project success criteria for stakeholders are shown in Figure 10.4. There are many more possible examples and they are obviously project-specific. For each project the aim should be to make the success criteria as measurable as possible. This often requires the use of attitude surveys to fix pre- and post-measures.

The 'reputation' of the project is important and often affects the way customers feel about the asset, new facility or new product after its completion. Projects that develop a poor reputation during delivery may suffer later when put to use by poor utilization, or worse, failure to achieve the revenues forecasted.

| | | |
|---|---|---|
| • Satisfied investor | • Happy operator | • High staff morale |
| • Strategic marketing opportunities developed | • Support for future projects is created | • Associated benefits are realized |
| • Friendly neighbours | • Interested customers | • Political support |
| • Contented regulator(s) | • Lobby group support | |

Figure 10.4   Stakeholder success criteria

## TECHNICAL

The rate of change in the world is accelerating as Toffler predicted in *Future Shock* (1970). He demonstrated the constant and accelerating progress of new technologies by measuring in human lifetimes. We now all know the statistics such as '80 per cent of all the scientists and engineers who have ever lived are alive today.' When new projects are conceived many important decisions are taken at the early conceptual and definition stages that will have a major impact on the final outcome of the deliverables, the timescale and cost. Few are greater than deciding which technology should be used. Should we use tried and tested technology? Or should we use the latest, without a proven track-record? These decisions will be driven by the business needs of the project owners, their risk profile and attitudes to technology. It will also be driven by what the competitors are doing. The one thing we can generally be sure of is that the more new, novel or innovative the technology, the more expensive it will be in terms of the final project outcome – time and money. There is a long history of innovative technology delaying and/or running over budget. The fact is that, particularly in IT, there has been a history of projects going forward with new technology that has been invented but not tested. The better rule for effective projects is to utilize tried and tested technology. The current wisdom is to move forward with tried and tested technology and utilize the 'latest' technology in the next version. Examples where the IT industry has been dogged failure due to the zealous use of the latest technology include the Nimrod Airborne Early Warning System, the London Ambulance Service, the air traffic control system, the passport system and many others.

Why should this be? Probably because people are over-optimistic about new technology. The London Underground Jubilee Line extension, with its planned 'moving block' technology, will not be delivered to the original specification and has already caused slippage and cost growth. It appears the technology was not proven at the time of procurement and is some way from being proven even now.

The motor industry uses four headings to describe the degree of innovation in a product for its assembly line workers that we might borrow for projects:

1. *Runners* (continuous process)   We do these all the time. All the project team members are completely familiar with this kind of project and their role in the delivery process.
2. *Repeaters* (batch process)   We do these from time to time, and can remember working on similar projects and the processes used. The team can flex the management processes to suit this type of project. We need a little more care than for a runner, but we anticipate few management problems.
3. *Strangers* (one-offs)   Team members do not recognize this type of project and have not done one like it before. It will need 'first principles' project management. However, we have undertaken many projects that are new to us and are experienced in managing them. We work from first principles and consult people who have worked on similar projects.
4. *Aliens* (absolutely new to us)   We have never seen this before and many components are new to us. None of the team know what it is or how to do it. We will have to apply a strict project management discipline and work from first principles, assuming very little. This is essential to coordinate the research, definition and implementation stages of the project. We will need a project manager experienced in managing innovative projects. We will involve our most experienced project staff, consult widely and recognize that this type of project has similarities to R&D projects.

As one climbs this ladder, the cost of managing the project will also escalate from perhaps as low as 2 per cent of the total project cost at the 'runners' end to as high as 30 per cent at the 'alien' end. This is the cost of the additional management required to manage projects of this nature.

One decision for the owner's team is the appropriate level of technology compared with the business purpose of the project. It is generally expensive to be the market leader who leads development of new technology, but some companies have made that their niche. I am told that BT has to re-invest its net worth every two or three years in new technology. A risky business indeed, but with big rewards. The alternative is to keep going with tried and tested technology. For example, the cable companies are tending to install fibre optic networks and digital switches. While no one would replace copper networks with more copper, there may be many years of life left in the old BT network. All network operators have the same problem: when to replace their networks. If they still work, why invest in modernizing them?

Another problem with investing in new technology is that it may become obsolete before the investors can recover their investment. Remember the 'rabbit' telephone. In the mid-1980s at BT's research division at Martlesham, I was shown a new type of portable telephone we would all be using shortly, which we would

**181**

carry with us and be able to use whenever we were in close proximity to a base station. Base stations were to be situated in or near public buildings. We would be billed as part of our home telephone account. The idea had been conceived to overcome the problem of vandalism to pay phones and the public perception that pay phones were unreliable. The whole idea from concept to market took about four or five years, by which time the scheme was being overtaken by mobile phones one could use anywhere. The 'rabbit' was killed off within six years at great cost to its investors.

Companies therefore have to look to their own technology risk profile and experience and choose accordingly, or recruit the skills needed to manage the higher risk. The perceived wisdom is that new technology projects with long paybacks are probably too risky for most of us. The solution is to undertake the transfer to the new technology in shorter, more certain steps, as a programme of projects. Most of the current thinking on project management focuses on the 'big gun' approach. In other words, define the required project outcome, plan for this and resist all project changes, save them up for the next version. It is difficult to adjust the aim of the project management team after project implementation has commenced, and it becomes exponentially harder as project completion nears. The solution would be some type of very dynamic project management methodology, with a total flexibility to keep changing direction as the ultimate goal was continuously redefined – a sort of 'guided missile' approach to the management of projects. This form of project management has yet to be developed as far as I am aware.

## CONCLUSIONS

Politics, economics, social issues and technology can all have a significant impact on the project outcome, often far greater than the effects of cost or time overruns to the deliverables of the project. The more complex these issues are likely to be on a project, the more experience and skills are required of the project management team and the more expensive relative to the total project cost the cost of managing it will be. The project managers, sponsors and other project management team members of these complex projects will need better 'soft' skills. Public relations and communication activities will need to be given greater emphasis throughout the project's life cycle. There will be a greater requirement for more effective consultation with all the stakeholders at the outset of the project, and managers will need to be given the appropriate training in all these areas.

## REFERENCES AND FURTHER READING

Handy, C. B. and Handy, E. (1999), *The New Alchemists*, Hutchinson, London.

Harpham, A. (1999), 'Why would a businessman study theology?', in J. Nelson (ed.), *Leading, Managing, Ministering – Challenging Questions for Church and Society*, MODEM/Canterbury Press, Norwich.

Harris, P. R. and Moran, R. T. (1996), *Managing Cultural Differences*, Gulf Publishing.

Latham, Sir Michael (1994), *Constructing the Team, Final Report of the Government/Industry Review of Procurement and Contractual Arrangements in the UK Construction Industry*, The Stationery Office, London.

Toffler, A. (1970), *Future Shock*, Pan, London.

## RELATED TOPICS

# 11 Managing the legal context

## Geoff Haley

This chapter looks at some of the legal constraints that project managers operate within and how those constraints need to be managed. It covers legal aspects of:

- procurement
- planning and enquiry
- the environment
- the law of tort.

Before looking at any other item of legislation covering project management, it should be stressed that none are more important than the Health and Safety Regulations. Failure to address health and safety issues can have a dramatic impact on the management of the project. These issues are therefore examined separately in Chapter 22.

## PROCUREMENT

When a government identifies a need for additional infrastructure it will generally procure that item by using some form of invited bid system. In any given infrastructure project a government will generally invite a number of parties to tender in competition for the project. There are various ways in which a government can do this, one of the most common being the World Bank procurement route. All projects funded by the World Bank must follow a detailed set of procurement rules. These rules set out how expressions of interests and proposals must be prepared and how the bidders are selected. The rules require that each bidder be assessed on clearly set out objective criteria. Similar rules are also used by the other multilateral agencies throughout the world such as the European Bank for Reconstruction and Development. The European Union also has a detailed set of rules regarding how infrastructure and services are procured.

## THE EUROPEAN PROCUREMENT REGIME

A series of European Community directives have established compulsory competitive tendering for contracts awarded by public bodies and utilities. The first set of directives (the Public Sector Directives) apply to public authorities including government, local authorities and quangos such as NHS Trusts.

The second set applies to public bodies and private companies operating in the utility sectors (the Utilities Directive): water, energy, telecommunications and transportation. Both sets of directives apply to contracts in respect of works, services and the supply of goods, provided certain value thresholds are met.

The general obligations laid down by the directives require projects to be advertised throughout the EU and to follow one of a number of fixed-award procedures:

- to employ objective criteria for qualitative selection of contractors and to award contracts on the basis of either the lowest price or the most economically advantageous tender; and
- to retrospectively notify the Commission of details of contract awards.

Broadly speaking, contracts for building works, supplies and services will be caught by the directives where the value of the contract exceeds the following thresholds.

### For public bodies

- Works contracts (building, maintenance, engineering and refurbishment): £3.6m
- Service contracts (management, architectural, quantity surveyors, accounting, building management, refuse disposal): £104 435
- Supplies contracts (in the case of certain public bodies including NHS Trusts): £104 435

### For utilities

- Works contracts (building, maintenance, engineering and refurbishment): £3.6m
- Service contracts: £311 947 (energy, water, transport sectors); £467 920 (telecom sector)
- Supplies contracts: £311 947 (energy, water, transport sectors); £467 920 (telecom sector)

It is worth noting that certain services are not subject to the full requirements of the regulations and awarding bodies or authorities are only obliged to place a notice in the Official Journal that a contract award has been made.

## CONSEQUENCES OF NON-COMPLIANCE

A failure to respect the competitive procurement procedures laid down by the Directives can result in an aggrieved third party raising a challenge to the award of a contract on the basis that it should have been given the opportunity to tender for the contract. This can result in calling a halt to the tender procedure, the setting aside of a decision and/or the award of damages to the aggrieved party as compensation for losses suffered by it as a result of a breach of the procurement regime.

Managers should be aware that challenges to public contracts in the USA and Australia are a regular occurrence and that contractors are becoming increasingly aware that tender rules and regulations can be used to great effect as a sword rather than as a shield.

The procurement regime seeks to ensure competition based on a transparent contract award procedure, free from discrimination. A practical step-by-step guide to a typical procurement exercise is set out below.

### Award procedures

Where the EC regime applies, contracts must be awarded using one of three procedures:

- The open procedure where there is no pre-selection of bidders.
- The restricted procedure where between five and twenty bidders must be considered.
- The negotiated procedure where the contracting authority consults the contractor(s) of its choice and negotiates the contract with one or more of them.

The timetable for carrying out procurement varies between the different types of procedures involved but will usually require a minimum of three months, whilst in complex cases a period of six to nine months is not unusual.

Contracts covered by the scope of the Directives must be advertised in the Official Journal of the European Community (OJEC). The notice must be sent to the OJEC in Luxembourg and be drafted in a prescribed format. The advertisement must state precisely the contracting body's or authority's requirements so that a potential contractor can decide whether to express an interest in tendering. Prior to advertising the project, generally speaking, there should be no problem in discussing the project informally with potential bidders provided this does not put any one of them in a privileged position, for example by divulging cost or pricing information to one and not to the others. Any information released to one potential bidder should be released to all other bidders once a shortlist of candidates has been selected.

### Pre-qualification appraisal

Where there is likely to be a large number of potential bidders, it is advisable to carry out a pre-qualification appraisal. This reduces the cost to bidders and also provides a reasonable and predictable chance of success for those who pre-qualify. Information sought from prospective bidders would include:

- a brief history of the bidder companies;
- a description of their general operations and experience in similar projects;
- independently audited financial statements and audited reports for the preceding three years; and
- information on proposed partners or subcontractors.

### Invitation to tender

Invitations to tender together with contractual documentation are then sent to selected or pre-qualified tenderers. The contract documents should be prepared at an early stage. They should contain a full, accurate and complete description of the requisite works, goods or services, using community standards and technical specifications when available to ensure that the tender is open to all potential contractors throughout the European Community.

The request for proposals needs to be designed in such a way as to enable proposals to be compared on a like-for-like basis, to encourage creativity and innovative proposals from the public sector and to elicit from bidders the relevant information required from them. Invitations to tender should also include expressly stated objective criteria for the selection of bidders and the award of contracts.

### Evaluation of tenders

Evaluation of tenders should be carried out on the basis of predetermined objective criteria and, particularly, the requirement that the contract should be awarded on the basis of the offer which is 'most economically advantageous' to the contracting authority. The main criteria for evaluating tenders would include such factors as:

- project understanding
- compliance with specification
- specific experience
- management qualifications.

Equally important is the need to find the most innovative and sound solutions in financing, technological, environmental impact and other matters. Negotiations should therefore be undertaken with one or more bidders by reference to their tendered bids before deciding upon the best and final offer and contract award.

### Contract award

The criteria for award will have been included in the tender documentation. The award should be made in accordance with the specified procedure and any time limits prescribed. A Contract Award Notice should be dispatched to Luxembourg for publication in the OJEC.

# PLANNING AND INQUIRY

Under most legal systems specific consents are required (such as planning permission to construct the facility) as a precondition to the commencement of construction of the works. Whether the public or private sector are better placed to obtain the consents depends on the type of project and the laws of the host county.

## PROJECT PLANNING IN THE UK

### Planning consent

Under Section 57(1) of the Town and Country Planning Act 1990, planning permission is required for the carrying out of any development of land. Except where the context otherwise requires, 'development' is defined by Section 55 of the 1990 Act as the carrying out of building, engineering, mining or other operations in, on, over or under land, or the making of any material change in the use of any buildings or other land. There are, inevitably, numerous exceptions to the requirement to obtain planning permission. However, if any development or alterations are carried out without permission, the local planning authority has the power to take enforcement action, which ultimately culminates in criminal sanctions.

### Enforcement action

Where a development is being or has been carried out without planning permission or in breach of the planning permission the local planning authority can issue an enforcement notice under the Town and Country Planning Act 1990, requiring the breach to be remedied within a specified time frame. Failure to remedy the breach is an offence and is subject to a fine.

## Planning authorities

At local level the administration of town and country planning is the responsibility of local planning authorities. In England and Wales there are two tiers of local planning authority:

- The County Councils, acting as county planning authorities.
- The District Councils, acting as district planning authorities.

The responsibilities of the county planning authorities are somewhat restricted and it is the district authorities that are responsible for the administration of the statutory provisions relating to the control of development.

## Planning procedure

The planning procedure has three main elements:

1. *The planning application* Where planning permission is required to authorize development, an application must be made to the local planning authority for the area in which that development is to be undertaken. This must be done in accordance with the Town and Country Planning Act 1990 and the Town and Country Planning (General Development) Order 1988.
2. *Notification to landowners* The application, setting out the nature of the development proposed, should be submitted on a form issued by the local planning authority. Prior to the lodging of the application, the applicant must notify the owners and agricultural tenants of any land comprised within the application site. The application must also be accompanied by a certificate stating that this has been done.
3. *Bad neighbour developments* Where an application relating to a form of development falls within the category of developments loosely described as 'bad neighbours' (those forms of development defined in the General Development Order which will generally have significant impact on amenity and environment) there is an obligation for the applicant to advertise the application in a newspaper circulating in the locality. The applicant must also erect a notice on site containing a statement that any person wishing to make representations to the local planning authority may do so and that the local planning authority is bound to consider any representations received before the end of 21 days from the date of application.

## Use of planning conditions

A local planning authority, on consideration of the planning application, may under Section 70(1) TCPA 1990:

- grant planning permission unconditionally;
- grant planning permission subject to such conditions as they think fit; or
- refuse permission altogether.

The planning authority may attach such conditions 'as they think fit', but these conditions must serve some useful purpose, having regard to the object of planning legislation, and must not offend against the general law. The area of discretion of the local planning authority in attaching conditions to a grant of planning permission remains, however, fairly wide. Nevertheless, it is important that the conditions (reasons for which must be stated) satisfy the following criteria:

1. A condition must serve some useful planning purpose, that is it must fairly and reasonably relate to the provisions of the development plan and to planning considerations affecting the land.
2. A condition must fairly and reasonably relate to the permitted development, that is it must relate to the actual purpose for which the permission was sought.
3. A condition must not be manifestly unreasonable – a condition which is wholly unreasonable is open to scrutiny by the Courts.
4. A condition may be imposed restricting the use of premises according to the personal circumstances of the occupier.
5. Conditions may be void for uncertainty, that is if no sensible or ascertainable meaning can be assigned to the condition.

### Compulsory purchase orders

Where it is unlikely that the site of a proposed development can be assembled by agreement, consideration must be given to the use of compulsory powers of acquisition to consolidate the area of land needed. The making of or, indeed the threat of a compulsory purchase order can assist in the following ways:

1. The assembly of the requisite land under the order.
2. The inducement to reluctant owners to dispose of land.
3. The removal of adverse third party interests, such as tenancies, from the title of land within the freehold ownership of the developer.

# ENVIRONMENTAL LEGAL

## BACKGROUND TO INTERNATIONAL ENVIRONMENTAL POLICY

By its very nature environmental pollution knows no frontiers. Environmental issues are challenging the sovereignty of states and the sanctity of agreements. Concepts of liability for ecological damage, environmental impact assessment, the transport of hazardous waste and the desirability of sustainable development are now worldwide concerns.

International laws and treaties are not binding on states until ratified by them. However, as an influence of local regulations and an indicator of future developments in environmental policy, international environmental laws must be included in any review of relevant legislation. Many nations, of course, have a federal system of laws of which cognizance must be taken. There are also wider regional arrangements, many of which, although primarily economic in essence, have environmental aspects, such as the North American Free Trade Agreement and, of course, the European Union.

## EUROPEAN ENVIRONMENTAL POLICY

Since 1987 the Treaty of Rome has had a separate environment title, according the environment a high level of protection. It is underlined by the now familiar tripartite structure of environmental policy, namely that preventative action should be taken even if full proof of damage has not been established, that pollution should be tackled at source rather than after the event and that the polluter should be made to pay.

The Maastricht Treaty, which was eventually ratified in 1993, introduced the concept of sustainable development (Chapter 12), amending Article 2 of the Treaty of Rome to include 'promotion of sustainable and non-inflationary growth, respecting the environment', that is ensuring that environmental issues were not sacrificed to economic growth.

## ENVIRONMENTAL ISSUES AFFECTING THE CONSTRUCTION INDUSTRY

The following is a list, in no particular order, of the main issues likely to impinge on a major project from the design stage through construction, handover and finally into operation:

● Visual impact and land use planning
● Archaeological effects
● Nature conservation and agricultural disturbance

- Ground water and hydro-geology
- Pollution of water, of the atmosphere, of the soil
- Coastal hydrography and marine ecology
- Disposal of soil and sediment
- Pollution by noise, smell, vibration and light
- Dangerous substances and accident hazards
- Energy supply and availability of natural resources.

There are others issues not mentioned above which may affect individual projects but it is interesting to note by way of practical example that the environmental impact assessment for the Channel Tunnel Project identified 18 distinct areas of environmental impact each of which required specialist reports within the assessment. Some of these aspects are now considered in more detail.

## ENVIRONMENTAL IMPACT ASSESSMENT (EIA)

At the international level, the 1991 ESPOO Convention on Environmental Impact Assessment in a Transboundary Context considers the cross-boundary effect of major development proposals, requiring prior notification to states which may be affected and enabling such states to require consultation with the developing state. Article 3(1) includes affected activities such as power stations, construction of motorways and express roads, airport runways, and dams and reservoirs.

At European Union level the requirement to provide a statement of the likely environmental impact for certain projects was established by EC Directive 85/337/EEC: Assessment of the Effects of Certain Public and Private Projects on the Environment.

EIA involves the systematic examination of the likely effects on the environment of a proposed development and it incorporates into the decision-making process the results of that examination. The Directive makes assessment mandatory for Annex I developments including such projects as oil refineries, nuclear power stations, airport runways, motorways and express roads. Projects outlined in Annex II, such as agriculture, mining, waste material and chemicals, require an assessment where there is likely to be a significant impact on the environment.

Directive 97/11/EC substantially amended Directive 85/337/EC by providing guidance on when environmental impact is 'significant', making it mandatory to consider alternative sites, and to define the scope of EIA to avoid developers supplying a bare minimum of information.

Apart from legislative requirements, environmental impact assessment is a useful tool for the identification of practical measures to reduce impact and disturbance when developing the design, and acts as a predictor for problems that may arise during the construction stage.

## SITE SUITABILITY

For projects in urban areas there is an increasing likelihood that funders at government level will attempt to direct developers towards sites which have been used previously (brownfield) rather than to unused areas (greenfield sites). Contamination of land from industrial residues, whether directly from on-site operations or the landfilling of waste, is a serious problem worldwide. One of the most noticeable knock-on effects on commercial transactions in land has been the risk of liability for contamination whether directly through broken deals or indirectly through banks and other funders refusing to lend on land offered as security. This has been particularly noticeable in the USA where the Superfund regime has caused a virtual shutdown in contaminated land dealings.

Land contamination is a major issue in Europe, particularly the further east one goes. At present there is virtually no central policy from Brussels on contaminated land except a 1993 green paper which went no further, although there are signs that the Commission still intends to tackle this problem. The costs of remedying soil pollution can be enormous. However, these are likely to be outweighed completely by the costs of responding to an environmental damages claim that might be brought against the owner of a site who is still regarded as the primary target for legal liability in many Member States.

In the UK s.57 of the Environment Act 1995, which was implemented in July 1999, seeks to address the problem of contaminated land and aims to prevent future contamination and develop contaminated sites. With this, the implementation of new regulatory measures will have to be addressed where existing contamination presents unacceptable risks. As a result the regime should contribute significantly to the redevelopment of brownfield sites and return contaminated land to beneficial use. Under the provisions local authorities and environment agencies will be responsible for inspecting land to determine if it falls into the definition of contaminated land, and will have to work with other organizations to develop understanding and solutions.

## ENVIRONMENTAL ISSUES DURING THE CONSTRUCTION OF PROJECTS

### Soil and sediment disposal

In the past this has usually been a question of physical practicalities of disposing of very large volumes of extracted soil or dredging. With developing concern and legal constraints over the disposal of some types of waste (and construction waste is for the most part included) there is a likelihood that if the extracted material is contaminated considerable operational difficulties may arise. The problem is of particular concern for tunnels where large quantities of soil may have to be moved a considerable distance away from the nearest acceptable deposit point. If the tunnel is proceeding under land currently or previously used for industrial processes, extracted material runs a high risk of containing heavy metals and other soil pollutants, and if the material is water bearing there is an immediate problem of leachate.

Various international conventions seek to reduce and ultimately prohibit the dumping of various substances at sea. These include the 1973 MARPOL Convention, the UN Convention on the Law of the Sea (UNCLOS), which finally came into force in November 1994, and, on a more regional basis, the Oslo, London and Paris Conventions and the North Sea Conferences. These are reflected in a number of important, more local regulations.

### Blasting and piling

Noise and vibration are two of the main environmental effects. Dust also can be a considerable problem from these operations and provision to reduce dust nuisance by water spraying and covering exposed surfaces may well be insisted on. Dilapidation surveys may also be required prior to commencement if there is a risk of blasting damage.

### Ventilation

This can be a serious problem with tunnels and other underground workings, especially for longer tunnels where provision may have to be made for collection of vehicle, compressor and other exhaust gases which at the collection and venting points are likely to exceed EU or other limits. Accordingly, filtration systems may be required. Controls over emissions of sulphur dioxide, carbon monoxide, nitrous oxide and diesel particulates are tending to increase at international and regional levels.

### Drainage

With growing emphasis on water pollution standards and disposal of waste water, general site drainage and sanitation will require consideration. The latter may be more of a problem in the case of temporary sites because there will not necessarily be any long-term sewerage provision for the future life of the project (if for example it is a bridge or tunnel).

Should there be any need to establish waste disposal sites, consideration will have to be given to the collection of leachate and tankering it off site. Silt arising from construction is increasingly being regarded as a serious water pollutant. There have been several notable prosecutions of construction companies for environmental damage from this cause.

While point source discharges to water systems are in many countries now well regulated, diffuse water pollution (with no discernible discharge point) continues to be a major constituent of marine pollution. One area giving the most concern is rainwater run-off from motorways, bridges and other large surface area developments. Balancing ponds to contain water run-off, rubber particles and polycyclic aromatic hydrocarbons are now a requirement of modern motorway design.

The European Union has treated waste water very seriously through the implementation of Directive 91/271, which governs the collection and treatment of waste water, the adverse effects on drinking water and ecological disturbances. Failure by Member States to comply with the Directive will result in a formal notice, which will require comments from the competent national authority explaining the impact on public and private projects. Ultimately the Member States could be referred to the European Court of Justice for failure to implement the Directive. Such a failure was illustrated by the UK which did not implement Directive 91/676 concerning the protection of waters against pollution caused by nitrates from agricultural sources, which resulted in the UK being referred to the ECJ.

### Lighting

Provision will be required for construction lighting for night-time and poor visibility operations and, of course, a finished project may have to be permanently lit. Security lighting will be required for high hazard areas, transport pounds and other isolated parts of construction sites. Increasingly, use of high intensity lighting has created a concern over the unacceptable effects of light pollution particularly for adjacent residential areas and also from a visual impact point of view where developments take place in rural areas where night-time lighting patterns are traditionally at a very low level.

### Transport

Both on- and off-site transport produces noise and particularly air pollution considerations. In some Member States (the UK is one example) permits may be required for transporting waste material although normally there is an exemption for on-site transfers. There are increasing restrictions on the transport of hazardous waste, particularly in a transboundary context.

## Noise pollution

Construction sites are inherently noisy and are often located in otherwise quiet residential areas. Twenty-four hour operation is the rule rather than the exception. As a result, construction noise has become a major EU concern and there are fifteen or more Directives in force establishing maximum noise emission levels for everything from tower cranes to compressors. Much of this legislation is implemented through health and safety rules. Early identification of main noise sources is essential at the planning stage so preventative measures can be incorporated in the design. Earth moundings and other forms of blanketing or baffles can help to reduce the impact – an obvious candidate for cut and fill provision.

## Nature conservation

A significant concern is the possibility of harm to habitats, flora and fauna from construction activities or from the eventual use of the project itself. However, the reverse is also true in that on motorways and bridges, large animals can present considerable hazards to drivers. Provisions should therefore be made to avoid too much disruption.

## Rehabilitation

At the completion of the project various ancillary matters may have environmental aspects. Re-establishment of interrupted land uses will often be required. Landscaping to restore previous visual integrity as far as possible is often an important condition applied at the planning stage. This may well give rise to associated problems such as the use of pesticide sprays for controlling weed growth etc. In addition there will be the question of removing temporary buildings, clearing the site of all residues of toxic materials and other hazardous substances. For long-term construction projects, demolition of buildings may itself produce additional pollution risks where ground has hitherto remained undisturbed.

## THE EFFECT OF ENVIRONMENTAL ISSUES ON CONTRACTS AND CONTRACTORS

The environmental lobby is powerful and contractors and project designers who dismiss the environmental factor do so at their peril. 'Mainstream' pollution – atmospheric, water, waste, noise – is increasingly regulated but the fiercest battles are more likely to be over habitats and amenity protection and in respect of the longer-term 'downstream' diffuse effects on general ambient environmental quality. High risk target areas in the future will be traffic generation, energy consumption, resource protection and the concept of sustainable use and development.

Third parties are likely to be accorded greater rights to intervene in environmental conflicts. The public will have access to more and more information on the environment and on related health and safety and planning aspects, giving it the opportunity to exploit that information to bring damages claims, lodge interdictory procedures to suspend or stop project construction and require reviews of administrative decisions.

As the 'zero impact' approach continues to be demanded, so developers of large projects will have to adopt a precautionary approach, facing up to environmental issues at the inception of the planning process. This is already required in specific areas for both environmental and health and safety requirements, as has been seen above, but for other issues a general environmental ethic will be mandatory.

There will be an increasing need to include within the multidisciplinary team approach the use of not only designers, planners and engineers, but environmental consultants, lawyers and risk management consultants. Contract documentation will increasingly stipulate environmental constraints. This is happening already. Transmanche Link, as contractor for the Channel Tunnel, was required to design and construct the project 'to reduce and avoid all harmful effects on the environment' and to have in place the necessary staff to coordinate the incorporation of environmental aspects during construction. These requirements should not be seen to produce only negative effects. Observance of sound environmental practice can provide considerable advantages to the industry itself. The following are discernible as benefits:

1. Identification of environmental problem areas at the design stage will act as an 'early warning' system for possible delays at the construction stage.
2. Reduction in costs to the client – environmentally progressive engineering techniques are often cheaper than traditionally engineered schemes.
3. Adoption of a 'due diligence' approach to environmental issues throughout the development and life of a project will go a long way towards saving the potentially horrendous costs of a civil liability damages claim (or a regulatory penalty). As the tendency develops for major projects to be developed on a build/own/operate basis, so the risk of liability for environmental damage will attach to the company or consortium involved. Thus the need for constant consideration to be given to the impact of the environment on a full 'life cycle' basis.

# LAW OF TORT

Over the last few decades the law of tort affecting the construction industry has experienced some radical shifts. Through the 1970s and 1980s a long list of cases culminating with *Junior Books* v. *Veitchi* (1983) established a body of law that gave rise to duties and liabilities independent of any contractual link. Contractors and designers owed a duty to those who were affected by their work and any breach of those duties would give the person affected a direct right of action against the wrongdoer. The reasoning behind the protection afforded by the common law, through the tort of negligence, was to protect third parties who acquired an interest in land and subsequently found they had no power or rights of action against previous or current contractors and designers operating on the land in question. The doctrine of privity of contract – the doctrine that provides that only the parties to the contract may enforce the rights and the liabilities under it – constitutes a bar to recovery by any third party, such as a lending institution or a purchaser against contractors and designers.

However, in 1989 the House of Lords in *D&F Estates* v. *Church Commissioners* (1989) and later in *Murphy* v. *Brentwood DC* (1991) reversed a trend which many had thought was here to stay. Through these cases it became clear that tort would not protect third parties who had suffered economic loss at the hands of contractors or designers. Thus loss, other than personal injury or physical damage, deriving from defects negligently caused by contractors or designers was not recoverable in tort. The legal void created by these decisions has since been filled, to a certain extent, by 'duty of care' letters which are now well known under the heading of 'collateral warranties'. The essential features of collateral warranties are:

- they enable rights to be given to any person who has an interest in a building but who was not a party to the contract for its design and construction;
- those rights lie directly against the persons who were responsible for the design and construction of the building – they are not dependent on the solvency of intermediate parties;
- collateral warranties can be tailored to match precise circumstances – the nature of the person receiving them, insurance cover held by the party giving them and so on.

The pre-eminent standard form in this field is the British Property Federation's (BPF) Consultant/Funder Warranty Agreement, 'CoWa/F'. It was followed in 1992 by the form 'CoWa/P and T', the more controversial equivalent for Purchasers and Tenants. However, many doubts continue regarding both the form and the efficacy of collateral warranties generally. The construction industry has for some time suggested that insurance-based coverage of post-construction defects rather than a liability inherent in the present system, including collateral warranties, may well be preferable.

As a result of the many problems linked to contractual warranties the Law Commission published a consultation paper in 1996 that proposed reform of the doctrine of privity of contract. The consultation paper gave third parties the right to enforce a contract even if they do not have a direct contract with the person with whom they are in dispute. At the time this consultation paper was severely criticized by the construction industry which believed it would lead to enormous uncertainties which in turn would lead the industry to increase construction costs as a result of its increased liability. In spite of this, the Contracts (Rights of Third Parties) Act 1999 received Royal Assent on 11 November 1999 and came into force on the same day. However, the Act is not retrospective and, unless the contract expressly states otherwise, it will not apply to any contract entered into within the six-month period starting on 11 November 1999. After that date it will apply to all contracts subject to exceptions unless specifically excluded.

## REFERENCES AND FURTHER READING

RIBA, ACE and RICS (1990), *Consultant/Funder Warranty Agreement, CoWA/f*, Royal Institute of British Architects/Association of Consulting Engineers/Royal Institution of Chartered Surveyors, London.

## RELATED TOPICS

| | |
|---|---|
| Health and safety | Chapter 22 |
| Environmental management | Chapter 12 |

# 12 Managing the environment

## Rodney Turner

In Chapter 10 Alan Harpham introduced the concept of PESTLE analysis (political, economic, social, technical, legal and environmental analysis) as a way of assessing the impact of the project's context on the project, and the project on its context. Alan Harpham discussed the first four of these (the PEST of PESTLE) and Geoff Haley discussed the legal issues in Chapter 11. We now come to the impact of the project on its environment, and the environment on the project. Let me reinforce at this point that I do differentiate between the context and the environment:

- The 'context' I use to describe the complete situation within which the project exists, the political, economic, social, technical, legal and environmental pressures acting on it.
- The 'environment' I limit to the physical surroundings of the project, which for almost all, but not every, project is the Earth's biosphere.

I know many people use the word 'environment' to describe what I have called here context, and often it does not matter, but there are times when it is important to be clear what one means.

In this chapter I describe how to develop an environmental strategy for the organization and its projects, some of the environmental principles used when considering environmental impacts, how to cost environmental impacts into the appraisal of projects, how to conduct an environmental impact analysis, and a procedure for obtaining consents.

## DEVELOPING AN ENVIRONMENTAL STRATEGY

Pollock (1995) gives a four-step process for developing an environmental strategy:

1. Develop understanding.
2. Measure and improve performance.
3. Maintain positive attitudes.
4. Review progress and decide next steps.

## DEVELOP UNDERSTANDING

The first step is to obtain commitment of people in the organization to improving environmental performance, to obtain the right attitudes (see Figure 5.2). Frequently asked questions are:

- Is it necessary?
- Do we actually have an impact?
- Can we afford it?

### Is it necessary?

Well, 'Yes!', not only to protect the environment, but for legal, social and commercial reasons. Most of us are now aware of the nightmare scenarios that are painted, of rising atmospheric temperatures, rising sea levels and rising incidences of skin cancer. Many of the doom-mongers have been proved wrong in the past. A report produced in the early 1970s by an organization called the Club of Rome predicted that the oil would run out in the early 1980s. There are now greater reserves than ever. But even if some of the predictions are just one-tenth right, there is enough to be concerned about. Later I describe two principles, the Precautionary Principle and the Principle of Sustainable Development, both of which suggest that we should not do something if we are not aware of its impact and that we have an ethical duty to our grandchildren to leave them a world they can live in. Even if we are unconvinced by those arguments, there is a body of national, European and international legislation that imposes significant constraints on what we can do. Figure 12.1 shows Acts of Parliament in the UK, but most developed countries have similar legislation, some of it required in Europe by EU directives, and some countries have even more severe legislation. More requirements are given in Chapters 11 and 22. However, it is also a common principle that public opinion runs ahead of legislation, that politicians respond to public opinion rather than lead it (see Chapter 11 of Turner, Grude and Thurloway 1996, and Chapter 45). Hence our customers, shareholders, employees and other stakeholders all have attitudes which we cannot ignore. Figure 12.2 offers a checklist of potential pressures that may require us to improve our environmental performance.

| Reach | Legislation |
|---|---|
| UK | Alkali Act |
| | Control of Pollution Act 1974 |
| | Health and Safety at Work Act 1974 |
| | Environmental Protection Act 1990 |
| | Integrated Pollution Control Act 1991 |
| | Water Resources Act 1991 |
| | Control of Industrial Major Accident Hazard Regulations 1984 |
| | Town and Country Planning (Assessment of Environmental Effect) Regulations 1988 |
| | Planning Policy Guidelines |
| | Green Paper on Environmental Liability for Damage caused by Pollution |
| European | Construction Products Directive |
| | Emissions Directive |
| | Environmental Impact Assessment Directive |
| | Hazardous Waste Directive |
| | Integrated Pollution and Protection Directive 1992 |
| | Noise Limits Directive |
| | Single European Act – Polluter Pays Principle |
| International | Environmental Protection Agency |
| | Montreal Protocol |
| | Rio de Janeiro and Berlin conferences |

**Figure 12.1   Environmental legislation**

| Pressures for environmental change | Low | | | | | High |
|---|---|---|---|---|---|---|
| Government | 1 | 2 | 3 | 4 | 5 | 6 |
| Pressure groups | 1 | 2 | 3 | 4 | 5 | 6 |
| Public awareness | 1 | 2 | 3 | 4 | 5 | 6 |
| Local communities | 1 | 2 | 3 | 4 | 5 | 6 |
| Public relations | 1 | 2 | 3 | 4 | 5 | 6 |
| Green consumers | 1 | 2 | 3 | 4 | 5 | 6 |
| Competitors | 1 | 2 | 3 | 4 | 5 | 6 |
| Employees | 1 | 2 | 3 | 4 | 5 | 6 |
| Insurers | 1 | 2 | 3 | 4 | 5 | 6 |
| Capital markets | 1 | 2 | 3 | 4 | 5 | 6 |
| Shareholders | 1 | 2 | 3 | 4 | 5 | 6 |
| Uncovering risks | 1 | 2 | 3 | 4 | 5 | 6 |
| Crises | 1 | 2 | 3 | 4 | 5 | 6 |
| Ethics | 1 | 2 | 3 | 4 | 5 | 6 |

**Figure 12.2   Pressures for performance improvement**

## Do we actually have an impact?

To determine the impact of the organization or a project, you need to consider the inputs and the outputs. The processes tend only to have an impact through the inputs and outputs. Figure 12.3 contains a potential checklist of impacts.

## Can we afford it?

Well, 'You have to!' But in fact there is substantial anecdotal evidence that environmental awareness pays. The question reduces to a cost–benefit analysis. The section below on environmental accounting and costing shows how the cost of environmental impact and awareness can be built into project appraisal. There are also other costs associated with conducting environmental impact assessments and the consent process, but those are often required by law. Benefits can come from reduced costs and increased income. Often environmental hygiene reduces waste and other inputs and outputs listed in Figure 12.3, reducing costs and hence making savings greater than the cost of implementing the environmental policies. A Japanese steel company felt it was not attracting the right quality graduate engineers because of its working environment, so the company improved the environment so people could wear white overalls. Energy consumption dropped 30 per cent. Other benefits can arise from:

- attracting the green consumer;
- attracting the green investor;
- meeting the environmental requirements of potential clients;
- reducing insurance premiums;

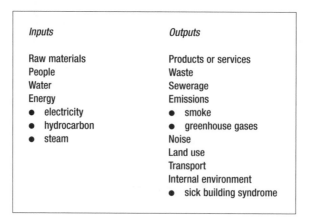

**Figure 12.3    Input–output model of environmental impacts**

- improving staff commitment and satisfaction;
- being better integrated with the local community;
- reducing energy consumption;
- reducing waste disposal costs;
- avoiding fines.

In the early 1980s I worked with ICI in North East England. There was a proposal to store low and medium level nuclear waste in a redundant mine on the site. This would have cost ICI nothing and generated rental. Local house prices started to fall, so the local population was paying for the proposal, and as the support of the local community was essential to ICI it did not go ahead with the scheme.

## MEASURE AND IMPROVE PERFORMANCE

The British Standard for environmental performance, BS7750, suggests a twelve-step process or environmental management system, EMS, for measuring and improving environmental performance.

1. *Initial review* Review environmental performance and construct an input–output model.
2. *Strategy* Develop a strategy based, perhaps, on the sixteen-point charter issued by the International Chamber of Commerce (Figure 12.4).
3. *Organization and personnel* Gain commitment of all people in the organization, from top to bottom. Develop positive attitudes.
4. *Register of regulations* Keep a list of relevant regulations, as per Figure 12.1.
5. *Register of effects* Record your input–output model as per Figure 12.3.
6. *Objectives and targets* Set aims and objectives for improvement. Objectives should be SMART: specific, measurable, achievable, realistic and time-framed.
7. *Management action plans* Develop project plans for the achievement of each objective, including a milestone plan and responsibility chart.

| | |
|---|---|
| 1. Integrated management | 9. Research |
| 2. Employee education | 10. Precautionary approach |
| 3. Products and services | 11. Contractors and suppliers |
| 4. Facilities and operation | 12. Emergency preparedness |
| 5. Corporate priority | 13. Transfer of technology |
| 6. Process of improvement | 14. Contributing to the common effort |
| 7. Prior assessment | 15. Openness to concerns |
| 8. Customer advice | 16. Compliance and reporting |

Figure 12.4   Sixteen-point charter for sustainable development

8. *Management manual*   Record everything so far in a manual and put on wide circulation, including the intranet. Make sure people refer to it.
9. *Organizational control*   Control the implementation of the improvement projects.
10. *Record*   Monitor what is achieved.
11. *Audits*   Audit the effectiveness of the improvement projects and make appropriate improvements.
12. *Review*   Review progress annually.

## MAINTAIN POSITIVE ATTITUDES

Step 3 and Figure 5.2 suggest it is important to develop and maintain positive attitudes. This can be achieved by the seven steps below:

1. Seek senior management support and involve it in the process.
2  Hold regular meetings of interested people, including environmental hygiene circles.
3. Network with people in other organizations.
4. Run competitions and offer awards for suggestions.
5. Involve the local community.
6. Maintain internal communications.
   - newspapers
   - company magazines
   - notice boards
   - intranet.
7. Involve the functions of the organization:
   - marketing
   - finance
   - human resource management.

## REVIEW PROGRESS AND DECIDE NEXT STEPS

In the annual review, you will want to ask yourself the questions:

- How did we do?
- Where do we go next?

### How did we do?

You will obviously review progress against your objectives, but other measures of improvement include:

- environmental initiatives suggested;
- environmental initiatives achieved;
- staff attending environmental courses;
- staff requesting information;
- hits on the intranet page;
- support from senior management;
- customer satisfaction;
- benchmarking against competitors;
- feedback from network contacts.

### Where do we go next?

Again, you will obviously set objectives for greater improvement, but as you move up a learning curve that will be increasingly more difficult. Improvements will become increasingly more costly. You will need to work to maintain what you have achieved and to maintain positive attitudes, and that may eventually become more important than achieving new improvements. You may start to ask deeper questions like:

- Why does it have to be like this?
- How can we change attitudes on a wider stage:
  - the local community?
  - nationally?
  - globally?
- Are we masters of our destiny or creators of our doom?

## ENVIRONMENTAL PRINCIPLES

In making decisions about what options there are in the design of our projects, and their impact on the environment, there are four principles which can guide our thinking:

1. Sustainable development
2. The precautionary principle
3. BPEO, BATNEEC and IPC
4. The polluter pays

### SUSTAINABLE DEVELOPMENT

Sustainable development is defined as:

Development which meets the needs of the present generation without compromising the ability of future generations to meet their needs.

(Bruntland 1987)

Many of the examples of unsustainable development from both rich and poor nations are of agricultural land taken out of production in ways that mean they can never be returned to agriculture:

- Covered in tarmac, housing and industrial sites throughout the western world.
- Made unusable through poor irrigation practices resulting in soil salinity which cannot be economically reversed in developing nations.
- Mined for minerals.

In the former Soviet Union poor irrigation practices resulted in the Aral Sea halving in size so that former fishing villages were 80 kms from the coast, and the salinity of the sea rising and killing most of the fish.

Our grandchildren and their grandchildren need the land for development and so we have a moral duty to use it in such a way that it continues to be reusable. If that increases the cost of our projects, then so be it.


## THE PRECAUTIONARY PRINCIPLE

Sometimes when faced with various options we do not know what the impact of some of them will be. Some people say that it is acceptable to carry on doing things until we know for certain that the impact is bad. However, the view that is rapidly gaining credence is the opposite, that we should not do things if there is any risk that they may damage the environment until we know for certain what the consequence is, and that we know it is acceptable (sustainable).


## BPEO, BATNEEC AND IPC

The concepts of best practical environmental option (BPEO) and best available technique not entailing excessive cost (BATNEEC) are defined within the UK's Environmental Protection Act 1990:

1. BPEO applies at the strategic level, when governments or companies make decisions about what projects they will and will not do. For instance, in disposing of waste the government may choose between landfill and incineration. In deciding transport policy it will choose between road and rail. Several years ago, Shell needed to dispose of a redundant North Sea oil rig, and was deflected from the BPEO by Greenpeace, which later admitted it was wrong.

2. BATNEEC applies at a tactical level, once a project is underway, when deciding what options will be carried forward for design and implementation. If a design option is likely to have an impact on the environment, then alternative design options should be considered and compared. The difference in cost between the initially proposed option and the next best alternative can be calculated and then the simple question asked, 'Is that extra cost worth spending to protect the environment?' Sometimes the extra cost can be justified not just through the protection to the environment but through the benefits listed above. Sometimes the comparison will result in improvements to the original design which will reduce the impact on the environment. Sometimes the analysis shows that the originally proposed option was the best and the cheapest.

Integrated pollution control (IPC) is also defined in the UK's Environmental Protection Act 1990. Its main objectives are:

- to prevent or minimize the release of prescribed substances, and to render harmless those substances which are released;
- to develop an approach to pollution control which considers discharges from industrial processes to all media in the context of the environment as a whole.

Organizations are regularly fined for harmful discharges. This is not so much a technique to help us consider options and then choose the optimum in terms of cost and impact; it lays down minimum requirements for pollution control.

## THE POLLUTER PAYS

This is a principle that receives a lot of lip-service, but its application falls well short. Environmentalists have long argued that if the true environmental impact of road transport were taken into account, rail transport would often be preferred. A motorway covers more agricultural land than a railway, it consumes more agricultural land in the mining of aggregates for its construction, and cars pump more carbon into the air per passenger mile than trains. In the late 1990s the Labour Government increased the price of petrol year on year, but the money raised was not used to reduce the pollution effect of road transport. If the polluter were truly to pay, it would shift the balance perhaps for BPEO and BATNEEC.

## ENVIRONMENTAL ACCOUNTING AND COSTING

In choosing options under BPEO or BATNEEC, we need a way of providing a perceived benefit to environmental protection or disbenefit to the environmental damage we cause, so that cost–benefit analysis can be conducted on the various options. Various methods have been developed to do this (Turner 1995).

1. *The contingent valuation method* This involves asking people what they would pay for an environmental improvement or accept in compensation for a disbenefit. In the example of ICI and the storing of nuclear waste described earlier, the local population would have wanted compensation for the loss of value of their houses. The fall in the price of houses provided a clear indication of the contingent valuation.

2. *The travel cost method* For national parks and other public amenities which may be damaged we can find out how many people visit per year, and the time and cost of travelling there. The estimated value of people's leisure time (what they would pay for alternatives) and the cost of travelling to the site can provide a guide to the annual value of the site.

3. *The hedonic pricing method* Hedonic comes from the Greek word meaning pleasure. We try to evaluate the pleasure people receive from the environment. How much is their leisure time worth? What is the reduction in perceived pleasure in living somewhere reflected in the reduction of house prices? The latter applies to road and rail schemes as much as the ICI example above.

4. *The least cost alternative method* Sometimes when applying BPEO or BATNEEC you are reduced to comparing the cost of two alternatives and asking, 'Is the environmental damage I am doing worth that much?', thus making a subjective assessment. This could have been applied to the M3 motorway extension over Twyford Down, near Winchester. The damage done can *never* be reversed (sustainable development) and it is ugly. (This project is, of course, an example of government not subjecting itself to the laws it imposes on the population).

## ENVIRONMENTAL IMPACT ANALYSIS

There are many reasons why an environmental impact assessment (EIA) may be desirable or even essential as part of the feasibility or design process for a project:

1. It is required by law in some instances, especially in the WETT industries (water, energy, telecommunications and transport).

2. It may be a requirement of obtaining planning permission or consents, or it may facilitate that process.

3. It may help persuade the local community that the project does not have the

impact it fears, especially as part of a stakeholder management strategy (see Chapter 42).

4. It may help you consider various options under BPEO or BATNEEC analysis.

A booklet has been produced for the UK by the former Department of the *Environment entitled Environmental Assessment – A Guide to Procedures*, which spells out how and when to carry out an assessment under the Town and Country Planning (Assessment of Environmental Effects) Regulations 1988. It gives guidance on when an assessment is essential or desirable, and how one should be conducted. This booklet reflects a directive issued by the European Union in 1987, which requires an EIA to be conducted for certain types of developments.

There is no specified requirement of what an EIA should include and who should be involved in its preparation. However, if we examine what should be included in an EIA we can then consider who should be involved in its preparation.

## CONTENTS OF AN EIA

It is likely that an EIA will include some or all of the following:

1. A full description of the development, including information about the site, design, size and scale, and other information considered relevant. This may include drawings and artists' impressions.
2. A description of the significant effects of the development on the environment, including its impact on people, flora, fauna, air, water, soil, climate, landscape, cultural heritage and so on. This may include an input–output module for the project prepared as suggested earlier. This should be supported by data and further drawings and artists' impressions.
3. Where significant environmental effects have been identified, a description of measures taken to reduce them. This should include alternatives considered under BPEO and BATNEEC and an explanation why the option chosen was preferred.
4. A summary in non-technical terms of all the above information for the layperson.

This last item is essential. Unfortunately for developers, the public has become more active in its resistance to developments. Although people are better educated, and therefore better able to formulate their position and widely publicize it, they still do not always understand scientific or engineering principles. Objectors are therefore able to cause substantial damage through their ignorance of all the scientific or other facts, or their misrepresentation of them to the public. Examples include:

- Greenpeace stopping Shell from finding the best solution for disposing of the Brent Spar North Sea oil rig.
- Protestors killing a uranium mining project in Canada by asking at the planning enquiry what the level of radiation would be in the waste water. The developers gave an exact answer, and even though the level was less than that in rain-water, the protestors argued than anything other than zero (impossible to achieve) was unacceptable.

It is the fault of developers if they do not produce their assessment in layperson's terms and explain the project fully to the local community.

## CONDUCTING AN EIA

The preparation of an EIA should be a collaborative exercise involving the project manager, planning authorities, statutory consultative bodies and other interested parties, especially the local community. Depending on the project and its impact, some statutory authorities need to be consulted by law. These include:

- the Nature Conservancy Society
- the National Rivers Authority
- HM Inspectorate of Pollution
- the Health and Safety Executive
- local planning authorities.

Non-statutory or non-governmental bodies which may be consulted include:

- the Royal Society for the Prevention of Accidents
- the Royal Society for the Protection of Birds
- the National Trust
- the Heritage Trust
- the Royal Society for Nature Conservation

as well as local groups such as conservation and civic societies. Obviously the more widely you consult, the more it costs, but the less risk there will be a hitch in obtaining consents.

## OBTAINING CONSENTS

Almost all developments require some form of consent. Under the UK's planning regulations, a development is defined as:

the carrying out of building, engineering, mining or other operations in, on, over or under land, or making of any material change in the use of buildings or other land.

Consent will usually be awarded by a local planning authority, a district or unitary authority. However, the Secretary of State for the Environment, Regions and Transport can request to scrutinize any application, and the applicant can appeal to the Secretary of State against rejection. Sometimes consent is obtained via an Act of Parliament. A Private Members Bill is introduced in November and the result is known 14 months later. For major developments, a public enquiry is also required. A major proposal is defined by:

> the development proposal is of major public interest because of its national or regional implications, or the extent or complexity of the environmental, safety, technical or scientific issues involved, and where for these reasons there are a number of third parties involved as well as the applicant and the Local Planning Authority.

## MANAGING THE PROCESS OF CONSENT

The consent process breaks into two stages.

### Stage 1: Pre-consent

During the first stage, the project and consent application are formulated, up to the decision to make the application for consent. During this stage:

- the project is defined;
- consent and other key factors are identified;
- risks are analysed and reduction strategies are formulated;
- mitigators to obtain local support are identified;
- a consent strategy is developed;
- local consultations are planned and begun;
- the potential application is reviewed;
- the decision is taken to abandon the application, to redefine the project or to proceed with the application.

There are two possible strategies for local consultations:

1. *Define and inquire*   The project formulation is undertaken entirely within the sponsor's organization, only being made public when the consent is applied for.
2. *Consult and refine*   Consultation with affected parties begins early, to obtain their input while significant options remain open.

### Stage 2: Consent application

During the second stage, the application is made. During this stage the project team are mainly involved with managing external relationships. During this stage:

- the consent strategy is finalized;
- the application is submitted;
- the inquiry is planned for and held if necessary;
- risk assessment is continued;
- local consultations are continued;
- the outcome is assessed;
- the decision is taken to abandon the scheme, redefine it or to proceed to construction.

## THE RISKS AND COSTS OF OBTAINING CONSENT

Clearly the above procedures can entail considerable cost and there is always the risk that consent will not be granted. Costs can arise from:

- drawing up the case, including the preparation of an EIA;
- the holding of an enquiry, including legal fees, attendance, inspection, etc.;
- idleness of the project team between the completion of design (required for the consent) and commencement of work (after consent has been obtained) – errors of communication can arise at this time;
- conditions attached to the consent;
- mitigators to the local community to induce their acceptance of the development;
- delays as a result of redesigning the proposal to meet the requirements of planning authorities;
- lost commercial value of information disclosed to the public;
- delayed return on investment from delay to the start of the revenue stream;
- wasted effort if consent is refused.

Against this, if consent is awarded, the project will be well scrutinized from many viewpoints and so the chances of error in the design are very much reduced, making the proposal more robust and increasing the chance of success.

## REFERENCES AND FURTHER READING

Bruntland, H. G. (1987), *Our Common Future*, Oxford University Press, Oxford.
European Construction Institute (1995), *Total Project Management of Construction Safety, Health and Environment*, 2nd edition, Thomas Telford, London.
Pollock, S. E. (1995), *Improving Environmental Performance*, Routledge, London.
Turner, J. R. (ed.) (1995), *The Commercial Project Manager*, McGraw-Hill, London.

Turner, J. R., Grude, K. V. and Thurloway, L. (eds) (1996), *The Project Manager as Change Agent*, McGraw-Hill, London.

Wathern, P. (1988), *Environmental Impact Analysis, Theory and Practice*, Unwin Hyman, London.

## RELATED TOPICS

# 13 Projects for shareholder value

## Rodney Turner

Projects are undertaken to add value to the sponsoring organization. In the private sector this ultimately means increasing the value of shares to holders of equity in the company. In the public sector value comes more from reducing costs, but similar principles apply. In the next chapter Stephen Simister explores the concept of value, the relationship between function and cost, and the techniques of value analysis. In this chapter I consider the view of the outside world, and particularly the view of the owners of equity in the sponsoring organization. They own shares in a company with a view to wealth creation. We need to consider how to choose and control projects to optimize the objective of wealth creation, and in particular we need to consider the relative impacts of time, cost and functionality on the achievement of that objective. Traditionally, projects are said to be successful if they are completed to time, cost and quality. Certainly, the earlier a project is completed, the more cheaply and the greater the functionality, the greater is its contribution to shareholder value. However, the relative impacts of time, cost and functionality are often unknown.

This chapter uses shareholder value analysis to assess the impact of projects on the sponsoring organization, and the relative impacts of time, cost and functionality. First, it is necessary to enhance shareholder value analysis to make it more appropriate for the analysis of projects. It is shown that the impact of projects on their parent organization can be predicted from eight financial ratios linked to eight value drivers, and the nature of the impact is different for different industries with different ratios. The different impacts are analysed for ten of the UK's top 100 companies. To assess and manage projects appropriately, managers need to understand these different impacts, and in their annual appraisal project managers should be judged by the contribution of their projects to the value of the organization.

## LINKING PROJECT SUCCESS, PERFORMANCE AND APPRAISAL

Many people judge project success by whether a project contributes value to the sponsoring organization (Wateridge 1995, 1996, 1998). Further, if the project team coordinate their efforts to deliver value to the sponsor, it increases the chance of achieving a successful outcome. The most significant contributor to project success is to agree the success criteria with the stakeholders at the start of the project and to coordinate their efforts to deliver those agreed criteria as the project progresses (see Chapter 5). This may require individual team members to sub-optimize the parameter that interests them (time, cost or functionality) to achieve an overall optimum for the project.

However, usually no guidance is given to project managers and their teams about the appropriate balance between these three parameters, the so-called 'triple constraint'. Many project managers are judged in their annual performance reviews by how many of their projects were completed on cost and time, and so that becomes their main focus. Perhaps they should be judged on the potential of their projects to create value for the organization, which may require greater focus on functionality.

Net present value (NPV) has traditionally been used to assess the value of a project (see Chapter 27). It is assumed that the NPV of a project represents its contribution to the value of the parent organization. However, it has not been possible to prove conclusively that NPV is correlated to shareholder value creation (Woods and Randall 1989). The technique has other weaknesses (Mehari 2001). Its application is independent of the financial ratios of the sponsoring organization, and it favours projects from parts of the business with high indirect costs and low direct costs, in direct contradiction to conventional management thinking. Businesses with high indirect costs are more exposed to business cycles and are less able to control total costs. Further, and strangely, even though it is used to appraise projects, NPV is not used as a project control tool to compare alternative recovery strategies for projects in difficulty (Gardiner and Stewart 2000). It is not used to determine the appropriate balance between time, cost and functionality to maximize wealth generation of the project.

A modern technique of investment appraisal analyses a project's contribution to the value of equity of the parent company, the shareholder value (Mills 1994; Mills and Turner 1995). Shareholder value analysis (SVA) calculates a company's value as the net present value of future dividends, paid out of free cash flow after profit has been used to pay tax and reinvest in the business. It estimates future free cash flow in terms of eight value drivers. SVA suggests that the contribution of a project to the value of the firm is the NPV, and so its contribution to shareholder value is NPV less new debt required to finance the project. The eight value drivers alone cannot be used to determine the performance of projects undertaken by the organization. However, the value drivers can be calculated from eight traditional financial ratios, which can in turn be used to predict the NPV of projects. Using the financial ratios, it is possible to identify a generic project for an organization and analyse the relative impacts of variations in time, cost and functionality to determine how these differ for different organizations, with different financial performance.

In this chapter I introduce the financial ratios and show how they can be used to predict the shareholder value of a company and to determine the NPV of a generic project. I use the model for net present value of a generic project to analyse the impact of changes in time, cost and functionality on the net present value, and hence the shareholder value of the organization. I use ten of the UK's top 100 companies as examples to show how the impact varies between companies with different ratios. I then do a more detailed analysis on two of the organizations to give a broader feel of the impacts and to provide a basis for extrapolating the data for the other companies. The two organizations, Zeneca and ICI, used to be the same company until their demerger in the early 1990s. This analysis perhaps illustrates the pressures that led to the demerger.

## SHAREHOLDER VALUE ANALYSIS

Shareholder value analysis calculates the value of shares in a company as the net present value of future dividends. Future dividends are paid out of free cash flow, which is profit, less tax, less money reinvested in the business (Mills 1994; Mills and Turner 1995):

Dividends   =   Free cash flow

          =   Profit – tax – capital invested in the business

Future free cash flow is calculated from eight parameters, called value drivers. There are three operational drivers used to estimate future cash generated by the business:

D1 sales growth rate

D2 operating profit margin (or operating costs as a percentage of turnover)

D3 cash tax rate

and five investment drivers used to calculate the amount of cash invested in the business, and at what cost and over what planning period:

219

D4 replacement fixed capital employed, RFCE (assumed equal to depreciation)

D5 incremental fixed capital employed, IFCE (required to generate sales growth)

D6 incremental working capital employed, IWCE (also required to generate sales growth)

D7 cost of capital

D8 planning period

There is no replacement working capital investment, that is revenue, paid out of operating costs. The contribution of a project to shareholder value is the NPV minus new debt required to finance the project. It is not possible to calculate the NPV of a project, and hence its influence on shareholder value, directly from the eight value drivers. However, it is possible to calculate the value drivers and the NPV of projects from the following financial ratios:

R1 direct cost to turnover      = direct costs/turnover

R2 indirect cost to turnover      = indirect cost/turnover

R3 depreciation to turnover      = depreciation/turnover

R4 rate of depreciation      = depreciation/fixed capital employed

R5 fixed capital employed to turnover      = fixed capital employed/turnover

R6 working capital employed to turnover      = working capital employed/turnover

R7 debt to capital employed or debt equity ratio

R8 interest rate on debt

The value drivers D2 to D7 can be calculated from ratios R1 to R6 as follows:

$$D2 \quad = \quad 100\% - R1 - R2 - R3 - R8 * R7 * (R5 + R6)$$

$$D3 \quad = \quad R4/R5$$

$$D4 \quad = \quad Sales * R3$$

$$\quad = \quad Turnover * R4$$

$$D5 \quad = \quad D1 * R5$$

$$D6 = D1*R6$$

$$D7 = (1-R7)*RE + R7*R8$$

$$RE = \text{return on equity expected by shareholders}$$

D1 and D8 are assumed from the company's strategic plan, and D7 is the weighted average cost of capital, calculated from R7, R8 and assumed returns expected by holders of equity, RE. The analysis takes the turnover in a base year, and an assumed rate of growth, to calculate shareholder value. Figure 13.1 shows the calculation for a UK company from the pharmaceutical industry, Zeneca, using figures obtained from the 1997 annual report. This calculation assumes a constant debt equity ratio. It is also possible to do the calculation assuming constant debt. The latter gives an answer about 3 per cent smaller. Figure 13.2 contains the ratios for ten of the UK's top 100 companies, using figures obtained from their annual reports for 1996 or 1997. This table also includes the calculated shareholder value for each of these companies using a six-year planning period. The final column shows the amount the companies were trading above or below the calculated figure in the middle of 1998, immediately before the strong rise of the stock market through to the middle of 1999 (a positive figure indicates that the market capitalization was that percentage greater than the shareholder value calculated).

The direct costs include costs of sales, materials and labour where included. They also include duties for liquor sales and oil and gas products, and research and development costs. Figures in annual reports are quoted inclusive and exclusive of duty. The calculation can be performed either way. Since the model is linear, the same answer is obtained. (Elsewhere, I have performed the calculation on the Norwegian state oil company, Statoil, as a comparison to BP. In Statoil's annual report at least, the distinction between duty, corporation tax and owner's dividend appears somewhat unconventional.) It is usual to treat research and development as a sunk, and therefore indirect, cost. However, this distorts the investment appraisal process, favouring products with high research and low production costs over products with low research and high production costs. Some firms make R&D a direct cost by charging an internal royalty. It can be argued that as part of the investment appraisal process, research costs should be treated as a direct cost if the comparison is between making the product as opposed to licensing its production elsewhere. I also believe that it should be included as a direct cost, because in deciding to invest in a product from a part of the business with high research costs, the firm commits itself to ongoing research in that area to support that business.

221

| | Ratios | Year | | | | | | |
|---|---|---|---|---|---|---|---|---|
| | | 0 | 1 | 2 | 3 | 4 | 5 | 6 |
| Sales growth rate (assumed) | 12.0% | | 12% | 12% | 12% | 12% | 12% | 12% |
| Sales | | 100.00 | 112.00 | 125.44 | 140.49 | 157.35 | 176.23 | 197.38 |
| Direct costs (R1) | 50.5% | (50.50) | (56.56) | (63.35) | (70.95) | (79.46) | (89.00) | (99.68) |
| Indirect costs (R2) | 24.5% | (24.50) | (27.44) | (30.73) | (34.42) | (38.55) | (43.18) | (48.36) |
| Interest (from R7 see below) | | (1.50) | (1.68) | (1.88) | (2.11) | (2.36) | (2.64) | (2.96) |
| Depreciation (R3) | 10.0% | (4.15) | (4.65) | (5.21) | (5.83) | (6.53) | (7.31) | (8.19) |
| | | ===== | ===== | ===== | ===== | ===== | ===== | ===== |
| Operating profit | | 19.35 | 21.67 | 24.27 | 27.19 | 30.45 | 34.10 | 38.19 |
| Cash tax rate (D3) | 35.0% | 6.77 | 7.59 | 8.50 | 9.51 | 10.66 | 11.94 | 13.37 |
| | | ===== | ===== | ===== | ===== | ===== | ===== | ===== |
| Profit after tax | | 12.58 | 14.09 | 15.78 | 17.67 | 19.79 | 22.17 | 24.83 |
| Add back depreciation (R3) | | 4.15 | 4.65 | 5.21 | 5.83 | 6.53 | 7.31 | 8.19 |
| | | ===== | ===== | ===== | ===== | ===== | ===== | ===== |
| Operating cash flow | | 16.73 | 18.73 | 20.98 | 23.50 | 26.32 | 29.48 | 33.02 |
| Less RFCE (R3) | | (4.15) | (4.65) | (5.21) | (5.83) | (6.53) | (7.31) | (8.19) |
| Less IFCE (R5) | | (2.29) | (2.57) | (2.87) | (3.22) | (3.60) | (4.04) | (4.52) |
| Less IWCE (R6) | | (0.50) | (0.56) | (0.62) | (0.70) | (0.78) | (0.88) | (0.98) |
| | | ===== | ===== | ===== | ===== | ===== | ===== | ===== |
| Free cash flow | | 9.79 | 10.96 | 12.28 | 13.75 | 15.40 | 17.25 | 19.32 |
| Cost of capital (D7) | 6.0% | 6.0% | 6.0% | 6.0% | 6.0% | 6.0% | 6.0% | 6.0% |
| Discount factor | | 1.00 | 0.94 | 0.89 | 0.84 | 0.79 | 0.75 | 0.70 |
| PV of free cash flow | | | 10.34 | 10.93 | 11.55 | 12.20 | 12.89 | 13.62 |
| Cumulative PV | | | 10.34 | 21.27 | 32.82 | 45.02 | 57.92 | 71.54 |
| | | | | | | | | |
| Residual free cash | | | | | | | | 24.83 |
| Residual value | | | | | | | | 413.77 |
| | | | | | | | | ===== |
| PV of residual value | | | | | | | | 309.19 |
| Cumulative PV | | | | | | | | 71.54 |
| | | | | | | | | ===== |
| Value of company | | | | | | | | 380.73 |

CAPITALIZATION

| | | 0 | 1 | 2 | 3 | 4 | 5 | 6 |
|---|---|---|---|---|---|---|---|---|
| Fixed capital employed (R5) | 41.5% | 41.50 | 46.48 | 52.06 | 58.30 | 65.30 | 73.14 | 81.91 |
| Incremental FCE (R5) | | 4.98 | 5.58 | 6.25 | 7.00 | 7.84 | 8.78 | 9.83 |
| IFCE paid from equity (1–R7) | 46.0% | 2.29 | 2.57 | 2.87 | 3.22 | 3.60 | 4.04 | 4.52 |
| Working capital empl'd (R6) | 9.0% | 9.00 | 10.08 | 11.29 | 12.64 | 14.16 | 15.86 | 17.76 |
| Incremental WCE (R6) | | 1.08 | 1.21 | 1.35 | 1.52 | 1.70 | 1.90 | 2.14 |
| IWCE paid from equity (1–R7) | 46.0% | 0.50 | 0.56 | 0.62 | 0.70 | 0.78 | 0.88 | 0.98 |
| | | | | | | | | |
| Total capital employed | | 50.50 | 56.56 | 63.35 | 70.95 | 79.46 | 89.00 | 99.68 |
| Debt (R7) | 54.0% | 27.27 | 30.54 | 34.21 | 38.31 | 42.91 | 48.06 | 53.83 |
| Equity (1–R7) | 46.0% | 23.23 | 26.02 | 29.14 | 32.64 | 36.55 | 40.94 | 45.85 |
| | | | | | | | | |
| Interest (R8) | 5.5% | 1.50 | 1.68 | 1.88 | 2.11 | 2.36 | 2.64 | 2.96 |

Figure 13.1   Shareholder value analysis for Zeneca

| Sector | Name | Direct costs R1 %T | Indirect costs R2 %T | Depreciation R4 %FCE | FCE/ sales R5 %T | WCE/ sales R6 %T | Debt/ CE R7 % | SVA6Y %T | Capitalization /SVA % |
|--------|------|------|------|------|------|------|------|------|------|
| Pharmaceutical | Glaxo | 33.0 | 27.0 | 10.5 | 45.5 | 5.5 | 49.0 | 680 | 11.9 |
| Breweries | Guinness | 40.0 | 28.5 | 5.0 | 93.5 | 51.0 | 35.0 | 310 | 24.7 |
| Media | Reed Elsevier | 38.5 | 34.5 | 3.0 | 85.5 | 18.0 | 77.5 | 394 | −17.6 |
| Pharmaceutical | Zeneca | 50.5 | 24.5 | 10.0 | 41.5 | 9.0 | 54.0 | 380 | 21.7 |
| Stores | Marks & Spencer | 76.5 | 8.5 | 4.5 | 46.0 | 25.0 | 18.0 | 190 | 11.4 |
| Chemicals | BOC Group | 59.5 | 20.0 | 8.5 | 90.0 | 12.5 | 37.0 | 139 | −13.9 |
| Electricals | GEC | 66.0 | 22.5 | 22.5 | 16.0 | 8.0 | −83.0 | 148 | 21.7 |
| Engineering | British Aerospace | 84.0 | 6.5 | 8.0 | 32.5 | 7.5 | 40.0 | 104 | 20.5 |
| Stores | Sainsbury's | 91.5 | 2.0 | 0.0 | 44.0 | 7.5 | 46.0 | 74 | −34.6 |
| Chemicals | ICI | 72.0 | 19.0 | 6.0 | 54.0 | 15.5 | 71.0 | 40 | 61.9 |

**Figure 13.2  Ratios and shareholder value for ten UK FTSE100 companies**
*Source*: Company reports

## THE GENERIC PROJECT

It is possible to identify a generic project for an organization, one that has the same financial ratios as the company as a whole, to perform notional investment appraisal and to analyse the relative impact of variations in time, cost and functionality on that generic project. Figure 13.3 contains the calculation of net present value (NPV) for the generic project in Zeneca. Starting with an initial fixed capital investment of 100 units, all other figures can be determined using the financial ratios. It is then also possible to calculate the contribution of the generic project to increased shareholder value assuming:

A1 – no new debt is required to finance the project, that is it is financed out of retained profit, in which case the increase in shareholder value is equal to the NPV;

A2 – new debt is required at the average rate of debt to capital employed, in which case the increase in shareholder value is NPV less R7;

A3 – 100 per cent new debt is required, in which case the increase in shareholder value is NPV minus 100.

Figure 13.4 shows the contribution to shareholder value of the generic project in the ten companies in Figure 13.2 for a project with initial investment of 100 units, with each of the assumptions A1 to A3. All projects have a life of six years, except Sainsbury's, which needed a life of ten years to show positive NPV. Using the generic project it is possible to calculate the effect of changes in time, cost and

| | Ratios | Data | | | | Year | | | | |
|---|---|---|---|---|---|---|---|---|---|---|
| | | | 0 | 1 | 2 | 3 | 4 | 5 | 6 | |
| Fixed capital (R5) | 41.5% | 100.00 | 100.00 | 0.00 | | | | | | |
| Working capital (R6) | 9.0% | 21.69 | 21.69 | | | | | | | |
| | | | ===== | ===== | ===== | ===== | ===== | ===== | ===== | |
| Sales | | 240.96 | | 240.96 | 240.96 | 240.96 | 240.96 | 240.96 | 240.96 | |
| Cost of sales (R1) | 50.5% | 121.69 | | 121.69 | 121.69 | 121.69 | 121.69 | 121.69 | 121.69 | |
| | | | ===== | ===== | ===== | ===== | ===== | ===== | ===== | |
| Profit | | | | 119.28 | 119.28 | 119.28 | 119.28 | 119.28 | 119.28 | |
| | | | ===== | ===== | ===== | ===== | ===== | ===== | ===== | |
| Cash flow | | | (121.69) | 119.28 | 119.28 | 119.28 | 119.28 | 119.28 | 119.28 | |
| Discount factor (D7) | 6.0% | | 1.00 | 0.94 | 0.89 | 0.84 | 0.79 | 0.75 | 0.70 | |
| Present value | | | (121.69) | 112.53 | 106.16 | 100.15 | 94.48 | 89.13 | 84.09 | |
| | | | ===== | ===== | ===== | ===== | ===== | ===== | ===== | |
| Net present value | | | (121.69) | (9.16) | 97.00 | 197.14 | 291.62 | 380.75 | 464.84 | |
| Shareholder value, A1 | | | | | | | | | 464.84 | |
| Shareholder value, A2 | | | | | | | | | 410.84 | |
| Shareholder value, A3 | | | | | | | | | 364.84 | |

Figure 13.3   Analysis of the generic project for Zeneca

| Name | $\Delta$SV Proj A1 | $\Delta$SV Proj A2 | $\Delta$SV Proj A3 | $\Delta$SV $\Delta$S 10% A4 | $\Delta$SV $\Delta$S 10% A5 | $\Delta$SV $\Delta$C 10% A6 | $\Delta$SV $\Delta$C 10% A7 | $\Delta$SV $\Delta$C 10% A8 | $\Delta$SV $\Delta$T 10% A9 | $\Delta$SV $\Delta$T 10% A10 | $\Delta$SV $\Delta$T 10% A11 | $\Delta$SV $\Delta$T 10% A12 |
|---|---|---|---|---|---|---|---|---|---|---|---|---|
| Glaxo | 612 | 563 | 512 | 73 | 109 | 10 | 15 | 20 | 6 | 18 | 17 | 20 |
| Guinness | 161 | 126 | 61 | 32 | 53 | 10 | 14 | 20 | 4 | 9 | 8 | 11 |
| Reed Elsevier | 232 | 155 | 132 | 36 | 58 | 10 | 18 | 20 | 4 | 10 | 9 | 11 |
| Zeneca | 464 | 410 | 364 | 58 | 118 | 10 | 15 | 20 | 5 | 19 | 18 | 21 |
| Marks & Spencer | 97 | 79 | (3) | 25 | 107 | 10 | 12 | 20 | 5 | 18 | 17 | 19 |
| BOC Group | 94 | 57 | (6) | 13 | 55 | 10 | 14 | 20 | 3 | 10 | 9 | 11 |
| GEC | 895 | 978 | 795 | 104 | 308 | 10 | 2 | 20 | 11 | 49 | 48 | 50 |
| British Aerospace | 119 | 79 | 19 | 25 | 141 | 10 | 14 | 20 | 7 | 25 | 24 | 26 |
| Sainsbury's | 25 | (21) | (75) | 14 | 167 | 10 | 15 | 20 | 7 | 18 | 17 | 19 |
| ICI | 123 | 52 | 23 | 26 | 91 | 10 | 17 | 20 | 4 | 15 | 15 | 17 |

Figure 13.4   Shareholder value of the generic project and the impact of variations in
project performance

functionality on its out-turn. In all cases the change is calculated as an absolute
figure. Since the model is linear, the absolute figure is independent of
assumptions A1 to A3. The following assumptions are made.

## FUNCTIONALITY

Loss of functionality reduces either sales volume or sales price, or both. Both result in a loss in turnover. If there is a loss in sales volume, then presumably it will be possible to achieve some savings in direct costs, and hence direct costs might be treated as variable. If there is a loss in sales price, then there will be no reduction in costs, and so they will need to be treated as fixed. The two extremes of treating direct costs as fixed and variable were considered. In any given case it is expected that the actual outcome will be somewhere in between. So:

A4 – 10 per cent reduction in sales, all costs variable;

A5 – 10 per cent reduction in sales, all costs fixed.

## COST

I assumed possible overspend of fixed capital only. Overspend can be paid for out of equity or new debt. I investigated paying for it out of equity only, debt only and debt and equity at the given debt : equity ratio. So:

A6 – 10 per cent increase in capital cost, no additional debt;

A7 – 10 per cent increase in capital cost, additional debt at the standard debt to capital employed ratio;

A8 – 10 per cent increase in capital cost, funded entirely from debt.

## TIME

When a project is delayed, loss in NPV or shareholder value comes from two sources. First, the delay will almost certainly lead to an increase in capital cost. Projects that are delayed usually cost more, through rework and an increase in time dependent costs. Second, there may be loss of sales. Here two assumptions are possible. One is that there is a loss of sales in year 1, but these are regained at the end of the project life. There will be a small loss of NPV, because the time value of sales in year 7 is less than year 1. The other is that the sales lost in year 1 are lost for all time. This will occur if there is a limited market window or delay allows a competitor to capture market share (in which case the loss may be even greater still). I made one of four possible assumptions when considering a delay to a project:

A9 – the start of the project is delayed, but all the cost is spent in the original period and there is no overspend. All sales lost in year 1 are regained in year 7;

A10 – the start of the project is delayed, but all the cost is spent in the original period and there is no overspend. All sales lost in year 1 are lost for ever;

A11 – the start of the project is delayed, and the expenditure of the project is spread over the extended time period, but there is no overspend, that is the same amount of money is spent over a longer period. All sales lost in year 1 are lost for ever;

A12 – the start of the project is delayed, the expenditure is spread over the longer period and there are some time dependent costs. I assumed that 25 per cent of the costs were time dependent. The resulting overspend could be paid for out of a mixture of debt and equity, at the standard ratio. All sales lost in year 1 are lost for ever.

## IMPACT OF PROJECT PERFORMANCE

Figure 13.4 shows the impact of underperformance of functionality, cost and time on the generic projects from the ten companies. In all cases, except Sainsbury's, I assumed that the project has a six-year life. In high cost, high capital companies, a longer project life may be more appropriate. For Sainsbury's I had to assume a ten-year project life to obtain positive net present value. From this data we can conclude the following:

1. Loss of sales (functionality) always has a greater impact than time or cost. As would be expected, the impact is more severe if the sales costs are fixed. It is essential that companies with high costs are able to control their costs if there is a loss of sales. For companies with high sales to capital employed and low costs, the impact of loss of sales is very much more severe than overspend or delay, and so it is essential to achieve the functionality. Delay or overspend may be appropriate to maintain functionality (as long as the delay does not itself result in loss of sales). For companies with low sales to turnover and high costs, keeping a control on costs and timescale is almost as important as maintaining functionality.
2. Columns A6 and A8 contain the same numbers in absolute terms for all companies, because the model is linear. The figure in column A7 lies between, dependent on the debt equity ratio (except for GEC which has a cash mountain). In low sales to turnover companies (capital intensive companies), capital cost is almost as important as sales if they can control their costs of sales.
3. Comparison of columns A10 and A11 shows that delaying expenditure without losing sales actually results in an improvement of NPV and shareholder value. (One project where this was observed in practice was the construction of the Thames Barrier (Morris and Hough 1987).) Comparison of columns A1 and A12 shows that for all companies, the impact of lost sales resulting from a

delay is greater than the impact of any resulting overspend. Column A9 shows that the impact is less marked if the sales are delayed rather than lost, (which will be the case in the public sector where the revenues are cost savings).

4. The relative impact of delay and overspend is dependent on the financial ratios of the company. Delay has more impact in capital intensive companies with high costs, because sales are needed to pay for the investment.

All these results suggest that it is more important to obtain the correct functionality for a project than to finish rigidly on cost and time.

## COMPARISON OF ZENECA AND ICI

Zeneca and ICI are two companies which were demerged in the early 1990s from the then one company ICI. Figure 13.5 contains a more specific list of variations of project performance to compare the impact on the value of each company. It can be seen that the impacts are quite diverse. This raises the question of how was it possible to make rational comparisons of projects from different parts of the business when they were the same company. The assumption must be that projects from the part of the business that is now Zeneca will have always won out in competition for scarce resources. The part of the business that is now ICI was being milked to invest in Zeneca, meaning it would have been gradually run down if the two businesses had not been split. In the mid-1980s I was employed by ICI to do investment appraisal of projects from the petrochemical industry. I found that my projects, with high operating costs but low indirect costs could not compete against projects from less profitable parts of the business with high indirect costs but low operating costs.

| Variation in project performance parameter | Impact on Zeneca | Impact on ICI |
|---|---|---|
| Generic project NPV, for initial FCE investment of 100 units | 464 | 123 |
| Sales down 10%, direct costs variable, A4 | NPV down 13% | NPV down 21% |
| Sales down 10%, direct costs fixed, A5 | NPV down 25% | NPV down 75% |
| Sales loss for break-even, direct costs variable | 80% | 50% |
| Sales loss for break-even, direct costs fixed | 40% | 13% |
| Fixed capital overspend 10%, A7 | NPV down 02% | NPV down 09% |
| Fixed capital overspend for break-even, A7 | 460% | 125% |
| Delay of 1 month, assumption A12 | NPV down 05% | NPV down 14% |
| Delay of 1 year, A12 | NPV down 53% | NPV down 159% |

Figure 13.5  Comparison of the impact of variation in the performance of the generic project in Zeneca and ICI

## CONCLUSIONS

The following conclusions can be drawn:

1. It is important for project managers to understand the impact of loss of functionality on the performance of their projects, and to balance the need to obtain the appropriate functionality against a desire to finish rigorously on cost and time.
2. Project managers should be judged in their annual performance appraisal not just on how many of their projects were finished on cost and time, but also on the ability of their projects to generate sales. Given the results of this chapter, greater weighting should be given to sales potential than cost or time performance, but the appropriate weightings will vary from company to company dependent on the financial ratios.
3. Understanding the impact of financial ratios on the performance of their projects will help project managers weigh up conflicting demands for performance on cost, time and functionality. Perhaps project managers could be judged against their performance compared to the generic project for their organization.
4. When undertaking investment appraisal, and comparing competing projects in a portfolio, research costs, although sunk, should be treated as direct costs, because:
   - to stay in the business, the company needs to conduct ongoing research;
   - without conducting future research the company will lose shareholder value;
   - the research cost should be treated as a lost royalty payment.
5. Shareholder value analysis can provide an investment appraisal technique, which, when coupled with appropriate risk analysis, can show the risk associated with high fixed costs. It can also provide a control tool to allow constant monitoring of the impact of project decisions on shareholder value to optimize owner's wealth. This would allow comparison of the impact of project decisions on time, cost and functionality, and their differential impact on shareholder value.

## REFERENCES AND FURTHER READING

Gardiner, P. D. and Stewart, K. (2000), 'Revisiting the golden triangle of time, cost and quality: the role of NPV in project control, success and failure', *International Journal of Project Management*, **18** (4).

Mehari, M. A. (2001), 'Re-examining project appraisal and control: developing a focus on wealth creation', *International Journal of Project Management*, **19**.

Morris, P. W. G. and Hough, G. (1987), *The Anatomy of Major Projects: A Study of the Reality of Project Management*, Wiley, Chichester.

Mills, R. W. (1994), *Strategic Value Analysis*, Mars Business Associates, Henley-on-Thames.

Mills, R. W. and Turner, J. R. (1995), 'Projects for shareholder value', in J. R. Turner (ed.), *The Commercial Project Manager*, McGraw-Hill, London.

Turner, J. R. (1999), *The Handbook of Project-based Management*, 2nd edition, McGraw-Hill, London.

Wateridge, J. F. (1995), 'IT projects: a basis for success', *International Journal of Project Management*, **13**(3).

Wateridge, J. F. (1996), 'Delivering successful IS/IT projects: 8 key elements from success criteria to implementation via management, methodologies and teams', Ph.D. thesis, Henley Management College and Brunel University.

Wateridge, J. F. (1998), 'How can IS/IT projects be measured for success?', *International Journal of Project Management*, **16**(1).

Woods, J. C. and Randall, M. R. (1989), 'The Net Present Value of future investment opportunities: its impact on shareholder wealth and implications for capital budgeting theory', *Financial Management*, **1**.

## RELATED TOPICS

# Part III
# Functions

# Part II

## Functions

# INTRODUCTION TO PART III

In Part III we consider the systems for managing the delivery of the project's product or facility. We first need to define the facility, the functionality expected, how it will be delivered by the components of the facility and the quality or finish. We then define who will do the work of the project and how they will be organized. We define systems for managing cost and time, and how the resources are scheduled. Finally we consider the risks and how they are managed, and in particular the risk to the health and safety of the project workers.

### Chapter 14: Managing scope – functionality and value

In Chapter 14 Stephen Simister sets the scene for Part III. Projects are undertaken to deliver value for the sponsor. To deliver value, the facility produced by the project must perform certain functions. One definition of the value is the ratio between the functionality and the cost of delivering it. Value management (and the related topic of value engineering) is a structured technique for managing this relationship and ensuring that the project delivers value. This chapter describes the value management process.

### Chapter 15: Managing scope – configuration and work methods

Configuration management is a technique for managing the functionality of the facility produced by the project and the work methods to deliver it. The facility is broken into components, and the functionality of each component defined. This decomposition is known as product breakdown. The way the components make up the facility is known as the configuration. Through the processes of configuration management, the project team manage the breakdown, the functionality of each component and their configuration into the facility to provide

233

the total functionality. This process is linked to value management since the control of the total cost of the facility will be part of the value management process. Each component should provide value commensurate with the total value required from the facility. The techniques of configuration management can also be used to manage the work methods, that is the methods of making each component and building them into the facility, and this is also described. Goal Directed Project Management is a structured technique for managing both the product breakdown and work methods in a way consistent with configuration management. The technique is introduced. Finally, a link is made between the work methods identified by configuration management and the management of resources and progress described later.

### Chapter 16: Managing quality

It is necessary to define not only the functionality of the facility, but also the quality of finish. This covers many attributes or service levels required. In this chapter quality of projects is considered. A five-element model for delivering quality is described and we consider whether quality is free on projects. Several techniques for solving quality problems are also explained.

### Chapter 17: Managing organization – structure and responsibilities

Having decided on the configuration and work methods, we must define who will be involved in the project, their responsibilities and how they will be managed. In Chapter 17 Erling Andersen describes how to create a project organization. He identifies two levels of the project organization question – how will the project be integrated into the parent organization, and how will the project team be structured and managed? He discusses the issues involved. He then describes the use of responsibility charts to define people's involvement in the project.

### Chapter 18: Managing cost

In Chapter 18 Dennis Lock discusses how to manage the cost of the project. He starts by giving some definitions and sets out the principles of project cost management. He then describes methods of estimating costs and the development of cost budgets. In the rest of the chapter he explores methods of monitoring costs. He describes simple methods, using graphs and milestones, and ends with the earned value technique which can be used to monitor both cost and time on a project.

## Chapter 19: Managing the schedule

In Chapter 19 Dennis Lock describes how to calculate the schedule of the project. He explains the use of calendars and then three techniques for determining and representing the schedule: bar charts, activity-on-arrow networks and precedence networks. He then discusses several issues for optimizing the schedule.

## Chapter 20: Managing resources

One of the issues for optimizing the schedule discussed at the end of Chapter 19 is the use of resources and the need to balance their inputs. Dennis Lock explains those issues fully in Chapter 20. He describes principles of resource scheduling and the role of critical path networks in resource scheduling and the resolution of conflicts. He discusses the use of computers in resource scheduling, and how the outputs are used to manage the work of the project, including the resource input. He ends with some additional issues, such as the use of calendars, multiproject scheduling and scheduling resources in small departments.

## Chapter 21: Managing risk

In Chapter 21 Chris Chapman and Stephen Ward consider how to manage the risk inherent in the work of projects and the uncertainty in all estimates. They describe a nine-step risk management process (RMP) developed by the UK's Association for Project Management Special Interest Group on Risk Management and published as the *Guide to Project Risk Analysis and Management* (PRAM).

## Chapter 22: Managing health and safety

In Chapter 22 Jim Pearce discusses a specific risk issue, health and safety. He gives an introduction to occupational health and safety and describes benefits from its management. He then considers the identification and management of risks to safety. He describes the role of occupational health and safety on projects and suggests how to develop a safety policy.

# 14 Managing scope – functionality and value

*Stephen Simister*

The scope of a project can only be managed if it has been clearly defined from the outset. The pressure for changes to be made during implementation can invariably be traced back to an inadequately defined statement of need from the client (Wright 1998). Client organizations are by their very nature multi-faceted. Determining the exact requirements for a project from such organizations requires a clear framework within which decisions can be made. Structuring this framework at the outset of the project will ensure not only that the scope is adequately defined, but also that it can be managed during the project life cycle. The project definition acts as a benchmark against which all future decisions can be judged.

Clients should progress through a series of stages in determining the project definition, producing the following documents at successive steps:

- Client's business case: the financial *raison d'être* for the project.
- Project specific statement of need: an outline document setting out what is required to fulfil the business case.
- Strategic project brief: an outline document stating how the project will fulfil the statement of need.
- Project definition: a document setting out the exact details of the project, its scope.

The framework produced by this procedure enables both the functionality and the value of the project to be expressly defined and monitored.

In this chapter I consider the concept of value and how it is produced by the functionality of the facility delivered by the project. I define value as the relationship between function and cost, and introduce the concept of value management. I then describe a five-step process used in each value management workshop for defining the functionality of a project and managing its associated value.

237

# UNDERSTANDING VALUE

The term 'value' is used rather loosely and often the context of its use can change its meaning. Primarily we are interested in value as it relates to a project. It is useful, however, to examine value at an organizational level as ultimately projects have to contribute at this level.

## SHAREHOLDER VALUE

The phrase 'shareholder value' became part of the business vocabulary during the 1990s. There are two reasons for this development:

1. Big investors, particularly in America and Britain, became more activist about company performance. It was once rare for top executives to be punished for failing to deliver returns; now it is common.
2. A more cynical motive is that companies like shareholder value as a measure of performance because it is relatively easy to achieve. Recent stock market history has seen a steady rise in shares value almost regardless of how well companies are doing.

Shareholder value had no clear definition but was generally taken as a measure of whether a company had created (or destroyed) wealth for its shareholders. In recent years a more reliable measure has been sought and two methods have been developed: market value added (MVA) and economic value added (EVA). (In the last chapter we met a third method, shareholder value analysis, SVA.)

### Market value added (MVA)

As a system of analysis MVA aims to strip out most of the anomalies created by accounting standards to paint a truer picture of shareholder value. The basic calculation is to take the amount of money entrusted to management, measured by adding up money raised through shares issued, borrowing and retained earnings. That gives a measure of how much outsiders have given to the company in the years since it was founded. Then take the current value of the company's shares and debt, as a measure of how much money the investors could take out of the business. The difference is the MVA, which measures how the executives running a company have fared with the capital under their control since the company was established. If the MVA is positive, value is being created for investors, if negative, investors' money has been destroyed.

### Economic value added (EVA)

EVA takes the after-tax operating profit for a company and compares it with its cost of capital. Cost of capital is an economic concept that includes far more than just the interest paid to the bank and the dividend to shareholders. For each company the cost of capital varies, sometimes quite widely. Some industries are naturally more risky than others; investors will accept lower returns from an established food group than from a young software company because it is more likely the food group will generate stable returns while it is quite likely that the software company will stumble. The EVA figure represents the difference between the profit a company makes and the cost of its capital. The idea is that it is not good enough for a company just to make a profit from its business. It also has to make enough to cover the cost of its capital. If it is not covering the cost of its capital, plus a reasonable margin on top, then the logical conclusion is that it would have been better if investors' money had been placed elsewhere, or that a new management team should be brought in to make better use of the capital. (SVA, described in the last chapter, is effectively the net EVA discounted and summed over a number of years.)

If a company is consistently generating EVA every year, over time its MVA should start to rise. Conversely, if its EVA is negative, in time its MVA will start to fall. MVA is a great guide to where a company has come from, but EVA is a better guide to where it is going. Of course, shareholder value relates to those people who effectively own the company. What of the value of those who use a company's products or services – the customers?

## CUSTOMER VALUE

There is considerable debate within the business world on whether companies should deliver value for their shareholders or customers. There is no simple answer, but new techniques such as 'lean production' are designed to produce unique value for the customer. Project duration and cost are considered in 'project-as-production system' terms, making concern for total cost and duration more important than the cost or duration of any activity. Coordination is accomplished by the central schedule while the details of workflow are managed throughout the organization by people who are aware of and support project goals (as opposed to activity or local) performance. Value to the customer and throughput, the movement of information or materials to completion, are the primary objectives. Improvements result from reducing waste, the difference between the current situation and perfection (defined as meeting the customer's unique requirements in zero time with nothing in stores). Lean thinking focuses attention on how value is generated rather than how any one activity is managed. Whereas traditional project management views a project as the combination of activities, lean thinking views the entire project in production system terms, that is as if the project were one large operation.

## PROJECT VALUE

Organizations add value to their business through a series of processes. Increasingly such processes are undertaken within the context of a project. It is the cumulative effect of projects that decides the success or failure of a company to deliver value to both its customers and its shareholders. To create and sustain competitive advantage in the form of either effective differentiation and/or cost savings, organizations need the help of their suppliers. The supply chain has recently received considerable attention in the business press. Its prominence is raised here because projects bring together a range of suppliers. Increasingly these suppliers can add value to a project only if there is cooperation between them.

## DEFINING FUNCTIONALITY AND VALUE

One of the techniques traditionally used to define functionality and value is value engineering. Value engineering originated in the USA during the Second World War. Lawrence Miles of General Electric is credited with inventing it as a way of identifying alternative materials to replace those that were in short supply because of the war. Miles developed a technique that could focus on what something did, that is the function, rather than what it was. By focusing on the function of components Miles found alternative solutions which were often cheaper than the original method. Value engineering was identified as a method of reducing procurement costs by the US Navy in 1954. Since then practically all US Federal procurement requires the use of value engineering to demonstrate value in the procurement process. In value engineering value is defined as:

$$\text{Value} = \frac{\text{Function (what does it do?)}}{\text{Cost (how much does it cost?)}}$$

Figure 14.1 shows a number of connotations available for increasing value.

Value engineering is useful in situations where the functionality of a product can be clearly defined, typically during the design phase. This has its limitations and another technique has been developed to overcome these limitations – value

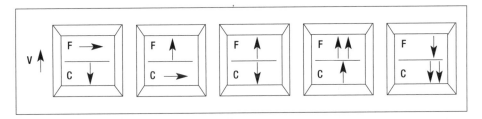

**Figure 14.1   How value is increased**

An arrow pointing upwards indicates an increase in that item (either F (function) or C (cost). An arrow pointing downwards means a decrease and an arrow pointing left means the item remains the same; a double arrow represents a greater increase (or decrease) than a single arrow. So it is possible to increase cost slightly but this leads to an even bigger increase in function, hence value is increased.

management. Within many European industries there is a growing view that value engineering is a special case of value management. Value management uses similar tools to value engineering but it is the scope of the technique that makes it so different. Value management is primarily concerned with ensuring that the client needs are clearly defined and that a true scope of work is produced for the project. Value management is the entire process and should commence during the early stages of a project, as shown in Figure 14.2. Value engineering is one of the techniques that can be applied in the value management process during the later stages of a project.

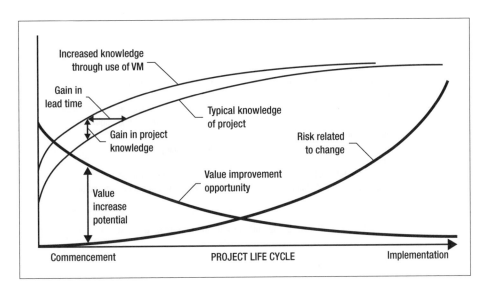

**Figure 14.2   The benefits of value management (VM)**
*Source*: Adapted from Thiry (1997)

241

To utilize value management to its full effect it needs to be undertaken at the concept or briefing stage of the project. At this stage the technique is used to define the project's requirements, that is the criteria that will guide the project throughout its entire life. During a project many changes can take place and a high level set of principles needs to be maintained so any changes can be tested and their suitability judged. Without such principles it is all too possible for a project not to meet all the expectations of the client. By having a benchmark against which to judge changes the project team can ensure that the project will meet the client requirements. Value management has been demonstrated to produce such benchmarks.

Some of the books and articles on value management may leave you with the impression that it is applied once in a project's life. This is not the case. Value management is a process which can be used throughout a project's life. What happens is that various tools and techniques are available which are applied at different stages to meet the particular requirements of that stage. In this section we are focusing on how the project requirements can be defined. This is the first stage at which value management should be used. Value management at this stage is concerned with producing the client's statement of need as shown below. The benefits of undertaking value management can be quantified in both hard and soft terms, as shown in Figure 14.3.

| Hard benefits | Soft benefits |
|---|---|
| ● Optimum balance between expectation and resources | ● Increased problem understanding |
| ● Identification of maximum revenue opportunities | ● Clear scope definition |
| ● Improvement of capital productivity | ● Sharing of objectives and purpose |
| ● Avoidance of unnecessary costs and over-specification | ● Development of team spirit |
| ● Consideration of both capital and life cycle costs | ● Flexibility of solutions |
| ● Optimal development/design solutions | ● Helpfulness of team |
| ● Effective management of change | ● Modelling of complex situations |

Figure 14.3   Hard and soft benefits of value management

A recent study of a construction project in the UK carried out by the National Audit Office indicated that without this statement of need projects have no baseline to act as a guide through the life of the project. The main findings from this study are shown in Figure 14.4. This example illustrates the importance of ensuring that the client produces an initial statement of need and that the constructional professionals who advise the client understand the true nature of the statement.

## THE VALUE MANAGEMENT PROCESS

The value management process maps directly onto the project management process. Value management is undertaken as a series of workshops which can be considered as intervention points at strategic stages in the life of a project (Figure 14.5). The number and exact timing of intervention points will depend upon the project, and workshops can be combined where required. Typical deliverables from the workshops are as follows:

- *VM1*  One of the prime purposes of a workshop at this stage is to present in clear and objective terms the mission of the project and its strategic fit with the corporate aims of the client organization.
- *VM2*  The aim of this workshop is to convert the output from VM1 into a project scope document which defines and specifies the performance of the various elements of the project.
- *VM3*  Once the scope is defined the project team can begin to test various design options against agreed criteria and determine the most appropriate solution.
- *VM4*  This workshop can act as a catch-all, refining the final stages of concurrently designed elements or dealing with changes in project requirements.

A typical value management workshop consists of a five-step process referred to as a job plan. The generic outputs of each of the steps for the early stages of a project are given in Figure 14.6. In utilizing value management for the early stages of a project the main technique used is facilitated decision-making within a workshop environment. The five-step process is used to structure the agenda for each workshop and, depending on the stage of the project and required outputs, various tools and techniques may be used in each of the steps.

The Natural Environment Research Council (NERC) is a non-governmental public body established by Royal Charter in the UK. The Oceanography Centre was financed by the Council and by Southampton University. The Oceanography Centre at Southampton will enhance and promote the important oceanography studies of the NERC and the University. The project was a major event for the NERC. They created a new type of facility and were faced with their largest ever capital construction project. The Council were aware of potential risks and took action to address them. They used an appropriate contract strategy, tried to complete design before they went to tender, and limited client changes during construction. They also undertook the work on the foundations separately in order to avoid delays. Initial indications are that users are broadly content with the building. Nevertheless, despite the Council's efforts, there were significant time and cost overruns, caused primarily by poor project management. The project was completed about twenty-two months later than planned, and the final cost has not been determined because of a dispute with the main contractor. If the main contractors pursue a claim against the NERC, and are successful, the budget of £49 million could be exceeded by a substantial amount. The National Audit Office were asked by the UK government to investigate the project and explain some of the problems which occurred with it, the main findings were:

- while some problems on this project remain outstanding, the Council has, since 1993, taken steps to improve their management of capital schemes
- many of the objectives for the building were not defined precisely in the brief and it is difficult to assess how far they had been achieved
- the users were broadly content with the building, even though some of the facilities that they specified were not provided
- the project team did not present alternative designs to senior management to meet the requirement of a 125-year life of the structure, and gave them little information on the costs and benefits of the chosen design
- the Council did not make sufficient use of professional assistance in the briefing and design stages. Although they commissioned a value management review, it was too late to affect the cost or design
- the Council considered the project's main priorities were cost and quality
- inadequacies in the budget, poor control over fees and uncertainty in the design before awarding the construction contract were the main causes of the cost overrun as a whole
- there was no contingency for development so cost increases meant cuts to the project
- fees doubled from £4.3 million to £8.6 million. This was due to the extension of the design period to accommodate fundamental changes, the delay in construction and the consultants' claims for additional work
- the Council did not make one person responsible for ensuring delivery of the project to time and budget – responsibility for project management fell on Council staff who lacked the necessary training and expertise
- the Council limited their choice of consultants to firms who had worked for them in the past but on smaller projects
- in the NAO's view the Council should have considered a wider range of firms.

The National Audit Office concluded that this project illustrates many important lessons, especially for small organisations not experienced in managing major construction projects.

**Figure 14.4   How things go wrong – report of the National Audit Office on the construction of the Southampton Oceanography Centre, 4 February 1998**

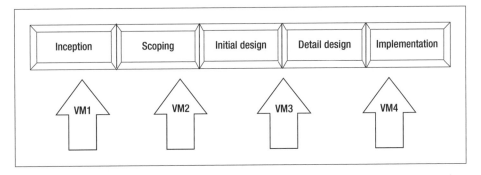

**Figure 14.5   Value management workshops during the project life cycle**

| | |
|---|---|
| 1.   Information | An information gathering process that focuses attention on the client's business drivers for the project. Particular importance is given to the use of facilitated workshops. |
| 2.   Speculation | Creative thinking techniques are used to generate alternative ways to provide the business drivers identified in Step 1. |
| 3.   Evaluation | The solutions generated are evaluated in terms of their feasibility and cost. Ideas are combined and consolidated to produce a list of, say, five or six ideas which are worthy of further consideration. |
| 4.   Development | The surviving ideas are developed in detail, ensuring that all of the interfaces with the client's business are fully accounted for. |
| 5.   Recommendation/implementation | The most suitable solution is identified and a formal recommendation made to the client for implementation. |

**Figure 14.6   Generic outputs for a value management workshop**

## STEP 1: INFORMATION

Think about the early stages of a project. The client is aware that there is a problem but does not know the exact nature of that problem. This obviously makes trying to define the project requirements very difficult. To define the project's requirements you need to have a clear understanding of the problem you are trying to solve. The client may know that it needs more office accommodation. So should you provide a building for 200 people or 300? Should you use this opportunity to re-engineer some of the business processes and relocate staff to other areas, or consolidate organizational functions in existing office accommodation? There are a multitude of questions the client needs to ask itself and then brief the project team accordingly. Value management is used to allow the client a forum for providing the answers to some of the questions that need asking.

At the early stages of the project the information is typically not held in documents but is held in the minds of people. The complex issues that gave rise to the need for a project are often locked up in the minds of the people who are running various functional departments within a company. To get the true picture of the problem this information needs to be extracted and documented in such a fashion as to be available to the project team.

The most appropriate method to get to the core information is to use a facilitated workshop. The facilitated workshop brings together all the key stakeholders from within the client organization and the project team and at this stage in the project life cycle would be a VM1 type (see Figure 14.5). The workshop will typically last for two days and is used as a forum for obtaining the core information that will form the client's statement of need. Typically the facilitator is not a member of the project team. This person is an expert in the value management process and focuses on managing the process of the workshop and not its content. This facilitator will provide a structure around which the stakeholders can discuss the key elements of the problem that the potential project is aimed at solving. To commence the workshop the facilitator will ask each of the stakeholders in turn to outline their objectives, constraints and risks for the project. This information is listed on flip charts by the facilitator under these three headings.

This basic information is then used as a starting point for facilitated discussion. This initial workshop will often be the first time that the key stakeholders have all met at the same time to discuss the project. The workshop provides the time needed to discuss the project properly. It is often the case that senior executives are not prepared to take time out of their busy schedule to discuss a project which could be vital to the future well-being of their company. They will, however, be forced to make time later on should the project go wrong. Once there has been discussion on the objectives, constraints and risks of the project, the next phase is to organize this information into a graphical representation called a value tree.

The value tree is a way of organizing the information so that people can visualize which are the most important elements of the project. Another key feature of the value tree is that ability to show the scope of the project. Often there are elements of a project upon which the client cannot decide until some initial design and costs work has been undertaken. By making explicit the areas which the client would like to include but are currently considered outside the scope of the project, the design team have a clearer remit upon which to work. A value tree for a new health centre is shown in Figure 14.7. The value tree demonstrates that whilst the internal layout of the health centre is important, its actual physical location in the community is of paramount importance. While this is ultimately a decision for the client to make, it reinforces to the design team that the facility

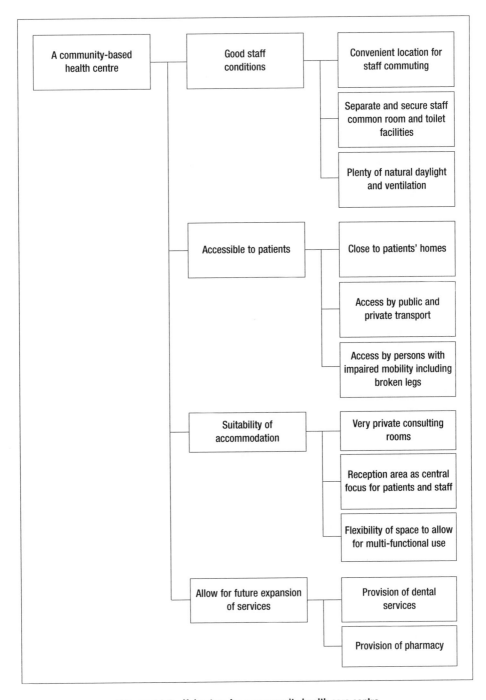

Figure 14.7    Value tree for a community health care centre

they are designing has to be used by people with whom they will not have any contact. All information is second hand, being provided by the doctors who will work out of the health centre. One of the features of value management is the highlighting of such issues. It may be appropriate in this instance for some of the patients who use the health centre to be interviewed to find out what they would like to see in the building.

During later stages of the project in a VM2 or VM3 workshop, a variant of the value tree is used called function analysis and systems technique (FAST). The concept in FAST diagrams is similar to that in value trees but more emphasis is given to defining functions.

Following on from this information step, the next step is to generate ideas as to how some of the elements identified in the value tree can be provided.

## STEP 2: SPECULATION

During this step the team focus on generating ideas as to how to provide the key elements identified in Step 1. For instance, are five consulting rooms adequate or should four be provided and provision made to provide a fifth at a later date? The principal feature of the speculation step is to stimulate creativity. The four golden rules are:

- suspend judgement – no criticism or evaluation (that comes during the next step);
- freewheel – the odder the ideas the better;
- quantity – the more ideas the better;
- cross-fertilize – combine and improve on the ideas of others.

The main technique used in the speculation workshop is brainstorming, where the team generate ideas, which are written on flip charts. Creative thinking is essential to this step if the use of the same old ideas to solve design problems is to be avoided. A constrained, conservative environment is detrimental to innovation, as shown in Figure 14.8. It is therefore necessary to ensure that the opposite environment prevails. Once the ideas for providing the key elements have been generated the next step is to evaluate them.

## STEP 3: EVALUATION

In the evaluation step, ideas are sifted to identify those that might be worth investigating further. It takes time and money to develop ideas and therefore only the most promising can be chosen. During the speculation step it is easy to generate as many as two hundred ideas; these must now be pruned down to about twenty that will be developed further.

| 1895 | 'Heavier than air flying machines are impossible.' | Lord Kelvin, President, Royal Society, UK |
| 1899 | 'Everything that can be invented has been invented.' | Charles Duell, Director US Patent Office |
| 1923 | 'There is no likelihood man can ever tap the power of the atom.' | Robert Millikan, Nobel prize winner in Physics |
| 1975 | 'There will not be a woman prime minister in my lifetime.' | Margaret Thatcher |

**Figure 14.8   The need for creative thinking**

Justification is the keyword of the evaluation step. The exercise should focus on justifying why an idea should be developed and, if no justification can be found, then it can be rejected. This process ensures that ideas are not simply dismissed because they will not work: the dismissal must be justified by a rational explanation of *why* they will not work.

## STEP 4: DEVELOPMENT

During this step the ideas that survived the evaluation step are developed further. Sufficient development work needs to be done to refine potential solutions to the point where they can either be rejected or taken further still and perhaps be incorporated into the client's brief. The amount of time and effort expended on any one proposal is only sufficient to allow the client to decide what its brief will contain.

## STEP 5: RECOMMENDATIONS/IMPLEMENTATION

This is the final level of the five-step job plan. The findings of the value management exercise are written up into a formal report for presentation to the client. The purpose of the report is to provide an accurate record of the exercise for future reference. The report will often form the basis of the client's statement of need and therefore its accuracy is paramount. This report can be used in later VM studies to ensure consistency of decisions and to act as an audit trail.

The five-step job plan allows the client to define its project in such a manner as to ensure that there is little room left for ambiguity during the later phases of the project. It is the structure of the five-step process that ensures all decisions are made in a consensus manner and against agreed, common criteria.

It has only been possible to provide a brief overview of the value management process. For a more detailed analysis reference should be made to Connaughton and Green (1996), Norton and McElligott (1995) and Male *et al.* (1998).

## SUMMARY

If project teams are to deliver successful projects they need to know what the client means by successful. Successful is invariably measured in terms of 'Does the project meet the needs of client?' and 'Does the client believe it has received value for money?'

The scope of a project can only be managed effectively on the client's behalf if the scope itself is adequately defined in the first place. Clients are increasingly seeking guidance from their project teams concerning how projects can enhance their businesses processes. Project teams need to respond to this challenge positively and take on board new responsibilities and techniques to deal with this situation.

## REFERENCES AND FURTHER READING

Connaughton, J. and Green, S. (1996), *Value Management in Construction: A Client's Guide*, CIRIA, London.

Male, S., Kelly, J., Fernie, S., Gronqvist, M. and Bowles, G. (1998), *The Value Management Benchmark: A Good Practice Framework for Clients and Practitioners*, Thomas Telford, London.

National Audit Office (1998), *Construction of the Southampton Oceanography Centre, Southampton UK*, The Stationery Office, London.

Norton, B. R. and McElligott, W. C. (1995), *Value Management in Construction: A Practical Guide*, Macmillan, Basingstoke.

Thiry, M. (1997), *Value Management Practice*, Project Management Institute, Sylva, NC.

Wright, I. C. (1998), *Design Methods in Engineering and Product Design*, McGraw-Hill, London.

## RELATED TOPICS

# 15 Managing scope – configuration and work methods

*Rodney Turner*

In the last chapter Stephen Simister defined value as the relationship between functionality and cost. He described how the project manager and the team manage functionality through a breakdown of the facility that the project delivers (Figure 14.7). Configuration management is a technique by which that functionality of the individual components, and the functionality of the total facility through the configuration of the components, can be managed. The work methods by which each component is made and built into the facility can also be managed using the technique. In Chapter 4 I introduced the goals and methods matrix (see Figure 4.1), saying that on some projects the goals, or the methods of achieving those goals, are uncertain. What this means is that, although the high levels of the component breakdown are known, the functionality of the components and their further breakdown are uncertain, as is the precise way they are configured into the facility. If you try to manage the project assuming the functionality is known, or the configuration or work methods are known, you are likely to fail, because you are doing nothing to clarify your understanding. What you must do is to manage the refinement of the specification, or the further development of the product or work breakdown structures, in a controlled way to gain the agreement of all stakeholders as the project progresses. This is configuration management. The stories are legion of projects where the project team have isolated themselves for the duration of the project, and then at the end delivered a product that is rejected by other stakeholders. Configuration management attempts to avoid that, by gaining agreement of the stakeholders to the configuration and functionality of the facility delivered by the project and the work methods by which they are delivered, not only at the start of the project, but right through and up to the end.

In this chapter I discuss configuration management. I describe four steps of configuration management and I suggest a change control procedure to support the process. Change control is an essential part of configuration management, but

251

only part of it. Gaining the continual agreement of the stakeholders to the configuration and functionality of the end product is the main aim. I also show how the emphasis of configuration management changes through the life cycle from agreeing the specification to delivering the agreed specification. Goal Directed Project Management, a technique that supports configuration management, is described. Finally the definition of the work methods identified by configuration management is linked to the management of resources and implementation and progress control, described in Chapters 20 and 26 respectively.

## THE FOUR STEPS OF CONFIGURATION MANAGEMENT

Figure 15.1 illustrates the concept of configuration management. When we start the project we may be uncertain about:

- the exact component breakdown of the eventual facility;
- the exact specification of the components and the total facility;
- how the individual components will be made and built into the total facility.

This is illustrated in Figure 15.1 by showing that we cannot precisely specify the goals or methods of delivering them. All we can say is that they lie within certain bounds. We agree those bounds as well as we are able with all the stakeholders and freeze the definition in a baseline. We work to that baseline for a period of time and refine our understanding of the goals and work methods. At predetermined review points we agree the refined definition with the stakeholders, and then freeze the revised definition as a new baseline. We continue this process until we deliver a fully agreed product at the end of the project. If at some point we cannot reach agreement, then either the previous specification was wrong or the refinements since the last agreement were wrong. In the former case we will need to change the specification; in the latter case we may need to repeat the last step in the process. Neither of these options will cost very much if the lack of agreement is identified early in the process. This can be achieved by holding the reviews reasonably frequently, especially in the design stages of the project. Both recovery mechanisms can be expensive if the lack of agreement emerges later in the life cycle (leading to the stories mentioned above).

There are four steps in the configuration management process (Figure 15.2). The first column in the figure contains terms commonly used in the configuration management; the second column tries to express steps using concepts developed elsewhere in this book.

252

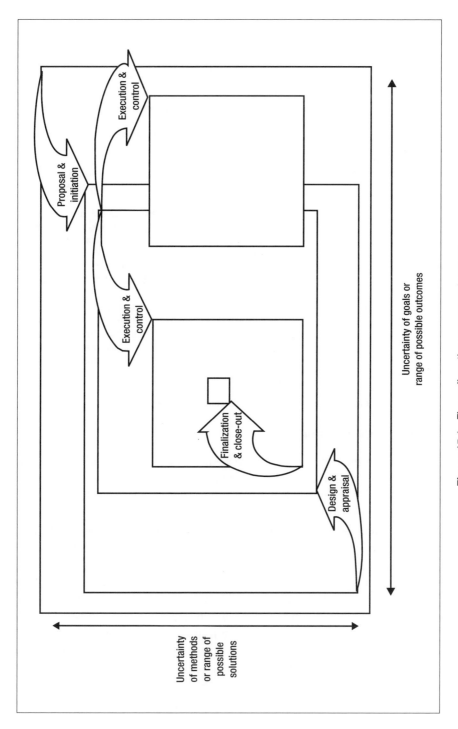

**Figure 15.1   The configuration management process**

253

| Step | Action |
|---|---|
| 1. Configuration identification | Develop a product breakdown of the facility to the current level of definition (perhaps as part of the value management process).<br>Identify the specification of the components in the breakdown, and of the total facility. |
| 2. Configuration reviews | Meet with all the project stakeholders to agree the current definition. |
| 3. Configuration control | If agreement is achieved:<br>● repeat steps 1, 2 and 3, developing the breakdown and specification further, until the facility is fully defined<br>If agreement is not achieved either:<br>● cycle back to the configuration as agreed at a previous review and repeat steps 1, 2 and 3, redoing the last steps of breakdown and specification, until agreement is achieved; or<br>● change the specification last obtained by a process of change control to match what people think it should now be. |
| 4. Status accounting | Memory of the current configurations, and all previous ones, must be maintained, so that if agreement is not reached at some point, the team can cycle back to a previous configuration and restart from there. Also memory of the configuration of all prototypes must be maintained. |

**Figure 15.2   The four steps of configuration management**

## CONFIGURATION IDENTIFICATION

Figure 15.3 represents the configuration identification of this book. There are seven parts, and within each part several chapters. There are also three components (the Preface, Chapter 1 and Index) not associated with parts, and therefore at the second level of breakdown where there is no first level. At whatever level of breakdown, I can write a specification of the components, and work methods for how they will be delivered. On the one hand, you might say that in this particular case the definition of the work methods is easy – write text. However, I might say that here the identification of the author is the work method, and I cannot do that until the specification of each chapter is determined. The definition of sections and subsections within each chapter could be said to be a further level of component breakdown, but in reality also helps to define the method of writing each chapter. At the time of writing, I still do not know precisely how many chapters there will be in each part. I therefore have an initial specification of each part (from the Body of Knowledge in Chapter 1 which is written), but that needs further refinement. I also still need to identify some of the

254

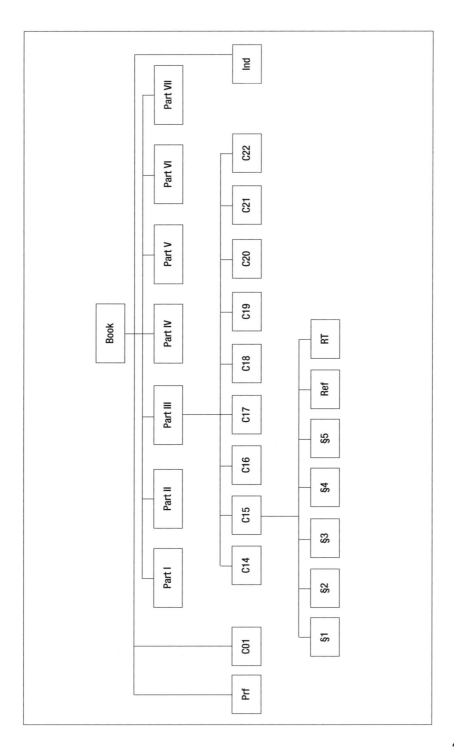

**Figure 15.3** Configuration identification (product breakdown) of this book (this part, this chapter)

authors, and agree with them the precise specification of the chapter they are to write, and the section and subsection breakdown.

## CONFIGURATION REVIEWS

At predetermined points, the team will meet with the project stakeholders to agree the current definition of the configuration. The stakeholders may include:

- the sponsor, representing the project's financiers;
- the champion and others representing the users or operators;
- representatives of the consumers, perhaps the marketing department;
- trade union or staff council representatives;
- representatives of the local community.

These reviews are automatically built into the PRINCE 2 process as end of stage reviews and they are required by ISO 10,006.

## CONFIGURATION CONTROL

If agreement about the current configuration is obtained, then its further definition and refinement can continue. If agreement is not obtained, then one of two problems has occurred:

- an early definition was wrong and needs to be changed;
- the work to come from the last definition is wrong.

If an earlier definition was wrong, it can be put right through change control. If the work to reach the present position was wrong, then you must return to where the configuration was agreed and redo the work from that point. Hopefully, it was the last definition that was right, and so it will only be necessary to cycle back to there. Sometimes, the problem can be at an earlier definition. The further refinement can help identify earlier weaknesses and the problem may have occurred earlier in the project.

If both of these types of problems are discovered at the design stage, their correction can be fairly simple. At the design stage a change may cost nothing and cause no delay. Repeating the work will cost additional design effort and build in a delay. But you have to ask yourself, what is more important, the functionality which will generate revenue and provide the value, cost or time, or some other parameter? Unfortunately, the answer to this question is not always clear-cut, which is why the success criteria need to be agreed before you start (see Chapter 5). If the problems are discovered during implementation, then their correction can cause considerable rework, with resulting additional costs and delay.

As an example of the problem that can occur, I might have specified Times Roman as the font for this book. If an influential stakeholder wants Bookman, then I check the previous specification where it says a printer's font is required. Both Times Roman and Bookman are printer's fonts, and so the wrong interpretation was put on the previous specification. Alternatively the stakeholder may want Courier. Courier is a typeface, and so the previous specification which said printer's font was wrong. Now we must change that to read typeface and specify Courier.

## STATUS ACCOUNTING

If a problem is found, then it will be necessary to refer back to the previous specifications. Unfortunately, as people refine the specification they tend to lose the memory of what the previous specification was. When a problem is then discovered, it is impossible to cycle back. At each review, the current status of the specification must be filed. Also, if prototypes are being developed, the precise specification of each prototype must be recorded through all its stages of development.

With the status accounting of this book, I have a version of the contents where this is Chapter C2, the second chapter in the third part, and another where it is Chapter 15. The former lets me make changes to earlier parts and not interrupt the definition of this chapter. I also keep the author's draft of each chapter, so I can check back against the changes I make in my edit.

## CHANGE CONTROL

Changes are an essential part of the configuration management process. The whole point is to refine our understanding of the design of the facility produced by the project and the method of delivering it. Hence you must have a subsidiary process for change control. I am not a great believer in bureaucracy, but one bit I do believe in is a change control form. If everybody proposing a change is asked to fill in a change control form, then many changes will evaporate at that point. The change will not be worth the time to fill in the form. Figure 15.4 is a suggested change control form.

### Key stakeholders

The first row contains space for the name of the project and key stakeholders. You may add more. Every stakeholder must sign off every issue of the change control form.

| | | |
|---|---|---|
| | Euro Projex<br>The European Centre for Project Excellence | |
| Project<br>Sponsor<br>Champion<br>Manager<br>Marketing | | Signature |
| Change no.<br>Issue<br>Date<br>Proposer | | |
| Description of<br>change | | |
| Impact | | |
| Benefit | | |
| Cost<br>● direct<br>● indirect<br>● rework | | |
| Appraisal<br>● NPV<br>● IRR<br>● payback | | |

**Figure 15.4   Example of a change control form**

### Status accounting information

The next row contains the status accounting information for the change control form.

### Description of change

A description of the change follows. The nature of the change and its effects must be explained. Why the change is beneficial must also be explained.

258

## Impact

The full impact of the change must be described. It should be explained what new work is required, and what rework and scrapping of previous work is needed. There may be other indirect impacts, on quality or on the ability to do work elsewhere.

## Benefit

A monetary value should be put on the value of the change.

## Cost of the change

Likewise a monetary value must be put on the cost. This should include the cost of the direct work, indirect work and rework necessary.

## Appraisal

The change should be appraised using standard techniques (see Chapters 27 and 28 for changes of far-reaching impact). Changes will usually be required to meet higher hurdles than the project itself. The reasons for this are that:

- many changes are 'nice to have', and so should be subjected to greater rigour – changes to avoid show-stoppers will have infinite IRR (internal rate of return) and therefore have no problem being accepted;
- the benefits are usually over-egged and the costs understated.


## CONFIGURATION MANAGEMENT THROUGH THE LIFE CYCLE

The cost of making changes increases throughout the life cycle. Many industries have a rule of thumb that the ratio of the cost required to make a change from feasibility to design to execution to close-out is:

$$1 : n : n^2 : n^3$$

For shipbuilding these ratios are said to be $1 : 3 : 9 : 27$, and for information systems $1 : 10 : 100 : 1000$. The impact and rework is greater in the later stages of the project and delays are more expensive. Once execution is underway, and money is being spent in earnest, delays increase the financing costs of a project. Hence it is preferable if the specification is agreed by the end of feasibility, and essential it should be agreed by the end of design. Thus the emphasis of configuration management changes at the transition from design to execution. During feasibility and design the emphasis is on agreeing the specification. And longer may be spent ensuring that it is right. During execution and close-out the emphasis of configuration management is on checking the specification of the product as it is delivered. As each chapter of this book is written by the author I check it against what I intended for that chapter, as each part is produced I check that, and at the end I check the complete book. The configuration identification becomes the test procedure for the facility as it is produced.

## GOAL DIRECTED PROJECT MANAGEMENT

Goal Directed Project Management (Andersen *et al.* 1995) is a technique that supports the configuration management process. It consists of two simple documents:

1. The milestone plan, which shows:
   - the intermediate delivery of components of the facility;
   - the intermediate delivery of assemblages of the components;
   - the final delivery of the full assembly of the facility;
   - intermediate review points at which the definition of future milestones is agreed;
   - completion of life cycle stages at which one team accept the intermediate design or products handed over from the team working on the previous stage.
2. The responsibility chart, used at two levels to show:
   - at the milestone level, the work methods to deliver the milestones as a whole, by showing departments and functions involved and their roles and responsibilities;
   - milestone by milestone, the work methods to deliver each milestone, by showing the activities required, the people involved and their roles and responsibilities.

Figure 15.5 shows the application of the approach and the use of the forms. (It is assumed that the project definition, as described by Stephen Simister in Chapters 14 and 25, has been done, and so the definition of the total facility is known.) Figures 15.6, 15.7 and 15.8 show the use of the forms for the planning of a project to deliver the systems and procedures required to operate a warehouse to supply materials to several related factories operating in three counties in South East England. You will see that early milestones are designed to gain agreement to the design of the systems and procedures, and the later milestones are designed to confirm delivery of the agreed systems and procedures, and to commission them. Erling Andersen describes the use of symbols in the responsibility chart to describe roles and responsibilities (and hence work methods) in Chapter 17.

| Managing | Products and functionality | Organization and work methods |
|---|---|---|
| Management level Contract between the project team and the organization | Milestone plan <br> ● what the project will deliver <br> ● when the project will deliver <br> ● gaining agreement to it | Project responsibility chart <br> ● who will support the project <br> ● what support will they give <br> ● what will they do |
| Detail level Contract between the project team members | | Activity responsibility chart <br> ● activities to deliver each milestone <br> ● who will do it and when |

Figure 15.5  The use of the forms in Goal Directed Project Management

## DEVELOPING THE MILESTONE PLAN AND RESPONSIBILITY CHART

Since the objective is to gain the agreement of the wider project team to the intermediate products and the method of their delivery, it is essential that the milestone plan and responsibility charts are developed in group working sessions. It is suggested that the milestone plan and project responsibility chart are developed in a project start-up workshop (see Chapter 24) to which appropriate managers are invited. The ideal number of people is around eight and they may include:

- the project champion (a senior user arguing the project's case)
- the project manager
- work area managers
- managers of groups or sections providing resources
- a planner from the project support office
- somebody who has worked on a similar project in the past
- a facilitator of the group dynamic.

To create a milestone plan, starting from the project definition report (see Chapter 14), a four-step process is suggested:

1. Brainstorm potential milestones.
2. Rationalize the list down to 12–24 by:
   - rejecting milestones as not relevant;
   - combining milestones;
   - incorporating milestones as activities of others.
3. Group the milestones into 3 or 4 areas of work:
   - Andersen *et al.* (1987) describe these as result paths.
   - A whiteboard or flip chart is useful for this.

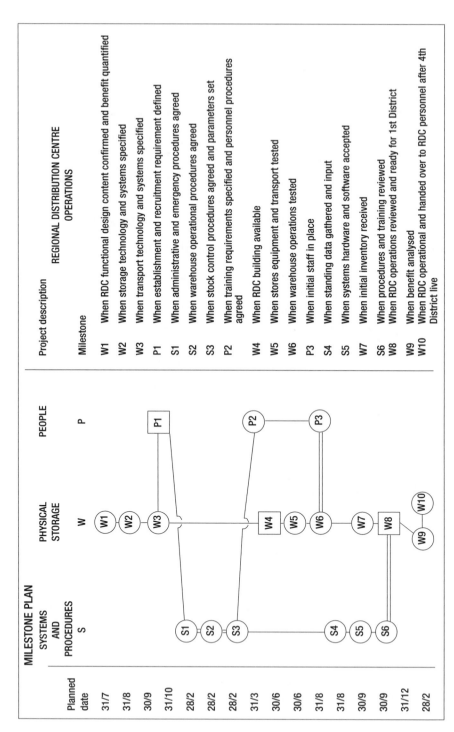

MILESTONE PLAN

| | SYSTEMS AND PROCEDURES S | PHYSICAL STORAGE W | PEOPLE P |

Project description

REGIONAL DISTRIBUTION CENTRE OPERATIONS

| Milestone | |
|---|---|
| W1 | When RDC functional design content confirmed and benefit quantified |
| W2 | When storage technology and systems specified |
| W3 | When transport technology and systems specified |
| P1 | When establishment and recruitment requirement defined |
| S1 | When administrative and emergency procedures agreed |
| S2 | When warehouse operational procedures agreed |
| S3 | When stock control procedures agreed and parameters set |
| P2 | When training requirements specified and personnel procedures agreed |
| W4 | When RDC building available |
| W5 | When stores equipment and transport tested |
| W6 | When warehouse operations tested |
| P3 | When initial staff in place |
| S4 | When standing data gathered and input |
| S5 | When systems hardware and software accepted |
| W7 | When initial inventory received |
| S6 | When procedures and training reviewed |
| W8 | When RDC operations reviewed and ready for 1st District |
| W9 | When benefit analysed |
| W10 | When RDC operational and handed over to RDC personnel after 4th District live |

| Planned date | |
|---|---|
| 31/7 | |
| 31/8 | |
| 30/9 | |
| 31/10 | |
| 28/2 | |
| 28/2 | |
| 28/2 | |
| 31/3 | |
| 30/6 | |
| 30/6 | |
| 31/8 | |
| 31/8 | |
| 30/9 | |
| 30/9 | |
| 31/12 | |
| 28/2 | |

Figure 15.6   Milestone plan for the warehouse project

## PROJECT RESPONSIBILITY CHART

Project: **RDC OPERATIONS**

Period: MONTH / QTR.

Issue/Date: A 4/8  
Approved by: MJE

**Legend**

- X – eXecutes the work
- D – takes Decision solely
- d – takes decision jointly
- P – manages Progress
- T – provides Tuition on the job
- C – must be Consulted
- I – must be Informed
- A – available to Advise

**Companies/Departments/Functions/Type of Resource**

| No. | Principle/Milestone Name | Project Manager | Supplies Project | Personnel Project | Systems Project | Finance Project | C.O.R's | Regional Supplies Manager | Director of Estates | Director of Finance | Consultants | DEC/McKeowns | Stores Equipment Manufacturers | DHA/DITS | RHA Audit | RDC Personnel |
|---|---|---|---|---|---|---|---|---|---|---|---|---|---|---|---|---|
| W1 | RDC design & functional content | XD | Xd | | I | | | IC | I | | CX | | | | | |
| W2 | Storage tech & systems spec. | XD | Xd | | Xd | | | IA | I | | CX | C | | I | C | |
| W3 | Transport tech & systems spec. | Xd | Xd | | I | X | | ID | I | d | C | C | | I | | |
| P1 | Establishment & recruit defined | DX | X | CI | I | I | CI | CI | | I | A | | | | | |
| S1 | Admin & emergency procedures | D | Xd | | I | | A | IA | | I | A | C | | | C | |
| S2 | Warehouse operational procedures | D | Xd | | C | | | | | | A | C | | C | C | |
| S3 | Stock control procedures | D | Xd | | C | I | Xd | | | | A | C | | C | C | |
| P2 | Training req. & personnel procedures | D | Xd | Xd | Xd | Xd | | I | | | A | A | A | | | |
| W4 | RDC building handed over | IC | I | I | I | I | | I | XD | | | | Xd | | | |
| W5 | Stores equip. & transport tested | D | Pd | | I | | | | | | A | X | | I | | DX |
| W6 | Warehouse operations tested | | Xd | Xd | Xd | Xd | Xd | | | | | | | | | DX |
| P3 | Initial staff recruited & trained | | Xd | Xd | Xd | Xd | | XI | | XI | A | X | | I | – | |
| S4 | Standing data input | D | Xd | Xd | Xd | Xd | | | | | | C | | | | |
| S5 | Systems hard/soft accepted | PD | Xd | Xd | Xd | Xd | CI | | | | | X | | | Xd | |
| W7 | Initial inventory received | XD | XD | | I | I | | | | | | | | – | – | PX |
| S6 | Procedures & training reviewed | Xd | Xd | Xd | Xd | Xd | | | | | A | X | | – | – | DX |
| W8 | Operations reviewed & ready | Xd | Xd | | Xd | Xd | | | | I | A | X | | | | |
| W9 | Benefit analysed | D | Xd | Xd | Xd | Xd | | | | I | | | C | | | |
| W10 | RDC operational & handed over | DX | X | X | X | X | | | | I | | | | I | | DX |

**Figure 15.7  Project responsibility chart for the warehouse project**

263

**ACTIVITY SCHEDULE**

Project: RDC OPERATIONS

Milestone No./Name: W2: Warehouse storage technology and design

Issue/Date: A 1 JUL

Approved by: DHS

SCALE : TWO DAYS

Legend:
- X – eXecutes the work
- D – takes Decision solely
- d – takes decision jointly
- P – manages Progress
- T – provides Tuition on the job
- C – must be Consulted
- I – must be Informed
- A – available to Advise

Named Functions/Named Persons/Named Resources

| Work Cont D | No. | Activity/Task Name: | DAVID | JOHN | WAREHOUSE DESIGNERS | MIKE | ARCHITECTS | DENNIS | GILLIAN | PETER | GEOFF |
|---|---|---|---|---|---|---|---|---|---|---|---|
| 18 | 1 | Identify stock range | C | X | X | I | | I | | | |
| 18 | 2 | Identify stock volumes | | X | X | | | | | | |
| 18 | 3 | Identify sortation data | C | CX | X | | | | | | |
| 18 | 4 | Identify picking volumes | C | CX | X | | | | | | |
| 9 | 5 | Identify picking solution | C | C | X | | | | | | |
| 9 | 6 | Identify sortation solution | C | C | X | | | | | | |
| 12 | 7 | Match picking/sortation | I | X | X | | | | X | | |
| 9 | 8 | Select designs solution | DX | dX | CX | I | | | X | | I |
| 27 | 9 | Select equipment types | DX | dX | CX | I | I | | | I | I |
| 3 | 10 | Detail equipment costs | | X | X | | I | | | I | I |

Figure 15.8  Activity responsibility chart for the warehouse project

264

4. Sort the milestones into sequence and draw their logical dependency:
   - This gives both a milestone plan and a precedence network for the project (see Chapter 19).

A similar process is used to develop the responsibility chart at the project or activity level. The chart at the project level will be developed by the same team as did the milestone plan, but a different team may develop the chart at the activity level. Then it will be the actual people working on the milestone. The process involves the following steps:

1. Using a flip chart, whiteboard, overhead projector or PC with a beamer, draw a grid.
2. Enter the names of products or components in the rows:
   - Milestones at the milestone level
   - Activities at the activity level
3. Enter the names of the resources involved in the columns:
   - Companies, functions, departments, groups at the milestone level
   - Named individuals involved in the milestone at the activity level
4. Enter the roles and responsibilities of the resources in the body of the matrix:
   - Use the symbols suggested by Erling Andersen in Chapter 17.

The body of the responsibility chart defines the work methods at that level, as opposed to the names of the rows which define the components of the facility. The charts over several levels define a *work breakdown* structure for the project, as opposed to the *product breakdown* structure defined by the configuration of the facility into components.

## MANAGING SCOPE OF WORK

In this chapter and the last we have defined the scope of the project very much by the functionality of the product or facility it will deliver and the decomposition or configuration of that facility into components. This is a recommended principle of project management, that you should define the plan (at least at the higher levels) in terms of the products the project will produce, rather than the work to deliver them. That gives a much more stable and robust plan, as the definition of the products (at least the components if not their precise specification) is more stable than the work required to deliver them. However, in the process of defining the configuration of the facility we have also defined the work methods required to deliver it.

The actual management of that work is not covered in this chapter. It is more natural to discuss that later, especially when discussing the management of the resources to do the work (Chapter 20) or the implementation and control of progress (Chapter 26).

## REFERENCES AND FURTHER READING

Andersen, E. S., Grude, K. V. and Haug, T. (1995), *Goal Directed Project Management*, 2nd edition, Kogan Page, London.

CCTA (1996), *Prince 2: Project Management for Business*, The Stationery Office, London.

ISO (1997), *ISO 10,006, Quality in Project Management*, International Standards Organization, Geneva.

## RELATED TOPICS

# 16 Managing quality

## Rodney Turner

People have traditionally said that the three measures of the success of projects is that they should be completed to time, to cost and to quality. However, when asked what they mean by quality, they are uncertain, and when asked how they manage it, they are even more uncertain. When you say to these people that the facility delivered by the project needs to perform in order to generate revenue, and hence pay for the project, they say performance and functionality are included in quality. In Chapter 14 Stephen Simister described how to design functionality and value into the facility and in Chapter 15 I described the use of configuration management to deliver that functionality. This could reduce the definition of quality to a very narrow view, the 'finish' of the facility. In this chapter I take a somewhat wider view of quality and describe its management. I examine what we mean by quality in the context of a project, describe a five-element model for managing quality and consider whether quality on projects is free. I also describe some tools for diagnosing quality problems.

## QUALITY IN THE CONTEXT OF PROJECTS

There are several definitions of what we mean by good quality in the context of projects:

- Meets customer requirements.
- Meets the specification.
- Solves the problem.
- Fit for purpose.
- Satisfies or delights the customer.

The customer will have an idea of the problem they are trying to solve and will formulate a solution. That will become their requirements. The customer will attempt to enunciate their requirement and a designer will try to capture that in a specification. When the project is delivered, it should be delivered in accordance with the specification. If there have been no mistakes in the preceding steps, the facility delivered will solve the problem, that is it will be fit for purpose and it will delight the customer.

Are these definitions the same thing? Well, hopefully, yes, but of course the phrase 'If there have been no mistakes in the preceding steps' says it all. The chance is small that each step is performed correctly. It is unlikely that:

- the customer will solve their problem exactly;
- they will covert their mental map into words that reflect them;
- the person writing the specification will hear exactly what the customer said and record it correctly.

Hence the chance the facility solves the problem and satisfies the customer, let alone delights the customer, is vanishingly small. Thus, the standard definition of quality is taken at the end of the chain, the facility should be fit for purpose, it should solve the problem required of it and (hopefully) thereby satisfy the customer. This requires acceptance that the specification may be imperfect and therefore needs some refinement. This gives us a dilemma. Traditional project managers think that the specification is sacrosanct and therefore must not be changed. However, if it is imperfect, then the facility may not solve the problem. On the other hand, if the specification is changed constantly, the project will never finish. Thus it must be changed, but changed sparingly, using the techniques of configuration management described in Chapter 15. The specification will define the finish expected. It will cover such issues as:

- the required functionality of the facility and its components;
- design standards it is required to meet;
- the time and cost it should be delivered at;
- various 'abilities' such as availability, reliability, maintainability and adaptability.

## A FIVE-ELEMENT MODEL FOR QUALITY

Figure 16.1 shows a five-element model for delivering good quality:

- The quality of what: the product or the management processes?
- Quality assurance and quality control
- Attitudes

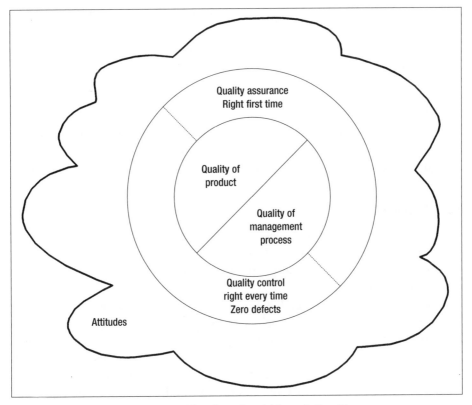

**Figure 16.1  Five-element model for project quality**

## QUALITY OF THE PRODUCT

It is the product that meets the criteria of the previous section. It is the product that provides the functionality, solves the problem and generates revenue. It is the quality of the product that is the ultimate arbiter of the quality of the project.

## QUALITY OF THE MANAGEMENT PROCESS

However, there is no doubt that following well-defined, previously proven successful ways of delivering the project increases the chance of delivering a successful solution. Part of the quality assurance of the product is following standard procedures for its delivery. However, the procedures must not be rigid rules, slavishly followed as more important than the quality of the product. I dealt with this issue in Chapter 4. What is important is that for this project you design a process or procedure that converts inputs into desired customer outputs that meet the need of the particular customer requirement (Chapter 6). That means taking the firm's standard procedures, which are flexible guidelines to best practice, and tailoring them to the needs of this project. Then at the end of the project you should audit the process to determine how you did and change the firm's standard procedures to encompass new learning.

## QUALITY ASSURANCE

Quality assurance is about taking steps to ensure that the product as delivered, and the management process, is 'right first time'. The best result, in terms of time, cost and quality, will be obtained if the product is delivered correctly at the first attempt.

## QUALITY CONTROL

Human beings are fallible and a last line of defence needs to be built in to check the product as it is delivered and the management process as it is implemented. This is necessary to ensure that the product the project produces is 'right every time' with 'zero defects'.

There is a major difference between projects and production in the balance between quality assurance and quality control. In production, millions of products are produced. The production can be sampled, every one-hundredth item destructively tested and using the techniques of statistical process control it can be determined when the production is going off specification. With a project, you cannot destructively test every one-hundredth product. You only produce one. Wrong once means wrong every time. Destructively testing the one is 100 per cent of the production. This pushes the emphasis back on to quality assurance, making sure the one that is made is right first time, and not relying on quality control. It also pushes the emphasis of quality control on to ensuring that the process is correct at the early stages, on to making sure that the early components produced are right. If you get it right from the start, you find that a momentum of quality builds up.

## ATTITUDES

We met attitudes in Chapter 5 when we discussed project strategy. Having the right attitude towards achieving success is an important element of achieving that success. Having all the stakeholders believe in the project from the start is an important contributor to project success. That was demonstrated in Chapter 5. And these attitudes are not solely the responsibility of senior management, middle management or junior management. It is the responsibility of all management, working together and doing their part for project success.

Figure 16.2 shows the four quadrants of quality, combining the first four elements of our model.

## QUALITY ASSURANCE OF THE PRODUCT

I cannot stress enough that the more you use previous experience, standards and qualified personnel, the more you increase the chance of success. The more you start with a blank sheet of paper, the more you increase the chance of failure. You also need to build in checks and balances. A well-defined specification, reviews and change control (the configuration management process) all help to gain agreement and focus on quality.

## QUALITY CONTROL OF THE PRODUCT

There is a standard three-step control process. As you work to produce results, you:

- monitor what you are achieving;
- compare that to your plan; and
- take action to recover progress.

For quality this means you should have a plan for the quality of each component in the product breakdown, a plan for the quality of how those are configured into the facility and a plan for the facility. As you deliver each component, you check its quality, as you configure the components, you check their quality, and you

| Quality of | The product | The management process |
|---|---|---|
| Quality assurance | • Previous experience<br>• Well-defined specification<br>• Standards<br>• Design reviews<br>• Qualified resources<br>• Change control | • Previous experience<br>• Well-defined process<br>• Standards<br>• Health checks<br>• Qualified managers<br>• Stable processes |
| Quality control | 1. Monitor<br>2. Compare<br>3. Correct<br>   • each component<br>   • their configuration<br>   • the facility | 1. Monitor<br>2. Compare<br>3. Correct<br>   • processes<br>   • reports<br>   • results |

Figure 16.2 The four quadrants of project quality

271

check the quality of the total facility. You do not wait until you deliver the facility and then check it. That is wrong the only time. You build up a momentum of quality from the first component to carry you through. That is a good attitude.

## QUALITY ASSURANCE OF THE MANAGEMENT PROCESS

The standards are now company standard processes, perhaps based on PRINCE 2 or ISO 10,006 (Chapter 6), tailored to the needs of this project and the facility it produces. The procedures also need to be configured as an integrated approved whole.

## QUALITY CONTROL OF THE MANAGEMENT PROCESS

The application of the three-step control process means conducting health checks and audits as described in Chapter 9.

# IS QUALITY FREE?

It has been claimed that improved quality is cheaper in the medium term than poor quality (Crosby 1979). Crosby's argument is as follows. There are three components of the cost of poor quality:

1. The cost of the assurance procedures.
2. The cost of the control procedures.
3. The cost of dealing with failures: scrap, rework, repairs under guarantee.

To reduce the total cost, you must first increase the cost of the assurance procedures. Initially there will be no impact on the other two. However, with time the number of failures will begin to fall, and hence their cost. Later, you can reduce the amount of control effort, as your confidence of getting it right increases. Later still, you can start to reduce the amount of your assurance effort. With time, the total cost of quality will drop below what it was initially and will eventually pay back the increased cost of assurance made initially. If you are a project-based organization, undertaking many projects over a period of time, you will find that over time the cost of your projects reduces – the quality improvement is free. The problem is that the whole cycle can take five years. The improvement takes longer than the first project on which it was implemented. The quality improvement is not free on the first project, just eventually for the organization as a whole.

A further problem arises if you are a contractor doing bespoke work for other organizations. Who pays for the initial effort, you or your clients? It was to overcome this problem that clients and contractors tried partnering during the early 1990s. Under multiproject partnering, clients and contractors agreed to work together through the five-year cycle. This proved not to be very successful as it coincided with a recession, and whereas before the recession it was favourable to clients, during the recession it was favourable to contractors, and clients wanted to be released from their commitments. What proved more successful was single-project partnering, where clients and contractors recognized that they had to work together again, so tried to maximize their joint learning from every project.

Although quality is not free on the first project, the quality of the facility that results from the first project can reduce its life cycle cost, that is the reduced maintenance costs outweigh the increased capital cost. Hence even though the project costs more, it can be worthwhile to put the increased effort into the increased quality of the project.

## DIAGNOSTIC TOOLS FOR SOLVING QUALITY PROBLEMS

There are many tools to help diagnose quality problems, but three of the most powerful are:

- Pareto analysis
- cause and effect diagrams
- structured problem-solving cycle.

### PARETO ANALYSIS

Pareto analysis, named after an Italian economist, assumes that 80 per cent of occurrences, here quality problems, result from 20 per cent of causes, and 20 per cent of occurrences result from 80 per cent of causes, the so-called 80 : 20 rule. Thus rather than trying to solve the vast majority of causes that result in just a few of our problems (the insignificant many), the suggestion is that you should identify and solve those 'vital few' causes which result in the majority of problems. As you eliminate the vital few causes, you can concentrate on the next most significant, but with decreasing impact. This is akin to a learning curve, where gaining greater and greater improvement requires proportionally greater and greater effort. This last sentence is a bit pessimistic, but the concept of concentrating your effort on those few causes which lead to the majority of problems is a very powerful means to produce quick, cost-effective returns.

## CAUSE AND EFFECT DIAGRAMS

Cause and effect diagrams attempt to trace back problems, as perceived through the symptoms or effects we see, to their root causes (Figure 16.3). They are sometimes called fish bone diagrams, because of their shape, or Ishikawa diagrams, after the man who first promoted their application to the solution of quality problems. They are constructed by repeatedly asking the question 'Why?' or 'What?' A certain effect is perceived, so we ask, 'Why does it happen?' or 'What causes it?' Once we have identified the main causes, we repeat the questions to find underlying sub-causes and so on, until we have identified the root causes of the effect we perceive. Obviously, when coupled with Pareto analysis, we will try to identify the vital few causes of the majority of our problems.

## STRUCTURED PROBLEM SOLVING

Having identified the 'vital many' causes of our problems, we will wish to eliminate them. A structured problem-solving technique can help. Turner (1999) suggests a ten-step process of three phases to aid problem-solving and decision-making and taking:

1. Decision making:
   - identify the problem
   - gather relevant data
   - identify the causes
   - generate possible solutions
   - evaluate the solutions.
2. Decision taking:
   - choose one of the solutions for implementation.

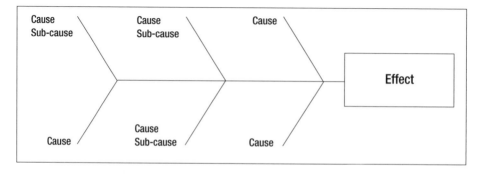

**Figure 16.3   Cause and effect diagram**

3.  Implementation:
    ● plan implementation
    ● communicate the plans
    ● implement
    ● monitor the results.

## REFERENCES AND FURTHER READING

CCTA (1996), *Prince 2: Project Management for Business*, The Stationery Office, London.
Crosby, P. B. (1979), *Quality is Free*, McGraw-Hill, New York.
ISO (1997) *ISO 10,006, Quality in Project Management*, International Standards Organization, Geneva.
Turner, J. R. (1999), *The Handbook of Project-based Management*, 2nd edition, McGraw-Hill, London.

## RELATED TOPICS

| | |
|---|---|
| Success criteria and strategy | Chapter 5 |
| Procedures, PRINCE 2 and ISO 10,006 | Chapter 6 |
| End of project reviews | Chapter 9 |
| Project health checks | Chapter 9 |
| Functionality and value | Chapter 14 |
| Configuration management | Chapter 15 |

# 17 Managing organization – structure and responsibilities

*Erling Andersen*

A project has at the outset no resources. To achieve its objectives, a project needs competent and motivated people working tightly together in an organized manner. The project itself must create an organization of people well suited to meet its challenges. This means building an organizational structure, establishing the formal relationships of the organization and clarifying the responsibilities of the individuals and organizational units involved. There are two basic topics to be approached when deciding the organization structure of the project:

- The external structure: the relationship between the project and its parent organization (base organization).
- The internal structure: the relationships between the project manager and the project participants and between all the project participants themselves.

There is no one right way to organize a project. The choice of project organization depends on many factors, including the nature of the task and the length and size of the project. In this chapter I present the different options. First, I describe different approaches to the external structure, before discussing which one to choose in a given situation. I then describe how to form the internal structure.

## EXTERNAL ORGANIZATIONAL STRUCTURES

There are three different external organizational structures (Jessen 1996):

- The 'fully incorporated' project organization
- The 'split authority' project organization
- The 'full authority' project organization

The fully incorporated project is established as part of an existing department or division in the parent organization. The project organization does not affect the basic structure of the parent organization. A line manager from the actual department or division usually heads the project. The project participants are mostly recruited from the same organizational unit, even if others might be involved. This kind of structure is of interest when the scope of the project is restricted to this one department. Actually, the task of the project could have been solved as part of the regular work of the parent organization, but organizing the task as a project may give it extra attention and effort. The problem of using this structure arises from the fact that the task of a project is seldom restricted to one part of the organization, meaning that the project does not consider all the factors important to the whole organization. That is what we call sub-optimization. There is also a danger that the project is so intertwined with daily work that it does not receive the desired attention.

A split authority project is where the project members are partly or 'fractionally' allocated to the project. They are recruited from different parts of the parent organization. The project participants remain in their regular position in the parent organization during the project period. Project work and duties in the parent organization have to be done simultaneously, and the project members have to divide their time between the two. They will have two bosses at the same time, both the project manager and the line manager. The project manager will be in a position of split authority, sharing the authority with the line manager. The split authority project organization is an example of a matrix organization. We discuss the pros and cons of such an organizational structure below.

A full authority project is organized completely outside the parent organization. The project participants are 100 per cent allocated to project work. The project manager is able to exercise full authority over the project participants. This kind of organizational structure is also called the pure project organization. We discuss it in more detail later.

In practice mixed forms of organizational structure may appear. In some projects we might have some participants who are working part time for the project and others who are fully allocated to the project. This might be called a hybrid organizational structure.

## THE SPLIT AUTHORITY AS A MATRIX ORGANIZATION

A matrix organization is an organizational structure well known from the general organizational theory. It means a combination of:

- functional departments which provide a stable base for specialized activities and a permanent location for members of staff;
- units that integrate various activities of the different functional departments.

A certain company might be organized as a matrix consisting of functional departments, on the one hand, and territories (geographical division) or products on the other. If projects are the units in the matrix, we have a split authority project organization. We know from organizational theory that the development of an effective matrix organization takes time and a willingness to learn new roles and behaviour. The most important advantages of applying a matrix organization to project work are:

- every project has reasonable access to the entire reservoir of competence within the company; it makes specialized functional assistance available to all projects ;
- the project participants know at all times the problems and potentials of the parent organization; they maintain a close contact to the parent organization during the project;
- better use of the resources of the company; it makes possible the maximum use of a limited pool of functional specialists;
- there is little anxiety among the project participants about what happens when the project is completed; they all have their 'home' in the parent organization.

The main advantage of a matrix organization is the access for all projects, large and small, to all the human resources of the company. The project could consider the company as a resource pool, from which it can draw the best available experts. Since the project may need the actual expertise for a rather short time, it might be easier to arrange this in-house than engaging external consultants. Besides that, the in-house people are much more familiar with the company, which means that their input to the project work is more relevant. Sometimes the project may need to go outside the company to find competent and qualified personnel, but only after it has evaluated the availability of the internal resources. The matrix organization has its disadvantages:

- There is ambiguity of authority; a project participant has two bosses.
- The project participant experiences a conflict between the demands for time and work from the parent organization and the project; the individual is confronted with a workload that is much greater than the time available.

When people are asked to join a project and at the same time keep their position in the parent organization, they are usually promised some reduced workload in their permanent job. Practice shows that it is difficult to live up to this promise to its full extent. There are good reasons for that. It is difficult to find other people who on short notice and for a short while can do the job in a way that really lessens the burden of the permanent holder of the job. The problem that arises from this is that the project participant gets a very heavy workload. In the beginning of the project the person works hard to master the demands of both jobs. In the longer run the motivation for project work dwindles.

## TASK CULTURE VERSUS ROLE CULTURE

In a matrix organization people do work for the project and parent organization at the same time. It is of great importance to understand that these two organizations represent different organizational cultures. The line organization is based on a role culture, while the project should be stamped as a task culture (Graham 1989). Working in these different cultures requires different attitudes and behaviour. It might be difficult for a person to move between the two jobs and adapt to the different cultures. However, the success of the project depends on the ability of the project manager to create a task culture, which is quite different from the role culture. The role (or bureaucracy) culture of the parent organization is characterised by the following features:

- The organization is created to handle routine jobs and repetitive tasks.
- Each person is doing his or her job as described by procedures or job descriptions; they should not get involved in tasks which are outside their domain.
- The influence and power of a person is determined by his or her position in the hierarchy or by the job title.
- All tasks should be treated according to prescribed rules; logic and rationality is the general principle of the management.

The task culture of the project, on the other hand, has the following features:

- The organization is created to handle a unique task.
- The task requires innovative behaviour and cooperation between functional specialists.
- Knowledge and expertise constitute power and influence on the results of the project.
- The general principle of the management is to get the job done.

Many project participants, who are used to the role culture, have problems adjusting to the demands of the task culture of the project. They believe that they are appointed to the project because of their position in the parent organization and act accordingly. They do not fully grasp that the main reason for their participation in the project is that they possess certain knowledge and experience of value to the project. They also have problems adjusting to the creative and innovative atmosphere of the project. The good project manager strives to create a task-oriented culture within the project.

## THE FULL AUTHORITY PROJECT ORGANIZATION (PURE PROJECT ORGANIZATION)

This kind of project is organized as an unit separate from the parent organization. It is a self-contained unit with its own staff, who work full time for the project. The most important advantages of this organizational structure are:

- the project manager has full line authority over the project and its human resources; all members of the project workforce are directly responsible to the project manager;
- the principle of unity of command exists; each subordinate has one, and only one, boss;
- the project participants have the project as their sole commitment; they can devote all their attention to project work.

The most pressing disadvantages are:

- it might be difficult to get access to certain kind of experts;
- there might be a tendency to keep certain experts on the project without being able to utilize them all the time;
- the project participants worry about what will happen to them when the project finishes;
- the project may take on a life of its own, without the modifying influence of people from the parent organization.

The pure project organization opens up for assembling a project team fully devoted to work on the tasks of the project. The most severe problem is access to and use of specialized experts. This is a lesser problem in a large project. In a small project it might be very difficult to attract the really good people and keep them occupied with the right kind of specialist task, when they are to spend all their time on this one project.

## CHOOSING AN EXTERNAL ORGANIZATIONAL STRUCTURE

Several factors might be taken into consideration when deciding which organizational structure is the most suitable. Some of the most important factors are discussed below:

### The size of the project

A large project would usually need a pure project organization; the size of the project dictates that the project needs a lot of resources on a full-time basis.

### The duration of the project

Long duration projects are more exposed to the danger of living their own life than projects of short duration. That is an argument for a matrix organization. However, long-lasting projects are often large, which is a factor pointing toward the pure project organization.

### The nature of the tasks of the project

The objective of many projects is to create changes within the parent organization. Such projects would benefit from a matrix organization. It is much easier to gain acceptance for changes when people who are affected by them are taking an active part in the preparations. This argument for a matrix organization does not hold when the project is supposed to deliver a physical product (like a bridge or a road) according to an agreed specification.

### The importance of time, costs and quality

A time critical project should be organized with full authority to the project manager. A matrix project might be more cost-efficient than the pure project organization since it has the advantage of utilizing experts from the parent organization at exactly the right time for the project and to the extent necessary. The same reasoning may be applied to the quality factor. We could also add that people from the parent organization would have a better understanding of what kinds of quality parameters the project should focus on.

### The competence and availability of personnel

As we have seen, there are many good reasons for establishing the project as a matrix organization with involvement of key people from the parent organization. However, this presupposes that the parent organization has a staff of competent people within the working area of the project and that they are allowed to use their time on the project as agreed upon.

## INTERNAL ORGANIZATIONAL STRUCTURES

The internal organization of a project should show how the project manager organizes the work of the project team. A team is a collection of individuals who work together to attain a goal. All their efforts must be coordinated. The project manager must establish the structure of the team, that is the rules of coordination – the rules governing the relationships of team members with the project manager and with each other. The structure and spirit of the team is of great importance for the success of the team.

## DIFFERENT INTERNAL STRUCTURES

There are various ways of developing an internal organization structure for a project. One is a traditional, task hierarchical structure. However, I stressed earlier the importance of creating a new spirit, a task-oriented culture within the project which is different from the traditional culture of a hierarchical organization. It would not be easy to create this new culture if the project organization were structured in the old-fashioned way. Frame (1995) suggests that a project team might be structured in other ways:

- Isomorphic team structure
- Speciality team structure
- Egoless team structure
- Surgical team structure

I discuss the hierarchical approach and Frame's four structures in turn.

### Task hierarchical structure

The team may be structured in a hierarchical way. The internal structure of the project would then be rather similar to the organizational structure of many parent organizations. This hierarchical structure might be used in large projects that require a traditional authority system. It might also be of interest to routine projects which more or less do the same as previous projects and where the need for creative innovation and variety is small. Each team member should do his or her job without bothering about the others.

### Isomorphic team

Figure 17.1 illustrates the isomorphic team structure. Under an isomorphic structure, the project is organized in a way that reflects the physical structure of the deliverable – the thing that is produced. The word isomorphic is a combination of the Greek 'iso', which means equal or same, and 'morph', which means form and shape. Two things are isomorphic when they can be said to have the same shape or structure. An isomorphic organizational structure might be used when the task of the project is to implement a new IT system. A successful implementation requires the installation of the software package, the training of future users and even some organizational changes in the parent organization to better utilize the potentials of the software. We would have an isomorphic

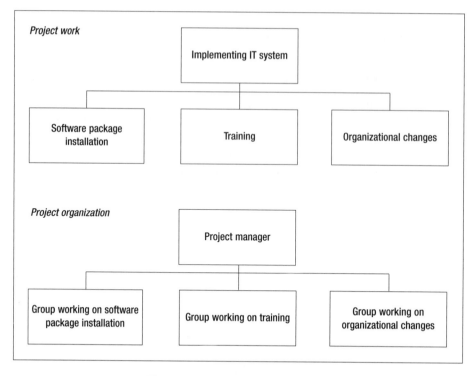

*Project work*

Implementing IT system

Software package installation

Training

Organizational changes

*Project organization*

Project manager

Group working on software package installation

Group working on training

Group working on organizational changes

**Figure 17.1   Isomorphic team structure**

structure if the project were organized as three groups: one dealing with the software, one with training and one with the organizational changes. All three groups report to the project manager.

The isomorphic structure has several advantages. It is organizationally simple. It is easy to see who is responsible for each part of the deliverable. If the different parts are independent, this approach allows for parallel work. In that way it could turn out to be a highly effective organization. However, usually the different pieces of the deliverable are seldom independent of each other and that constitutes the main problem of an isomorphic structure. There is a great risk that the efforts of the different working groups will not be sufficiently coordinated. The main task of the project manager would be to secure the coordination of the different working groups.

The isomorphic team structure borrows features from the traditional hierarchical functional organization, even if the intention is clearly a flatter structure than we would find in the parent organization. It has at maximum three levels: the project manager, the group leaders and the rest of the team.

## Speciality team

The speciality team structure is illustrated in Figure 17.2. It is more like a matrix structure. Under the speciality team, all project members have a speciality or a special field of competence, which is the main reason for their participation in the project, and each team member may work on different deliverables or different aspects of a specific deliverable. Their orientation would therefore tend to be more oriented toward their speciality than toward the deliverables. For each project task the project manager would put together a group of specialists who would execute it. The project manager might draw on the same people, the same kinds of specialists, for several different tasks.

The main advantage of this structure, as we find in all matrix organizations, is the better utilization of the specialists – the sharing of competence between different tasks. The problem, also well known from earlier, is that a certain specialist will have many different assignments which all compete for the limited time available. The efforts of the project manager should be directed towards putting together working groups that have the right combination of specialists and ensuring that all the members of the team have an acceptable workload.

## Egoless team

The egoless team structure is illustrated in Figure 17.3. The egoless team structure is as close as you can get to a completely flat organizational structure. There is no obvious leader and the work of the team is a truly collaborative effort. Decisions are achieved through consensus. Project tasks are based on inputs from most of the team members. This structure demands high level interactivity and communication among project members.

The strong point of an egoless team structure is that there is no boss who can impose his or her own subjective beliefs on the work of the project. All decisions are based on the knowledge and experiences of the team members themselves. In a positive and secure atmosphere they should be able to build on each other's viewpoints, which will create a result that is much better than that achievable by one person alone. The objection to this structure is that project work will not function without strong leadership. This criticism is certainly not without foundation. However, the egoless team may function and achieve good results in some projects. It might be most suitable when the project is confronted with a complex, ill-defined problem, and we can put together a small project team with people who know each other well and are creative and opposed to being told what to do. An egoless team is certainly a challenge to all the team members.

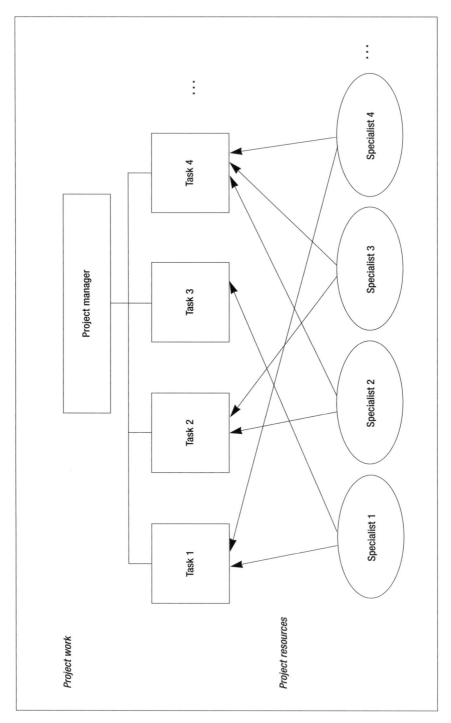

**Figure 17.2   Speciality team structure**

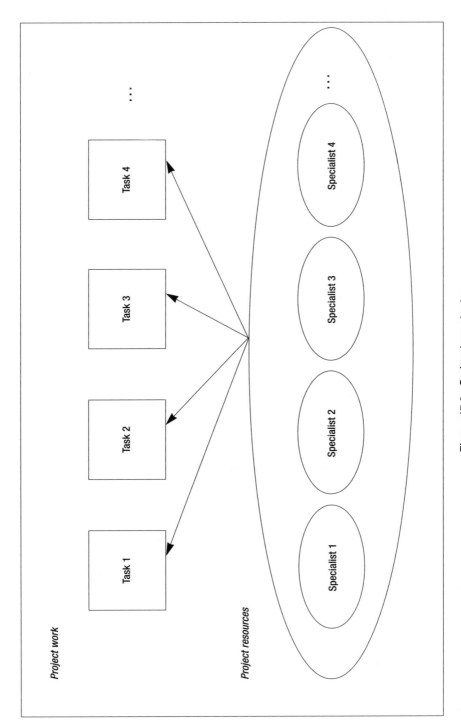

**Figure 17.3   Egoless team structure**

## Surgical team

The surgical approach to team structure (Figure 17.4) stands in direct opposition to the egoless approach. In an egoless team, it is the group effort that counts. In the surgical approach, one individual is given total responsibility and all focus is on this person and his or her abilities. The term is derived with reference to the situation of a surgeon, who during an operation has full authority in all subject matters and the full responsibility for what happens to the patient. In the surgical structure, the project manager is the most skilled and capable person on the project. The project manager manages the project team and at the same time decides on all professional matters of importance. The instructions to the subordinates are often detailed, allowing for very little freedom to determine how to conduct the work. The main task of the team members is to support the project manager and work according to his or her detailed instructions.

The advantage of the surgical team structure is that one person is in charge of all professional matters and is very capable of handling them; consequently the project will produce a a very well-integrated product. All parts of the deliverable will fit together perfectly. This approach might be of interest to projects that demand a high degree of creativity, for example a design project, and have access to an extraordinarily talented person to direct the creative process. The disadvantage is obvious; it is very difficult to find a person who can play the role of the leader. When we choose this approach, we might find out that the chosen person is not able to handle the challenge. In today's knowledge society, some team members with excellent professional background themselves may object to being treated as assistants or helpers.

I have now described five approaches to the internal structuring of a project, the traditional hierarchical organization and the four suggestions of Frame (1995). This is not an exhaustive list. Alternatives exist, but there is no one perfect structure. All the structures have advantages and disadvantages. Turner (1999) shows how the different structures suggested by Frame are appropriate at different stages of the project life cycle (Figure 17.5). Whatever structure we choose, we have to be aware that there are problems that will not be tackled and which will need the special attention of the project manager.

## RESPONSIBILITY CHART

In a hierarchical organization each person's responsibility is defined by his or her position in the hierarchy. When we have a flatter organization, or a completely flat organization, the responsibility of each person is not so clear. We need to define the obligations of each project member. The responsibility chart (Figure 17.6) is

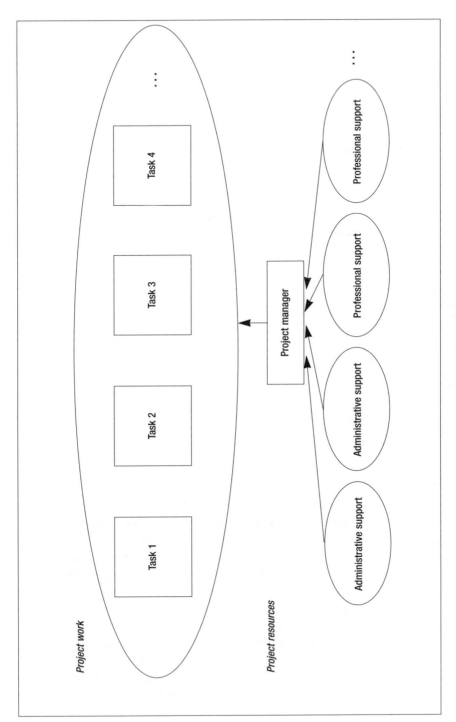

**Figure 17.4   Surgical team structure**

| Life cycle stage | Work culture | Team type |
|---|---|---|
| Feasibility | Laissez-faire | Egoless |
| Design | Democratic | Speciality |
| Execution | Autocratic | Isomorphic |
| Close-out | Bureaucratic | Surgical |

**Figure 17.5** Appropriate team structures at different stages of the project life cycle
*Source*: Turner (1999)

| | Ashley (project manager) | Ben (manager) | Cynthia (production) | David (sales) | Elisabeth (controller) | Frank (consultant) |
|---|---|---|---|---|---|---|
| Draw up draft of questionnaire | X/P | | | | | T |
| Gather views on questionnaire | P | | C | C | A | X |
| Determine final form of questionnaire | X/P | D | | | | |
| Set up mailing list, send out questionnaire | X/P | | | | | |
| Process the replies | X/P | | | | | X |

**Figure 17.6** The responsibility chart (symbols defined in text)

a useful tool to express what is expected of everybody in a project. It should be considered a necessary supplement to the organizational structure. The organizational structure determines the organizational principles which are to be applied in substantiating the relationships between all participants of the project. The responsibility chart can be used to make the organization 'tailor-made' for the actual project task. Because every project is unique, it is important that an organization be specially formulated for each individual project. The responsibility chart can be used for this purpose.

In its basic version, a responsibility chart is a matrix with rows representing activities and columns representing the people involved in the project. For each activity the chart assigns different responsibilities to the relevant persons. The chart may allow for many different types of responsibilities. The following set might be sufficient in most cases (each type of responsibility is referred to by a letter):

| | |
|---|---|
| X | EXecutes the work |
| D | Takes Decisions solely or ultimately |
| d | Takes decisions jointly or partly |
| P | Manages work and controls Progress |
| T | Provides Tuition or coaching on the job |
| C | Must be Consulted |
| I | Must be Informed |
| A | Available to Advise |

The responsibility chart in Figure 17.6 is a lot simpler than it would be in a real-life project. It here serves the purpose of illustrating the different aspects of a chart. We are looking at one part of a project. The task is to conduct a survey. The rows of the chart show the different activities. The columns show the people involved in these activities. The chart states the different responsibilities. In each row only one person can have the letter P. There must be one person who is in charge of the activity and has the main responsibility for the progress of the work. This person has the responsibility of ensuring that the activity is done on time and within budget. The person who has managerial responsibility (letter P) may at the same time do some work (letter X). The combination P/X is quite common in small projects.

Establishing the responsibility chart is a process that should involve all the participants of the project. This work clarifies the responsibilities of all team members and the responsibility chart serves the role of a contract of what has been agreed to.

It can also be advantageous to use a responsibility chart on a higher level. Andersen, Grude and Haug (1995) suggest using a responsibility chart to clarify the responsibilities of the involved parties in achieving the milestones of the project.

## REFERENCES AND FURTHER READING

Andersen, E. S., Grude, K. V. and Haug, T. (1995), *Goal Directed Project Management*, 2nd edition, Kogan Page, London.

Frame, J. D. (1995), *Managing Projects in Organizations*, revised edition, Jossey-Bass, San Francisco.

Graham, R. J. (1989), *Project Management as if People Mattered*, Primavera Press, Bala Cynwyd, PA.

Jessen, S. A. (1996), *The Nature of Project Leadership*, revised edition, Scandinavian University Press, Oslo.

Turner, J. R. (1999), *The Handbook of Project-based Management*, 2nd edition, McGraw-Hill, London.

## RELATED TOPICS

# 18 Managing cost

## *Dennis Lock*

Successful management of project costs is a complex process that cannot be left solely to the responsibility of the project manager. It embraces many aspects of contractual and commercial management that usually fall within the remit of other managers in the project organization. These other aspects, such as the management of cash flow, contract payment terms and dealing with contractors are dealt with in Parts V and VI. This chapter concentrates on initial cost estimating and budgeting, and on some of the cost analysis tasks that typically fall under the direct control of the project manager.

## COST DEFINITIONS

It is generally understood in accounting circles that the word 'cost' should never be used without a qualifying adjective. It must always be made clear what kind of cost is meant. There are many ways in which costs can be described, but it will be useful to outline some of the terms with which the project manager should be acquainted. There is no need to explain self-explanatory terms (such as labour costs and material costs) so the following list has been limited to a few that may not be familiar to all readers.

### Below-the-line costs

Various allowances that are added once a total basic cost estimate has been made are often known collectively as 'below-the-line' costs. These might include allowances for cost escalation, exchange rate fluctuation and other contingencies.

### Cost escalation

Cost escalation is the increase in any element of project costs caused by wage and salary awards and inflationary pressures on prices of purchased materials and equipment. It is usually expressed as an annual rate per cent.

### Direct costs

Costs that can be attributed directly to a job or project task are termed direct costs. If a person spends two hours in the manufacture of a component for a particular project, that person's time can be classed as direct because its cost can be identified, recorded and charged direct to the project. Similarly, the costs of materials, components and expenses directly attributable to a particular project can be classed as direct.

Direct costs are also likely to be *variable costs*. Variable costs are those which vary in proportion to the level of work actually taking place on the project. If work stops, so do the direct or variable costs. If the work rate is increased with the use of more resources, then the variable cost rate will also increase.

### Fixed costs

See *Indirect costs*.

### Indirect costs (overhead costs or overheads)

Facilities and services such as factory and office accommodation, management, personnel and welfare services, training, cost and management accounting, general administration, heating, lighting and maintenance all attract costs that must generally be incurred in running a business. Except in the case of an organization set up specially to fulfil only one project, these general costs cannot usually be allocated directly to one job or project. They are therefore termed indirect costs, often called overhead costs or simply 'overheads'.

Most indirect costs are also likely to be *fixed costs*. Costs are said to be fixed when they remain substantially unchanged and continue to be incurred irrespective of the level of project activity. Indirect management salaries are an example.

### Standard costing

Standard costing is a system in which cost data are compiled using standard rates for labour and materials. Standard rates are realistic mean rates. For example, all design engineers in a company might always be charged at the same standard hourly cost of £$x$, even though individually some engineers might be paid far less and others far more than £$x$. In projects, standard costs are typically used in cost estimates, budgets and for subsequent cost collection (from time sheets and material stores issue requisitions). This eliminates the need to consider day-to-day fluctuations in materials prices or salary differences between individual staff of the same trade or professional discipline.

From time to time the current cost rates are reviewed by the organization's accountants and compared against the standard rates in use. Any differences will give rise to a set of variances. When these variances become significant (usually as a result of cost inflation) new standard cost rates must be introduced.

### Variable costs

See *Direct costs*.

### Variance

A variance is any difference between a planned or budgeted quantity and the quantity actually measured after the event. It is usually used in connection with costs but it can also describe a deviation from the project schedule. Negative variances are especially important quantities because, provided they are detected and reported sufficiently early, they highlight problems where corrective action is needed. Variance analysis and reporting therefore satisfy the principle of management by exception.

## PRINCIPLES OF COST MANAGEMENT

Project cost management begins long before a project starts. It is a widely misunderstood function. Much of the activity often described as cost control or cost management is really nothing more than historical cost reporting, carried out too late to have any effect on costs that have already been incurred or committed.

### CHECKLIST OF COST MANAGEMENT FACTORS

The following list contains some of the factors that contribute directly or indirectly to effective project cost management. Items are not listed in any particular order of significance.

1. Full definition of the project and the scope of work involved.
2. Careful assessment of technical and commercial risks, with strategies for minimizing their possible effect.
3. Competent project manager.

4. Cost awareness by all project participants throughout the life of the project.

5. A project organization in which everyone is made aware of his or her project responsibilities.

6. A project work breakdown structure which yields work packages of manageable size.

7. Cost budgets, divided so that each work package is given its appropriate share of the total budget.

8. A code of accounts system which can be aligned with the work breakdown structure. As far as possible this should be compatible with other systems, such as drawing numbers and codes used in the organization's management information system.

9. A cost accounting system that can collect costs as they are incurred and allocate them with little delay to their relevant cost codes.

10. A prioritized work schedule, sufficiently detailed to allow the assignment and progressing of individual tasks from the work breakdown.

11. Effective management of well-motivated staff, to ensure that progress meets or beats the work schedule.

12. A method for comparing actual and planned expenditure for individual tasks, and for extrapolating the results to cover the whole project.

13. Willingness to commit additional resources or to take other measures promptly to bring late critical tasks back on schedule.

14. Effective supervision and quality control of all activities to aim at being right first time.

15. Supervision of staff time sheets so only legitimate times are booked to various cost codes.

16. Proper drafting of specifications and contracts.

17. Discreet investigation to confirm that the customer is of sound financial standing, with sufficient funds to make all contracted payments.

18. Similar investigation, not necessarily so discreet, of all significant suppliers and subcontractors (especially those new to the contractor's experience).

19. Effective use of competitive tendering for all purchases and subcontractors to ensure the lowest costs commensurate with quality and to avoid committing costs that would exceed estimates and budgets.

20. Proper consideration and control of modifications and contract variations, including charging all justifiable claims for price increases to the customer.

21. Avoidance of all non-essential changes, especially those for which the project customer will not pay.

22. Avoidance, as far as possible, of unbudgeted dayworks (particularly on large construction contracts).

23. Where dayworks are unavoidable, proper authorization and retention of daywork sheets.
24. Proper control of payments to suppliers and subcontractors to ensure that all invoices and claims for progress payments are neither overpaid nor paid too soon.
25. Recovery from the customer of all incidental expenses allowed for in the contract charging structure (for example expensive telephone calls, special printing and stationery, travel and accommodation).
26. Proper invoicing to the customer, especially ensuring that claims for progress payments or cost reimbursement are made at the appropriate times and at the correct levels, so that disputes do not arise which could delay payments.
27. Effective credit control to prevent payments from the customer becoming long overdue.
28. Internal security audits to help prevent losses through theft or fraud.
29. Regular cost and progress reports to senior management, highlighting potential schedule or budget overruns in time for corrective action to be taken.
30. Cost-effective design, perhaps using value engineering.
31. Prompt action at the end of the project to close off the accounts to prevent unauthorized time bookings and other items being charged to the project.

That long list can not be guaranteed as complete, but it includes the most obvious and important aspects of project cost management.

## MINIMIZING INDIRECT COSTS

Indirect costs are a true burden on project costs and must be incurred for every active day of the project life cycle. If the project overruns on time, it is almost inevitable that the indirect costs will overrun in direct proportion. If an organization is structured and managed so that its indirect cost rates are high, then that organization will be at a disadvantage when it seeks new work against its competitors in a price sensitive market. There are at least three ways in which indirect costs can be minimized.

1. *Reclassify some indirect costs as direct* Companies differ in their interpretation of direct and indirect costs, so one might class a particular cost item as direct while another classes it as indirect. For example, printing and stationery costs are typically indirect but special printing and stationery for a project may be accepted as a direct charge by the client. It might be possible to treat items such as international telephone calls, travel costs and other administrative expenses associated with a particular project in such a way that

they can be recorded and billed to the client. Whether or not the client will accept all these charges can be a matter for negotiation when the contract is made. Although the amounts for individual items may appear small, in total they can often result in significant saving.

2. *Completing work on or ahead of time*   If work can be completed on time, the associated indirect costs should be on budget. Let the work run late, and additional indirect costs must be absorbed.

3. *Reviewing indirect salary costs and expenses*   Many aspects of indirect cost reduction apply to any organization and are not restricted to project management. They involve running a 'lean organization' in which every manager and administrative member of staff is seen to fulfil an essential role, with unnecessary layers of management and wasteful administration jobs stripped out. Other expenses have to be controlled by the effective management of accommodation and other assets and by eliminating waste.

Some of these cost reductions call for drastic and unpopular management action. Others can be achieved with less pain. For example, some years ago installation of a telephone call-logging device immediately halved my employer's £100 000 annual communications bills by eliminating fraudulent use. Of the remaining £50 000, we were able to identify £25 000 worth of calls with particular projects and charge them to clients. So, for a small installation cost and very little management effort, we cut the company's annual overheads by £75 000.

## COST OF MATERIALS AND PURCHASED ITEMS

Purchased materials and equipment typically account for a large proportion of total project costs, yet management of the purchasing function is given little or no attention by many project management writers. Once a purchase order has been issued at a price over the budgeted amount it is too late to do anything about it. When the cost accounting system eventually picks up the costs of these purchases, when the invoices are paid, any over-expenditure will come to light as a nasty delayed shock. The costs of bought-out materials and equipment are committed irrevocably when each order is issued. The cost planning and reporting systems should, therefore, use data which are based on committed costs. That means considering the budgeted and actual cost of every purchase at the time when the purchase order is signed. Procedures should include adequate quality controls for producing accurate and unambiguous materials and equipment specifications. Sound purchasing methods are obviously important. These will almost certainly involve competitive tendering and careful analysis of bids. Clear authorization procedures should be in place, so that every purchase order is properly checked before final approval by an authorized signatory. Purchasing of equipment and materials is dealt with in Chapter 35.

## COST ESTIMATING

The most obvious reason for producing cost estimates is to assist in pricing decisions. However, cost estimates are necessary for all projects, including in-house projects and those sold without fixed prices. They are essential for funding and budgeting, for establishing outline resource requirements and for subsequent cost control.

### ESTIMATING ACCURACY

It is clear that the better the project can be defined at the outset, the less chance there should be of making estimating errors. It can sometimes be convenient to classify project cost estimates according to the degree of accuracy expected. Different organizations have their own ideas, but here is a typical arrangement.

- *Ballpark estimates* are estimates made when information or time is scarce. They are valuable for preliminary checks on resource requirements and for screening enquiries for possible tender preparation but are otherwise unreliable. It has been known for a manager to pick up a pile of drawings, weigh them thoughtfully in the hand and declare 'This project will cost £x million.' Some people have an extraordinary gift for that sort of thing, but such estimates are obviously unlikely to prove accurate. A well-reasoned ballpark estimate might achieve an accuracy of ± 25 per cent, given a fair wind, a great deal of luck and intuitive judgement.
- *Comparative estimates*, as their name implies, are made by comparing work to be done on a new project with similar work recorded on past projects. They depend on an outline project definition that enables the estimator to identify all the major tasks and assess their size and complexity. The other important requirement is access to cost and technical archives of past projects that contain comparable work packages or tasks. The estimators will adjust costs to allow for the effects of cost inflation since the relevant past projects. Accuracy must depend very much on the degree of confidence that can be placed in the proposed new design solutions, on the working methods eventually chosen and on the closeness with which the new project tasks can be matched with those of previous projects. It might not be possible to achieve

299

better than ±15 per cent accuracy but comparative estimates are often used as a basis for pricing tenders.

- *Feasibility estimates* can only be derived after the completion of preliminary project design. Quotations must then be obtained from the potential suppliers of expensive project equipment or subcontracts. Material take-offs or other schedules should be available to assist with estimating the costs of materials. The accuracy confidence factor for feasibility estimates should be better than ±10 per cent. This class of estimate is often used for construction tenders. The construction industry has the benefit of published cost tables, which give expected cost rates for a comprehensive range of construction activities based on the quantities involved.

- *Definitive estimates* cannot usually be made until most design work has been finished, all major purchase orders have been placed at known prices and work on the project construction or manufacture is well advanced. Estimating accuracy should obviously improve with time as actual recorded costs replace their corresponding estimates. Estimates become definitive when their accuracy can be accepted as ±5 per cent or better. Subject to good cost accounting, the figures for actual project costs and the definitive project estimate should converge at the end of the project.

The degrees of accuracy quoted in these examples are about as good as could ever be expected. It is very likely that many organizations will assign wider limits. It is also possible to find asymmetric limits, skewed about zero. A company might, for example, work on the assumption that its ballpark estimates are accurate to within +50 or -10 per cent.

## TABULATION

Project cost estimates should be tabulated to conform with the work breakdown structure. This will help to ensure that comparisons can readily be made between the estimates and the cost accountant's records of the actual costs eventually incurred, on a strict item for item basis. This is essential as part of the cost reporting and control functions. As experience builds up over a few years, records of estimates and corresponding costs can be used in comparative estimating for future projects, but only if all estimating and cost data are held in files structured to a common, sensible coding system. Using the work breakdown structure as the basis should automatically place all the cost estimates in a hierarchical structure. One estimating subset can be allocated to each main project work package or group of tasks. All the subsets can then be rolled up to give the estimated net total project cost.

## TABULATION FOR MANUFACTURING PROJECTS

A suggestion for a manufacturing project tabulation is given in Figure 18.1. This is just an example; there will, of course, be considerable variations in practice. One page or subset should be allocated to each manufactured assembly, work breakdown package or main component. Each row on the tabulation carries a project task, which might be a design job, the manufacture of a component or assembly, or perhaps the provision of special tooling or a jig. Totalling relevant columns should give the commitment expected from each department, and these results can be used to help with departmental budgeting and in making coarse assessments of resource requirements. A project summary page can then be arranged on which each row will correspond to one work breakdown package or other estimating subset.

The upper headings used in Figure 18.1 are all self-explanatory except, perhaps, for the item 'Case' at the top right-hand side. This is used when cost estimates have to be made for different proposed versions of a potential project. Each version can be given its own unique case number, so that there should be no subsequent confusion in finding the correct cost estimate that applies to the project version that is actually chosen and authorized.

Our example allows six different standard cost grades of labour to be shown. A few more grades might be needed in practice, but the number of columns has had to be limited here to maintain clarity within the space available.

The tabulation allows for overheads to be recovered as a percentage levy on the direct labour cost. Materials are estimated at cost, but with a small handling charge added to cover the cost of order preparation, storage and other administration. These arrangements will vary from one organization to another.

## DETAILED TABULATIONS FOR MATERIAL COSTS

Material cost estimates are often compiled separately from labour costs, perhaps using bills of materials, parts lists or material take-offs to carry the necessary level of detail. The method depends particularly on the industry. Special attention must be given to purchases, however, where commercial and transport transactions cross national frontiers.

Figure 18.2 is a slightly simplified version of a format used by a company engaged in very large international mining and minerals projects. Arranged in subsets according to main packages of the work breakdown structure, the aim is to show the total cost of each purchase, including all expenses needed to get the materials delivered to the project site. In the example shown, the project contractor always insists that suppliers quote to supply FOB (free on board). This

# COST ESTIMATE

Estimate for:

Project number
or sales reference:

Compiled by:

Estimate number:
Case:
Date:
Page:                of

| 1 | 2 | 3 | 4 | 5 | 6 | 7 | 8 | 9 | 10 | 11 | 12 | 13 | 14 | 15 |
|---|---|---|---|---|---|---|---|---|---|---|---|---|---|---|
| Cost | Item | Qty | Labour times and costs by department or standard grade | | | | | | Total direct labour cost | Overhead cost % | Standard or net cost | Materials Burden % | Longest delivery (weeks) | Total cost 10+11+ 12+13 |
| | | | Hrs | £ | Hrs | £ | Hrs | £ | Hrs | £ | | | | | |

Figure 18.1  A general purpose cost estimating form for manufacturing projects

## COST ESTIMATE FOR MATERIALS AND PURCHASED EQUIPMENT

Estimate number:
Case:
Date:
Page          of

Project number
or sales reference:

Compiled by:

Estimate for:

| Cost code | Description | Spec No. (if known) | Proposed supplier | Unit | Unit cost FOB | Quoted currency | Exchange rate used | Converted FOB cost | Qty | Project FOB cost | Ship mode | Freight cost | Taxes/ duties | Delivered cost |
|---|---|---|---|---|---|---|---|---|---|---|---|---|---|---|
| | | | | | | | | | | | | | | |
| | | | | | | | | | | | | | | |
| | | | | | | | | | | | | | | |
| | | | | | | | | | | | | | | |
| | | | | | | | | | | | | | | |
| | | | | | | | | | | | | | | |
| | | | | | | | | | | | | | | |
| | | | | | | | | | | | | | | |
| | | | | | | | | | | | | | | |
| | | | | | | | | | | | | | | |
| | | | | | | | | | | | | | | |

Total delivered materials and equipment costs this page

**Figure 18.2   Cost estimating form for purchased materials where international transport is involved**

303

means that supplier's price in each case includes packaging the goods and delivering them on to a ship or aircraft. Thereafter the buyer must pay all freight, insurance and agents' charges plus destination port charges, import duties and taxes. Columns have therefore been provided in the tabulation for these items. The column headed 'Ship mode' is simply to indicate whether the main part of the journey is to be by sea, air or road. FOB is one of a set of internationally recognized abbreviations for international terms of trade known as Incoterms. These are regulated and published by the International Chamber of Commerce.

## PROJECT CURRENCY

Most large projects involve transactions in foreign currencies. This can give rise to uncertainty and risk when exchange rates fluctuate. Some mitigation of this effect can be achieved if the contract includes safeguards or if all quotations can be obtained in the home currency of the project contractor. Otherwise it must be a matter for skill, careful judgement and foresight. A glance at Figure 18.2 will show that columns have been allocated for the conversion of foreign exchange rates. In large projects costs will typically arise in different countries and are likely to be quoted or incurred in a variety of currencies. This can greatly complicate the estimator's job, and any subsequent attempt at using the total estimate for budgeting and cost management. A common solution to this problem is to convert all costs into one currency, which might then be called the project control currency. The project control currency is likely to be that which applies in the country of the contractor's head office, but it might instead have to be a currency convenient to, and specified by, an overseas client. Whether or not the contractor wishes to disclose the exchange rates used in reaching its final cost estimates, the rates used for all conversions must be shown on all estimate tabulations and similar internal documents.

## SOURCES OF LABOUR ESTIMATES

Records from past projects have already been mentioned as a basis for comparative estimating. In some industries, particularly those associated with construction, published tables can be consulted. Estimates of labour times where no previous records exist are more difficult to obtain. Theoretically, they are best made by the managers who will eventually be responsible for working within the resulting budget limits. But not everyone has good estimating ability.

## PERSONAL ESTIMATING ABILITIES

Project cost estimating is not an exact science. Much of the process, particularly when estimating labour times, has to rely on the subjective judgement of individuals. If any ten people were to be asked separately to judge the time needed for a particular project task, it is hardly conceivable that ten identical answers would be received. Repeat this exercise with the same group of people for a number of different project tasks, and it is likely that a pattern will emerge. Some people will tend always to estimate on the low side. Others might give answers that are consistently high. The person collecting project cost estimates needs to be aware of this problem. In fact, just as it is possible to classify estimates according to confidence in their accuracy, so it is possible to classify the estimators themselves. I evolved the following classifications when dealing with estimates for design and manufacturing times on fairly large engineering projects.

- *Optimistic estimators* usually understate the time required for tasks. A person asked to estimate the time needed for a design task might, for example, say 'three weeks' when the initial task will actually take four weeks. It is likely that still more work will be needed later on as corrections have to be made to the drawings (sometimes called after-issue work). Most estimators are optimists.
- *Pessimistic estimators* always underestimate and demand too much time and too many resources. Such people might be seeking to build empires. Fortunately they are less common than the optimists.
- *Inconsistent estimators* lack the capability and skill to understand what is required of a task.
- *Accurate estimators* are too rare to be considered.

The person responsible for compiling the final project cost estimate will learn to recognize these personal characteristics. It might even be necessary to apply a correction factor to some of the raw estimates.

## BELOW-THE-LINE COSTS

When the costs for every work package have been estimated, adding them all together should give the total cost for the project. It is true that this should give the basic net cost but, for most projects, additional costs also have to be taken into account. So a line can be drawn under the net total cost, and below that line two or three important additions are usually needed.

## CONTINGENCY ALLOWANCES

A common source of estimating errors is the failure to appreciate that additional costs are almost bound to arise as the result of design errors, problems in the physical execution of the project, material and component failures, construction site difficulties and the like. The extent of these additional items will depend on many factors but performance on previous similar projects can give an indication of what to expect. For a straightforward project, not entailing undue risk, a contingency allowance of 5 per cent of the net project cost might be appropriate. It might have to be higher, but contingency allowances usually have to be applied with restraint in order to maintain competitive project pricing.

## COST ESCALATION

Every year wages and salaries increase, many raw materials and bought-out components cost more and indirect costs rise in a process we all know as inflation. The effect on a project that is estimated, quoted and carried out within a short period is not likely to be significant in a country with a stable economy and low annual rate of inflation. In other cases, however, and especially for projects with a life cycle covering several years, the effects of inflation can be significant. There are three complementary ways in which this problem can be tackled.

1. The validity of the price quoted must be limited to a specified period. That should prevent a customer from being able to accept a quotation based on cost estimates that have become outdated through long delays in signing the contract.
2. Another action for countering cost inflation is to write a cost escalation clause into the contract. The contractor should then be able to agree a price addition with the client if there are increases in wages and materials that are recognized as being outside the contractor's control.
3. A cost escalation allowance can be made below the line in the project estimate. Depending on the method used, this can be quite a complex calculation. Once a percentage annual escalation rate has been agreed, the most accurate method is to look at each cost element in turn, decide when that cost is likely to be incurred, and then work out the likely additional costs according to the predicted elapsed time and the escalation rate.

## PROVISIONAL ITEMS

It often happens, particularly in construction contracts, that the project contractor foresees the possibility of additional expense if certain pre-identified difficulties arise when work actually starts. For example, a client might specify that certain materials salvaged during demolition of a building are to be reused in the construction of a new replacement building. So, the cost of those materials should be free to the new project, they will not appear in the net project estimate and they will not be incorporated in the quoted price. The contractor might wish to make provision in case the salvaged materials are found to be unsuitable for reuse. To allow for that risk, a provisional item can be added below the line to cover the estimated cost of providing new materials. It is not unusual for a project proposal to include several items priced as provisional sums.

## COST BUDGETS

The initial project budgets must be derived from the cost estimates used when the tender or internal project proposal was prepared. These denote the authorized level of expenditure for all departments engaged on the project. Ideally the departmental managers, even if they did not provide the cost estimate data, should have had prior opportunity to approve the estimates and accept commitment to them.

### BUDGET BREAKDOWN

The total budget should be spread over the project work breakdown structure so that there is a specified budget for each work package and, within those work packages, a budget for each task. Each of these budget elements must have a unique cost code against which manpower time sheet data, material costs and all other direct expenses can be collected and accumulated.

### LABOUR BUDGETS

It is often said, with good reason, that managers should be given their work budgets in terms of man-hours rather than as the resulting costs of wages and overheads. The argument is that a manager should never be held accountable for meeting targets where he or she has no authority to control the causal factors. Project managers are rarely responsible for general increases in wages and salaries or for company overhead expenses. They are, however, responsible for progress and (through supervision) the time taken to complete each task. It is assumed here, therefore, that each manager will be given, and will be expected to observe, the man-hour budget for every work package under his or her control.

### BUDGETS FOR PURCHASES AND SUBCONTRACTS

Budgets for purchases and for subcontracts have to be expressed in the appropriate project currency. Relevant packaging, transport, insurance, duties and tax must be included. When these budgets are set out as time-scaled graphs, there are three possible options on how the timing should be determined. Depending on which option is chosen, the graphs will be displaced in time by several months. The options are as follows:

1. The earliest option, the time when each cost is committed by the signing of a contract or the issue of a purchase order.
2. The middle option, the time when payments have to be made against suppliers' and subcontractors' invoices.
3. The final option, the time when the materials are withdrawn from stores for use on the project.

The first of these is most appropriate for cost control. The second is relevant to cash flow prediction and funding. The third is of more interest for historical cost accounting.

### BUDGET ADJUSTMENTS FOR BELOW-THE-LINE ALLOWANCES

All budgets should initially be based on net project estimates, with below-the-line allowances excluded. Below-the-line items, especially contingencies, should be regarded as carefully guarded reserve budgets. Subject to an effective authorization procedure, appropriate sums can be 'drawn down' from these reserves from time to time to augment the control budget as legitimate needs arise.

### BUDGET CHANGES

Budgets on most projects are not static. They change each time a customer-requested change results in an agreed change to the project price. At any time it should be possible for the budget to be stated in terms of its initial amount, additions (or deletions) subsequently approved by the client and, therefore, the total current authorized budget.

## COST MONITORING USING SIMPLE GRAPHS

When project work starts, the project manager and others will want to know whether the rate of expenditure is in line with the plan. One common method is to draw a graph of budgeted costs against time and then compare the actual costs against it periodically.

## DRAWING A TIME-SCALED BUDGET GRAPH

The simplest way to draw a budget graph is to consult the schedule to find the project's start and finish dates, assume that expenditure is zero at the start, put a point representing total expenditure on the completion date and then join the project start and finish points with a straight line budget. That idea can obviously be dismissed at once because it makes the wrong assumption that expenditure will be linear.

It is necessary, therefore, to examine the elements of a budget in more detail. Each work package or, better still, each task should first be positioned in the time frame by reference to the detailed project plan. Then, using a cumulative build up of budgeted costs, a curve can be plotted that should reflect more realistically the planned rate of expenditure. When authorized changes affect the project budget, the curve should be stepped up or down by the appropriate amounts at the relevant dates. Cumulative project expenditure typically follows an S-shaped curve, starting with a low rate, then moving through a centre period of high activity until, finally, the rate slows down and the curve becomes asymptotic to the final cost.

## DATA SOURCES

Two points need to be made about the sources for the budget and actual cost data:

1. Care should be taken to ensure that the budget basis and actual cost basis correspond, so that like is compared with like. This applies not only to the selection of tasks or work packages, but also to the times when the relevant costs are to be considered.
2. The sources of actual cost data must allow collection as soon as possible in the project life cycle, so that adverse trends can be picked up in time for corrective action.

Direct labour costs should be considered as soon as the periodical time bookings can be analysed. Common practice is to collect and analyse time bookings weekly. The accounting system should be capable of allocating and costing these with little or no delay, provided there are no communication difficulties in collecting them. Any processing delay, at the outside, must not be allowed to exceed three or four days if the data are to be used effectively.

Claims expected from contractors and subcontractors should be budgeted at the times when they are planned to arrive. This information can be calculated by comparing the relevant tasks on the project schedule and the terms of payment agreed for the contracts. The collection of actual cost data for these claims should be possible at any time by adding the value of payments already made to claims received but not yet processed. Some contractors, however, can be very late in submitting claims, in which case provisional allowances (accrued costs) will have to be added to the actual cost data to avoid errors of omission.

Purchases of materials and equipment must be budgeted to coincide with the planned purchase order issue dates. For comparison, committed rather than actual invoiced costs have to be collected and accumulated. This means adding the values of all purchase orders as they are issued. Although it is the resulting invoices that will determine the actual final costs, that information will not be available in time for use in any cost control decisions. Indeed, such invoices sometimes continue to arrive after project completion.

## A SIMPLE EXAMPLE

The dotted curve in Figure 18.3 is an example of a planned cost curve (a time-scaled budget). This is for a construction project planned to last for 56 weeks with a net budget of £1 450 000. The curve has been plotted at four-weekly intervals. Now imagine that you are the manager of this project. You want to compare the actual project costs with the budget graph throughout the life of the project.

Your first task must be to establish the sources of your actual cost data. You should expect to receive direct labour cost reports from your accountant or your organization's management information system after prompt analysis of the time booked by the personnel involved. For contractors' claims you will probably have the services of a project cost engineer or a contract administration department. Your purchasing organization is likely to be the best source for the total value of materials and equipment costs committed at any given time.

Now consider Figure 18.3. Every four weeks you or, if you are fortunate, your administrative assistant plots the actual cumulative cost of the project on the same axes as your budget graph. It is now just past the end of week 28. You note, with satisfaction, that expenditure is running consistently below budget. The planned expenditure by the end of week 28 is £350 000 and the actual expenditure is only £280 000. There are managers who would be well satisfied with this state of affairs but what can *you* deduce from this? In fact, not a great deal. Only one thing is certain, which is that the project started late. Low spending at the start indicates insufficient input of resources in the very early weeks. In order to deduce more about the true cost performance at week 28 you need to know what has been achieved.

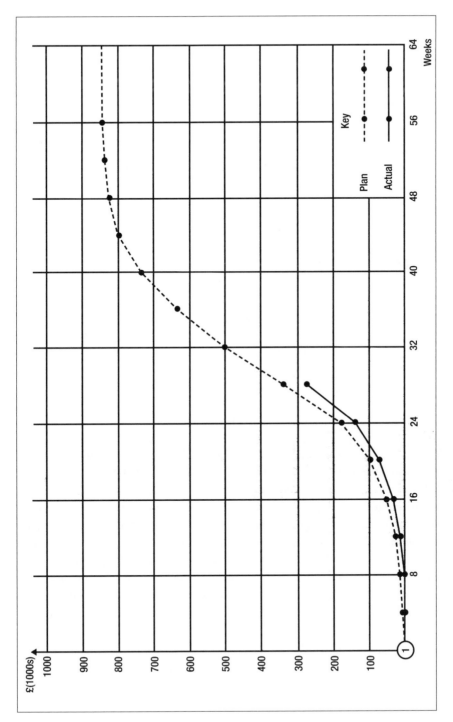

Figure 18.3  Comparison of actual costs against budget using simple graphs

311

The significance of the $S$ curve alone for assessing cost performance is, therefore, coarse and very limited. A method is needed that brings some measure of related achievement into the argument and which can provide answers to all the following questions:

1. How much have we spent to date?
2. What should we have spent to date?
3. What have we achieved so far?
4. What should we have achieved?
5. What implication do the answers to these questions have for the final cost of the project?

Milestone monitoring can provide the answers to at least some of these questions.

## MILESTONE MONITORING

Milestone monitoring (or milestone analysis) is one of the simpler methods by which managers can compare actual costs and progress with a project budget and schedule of work. The method is neither the most effective nor the most detailed, but it has the merit of needing only a modest amount of effort to set up and maintain. It also has the advantage of being useful where the project plans and work breakdown structure are not available in great detail.

### IDENTIFYING MILESTONES

The first step in milestone analysis is obviously to decide what milestones are. This is done by identifying certain key activities or events which lie at the boundaries between significant phases of the project. Put another way, a milestone denotes a particular, easily recognized stage in the progress of a project towards completion. The start and finish of the project are two obvious examples. Others might be the customer's acceptance of the final design, the issue of a package of drawings or the day when work starts on a construction site.

Ideally, milestones should coincide with the completion of packages from the work breakdown structure. That approach will be assumed in the remainder of this discussion. For each milestone, two essential pieces of information are needed:

1. The date for which the milestone is planned.
2. The associated budget cost. In the simplest method (described here) this is taken as the budgeted cost of all the project work and expenditure at the milestone date.

## PLOTTING THE MILESTONE GRAPHS

### The milestone/budget curve

With all milestone data available, the milestone/budget curve can be plotted. There is more than one method for doing this, but the simplest is to start by drawing the time-scaled budget graph (the $S$ curve) in the same way as in the previous example. Then the date for each milestone can be indicated by placing a symbol at the relevant points on the graph. Graph legibility will be greatly enhanced if all the milestones are identified by simple codes. If, for example, the planned milestones are numbered 1, 2, 3, etc., the corresponding symbols on the graph can use the same numbers, so avoiding the clutter of too much data in a small space.

### Plotting the actual results

As milestones are delivered, actual cumulative costs are plotted on the same axes as the graph of planned costs. Symbols for completed milestones can be added to the actual cost graph on the dates when the milestones are achieved. To be able to plot these results for comparison against the plan, two further facts must be established for each completed milestone:

1. The date on which the milestone was actually achieved.
2. The actual project expenditure incurred or committed up to that date.

### MILESTONE EXAMPLE

The simple example now described uses the same construction project and the same cost data as that introduced in the previous case. Figure 18.4 illustrates the milestone monitoring process. As in the previous case, the dotted curve represents the time-scaled budget and the solid line is the plotted actual expenditure up to the end of Week 28. Milestones have been added to the budget curve at their planned times. Milestone achievement dates are shown by the black diamonds on the actual cost curve. Cost and progress data for the milestones are set out separately in Figure 18.5.

### INTERPRETING THE RESULTS

The best way to appreciate the use of this method is to imagine yourself, as project manager, observing the relationship between the planned and actual graphs as the project weeks go by. Your first reaction must be frustration at the late start of the project. In milestone language, Milestone 1 has been delayed by

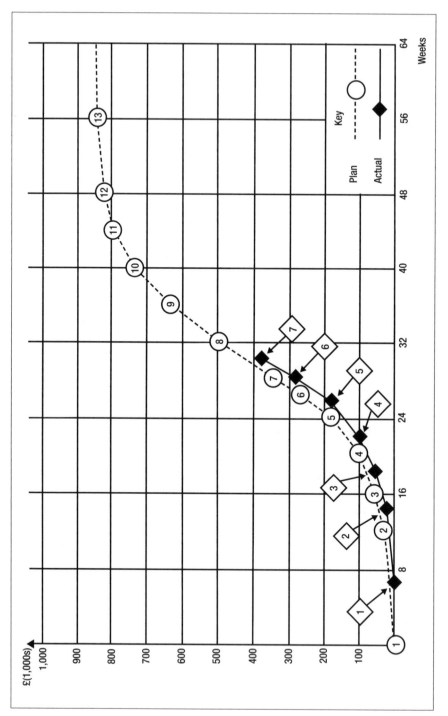

Figure 18.4 Comparison of actual costs against budget using milestones

314

| Milestone description | Schedule (week number) | | Cumulative cost £(1000s) | |
|---|---|---|---|---|
| | Plan | Actual | Budget | Actual |
| 1  Project start authorized | 0 | 6 | 0 | 0 |
| 2  Design approved | 12 | 14 | 25 | 20 |
| 3  Drawings issued for building | 16 | 18 | 60 | 55 |
| 4  Foundations completed | 20 | 22 | 100 | 100 |
| 5  Drawings issued for services | 24 | 26 | 180 | 180 |
| 6  All equipment for services ordered | 26 | 28 | 275 | 285 |
| 7  Walls built to eaves | 28 | 30 | 350 | 380 |
| 8  Windows and doors finished | 32 | | 500 | |
| 9  Roof on, building watertight | 36 | | 630 | |
| 10  Wiring and plumbing finished | 40 | | 730 | |
| 11  Services installed and tested | 44 | | 795 | |
| 12  Internal finishes completed | 48 | | 825 | |
| 13  Site and building handover | 56 | | 845 | |

Figure 18.5   Milestone data measured at Week 28 of the example

six weeks. However, it can be seen from the graphs, and from the table in Figure 18.5, that progress has improved as the project proceeds. Four weeks of the initial slippage were recovered, so that milestone achievement dates are now generally falling two weeks behind schedule.

How do these results relate to costs? Although the graph of actual costs is running consistently below the budget line, comparison between the planned and actual milestone performance gives a more revealing picture. Look at Milestone 5. Although completed two weeks later than plan, the budgeted and actual costs are practically in line. The situation has deteriorated somewhat by the time Milestone 6 has been achieved. Now, not only is the programme running two weeks late, but the costs are starting to exceed those budgeted. At Milestone 7, the two-week lag remains and the actual cost to achieve this milestone has been £380 000 against a budget of £350 000. The graphs show that this divergence between planned and actual costs is increasing with time. Unless effective action can be taken to reverse this trend, the project is likely to be completed at no profit or even at a loss.

## VALUE OF THE MILESTONE METHOD

The milestone method is not perfect. It is a compromise between attempting no comparison at all between planned and actual cost performance and committing the considerable effort needed for full-scale earned value analysis (which is outlined in the following section of this chapter). The principal disadvantages of milestone analysis can be summarized as follows:

1. The quantities measured tend to be rather coarse, at intervals which might be too infrequent.
2. Analysis is historical rather than predictive, so results may be obtained too late for the most effective action to be taken to reverse bad trends.
3. Work in progress is not properly considered or is not considered at all.

However, the method involves comparatively little effort and is a considerable improvement on the simple comparison of actual and budget cost graphs. It may, therefore, be attractive and useful to the project manager who has insufficient time and resources for carrying out more detailed analysis and prediction.

## COST REPORTING BASED ON EARNED VALUE

### THE CONCEPT OF EARNED VALUE ANALYSIS

Earned value analysis is an analytical method for comparing actual performance against planned performance in considerable depth of detail. Although the name is fairly new, the concept is not and many writers were describing it as long ago as the 1950s and 1960s under other names (in my own case as achievement analysis). As a predictive tool it can be regarded as the missing link between historical project cost reporting and active cost management. There is more than one approach to the method, but the procedure generally followed is outlined in Chapter 26.

At each review date the process aims to discover the true earned value achieved for all tasks completed or in progress. The results allow a cost performance index (CPI) to be calculated. This factor can be used to adjust the cost estimates for all remaining work (costs remaining to completion) on the assumption that the standard of cost performance achieved up to the review date will continue unchanged to the end of the project.

### REPORT TABULATION

Figure 18.6 shows a fairly typical layout for a project cost report based on earned value analysis. The number of pages in the complete document will obviously depend on the size of the project, but pages should be grouped logically in sets according to the work breakdown structure. Page totals can then be summarized on a sheet for the total project, at the top level of the work breakdown, and it is only this summary (sometimes called a rolled-up summary) which is likely to be used in project cost reports to the more senior management. A column-by-column examination of the tabulation will explain the procedure in more detail.

316

# PROJECT COST REPORT SUMMARY

Project title:

Project number:

Page     of

Report date:

| A Item | B Cost code | C Original budget | D Authorized budget changes | E Authorized current budget C+D | F ACWP | G BCWP (assessed) | H CPI G/F | J Forecast costs remaining (E–G)/H | K Forecast costs at completion F+J | L Forecast variance at completion E–K |
|--------|-------------|-------------------|------------------------------|----------------------------------|--------|-------------------|-----------|-----------------------------------|-----------------------------------|---------------------------------------|
|        |             |                   |                              |                                  |        |                   |           |                                   |                                   |                                       |

Sheet summary

**Figure 18.6   Project cost report summary based on earned values**

317

## Column A

The choice of items listed in this column will depend on where the particular page fits into the work breakdown structure. At the project summary level only the major work packages would be listed, but at lower levels it would be necessary to list all the tasks.

## Column B

The preferred choice for this column is to show the relevant item cost code from the project organization's coding system. In some projects, however, project clients expect to receive these reports (perhaps after suitable editing) and they have a habit of preferring to see codes that relate to their own system. This will be particularly true where the project manager and client work closely together in the periodical release of project funding by the client. It may, therefore, be necessary to arrange for two coding systems to be used on the same report.

## Column C

The original budget for the project, before any changes, is shown in this column. A decision will have to be made as to whether this will include all below-the-line allowances. Usually it is safer to exclude these until they can be added as authorized budget changes.

## Column D

This column is used to show the total budget changes authorized up to the report date. These changes might arise from the release of amounts held in reserve as contingencies or other below-the-line estimates but are more likely to come from authorized changes requested by the customer or client.

## Column E

This column gives the current budget. This should be the original budget plus amounts authorized by subsequent customer-funded changes or release of below-the-line allowances.

## Column F

The actual cost of work performed (ACWP) is entered here. For each item this usually means all direct labour and expenses used to the review date, plus the total value of all purchase orders issued and the value of any contractors' claims paid or awaiting payment. These costs must be entered for all items that have incurred costs, whether or not they are completed. Thus these costs include work in progress.

## Column G

The entries in Column G require careful attention. For each item the budgeted cost of work performed (BCWP) is wanted, measured at the review date. It is here that the concept of earned value is introduced. For any item, one of three conditions might apply at the review date:

1.  Work may not have been started, so that there is no earned value and BCWP is zero.
2.  The item might be finished, in which case maximum value has been earned. The BCWP for a completed item is equal to its current authorized budget (Column E).
3.  For every item which has been started but not finished, the earned value has to be assessed. There are several methods, but one way is to judge the percentage completion for the item. The BCWP can then be taken as that percentage of the current authorized budget.

## Column H

This column is optional and many companies do not include it. When the BCWP is divided by the corresponding ACWP a cost performance index (CPI) is obtained. This is an indicator of how efficiently money is being spent on each item. A CPI of less than one for a completed item means that the item's authorized budget has been exceeded. Similarly, when measured during work in progress a CPI of less than one means that the assessed earned value is less than the costs so far incurred.

## Column J

When £40 000 has been spent on a task out of a total budget of £100 000 a reasonable question to ask is 'How much will the work remaining cost? Will it exceed or lie within the £60 000 budget remaining?' This question should be asked for every item and for the whole project. Here are three conditions that could apply to any item.

1.  The item has not started. There is no earned value. The costs remaining should, therefore, be the whole of the authorized budget. If, however, the average CPI for the project is less than one, indicating overspending, the project administrator might decide to divide the budget by the CPI to make a more realistic prediction of the likely cost to complete. This is not, of course,

an increase in the authorized budget. It is simply a way of attempting to face and report facts. If current performance on other tasks is taken as the norm, this task too is likely to exceed its budget.

2. The item is finished. In that case there should be no cost remaining.
3. The item is in progress. Then the first step in deciding the remaining cost is to start with the value earned to date (BCWP) and subtract that from the total value (the current budget). That gives the remaining value to be earned. That figure must be divided by the CPI to adjust the remaining estimate in the light of the cost performance actually being experienced.

## Column K

Adding the forecast costs remaining to completion and the costs actually incurred to date should predict the total final cost.

## Column L

This column shows the difference between the authorized current budget and the predicted final cost.

## EFFECTIVENESS OF THE EARNED VALUE METHOD

It is easy to place too much reliance on earned value analysis predictions. Results are likely to be flawed for several reasons. Here are some of them:

- It is difficult to assess accurately the amount of work achieved on many kinds of tasks.
- Difficulty is likely to be greatest when a task has just started, so that prediction errors will be greatest at the times when they are most needed, which is early enough in the project for corrective action to be effective.
- The project manager will not find it easy to get everyone's cooperation in supplying complete and reasonably accurate data at the review dates.
- A considerable amount of clerical effort is needed to maintain the database and carry out the calculations. It is unlikely that such effort will be free of errors.
- If a computer is used to process the data, rubbish can more easily result than not. Suppose that work on a particular task is scrapped. The BCWP and CPI for that task both revert to zero at the point where the task is stopped and restarted. Dividing the remaining budget by the CPI gives infinity. So the project administrator must choose a different basis for calculating the CPI. One option is to calculate the CPI for the whole project and use that.

These observations are not intended to deter the reader from implementing an earned value system, but the difficulties in making it work should be realized.

## REFERENCES AND FURTHER READING

Barnes, M. (1990), *Financial Control*, Thomas Telford, London.
Bull, J. W. (1992), *Life Cycle Costing for Construction*, Blackie Academic, London.
Carter, R. and Wheeler, R. (1995), *How to Cut Costs by 20%*, Kogan Page, London.
Fleming, Q. W. and Koppelman, J. M. (1996), *Earned Value Project Management*, Project Management Institute, Upper Darby, PA.
George, D. J. (ed.) (1988), *A Guide to Capital Cost Estimating*, 3rd edition, Institution of Chemical Engineers, Rugby.
Kwakye, A. A. (1994), *Understanding Tendering and Estimating (for Construction Industry and Architects)*, Gower, Aldershot.
Smith, N. J. (ed.) (1995), *Project Cost Estimating*, Thomas Telford, London.
Stewart, R. (1991), *Cost Estimating*, 2nd edition, Wiley, New York.
Sweeting, J. (1997), *Project Cost Estimating: Principles and Practices*, Institution of Chemical Engineers, Rugby.
Wearne, S. H. (1989), *Control of Engineering Projects*, Thomas Telford, London.

## RELATED TOPICS

# 19 Managing the schedule

## Dennis Lock

Most people would agree that scheduling ranks high in the skills needed for successful project management. It is required to:

- ensure that the project is delivered at a time to make a worthwhile profit;
- coordinate the activities of the resources working on the project (Chapter 20);
- schedule expenditure.

During the first half of the twentieth century the principal scheduling tool was the bar chart. These diagrams are often called Gantt charts after the American engineer, Henry Gantt, who developed them for production scheduling in a munitions factory towards the end of the First World War. Gantt charts continue to be popular today, mainly as a tool to communicate the schedule to the people working on the project (Chapters 20 and 25). However, the amount of information they can convey is limited, both in terms of the practical number of project tasks and in the way in which those tasks can be shown to interrelate. In the 1950s a new family of techniques emerged which overcame these limitations. These were all based on the use of diagrams called critical path networks. As with Gantt charts, the exploitation of these critical path diagrams was accelerated and publicized following their successful use on high priority military projects in America. Several early versions of the critical path method can, however, be traced back to a number of different sources in Europe as well as America. Morris (1997) gives a full historical account of all these developments but here we shall concentrate on two versions of the critical path method in common use at the beginning of the twenty-first century.

## PREPARATION FOR SCHEDULING

The scheduling process is followed through this chapter using a small project (the furniture project) as a case study. A medium-sized furniture company wishes to embark on a project to add two new items of furniture to its catalogue. These are a desk with a single drawer and a simple but comfortable chair. The desk design is expected to be straightforward but the company's marketing manager has asked for an anatomical study to be conducted on statistical data to determine the ideal size and shape for the chair. The person in charge of this project is a senior design engineer, who will be assigned as project leader. She is able to draw on various people throughout the company from time to time to join her small team as she needs them, so that finding resources for this small project should present no problem. The project scope covers design, manufacture and evaluation of one prototype desk and chair set.

## PROJECT WORK BREAKDOWN AND TASK LIST

The project leader knows that one of her first tasks is to make a project schedule. She has decided to start by listing all the known tasks or activities (the words task and activity are used synonymously throughout this chapter). The list divides into three parts:

1. General project tasks
2. Tasks connected only with the chair
3. Tasks connected only with the desk

The list is set out in a very simple form of work breakdown structure. Had the project been bigger, this division into separate parts or work packages would have been more necessary and significant. The completed task list is given in Figure 19.1.

## ESTIMATING THE TASK DURATIONS

In consultation with her colleagues, the project leader must estimate how long each task is likely to take. Each estimate is for the total time expected to elapse between starting a task and finishing it. That time is irrespective of the number of people needed if, indeed, any people are needed at all. Each duration estimate must include non-productive time, such as waiting for glue to set during assembly. These duration estimates, therefore, serve a different purpose from those made for cost estimating. They are concerned primarily with task times as they collectively determine the length of the project life cycle. This furniture is to be made in the company's prototype workshop. The workshop manager should, therefore, be asked to estimate all the workshop task durations. For the times needed to buy all the materials, the project leader should ask the purchasing

| Activity number | Activity description | Duration (days) | Preceding activities |
|---|---|---|---|
| | *Chair* | | |
| 01 | Anatomical study for chair | 15 | None |
| 02 | Design chair | 5 | 01 |
| 03 | Buy materials for chair seat | 6 | 02 |
| 04 | Make chair seat | 3 | 03 |
| 05 | Buy chair castors | 5 | 02 |
| 06 | Buy steel for chair frame | 10 | 02 |
| 07 | Make chair frame | 3 | 06 |
| 08 | Paint chair frame | 2 | 07, 21 |
| 09 | Assemble chair | 1 | 04, 05, 08 |
| 10 | Apply final finishes to chair | 2 | 09 |
| | *Desk* | | |
| 11 | Design desk | 10 | None |
| 12 | Buy steel for desk frame | 10 | 11 |
| 13 | Make desk frame | 5 | 12, 15 |
| 14 | Paint desk frame | 2 | 13, 21 |
| 15 | Buy wood and fittings for desk | 5 | 15 |
| 16 | Make desk drawer | 6 | 15 |
| 17 | Make desk top | 1 | 15 |
| 18 | Assemble desk | 1 | 14, 16, 17 |
| 19 | Apply final finishes to desk | 2 | 18 |
| | *General activities* | | |
| 20 | Decide paint colours | 10 | None |
| 21 | Buy paint and varnish | 8 | 20 |
| 22 | Final project evaluation | 5 | 10, 19 |

**Figure 19.1    Task list for the furniture project**

manager, but she should herself know how much time to allow for the design tasks.

## UNITS OF DURATION AND THE PROJECT CALENDAR

A project schedule is likely to be expressed in time units of days, weeks or months, the choice depending on the size and duration of the project. The furniture project is small and simple, so the project leader has decided to estimate every task in days. She knows that her company normally works a five-day week, so that an estimate of five days' duration really means five weekdays (equivalent to a calendar week). If the schedule is eventually entered in a computer for processing, it is likely that the default calendar in the project management software will also assume a five-day week.

## Public holidays

If the furniture company is to shut down for public holidays, or for any other general holiday, the weekdays affected will have to be removed from the default calendar to prevent tasks from being scheduled during the holiday period.

## Alternative calendars

Project management software will usually allow the planner to create one or more special calendars. One of these can be assigned to an activity in place of the default calendar to overcome the following kinds of problems:

- When a task can be allowed to occupy six or seven days a week instead of being limited to the five weekdays in the default calendar.
- When a task is to be performed over more than one shift in a 24-hour period.
- Where the duration can include passive time that can span a weekend, such as watching the grass grow.
- Where the schedule calls for tasks to be performed in parts of the world with different public or religious holidays or working weeks.

Special calendars are explained at length in Chapter 20.

## Conversion of numbers to calendar dates

Project schedules are often compiled before the start date of the project is known. In those cases it is not possible, therefore, to put calendar dates on the schedule. All the examples in this chapter use day numbers or week numbers. In practice, day numbers or week numbers are inconvenient and mean little unless they can be related to the calendar. In any case, conversion of times to calendar dates from a schedule containing only numbers is tedious, time-consuming and prone to human error. For the furniture project it is assumed that the project leader will eventually use a computer to process the schedule. When the start date has been decided, the computer will base its calculations from that date and convert all day numbers into calendar dates before printing out the various reports.

## TASK SEQUENCE

The project leader must decide the sequence in which the tasks are to be done. She must consider each task in turn and note which tasks, if any, precede it. For example, the chair design cannot start until the anatomical study has been completed. Before the chair frame can be painted, two other tasks must have been finished, namely to make the frame and buy the paint. These relationships are difficult to show clearly in a simple list. However, all the tasks have been given identification numbers, and this has simplified the project leader's problem. For every task in the furniture project list, she has entered the identification numbers of tasks that must immediately precede it in the extreme right-hand column of Figure 19.1.

## SCHEDULING THE FURNITURE PROJECT USING A BAR CHART

### SIMPLE BAR CHART

Figure 19.2 shows the result when the furniture project leader attempted to produce a working schedule using a bar chart. The purpose of such a schedule must be twofold:

- To inform her superiors in the company of the intended project timescale.
- For use as a progressing tool throughout the short life of this project.

The bar chart will succeed in the first of these two aims as soon as calendar dates can be substituted for day numbers. It is a good visual aid and sets out the intentions clearly. Every task is depicted graphically in its allotted time slot. The chart is easy to understand for project management experts and non-experts alike. From the project leader's viewpoint, however, the chart is of less value. Its most significant failing is that it does not show which tasks have to be finished before others can start. When the chart is first set up on an adjustable board or drawn on paper, the project leader can observe all the relationships indicated in the final column of the task list. This can be quite a mental challenge, but a person with suitable aptitude can do it, provided that the project is not too big. The real difficulties come when the schedule has to be updated. Then it is easy for errors to creep in.

### LINKED BAR CHART

A linked bar chart can be used to indicate task interdependencies. This has been done for the furniture project in Figure 19.3. However, even for this small project it has not been easy for the project leader to show every interconnection between different tasks. She did not find it possible in this case to show the link from the end of the task to buy paint and varnish to the two frame painting tasks. On a larger project this difficulty would have been more serious. The notation provided by this method is therefore inadequate, or at least extremely limited, even for the small furniture project.

There are computer programs which can plot linked bar charts quite well.

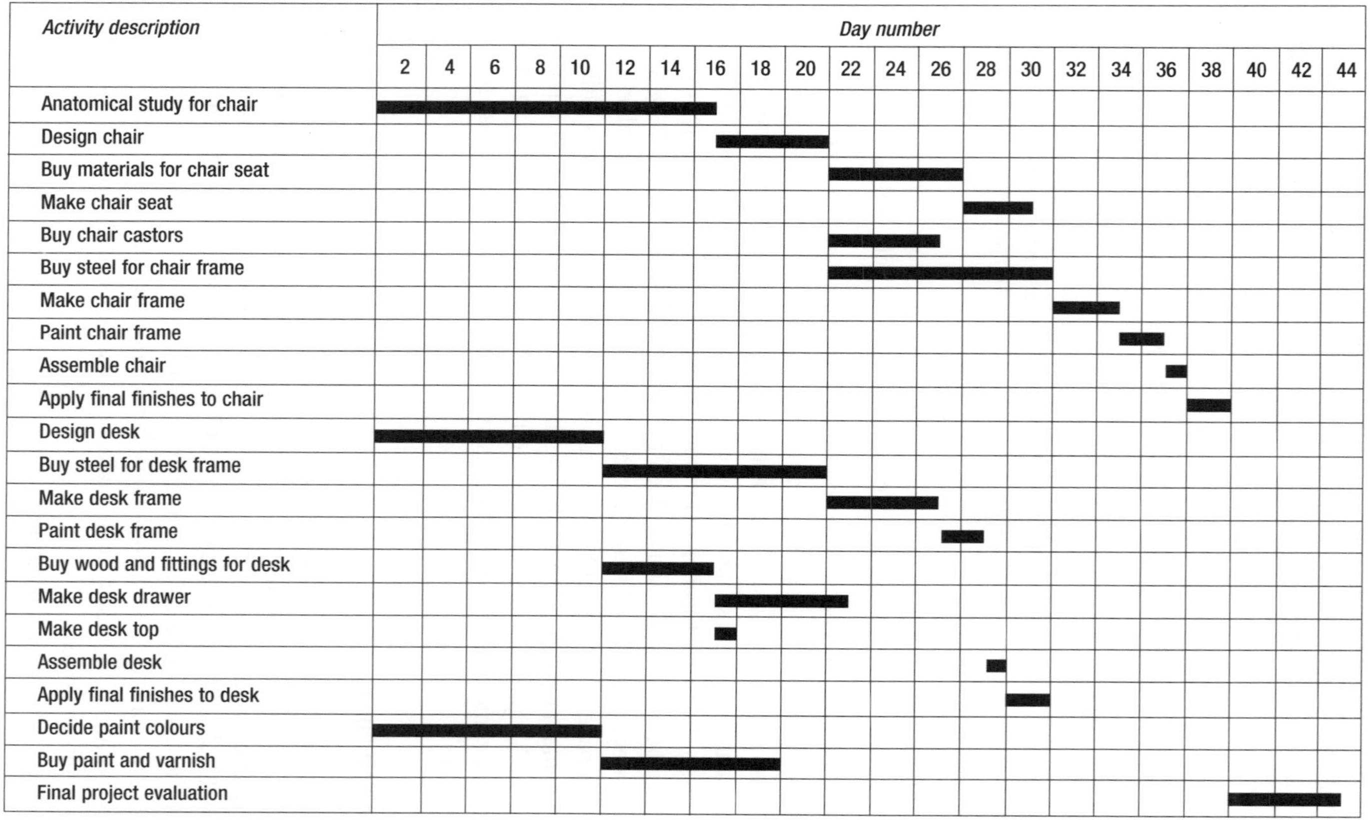

**Activity description** / **Day number**

2 4 6 8 10 12 14 16 18 20 22 24 26 28 30 32 34 36 38 40 42 44

Anatomical study for chair
Design chair
Buy materials for chair seat
Make chair seat
Buy chair castors
Buy steel for chair frame
Make chair frame
Paint chair frame
Assemble chair
Apply final finishes to chair
Design desk
Buy steel for desk frame
Make desk frame
Paint desk frame
Buy wood and fittings for desk
Make desk drawer
Make desk top
Assemble desk
Apply final finishes to desk
Decide paint colours
Buy paint and varnish
Final project evaluation

**Figure 19.2    Bar chart for the furniture project**

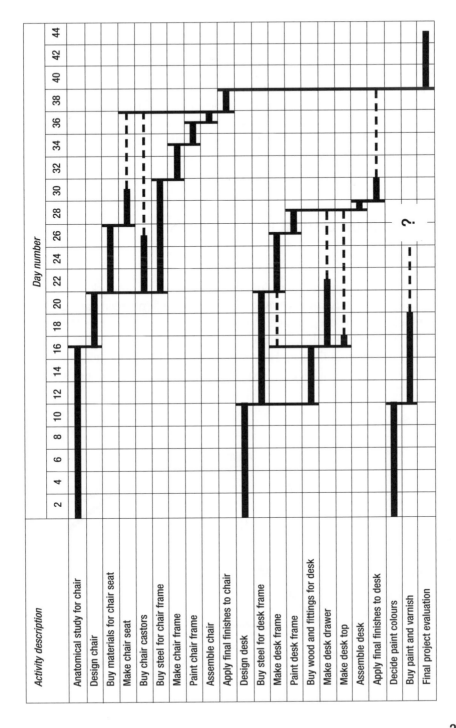

**Figure 19.3  Linked bar chart for the furniture project**

Microsoft Project is a notable example. These solve the problem of inflexibility associated with hand-drawn charts. Their value, however, remains limited because of the visual difficulty in trying to follow the paths of all the link lines on anything except the very simplest project.

The project leader must look for another scheduling method to overcome these problems. Her answer lies in using some form of critical path network. She has two variations from which to choose: activity-on-arrow and activity-on-node. Each of these methods has its advantages and disadvantages. Both will now be described, first in principle and then as the project leader applied them to her furniture project.

## ACTIVITY-ON-ARROW CRITICAL PATH NETWORKS

### THE NOTATION

All the essential notational elements of an activity-on-arrow network diagram are shown in Figure 19.4. Arrow networks (as they are often called) are easier to sketch quickly than precedence networks (described later). They lend themselves to rapid sketching, erasure and resketching on paper or other medium in front of an audience. They are, therefore, ideal tools for developing plans that embody the advice of experts at group brainstorming sessions.

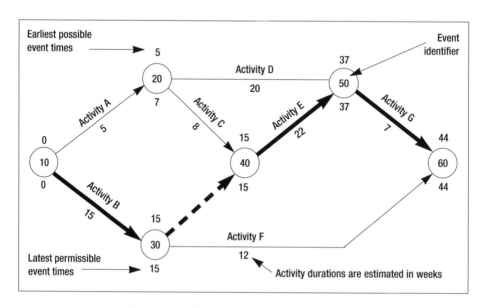

Figure 19.4   Notation for activity-on-arrow networks

Unfortunately they are not supported by most modern computer software. If a computer is going to be used, it will be necessary either to use precedence notation from the start or, as I often do myself, to sketch the network as an arrow diagram and convert it to precedence later, when the data are input to the computer. The conversion process is quick and easy. Having said that, precedence networks can be created quickly and easily using 3M Post-it Notes on a whiteboard or flip chart in a way that engages the audience interactively.

Network diagrams do not need to be drawn to scale and the length of an arrow has no significance. By convention, however, all network activities should progress from left to right. It is not strictly necessary, therefore, to draw arrowheads unless for some unavoidable reason an arrow has to be drawn running from right to left.

Every circle in the arrow diagram represents an event in a project, and the number written within the circle is simply a code or name that identifies the particular event. An event might be the start or finish of the entire project, the start of one or more activities, the finish of one or more activities, or (most likely) some combination of these. Events do not need to be numbered in sequence from left to right but, as here, planners often number in ascending order because this makes the job of finding a particular event on a very large network diagram far easier. The numbers in this example jump in intervals of ten: intervals of five or ten are often used so that, in the event of later activity insertions in the network, the left-to-right numbering sequence can be preserved.

Each arrow represents the activity needed to progress from one event (the preceding event) to the next (the succeeding event). An activity may be an active task (such as designing the desk in the furniture project) or a passive passage of time (such as waiting for materials to be delivered). Each activity takes its identification number from its preceding and succeeding events. Thus the activity from Event 10 to Event 20 would be identified as Activity 10:20.

No activity can start until all activities leading into its preceding event have been completed. Activities 20:50 and 20:40 cannot therefore start until Activity 10:20 has been finished or, in other words, until Event 20 has been achieved.

The dotted lines are dummy activities. These are not true activities and have zero duration, but they are real links (constraints) that form part of the logic. In our example, therefore, Event 40 will not be achieved until Activity 20:40 has been finished and, through the dummy, Activity 10:30 has also been finished. It can be seen that network notation clearly shows the interdependencies (constraints) between all the different activities in the project.

## TIME ANALYSIS AND THE CRITICAL PATH

Durations in the example in Figure 19.4 have been estimated in weeks and written below the activity arrows to which they refer. Activity 10:20 is therefore expected to take 5 weeks from start to finish.

### The forward pass

The small numbers written above the event circles in Figure 19.4 indicate the earliest time at which each event can be achieved. The earliest times for Events 20 and 30 are obvious, because these events cannot be achieved until the times estimated for their preceding activities have elapsed. The earliest times for all other events must be found by adding activity durations from left to right throughout the network, a process known as the forward pass. In each case it is the longest path that will determine the earliest possible time for an event. Dummies must be included in all paths. So, when looking at Event 40, for example, two paths must be considered. One goes through Events 10, 20, and 40 with a total path duration of 13 weeks. The other possible path leading into Event 40 runs through Events 10, 30 and 40 via the Dummy 30:40, with a total path duration of 15 weeks. So the earliest possible time for Event 40 is 15 weeks.

At Event 50, the path from Event 20 through Activity 20:50 is 25 weeks but the path from Event 40 is the longer, at 37 weeks. The earliest possible time for Event 50 is therefore 37 weeks. The forward pass must end at the final project event, which is Event 60. The earliest possible time for this event is week 44. This means that (provided the activity duration estimates are correct) this project cannot be completed in less than 44 weeks.

### The backward pass

The forward pass through the network has found the earliest possible time for every event and, through those results, the earliest possible start and finish time for every activity. The question now arises, what are the latest permissible times for those events and activities if project completion is not to be delayed? These times are found by a process known as the backward pass. The principal determinant must be the latest permissible time for the end event. In other words, what is the latest permissible finish time for the whole project?

It will be assumed here that the project must be finished as soon as possible, which is the case for most projects. This means that the latest permissible time for completing the project at Event 60 must be its earliest possible time. The result, week 44, is written below the event circle. Again taking the longest path in each case, we now have to work backwards through the network to find the latest permissible times for all the other events. At Event 50 the latest permissible time must be the latest time for Event 60 minus the duration of the connecting activity. That is, 44 minus 7 which is 37. The latest permissible time for Event 20, for example, is found by looking at the paths from Events 50 and 40. These, respectively give the results 37 minus 20 (17) and 15 minus 8 (7). So Event 20 must be achieved not later than week 7 if the project finish is not to be delayed beyond week 44.

### The critical path

When both the forward and backward passes have been made through any network, there will always be at least one path connecting events in which the earliest and latest times are the same. These events must be achieved at their earliest possible times if the project is to finish at its earliest possible time. No delay to any one of these events can be permitted. They are critical to the progress of the project. The path linking them from project start to finish is called the critical path. It is not uncommon to find a critical path that branches or a network with more than one critical path. The critical path in Figure 19.4 is shown in bold rules.

### Float

Float, otherwise known as slack (particularly in America), is the amount by which any event or activity may be delayed without delaying the whole project completion. All critical activities have zero float. Any attempt to impose a project finish time that is earlier than the earliest possible time calculated from time analysis will drive the system into a hypercritical state, with some or all events and activities having negative float values. If an arbitrary completion target at week 42 were imposed on the project network in Figure 19.4, for example, then all previously critical activities would have a float of minus two weeks. This, of course, means that the schedule is impracticable to implement unless it can be changed.

If an activity possessing float is delayed for any reason during the actual progress of a project, some or all of its float will be used up. Less float is then likely to remain for all the following activities, but this effect is not quite straightforward and depends on the position of the activity in respect to its surrounding activities. That position will determine the type of float, as explained in the following definitions.

### Total float

Total float is defined as the amount by which an activity can be delayed if all its preceding activities have taken place at their earliest possible times and all succeeding activities are allowed to wait until their latest permissible times. All non-critical activities possess total float. The total float of an activity is calculated by taking the latest permissible end-event time *minus* the earliest possible start-event time *minus* the activity duration.

The amount of time analysis information that can be shown on an arrow diagram is often limited and can be misleading for the beginner. This is seen at Activity 30:60, for example. Events 30 and 60 both lie on the project critical path but Activity 60, which joins them, is not critical and does not form part of the critical path. The situation soon becomes clear with a little thought. Event 30 is effectively fixed at Week 15, and Event 60 is fixed at week 44. So the time separating these two events is 44 minus 15 weeks, which is 29 weeks. Activity 30:60 can be allowed to take place anywhere within these 29 weeks without affecting the project completion time. Since it occupies 12 of the 29 weeks itself, it must possess 29 minus 12 weeks float, which is a total float of 17 weeks. Activity 30:60 is slightly special in another way because it possesses two other kinds of float. These are *free float* and *independent float*.

### Free float

Free float is the amount of float possessed by an activity when all preceding activities take place at their earliest possible times and all preceding activities can also still take place at their earliest times. Free float is the earliest possible end-event time *minus* the earliest possible start-event time *minus* the activity's duration. The result for Activity 30:60 is 17 weeks. Free float is far less common than total float. Many planners ignore it.

### Independent float

Independent float is the amount of float possessed by an activity if all preceding activities take place at their latest permissible times and succeeding activities can still take place at their earliest times. Independent float is calculated by taking the earliest possible end-event time *minus* the latest permissible start-event time *minus* the activity duration. The result for Activity 30:60 is again 17 weeks. Independent float is uncommon and is not usually featured in computer reports or considered by planners.

## ACTIVITY-ON-ARROW NETWORK FOR THE FURNITURE PROJECT

The project leader of the furniture project, after attending a two-day training course, learned how to draw arrow networks. On returning to her office she converted the tasks listed in Figure 19.1 to the arrow diagram shown in Figure 19.5. In this diagram she was able to show all the task interdependencies and to calculate the relative priorities of all the tasks (expressed in terms of total and free float). However, her superiors did not feel so comfortable with the new diagram and preferred the original simple bar chart.

The dummy connecting Event 13 to Event 15 is not strictly necessary. The additional event created by inserting the dummy (Event 13) does, however, provide space for showing the earliest possible completion time for Activity 6:13. More importantly, without the dummy, the activities for making the desk drawer and making the desk top would both be identified as Activity 6:15. By adding the dummy, the project leader has given both these activities different identifier codes. This distinction used to be very important when computer software was available for arrow networks. The problem does not arise with precedence notation.

The time analysis data become more useful for progressing the furniture project when they are set out as in the table shown in Figure 19.6, but the project leader would still not find the information very practical without knowing the start date for the project. Then the network can be processed by computer so that the table shows calendar dates instead of week numbers. The computer would also be able to sort the activities into a more useful sequence. For this project, sorting activities by ascending order of earliest start date will be most convenient for issuing and controlling work.

The computer brings flexibility to the scheduling process and is able to cope with changes in project scope or with rescheduling for any other reason. Further, the senior managers can still have their beloved bar charts, because modern project management software is able to plot bar charts from the network data. Before the furniture project leader can use the computer, however, she will have to learn how to draw the network using the precedence system.

## PRECEDENCE NETWORKS

Precedence networks are the most common form of activity-on-node networks. Here the network nodes (circles or rectangles) represent activities instead of events. There are no events depicted as such, although activity nodes with zero or unity duration can be placed to represent important events if the planner

**335**

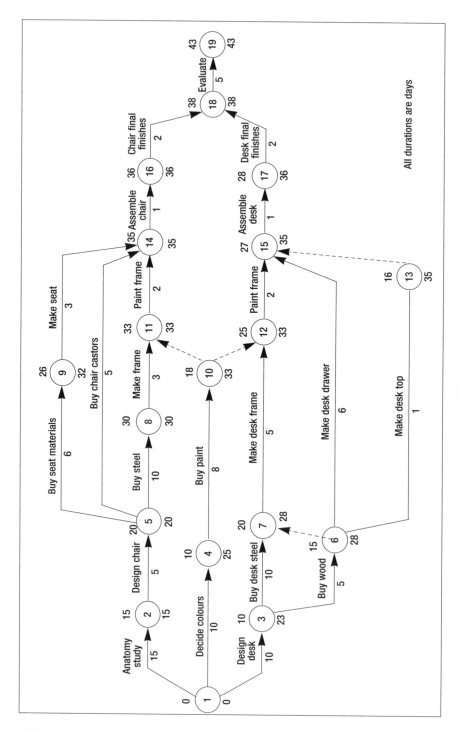

**Figure 19.5  Arrow diagram for the furniture project**

| Prec. event | Succ. event | Activity description | Duration (days) | Earliest start | Latest start | Earliest finish | Latest finish | Free float | Total float |
|---|---|---|---|---|---|---|---|---|---|
| 1 | 2 | 01 Anatomical study for chair | 15 | 0 | 0 | 15 | 15 | 0 | 0 |
| 2 | 5 | 02 Design chair | 5 | 15 | 15 | 20 | 20 | 0 | 0 |
| 5 | 9 | 03 Buy materials for chair seat | 6 | 20 | 26 | 26 | 32 | 0 | 6 |
| 9 | 14 | 04 Make chair seat | 3 | 26 | 32 | 29 | 35 | 0 | 6 |
| 5 | 14 | 05 Buy chair castors | 5 | 20 | 30 | 25 | 35 | 10 | 10 |
| 5 | 8 | 06 Buy steel for chair frame | 10 | 20 | 20 | 30 | 30 | 0 | 0 |
| 8 | 11 | 07 Make chair frame | 3 | 30 | 30 | 33 | 33 | 0 | 0 |
| 11 | 14 | 08 Paint chair frame | 2 | 33 | 33 | 35 | 35 | 0 | 0 |
| 14 | 16 | 09 Assemble chair | 1 | 35 | 35 | 36 | 36 | 0 | 0 |
| 16 | 18 | 10 Apply final finishes to chair | 2 | 36 | 36 | 38 | 38 | 0 | 0 |
| 1 | 3 | 11 Design desk | 10 | 0 | 13 | 10 | 23 | 0 | 13 |
| 3 | 7 | 12 Buy steel for desk frame | 10 | 10 | 18 | 20 | 28 | 0 | 8 |
| 7 | 12 | 13 Make desk frame | 5 | 20 | 28 | 25 | 33 | 0 | 8 |
| 12 | 14 | 14 Paint desk frame | 2 | 25 | 33 | 27 | 35 | 0 | 8 |
| 3 | 6 | 15 Buy wood and fittings for desk | 5 | 10 | 23 | 15 | 28 | 0 | 13 |
| 6 | 15 | 16 Make desk drawer | 6 | 15 | 29 | 21 | 35 | 14 | 14 |
| 6 | 13 | 17 Make desk top | 1 | 15 | 34 | 16 | 35 | 19 | 19 |
| 15 | 17 | 18 Assemble desk | 1 | 27 | 35 | 28 | 36 | 0 | 8 |
| 17 | 18 | 19 Apply final finishes to desk | 2 | 28 | 36 | 30 | 38 | 0 | 8 |
| 1 | 4 | 20 Decide paint colours | 10 | 0 | 15 | 10 | 25 | 0 | 15 |
| 4 | 10 | 21 Buy paint and varnish | 8 | 10 | 25 | 18 | 33 | 7 | 15 |
| 18 | 19 | 22 Final project evaluation | 5 | 38 | 38 | 43 | 43 | 0 | 0 |

**Figure 19.6   Time analysis data from the furniture project network**

337

wishes. The arrows joining the activity nodes are simply links, indicating the logical constraints. Hence, dummies are not needed.

## PRECEDENCE NOTATION

Some people find precedence networks more difficult to draw manually and so in the past they were less suited to brainstorming sessions than arrow networks. However, the invention of 3M Post-its and their use in project planning sessions means that it is often a precedence network that now results from a group planning session. Furthermore, they do have many advantages and, for all practical purposes, are mandatory if computer processing is required. The most commonly used elements of the method are shown in the simple example of Figure 19.7. The project represented here is the same as that in Figure 19.4.

Precedence time analysis is carried out by the same process as in arrow networks, but there is more room on the precedence diagram to show the results. For example, Activity F on the precedence diagram is the same as Activity 30:60 in Figure 19.4. In the precedence version, however, the total float of 17 days can

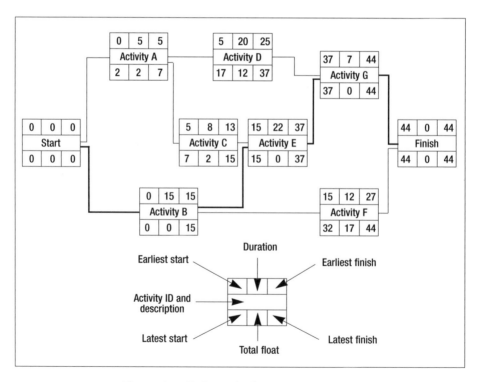

**Figure 19.7   Basic notation for precedence networks**

be shown on the diagram whereas this was hidden in the arrow network. The key on the precedence diagram shows the meaning of the numbers written in each activity box and no further explanation is needed here. Many people find precedence diagrams easier to understand than their arrow counterparts. This is partly because precedence diagrams closely resemble flow charts used by engineers and others. They also look more elegant and can be plotted successfully by many computer programs (although at least one very popular program fails badly in this respect).

## PRECEDENCE DIAGRAM FOR THE FURNITURE PROJECT

The precedence network for the furniture project is shown in Figure 19.8. Compare this with the arrow version in Figure 19.5. Most people would agree that the precedence version is easier to understand than its corresponding arrow network.

## COMPLEX CONSTRAINTS IN THE PRECEDENCE SYSTEM

The precedence method of networking allows the expression of complex relationships between different activities that cannot easily be shown in arrow networks. There are three complex relationships possible in addition to the normal (default) finish-to-start links. All four constraints are explained in Figure 19.9.

Many computer programs now just use the finish-to-start dependency, with:

- a negative value of $x$, a lead, representing that the start of the succeeding activity overlaps the preceding activity;
- a positive value of $x$, a lag, representing a delay before the start of the succeeding activity.

# CREATING PRACTICAL LOGIC

The furniture project leader used her project work breakdown and its resulting task list as the starting point for her network. This approach is widely taught and used, and is probably best, at least for the beginner. However, the best network logic is likely to result from a brainstorming session in which key project experts are allowed to participate. The task list remains important, but it has to be regarded as an incomplete checklist. The brainstorming session will help to identify activities that might otherwise have been forgotten and it should

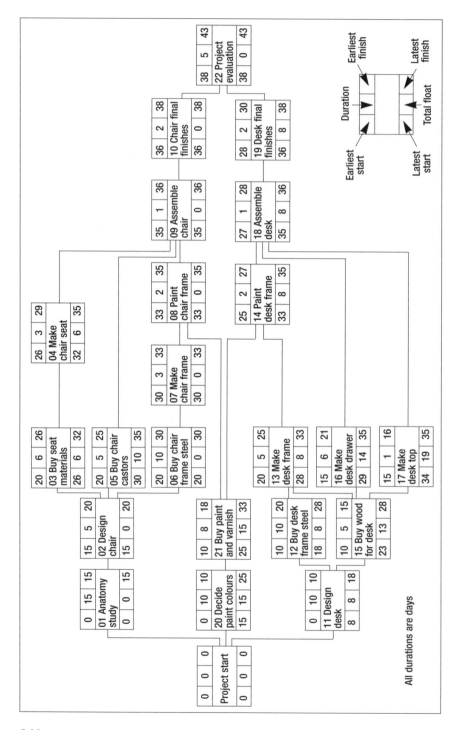

**Figure 19.8  Precedence diagram for the furniture project**

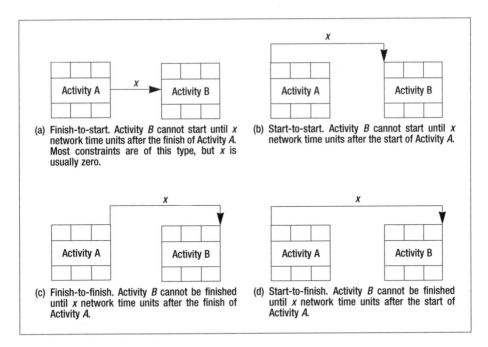

(a) Finish-to-start. Activity *B* cannot start until *x* network time units after the finish of Activity *A*. Most constraints are of this type, but *x* is usually zero.

(b) Start-to-start. Activity *B* cannot start until *x* network time units after the start of Activity *A*.

(c) Finish-to-finish. Activity *B* cannot be finished until *x* network time units after the finish of Activity *A*.

(d) Start-to-finish. Activity *B* cannot be finished until *x* network time units after the start of Activity *A*.

**Figure 19.9  Complex constraints**

certainly result in more practical network logic. For example, the task list is unlikely to include activities such as waiting for materials to be delivered or for key stage approvals during design. These tasks may not attract any cost, so they need not feature in work breakdowns made with cost estimating in mind. However, they can have great significance for the project timescale.

So, unless the organization has great experience in very similar projects, a good way to produce an initial network is to call a meeting of all those who will manage or execute work in the key areas of the project. (Project start-up is covered in Chapter 24.) A planning expert should be in the chair, and he or she should be so familiar with the networking technique that those who have never even seen a network diagram before will quickly absorb the concepts through the expert's example and guidance as the meeting proceeds. The chairperson will, from long experience, know the kinds of questions to ask in order to reveal tasks that might otherwise have been forgotten; questions that can seem obvious but are easily forgotten:

● 'Can this chair really be assembled before the frame has been painted?'
● 'Can you start to dig the foundations for this construction project the instant you arrive on site? How would you know where to dig? Surely you would need to do some marking out first? Will you not need to hire some machinery?'

341

A project network must do more than contain all the significant activities: it must also link them in a logical and practical way. Ask any two groups of people to draw a network for the same project and you will almost certainly get two different networks. That does not necessarily mean that one or both of these are wrong. There is usually more than one practical way of planning and executing a complex project. What is important is to strive for a plan that is seen to be achievable, efficient, practical and expressed in sufficient detail for work to be issued and followed up at short regular intervals.

## EARLY CONSIDERATION OF RESOURCES

Planners are often faced with the problem of resources when they estimate task durations. How can they estimate the duration of a task when they do not know if sufficient resources will be available at the time scheduled by time analysis? What effect will other activities have where they need the same resources? Suppose that a particular task might take two weeks if one person is employed but only one week if three people are used. Should the duration be estimated as one week or two? There are useful rules to apply when answering these questions. These are illustrated by the following examples.

### CASE 1

An activity will need the use of an electrician. So will several other activities in the same network. How can the planner estimate the duration of the activity when he or she does not know whether or not an electrician will always be available? The answer is to estimate the duration for the activity as if an electrician will be available whenever required, irrespective of the demands of other electrical tasks in the project. The planning process then goes through two logical, consecutive stages, as follows:

1. The computer will first establish time analysis data with no reference at all to resources.
2. The computer can now be commanded to carry out a separate resource scheduling calculation in which it attempts to start each task at its earliest possible time but will only do so if the electrician has not already been allocated to another task. Tasks with highest priority will have first claim on the electrician and will be scheduled next. Highest priority usually means least float.

The main point to grasp here is that the network should first be estimated without

342

considering possible resource conflicts. Resource scheduling is a subsequent, quite separate exercise.

## CASE 2

A single project activity calls for the use of one or more electricians. The planner knows that the electrical department usually has a total of ten electricians available to work on projects. The duration of the activity in question depends on the number of electricians used and would take six days if two electricians could be found but would extend to 15 days with only one. It is more efficient in this case to plan for the use of two electricians and write six days down as the estimated duration. The planner now sees a problem. No one knows how many of the ten electricians from the electrical department will be available for the activity because that must depend on when it takes place and on what else is happening at that time. The correct approach in this case is to estimate the duration as six days, using the optimum number of electricians and ignoring possible resource conflicts. Subsequent resource scheduling will take care of the actual resource consideration. In other words, the scheduling must be taken one step at a time, which means time analysis first and resource allocation as a quite separate second.

## CASE 3

An activity could be completed in 20 days with five electricians but this duration might be reduced to 15 days if eight electricians could be used. The planner knows that the company only employs a total of six electricians. Although the planner must ignore the claims on these electricians made by other tasks in the network, he or she must exercise common sense and avoid planning to use more electricians than the total available to the project. So the duration for this activity must be estimated as 20 days.

## NETWORK TOO BIG?

At one time network size was limited only by the length of the drawing paper roll available. Almost invariably drawn in arrow notation, networks containing several thousands of activities were fairly common. Although large networks are still sometimes necessary, modern networks tend to contain fewer activities for two principal reasons:

- Scrolling large networks across computer screens is not particularly convenient.
- Planners now recognize that very large networks can be too cumbersome and impracticable.

Projects, however, have not shrunk. So how do we still manage to include all the important activities with smaller networks? The answer is to break the plan down into a number of smaller, more easily manageable networks. This can often be achieved by drawing a separate network for each major work package from the work breakdown structure. However, the separate networks must be welded into a project whole. This is best achieved by linking them at suitably chosen interfaces.

Suppose, for example, that the furniture project scope were to be extended to include setting up a new production facility and running a nation-wide marketing campaign. The company management would be unwise to ask for one detailed network for the whole project. Instead, it would probably separate the project into three major work packages, each with its own leader, and each with its own network plan thus:

1. The furniture design and prototype project
2. The furniture factory project
3. The furniture marketing project

Computer software houses now cater for these hierarchical project arrangements and software is available that can combine subprojects within projects and/or all the projects being conducted in an organization or even a group of companies. The use of smaller subnetworks allows each to be planned under the direction of the manager responsible for the particular work package. Care must be taken, however, never to lose sight of the whole picture. This can usually be achieved by producing a summary network, which is a kind of umbrella plan covering the whole project in which most of the few activities contained each represent a whole subnetwork or major work package.

## TIMESCALE TOO LONG?

When time analysis is first carried out on a new network, the result is often a disappointment or even a shock. Taking the furniture project as an example, suppose that instead of the 43 days predicted the company's management wanted the project finished in only 30 days. What could the project leader do about this? First reactions are likely to be anger or despair and a 'can't be done' response. She can, however, consider three options.

1. She can review all the duration estimates and shorten some of them arbitrarily.
2. She can consider asking for more money and other resources.
3. She can review the network logic.

Options 2 and 3 can be combined for maximum effect. The process is sometimes called fast-tracking and, for consumer product development projects, reducing the 'time-to-market'. All of these options will now be discussed briefly.

## OPTION 1: REDUCE NETWORK DURATION TIMES ARBITRARILY

This option can usually be dismissed out of hand. If the original network was compiled using the best possible assessment of duration times, then writing in shorter times without good reason is likely to produce failure. The revised plan might look good on paper and please the senior management but, if it is not practicable, it should not be accepted. The result can only disappoint.

## OPTION 2: SPEND MORE MONEY

An activity can sometimes be shortened by putting in more effort. Perhaps two people could be used instead of one for a particular task. It might be possible to get materials faster, but at more expense, by changing suppliers or by using express freight. Additional equipment might be hired to speed a task. Although the use of planned overtime is never recommended, an exception might be made in the case of a critical activity. All of these actions are collectively known to planners as 'crashing'.

To achieve maximum effect at minimum extra cost, only critical activities should be considered for crashing. There is no point in wasting money to crash an activity that has a considerable amount of float. It is usually found, however, that crashing all the activities along the critical path shortens the path to the extent that it is no longer the path with greatest duration. In other words, when time analysis is carried out on the revised network, activities that were previously non-critical have themselves become the new critical path. So then those activities too can be considered for crashing.

If a network is crashed expertly and the process is repeated until the limit is reached, it is likely that many, if not most, activities will have become critical. That should result in a plan representing maximum time saving at minimum extra cost. Bear in mind, however, that this cost/time optimization is to some extent an artificial concept. The activity duration times are only estimates and it is unlikely that every task will be completed exactly according to plan. The network schedule should, therefore, be kept under constant review as the project proceeds and changed whenever necessary to maintain optimization. While reviews and updates are desirable for any plan, the process becomes most important when so many activities are critical.

## OPTION 3: REVIEW THE NETWORK LOGIC

A careful review of the original network logic can sometimes lop a considerable amount of time from the planned project duration. It might even be found that one or two activities can be omitted altogether (perhaps an approval stage could be removed, for instance). Although most network constraints assume that no activity can start before all its predecessors have been finished, it is sometimes practicable to allow activities to overlap to some extent.

For example, it might be possible to purchase materials before design is complete, because the designer will be able to tell the buyer what is required before the finished drawings are issued. Similarly, a limited amount of manufacture can sometimes take place before final issue of drawings. If a subcontractor is to be involved, advance notice can sometimes be given that will allow the subcontractor to reserve capacity and, perhaps, start ordering supplies. It is even possible, on occasion, to run activities completely in parallel instead of sequentially. Such measures can shorten the expected duration of a project considerably, but there is often a price to pay in the form of added risk.

The complex constraints of precedence notation are ideal for depicting overlapping activities. The start-to-start option is particularly useful in this respect (see Figure 19.9). Time analysis becomes more difficult but this is not a problem when the network is processed by computer.

## REFERENCES AND FURTHER READING

Lock, D. (2000), *Project Management*, 7th edition, Gower, Aldershot.

Lockyer, K. and Gordon, J. (1996), *Project Management and Project Network Techniques*, 6th edition, Financial Times, Pitman Publishing, London.

Morris, P. W. G. (1997), *The Management of Projects*, 2nd edition, Thomas Telford, London.

Spinner, M. P. (1992), *Elements of Project Management: Plan, Schedule and Control*, 2nd edition, Prentice Hall, Englewood Cliffs, NJ.

## RELATED TOPICS

# 20 Managing resources

## Dennis Lock

Project planning cannot usually be considered complete until all activities have been scheduled to take account of the organization's resources. The aim should be to plan so that these resources are never impossibly overloaded or left wastefully idle, while attempting to finish every project on or before its required completion date. This can be a complex process. The ideal schedule may not always be achievable, but this chapter offers some rules and techniques that can help to schedule resources sensibly and efficiently.

## WHAT RESOURCES TO SCHEDULE

In addition to time, the resources used by most projects include materials, accommodation, cash, plant and labour. We start by considering who needs to schedule resources, and what resources they can and should apply project management techniques to schedule.

### WHO NEEDS TO SCHEDULE RESOURCES?

Responsibility for scheduling resources may belong to the project manager, or it could be a problem for someone else in the management chain (see Figure 30.1). The person who acts only as project management consultant or adviser may be able to leave resource scheduling (with the likely exception of cash flow) to the contractors and subcontractors who employ the people to do the work. A managing contractor for a construction project will have to schedule work for its head office engineering staff but, again, can leave the day-to-day scheduling of most direct labour to the relevant subcontractors.

Companies most likely to benefit from detailed project resource scheduling are those who employ professional or skilled direct labour in significant numbers.

If temporary staff with the requisite skills can be engaged readily at short notice, scheduling may simply be a process of assessing future numbers (a crude form of manpower planning). The most complex and difficult resource allocation problems are found in those organizations where the labour force is largely permanent (and, therefore, relatively stable and inflexible) and where the people have valuable skills, training and experience that are peculiar to the company and its work.

## RESOURCES THAT CAN BE SCHEDULED USING PROJECT MANAGEMENT TECHNIQUES

Most of the examples in this chapter are illustrated using direct labour examples, where the resources are people with particular skills. The same techniques can, however, be applied to most other types of resources that are quantifiable in terms of simple units or numbers. These techniques can therefore be used to schedule hire plant, bulk materials, machine time, process plant capacities and so on. Accommodation is one possible exception because it is not a resource that can always be described and calculated adequately in terms of simple units of area, such as square metres. Area shape, height, means of access, lighting, power supplies and other services, materials handling facilities, and floor loading may have to be taken into account. In planning the use of assembly bays for the assembly and test of large machines, for example, one machine can sometimes be allowed to overhang another. This is just one example where different projects may be able to share common floor space. Such problems cannot be solved by simple arithmetic, but may need three-dimensional drawings, physical scale models or a sophisticated dynamic computer-aided design system.

## RESOURCES THAT SHOULD BE SCHEDULED USING PROJECT MANAGEMENT TECHNIQUES

It is usually a mistake to attempt to schedule every possible kind of resource to be used on a project. That leads to unnecessary complication, and just one attempt at the monumental amount of work needed will probably be enough to deter the planner from ever trying it again.

Consider, for example, an engineering department which designs special purpose machinery. The department is handling a continuous workflow for several projects. The engineering manager knows, from experience, that for every ten engineers working on mechanical design, one instrumentation engineer is needed to design the supporting pipework and lubrication systems. In this case it may only be necessary to schedule the mainstream engineers. If 100 engineers are going to be needed, the manager knows that ten instrumentation engineers must be provided to support them. This approach, which I have seen proved in practice, can be extended to many other types of resources (for example inspection personnel in relation to machine operators, paint oven capacity in relation to sheet metal machine capacity and so on). Similar arguments usually apply to most indirect staff, such as print room operators, purchasing clerks and those involved in the more general administrative and management activities. The old expression KISS – Keep It Simple, Stupid – applies. Do not attempt to schedule everything but concentrate on the scarce or key resources and let their dependent resources fall into place.

# RESOURCE SCHEDULING PRINCIPLES

## RESOURCE AGGREGATION

The practice of resource scheduling can be introduced by considering the case of just one department within an organization that is carrying out a project to build a chemical processing plant. The department concerned is responsible for pipefitting. The time data for these activities have been derived from a network diagram for the complete project. In practice, of course, all the other activities in the network would have to be scheduled, involving several other departments and resource types.

The upper part of Figure 20.1 shows a fragment of a bar chart. This has been derived from the project network, but has been edited so that it includes only pipefitting activities associated with the main plant control panel. For simplicity it has been assumed that each activity on the network will need one pipefitter for the whole of its duration. Every activity has been shown starting at its earliest possible time, as determined by network critical path analysis. The hatched extensions shown after some of the bars indicate the amount of total float available. The figures at the foot of the bar chart show the number of pipefitters needed each day to fulfil this schedule. This usage requirement is displayed to better effect by the histogram in the lower half of Figure 20.1.

This schedule has been obtained by the simple addition of resources with no regard to their availability. The process is, therefore, known as resource aggregation. It is common for managers to rely on such schedules, hoping optimistically to be able to start each task at its earliest possible time predicted by the network. The pattern of work, however, is going to be far from satisfactory, with high peak loads alternating with relatively idle periods. If the department in our project has only two pipefitters, the schedule is impossible.

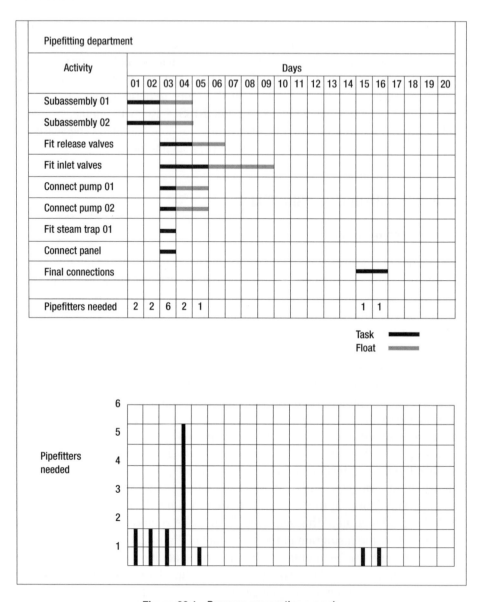

**Figure 20.1   Resource aggregation example**

## RESOURCE SCHEDULING

Figure 20.2 shows the same tasks as those displayed in Figure 20.1. However, some of the tasks have now been deliberately delayed by the planner, but not to the extent that their times will exceed the amount of total float available. Now the

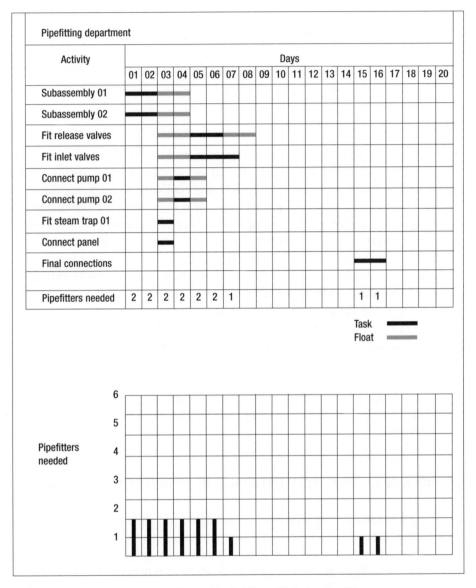

**Figure 20.2** **The workload of Figure 20.1 after smoothing**

work pattern expected from the pipefitters has become far more satisfactory. The peaks and troughs have been smoothed out. Attempts to obtain acceptable resource schedules are variously called resource smoothing, resource allocation, resource scheduling or resource optimization. These terms are not quite synonymous: the smoothing or optimization process aims at a more perfectly

353

smooth result than the simpler scheduling or allocation procedure. Most computer systems will not produce the smoothest possible work patterns but the results are likely to be acceptable and practicable, especially when it is remembered that all planning and scheduling relies at heart on estimates that are largely themselves subjective and, in many cases, open to question.

## USE OF CHARTS

It is easy to imagine the scheduling process, at least at the basic level just described, as being conducted by clerical or simple charting methods. An adjustable bar chart can be used, with task strips coloured to represent different resource types. The chart, probably mounted on a wall, allows the positions of all the strips to be adjusted, perhaps using slots, a plug-in grid or magnetic adhesion. Such charts were once common for planning departmental workloads, both for workpeople and for various processing facilities (such as machines in a workshop). Although charts are still an option to be considered in extremely simple circumstances (departmental holiday charts are an obvious case) they cease to be of any value when the amount of data to be considered is too great. Unlike a critical path network, it is not usually possible to show all the logical constraints between jobs on a chart and this is likely to lead to scheduling errors. Once the planner attempts to use more than a few different colours for coding, or tries to plan more than about 50 different tasks, the whole thing becomes tedious to set up, difficult to interpret and exceedingly difficult to reschedule. In the remainder of this chapter it is assumed that the planner has access to a suitable computer system.

## THE ROLE OF CRITICAL PATH NETWORKS IN RESOURCE SCHEDULING

Resource scheduling involves a series of decisions or judgements which, in turn, need a set of data. When a person or a computer attempts to place each activity at a sensible place in the project time frame, there are several questions which must be considered with respect to the project's critical path network:

1. What other activities must be completed before this activity can start?
2. What is the earliest date this activity could start, assuming that resources are available?
3. If there is a shortage of resources, for how long could this activity be delayed until resources become available?
4. If two or more activities requiring the same scarce resource could be started

on the same day, which should be started at once and which should be delayed? In other words, which activity has the highest priority?

## FLOAT AS A DETERMINANT OF PRIORITY

Critical path analysis will determine how much float each activity has at the start of the project. It is this float information that is vital to the subsequent resource scheduling process. Activities with float can be delayed, until their latest permissible dates if necessary, if resources are not available for them. Critical activities must obviously be started at their earliest possible dates if the project is to be finished at its earliest possible time. When two or more activities are competing for the same scarce resource, it is the activity with least total float that must be given priority.

## WHY RESOURCE CONSTRAINTS ARE NOT CONSIDERED INITIALLY

When a network is first drawn, the planner will have plenty to do identifying all the activities needed, specifying the logical constraints between them, estimating durations and carrying out time analysis. It is not possible to consider all potential resource constraints at that time, owing to the complexity of the task and the unsuitability of critical path networks for that purpose. It is always sensible to consider resource scheduling as a separate, subsequent process, carried out after the initial time analysis of the network has been drawn with no regard to resource constraints. A planner who happens to know a particular resource is scarce might be tempted to introduce special logic constraints to the network logic. Suppose, for example, a project organization only employs one instrument fitter and that the network contained ten instrument fitting activities. The planner could ensure that no two of these activities could be scheduled in parallel by the simple expedient of linking them all in series. However, that would indeed be a foolish approach, as the planner cannot know in advance about other critical issues:

- How can the planner know in advance the best sequence in which those activities, from different parts of the network, should take place?
- What would all those extra links do to the main body of the network logic?
- How would the planner be able to remember all those resource constraints if the network had to be changed?

The critical path network is therefore not usually the appropriate place for dealing with constraints arising from resource limitations. However, there is one important exception.

## AN EXCEPTION TO THE RULE

Although resource scheduling is usually an exercise that follows (but is not usually part of) network analysis, there are cases where the availability of resources will affect the initial network diagram.

Consider an activity on the network for the assembly by one or more fitters of a complex piece of electromechanical equipment. Suppose that the planner has been given the options for estimating the duration of this activity shown in Figure 20.3. Which option should the planner use for planning? The optimum solution appears to be to plan for the use of two fitters, who should finish the job in three weeks. The use of more than two fitters would certainly reduce the duration further but only at the expense of reduced efficiency and increased cost. We now have an activity that is going to use two fitters for three weeks. We know that other activities in the same network are also going to need fitters for varying durations at times as yet unknown. The experienced planner will not consider those other demands on fitters at this stage of the planning and scheduling process. That problem can be resolved later, by the separate procedure of resource scheduling.

Suppose, however, that the planner has been told that cost is less important than completing this project in the shortest possible time. If this assembly activity happened to be on the critical path, it might be thought justifiable to plan for the use of nine fitters. The planner knows, however, that the company only employs a total of five fitters and it can generally be assumed that one of those will not be available for project work at any time for a number of reasons. The planner would therefore limit the number of fitters assigned to this activity to four, and would estimate its duration at two weeks. So, although resources are generally not considered at the time of network preparation, common sense must play some part in deciding how resources should be assigned to each activity.

| Number of fitters | Time needed for assembly (weeks) | Works content (man-weeks) |
|---|---|---|
| 1 | 6.0 | 6.0 |
| 2 | 3.0 | 6.0 |
| 3 | 2.5 | 7.5 |
| 4 | 2.0 | 8.0 |
| 5 | 1.5 | 9.0 |

Figure 20.3   Scheduling data for a complex activity

## SPECIFYING THE RESOURCES NEEDED FOR EACH ACTIVITY

The above example illustrates that a preliminary step in resource allocation is to consider each network activity in turn and estimate not only its duration, but also the number of units of each resource type needed to complete the activity within that duration. This means that the planner must make a number of tactical decisions in which a balance is struck between planned activity durations and the numbers and types of resources required. These decisions must be recorded on the network so that the data can be used later for input to the computer for resource scheduling and to ensure that the original tactical intentions are followed when the work takes place. Both to save effort and to make best use of the limited space for showing data on the network it is usual to use a short code for each resource type. To give an example, BL might be used to indicate bricklayers and BM for bricklayers' mates or labourers. Then the simple coding '5D 2BL 2BM' on a network activity would mean that the intention is for the task to take five days using two bricklayers and two labourers.

# CONFLICT BETWEEN PROJECT TIME AND RESOURCE LIMITS

During the resource allocation process, it is often found that the resources available will not allow work to take place fast enough to complete the project within its target timescale. (I assume, for simplicity, that this target timescale is equivalent to the duration of the network critical path, the shortest possible time in which the project can logically be finished given ample resources.) Figure 20.4 illustrates the problem. The project is depicted as a balloon containing the resources. The resources can be regarded as an incompressible liquid so that the balloon can be changed in shape but its volume will remain constant. A project that uses resources is bounded by two principal limits, namely the level of resources available and the permissible project completion time. If the available timescale is reduced (for example if the client wants the project finished earlier), the time limit can be moved to the left until it hits the earliest possible time indicated by the network. However, the balloon will then be squeezed upwards to require a higher rate of resource usage. If, for any reason, the amount of resources available has to be reduced, then the balloon will be squashed flatter, and the project timescale must be extended to accept a later project completion date.

This argument gives rise to the terms 'resource-limited schedule' and 'time-limited schedule'. The planner often has to decide or be told which option is the more important: keeping within available resources at the risk of running late or

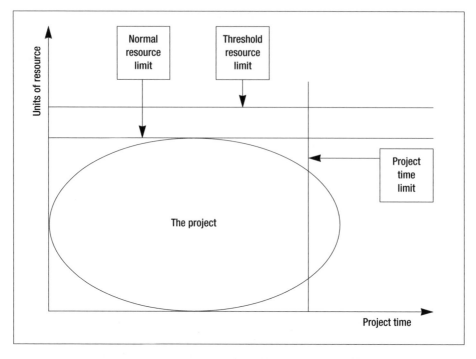

**Figure 20.4   Conflict between project time and resource limits**

running to time at the possible expense of having to hire extra labour. Computer systems will almost certainly require the planner to state whether time-limited or resource-limited rules apply before running the program.

## THRESHOLD RESOURCES

The use of so-called threshold resources can be one solution to the problem of a time-limited schedule where the known levels of available resources might prove to be inadequate. A simple case will illustrate the concept of threshold resources. Suppose that the number of test technicians normally available for project work is five. The planner will therefore set up the project in the computer system and will specify the availability of test technicians as five. The planner, however, has doubts that this number of technicians will be able to complete a new project in time and these doubts are confirmed when the time-limited schedule is first processed by the computer. The planner knows that three more senior (and therefore more highly paid) test technicians could be called in from another part of the organization to assist at times of crisis. Some computer programs will allow the planner to specify these additional technicians as a threshold resource. The threshold resource will be used by the computer only when activities would otherwise be delayed past their latest permissible finish times. Other sources of additional labour resources might be from external subcontractors or agencies supplying temporary personnel, or existing personnel may be expected to work extended hours or overtime (this last option is not to be recommended except in emergencies).

## SPLITTABLE ACTIVITIES

Activities can be specified as splittable or non-splittable. A splittable activity is one that can be interrupted and restarted later to release scarce resources temporarily for another activity that has higher priority. The split activity will be resumed later when resources are again available. The default condition of most software will regard activities as non-splittable.

# SCHEDULING PROJECT RESOURCES WITH A COMPUTER

In the early days of project management software, the capability of most programs was limited to time analysis. With two or three notable exceptions, close examination of those programs which did claim to be able to schedule resources revealed that they were capable only of resource aggregation. In recent years there has been a dramatic and most welcome change, so that practically every program now available has some sort of useful resource scheduling capability. Many programs are capable of excellent all-round performance and there is generally something to suit every project requirement and every purse. Advertisements announcing improved versions of existing programs and completely new products are regularly seen in project management journals. However, it always pays to check out the sometimes extravagant claims made in advertising material before committing time and money to a purchase, so that hard facts can be separated from optimistic fiction.

Most modern programs operate in the Microsoft Windows environment and therefore share some characteristics. These programs vary greatly, however, in their general approach, method of use, capacity, capability and flexibility. Some are relatively simple and can be put to work almost immediately, while those at the higher, professional end of the market need operators who have had at least some training. The remainder of this chapter must therefore be written in general terms and some of the features or characteristics described here will not apply to every available software package.

## INITIAL DATA PROCESSING

The first significant step in scheduling is time analysis. The computer digests the network input data and, on command, attempts time analysis. Backward and forward passes are made through the network and the computer will log any obvious input data errors and omissions (such as dangles and loops). When all known errors have been cleared, valid time analysis data can be calculated and written to the database. The following information is among that which will now be on file for each activity record:

- The activity ID (from the network)
- Activity description
- Duration
- Earliest possible start
- Latest permissible start
- Earliest possible finish
- Latest permissible finish
- Free float
- Total float
- Resources needed, by type and quantity
- Activity cost (either as a specified activity cost or as a derivative of the number of resource units multiplied by unit cost rates)
- Various codes allocated by the planner for later use in filtering and sorting data for reports

Although resource allocation is a separate, subsequent process after initial time analysis, modern computer systems are so fast in operation that the whole time analysis/resource allocation process can appear seamless.

## ALTERNATIVE COMPUTING APPROACHES

Considerable effort has been expended in the search for mathematically ideal project scheduling methods (aiming for perfect smoothing of all resource usage). However, mathematical optimization algorithms tend to overkill the problem and use large amounts of computational resources. In any case, even it were possible to slot all activities into a time frame with watch-maker precision, this would have certain disadvantages. Estimates of activity durations and the resources required are usually approximate and subjective. Reality varies from the estimates. The beautifully scheduled pieces therefore turn out to be a different size from those imagined and no longer fit exactly. For most practical systems the goal is to provide a good, usable schedule, not necessarily the mathematical optimum. There are two main approaches, based on either a 'parallel' or a 'serial' procedure. Both are heuristic, common sense techniques.

## Parallel scheduling

Parallel scheduling can be visualized as follows. Imagine a network with several possible start points. This network is to be scheduled on a day-by-day basis through the project. The following are the computing steps:

1. Consider day one and all the start activities of the network. Build an 'eligibility list', consisting of these activities.
2. Consider the activity with the highest priority from the eligibility list. Can it start yet? Is its earliest start less than or equal to the day being considered? If so, compare its resource requirements for its next day with the resource availability on day one of the project.
3. If all relevant resources are available in sufficient quantity, schedule the first day of that activity to occur on the first day of the project. If that completes the activity, then add all successor activities to the eligibility list.
4. Repeat the process for the activity with the next highest priority from the eligibility list, and so on until all eligible activities have been considered for that day.
5. Then move to the next day of the project. Any unallocated amounts of 'pool' resources are rolled over to day two. The actions described above are repeated for day two.
6. And so on until all activities in the project have been scheduled.

This process works more naturally when the planner has requested a resource-limited schedule, in which the resources available are confined within maximum limits but the time available to project completion can be extended indefinitely.

## Serial scheduling

Serial scheduling works by considering each activity in turn instead of each day of the project in turn. The computing steps can be visualized as follows:

1. Using resource data availability supplied by the planner, build two-dimensional tables of resource availabilities. For each resource there will be a table that records the amount of that resource which will be available for every day of the project.
2. Following time analysis, there will be a pre-sequenced list of the activities which comprise the project. Consider each activity in turn. Each will have an 'earliest feasible start' time, which will initially be the same as its earliest start as derived from time analysis.

3. The section of the resource tables between the activity's earliest feasible start and latest finish is scanned to see if the activity can be scheduled as a whole without splitting. If this is so, the activity is scheduled at the first available point. If not, then if the activity is splittable, an attempt is made to fit the activity in between its earliest feasible start and latest finish in sections. If this is impossible, an extra layer of resource availability is called in and the process is repeated for the activity, until it can be fitted in.
4. If an activity is scheduled at a point later than its early start, the earliest feasible starts of all successive activities are updated to be greater than the finish of the activity that has just been scheduled. When all this has been done for every activity in the network, the project has been scheduled.

Serial scheduling works more naturally under the time-limited option, where there is a fixed end date to the project but the resources can be exceeded if necessary.

### Serial or parallel?

Serial methods are more popular than parallel methods, for a number of reasons. Parallel scheduling tends to split activities rather more than serial. Ideally, a parallel scheduling algorithm would like to be able to split any activity into one-day sections, particularly if activities have complex resource requirements or if resource availability changes during the project. Parallel scheduling also tends to need more computer memory per activity (which can limit the size of network that can be calculated on a given computer).

### Dual completion target dates with serial scheduling

Serial levelling schemes sometimes have a feature which allows two target project completion dates to be specified. These are the desired project end date and a latest permissible (or secondary) end date. Resources are classified into two sections, 'important' and 'exceedable'. If the scheduling system would have exceeded the availability of an important resource (and its threshold level, if there was one), then the activity is allowed to delay itself past its latest finish as determined from initial time analysis. It is not allowed to delay past its secondary latest finish (that is its latest finish relative to the secondary end date for the whole project).

### PRIORITY RULES

The planner may be asked to specify a priority rule to be applied at the individual activity level. The range of options depends on the software used. A useful choice is to give highest priority to activities with least remaining float. Remaining float is the amount of total float left after the resource scheduling process has caused the planned start to be delayed.

## SPECIFYING AVAILABILITY LEVELS

The input data for any software package will include the establishment of a resources file, which lists all resource types and their availabilities and cost rates. For each resource type, the planner will be prompted to enter normal and threshold availability levels. These levels may vary as time proceeds, so that, for example, ten instrument technicians might be specified as the number available from 1 January 2001 to 30 June 2001, eleven from 1 July to 31 December 2001 and so on. A cost rate per unit of time can be given for each resource, with different levels for normal and threshold quantities.

Some caution is needed in deciding the availability levels that should be declared. Not all people in a typical department will be able to work on projects at any given time. Some will be ill, some on holiday, some away on training courses and so on. Others might be working on jobs that could not have been planned, such as rework from earlier projects or small but urgent tasks for customers. In short, there will always be unplanned activities or other reasons why the total workforce cannot be used for project work. My own solution to this problem has always been to reserve a small percentage of each resource for these unplannable activities (it might be 15 per cent) and to reduce the amount available for project work accordingly. If, for instance, there is a department of 60 engineers, all capable of doing similar work, the planner would specify only 51 as being available as the normal resource level for all project work.

### Alternative and summary resources

Project resources in short supply can sometimes be augmented by substituting other resources. For example, in a project using both senior and junior engineers, senior engineers might well be substituted for junior engineers to ease a temporary overload. Two different kinds of tools may be capable of carrying out a given process. One of these types may, however, be less efficient than another for this purpose, so that larger numbers of that particular type may be required if it is used as an alternative. These and other substitution possibilities can be specified in advance with one or two of the higher level software packages.

# OUTPUT REPORTS FROM RESOURCE SCHEDULING

Various reports can be produced from the resource schedule.

## WORK-TO LISTS

All readers who use project management software will be familiar with the typical time analysis report, an example of which is shown in the upper half of Figure 20.5. Imagine that this contains all the project activities to be carried out by the electrical department. The usual practice is to exclude, by filtering, all activities that have no relevance to the department. The activities which are included can be sorted in one of several ways, earliest start dates being commonly used. When given such reports, the electrical department manager will attempt to issue work at the earliest start dates, but must hold some activities back if all the electricians are otherwise occupied. Time analysis reports are calculated with no regard to resources and their use as control tools can be a hit and miss affair.

The lower half of Figure 20.5 shows a report format that is typical of a work schedule produced after resource scheduling. The result is, at first sight, similar to the simple time analysis tabulation in the upper half of the figure and it should certainly list the same activities. The most important difference is that the manager is given a set of scheduled start and finish dates for all project work for the department. These dates should be feasible working times because they have been calculated by the computer after consideration of the electricians as a resource. In other words, the computer is issuing work to the department at a rate commensurate with the department's resources.

## OTHER REPORTS

Many other reports, tabular and graphic, can be obtained from a resource scheduling program, especially if cost rates are given for each resource, and where estimated costs are specified for activities such as the purchasing of materials. Many of these reports can be printed using multiple colours and three-dimensional effects. These reports can include:

• a table listing the quantity of each type of resource needed for the project, spelled out day by day, week by week or for whichever duration units apply. Some reports have a column for the daily estimated project costs and can also show cumulative totals that increase with time until they flatten out at the scheduled project completion date to indicate the estimated total direct project cost;

**TIME ANALYSIS**

| | Report date | 15 Jan 2005 |
|---|---|---|
| Test project. Project number 1234 | Time now | 17 Jan 2005 |
| Department: Electricians | | Page 1 |

| ID | Activity description | Duration | Early start | Late start | Early finish | Late finish | Free float | Total float | Activity cost |
|---|---|---|---|---|---|---|---|---|---|

All activities for the electrical department listed here, sorted by order of early start date

**WORK-TO LIST**

| | Report date | 15 Jan 2005 |
|---|---|---|
| Test project. Project number 1234 | Time now | 17 Jan 2005 |
| Department: Electricians | | Page 1 |

| ID | Activity description | Duration | Early start | Scheduled start | Scheduled finish | Late finish | Remaining float | Resources |
|---|---|---|---|---|---|---|---|---|

All activities for the electrical department listed here, sorted by order of scheduled start date

**Figure 20.5   Time analysis and work-to list reports compared**

365

- resource histograms (see Figure 20.2);
- cash flow schedules;
- time/cost graphs;
- bar charts, using scheduled dates (a graphic form of the work-to lists).

## SOME RESOURCE TIMING PROBLEMS

Every project management program is governed by one or more working calendars.

### THE DEFAULT CALENDAR

The simplest calendar case is the default calendar. This will probably be specified as five eight-hour weekdays, with no work possible at weekends. This means that the computer will not include weekend days in time analysis calculations or reports. An activity with a duration of ten days will be shown as taking two calendar weeks. Adherence to the default calendar can produce some anomalies. One example would be an activity to cover the delay while paint dries or concrete cures. If the plan showed concrete being poured on a Friday, it would (illogically) not allow curing to begin until the following Monday because the weekend days are simply invisible for scheduling. There is more than one way of overcoming this problem. One is by using non rate-constant resource patterns (described later) and the other is by introducing a different calendar file.

### USE OF SPECIAL CALENDARS

All good project management software allows the planner to specify many different calendars, each with its own identifying file code. Activities will usually be planned using the default calendar but, by specifying the appropriate code, particular activities can be timed differently. In the case of the concrete curing activity mentioned above, a calendar could be set up that has seven working days in every calendar week, so that the concrete curing could proceed uninterrupted through the weekend.

### CALENDARS AND RESOURCES

The ability to specify multiple calendars enables the planner to solve many problems that can arise in resource scheduling. Here are some examples.

### Allowance for public holidays

Non-working days caused by public holidays can be taken out of the default calendar or by setting up a holiday file (the approach can depend on the software chosen). An international project will have activities performed in countries with different public holidays. It is only necessary to set up a calendar file for each country and then allocate the calendar file to each activity that is appropriate for the country in which it is to be carried out.

### Allowance for individual holidays

There are several ways for dealing with the scheduling problem of staff (resources) who will be absent at varying times for their personal annual leave. The most sophisticated project management software will allow a staff file to be set up which contains details of all individuals working on projects. Every person is filed under their own name. The file can include all kinds of data, including personal skills (in other words, the resource category), cost rate, employment history and planned holiday dates. That method is far from common and is beyond the capabilities of most project management software. Moreover, it tends to place responsibilities on the project administration function that should more rightly be those of the human resources department. The usual practical approach is to allow for staff holidays as a blanket reduction in the number of resources declared as available.

### Shift working

Some organizations operate two or three shift working for some of their staff, while others work normal office hours. This is another case where the introduction of multiple calendars can solve the problem. The planner just sets up different calendars for those activities which can take place outside normal working hours and then ensures that the activities are assigned to their correct calendars.

## RATE CONSTANCY

The most common method for specifying resource requirements when each activity is entered into the computer is to regard the application of each resource as constant throughout the duration of that activity. The planner will then be presented with this as the default, rate constant, option. Thus, when an activity has been estimated at a duration of five days and needing one labourer, the assumption is that one labourer will be employed on the activity constantly from start to finish. Even if the resource usage varies somewhat during the course of the activity, the rate constant option will probably be an acceptable compromise because any slight error would be swamped by all the other labouring activities in the total project.

There are occasions, however, when resources should be specified as non rate-constant. The timing problems of the concrete pouring and curing activities mentioned earlier in this section could be solved by this method. Suppose that the act of concrete pouring and mixing takes two days and that a further period of five days is needed for the concrete to cure sufficiently. The planner could proceed as follows to produce the desired scheduling result (provided that the default calendar covered weekends):

1. Combine the concrete pouring and curing as one activity.
2. Estimate the activity duration as seven days.
3. Specify the activity as non-splittable.
4. Declare the resource required as one labourer.
5. Specify the resource as non rate-constant.
6. When prompted by the computer, define the resource usage pattern as one labourer for each of the first two days, with zero resources needed for the final five days.

## MULTIPROJECT SCHEDULING

Most organizations work on several projects simultaneously (see Chapters 3 and 7). The projects might be at different locations and would almost certainly be represented by logically independent network diagrams. Such projects typically require resources to be provided from a common pool. Engineers, designers, laboratory facilities and corporate resources are all examples of common resources. All these projects therefore interact with each other in their demand for resources and this increases the complexity of resource scheduling.

It might be considered possible to schedule an individual project by setting aside resources specially for that project. This, however, would introduce the need to make arbitrary decisions and lead to inflexible and wasteful use of resources elsewhere. Multiproject scheduling (programme management) is the best approach to solving this problem. Geoff Reiss gave a detailed analysis of the way systems are used in Chapter 7. Here we focus on the resource scheduling issues. The method involves planning all projects in a computer model of the organization, where all relevant resources are scheduled and allocated to projects according to a set of rules specified by the planner and followed by the software. Provided suitable software is used, the process is relatively straightforward and should not be beyond the ability of a planner able to schedule resources for a single project.

## PROJECT PRIORITIES IN A MULTIPROJECT MODEL

When several projects are being scheduled against common resources, the question of the relative priorities of these projects must arise. There are several different ways of assigning priorities to projects. Two are discussed here.

### Using target project completion dates as the driver

In the ideal multiproject model priorities should fall out automatically if each project is given a target start date and target completion date. Then, even though there are unlikely to be any logical network connections between the different projects, all the time analysis data held on the common database can be used by the computer when deciding which competing activity should receive first claim on a scarce resource. It may be enough to consider the total float of the individual activities in the projects as being the criterion upon which they are scheduled. This is adequate if the projects are of roughly equivalent importance, so that a critical item in project A carries the same priority as a critical item in project B which shares the same start date. If this is not so, a process known as 'residual scheduling' may be appropriate.

### Residual scheduling

Here, the projects to be scheduled are taken one by one. All of the highest priority project is scheduled before any of the second priority project. The second priority project uses those resources remaining after the first project has finished and so on down the list. This tends to produce a resource utilization pattern similar to Figure 20.6. Residual scheduling is the opposite extreme from the strategy of giving each project essentially equal weight.

### Which option?

Some managers might find the ideal solution somewhere between the two extremes just described. Compromise solutions can be obtained by allocating only part of the total resource pool to the highest priority project. My own practice has always been to use the first of these two options, namely relying on the imposition of target start and finish dates for every project. Although many other options might be possible (depending on the capability of the software), I have always considered that the appropriate course is to decide priorities on the basis of delivery dates required by and promised to the customer, leaving the

**369**

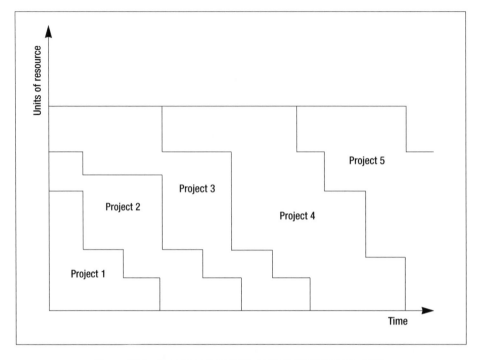

**Figure 20.6    Resource usage pattern typical of residual scheduling**

computer to undertake the extremely complex task of scheduling the many hundreds or thousands of activities.

## MANAGING THE MULTIPROJECT MODEL

It should be assumed that some form of access to the multiproject model will be available to several project managers and other senior project team members. The level of access allowed needs to be considered with some caution, balancing the great potential benefits against the risk of database corruption. The project management programs capable of handling many projects in a large multiproject model are themselves complex and need specialist training to achieve their maximum potential. It is unlikely that every person working on every project will have the necessary skills to interact with the software fully without introducing errors and corrupting the model. Some access limitations are therefore desirable.

It might be sensible, for example to allow project managers and senior staff to have access to the model for interrogation and for the entry of progress data, whilst blocking any action that would change the basic set-up parameters of the model. One useful approach (which I recommend) is to establish a small control

370

or coordination group to act as a system interface (Chapters 7 and 8). This group need only be one or two people strong. Any authorized project member can have access to the database to enter progress data or time sheet information or to view most of the reports produced by the system. Senior members of management or the sales organization can be given access to a copy of the model in which they can test the possible effects of new project opportunities in 'what-if?' testing at the strategic level. Any data corruption in this process will be limited to the copy. The concept of this management organization is illustrated in Figure 20.7.

## DETAILED WORK SCHEDULING WITHIN SMALL DEPARTMENTS

Project schedules govern the general rate at which work will reach various departments by providing achievable work-to lists. Each of these work-to lists will correspond to the network activity level of detail and will establish priorities at this level. Project scheduling should not be expected to cope with the finer level of detail needed for allocating work to individual people or for controlling manufacturing operations in a machine shop.

The production manager must rely on production control methods for timing and sequencing machining operations and the routeing of workpieces. But the project schedule will provide the framework within which production control schedules must work, by recommending start and finish dates and quantifying the priority for each network activity. Project scheduling can ensure that work is loaded to the production facility at a rate which is in line with its total capacity. This should enable the separate production control system to plan all the detailed machining and assembly operations within the project target dates.

The allocation of work to skilled individuals in departments according to their particular experience or aptitudes (for example an engineer with a special flair for gear design) must be left to departmental managers and supervisors. Project resource scheduling does not, therefore, remove or dilute the responsibility of supervisors and managers for allocating tasks within their departments. It is left to managers to decide which of their staff should be assigned to each job on their work-to lists. The purpose of the project schedule is always to ensure that no department is expected to work beyond its capacity.

## BENEFITS

The organization which successfully uses multiproject resource scheduling based on network analysis will enjoy many benefits. The data obtained can help

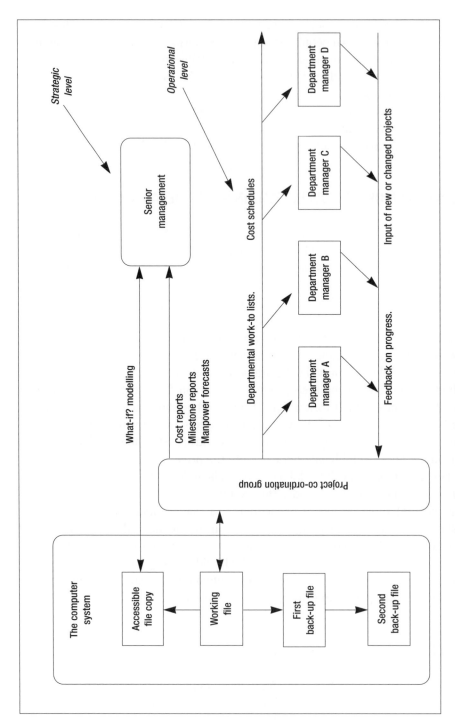

**Figure 20.7  Multiproject scheduling: framework for communication and secure control**

in strategic planning decisions and in recruitment (or redundancy) planning for the whole organization. New project opportunities can be tested in the multiproject model to help management to decide whether or not to bid for them. My own experience has been that greater efficiency, greatly reduced costs, earlier project completion dates and fewer crises can be expected for all active projects.

These rewards can be gained for relatively small cost, provided that appropriate software is chosen and that it is used sensibly by individuals who have been properly selected and trained. It is not necessary to set up a large planning group. One or two specially trained individuals with the appropriate skills and aptitude can cope with many projects. If it is to succeed, however, multiproject scheduling needs total commitment from all project managers and key staff, plus unqualified support from higher management.

Top management support must, of course, include some authorization of funds for the purchase of software and for the provision and training of planning staff. This aspect of management support is, however, of far less importance than the need to motivate, persuade or (in the last event) command every responsible person in the organization to follow the necessary procedures. The highest and most common risk of failure lies in the lack of this total and continuing commitment from all management levels. The multiproject model can only be established, remain valid and justify its investment if all project managers produce their project network plans before the project start dates and report changes and progress to the planning coordinator promptly and regularly.

## REFERENCES AND FURTHER READING

Lock, D. (2000), *Project Management*, 7th edition, Gower, Aldershot.
Reiss, G. (1996), *Programme Management Demystified: Managing Multiple Projects Successfully*, Chapman & Hall, London.

## RELATED TOPICS

# 21 Managing risk

## Chris Chapman and Stephen Ward

This chapter describes a project risk management process initially drafted for the *Association for Project Management (APM) Project Risk Analysis and Management (PRAM) Guide* (Simon *et al.* 1997) and further developed in another book and paper (Chapman and Ward 1997; Chapman 1997). As indicated in the acknowledgements, the basis of this chapter is the experience of a large number of organizations which have successfully used risk management processes (RMPs) for a number of years. This experience was compiled by a working party of 20 drawn from the APM Specific Interest Group (SIG) on Risk Management, a group of more than one hundred who represent a broad spectrum of organizations in the UK. The structured process provided by this chapter has become a standard because of this wide authorship and support, and it works well as a framework for discussion. All of those who contributed know it works well in practice, although we previously described it in different terms, with different emphasis. This process of synthesis also provided useful new insights.

A formal risk management process (RMP) should be applied at all stages in the project life cycle, by both clients (project owners) and contractors (other parties associated with a project). It is most easily explained, and applied for the first time, when implemented in a comprehensive manner on behalf of a client at a sanction stage. This chapter assumes that this is the perspective and stage of interest initially, revisiting these assumptions later.

Most specific RMPs are described in terms of phases (stages) which are decomposed in a variety of ways, some related to tasks (activities), some related to deliverables (outputs/products). The nine-phase structure used here is more detailed than most specific methods. A consequence of the additional detail provided by nine phases is clarification of the relative importance and role of aspects of the process which other specific RMP descriptions emphasize in varying degrees. This includes making explicit several very important aspects which none of the earlier descriptions addresses directly.

The methodology described here is comprehensive, encompassing all important aspects of all methods familiar to all the APM SIG authors. Shortcuts are possible and more sophisticated processes are also possible within the framework provided. Both are addressed in Chapman and Ward (1997). Illustrative case studies and other supporting material are provided in the APM Guide (Simon *et al.* 1997).

## THE RISK MANAGEMENT PROCESS (RMP)

The nine phases are discussed in a start-to-start precedence sequence. Once started all phases proceed in parallel, with intermittent bursts of activity defined by an iterative process interlinking the phases. Each phase is associated with broadly defined deliverables. Each deliverable is discussed in terms of its purpose and the tasks required to produce it. Significant changes in purpose underlie the boundaries between phases. Figure 21.1 summarizes the phase/deliverable structure, Figure 21.2 indicates in linked bar chart form the way effort expended in each phase might be focused over the life cycle of a typical RMP, and Figure 21.3 summarizes the phase structure in flow chart format. Other specific RMP descriptions can be mapped onto the nine-phase description provided here. For example, the four-phase SCERT (synergistic contingency evaluation and response technique) description (Chapman 1979, 1990) and the slightly different four-phase structure plus an initiation phase used by the UK Ministry of Defence (MOD(PE)-DPP(PM) 1991) align as indicated in Figure 21.4. Part of the purpose of the APM SIG PRAM Guide project was the provision of a standard process description and terminology to avoid the unnecessary confusion generated by slightly different descriptions of common concepts.

### THE DEFINE PHASE

All specific RMPs have a define phase, but much of it is usually implicit. Its purpose is to define project effort to date in a form appropriate for the RMP. It involves the following two steps:

1. Consolidate in a suitable form existing relevant information about the project which the RMP addresses. For example, project objectives should be clearly stated, project scope (including breadth and time frame) and strategy need to be defined, activity plans need to be set out at an appropriate, simple, overview level, associated timing and resource usage implications specified, and underlying issues like design and stakeholders' interests determined.

| Phases | Purposes | Deliverables (may be targets not achieved initially) |
|---|---|---|
| Define | Consolidate relevant existing information about the project. Fill in any gaps uncovered in the consolidation process. | A clear, unambiguous, shared understanding of all relevant key aspects of the project documented, verified and reported. |
| Focus | Scope and provide a strategic plan for the RMP. Plan the RMP at an operational level. | A clear, unambiguous shared understanding of all relevant key aspects of the RMP, documented, verified and reported. |
| Identify | Identify where risk might arise. Identify what we might do about this risk, in proactive and reactive terms. Identify what might go wrong with our responses. | All key risks and responses identified, both threats and opportunities, classified, characterized, documented, verified and reported. |
| Structure | Testing simplifying assumptions. Providing more complex structure when appropriate. | A clear understanding of the implications of any important simplifying assumptions about relationships between risks, responses and base plan activities. |
| Ownership | Client/contractor allocation of ownership and management of risks and responses. Allocations of client risks to named individuals. Approval of contractor allocations. | Clear ownership and management allocations, effectively and efficiently defined, legally enforceable in practice where appropriate. |
| Estimate | Identify areas of clear significant uncertainty. Identify areas of possible significant uncertainty. | A basis for understanding which risks and responses are important. Estimates of likelihood and impact in scenario or numeric terms, the latter including identification of assumptions or conditions, sometimes with a focus on 'show-stoppers'. |
| Evaluate | Synthesis and evaluation of the results of the estimate phase. | Diagnosis of all important difficulties and comparative analysis of the implications of responses to these difficulties, with specific deliverables like a prioritized list of risks or a comparison of base plan and contingency plans with possible difficulties and revised plans. |
| Plan | Project plan ready for implementation and associated risk management plan. | 1. Base plans in activity terms at the detailed level required for implementation, with timing, precedence, ownership and associated resource usage/contractual terms where appropriate clearly specified, including milestones initiating payments, other events or processes defining expenditure and an associated base plan expenditure profile. 2. Risk assessment in terms of threats and opportunities, prioritized, assessed in terms of impact given no response is feasible and potentially desirable, along with assessment of alternative potential reactive and proactive responses. 3. Recommended proactive and reactive contingency plans in activity terms, with timing, precedence, ownership and associated resource usage/contractual terms where appropriate clearly specified, including trigger points initiating reactive contingency responses and impact assessment. |
| Manage | Monitoring. Control. Developing plans for immediate implementation. | Diagnosis of a need to revisit earlier plans, and initiation of replanning as appropriate, including on a regular basis specific deliverables like the monitoring of achieved performance in relation to planned progress and prioritized lists of risk/response issues. Exception (change) reporting after significant events and associated replanning. A rolling horizon of detailed plans for implementation (base and contingency). |

**Figure 21.1  A generic risk management process structure (client perspective/sanction stage initiation)**

377

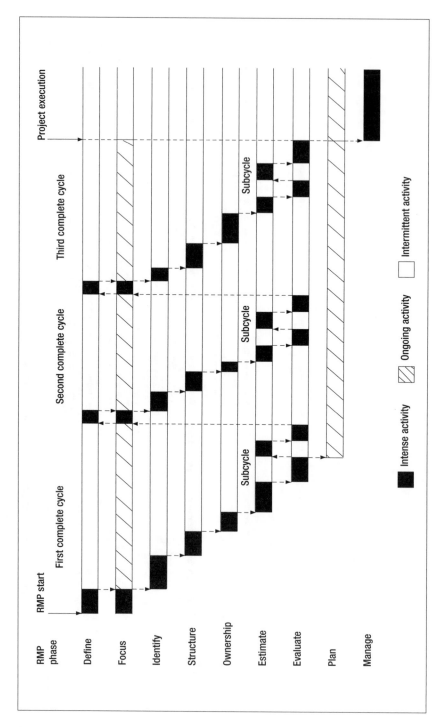

**Figure 21.2 An example of RMP focus over time (client perspective/sanction stage initiation)**
*Source:* Chapman (1997)

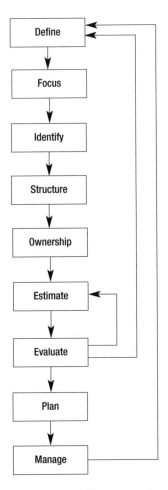

**Figure 21.3   Risk Management Process (RMP) phase structure flow chart**

2. Undertake project management activities to fill in gaps uncovered in the consolidation process. In principle such gaps should not exist, but in practice this is a crucial aspect of the RMP, a form of risk assessment of the project management process to date and response to any concerns.

Achieving both purposes of the define phase is essential, a basic foundation for what follows. The deliverables provided by the define phase may be a single document or parts of several documents. Whatever their form, a comprehensive and complete define phase should clarify all relevant key aspects of the project which the RMP addresses, in a manner accessible to all relevant client staff. The target deliverable is this clear, unambiguous, shared understanding of the project.

| APM (used here) | UK MOD (1991) | SCERT (Chapman 1979) |
|---|---|---|
| Define | Initation | Scope |
| Focus | | |
| Identify | Identification | |
| Structure | Analysis | Structure |
| Ownership | | |
| Estimate | | Parameter |
| Evaluate | | Manipulation and interpretation |
| Plan | Planning | |
| Manage | Management | |

**Figure 21.4   Risk Management Process (RMP) phase structure comparisons**

Six tasks are required to provide this deliverable, the first two of which are specific to the define phase and the last four common to all phases:

1. *Consolidate* Gather and summarize in a suitable form relevant existing information.
2. *Elaborate* Fill in the gaps, creating new information.
3. *Document* Record in text with diagrams as appropriate.
4. *Verify* Ensure that all information providers agree as far as possible, that important differences in opinion are highlighted and that all relevant providers are referred to.
5. *Assess* Value the analysis to date in context to ensure that it is 'fit for purpose' given the current status of the risk management process.

6. *Report* Release verified documents, presenting if appropriate.

Because aspects of the project may not be clearly defined when the RMP begins, and may take some time to be clearly defined, important and central aspects of the define phase may be ongoing. However, the initial concern of the RMP should be to make as much progress as possible with the define phase before moving on to later phases. The greater the level of unfinished business from the define phase, the lower the efficiency and effectiveness of the following phases. Figure 21.2 indicates the way effort expended on the define phase might be timed in a typical RMP. The bulk of the effort is at the outset, but there are further bursts of effort at the start of subsequent cycles through the process, three complete cycles being illustrated in Figure 21.2. Ongoing define phase activity throughout the process is another way Figure 21.2 might portray this phase.

Development of this phase in Chapman and Ward (1997) is structured around Figure 21.5, which uses an influence diagram to explore the relationships

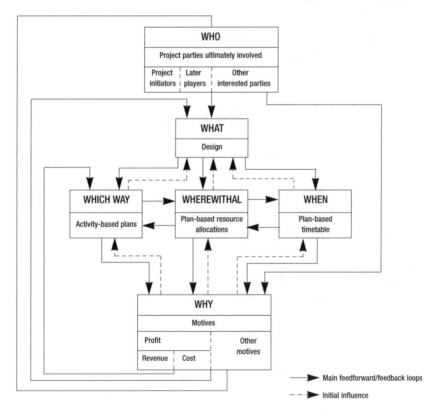

**Figure 21.5 The six W's**
*Source:* Chapman (1997)

between 'the six W's'. Ensuring that all six, and their interrelationships, are fully understood provides an insight of great value. It allows recognition, for example, that the best way to deal with some risks may be to abandon activities generating the risks and achieve objectives some other way, in the limit perhaps redefining success.

## THE FOCUS PHASE

All specific RMPs have a focus phase, although it may be given other titles. Its purpose is twofold:

1. To define RMP scope and strategy as distinct from the strategy of the project the RMP addresses.
2. To plan the RMP in operational terms as a project in its own right.

For example, if an RMP is being applied to test the viability of a new project, a purely qualitative approach may be appropriate. However, if an RMP is being used to assess budgets or bid prices, a fully quantitative (probabilistic) approach may be required, these differences having important specific method and resource requirement implications. Achieving both purposes of this phase is essential, as basic to what follows as the define phase. Some specific RMPs make more of this phase than others. For example, the MOD Risk Strategy Plan (1991) requires more formalization of both aspects of this phase than most. The deliverables provided by the focus phase may be a single document or parts of several documents. Whatever their form, a comprehensive and complete focus phase should clarify all relevant key aspects of the RMP as a project in its own right in a manner accessible to all relevant client staff. The target deliverable is this clear, unambiguous shared understanding of the RMP. As well as the repetitive common tasks (document, verify, assess and report), additional tasks are required to provide this deliverable:

1. *Scope the process* This task deals with issues like who is doing the analysis for whom, why is the formal project risk management process being undertaken (what benefits must be achieved) and what is the scope of the relevant risk.
2. *Plan the process* This task addresses issues like using what resources over what time frame, using what models and methods (techniques), what software and so on, and culminates in a 'tactical' plan for the risk management process, to make the process operational.

The focus phase may be largely concurrent with the define phase, but updating RMP plans will be ongoing. Figure 21.2 shows how the effort expended on the focus phase might be timed in a typical RMP, assuming bursts of activity linked to the define phase, and some ongoing activity. The define and focus phases may be thought of jointly as a higher level initiation phase as indicated in the UK MOD process (Figure 21.4). The define and focus phases are part of an even larger 'scope' phase in the SCERT process (Figure 21.4). They are separated here because they are concerned with very different deliverables, both of which are essential to what follows. Separation facilitates viewing the focus phase as a project in its own right, and applying all we know about good project management to this phase.

## THE IDENTIFY PHASE

All specific RMPs have an explicit identify phase, some using this designation, the UK MOD for example (omitting to worry about the identify/identification distinction). We cannot manage risk if we do not understand:

- where it is coming from, in terms of what detrimental effects might be experienced and the mechanisms underlying these effects;
- what we might do about it, in proactive and reactive response terms;
- what might go wrong with our responses, that is secondary risks.

All RMP methods emphasize a need to identify sources of risk at the outset. Some specific RMPs concentrate initially on impact or effects of these risk sources, leaving root causes or root sources until later. Some specific RMPs which defer the issue of root causes until later also defer the related issue of responses (to effects and root causes), and then only consider alternatives in relation to major risks. However, at least one response, even if it is 'do nothing and accept the risk' (which may not be feasible) must be identified and assumed in order to understand the impact of a risk later in the first pass (iteration) through the process. The RMP is iterative, with frequent loops back, so specific RMPs which in theory do things in different orders can prove much the same in practice. In addition to the four common tasks (document, verify, assess and report), identifying risks and responses involves two specific tasks:

1. *Search* For sources of risk and responses, employing a range of techniques such as pondering, interviewing, brainstorming and checklists.
2. *Classify* To provide a suitable structure for defining risks and responses, aggregating/disaggregating variables as appropriate.

The deliverables from the identification phase should include a risk list (log or register), indicating at least one assumed response, 'do nothing' being one option. The immediate deliverables may include a preliminary assessment of response options associated with these risks, but more detailed lists of response options may be deferred. The key deliverable is a clear common understanding of threats and opportunities facing the project. Opportunities (upside risks and more effective ways of proceeding in general) and associated responses need to be identified and managed with the same resolve as threats. Often RMPs are successful because the process of generating and reviewing responses leads to the identification of opportunities with implications well beyond the risks which led to their identification. Figure 21.2 indicates the way identify phase effort might be focused in a typical RMP, assuming significant preliminary assessment of responses at the outset of this phase and renewed response option identification effort later in areas where risks remain a concern.

## THE STRUCTURE PHASE

It is useful to decompose the UK MOD 'analysis' phase into four phases (structure, ownership, estimate and evaluate), because they each have different deliverables serving different purposes. All RMPs have a structure phase, usually part of another phase, like the UK MOD 'analysis' phase. Some aspects are necessarily integrated with earlier phases, like the structure implied by the lists of activity risks and responses. Other aspects are necessarily left until now, or later. In some specific RMPs structure is implicit, assuming a simple standard structure by default. In general we want the structure used for an RMP to be as simple as possible, but not misleadingly so. The purpose of the structure phase is to test simplifying assumptions and provide a more complex structure when necessary. Failure to structure can also lead to lost opportunities. For example, some responses (general responses) to particular risks can deal with sets of risks, possibly all risks up to that point in a project. It is important to recognize the opportunities provided by such general responses. Structuring involves three specific tasks:

1. *Refine classifications* This entails the review and development (where appropriate) of existing classifications – a 'new' response may be defined because the understanding associated with an 'old' one may be refined or a new classification structure may be introduced, distinguishing between specific and general responses for example.
2. *Explore interactions* This involves reviewing and exploring possible interdependencies or links between project activities, risks and responses, and seeking to understand the reasons for these interdependencies.
3. *Develop orderings* This concerns possible revisions to the precedence relationships for project activities assumed in the define phase. An ordering for risks is also needed for several purposes, including priorities for project

and process planning, and for expository (presentation) purposes. In addition, this step involves developing a priority ordering of responses which takes impacts into account, including secondary risks.

In terms of documentation, the structure phase involves the generation of a set of pictures or graphs, and defining associated mathematical models where appropriate, which captures all the key relationships in terms which are as simple as possible. The key deliverable of the structure phase is a clear understanding, on the part of the analysts and all users of the analysis, of the implications of any important simplifying assumptions about the relationships between risks, responses, base plan activities and all the other W's.

## THE OWNERSHIP PHASE

All RMPs have an ownership phase, with three purposes:

1. To distinguish the risks and associated responses the client is prepared to own and manage from those the client wants other organizations (such as contractors) to own or manage.
2. To allocate responsibility for managing risks and responses owned by the client to named individuals.
3. To approve, if appropriate, ownership/management allocations controlled by contractor(s) and third parties.

The first of these purposes should be achieved before moving on to the following phase of the RMP. Some organizations consider this first purpose as a part of project strategy, which the define phase will identify. Deferring achievement of the other purposes until later is usually appropriate, as indicated by Figure 21.2. This suggests modest effort initially, increasing in subsequent cycles as the first purpose is replaced by the second and third. The deliverables provided by the ownership phase are clear ownership and allocations of management responsibility, efficiently and effectively defined, and legally enforceable as far as practicable. The tasks required to provide this deliverable may be very simple or extremely complex, depending upon contract strategy. For expository purposes assume no fixed corporate contracting policy. In these circumstances the ownership phase involves two specific tasks:

1. *Scope the policy* This task addresses issues such as the objectives of the ownership strategy (the *why*), which parties are being considered (the *who*) and what kinds of risks require allocation (the *what*). It culminates in a policy for risk allocation issues.
2. *Plan the allocation* This task considers the details of the approach (the *which*

*way*), the instruments (the *wherewithal*) and the timing (the *when*). It transforms risk ownership policy into operational contracts.

Separate identification of this phase facilitates treating it as a project in its own right and applying to it all we know about good project management.

## THE ESTIMATE PHASE

All RMPs have an estimate phase, concerned with cost, time and other performance measures. However, it may be given alternative designations, like the 'parameter' phase of the SCERT process (Figure 21.4), or be embedded in a broader phase, like the UK MOD 'analysis' phase. It should have two purposes, which are related but important to distinguish:

1. To identify areas of the project 'reference plan' which *might* involve significant uncertainty, which need more attention in terms of data acquisition and analysis.
2. To identify areas of the project reference plan which *clearly* involve significant uncertainty, which require careful decisions and judgements by the client team.

A single pass to achieve the second purpose is not usually a cost-effective approach. We want to minimize the time spent on relatively minor risks and risks with simple response options, to use the time on major problems involving complex response options. To do this a first pass with a focus on the first purpose can be used, looping back until the second purpose can be achieved with confidence. Initial iterations can involve just the estimate and evaluate phases, illustrated in Figure 21.2 by one such loop (subcycle) within each of the two complete loops back to the define phase. Later more complete loops are effective, providing more attention to detail and some revisions in relation to the previous phase outputs in those areas where unresolved risk issues suggest it is worth applying more effort. Attempting to achieve the required outputs via a single pass is not effective, because it involves attention to detail which proves unnecessary in some areas, as well as skimped effort in areas where more effort would be productive. Part of the process of managing the RMP as a project in its own right is to respond to those areas where risk (threats or opportunities) is identified and better solutions required. The RMP has a clearly defined formal structure, but it cannot be applied in a mechanical manner. Most experienced risk analysts understand this, but many formal statements of RMP methodology do not make this important point clearly enough.

The deliverables provided by the estimate phase are estimates of likelihood and impact in terms of cost, duration or other project criteria identified earlier.

386

Some specific RMP methods suggest numeric probability distributions from the outset. Some suggest likelihood and criteria ranges associated with labels like High (H), Medium (M) and Low (L) initially, numeric measures later if appropriate. Most methods recognize that assessment of some risks may be best handled by identifying them as conditions, associated with assumptions, deliberately avoiding estimation in the usual sense. Most methods recognize that estimation in the usual numeric (or H/M/L label) terms may be a waste of time, best eliminated on occasion. For example, if on a first pass the concern is identifying and then managing any 'show-stoppers', 'estimation' reduces to looking for show-stoppers. The key deliverable of the estimate phase is the provision of a basis for understanding which risks and responses are important. Three specific tasks are required to provide this deliverable:

1. *Select an appropriate risk* As the basis of a process of successive estimation of a set of risks, select an appropriate place to start and assess each successive risk in terms of initial estimates and refinement of those estimates.
2. *Scope the uncertainty* Provide a simple numeric subjective probability estimate, based on the current perceptions of the individual or group with the most appropriate knowledge, to 'size' the risk.
3. *Refine earlier estimates* If the impact of the risk being estimated given chosen responses warrants, or the sensitivity of associated response decisions warrants, refine the initial scoping estimate. This may be undertaken in conjunction with refining the response-related decision analysis.

### THE EVALUATE PHASE

All RMPs have an evaluate phase, although it may be coupled with the estimate phase and embedded in a broader analysis phase, like the UK MOD 'analysis' phase, or it may be coupled with planning and management, as in the SCERT process. Its purpose is synthesis and evaluation of the results of the estimate phase, with a view to client assessment of decisions and judgements. The deliverables will depend upon the depth of the preceding phases achieved to this point, looping back to earlier phases before proceeding further being a key and frequent decision at this stage. For example, an important early deliverable will be a prioritized list of risks, while a later deliverable might be a diagnosed potential problem associated with a specific aspect of the base plan or contingency plans, and suggested revisions to these plans to resolve the problem. Specific loops back to earlier phases are not indicated on Figure 21.3, because they could be to any phase. The key deliverable is diagnosis of any and all important difficulties, and comparative analysis of the implications of responses to these difficulties. Generic tasks other than the three common tasks cannot be usefully defined at the level of generality used here, but specific tasks are discussed and illustrated in Chapman and Ward (1997). The evaluate phase should be used to drive the distinction between the two purposes of the estimate phase indicated earlier, that is a first pass can be used to portray overall uncertainty and the relative size of all contributing factors. Further passes are then used to explore and confirm the importance of the key risks, obtaining additional data and undertaking further analysis of risks where appropriate, before moving on to consideration of project decisions and judgements. However, to make these judgements as part of the evaluate phase, careful consideration has to be given to such judgements in the estimate phase, to capture both uncertainty 'in nature' (inherent in the project) and uncertainty related to our understanding of this inherent uncertainty.

## THE PLAN PHASE

All RMPs have a plan phase. It may be called that, as in the UK MOD process, or be coupled with ongoing risk management, as for the SCERT process. The plan phase uses preceding RMP effort to produce a project base plan ready for implementation and associated risk management plans (actions) for the project management process. Ensuring that these plans are complete and appropriate is the purpose of this phase. The plans are the deliverables. The specific tasks are reasonably obvious in relation to the specific deliverables. Some of the key specific deliverables any RMP plan phase should provide are as follows:

1. Base plans in activity terms, at the detailed level required for implementation, with timing, precedence, ownership and associated resource usage/contractual terms where appropriate clearly specified, including milestones initiating payments, other events or processes defining expenditure and an associated base plan expenditure profile.
2. Risk assessment in terms of threats and opportunities, prioritized, assessed in terms of impact given no response if feasible and potentially desirable, along with an assessment of alternative potential proactive and reactive responses.
3. Recommended proactive and reactive contingency plans in activity terms, with timing, precedence, ownership and associated resource usage/contractual terms where appropriate clearly specified, including trigger points (decision rules) initiating reactive contingency responses and impact assessment.

Proactive responses are built into the base plans, and reactive responses into the associated contingency plans, when they become part of the total project plans.

388

All phases of the RMP should be closely coupled with project planning in general, but the need for this coupling is perhaps particularly obvious in this phase. Most experienced risk analysts argue in favour of reaching the plan phase for the first time early in the RMP, much of the RMP time then being spent in iterative loops concerned with the development of project plans. Figure 21.2 assumes this is the case, showing three complete cycles being used to revise and reassess developing plans as well as refining analysis of risks and responses where this seems worth while. In practice early completion of the first pass may not be achievable, but the benefits of the RMP will be reduced as a direct consequence. Some specific methods suggest a formal separation between base plans (which are owned by the project planning function) and the risk management plans (which are owned by the risk management function). This can be required by organizational constraints, but it is not desirable. It highlights the practical need to separate project management and risk management in some organizations, but the general desirability of seeing risk management as an integral part of project management.

## THE MANAGE PHASE

All RMPs have a manage phase, ongoing as the project is implemented, concerned with monitoring actual progress of the project and associated risk management plans, responding to any departures from them and developing more detailed plans for the immediate future. One key deliverable is diagnosis of a need to revisit earlier plans, the basis of control, and initiation of replanning as necessary. Another is rolling development of plans ready for implementation. The specific tasks relate to the specific deliverables as in the evaluate and plan phases.

Some of the key deliverables that any RMP manage phase should provide on a regular cycle (monthly for example) include the following:

1. Measures of achieved performance in relation to planned progress.
2. A short prioritized list of risk/response issues requiring ongoing management attention, with recent changes in priority emphasized and trends assessed.
3. Related lower level, more detailed reports drawing appropriate management attention to all issues requiring action.
4. Appropriate replanning and exception/change reporting in response to significant events.

# ALTERNATIVE PERSPECTIVES

There are several alternative perspectives which can raise complex issues. These include the application of the RMP earlier or later in the project life cycle, the sharing of risk between clients and contractors, and possible shortcuts to the process. All three of these perspectives raise complex issues and only a few overview comments can be offered here.

## RMP EARLIER IN THE LIFE CYCLE

Implementing an RMP earlier in the project life cycle is in general more difficult, because the project is more fluid and less well defined. A more fluid project means more degrees of freedom, more alternatives to consider, including alternatives which may be eliminated for reasons unrelated to the RMP as the project matures. A less well-defined project means appropriate documentation is harder to come by and alternative interpretations of what is involved may not be resolvable. At a very early stage in a project's life cycle, just after conception, RMP can be like attempting to nail jelly to the wall.

That said, implementing an RMP earlier in the project life cycle is in general much more useful if it is done effectively. There is scope for much more fundamental improvements in the project plans, perhaps including a risk driven redesign or initial design of the product of the project. The opportunity aspects of RMP can be particularly important for early RMP implementation. It is important to be clear about project objectives, in the limit decomposing project objectives and formally mapping their relationships with project activities, because pre-emptive responses to risks need to facilitate lateral thinking which addresses entirely new ways of achieving objectives. Some broad general features of an RMP earlier in the project life cycle include such characteristics as it is usually less quantitative, less formal, less tactical, more strategic, more creative and more concerned with the identification and capture of opportunities.

## RMP LATER IN THE LIFE CYCLE

Implementing an RMP later in a project life cycle gives rise to somewhat different difficulties, without any compensating benefits. Contracts are in place, equipment has been purchased, commitments are in place, reputations are on the line and managing change is comparatively difficult and unrewarding. An RMP can and should encompass routine reappraisal of a project's viability. In this context early warnings are preferable to late recognition that targets are incompatible or unachievable. That said, better late than never.

As a general rule, the earlier the better. However, organizations that want to introduce an RMP and have some choice about which in the context of a range of possible projects to use as test cases would do well to start with a project that has been well managed to the project approval stage. Being thrown into the deep end may prove an effective way to learn to swim, but there are preferable alternatives.

## CLIENT AND CONTRACTOR RISK AND RMPS

Guidance associated with alternative perspectives and associated approaches to contracting are beyond the scope of this chapter, but it may be useful to make the following points:

1. If risk ownership is not clearly defined, a client's risks can be a contractor's opportunities.
2. Clients and contractors necessarily have different objectives, but a contract which leads to confrontation is perhaps the biggest single risk most projects encounter, a contract which seeks congruence in objectives being critical.
3. Clients and contractors both need to undertake separate RMPs, but should establish a constructive dialogue involving input to each other's RMPs; 'fixed' price contracts mitigate against this.
4. The trend towards 'partnering' and other forms of contracting which facilitate cooperative working is a trend to follow, but not blindly, when developing a comprehensive procurement strategy.
5. A carefully and thoughtfully executed RMP should address all the really difficult and sometimes obscure questions, like how contracts should be structured and defined, as well as the comparatively obvious ones like how much the project will cost, if for no other reason than that the answers to the simple questions usually depend upon the assumptions about the difficult ones.

## SELECTING SHORTCUTS

The comprehensive RMP outlined here should be understood as a cohesive, internally consistent, integrated process in full before attempting the shortcuts and modifications that are essential in most practical applications. Practical projects require shortcuts, but explaining how shortcuts should be selected is not a simple matter.

## CONCLUSIONS

The RMP outlined in this chapter is comprehensive in the sense that it is designed to include all specific methods in current use that the authors of the APM Guide were familiar with, to give the reader an overview. Separate chapters for each phase of the process and topics like using the process earlier or later in the project life cycle in Chapman and Ward (1997) give this overview more operational content and clarify its nature with examples. The APM PRAM Guide (Simon *et al.* 1997) elaborates in a different manner, including the use of case studies. Several key issues should be clear from the overview provided here:

1. RMPs are highly structured, but they do not imply a rigid 'paint by numbers' approach. Creativity, lateral thinking and imagination are stimulated by the process, not discouraged.
2. RMPs are in many important respects largely a formalization of the common sense project managers have applied for centuries. The RMP described here is not a new way of thinking, or the engine of an intellectual revolution, which requires a significant change in mindset to be appreciated.
3. The formalization involved in RMPs is central to capturing the benefit of RMPs, as part of the communication processes involved. The level and kind of communication RMP can generate can lead to significant culture changes within organizations. These changes can be quite fundamental, and they can be very complex.
4. Because RMPs might be concerned with very complex issues, it is important to 'keep it simple', adding complication only when benefit from doing so is perceived.
5. The iterative nature of the RMP is central to 'keeping it simple', using early passes of the process to identify the areas that need more detailed assessment in later passes.
6. A particularly useful insight that the focus phase of the APM process captures is the need to 'plan and manage the planning' as a project in its own right, using everything we know about 'planning and managing'. The distinction between 'planning' and 'planning the planning' is important, and making it explicit is very useful.
7. A particularly useful insight that the ownership phase of the APM process captures is the need to manage relationships as a project in its own right.
8. An exciting aspect of the direction this RMP definition and development is taking is its strategic flavour, moving away from tactical planning. It is driving project owners towards seeing project risk management as benefit management of selected projects, and understanding the connections

between individual project benefits and requirements as an output of a programme management approach to project management. Further, they are seeing programme management as a basis for strategic management. Finally, to close the loop, they are seeing project selection as an output of strategic management.

## ACKNOWLEDGEMENTS

Members of the APM SIG on Project Risk Management who were involved in the working party which contributed to the generic process definition described in this paper (and their organizations) are: Paul Best (Frazer-Nash); Adrian Cowderoy (City University, Business Computing); Valerie Evans (Ministry of Defence Procurement Executive); Ron Gerdes (British Maritime Technology Reliability Consultants Ltd); Keith Gray (British Aerospace Dynamics); Steve Grey (ICL); Heather Groom (British Aerospace Dynamics); Ross Hayes (University of Birmingham, Civil Engineering); David Hillson (PMP, Project Management & Professional Services Ltd); Paul Jobling (Mouchel Management Ltd); Mark Latham (BAe-SEMA), Martin Mays (Bae-SEMA); Ken Newland (Quintec Associates Ltd); Catriona Norris (TBV Schal); Grahame Owen (IBM); Philip Rawlings (Eurolog); Francis Scarff (CCTA, The Government Centre for Information Systems); Peter Simon (PMP, Project Management Professional Services Ltd); Martin Thomas (4D Management Consultancy); David Vose (DVRA, David Vose Risk Analysis).

National Westminster Bank colleagues suggested the particularly useful closure of the loop in point 8 in the conclusions.

John Wiley and Sons kindly agreed to the direct use of material from Chapman and Ward (1997) which makes up much of this chapter.

## REFERENCES AND FURTHER READING

Chapman, C. B. (1979), 'Large engineering project risk analysis', *IEEE Transactions on Engineering Management*, **EM-26**: 78–86.

Chapman, C. B. (1990), 'A risk engineering approach to project risk management', *International Journal of Project Management*, **8**(1): 5–16.

Chapman, C. B. (1997), 'Project risk analysis and management – PRAM the generic process', *International Journal of Project Management*, **15**(5): 273–81.

**393**

Chapman, C. B. and Ward, S. C. (1997), *Project Risk Management: Processes, Techniques and Insights*, Wiley, Chichester.

MOD(PE)-DPP(PM) (1991), 'Risk management in defence procurement', Reference D/PPP (PM) 2/1/12, published by and obtainable from the Ministry of Defence, Procurement Executive, Directorate of Procurement Policy (Project Management) Room 6302, Main Building, Whitehall, London, SW1A 2HB.

Simon, P., Hillson, D. and Newland, K. (eds) (1997), *Association for Project Management (APM) Project Risk Analysis and Management (PRAM) Guide*, APM Group Limited, Norwich.

## RELATED TOPICS

# 22 Managing health and safety

## Jim Pearce

Safety is defined as the result of controlling work activities to ensure that accidents are prevented. An accident is an uncontrolled or unforeseen event that is capable of causing one or more of the following:

1. Damage and other harm, such as ill-health, to people.
2. Damage to plant, equipment or premises.
3. Damage to the project, such as interruptions.
4. Damage to the external environment.

Although other names are sometimes used for accidents that do not cause actual personal injury (near misses, incidents, etc.), I prefer to use the term 'accident' to include all of these.

The objective of this chapter is to review the role of occupational health and safety (OHS) highlighting the demands placed upon the project manager to meet good practice and legal requirements (see Appendix 22.1). Above all, a positive common-sense approach is needed. All concerned with the project may be required to justify their actions and omissions before a court (see Appendix 22.2: Personal Responsibility).

## AN INTRODUCTION TO OCCUPATIONAL HEALTH AND SAFETY

Acceptable standards of occupational health and safety (like anything else worth while) do not happen by chance. They can only be achieved by a positive planned approach to all work activities. To help maintain consistent high standards a well-established and formal health and safety management system (HSMS) is required. This must ensure that OHS is an integral part of all corporate and hence project activities. It should establish clear responsibilities for management and further development of OHS standards and procedures to control specific risk activities. In general it will help ensure that the organization:

- identifies possible loss-producing situations, that is hazards, taking into consideration who could be hurt, both employees and non-employees;
- evaluates the risk associated with each identified hazard;
- checks the suitability of existing controls and identifies additional measures required;
- plans the implementation of these control measures;
- monitors and reviews OHS performance; and
- Maintains and where possible improves standards.

A hazard is defined as a property of a substance, equipment process or workplace environment that has the potential to harm persons, equipment or the workplace environment. In other words, it is a built-in property, an integral part of that item or situation. The Health and Safety Executive (HSE) in its publication *Successful Health and Safety Management, HS(G)65* (HSE 1997a) emphasizes the need for an effective HSMS:

> Organisations that are good at managing OHS create an effective framework to maximise the contributions of individuals and groups. Health and safety objectives are regarded in the same way as other business objectives.
>
> Disasters such as the sinking of the Herald of Free enterprise, the train crash at Clapham Junction and the fire and explosion on Piper Alpha provide vivid examples of the effect of giving insufficient attention or weight to OHS. In these, inadequate management decisions led to:
>
> 1. Unrealistic timescales for implementing plans, which put pressure on people to cut corners and reduce supervision
> 2. Work scheduling and rosters which failed to take account of the problems of fatigue
> 3. Inadequate resources allocated to training
> 4. Organisational restructuring which placed people in positions for which they had insufficient experience
> 5. Jobs and control systems which failed to recognise or allow for the fact that people would be likely to make mistakes and might have difficulties communicating with each other.

## THE COST OF HEALTH AND SAFETY

Health and safety can be expensive, but if ignored the lack of control could prove even more expensive. Sooner or later deficiencies will result in accidents and loss due to:

- injuries, damage, business interruption;

- shutdown as a result of prohibition notices;
- criminal prosecutions resulting in potentially unlimited fines or imprisonment;
- costly civil law claims for compensation.

The human and economic cost of failure should be a tremendous incentive to improve safety standards. Another HSE publication, *The Costs of Accidents HS(G)96* (1997), identified the following costs of poor OHS performance:

1. A construction site loss of over 8 per cent of the original tender price of £8 million.
2. An NHS hospital loss amounting to 5 per cent of annual running costs.
3. A transport company loss of 37 per cent of annual profits.

It also revealed that uninsured losses from accidents cost organizations between 8 and 36 times what they are paying in insurance premiums. Therefore, far from all the costs of failure being borne by the insurers, organizations are themselves bearing a substantial portion of the costs. In some cases these can make the difference between profit and loss. In the view of the HSE, investment in loss reduction contributes directly to profits and may yield a better return than a similar investment to improve sales and market share.

This view is held not only by safety professionals, but also by more successful organizations. For instance, the CBI recognizes that effective OHS management contributes to waste and cost reduction and promotes a positive corporate image. Managers should therefore acknowledge that OHS management makes a positive contribution to the success of the organization and grant it at least the same degree of importance as productivity and quality.

As the cost of failure can be high it makes sense to devise and implement suitable control systems. These must take into account relevant (minimum) legal requirements (see Appendix 22.1: The Legal Requirements). Some legal duties are absolute and must be complied with no matter what the cost or practicality. However, most are qualified by terms such as 'as far as is reasonably practicable' or 'suitable and sufficient'. This requires an assessment of effectiveness, reliability and cost relative to the scale of the foreseeable loss. The requirement to carry out assessments has been made explicit in the Management of Health and Safety at Work Regulations 1999 (MHSW) and other regulations such as the Control of Substances Hazardous to Health Regulations (COSHH) and the Construction (Design and Management) Regulations 1994 (CDM). They also require the introduction of suitable control measures.

## RISK ASSESSMENT

MHSW Regulation 3 requires every employer to assess the OHS risks to which employees (and non-employees such as the general public and the employees of contractors) are exposed as a result of its work activities. Identical responsibilities are placed upon the self-employed. Note this requirement does not require an employer to repeat any risk assessments carried out under other legislation, such as COSHH. Each assessment must be periodically reviewed to check its validity. Assessments should also be reviewed when there is reason, such as an accident or the introduction of new or changed systems, to doubt the validity of the original assessment. If an employer has more than five employees, the significant findings of these assessments must be formally recorded. When the assessment has been completed, its findings must be communicated to those who need to take control action, managers, employees and others.

### OBJECTIVES OF RISK ASSESSMENT

A risk assessment has the following objectives:

1. To identify the foreseeable hazards that might cause harm to employees or non-employees.
2. To evaluate the tolerability of the risks arising from these hazards.
3. To ensure that suitable measures are in place to protect exposed persons from harm (and to comply with relevant statutory duties).
4. To identify additional control actions required to minimize these risks. These protective and preventative measures should comply with those identified in current HSE and other authoritative publications.

### METHOD FOR RISK ASSESSMENT

Risk assessments should be undertaken by people who are:

- familiar with good practice and legal requirements;
- capable of analysing and evaluating the task, substance, persons, equipment and environmental (both workplace and external) factors;
- able to identify the need for further information on the risks, or to recognize their own limitations and know when to call for specialist advice;
- able to draw valid conclusions and make recommendations to improve risk control;
- able to make a clear record of the assessment. It should be borne in mind that

the organization could be challenged by the enforcing authorities or the courts to prove that the assessment was adequate (see Appendix 22.1).

A common-sense approach is often all that is needed. The extent to which the exercise goes beyond this depends on the complexity of the project and the identified risks. For complex and potentially high risk projects quantitative risk assessment techniques and possibly external consultants may be used. These techniques could include failure mode and effects analysis, event tree and fault tree analysis, and human action mode analysis. I have found it beneficial if workers required to exercise a significant degree of self-supervision carry out a basic task and environment risk assessment before commencing their work activity.

## A SIMPLE RISK ASSESSMENT TECHNIQUE

Figure 22.1 contains a risk assessment technique which could be useful. If it is necessary to guide and prioritize the implementation of control actions, the risk potential (R) can be estimated by assigning a rating to the potential loss severity (S), the frequency at which this could occur (F), the number of persons who could be affected (N) and multiplying these together.

$$R = S \times F \times N$$

## RISK CONTROL

Decisions concerning the reliability of control measures must be guided by reference to the preferred hierarchy of control principles established by the Regulations (Schedule 1), which is as follows:

1. *Eliminate risks* by substitution with the inherently less dangerous by:
   - use of less hazardous substances or equipment;
   - avoiding carrying out particular operations by using a contractor (see following section on risk transfer).
2. *Combat risks* at source using engineering controls giving priority to collective measures that protect both the operator and anyone else who could be foreseeably at risk by:
   - isolating operators from risk of exposure to hazardous substances by enclosing the process;
   - keeping all persons away from the danger zones associated with machinery by the provision of guards;

| | |
|---|---|
| Step 1 | Conduct an exercise to identify all the tasks involved in the project. These can then be organized into generic groups, so reducing the number of individual assessments needed. |
| Step 2 | Appoint small teams of trained and experienced people to examine the tasks and identify the associated hazards. These teams should include representatives of supervision. A manager should lead each team. |
| Step 3 | Identify how each task is carried out, as this will affect the risk potential. A variant of the hazard and operability studies technique can be used. In this, simple flow diagrams are examined to identify possible failure scenarios by asking 'what-if?' questions. (Workplace observation of established tasks is essential to identify all relevant activities.) This should enable required control actions to be identified. The effect of proposed control actions should be assessed to ensure that no additional risks have been introduced. |
| Step 4 | With established tasks, evaluate whether the risks associated with the identified hazards are adequately controlled or not. (At this stage it may be possible to identify more effective methods of risk control than those currently used.) If control is inadequate, additional measures must be identified and subsequently assessed to ensure that unnecessary risks are not being introduced. |
| Step 5 | A formal record should be made of the significant assessment findings. The assessment should be circulated to management and anyone affected by the risk. The formal record will assist in management reviews and subsequent reassessments. |

**Figure 22.1   A risk assessment technique**

- designing equipment and work procedures to minimize risk;
- as soon as possible, taking advantage of new technology to improve working conditions and methods.

3. *Minimize risk* by:
   - establishing safe systems of work;
   - lowering the number of people exposed and/or the scale of the operation;
   - adequately supervising work activities. The level of supervision required will depend on the level of the risk and the competence of the employee;
   - ensuring that employees are competent by supplying suitable training, information and instruction;
   - the use of appropriate personal protective equipment (PPE) when risks cannot be reduced to acceptable levels by other means. As far as is reasonably practicable the use of PPE should be accepted only as a temporary or emergency response measure.

## RISK TRANSFER

Can the cost of OHS be transferred to someone else? If risk elimination is not possible, risk transfer might certainly be an acceptable way of reducing the potential for loss to a tolerable level. However, remember that a level of risk acceptable to management may be significantly different to that which is tolerable to exposed persons. Methods of risk transfer include:

- subcontracting to a specialist supplier of products or services;
- insurance.

For most organizations Employer's Liability Insurance is compulsory. However, while it is possible to insure against the effects of negligence it is neither legal nor possible to insure against fines that the courts might impose.

There have been several instances where the cost of risk transfer has been expensive for the 'innocent' party. What if the damage was due to the negligence of a contractor? Can a claim be made against it? Contract conditions may be drafted so that damage to the occupier's buildings, contents and plant by fire (a common source of loss) is specifically excluded. Often the client is required to purchase insurance in the joint names of itself and the contractor. Contracts with subcontractors or suppliers often state that they accept no liability for loss of business or profit arising out of any damage caused by them. If liability is accepted, it may be only to replace unacceptable items or for extremely limited sums. The claim may also have to be made within a short period after the supply of the product or service. This is often too short for the damage to be discovered. Even when the specialist contractor has been engaged to supply both specialist plant and operators, the contract can be worded so as to transfer liability for any accidental damage to the client.

Is it, therefore, worth trying to transfer the risk to someone else? Yes, of course it is. The best commercial and technical option may be to use an external supplier. It is, however, necessary to ensure that any contractor used has an appropriate level of OHS competency. It is also advisable to consult a specialist risk manager at the earliest possible stage. Even if no external suppliers are used, it would still be good sense to consult a specialist risk manager to ensure that the project is adequately covered for:

- employers' liability;
- fire and other damage;
- product liability;
- consequential business loss;
- third party (public) liability; and
- environmental liability.

## HEALTH AND SAFETY MANAGEMENT SYSTEMS

The duty to conduct a formal risk assessment is a key requirement. This should provide the basis for satisfying Regulation 5 of the MHSW Regulations. This regulation requires that every employer shall make and implement such arrangements as are appropriate for the effective planning, organizing, control, monitoring and review of the protective and safety measures, that is to prepare an HSMS or safety plan. If there are more than five employees, these arrangements must be formally recorded. This is a similar requirement to that of §2.3 of the HSWA, which requires the establishment and revision as necessary of an OHS policy (see p. 405). As with the HSWA requirement an HSMS should provide practical organizational and risk control standards. These will help the employer or project manager to communicate requirements, ensure competency, monitor performance and hence control OHS. It should be recognized that the HSMS is a facet of the organization's management system. Here are some specific examples of this requirement in recent legislation:

1. The tender and construction phase safety and health plans required under the Construction (Design and Management) Regulations 1994 which implements (within the UK) the EU Temporary or Mobile Construction Sites Directive.
2. The Offshore Installations (Safety Case) Regulations.
3. The Railway (Safety Cases) Regulations.

However, the requirement is not entirely new. The Control of Industrial Major Accident Hazard (CIMAH) Regulations 1984 (replaced by the Control of Major Accident Hazard (COMAH) Regulations 1999) required that:

> A manufacturer who has control of an (specified) industrial activity . . . shall at any time provide evidence including documents to show that he has:
>
> 1. Identified the major accident hazards; and
> 2. Taken adequate steps to:
>    2.1. Prevent such major accident hazard;
>    2.2. Limit their consequences to persons and the environment (by establishing emergency plans); and
>    2.3. Provide persons working on the site with sufficient information, training and equipment to ensure their safety.

A possible drawback of these safety cases is that they focus on the prevention of major disasters, so it is possible for the organization to neglect more routine hazards. All actions taken to control risk should comply with the preferred hierarchy of control measures identified earlier.

# THE ROLE OF OCCUPATIONAL HEALTH AND SAFETY IN PROJECT MANAGEMENT

There are a few basic questions that should be answered before starting any project. These include the obvious:

- Can it be done? Is the project technically feasible?
- Do we have the technical capacity to do it?
- Have we got enough resources to do it?
- Is it worth doing? Will it be profitable?

However, there is one other important question, namely:

- Can it be done without an unacceptable degree of risk to the OHS of those working on the project or to anyone else who could be affected by it?

Whilst the main objectives of a project may be to get the job done, maximize efficiency, minimize costs and manage for profit, it must be recognized that actions to identify and prevent, or reduce, losses due to accidents are essential. OHS must never be regarded as an 'add on' function or an optional factor. Add ons are too easy to remove or nullify. To achieve acceptable standards, safety must be built in from the design concept stage. If this is done, it is more likely that an optimum mix of control measures and performance standards will be achieved for production, quality and OHS.

## PROJECT DESIGN OBJECTIVES AND RESPONSIBILITIES

The OHS objectives of a project are to ensure that it is, as far as reasonably practicable, safe and free from risks to health during:

- design, including any associated research and development;
- construction or installation;
- commissioning;
- setting (for example tool setting of machinery);
- use;
- maintenance and repair;
- modification;
- removal or demolition; and
- disposal.

The above must not only take into account normal conditions, but also meet any reasonably foreseeable misuse or emergency conditions. Responsibility for this lies with senior project managers, senior user (client) managers and their employees. To achieve this, the roles and levels of authority of all participants must be clearly defined, ideally in writing. In addition to the usual actions leading to project definition (see Chapter 25) the client should appoint a competent person (or organization) to act as project manager or planning supervisor. Amongst their responsibilities are to ensure that safety and health considerations are an integral part of the design process and to resolve any conflicts arising from various design requirements. As a result, specialist design requirements will be reconciled and translated into a plan that clearly communicates to implementors a set of established OHS performance standards. This plan should also address any hazards associated with the environment in which the project is to be carried out. Consequently, as many of the client's requirements as is reasonably practicable should be achieved in an economical and safe manner. In addition the product will be of good construction, sound material, adequate strength, be safe to use and without risk to health. The client through its project manager should take the following steps:

1. Assess and appoint competent designers.
2. Establish that OHS considerations are integral to all design stages from concept onwards.
3. Ensure that adequate sources of information are available using internal and external sources as appropriate.
4. Ensure that competent persons carry out design reviews and approve the design as meeting user (and OHS) requirements.
5. Establish a formal change procedure for approving modifications both during development and later on as a service to the client (see Chapter 15).
6. Provide a preconstruction OHS plan to the implementor (principal contractor) which will aid the development of a construction phase plan.
7. Ensure that risk assessment exercises are carried out at appropriate stages.
8. Establish a project technical file (including all drawings, specifications, calculations, operating and maintenance requirements, etc.) to be provided to the client. This would aid subsequent OHS management activity.

## HEALTH AND SAFETY FILE

Among the responsibilities specified by the Construction Design and Management Regulations (CDM) is the preparation of an OHS file appropriate to the characteristics of the project (see point 8 above). This duty is similar to the requirements to produce a technical file included in the so-called Product Directives. These set various requirements that must be met before specified types of products can be marketed within the European Community. In particular, these items must satisfy relevant 'essential safety requirements' (ESRs). ESRs have been produced to cover a number of cases, including use of machinery and hazardous substances, to name just two examples.

## PRODUCT LIABILITY

Managers of projects for the purpose of introducing new products into the marketplace may have to take into account the effects on OHS of domestic as well as occupational users. To provide for this, the EU has produced the Directive on Strict Product Liability. This was implemented in the United Kingdom by the Consumer Protection Act 1987. Strict liability means that there is no need to prove that the producer of a defective product was negligent. What has to be proved by the claimant is that:

- there was injury or damage;
- the product was defective; and
- the defect caused the injury or damage.

An article or substance is defective if the safety of the product is not to the standard that the consumer is entitled to expect. This will take into account all the circumstances including user instructions, accompanying warnings, etc. Amongst possible defences is the development risk defence. This means that the state of scientific and technical knowledge at the time of supply was not sufficient to enable the defect to be discovered. This defence reinforces the need to prepare a product technical file, to keep adequate records and to be prepared to respond in a prompt and positive manner to rectify any defects revealed through user experience. Organizations have been prosecuted for not informing customers when experience has identified previously unknown OHS risks.

## SAFETY POLICY

Every employer of five or more persons is required under §2.3 of the HSWA to prepare a statement of its OHS policy. The purpose of this policy document is very similar to that of a safety plan required by other legislation. It must state the organization's OHS objectives, define the responsibilities of its management and staff and set performance standards that can be used to guide and control implementation. Above all, it must be a working document reflecting a practical management system that helps all persons in the organization to meet personal and corporate obligations. Successful OHS policies are in three parts:

1. A general statement of policy that outlines the commitment of the organization and its management with respect to OHS.
2. Assignment of responsibilities to manage the ongoing development and planned implementation of the policy.
3. Specific arrangements for ensuring that adequate standards will be achieved and maintained. These will consist of procedures to:
   - ensure that management establishes and maintains (i.e. controls) the system;
   - guide cooperation/consultation with employee representatives;
   - ensure dissemination of OHS information;
   - ensure development and maintenance of employee competency;
   - guide the control of specific risks.

The last section should be written as internal codes of practice, setting both organizational and technical performance standards. These will aid monitoring, management review activities and modification as required. The safety policy, like a project safety plan, must be specific to the site or project. However, in multi-site organizations there is a need for a coordinated approach to ensure that high standards are achieved in a similar manner. All employees must have been thoroughly briefed on their responsibilities and the procedures by which they are to be implemented. The content of the three parts will now be examined more closely.

## GENERAL STATEMENT OF OHS POLICY

The purpose of the general statement is to set out a brief but explicit declaration of the organization's commitment to OHS. This should identify the senior executive responsible for coordinating the development and implementation of the policy. It should also include, amongst others, the following commitments:

1. Health and safety issues are just as important as any other organizational objective.
2. Legal requirements are to be considered as the minimum – not the optimum – standards.
3. The organization is committed to review and upgrade standards on a continuous basis.
4. The commitment to involve all staff in the development and implementation of OHS measures.

## DEFINING THE ORGANIZATION

The objective of this part of the OHS statement is to set out the chain of responsibility from executive management through to 'shop floor' employees. It should also define the role of specialist support staff such as the safety adviser.

The general functions of managers for formulating, planning and implementing the organization's policy should be clearly identified and, as appropriate, complemented by specific responsibilities for an established set of tasks. They should be described in sufficient detail to give positive guidance and also to aid performance monitoring by the individual's manager. The review of a person's OHS performance should be regarded as a routine activity to be conducted along with the appraisal of other operational responsibilities. It is recommended that job descriptions should make reference to OHS responsibilities.

## ARRANGEMENTS FOR IMPLEMENTATION

The objective of this part of the OHS policy is to provide procedures that set required standards of performance and give positive guidance on how to meet assigned responsibilities. It should include the following elements:

1. Activities designed to ensure that the management team are in *control* of the HSMS. These should include procedures guiding:
   - the formulation and development of the system;
   - risk assessment;
   - supervision of work activities taking into account the level of risk and the competence of the operators;
   - proactive monitoring activities such as planned inspections;
   - reactive monitoring through the reporting and investigation of accidents;
   - systematic audits of the HSMS; and
   - management review of the system covering:
     - an assessment of the degree of compliance with organizational procedures;
     - the identification of activities where procedures are absent or inadequate;
     - an assessment of the achievement of specific objectives;
     - an examination of accident, ill-health and incident data, accompanied by the analysis of both immediate and underlying causes, trends and common features.
2. The establishment of formal *cooperation* between the management team and employees by establishing an OHS committee which assists in monitoring both the implementation of the HSMS and its ongoing development.

**407**

3. The establishment of systems that guide the acquisition of OHS information and its systematic *communication* both within the organization and outside as required.
4. Activities designed to ensure that *competent* persons are recruited and the ongoing development of their capabilities to meet organizational needs via training.
5. The creation of specific *risk control systems* to meet operational needs, such as the use of fork-lift trucks, chemicals, noise, personal protective equipment, control of contractors, permits to work and so on.

Within all these procedures the following features should be evident:

1. A statement that the procedure is part of the organization's policy.
2. Assignment to a senior manager of responsibility for their development and monitoring of their implementation. This does not detract from the responsibility of those in charge of an area or activity to ensure that standards are achieved. Their responsibilities should also be defined.
3. Procedures should then detail the activities and standards needed to achieve adequate control, through consultation, communication and the competence of project personnel.
4. Arrangements for monitoring performance and management reviews.

## SAFETY MANAGEMENT SYSTEM AUDITS

It is strongly recommended that regular internal HSMS audits are conducted to check that existing procedures are satisfactorily implemented. These should be supported by regular (perhaps annual) verification audits to measure performance against HS(G)65 and other current good practice requirements, including legislation. These audits should be conducted by someone independent of the system and the organization's operational activities. This person could be from elsewhere in the organization or from an external consultancy. A number of proprietary audit systems have been developed to facilitate appraisals, including:

- CHASE: The Complete Health and Safety Evaluation System, from Health and Safety Technology Management Limited, Birmingham
- Five Star System, from the British Safety Council, London
- ISRS: International Safety Rating System, from the International Loss Control Institute
- QSA: The Quality Safety Audit, from the Royal Society for the Prevention of Accidents (RoSPA), Birmingham

Many audits include scoring systems to help evaluate the quality of the HSMS.

408

These are useful as they can help determine priorities. However, care should be taken that the system chosen examines the detail of the organization's HSMS and not just broad-brush concepts.

## ACKNOWLEDGEMENT

Extracts from *Successful Health and Safety Management, HS(G)65* (1997) are reproduced with the permission of the Controller of The Stationery Office.

## REFERENCES AND FURTHER READING

Bird, F. E. Jr. and Germain, G. L. (1985), *Practical Loss Control Leadership*, Institute Publishing, Loganville, GA.

Cooper, D. (1998), *Improving Safety Culture: A Practical Guide*, Wiley, Chichester.

European Construction Institute (1995), *Total Project Management of Construction Safety, Health and Environment*, 2nd edition, Thomas Telford, London.

Fife, I. and Machin, E. A. (1990), *Redgrave, Fife and Machin. Health and Safety*, Butterworths, London.

Greenburg, H. R. and Cramer, J. G. (eds) (1991), *Risk Assessment and Risk Management for the Chemical Process Industry*, Van Nostrand Reinhold, New York.

HSE (1992), *Offshore Installations (Safety Case) Regulations*, The Stationery Office, London.

HSE (1995a), *A guide to Managing Health and Safety in Construction*, The Stationery Office, London.

HSE (1995b), *Managing Risk – Adding Value: How Big Firms manage Contractural Relations to reduce Risk. A study*, The Stationery Office, London.

HSE (1997a), *Successful Health and Safety Management, HS(G)65*, 2nd edition, The Stationery Office, London.

HSE (1997b), *The Costs of Accidents, HS(G)96*, The Stationery Office, London.

Ridley, J. (1990), *Safety at Work*, Butterworth-Heinemann, London.

Smith, A. J. (1992), *The Development of a Model to Incorporate Management and Organizational Influences in Quantified Risk Assessment*, HSE Contract 614 Research Report, no. 38/1992, The Stationery Office, London.

Stranks, J. W. (1991), *The RoSPA Health and Safety Practice Handbook*, Pitman, London.

*The Health and Safety Factbook*, Professional Publishing, London (with updating service).

**409**

*Tolley's Health and Safety at Work Handbook* (1992), 5th edition, Tolley, Croydon.
Wells, G. (1997), *Major Hazards and their Management*, Institution of Chemical
  Engineers, Rugby.

## RELATED TOPICS

| | |
|---|---|
| Configuration management and change control | Chapter 15 |
| Managing risk | Chapter 21 |
| Project definition | Chapter 25 |

## APPENDIX 22.1: LEGAL REQUIREMENTS

Traditional United Kingdom safety legislation, such as the Factories Act 1961, the Shops, Offices and Railway Premises Act 1963 and their supporting regulations, was prescriptive in nature. It was a response to persistent serious accidents and concentrated on a 'safe place/safe machine' strategy. Employers were expected to meet minimum requirements based on what was good practice at the time each law was introduced. Unfortunately, as these requirements often did not keep pace with technology, many loopholes were created and many persons were not protected. Recognizing the need for a change of approach, and that human factors needed to be taken into consideration, the Health and Safety at Work etc. Act 1974 was introduced. This brought many aspects of common law into statute law. In particular, it required the provision and maintenance of safe systems of work (these being safe equipment, safe workplace, safe substances, plus safe person strategies linked together into safe working methods). The goal-setting nature of this Act has been re-enforced by legislation required by the European Union such as the Management of Health and Safety at Work Regulations 1992 and the Construction (Design and Management) Regulations 1994.

### COMMON LAW

Common law is based upon the duty of care. Failure to take reasonable care that your acts and omissions do not adversely affect your 'neighbours' is negligence. These failures could, if damage to persons, plant, property or business interruption results, lead to claims for compensation. Negligence can be defined as doing something that the reasonable person would not do or failing to do something that the reasonable person would do (in the prevailing circumstances (*Blyth* v. *Birmingham Waterworks Co.* (1856)). In occupational terms, a 'reasonable person', that is a 'competent person', is one who has sufficient theoretical and practical knowledge, skill and experience to be able to recognize faults, their significance in the particular circumstances and take control actions. He or she is also not too rash or too timid. A 'neighbour' is anyone who could be so directly affected by one's acts and omissions that one ought reasonably to have them in contemplation (*Donaghue* v. *Stevenson* (1932)). The doctrines of foreseeability and reasonableness are of paramount importance. In *Walker* v. *Bletchley Flettons Limited* (1937) the judge stated:

> The fact that an accident has never happened does not necessarily diminish the foreseeability of one, no more than does the occurrence of one accident yesterday increase the foreseeability of accidents in the future.

**411**

## THE HEALTH AND SAFETY AT WORK ETC. ACT 1974 (HSWA)

The HSWA sets duties on all persons concerned with occupational activities. This means not only the employer, but also employees, the self-employed, manufacturers, suppliers, designers, importers and, potentially, the general public. It should be read in conjunction with the Management of Health and Safety at Work Regulations 1999 and other subordinate Regulations. To fail to meet these responsibilities is a criminal offence that, in some cases, could result in unlimited fines and/or up to two years in jail.

The main duties lie with the employer (see Appendix 22.2: Personal Responsibility). This is to ensure, so far as is reasonably practicable, the health, safety and welfare of its employees (§2.1). In addition, each employer (or self-employed person) shall, so far as is reasonably practicable, ensure that its work activities do not adversely affect the health, safety and welfare of other persons (§3). They must also, in prescribed circumstances, supply information. All persons connected with non-domestic premises (§. 4) shall, so far as is reasonably practicable, ensure safe access and egress, and absence of risks to OHS arising from the use of plant or substances to persons who are not their employees. The employer's responsibility to its employees is further expanded in §2.2, by having to ensure that, so far as is reasonably practicable, the employer:

- provides and maintains safe plant and safe systems of work;
- provides and maintains a safe place of work with safe access and egress;
- provides and maintains a safe and healthy working environment;
- provides and maintains safe arrangements for the use, handling, storage and transport of articles and substances;
- provides each employee with information, instruction, training and supervision as is necessary to ensure OHS.

Section 9 requires the provision, maintenance and free replacement of any item specifically required to be provided by legislation. All the above are absolute duties and must be met (see *Lockhart* v. *Kevin Oliphant* (1992)). A permitted defence is that the dutyholder achieved a standard that was as far as was reasonably practicable.

### The meaning of 'so far as is reasonably practicable'

When a duty is qualified by the phrase 'as far as is reasonably practicable' the required standard of compliance is lower than that which is physically achievable (by current technology). It requires that the reasonably foreseeable losses arising out of the activity be calculated. These should be compared against the costs of control actions. All calculations must be done before initiating the activity.

A control action would be deemed unreasonable if the costs were grossly disproportionate to the loss, that is the risk must be insignificant in proportion to the sacrifice (*Marshall* v. *Gotham Co. Ltd* (1954)). Thus, there is a strongly implied requirement to conduct risk assessment. Failure to carry out this assessment is trusting to luck and a breach of legislation (see *R* v. *Board of Trustees of the Science Museum* (1993)). This assessment must be followed up by suitable control action. There is no obligation to eliminate the risk, only to reduce it to a tolerable (currently acceptable) level and by adequate supervision ensure that these standards are consistently achieved.

### Self-regulation

One effect of the HSWA is that employers or project managers can conduct their business in any way they wish, as long as they can justify their actions within the framework set by modern legislation. This freedom has been termed self-regulation. It is a demanding requirement and not a soft option. Judges' decisions, for example *Walker* v. *Bletchley Flettons Limited* (1937), have determined that there is a duty:

- to identify foreseeably dangerous items and situations;
- to take into account the reasonably foreseeable actions of persons, including forgetfulness, and to some extent wilfulness and stupidity; and
- to take into account circumstances that can be reasonably foreseen.

### When is something dangerous?

Something is deemed to be dangerous according to the following definition:

> In the ordinary course of human affairs, danger can be reasonably anticipated from its use not only to the prudent, alert and skilled worker intent upon his task, but also to the careless and inattentive worker whose inadvertent or indolent conduct may expose him to risk of injury or death.
>
> (*Mitchell* v. *North British Rubber Company Limited* (1945))

### Modern legislation sets objectives

The HSWA and its subordinate regulations are designed to set objectives, rather than specific standards, as these can easily be rendered redundant. These measures are often supported by dedicated approved codes of practice that, when offered in evidence by the enforcing authority, must be accepted as setting minimum reasonably practicable standards. In addition, the Health and Safety Executive (HSE) has published an extensive series of guidance notes and booklets. These, although not automatically admissible in court, provide official guidance to what is 'reasonably practicable' and have significant persuasive influence. It is worth noting that all recent guidance notes and booklets follow the management approach outlined in HS(G)65. Additional sources of information on acceptable standards include codes of practice published by various professional institutions, the British Standards Institution and other authoritative bodies.

## Interpretation

Managers must to be able to interpret the requirements of legislation. Fortunately, the Acts and Regulations themselves often provide definition clauses, and, of course, there are the associated ACoPs (Approved Codes of Practice) and various HSE guidance notes. In general a practical or 'normal meaning' common-sense approach is often required. For example, the term 'as applied' in HSWA §82.2 (dealing with the general interpretation of the Act) requires the application of current technology. Common practice will be taken into account, but beware – common practice is often not good practice. This mirrors the guidance provided in *Stokes* v. *GKN* (1968), where it was stated that the reasonable and prudent employer would:

- use proven, safe and recognized practices;
- keep reasonably abreast of developing knowledge; and
- not be too slow to apply it.

Although a self-regulatory approach is required there is still a need for specific and prescriptive guidance. This will be supplied by Regulations produced to meet the requirements as identified by EU Directives and the HSC. These will produce an increasing body of common standards throughout the Single European Market.

## The burden of proof

The onus of proving what was reasonably practicable does not lie with the enforcing authority. It is up to the accused (HSWA §40) to prove that it was not practicable or reasonably practicable to do more than was done to satisfy the requirement. This is a change from the usual UK criminal legislative position, where it is the responsibility of the accuser to prove guilt. The accused is required to prove that he or she exercised due diligence. That is:

- the hazards and risks had been identified;
- the best available technology not entailing excessive cost had been employed; and as a result
- the residual risk was as low as was reasonably achievable, that is the best OHS option had been implemented.

414

To prove this there is a need to keep records of significant risk assessment and decisions.

## UK IMPLEMENTATION OF EU DIRECTIVES

In the United Kingdom EU directives will be implemented by the HSWA supported by the following Regulations:

- Management of Health and Safety at Work Regulations
- Provision and Use of Work Equipment Regulations
- Manual Handling Operations Regulations
- Personal Protective Equipment at Work Regulations
- Health and Safety (Display Screen Equipment) Regulations
- Workplace (Health Safety and Welfare) Regulations
- Construction Design and Management Regulations, etc.

These Regulations amend and extend previous legislation. Features common to them include:

- the need to identify hazards and carry out a risk assessment;
- the need to control identified risks by means of recognized protective and preventative measures; and
- employers are expected to introduce arrangements for meeting these protective and preventative measures (which means planning, organizing, implementing, control monitoring and management reviews).

It should be noted that the 'due diligence' defence of 'so far as is reasonably practicable' has been excluded from the requirements of these directives and hence the Regulations. Their requirements are absolute and therefore must be met. It is to be hoped that the standard achieved will be interpreted in the light of current technology and what could be considered reasonable considering the circumstances.

## ENFORCEMENT

Health and safety requirements are enforced by inspectors managed by the Health and Safety Executive (HSE) or by environmental health officers appointed by local authorities. The HSE inspector most likely to be encountered by project managers will belong to the Factory Inspectorate. All inspectors appointed under the HSWA have wide-ranging powers to enable them to enforce the requirements of the Act. The most probable outcome of an inspector's visit will be a letter setting out various requirements. If necessary, the inspector will issue an *improvement notice.* This will require protective and preventative measures to be implemented within a specified period. When, in the opinion of the inspector, the circumstances give rise to immediate danger or risk of serious injury, a *prohibition notice* will be issued. This will prohibit specified activities until the situation has been remedied. It is possible to appeal against these notices within 21 days to an industrial tribunal. Failure to meet the requirements of an inspector or a notice is an offence, and when necessary an inspector can initiate prosecution. Depending on the degree of seriousness, cases will be heard either in a Magistrates' Court or a Crown Court (or their Scottish equivalents).

The Offshore Safety Act 1992 (OSA) allows magistrates (sheriffs in Scotland) to impose fines of up to £20 000 for a breach of §2.6 of the HSWA or breach of an improvement notice, prohibition notice or court remedy order. Individuals may be liable for a term of imprisonment not exceeding six months. It also widens the range of OHS offences for which a Crown Court (or its Scottish equivalent) can impose custodial sentences. These courts can imprison individuals for up to two years and/or impose an unlimited fine for serious offences or a breach of an enforcement notice or court remedy order, as well as for offences against earlier legislation (explosives, licensing regimes). Offences other than those outlined above will, under the Criminal Justice Act 1991, attract a fine of up to £5 000.

### THE MANAGEMENT OF HEALTH AND SAFETY AT WORK REGULATIONS

Figure 22.2 contains a set of Regulations which, together with the HSWA, form the framework for all OHS responsibilities.

| Regulation 3 | Requires all employers and self-employed to carry out suitable and sufficient risk assessments. See body of text above. |
|---|---|
| Regulation 4 | Outlines the principles of prevention that should be applied to control risks. |
| Regulation 5 | Requires the introduction of OHS arrangements to ensure risks are adequately controlled. See earlier in this chapter. |
| Regulation 6 | Requires the introduction of health surveillance when identified as necessary (by risk assessment) to aid the control of risks to health. |
| Regulation 7 | Requires the appointment of a competent person or group of competent persons to provide OHS assistance. See Appendix 22.3 covering the role of the OHS adviser. |
| Regulation 8 | Requires the establishment of appropriate emergency procedures. These could range from first-aid arrangements to full-scale disaster plans. They should be based on formal assessment, be fully documented, and form part of the safety plan or safety policy. (It should be noted that in the United Kingdom the Home Office has introduced the Fire Precautions (Places of Work) Regulations 1997 to meet fire emergency situations.) |
| Regulation 10 | Reinforces the requirement of §2.2 of the HSWA to provide information to employees. |
| Regulation 11 | Emphasizes the duties of two or more employers sharing a workplace to cooperate with each other to meet their duties under the relevant statutory duties. |
| Regulation 13 | Reinforces employers' duties under §2.2 of the HSWA to provide training, as necessary. It specifies circumstances where training is required and emphasizes the need to provide refresher training. |
| Regulation 14 | Reinforces the employee's duty not to interfere with preventative and protective measures. It also adds a new duty: to inform the employer of OHS problems and shortfalls in the protective arrangements of which employees become aware. |
| Regulation 15 | Requires the provision of operational OHS information to temporary workers and to any agency providing such workers. |

**Figure 22.2    The Management Of Health And Safety At Work Reguations 1999**

417

## APPENDIX 22.2: PERSONAL RESPONSIBILITY

The Health and Safety at Work Act, the Fire Precautions Act, the Environmental Protection Act and recent Regulations place responsibility on both the employer and individuals from directors to the shop floor. This is fair, as corporate responsibilities will only be achieved by the efforts of individuals on whom the organization must rely. The employer remains responsible for ensuring that managers and others who exercise discretion and judgement:

- are competent to do so;
- have been provided with clear guidelines; and
- meet set performance standards.

Responsibility for carrying out these duties is personal and cannot be transferred to any other person, especially the safety adviser. This role (see Appendix 22.3) should be recognized by all as being to advise the organization with authority and independence. In the eyes of the law, the obligations placed on a manager or individual do not extend beyond matters that are, in practice, within their control, or where authority to act has been delegated explicitly by the employer. Figure 22.3 lists four sections of HSWA which deal with personal responsibility.

An appeal under the Fire Precautions Act (*R.* v. *Boal* [1992]) clarified the interpretation of the term 'manager'. The Court of Appeal determined that there was no intention in §23 of the Act to impose criminal responsibility on anyone but those in a position of real authority within an organization. These were those with the power and responsibility to set corporate policy; there was no intention to 'strike at underlings'. This decision confirms that these sections are designed to deal with offences committed by senior persons, who can be described as being 'of the mind of the body corporate'. A case often quoted is that of *Armour* v. *Skeen* (1977). A worker repairing a bridge over the River Clyde fell to his death. Armour, as Director of Roads for Strathclyde Regional Council, was responsible for supervising the safety of council workers while on the roads. It was alleged that he had not prepared a written safety policy statement for road work and had failed to inform his staff of implications and requirements of the 1974 Act and of the need for adequate training and supervision. His defence, that he had no personal duty to carry out the council's statutory duty under HSWA §2.3, was rejected. This conviction was upheld on appeal. It is noteworthy that for failing to follow the terms of a prohibition notice, a director (Mr Rodney Chapman of Chapman Chalk Supplies Ltd) was not only fined £5 000 under §37, but also disqualified from being a company director for two years under a provision of the Company Directors Disqualifications Act 1986.

As a result of the sections of the Act described here, those concerned with

| §7 | Sets the general duty of employees to take reasonable care to ensure the safety of themselves and others from their acts and omissions. It also requires them to cooperate with others (employer, client, contractors, etc.) to enable them to meet their legal duties. |
|---|---|
| §8 | Requires all persons not to intentionally or recklessly interfere with or misuse anything provided in the interests of OHS.<br>(It is under § 7 and § 8 (and presumably under MHSW Regulation 11) that offences committed by employees would normally be pursued.) |
| §36 | Provides for circumstances where someone (e.g. an organization) commits an offence as the result of the acts or omissions of another person (e.g. an employee). That person may be charged with and convicted of the offence even if proceedings are not taken against the first person. This allows for a range of responses by the enforcing authority. If the organization responsible has acted with due diligence by:<br><br>● identifying the risks;<br>● establishing suitable control procedures;<br>● assigning responsibilities to competent persons who are aware of their roles, have adequate authority and are actively (and adequately) monitored by their managers;<br><br>the organization cannot be held responsible for the failure (*Tesco Supermarkets Ltd.* v. *Nattras* (1972)). If there are inadequacies on the part of the organization as well as those of the individual person, then both could face charges arising out of the failure. Several middle managers have been charged under this section of the Act. |
| §37 | Makes it a separate offence for a breach of any statutory provision to be committed with the consent, connivance or through the neglect of any director, manager, secretary or similar officer of an organization. There are almost identical provisions in §157 of the Environmental Protection Act 1990 and §23 of the Fire Precautions Act 1971. |

**Figure 22.3   Sections of the Health and Safety at Work Act dealing with personal responsibility**

management should note that they are always accountable for OHS standards. This accountability cannot be delegated. It will exist even when the manager is not physically present. It is important that managers ensure that the following procedures are implemented:

1. Hazards have been identified.
2. The risks have been evaluated.
3. Suitable protective and preventative measures have been established.
4. Operational responsibilities have been assigned to competent persons.
5. Proactive monitoring systems (physical inspections and audits) have been established.
6. Accidents are promptly and thoroughly investigated.
7. Necessary remedial actions are promptly implemented.
8. The safety management system is reviewed regularly by those responsible for its overall management.

419

# APPENDIX 22.3: SAFETY PRACTITIONER

MHSW Regulation 7 requires every employer to appoint sufficient competent persons to assist in undertaking the protective and preventative measures. In addition, Regulation 8 requires the employer to establish emergency procedures and nominate a sufficient number of competent persons to implement the evacuation aspects of these procedures. There is also a requirement to ensure that they are allowed sufficient time and facilities to enable them to fulfil their functions. The Regulations require that where there is a competent person in the employer's employment, that person shall be appointed to provide safety assistance in preference to a competent person not in his employment. Persons appointed can only be regarded as competent if they have sufficient training, experience, knowledge or other qualities to enable them properly to assist the employer in its duties. The safety adviser must be competent to advise on the action to be taken or (where so required) to implement such action. This requires suitable training, such as in the National Examination Board in Occupational Safety and Health's Diploma, and appropriate technical expertise.

## COMPETENCE AND DUTIES OF A SAFETY ADVISER

The following list has been adapted, with permission, from the *Criteria for a Registered Safety Practitioner*, published by the Institution of Occupational Safety and Health.

1. Assist management to identify the full range of hazards known and not previously encountered in the workplace by:
   - helping to draw up safety inspection systems and occupational health and hygiene survey programmes;
   - assisting in drawing up procedures for vetting the design and commissioning of new plant and machinery and the introduction of new chemicals into the workplace.
2. Assist in the assessment of the extent of the risks to which persons both inside and outside the workplace are exposed by:
   - maintaining an adequate OHS information database;
   - analysing data on injuries, dangerous occurrences and near misses in the workplace;
   - helping to assess the risks to third parties caused by products, services and pollutants;
   - arranging for quantitative risk assessments when appropriate.

3. Assist in the development of control strategies by:
   - helping the organization make judgements on what is reasonably practicable in minimizing particular risks and so ensuring legislative compliance;
   - assisting in the development of a framework of safe systems of work (including permit-to-work systems);
   - helping to set strategies for risk reduction for particular problems;
   - assisting in setting up strategies for assessing health risks as required by, for example, the Control of Substances Hazardous to Health Regulations;
   - contributing to the development of strategies for eliminating or reducing risk, in cooperation with other professional staff and with line management;
   - helping to analyse training needs and develop training strategies.

4. Assist in the implementation of control programmes by:
   - helping in setting safety objectives;
   - helping to set control programmes for the use of personal protective equipment;
   - organizing and reviewing emergency and disaster planning procedures;
   - providing hazard information to managers, workers and others;
   - assisting in the organization and running of safety education and training programmes.

5. Assist in monitoring and evaluating the success of control programmes by:
   - helping to set up systems for the regular collection of information on injuries, diseases and dangerous occurrences, near misses and the state of the workplace environment;
   - helping to analyse such information to establish whether objectives are being met and whether there is improvement or deterioration in performance;
   - assisting in ensuring that the audit, survey and inspection procedures in the organization are carried out;
   - participating in the investigation of injuries, diseases and dangerous occurrences and near misses to see whether improvements to systems of work or equipment are needed;
   - encouraging prompt remedial action to be taken to rectify deficiencies.

6. Help maintain an adequate organizational framework for safety and health programmes by:
   - assisting in the preparation and revision of the organization's OHS policy;
   - helping to establish effective safety committees and effective cooperation with workplace employee safety representatives;
   - managing the work of subordinate safety and health staff (in larger organizations);

- cooperating effectively with other professional safety and health staff;
- influencing engineers, architects, buyers, members of elected bodies and others on safety issues;
- helping to set up and maintain effective safety and health information systems, including access to outside sources;
- helping to maintain satisfactory relations with safety and health enforcement agencies, and other relevant outside bodies (e.g. insurers, trade associations, etc.).

In addition the employer should ensure that the person or persons appointed have adequate resources and sufficient seniority and independence of action in the organization.

# APPENDIX 22.4: CONSTRUCTION HEALTH AND SAFETY

The Construction (Design and Management) Regulations 1994 (CDM) set out the responsibilities of the client, the planning supervisor and the principal contractor. These require the client to appoint a competent person or organization to act as planning supervisor as well as competent designers and a competent principal contractor. The duties of the planning supervisor include the following:

1. Assisting as necessary in the assessment and appointment of competent designers.
2. Coordinating the design process to ensure that risks have been identified and that the design takes the general principles of risk control into account, by:
   - ensuring technical and/or organizational aspects are decided, in order to plan the various items or stages of work which are to take place simultaneously or in succession;
   - assisting in estimating the period required for completing such work or work stages.
3. Drawing up or causing to be drawn up an OHS plan setting out in detail the hazards associated with the construction process and those associated with the site.
4. Preparing an OHS file appropriate to the characteristics of the project, containing relevant information that should be taken into account during any subsequent works.
5. Assisting in the assessment and appointment of an organization that will act as the 'Principal Contractor'.
6. If required by the client, to act as their 'on-site adviser' and monitor progress and OHS standards.

During project execution the responsibility for OHS rests mainly with the principal contractor. However, the client has a responsibility to monitor standards to ensure that the project activities are not endangering third parties. Failure to do so can and has resulted in the client being successfully prosecuted. The main responsibilities of the principal contractor are as follows:

1. Draw up a 'construction phase' OHS plan.
2. Select and coordinate the activities of subcontractors ensuring that they have the relevant competencies and information to perform assigned tasks safely.
3. Monitor and coordinate OHS and operational provisions to ensure that all persons:
   - apply the preventative and protective principles in a consistent manner;
   - where required, follow the safety and health plan referred to above;

- make, or cause to be made, any adjustments required to the safety and health plan and provide information to the planning supervisor to take into account the progress of the work and any changes that have occurred;
- organize cooperation between subcontractors and the self-employed, including successive employers on the same site;
- coordinate their activities and information flow, with a view to protecting workers and preventing accidents and occupational health hazards;
- coordinate the arrangements for checking that working procedures are being implemented correctly;
- take all necessary steps to ensure that only authorized persons are allowed on the construction site.

# Part IV
# Process

# INTRODUCTION TO PART IV

In Part IV we consider the processes by which the project's products or facility are delivered. We explain what the life cycle is, why it is an inherent part of project management and its implications. We then describe three stages of the life cycle: start-up, definition, and implementation and control.

### Chapter 23: Managing the project life cycle

In Chapter 23 Chris Dawson describes the project life cycle. The modern approach is to view the life cycle as a process; the project is a process to convert inputs into desired customer outputs. Chris Dawson differentiates between two life cycles: the project management life cycle, the process by which the project is planned and executed, and the product life cycle, the process by which the inputs are physically converted into the outputs. He describes the subprocesses in the project management life cycle and the overlap between the project and product life cycles. He ends by discussing network models of the life cycles.

### Chapter 24: Managing the project start

Roland Gareis describes project start in Chapter 24. This is not strictly a stage of the life cycle, as start-up can be conducted at the start of every stage. A project is a social system, which exists in its context, and it must be integrated into that context. The objectives of start-up are considered, and the methods, timings and design. A benchmarking process to provide quality check is briefly described.

### Chapter 25: Proposal, Initiation and feasibility

Stephen Simister describes the project definition stage in Chapter 25. He describes the essential features of the proposal, initiation and feasibility stages of the project and provides a detailed description of the elements of a feasibility study.

### Chapter 26: Managing implementation and progress

In Chapter 26 Dennis Lock examines implementation and progress monitoring and control. He introduces an essential framework for implementation and progress measurement, and then discusses the need to communicate the plan. He describes the key issues of start-up as they relate to implementation and progress measurement and discusses how to manage progress in several functions. He also considers higher levels of progress measurement and some special cases. He then describes methods of progress measurement and control, in particular the earned value method, change control and progress reporting.

### THE MISSING CHAPTER: PROJECT CLOSE-OUT

It was intended at this point to include a chapter on project close-out. However, I could not find an author. I could have written a chapter myself, paraphrasing Chapter 13 of my book, *The Handbook of Project-based Management* (Turner 1999). However, I decided to leave the chapter out, almost as a homage to the reason why I was not able to find an author. In an article in the *International Journal of Project Management*, Thermistocleous and Wearne (2000) reviewed the number of papers that have appeared in the *International Journal of Project Management* and the *Project Management Journal* on topics from the Body of Knowledge. In nearly 20 years of *IJPM*, and 25 of *PMJ*, there has been not one paper on project close-out. There were about 250 papers in *IJPM* in that time, covering 500 topics. There are about 50 topics in the Body of Knowledge, so each one was mentioned on average ten times in that period, but not once was project close-out mentioned. As editor of *IJPM*, during 1997 and 1998 I conducted an exercise to determine the areas of interest of the members of the International Editorial Board and the other referees. I asked each person to chose five topics from a similar list. One hundred people responded and so 500 selections were made, with an average of ten selections per topic. *Not one person nominated project close-out.* Nobody is interested in project close-out as a research topic. Everybody seems to enjoy the thrill of the chase, but not the final kill. I am therefore leaving this chapter out, as a message to people – 'We need research on project close-out.' As Eric Gabriel once said to me, 'Everybody remembers ineffective project close-out; nobody remembers effective project start-up.'

## REFERENCES

Thermistocleous, G. and Wearne, S. H. (2000), 'Project management topic coverage in journals', *International Journal of Project Management*, **18**(1).

Turner, J. R. (1999), *The Handbook of Project-based Management*, 2nd edition, McGraw-Hill, London.

# 23 Managing the project life cycle

*Christian Dawson*

A project is a complex process that has three dimensions and can, therefore, be viewed from three different angles:

1. A project can be viewed as a number of stages through which it is seen to progress to completion. This 'stages interpretation' now tends to have been superseded by a process perspective in which a project is viewed as a multifarious process consisting of subprocesses that interact with one another. While this perspective can be rather complex, it is possible to visualize the project process in simple terms using diagrammatical project management techniques. These techniques include familiar activity networking techniques (such as PERT and CPM), Gantt charts, breakdown structures, organizational charts and so on.
2. A project can be viewed from the different management levels at which it is planned and controlled. These levels focus on either long-term or short-term goals and the ways in which projects integrate into organizations, business areas and markets. From this perspective we can also see the broader environmental impacts of projects and their industrial context.
3. From the third perspective a project is seen to be composed of five elements that require managing and controlling throughout the entire life cycle: time, cost, quality, scope and resources. While scope is sometimes interpreted as an aspect of quality and subsumed within it, identifying scope as an element in its own right enables it to be managed and controlled more easily. All projects contain these five elements to a greater or lesser extent. Trade-offs and attention to these elements vary throughout the project life cycle, and also from one project to the next.

A factor subsumed in each of these perspectives is risk. Because of the unique nature of projects, risk is inherent throughout all levels of a project, all elements of a project, and within the project processes themselves. Managing risk was discussed in detail in Chapter 21.

In addition to the three perspectives one can also focus on the numerous support elements that help people deal with the complexities of the project process. These support elements include techniques, methods, guidelines, models and software tools, and are often studied in their own right, although they must be applied in context to address the needs of each of the perspectives introduced above.

This chapter focuses on the project management life cycle from a process perspective and examines how this process and its subprocesses are managed and controlled.

## PROCESS MODEL

At a holistic level, the project management life cycle can be represented by a simplistic process model. Such a model shows the life cycle as a process that takes a set of inputs, acts upon them through a coherent set of activities and produces a consequential set of outputs. This process is well represented by the meliorist model (Figure 23.1). The meliorist model shows how a project transforms an existing situation, $S_A$, into a desired situation, $S_B$, by performing a set of actions that represent a project. This desired situation may mean different things to different people; the project's sponsor, the project manager, the users and so on. The desire to move to $S_B$ might stem from the fact that situation $S_A$ is currently unacceptable and a project is seen as a solution to this problem. This problem may not yet exist but may be anticipated in the future. Before the problem arises something, a project, must be done to avert it. Alternatively, while

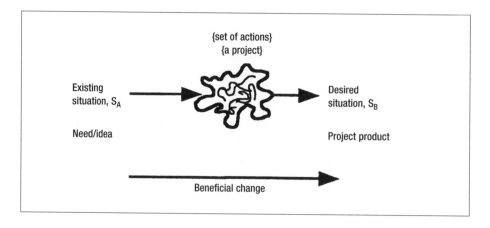

**Figure 23.1  The meliorist model interpretation of the project process**

situation $S_A$ may be satisfactory, there may be a more appealing situation at $S_B$ to which people are drawn. In this case there is a 'pull' towards an appealing $S_B$ rather than a 'push' from an unsatisfactory $S_A$. Whichever the case, a project's objective is to bring about some form of beneficial change, whatever this happens to be.

## PROCESSES

There is more to a process than a mere collection of tasks or functions. A process is a coherent series of activities that takes a collection of inputs and creates a set of outputs. A process should be capable of improvement, it should be supported by tools, it should be measurable and it should be repeatable (Down *et al.* 1994). It is by its inputs and outputs that a process is identified and defined. In project management terms, these inputs and outputs are represented by either documents or documentable items. No item should be produced from such a project process without being documented in some way or another.

The input to the meliorist model introduced above would be a documented idea for a project, a documented problem that requires resolution, or a set of documentation from a previously completed product phase. The output from this holistic model is the project's documented product. A project's product is not necessarily a physical object but a product in the most general sense of the word. It might be a new organizational structure, a new set of management procedures, an industrial plant, a bridge, a set of aircraft designs, a set of quality standards and so on.

While inputs and outputs are crucial to the understanding of processes, another of their key features is that they must consist of a *coherent* series of activities. The key term within this definition is coherent. A process must consist of activities that interrelate and combine effectively with one another and it must be understood and manageable. A process that is merely identified as a number of muddled, connected activities will be inefficient, difficult to manage and unrepeatable. This is not to imply that projects are repeatable. Projects are unique endeavours that bring about beneficial change. The project management process that is used to manage a project that achieves this aim should itself be repeatable and be applicable in many project scenarios. In this way project success through successful project management processes can be achieved again and again.

## PRODUCT AND PROJECT PROCESSES

While the meliorist model provides an interesting academic interpretation of the project management process, it provides little information, explanation or technique that can be utilized. It is the subprocesses within this model that are more valuable and require closer scrutiny and explanation. Looking in more detail at these subprocesses, the Project Management Institute identifies two categories into which project processes can be classified (PMI 1996: 27):

- Project management processes
- Product-oriented processes

Project management processes are those processes that deal with managing and controlling the project as a whole. That is, they represent the work a project manager performs to hold a project together on a daily basis: defining work, organizing resources, planning, scheduling, controlling, motivating, delegating, etc. Product-oriented processes are those concerned directly with developing the project's product. These are the processes performed by the project's resources, which are managed and controlled by the project management processes. A project's resources cover everything used in a project, predominantly those resources used to develop the project's product. These resources include staff, contractors, equipment, machinery, computer access time, rooms, consultants, plant, software, hardware, etc.

## LIFE CYCLES

Before looking in more detail at projects from a process perspective, the stages interpretation will be discussed. What is sometimes unclear is the scope of a product's life cycle that such a stages interpretation encompasses. For example, Field and Keller (1998) discuss whether a feasibility study is part of this cycle. Towards the latter stages of the project process it is arguable whether a project would encompass operation, maintenance and retirement of the project's product. However, many projects exclude these activities as they occur after the project is signed off. For example, when building a bridge, while the project's sponsor may be concerned with future maintenance, the project manager would only be concerned with completing the bridge on time and within budget. The problem arises because of a confusion between the project and product life cycles. A product life cycle can span several years – from the time the idea for the product is formed to the time the product is finally phased out, retired and replaced. A project, on the other hand, progresses through a set of stages that occur within a much more limited period. A project is unlikely to encompass the broad life cycle of the product and is usually focused on the initial development of a new product.

## PROJECT MANAGEMENT STAGES

The number of stages into which projects can be categorized varies, and many authors identify different numbers and different levels of detail. Weiss and Wysocki (1992), for example, identify five distinct stages as definition, planning, initiation (organize), control and close. The previous edition of this book (Lock 1994) identifies ten distinct stages of project management and Turner (1999) defines four such stages as germination, growth, maturity and metamorphosis. For the purposes of this chapter, Weiss and Wysocki's five-stage interpretation will be used.

Unlike the process interpretation, classifying project activities into stages can confine them to temporal frameworks and can ignore interrelationships, interactions and possible repetition of work.

## PRODUCT LIFE CYCLE

The product life cycle is much broader in terms of its general scope than the project life cycle might be. Not only is it difficult at times to determine when a product is 'finished' but it is also difficult to define just when its development started. Does one, for example, include in the product life cycle activities such as development of the initial product idea? To overcome this problem it is possible to define a broad set of stages that encompasses the entire spectrum of activities that occur in a product's life time. Such a definition is shown in Figure 23.2. This definition covers operation and eventual retirement of a project's product. Analysis refers to the initial investigative work on a project's product – its idea, feasibility, definition and planning. Synthesis encompasses the work on the product itself – its development. Operation represents the implementation, use

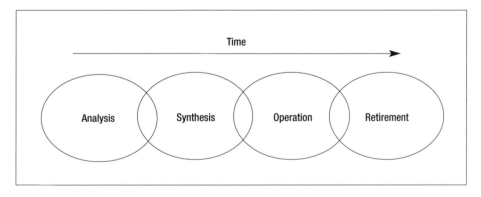

**Figure 23.2   The product life cycle**

and maintenance of the project's product, and retirement represents the final withdrawal and replacement of the product. These stages are not mutually exclusive and common activities occur at the overlaps between each stage. For example, between operation and retirement, a phased implementation of a new system would lead to a reduced operation of the existing system and the initial pilot running of the new one.

## PRODUCT DEVELOPMENT PHASES

One other important aspect of the product life cycle is to identify the phases through which a product is developed. Phases are elements of a product's work breakdown structure. They identify the actual work that will be performed to achieve the product's objectives. While product life cycle stages represent abstract categorizations that attempt to classify work in particular time frames, phases represent key developments of the actual work itself. For example, a project to develop a motorway might be split into a number of phases: Phase 1: build motorway between junctions 1 to 3; Phase 2: build motorway between junctions 4 to 5; Phase 3: construct a new junction at 5A and so on. Each of these phases is a project in its own right and would be planned and managed as such.

## THE PROJECT/PRODUCT OVERLAP

Although the project and product life cycle have been defined separately it is important to be aware of the relationship between them. A project can be a small part of a larger product development – representing the development of one phase of the product. Alternatively, a project may wholly encompass the entire product life cycle. Each phase of a product development should be managed as a mini project and consequently should be managed through the five stages of the project life cycle. Figure 23.3 provides an interpretation of this issue. In this figure two projects are shown:

1. Project A represents a small project to complete the initial feasibility study and design for a system – Phase 1 of the product's development. This project is managed and pursued just like any other project. The project's product in this case would be the completed analysis, design and feasibility documentation for the larger product.
2. Project B is a medium-sized project to investigate, design, develop and implement a system. This project would be concerned with integrating the system into its working environment and setting up operational procedures. This project encompasses Phases 1 and 2 of the product's development.

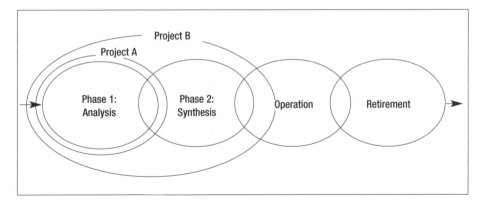

**Figure 23.3   Projects as part of the product life cycle**
*Source:* Adapted from PMI (1996)

This interpretation of project and product can be compared with Boehm's (1988) spiral model within the software development industry. In this model the product is seen to develop through a series of phases: requirements, development, integration and maintenance. Each of these 'phases' is completed in turn through a four-stage process: determine objectives, evaluate alternatives, develop, plan next phase. Thus, each phase of a system's development can be interpreted as a mini project with its own budget, goals and timescales.

# PROJECT PROCESSES

## PROJECT MANAGEMENT PROCESSES

While stages represent the high level states through which projects progress, project management processes represent the series of actions that are performed to bring about a project's result (PMI 1996: 27). In reality project management activities occur in parallel with each other, they might be repeated and they might occur at different stages of the project process. By classifying activities from a process perspective the temporal problem of the stages interpretation diminishes. There are six project management process groups that occur within a project's life cycle. These are shown in Figure 23.4 (adapted from PMI's PMBoK, 1996). Rather than looking at the activities that are performed within a particular stage of the project life cycle, and at the order in which these activities are performed, the process perspective identifies the processes that are performed irrespective of project stages. These processes would be repeated for each phase of a product's development. [This part of the handbook describes initiation processes, definition

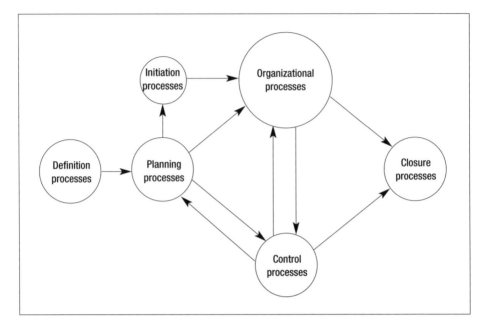

**Figure 23.4   Project management processes**

process and control processes. Planning and organizing processes are covered in the previous part when considering the functions planned and organized. The absence of closure processes is explained in the introduction to this part.]

### Definition processes

Definition processes (Chapter 24) are those used to investigate the feasibility of the project or product phase, identify a problem that needs resolving, define the project in terms of goals and objectives, submit a project proposal and obtain project go-ahead. They might also involve arranging finance, planning permission, sorting out environmental issues and contracts, negotiating legal problems, identifying the project's goal and objectives, defining the project in specific and general terms, and committing to the project.

### Planning processes

Planning processes (Chapters 14 to 22) are those used to prepare workable plans and identify how the project will fulfil its business needs. Project planning involves identifying the work that needs to be performed to complete the project successfully, deciding on how to approach this work, estimating and scheduling work and resources, budgeting and planning cash flows for the duration of the project and defining standards that need to be maintained. Planning processes also involve scope planning and definition, and activity planning and sequencing. It is during these processes that project management tools and techniques are applied with enthusiasm. These include techniques such as Gantt charts and activity networks, work breakdown structures, organization structure charts, responsibility matrices and so on.

## Initiation processes

Initiation processes (Chapter 24) relate to a project's set-up and start-up. They are important as they include motivating staff, communicating the plan, arranging staff and resources into a work routine, setting up communications strategies, allocating rooms and work areas, assigning work to resources and starting the project with a kick-off meeting or launch workshop. They have a particular impact on the motivation, confidence and understanding of a project's workforce. Failure to motivate staff and provide them with a clear view of the project's goal may well lead to a poor team performance that is difficult to rectify later.

## Control processes

Control processes (Chapter 26) focus on the four elements of time, cost, quality and scope as the project progresses. Control processes are those concerned with monitoring these elements with respect to project plans, trading them off against one another, identifying variances and taking corrective action where necessary. Any changes introduced through a project's control processes must be communicated and coordinated across the project as a whole.

## Organizational processes

These concentrate on coordinating and organizing the fifth project element – the resources that do the work to develop the product. While control processes focus on more abstract project elements, organization focuses on the project's resources and actually getting the work done.

## Closure processes

The final set of processes relates to closure activities. These processes cover those activities concerned with getting the project's product accepted and bringing about the project's completion in an orderly fashion. The project's product must be integrated into the organization, system or environment into which it was designed to fit, resources must be disbanded and reassigned and commission testing must be undertaken.

This process interpretation identifies the interactions between processes through the transfer of documents and documentable items. In Figure 23.4 the interconnecting arrows between the processes represent this flow of items. Thus the output from one process serves as an initiating input to another. For example, from a project's definition processes a product definition document will be produced. This will form the basis from which project plans can be drawn up by certain planning processes.

## PROCESS OVERLAP

Figure 23.4 shows the relationship between processes and how documents and documentable items pass between them. However, this figure appears to imply that each process is discrete and occurs only when another set of processes have completed and created an instigating input. This seems to return to the distinct stages interpretation of projects. However, this is not the case as process groups overlap with one another and occur simultaneously. Figure 23.5 shows an interpretation of this overlap. In this figure it is clear that project management processes do not happen in isolation but overlay one another and occur simultaneously throughout the project life cycle. For example, while definition processes start well before anything else, there is a time when they are performed simultaneously with planning processes. Planning processes in turn continue until almost the very end of a project (its closure). This happens because replanning may be necessary as schedules are missed or resources change.

## PROCESS ACTIVITY LEVELS

Figure 23.6 (adapted from PMI 1996) presents the intensity of overlap between process groups and shows the level of activity within each group throughout the life cycle. Note this activity level represents project management activity not product-oriented activity. Thus it represents the intensity of project-focused activity performed by the project manager. Figure 23.6 also presents project management activity for the entire duration of a project. This is the sum of individual project process activities. Notice how total project-oriented activity remains 'relatively' consistent once a project is underway. It is only during the initial definition and final closure processes that project management activity declines.

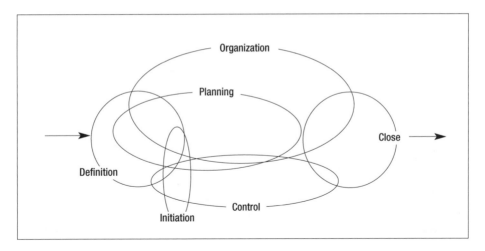

**Figure 23.5  Overlapping representation of project management processes in the life cycle**

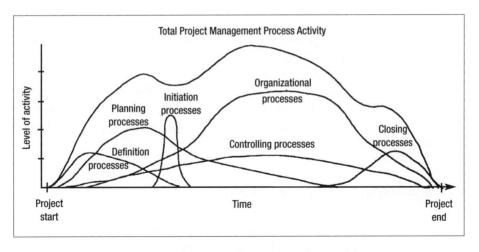

**Figure 23.6  Level of activity of project management processes**
*Source*: Adapted from PMI (1996)

## PRODUCT PROCESS ACTIVITY

The level of effort directed towards developing the actual project's product only picks up during the central 80 per cent of the project life cycle. This is shown in Figure 23.7, which reveals the level of activity directed towards the development of the product by the project resources. This increased activity roughly coincides

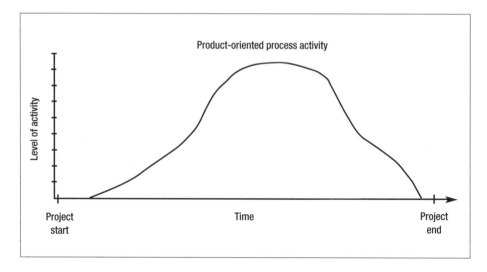

**Figure 23.7    Level of activity on product development processes during the course of a project**

with the peak of project-oriented process activity within a project. During a project's definition and planning stages no product development activities are performed. It is only when a project's initiation, organization and control processes are performed that resources focus on getting the job done. Once underway, work on the project's product intensifies. This work is completed before the project's final closure which remains the concern of the project manager.

## EXTENDED PROCESS LIFE CYCLE MODELS

The previous sections of this chapter aimed to set within context project management processes. This has been achieved by moving away from the stages interpretation of projects. The move towards a process interpretation can be likened to the ideas introduced by business process re-engineering (BPR) during the 1990s in which organizations are viewed from a process rather than a functional perspective.

### PROJECT LIFE CYCLE PROCESS MODELS

The project process model in Figure 23.4 is stable at this top level, because the processes involved with project management should be clear and follow a

442

repeatable model such as the one identified. On the other hand, the product development process is not fixed. This process is product dependent as the product might well be difficult to define as, for example, in research and development projects. Some flexibility in the product development process is therefore required. This flexibility can be introduced and managed in two ways. First, by identifying alternative routes through the product development process and, second, by using flexible planning techniques that allow plans to evolve as projects progress. Rolling wave planning is just such a technique. Rolling wave planning (Turner 1999; CCTA 1996) provides a broad plan that the project will follow, leaving any details until each phase of the product life cycle is tackled. Thus, project planning activity ebbs and flows like a rolling wave throughout the entire life cycle of the project. In this case what happens to the project's product at each stage of the product life cycle is unclear at the initial stages. Rolling wave planning allows plans to be firmed up as a project progresses and more is learnt about the product.

## HYBRID PROCESS MODELS

The alternative is to attempt to identify any potential routes through the product development process at a much earlier stage. This technique can be achieved by using hybrid models that combine all potential development routes into one model at the start. This has an advantage over rolling wave planning in that potential trouble spots, repetition and alternatives are explicitly identified early on. Thus contingency plans can be put into effect sooner and more accurate assessments of risks can be made.

One of the main characteristics of projects that separate them from ordinary day-to-day operations within a company is that they are unique. The uniqueness of projects introduces problems for project management as it implies that a repetitive, consistent product process model cannot be used 'off the shelf'. Such a process would need adopting and adapting to each new project situation. An alternative is to use hybrid processes that implicitly incorporate flexibility into their structure. Hybrid processes combine several product process models. They identify complex process structures at several levels. These models can be relatively flexible in their lower levels but relatively stable at the top.

## EXAMPLE

As an example, the software development life cycle is presented. Figure 23.8 shows a simplified version of this life cycle. This model is an extract from the broader life cycle phases of the software development process:

**443**

1. Requirements definition is the documentation produced by the users identifying their needs for a system.
2. This is interpreted by the software developer (systems analyst) to produce a requirements specification. A requirements specification aims to remove any inconsistencies and ambiguities from the users' requirements definition in order to provide a firm, clear specification of what the users need from the system. This is sometimes referred to as a functional specification or a system specification.
3. Now that the users' needs have been clearly specified it is possible to put together a detailed design for the system that will address those needs. This results in the design specification.
4. From this design the system can be developed and implemented (system development and implementation).

Looking more closely at this process it is clear that feedback and repetition *may* take place as indicated by the arrows. Figure 23.8 actually identifies a hybrid process. In this model the conventional software development life cycle has been combined with a throw-away prototyping model and an evolutionary prototyping model. The process now consists of potential alternative development routes. For example, once the requirements specification has been drawn up the systems analyst may wish to check that these are a fair representation of the users' needs by producing a disposable prototype. This prototype is presented to the users to check their satisfaction with the proposed system and confirm that their needs have been correctly identified. This may result in modifications to the requirements specification and the development of another throw-away prototype.

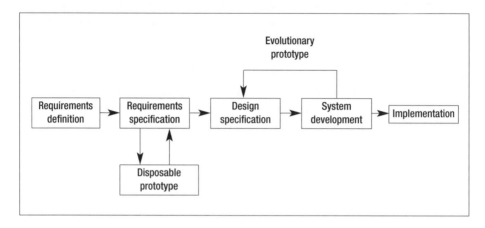

Figure 23.8 An example of a software development process model

444

The evolutionary prototyping model is represented by the feedback loop from the system development to design specification. A subset of the final system will be developed from the initial design. This is presented to the users to obtain feedback. The users may or may not be satisfied with this system. If they are not, changes are made to the design (the design specification revisited) and the system is redeveloped in line with these changes. Once again loops through the process may or may not occur. Depending on the nature of the customer and system being developed, there will be more or less chance of these loops being followed.

## MANAGING THE PROCESS LIFE CYCLE

### PROJECT MANAGEMENT TECHNIQUES

To manage the project management process it is necessary to represent this process in some way. The most common way of visualizing projects is through the use of Gantt charts (bar charts) and activity networks (see Chapter 19). While Gantt charts are useful for managing and controlling time and resources, activity networks provide a useful means of managing project activities by identifying their relationships and sequencing. Figure 23.9 summarizes the different kinds of activity networks available. PERT and CPM are terms commonly used to refer to such networks. This is highlighted in Figure 23.9 which shows how PERT and CPM apparently refer to a number of different representations and complexities. CPM* and PERT* show the extended use of these terms when referring to more complex activity networks.

| Increasing Complexity | | Representation | | |
|---|---|---|---|---|
| | | AoA | AoN | PDM |
| | DANs | CPM | CPM* | CPM* |
| | PANs | PERT | PERT* | PERT* |
| ↓ | GANs | GERT/VERT | – | – |

Figure 23.9   Activity network representations

Since their inception in the late 1950s activity networks have become an invaluable aid to planning and managing all kinds of projects throughout industry. At that time the activity network originated in two very similar forms: PERT (program evaluation and review technique) and CPM (critical path method). Activity networks began initially by representing the tasks in a project by arrows connecting nodes or events. Consequently these networks are sometimes referred to as activity-on-the-arrow (AoA). An alternative representation soon developed in which the activities were represented by nodes and their relationships were represented by interconnecting arrows. This representation is called activity-on-the-node (AoN) and is logically equivalent to the AoA representation. In both these cases it is implicit within the network structure that all tasks must finish in sequence for a project to complete successfully. It is possible to extend the logic of the AoN representation by introducing constraints between the finish times and start times of connected activities. The precedence diagram method (PDM) does this by introducing finish-to-start delays, start-to-finish delays, start-to-start delays and finish-to-finish delays (see Chapter 19).

Not only can activity networks be split according to their representation but they can also be classified according to the characteristics of the tasks themselves. CPM belongs in the simplest of these three categories – the deterministic activity network (DAN). DANs are used to manage projects in which the tasks are well understood and complete in recognized times. Thus, each task is represented by a single duration estimate. However, in many projects it is difficult to accurately predict the duration of tasks. Probabilistic activity networks (PANs), such as PERT, assist in these situations. In these cases activity durations are represented by probability distribution functions that are usually based on three time estimates (most likely, optimistic and pessimistic). Due to the stochastic nature of the activity durations, PANs tend to be difficult to analyse unless Monte Carlo simulation is employed. It is usual, therefore, for managers to focus on the critical path of these networks – the path that has the longest duration.

To take these networking techniques one stage further requires their logic to be redefined. Generalized activity networks (GANs) represent this advancement. Development of GANs began in 1962 and the most common form is the graphical evaluation and review technique or GERT (Pritsker and Happ 1972). More recent developments include the venture evaluation and review technique or VERT (Moeller and Digman 1981; Kidd 1991) and an AoN GAN developed by Dawson and Dawson (1995). GANs differ from other activity networks in their definition of task input and output characteristics. PERT and CPM networks insist on a deterministic structure which implies that all activities must occur, in sequence, for a project to complete successfully. GANs, on the other hand, allow either

**446**

deterministic or probabilistic branching to be defined. An interesting facet of GANs is their ability to handle loops. If loops are formed in ordinary networks, activities appear to be unable to begin until after they have completed. The probabilistic nature of the GAN, on the other hand, allows feedback from activities to earlier stages in a project life cycle.

## EXAMPLE

As an example of GANs we will use the hybrid process model of the software development life cycle introduced earlier. On the surface this might appear as a linear process with each phase succeeding the previous one. At this top level it can be planned using conventional project management techniques such as PERT and Gantt charts. A simple example of this plan is presented in Figure 23.10. Unfortunately, as discussed, ordinary activity networks cannot plan for the repetitive loops identified in this process. These loops would have to be implicitly planned using probability distribution functions of PERT. In this case the throwaway prototype used to elicit the requirements specification at stage two has been implicitly planned into this phase of the life cycle. The PERT network would include an optimistic estimate of no prototype development, an expected estimate of one prototype development and a pessimistic estimate of two.

Figure 23.11 provides a GAN interpretation of this hybrid process model. Now it has been possible explicitly to identify probabilistic branches and loops. These loops may have their repetitions defined. For example, within one department only one disposable prototype is ever developed. Alternatively, it may be unclear how many times each of the loops might be performed and each loop may have, say, a 40 per cent chance of occurring each time. This figure may be calculated from experiences with past projects and may be decreased each time the loop is performed. Figure 23.11 is a much more accurate representation of the software development process model. Loops can now be clearly identified and some form of analysis can be made to predict likely results from this project. Such analyses are likely to include Monte Carlo simulation which will provide probability distributions indicating the likelihood of completing the project within particular time limits.

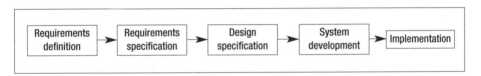

**Figure 23.10** **Ordinary activity network representation of example software process**

**447**

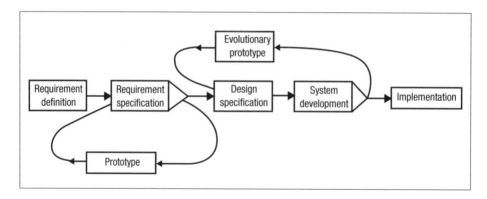

Figure 23.11   GAN representation of example software process

## SUMMARY

Projects can be viewed from three perspectives: their elements, their levels and their processes. These processes are either product-oriented or project-oriented. While the project processes are relatively consistent and should be repeatable from one project to the next, the product development process is not. Managing the product process can thus be improved by incorporating flexibility into project plans. This might be achieved by rolling wave planning techniques or by combining several product models into one hybrid process. Such a process is difficult to manage using conventional project management techniques such as PERT and CPM. A more flexible technique such as a GAN can cope with these uncertainties.

## REFERENCES AND FURTHER READING

Boehm, B. W. (1988), 'A spiral model of software development and enhancement', *Computer*, May.

CCTA (1996), *PRINCE 2: Project Management for Business*, The Stationery Office, London.

Dawson, C. W. and Dawson, R. J. (1995), 'Generalized activity-on-the-node networks for managing uncertainties in projects', *International Journal of Project Management*, **13**(6), pp. 353–62.

Down, A., Coleman, M. and Absolon, P. (1994), *Risk Management for Software Projects*, McGraw-Hill, London.

Field, M. and Keller, L. (1998), *Project Management*, Thomson Business Press, London.

Kidd, J. B. (1991), 'Do today's projects need powerful network planning tools?', *International Journal Production Research*, **29**(10).

Lock, D. (1994), *The Gower Handbook of Project Management*, 2nd edition, Gower, Aldershot.

Moeller, G. L. and Digman, L. A. (1981), 'Operations planning with VERT', *Operations Research*, **29**(4), pp. 676–97.

PMI (1996), *The Guide to the Project Management Body of Knowledge*, Project Management Institute, Upper Darby, PA.

Pritsker, A. A. B. and Happ, W. W. (1972), 'GERT: Graphical Evaluation and Review Technique Part I. Fundamentals', *Journal of Industrial Engineering*, **17**, pp. 267–274.

Turner, J. R. (1999), *The Handbook of Project-Based Management*, 2nd edition, McGraw-Hill, London.

Weiss, J. W. and Wysocki, R. K. (1992), *5-Phase Project Management, A Practical Planning and Implementation Guide*, Addison-Wesley, Reading, PA.

## RELATED TOPICS

# 24 Managing the project start

## Roland Gareis

Project management is a business process of the project-oriented organization (Figure 24.1), which includes the subprocesses of project start, continuous project coordination, project controlling, management of a project discontinuity and project close-down (Chapters 6 and 23). In projects, the project management process is performed in addition to the work or contents-related processes required to achieve the project results. Contents-related processes, that is the work of an engineering project, are engineering, procurement, logistics, construction, etc. The project management process starts with the formal project assignment and ends with the acceptance of the project results by the project owner (Figure 24.1). The objectives of the project management process are:

- to successfully perform the project according to the project objectives;
- to manage project complexity and project dynamics;
- to continuously adjust the project boundaries;
- to manage the project–context relationships;

by efficiently performing the project management subprocesses.

The project start is the most important project management subprocess, because it establishes the bases for the other project management subprocesses, such as the project plans, the project communication structures and the relationships to relevant environments. For the project start process objectives, functions, methods, responsibilities and deliverables can be described, which allow measurement of the quality of the project start process. The perception of projects influences the management of the project start. By defining projects as temporary organizations the formal establishment of a temporary organization and its integration in the company organization is emphasized.

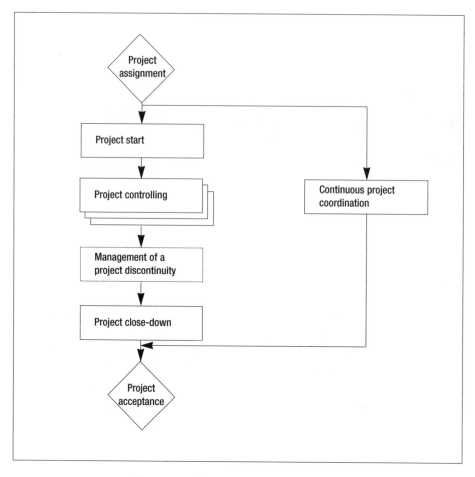

**Figure 24.1   The project management process**

## PROJECTS ARE TEMPORARY ORGANIZATIONS

The project management approach applied in the project start process is determined by the way projects are perceived. The traditional perception of projects as complex, goal-determined and risky tasks (Chapter 4) supports above all the use of project planning methods in the start process. Typical examples for such planning methods are the work breakdown structure and CPM, as techniques for both scheduling and supporting resource and cost plans (Chapters 18, 19 and 20). Due to the dynamics of projects, methods of risk management are used too.

For the performance of work packages in the traditional project management

452

approach above, the distribution of formal responsibilities between the project manager and line management is important. The pure line project organization, the matrix project organization and the influence project organization are suggested as relevant alternatives (Chapter 17). In the matrix project organization, the planning and the control of the project progress, schedule and costs are considered as responsibilities of the project manager.

A more advanced definition considers a project as a temporary organization for the performance of a relatively unique process of high complexity resulting in a specified object. Projects become instruments to further differentiate company organizations. In addition to the permanent base organizations of companies, such as divisions, business units and departments, which perform repetitive processes of low or medium complexity, temporary project organizations are applied too.

According to social systems theory, organizations – and consequently projects – can be perceived as social systems. On the one hand, social systems differentiate themselves from social environments and, on the other hand, they relate to these environments. Relevant project environments are customers, suppliers, public authorities, the media, etc. (Chapter 10). In addition to this social context, further context dimensions of projects are the pre- and the post-project phase and the relationships of projects to the strategies of companies (Chapter 2 and 13). Projects as social systems are not trivial, having expectable input–output relations (Chapter 6), but are characterized through their complexity and dynamics.

## OBJECTIVES OF THE PROJECT START PROCESS

Based on the perception of projects as temporary organizations (and as social systems) the following objectives can be defined for the project start process:

1. Development of the 'Big Project Picture' by agreeing on the project boundaries.
2. Formal establishment of the project as a temporary organization.
3. Appropriate integration of the project into the company organization.
4. Development of a specific project culture.
5. Establishment of communications between the project and other projects, the base organizations and relevant project environments.
6. Transfer of information about decisions and documentation of the pre-project phase into the project and clarification of expectations about the post-project phase.

7. Development of appropriate plans for managing the project complexity and dynamics.
8. Definition of communication structures and deliverables for the other project management subprocesses.
9. Communication of the results of the project start process by an initial project marketing.

## THE 'BIG PROJECT PICTURE'

Project boundaries define what belongs to a project and what does not. The boundaries of a social system are determined through its sense. Sense is assigned to a project through the definition of project goals, whereby all closely coupled goals have to be considered. The delimitation of goals, which are to a high degree dependent on the project goals, endangers the quality of the project.

Therefore, in an IS/IT project, for example, one should consider not only the goals of software design, software development, hardware and software implementation and possibly a pilot application, but also the goals of implementing the appropriate organization and recruiting and training the personnel required for the use of the new IT system, (the PSO project – Chapter 4). All these goals are closely coupled and should therefore be managed by one (project) organization. Apart from the definition of the project scope of work the construction of the project boundaries is achieved by agreeing on the project start and end events, as well as by agreeing on the project budget and on central project roles.

## SPECIFIC ORGANIZATIONAL DESIGN

The perception of projects as temporary organizations especially encourages the awareness that every project requires a specific organizational design in the project start process (Chapter 17). The organizational design of projects goes beyond the definition of responsibilities for the project manager. Project specific roles are to be defined, particularly the role of the internal project owner, project specific communication structures have to the agreed on, and rules and norms for cooperation in the project team have to be developed. Important communication structures in projects are project-related workshops (for example project start workshops, project controlling workshops and project close-down workshops) and project team meetings. The authority to make project-related decisions has to be delegated to the project team. The team members have to be empowered. No more control activities of line managers are required. These are too expensive and too time-consuming. The matrix project organization is dead!

454

## PROJECT CULTURES

The establishment of a project specific culture is one of the objectives of the project start process. Instruments for the development of a project identity are a project name and a project logo, project specific values, a project mission statement and a specific project language (see Chapter 40). The project culture development requires special competences, such as symbolic management, from the project manager and the project team.

## THE RELATIONSHIPS OF THE PROJECT TO ITS CONTEXT

The social context of a project is defined as its social environments. The relevant contexts are constructed in a project environment analysis (see Chapter 10). 'Relevant' for a project are those contexts that can influence the project success. They can be differentiated in external project environments (for example clients, partners, suppliers, media, etc.) and internal project environments (for example project owner, project team). Viewing the project owner and the project team as internal project environments, means that appropriate attention is given to these environments. Further dimensions of the project context are the contribution of a project to meet the company's strategies (see Chapter 2) as well as its relationships to other projects of the company (see Chapter 3). These relationships can be of synergetic or conflictive nature. Interim results of a project can, for example, be a prerequisite for the further performance of a project. In the project start process all these relationships need to be analysed, and strategies and measures for their management have to be defined.

## THE INFLUENCE OF PRE- AND POST-PROJECT PHASES ON PROJECT STRUCTURES

By the definition of the project start and end events, the pre-project phase and the post-project phase become project context. Projects normally have a long history. Information about the cause, which led to a project, as well as decisions made before formal project start are of great importance for the comprehension of the project goals and for the development of the project structures. The post-project phase is also important in temporary systems. The post-project phase has to be planned and the expected actions and decisions in the post-project phase need to be considered in the development of the project structures. The awareness about the necessary conclusion of the project and temporary environmental relations leads to a specific project identity.

## BUILDING UP PROJECT COMPLEXITY

According to Ashby's law of 'requisite variety', an appropriate complexity has to be built up in a social system to enable it to relate to its (infinitely) complex environment. The simultaneous application of different project management methods, such as the work breakdown structure, the schedules, the project environment analysis, etc., allow the build-up of adequate project complexity in the project start process. The project management methods are not just planning tools, but instruments to support and structure the project communications.

## ESTABLISHING THE BASIS FOR OTHER PM SUBPROCESSES

The agreements made, the project culture established and the project plans developed become the basis for performance of the further project management subprocesses. In the project start process, the basic structures for the other subprocesses, that is the project coordination process, the project controlling process, the project discontinuity management process and the project close-down process, have to be defined. The communication structures for the different subprocesses and the deliverables for each subprocess have to be agreed on. For the different workshops and meeting types goals have to be defined, the participants have to be fixed and their frequency and durations have to be planned. Deliverables for the project controlling process include project progress reports and updates of the project plans; deliverables for the project close-down process include final project reports and 'as-built' plans.

## PROJECT MARKETING AS A PROJECT MANAGEMENT FUNCTION

A project is by definition unique and complex, and representatives of the relevant project environments must be kept informed about the project objectives and structures. Possible instruments for initial 'project marketing' in the project start process are project presentations, a first issue of a project newsletter, information about the project in the company newsletter, a project private viewing and, most importantly, informal conversations about the project.

# TIMING OF THE PROJECT START PROCESS

The start event of the project start process is the assignment of a project to the project team by the project owner. Before this formal project assignment is given, no project account can be established, which means that the project manager and the project team members cannot spend any resources on the project. The end event of the project start process is the filing of the initial project management documents, developed in the project start process (see Figure 24.2).

By defining the project assignment as the project start event the assignment preparation process becomes a context of the project. Based on the preparation of a project proposal in the project assignment process, it has to be decided whether a given problem should be worked on or not, and in which organization form (base organization, project or programme) it should be worked on. If a project is proposed as the appropriate organization form, rough project plans have to be part of the proposal. These rough project plans can be used as the basis for the detailed project planning in the project start process.

For contracting projects the formal project assignment by the (internal) project owner might be given before the contract with the (external) client is formally established, at the time the contract is established or afterwards. So the timing of the project assignment has to be clearly differentiated from the timing of the establishment of a contract between a contractor and a client.

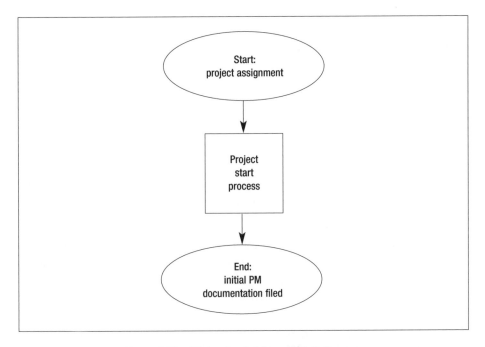

**Figure 24.2   Start and end of the project start process**

## FUNCTIONS, METHODS, RESPONSIBILITIES AND DELIVERABLES OF THE PROJECT START PROCESS

By structuring the project start process in phases and functions, by assigning organizational responsibilities to these functions, by defining the project management methods to be applied and by defining deliverables to be achieved, the project start process can be described. The project start process can be structured in a number of phases:

- Planning the project start
- Preparing the project start
- Performing the project start communications
- Following up the project start communications

The detailed functions to be performed and the responsibilities of the project roles of project owner, project manager, project team and others can be documented in a responsibility matrix (Chapter 17) (Figure 24.3).

## DESIGN OF THE PROJECT START PROCESS

For the design of the project start process the following elements may be considered:

- Project start communication forms and start workshop
- Standard project plans
- IT tools
- Project coaches
- Checklists for the project start

### THE PROJECT START WORKSHOP

Communication forms to be combined in the project start process are individual talks between the project manager and project team members, kick-off workshops and project start workshops (Figure 24.4):

- In an individual meeting, direct communication between the project manager and an individual project team member takes place. The objective of such a communication is to mutually provide information relevant to the project. This one-to-one communication provides orientation, but might lead to a 'subjective perception' of the project.
- A kick-off meeting is a one-way communication, in which project information is provided to the project team by the project owner and the project manager.

458

| Activities / Responsibilities | Project owner | Project manager | Project core team | Project team | Members of the project team | Project coach | Externals | Documents |
|---|---|---|---|---|---|---|---|---|
| **Planning the project start** | | | | | | | | |
| • Check: internal project assignment and results of the pre-project phase | | | R | | | | | |
| • Selection of starting form of communication | | | R | | | | | |
| • Selection of project team members (and of a project coach) | | | R | | | | | |
| • Selection of methods and form of documentation of PM to be used | | | R | | | | | |
| • Agreement with the project owner | C | | R | | | | | 1 |
| **Preparing the project start** | | | | | | | | |
| • Hiring of a project coach (option) | | | R | | | (C) | | |
| • Preparation of starting communications I, II … | | | R | | | (C) | | |
| • Invitation of participants | | R | | | | | | 2 |
| • Documentation of the results of the pre-project phase | | | R | | C | (C) | C | |
| • Drafts for planning, organizing and marketing of the project | | | R | | C | (C) | C | |
| • Developing of information material for starting communications | | | R | | C | (C) | C | 3 |
| **Performing the project start** | | | | | | | | |
| • Distribution of information material to the participants | | R | | | | | | |
| • Performance of start communication I | C | | | R | | (C) | C | |
| • Draft of PM document 'project start' | | | R | | | (C) | | |
| • Performance of start communication II | C | | | R | | (C) | C | |
| **Following-up the project start** | | | | | | | | |
| • Completion of the PM document 'project start' | | | R | | | (C) | | |
| • Agreement with project owner | C | R | | | | | | 4 |
| • Project marketing: first informations | C | | | R | | (C) | C | |
| • Distributing and filing of PM document 'project start' | C | R | | | | | C | |
| **Performing first work packages (parallel)** | | | | | | | | |

*Key:*
R   Responsible
C   Cooperation
I   Information

*Documents:*
1. List of methods of project management to be used
2. Invitation for participants to workshops concerning the project start
3. Information material for the start of the project workshop
4. Project management document 'project start'

**Figure 24.3   Project start responsibility matrix**

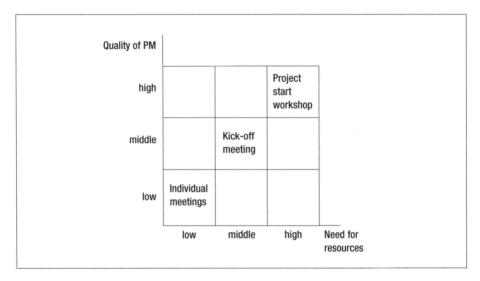

**Figure 24.4  Communication forms for the project start process**

- A project start workshop is an interactive communication form, in which a common 'Big Project Picture' is developed in a communication process of the project team, project owner and representatives of relevant environments.

In large and complex projects, several start workshops and/or kick-offs with different target groups might be necessary. After a project start workshop with the project team members of a contractor, another workshop with the project team members of the client might be organized. A typical agenda of a project start workshop is shown in Figure 24.5.

- Introduction
- Expectation of the project owner, project team, partners, subcontractors, consultants, etc. regarding the project
- Information about the project assignment, and results of the pre-project phase
- Classification of the project objectives and objects of consideration
- Finalizing the project plans and the project organization
- Presentation of achieved results to the project owner
- Planning the next steps

**Figure 24.5  Agenda for a project start workshop**

Rodney Turner suggests another agenda with timings (Figure 24.6). This is a long two days or a comfortable three days. One set of timings starts at 4.00 p.m. on the first day, and finishes with dinner on the third day; the other starts at 10.00 a.m. on the first day and finishes with lunch on the third day. It never works quite as smoothly as the timings given, and there is contingency built in. The workshop should be held off-site, away from the distractions of the office. Back in the 1980s that meant we were completely isolated, and people could focus on the task at hand. Now you have to insist that mobile phones are left in the bedrooms. Holding the workshop off-site in a hotel also helps team building (Chapter 40). The team can relax together in the evening and get to know each other.

| Agenda item | Duration (hours) | Timetable 1 | Timetable 2 |
| --- | --- | --- | --- |
| Success criteria | 1.5 | 1: 16.00 | 1: 10.00 |
| Definition | 1.5 | 1: 17.30 | 1: 11.30 |
|    purpose | | | |
|    scope | | | |
|    objectives | | | |
| Milestone plan | 3.0 | 2: 09.00 | 1: 14.00 |
| Responsibility chart | 2.0 | 2: 14.00 | 2: 09.00 |
| Calculate durations | 0.5 | 2: 16.00 | 2: 11.00 |
| Schedule milestones | 0.5 | 2: 16.30 | 2: 11.30 |
| Quality plan | 1.0 | 2: 17.00 | 2: 14.00 |
| Risk analysis | 2.0 | 3: 09.00 | 2: 15.00 |
| Activity plans | 1.0 | 3: 11.00 | 3: 09.00 |
|    early milestones | | | |
| Control plan | 1.0 | 3: 12.00 | 3: 10.00 |

**Figure 24.6   Agenda and timings for a project start workshop**

## STANDARD PROJECT PLANS

If a project-oriented organization performs the same project types repetitively (such as contracting projects performed by an IT company), standard project plans for these project types can be developed. Standardization is an instrument of organizational learning. Examples of project plans that can be standardized are:

- work breakdown structures
- object breakdown structures
- project milestone lists
- project organization charts
- project responsibility matrices.

The efficiency of the start process can be improved by applying standard project plans. Of course, the standards need to be adapted for the specific requirements of a given project. Even when standards are applied, the development of a project specific culture should be pursued.

## THE APPLICATION OF IT TOOLS

Especially in virtual project organizations, with project team members from different companies distributed at different locations, the design of an appropriate IT infrastructure for the project is one of the challenges of the project start process (Chapter 8). The choice of project management software and office software has to be made and implemented, and access to the required hardware made available for everybody. Further, decisions have to be made about the application of new communication tools such as video-conferencing.

## PROJECT COACHING

Projects more frequently become an object of consideration for consultancy. Project coaching can be defined as the project management consultancy of a project. Because of the social complexity of the project start process, the coaching of it provides important support for the project. The project coaching might include the following services:

- Supporting the transfer of know-how from the pre-project phase into the project.
- Supporting the organizational design of the project.
- Supporting the development of the project plans.
- Moderating project start meetings and the project start workshop(s).
- Supporting the documentation of the project start process.

The project team have to decide if they want to engage a project coach for the project start process. The project coach is a project external role, which might be recruited either from within the project performing companies or from an external consulting company.

## CHECKLISTS

Various checklists can be used for the performance of the project start process including:

- a checklist for the preparation of a project start workshop;
- a checklist of required project management methods; and
- a standard project handbook.

462

As an example a list of contents of a standard project handbook is shown in Figure 24.7.

```
Project Management
1           Project coordination
1.1         To-do list
2           Project start
2.1         Project organization and culture
1.2.1       Project assignment
1.2.1       Project communication structures
1.2.1       Project responsibility matrix
2.2         Project context
2.2.1       Pre-project and post-project phase
2.2.2       Project environment graph
2.2.3       Project environment relations
2.2.4       Project marketing
2.3         Project planning
2.3.1       Project objectives
2.3.2       Work package specifications
2.3.3       Project milestones
2.3.4       Project bar chart
2.3.5       Project cost plan
2.3.6       Project personel resources
2.4         Project risk analysis
2.4.1       Project risk analysis
2.4.2       Project scenarios
2.4.3       Alternative project plans
3           Project controlling
3.1         Project progress reports
3.2         Minutes of project controlling meetings
4           Project close-down
4.1         Project close-down reports
```

Figure 24.7   List of contents of a standard project handbook

## PROJECT START AND PROJECT TYPE

Projects can be differentiated by industries, goals, the extent of implementation, the degree of repetition, the type of project owner and their relationship to company processes (Figure 24.8). From different project types arise different challenges and potentials for the design of the project start process.

- A conception project and a realization project build a chain of projects. In the conception project rough plans for the consecutive realization project are

**463**

| Differentiation criteria | Types of projects |
|---|---|
| Project goals | Contracting projects, marketing projects, organizational development projects, etc. |
| Extent of implementation | Conception projects and realization projects |
| Degree of repetition | Unique and repetitive projects |
| Type of project owner | Internal and external projects |
| Complexity | Projects of higher and lower complexity |
| Relation to company processes | Projects for the realization of primary, secondary and tertiary processes |

**Figure 24.8   Differentiation of project types**

already developed. These form the basis for project planning in the project start process of the realization project.

- For repetitive projects project management methods can be standardized. Standard project plans can be applied in the project start process. In unique projects more creativity is required. Specific working forms and creativity techniques have to be applied in the project start process of unique projects.
- In an external project of a contractor, representatives of the client have to be actively involved in the project start process. Usually they become members of the project owner group as well as of the project team. Further, external projects are based on a comprehensive bidding and negotiating process, in which decisions regarding the structure and the culture of the following contracting project are made (e.g. decisions regarding nominated subcontractors).

Rodney Turner writes that the approach to project start depends on how well the goals and the methods of delivering them are defined (Figure 24.9, after Figure 4.1).

**TYPE 1**

The goals and methods will be well understood if this is a project that is very similar to ones done in the past. The emphasis will be on adapting well-understood processes to this project, using specialist implementers. The facilitator will therefore probably be an expert in this type of project. The project manager's role will be that of a conductor, leading the team through a well-defined score and imposing his or her interpretation.

| | | Type 2 | Type 4 |
|---|---|---|---|
| | No | Invite many disciplines<br>Brainstorm techniques<br><br>*Experts in work*<br><br>COACH | Invite many disciplines<br>Problem-solving and strategy<br><br>*Experts in teams*<br><br>EAGLE |
| Goals<br>well<br>defined | Yes | Type 1<br><br>Invite specialists<br>Tailor known techniques<br><br>*Experts in work*<br><br>CONDUCTOR | Type 3<br><br>Invite specialists<br>Agree end stage milestones<br><br>*Experts in teams*<br><br>MASTER MASON |
| | | Yes | No |
| | | Methods well defined | |

Figure 24.9   Start-up and the goals and methods matrix (see Figure 4.1)

## TYPE 2

The goals are well understood, but they are novel, so it is not yet known how best to achieve them. The emphasis will be on brainstorming the techniques, using multidisciplinary teams comprising people who may be able to contribute to the process. The facilitator may again be an expert in this type of work, somebody who can advise how similar tasks have been done in the past. The project manager will be a coach. The objective might be to get the ball into the goal at the end of the field as many times as possible in the next 90 minutes (very clear). How is completely unknown. The coach instructs the team in standard plays, but then can only shout instructions from the sideline as the game unfolds.

## TYPE 3

The specification of the goals is now unclear, but a well-defined life cycle will be followed in defining them. The emphasis is on agreeing milestone and stage review points at which progress towards the definition of the goals is reviewed, and agreed. Specialist teams who have done similar things in the past are invited

**465**

as they have experience in the standard life cycles to be followed, but the facilitator is someone who can guide the team in their problem-solving. The project manager is a master mason. Exactly what the cathedral will look like or how it will stand up is not known at the start. But the team will follow defined stone crafting techniques, under the guidance of the master mason, to put it up.

## TYPE 4

Neither the goals nor the methods are known. What is known is the business problem to be solved, and so the emphasis is on solving that problem, identifying the deliverable that will solve the strategic problem and then treating the project as Type 2, once the deliverables are defined. Multidisciplinary teams will be invited again to give a broad range of views about possible solutions to the problem, but the facilitator will be somebody who can guide the team in their problem-solving. The project manager must be an eagle, able to hover above the project and see it in the context of the business, but then able to spot small details and swoop down to deal with them, before returning to hover above the project again.

## QUALITY OF THE PROJECT START PROCESS

By evaluating the deliverables and the design of a project start process its quality can be measured. As mentioned above, deliverables of the project start process are the documents resulting from the initial application of the project management methods in the project, such as the work breakdown structure, the project organization chart, etc. The design of a project start process can be evaluated on the appropriateness of the communication forms applied, the IT tools implemented, etc. and the costs and time spent on this project start process. In a benchmarking of the project start processes of nine Austrian companies in 1998 the project start practices of these companies were compared and related to the 'best theory' as a defined benchmark (Gareis and Huemann 1998). The deliverables resulting from the design of the project organization in the different companies are shown in Figure 24.10.

## CONCLUSIONS

The project start process is characterized by the pressure to start the work as soon as possible, but there will be different expectations in the project team regarding the project objectives and social uncertainty because the project team

466

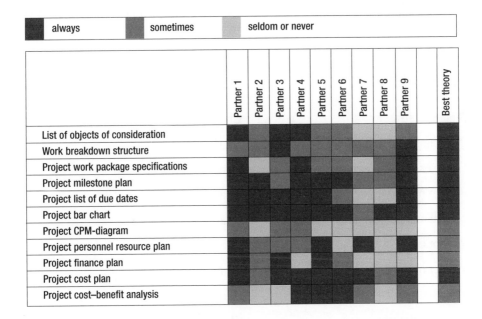

**Figure 24.10** Results of benchmarking the project start process (example)

members do not know each other (in the new project roles). If this time pressure leads to a project start without appropriate project management provisions, the following might result:

- Unrealistic and unclear project objectives
- Unclear project role definitions
- A lack of project specific rules and values
- No comittment regarding the project plans
- Little sensibility regarding the management of the project environment relationships
- Consequent poor project performance

This is why a professional project start is a must!

## REFERENCES AND FURTHER READING

Fangel, M. (1998), 'Best Practice of Project Start-up', in A. Hauc (ed.), *Proceedings of the IPMA 14th World Congress on Project Management, Ljubljana, June 1998*, International Project Management Association, Zurich.

Gareis, R. and Huemann, M. (1998), 'International Research Project PM-

Benchmarking: Benchmarking the PM-Process', *Project Management: The Professional Magazine of the Project Management Association Finland*, **4**(1).

## RELATED TOPICS

| | |
|---|---|
| Business strategy | Chapters 2 and 13 |
| Programme management | Chapter 3 |
| Features of a project | Chapter 4 |
| Project management processes | Chapter 6 |
| The virtual project support office | Chapter 8 |
| Project context | Chapter 10 |
| Project organization | Chapter 17 |
| Managing cost | Chapter 18 |
| Scheduling time | Chapter 19 |
| Scheduling resources | Chapter 20 |
| Project life cycle | Chapter 23 |
| Team motivation and commitment | Chapter 40 |

# 25 Proposal, initiation and feasibility

*Stephen Simister*

Most projects are born out of good ideas. For instance, James Dyson decided it would be a good idea to produce a vacuum cleaner without a dust bag and it took him over fifteen years to get his product to market. Of course, not all good ideas become projects. There has to be a structured appraisal of the idea to ascertain the necessary level of resource that should be expended exploring its feasibility.

A typical four-stage project life cycle is shown in Figure 25.1. The first stage is proposal and initiation, which deals with the definition of the project and its contextualization. In terms of cost, the majority of a project's expenditure occurs in execution and control, but the greatest influence over cost is during proposal and initiation. Decisions made here have a lasting impact on later expenditure. The ability to influence costs falls off rapidly during design, so changes made later are impossible to implement without incurring considerable additional cost. During proposal and initiation the critical success factors of the project are determined. It is at this stage that we set the bases for the project's success by determining the strategy for its management. It is also important to document the decision-making process so options that were not considered viable do not suddenly reappear later in the project life cycle.

A typical flow chart for the early definition of a project is set out in Figure 25.2. Although three (sub-)stages are shown in the flow chart they are often difficult to

| Stage | Name |
|---|---|
| Germination | Proposal and initiation |
| Growth | Design and appraisal |
| Maturity | Execution and control |
| Metamorphosis | Finalization and close-out |

Figure 25.1    A typical four-stage project life cycle

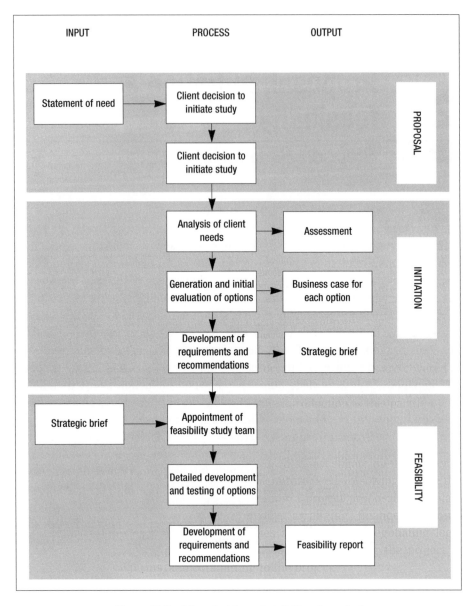

INPUT  PROCESS  OUTPUT

Statement of need → Client decision to initiate study

Client decision to initiate study

PROPOSAL

Analysis of client needs → Assessment

Generation and initial evaluation of options → Business case for each option

Development of requirements and recommendations → Strategic brief

INITIATION

Strategic brief → Appointment of feasibility study team

Detailed development and testing of options

Development of requirements and recommendations → Feasibility report

FEASIBILITY

**Figure 25.2  A flow chart for early definition of a project**

delineate in practice. There is a general merging and fluidity between them. While this is acceptable, it is important to remember that the process should be forward moving. Hence, once an end of stage milestone has been reached, it is not revisited unless an obvious and detrimental mistake has been made. It is not uncommon for unfavourable options to be constantly re-evaluated just because they have support at senior level. This is a waste of resources and adherence to a structured process should prevent this happening.

In this chapter, I discuss each of the three stages in turn.

## PROPOSAL

The project has to start somewhere. It is interesting to note that many organizations could not pinpoint the exact circumstances or time that a project comes into being. The proposal stage is all about turning ideas into a structured appraisal process that could lead to a project being undertaken. Resources will be expended just by investigating the validity of an idea.

The commencement of the proposal stage is the provision of a statement of need by the proposer. This statement of need should outline in broad terms the needs that must be satisfied to provide the required business benefit. Preparing a statement of needs is very important as this document becomes the basis upon which future decisions will be made.

Based on this statement of need a decision will be made as to whether resources should be committed to study the requirements further. If further study is justified then a project sponsor should be appointed. This person becomes responsible for guiding the project through to its conclusion. The sponsor is the interface between the project team, who will undertake various tasks, and the end-users of the project. Once the sponsor has been appointed the project moves from the proposal stage into the initiation stage.

## INITIATION

The setting of clear, unambiguous objectives is key to project success. The objectives and initial definition of the scope can be determined using various techniques described elsewhere in this book (Chapters 14 and 15). People can have covert objectives that differ from the project's stated objectives. Even the sponsor can have a hidden agenda. Hence the interpretation of the sponsor's requirement is unlikely to be the subject of unanimous or even objective judgement. This makes even the first step difficult, and means it must be done in a way that leaves little margin for misunderstanding. The use of a project definition workshop (Chapters 14 and 24) is a powerful medium for flushing out covert objectives.

Having defined the project's objectives, we can set constraints for its cost and duration, and the performance of the facility. The purpose indicates parameters for the facility's value and the time window in which it has that value, and from these we determine the maximum cost and latest completion date of the project. The value of the facility depends on the completion date: the later completion, the lower the value. The decrease in value represents two things: revenues from the facility having lower present value, and lost revenue if the product has only a limited life (Chapter 27). This decrease may allow several build programmes, with an optimum achieved in some optimum time window (Turner 1999). There may be some indication at this stage whether these times and costs are realistic for achieving the objectives set, but it is not until the feasibility study is completed that you can begin to match the costs to the definition of the work to be done.

It is during the initiation stage that the business case for the principal options is developed in order for a decision to be made as to which of the principal options will go forward to the feasibility stage. Up until the end of the initiation stage only a very limited amount of resources will have been expended investigating the proposal. Once the decision to go into a feasibility study is taken, the amount of resources required increases considerably. Therefore the decision to go into the feasibility study should be a gateway to ensure that scarce resources are being used in the most effective manner. The main output of this stage is the strategic brief that forms the starting point of the feasibility study.

## THE FEASIBILITY STUDY

During the feasibility study the range of possible options is examined and potential issues identified. The aim is to narrow down the range of options, provide an assessment of each one remaining and propose solutions to issues confronting the project. The feasibility study is where the project is really defined. It is at this stage that the critical success factors are often determined.

### AIMS OF THE FEASIBILITY STUDY

Feasibility studies involve time and money and so it is essential they are well managed. By understanding the aims of the study and the criteria for its success, we can focus our effort. The objectives of the study will be specific to the project, but the following are usually significant:

- Exploring all possible options for implementing the project.
- Achieving a clear understanding of the issues involved.

- Producing enough information to be able to rank the options.
- Obtaining a clear picture of the way forward.

### The options

As many ideas as possible should be explored within clearly defined boundaries. Each option must be thoroughly reviewed against a consistent set of criteria to determine whether it can be improved, within the limitations of market and technical conditions. The strategic brief can act as a guide to the study, but it should not stifle imagination and creativity.

### The issues

The feasibility study must give a clear understanding of the issues. In particular, associated with each option still being considered should be: estimates of costs and revenues; an understanding of the views and objectives of the various sponsors and institutions involved; confirmation of both technical and financial viability; and estimates of the likely economic and financial returns.

### Ranking the options

The study should produce enough information to rank options. The criteria used are based on the strategic factors such as cost, programme and benefit to the business. Their weighting in the ranking of options depends on the sponsor's requirements.

### Recommendations

The study should result in a clear idea of future stages. It helps to think of the feasibility study as a funnelling and filtering exercise, directing a wide range of possible ideas into a much narrower range of options, with those that clearly fail to meet objectives sifted out. The study should aim to provide clear documentary evidence as to why a particular option has been singled out for taking forward. If a range of alternatives is selected then the feasibility study should also provide guidance as to how these alternatives are narrowed down even further.

### THE FACTORS ADDRESSED

The study must provide an understanding of factors influencing success, and assess the advantages and disadvantages of each option to enable them to be ranked. The following factors influence feasibility.

473

## Market conditions

Expectation of returns depends on satisfying demand for the project's product at a certain price level. Usually neither future demand nor future prices can be predicted very accurately. If there is a limited portfolio of potential buyers, or the market is volatile, or demand is price-sensitive (as with commodity products), the project is vulnerable to many adverse circumstances over which the project manager has little influence. However, the existing market environment provides a wealth of information on which to base sales forecasts, establish price structures, understand potential purchasers and consumers, evaluate expected trends in demand and the actions of potential competitors, and learn about the expected quality of the product or service.

## Supply considerations

Existing supply conditions are also important sources of information. The feasibility study should assess the cost, quality and availability of capital equipment, raw materials and labour. Different technical options should also be explored and specialist technical advice obtained on their feasibility.

## Financial prospects

The profitability of the project can be analysed by applying economic evaluation techniques. The financial feasibility also depends on whether the expected return from a project is sufficient to finance debt and provide shareholders with an adequate return to compensate them for their risk. Financial feasibility is influenced by economic conditions such as interest and exchange rates prevailing when costs are incurred and income received. The approach differs for projects in the private or public sector. The latter often take account of non-monetary benefits and costs, as well as factors such as environmental impact. Shadow prices are used where the market price is considered not to reflect the economic cost or benefit of an input or output of the project. The private sector usually places more weight on purely monetary return, although legislation, tax benefits or subsidy, and public relations considerations may encourage it to place value on non-monetary factors.

Adequate consideration must be given to risk and uncertainty. Risk and uncertainty cannot be eliminated, but they can be managed and reduced by prudent project design and management, and taken into account in comparison of project options. You should also remember that the shareholders' evaluation of the project, and hence the share price of the company, depends on their assessment of the risk.

## INITIATING THE STUDY

The following five steps are required in setting up a feasibility study.

### Management team

Appoint an experienced manager and management team. The make-up depends on the nature of the project. For the feasibility study, it should include technical, financial and marketing expertise, and for larger projects may also have economists, legal and environmental experts, human resources experts, etc. It is essential that a good balance is struck between specialists, as assessment of the options may be biased if one specialism dominates. For example, if technical experts dominate, they may emphasize technically exciting options that may not provide the required financial return. It is often helpful to limit the size of the core management team, as far as the size of the project allows. Compact teams are usually easier to organize and coordinate than larger groups. The manager of the study will usually not be the project manager for subsequent stages. However, it is a good idea for the latter to be a member of the management team for the study, and thus have greater ownership and commitment to the results of the study, the decisions made and the strategy set.

### Scope the study

Examine the scope of the study to assess the work involved and any constraints imposed (quality, cost, time, etc.). The manager must determine exactly what the decision-makers require to guide them in their choice of the project options and in what form the information is needed. A work plan with the delivery time and content of interim and final reports should as far as possible be agreed in advance with the decision-makers. Remember, project management is fractal management; the study needs planning as much as the implementation of the project.

### External advisers

Appoint external advisers to supplement the expertise of the core team. It might also be necessary to obtain certain permission and consents, if only on a provisional basis. It would be prudent, for example, to obtain outline planning permission for any construction work envisaged in the project.

### Plan the study

Draw up a plan for the study, including a milestone plan and responsibility chart (Chapters 15, 17 and 24). The milestone plan should identify key stages for the study: interim and final reports, meetings, data collection, etc. The plan can highlight different lines of enquiry involved and their interdependence, enabling the different aspects of the study to be coordinated. It should be robust, but sufficiently flexible to cope with any unexpected changes. Adequate allowance should be made for the time required to request and collect data as well as processing and interpreting results.

### Schedule the study

Set the timetable and budget for the study. These must be sufficient to enable options to be properly explored and refined, without endangering the feasibility of the whole project. It is important to budget for an adequate exploration of the options without going to the depth of investigation required for the design and appraisal stage.

The project definition workshop (Chapter 24) can be used to undertake the last two steps, as well as developing the initial project definition and strategy.

### MANAGING THE STUDY

Once it has been planned, the following are the three main elements of managing the feasibility study.

### Organization

This involves the adoption of a clearly focused but flexible structure based around the milestone plan. The team should be aware of what is expected, and by when. They should understand how they fit into the study framework, and to whom they should report. Hence, roles and responsibilities must be clearly defined. The responsibility chart is the tool that effectively achieves this.

### Implementation

This requires efficient communication within the team. The manager should maintain frequent contact with sponsors to ensure that the study remains on target and that any change in requirements is identified. The team should maintain good internal communications to ensure that delays are reported, to minimize knock-on effects, to avoid duplication and to confirm all information received has been made available to all members of the team. It is particularly important that good communication is maintained between team members in different fields of expertise to take account of any interdependencies.

476

### Control

This is the responsibility of the manager who must ensure that milestones are being reached on time and that the milestones adopted lead to punctual report delivery. Likewise, costs should be monitored to ensure that the study remains within budget. Control involves monitoring of timing and budgets, and rapid and effective corrective action when targets are not met, either by revising targets or by restructuring present plans within the existing targets. The detail of how work is assigned to people and their progress monitored and controlled, during the feasibility study or any other stage, is discussed later in the book.

### Completing the study

The feasibility study should act as a springboard for the next phase in the project life cycle – design and appraisal – ensuring that it is able to commence in a focused way. The end product should therefore comprise a clear, concise report, the project definition report, which presents the original specification and objectives, with the conclusions and recommendations for use in the next stage. The report should highlight advantages and disadvantages – cost, revenue, strategic considerations, economic benefits, etc. – for each of the options which deserve further consideration and the proposed solutions to issues confronting the project. Furthermore, the report should indicate sensitivities to variations from the assumed base case.

Once again, the feasibility study is an important step in the project process. If the study finds that the project is not economically or technically viable it should clearly state this and allow the project to be closed down in a controlled manner. The feasibility is a gateway through which the project must pass. Once the project passes into the design and appraisal stage the amount of resources committed to it will be quite considerable.

## CONCLUSIONS

This chapter has explained what should happen during the proposal, initiation and feasibility stages of a project. For a project to succeed it must be built on strong foundations which are laid during these stages. It is difficult to conduct a thorough investigation during the early stages of a project as this is when the amount of information available is minimal. However, decisions must be made to enable the project to progress forward. This dichotomy is what generally leads to project failure.

The early stages of a project are crucial to its success and the appropriate resources must therefore be allocated to these stages. Careful execution of these stages will pay handsome dividends during the later stages as is outlined in the proceeding chapters.

## REFERENCE AND FURTHER READING

Turner, J. R. (1999), *The Handbook of Project-based Management*, 2nd edition, McGraw-Hill, London.

## RELATED TOPICS

| | |
|---|---|
| Project success and strategy | Chapter 5 |
| Processes and procedures | Chapter 6 |
| Functionality and value | Chapter 14 |
| Configuration definition | Chapter 15 |
| Responsibility charts | Chapter 17 |
| Project life cycle | Chapter 23 |
| Project start-up and definition workshops | Chapter 24 |
| Project appraisal | Chapter 27 |

# Managing implementation and progress

*Dennis Lock*

This chapter starts with the basic assumption that progress needs managing. The importance of delivering all project commitments on or before the promised dates should be obvious. A project is unlikely to be considered successful if it is completed later than the time agreed between the project contractor and the project owner. A project for the manufacture of a machine cannot be counted a success if late delivery of the machine causes the owner to suffer delayed start-up, loss of market share and reduced revenue. The Olympic Games are a failure if the athletes are asked to come two weeks late. It is a general rule that any extension of a project beyond its originally agreed timescale must lead to extra expenditure or losses, simply through the indirect or time-dependent costs, such as the cost of the money and other resources (accommodation, people, materials) locked into the programme. Further, a late project is likely to have a knock-on effect and cause the starts (and therefore the finishes) of subsequent projects to be put at risk of delay. No one should argue with the assumption that project time is a vital, irreplaceable and expensive resource. All project resources should be managed effectively and time is no exception.

## ESSENTIAL FRAMEWORK OF PROGRESS MANAGEMENT

To give a project some chance of being carried out according to the client's wishes, the management methods and structure have to be suitable. If any of the following conditions is not met, progress will be difficult or impossible to manage effectively. Some of these conditions may seem very obvious but they are not always fulfilled in practice.

### Project definition (Chapters 14 and 25)

The project specification and objectives have to be clearly defined. The project manager must be in no doubt about what he or she is expected to deliver and those deliverables must be feasible given the resources and time available.

### Control of changes (Chapter 15)

Uncontrolled changes can wreak project havoc. They must be properly considered and controlled if delays and overspending are to be avoided.

### Organization (Chapters 17, 20, 33 and 40)

The project organization must be led by a competent project manager and should be appropriate to the size and nature of the project, with effective downward, upward and lateral communications.

### Supportive management (Chapters 41, 42 and 43)

The project manager is not a stand-alone system. He or she cannot operate in isolation. One essential requirement is the material and moral support of higher management.

1. Material support includes the authorization of funds necessary for managing and executing the project. The project must not be allowed to fail through lack of essential resources and facilities (such as people, equipment and accommodation).
2. Moral support is at least as important as material support. It can take many forms. Here are some examples:
   - Appropriate and generous delegation of authority and responsibility to the project manager.
   - Enforcement of project management procedures and systems throughout the organization.
   - Interceding with managers inside the organization in support of the project manager – one example could be the resolution of priority conflicts.
   - Interceding at higher management level outside the project organization – a common example is when a project manager has no success in obtaining essential materials from a key supplier; dialogue between the two organizations at higher management level can sometimes produce results.
   - Encouragement of individual development through training and further education.

- Physical presence – occasional attendance at progress meetings and visits to workplaces or a project site to lend encouragement.

### Customer partnership (Part VI)

The customer (or client or owner) must act responsibly and cooperate with the project contractor. This means:

- paying valid claims for payment promptly;
- avoiding unnecessary changes;
- giving design approvals without delay;
- generally appreciating the problems that face the contractor.

There should be an atmosphere of partnership rather than confrontation. Concurrent engineering is a good example of such partnership, where customer and contractor work together in a search for mutually beneficial project strategies.

### Competence of people in organizations (Chapter 39)

The success of a large project depends on the competence of many people throughout the organizations of subcontractors, suppliers of equipment and materials, service companies, government departments, the customer and the project contractor. Some of these people will be competent. Others might be less so. We have to assume that most are capable of performing their jobs properly if project progress is to be assured. Although the project manager will not have direct control over the people in external organizations, control can be exercised by the careful choice of those organizations.

### Allocation of responsibilities (Chapters 15 and 17)

People must know what is expected of them. One tool that can assist the project manager to allocate responsibilities is the linear responsibility matrix (described in Chapter 17). The responsibility matrix is best suited to deal with task categories rather than listing all the detailed tasks themselves. For example, it can show the person or body responsible for approving new designs in general, but it is not the place in which to list all the drawings that carry those designs.

### Workable schedule (Chapters 19 and 20)

The project schedule is the key document for managing progress. Larger projects will probably have to be broken down into smaller work packages using a hierarchical, coded work breakdown structure. Here are some characteristics of the ideal plan for a project or for each of its work packages:

- All significant tasks included.
- Tasks placed in logical sequence, preferably as a critical path network.
- Estimates of duration as realistic as possible.
- Scheduled to use resources at feasible rates.
- Flexible to authorized changes and progress, so that it can be kept up to date.
- Divided into separate work-to lists for departments or work groups.

### IMPOSSIBLE?

With all these imposed conditions perhaps it is a wonder that any project ever gets finished on time. And, so far, we have not even thought about all the other things which can go wrong accidentally, as seen in any insurance company's catalogue of disasters: fire, storm, civil commotion, war (civil or otherwise), strikes, lockouts, objects dropped from aircraft, other natural disasters, unnatural disasters, and so on *ad infinitum*. What chance does any project ever have of being finished on time? Many do, of course, finish late.

Progress management seeks to start and finish every task in accordance with the project plan. It should foresee and forestall possible risks, monitor work in progress, identify current problems and (above all) must take corrective and timely action against significant delays.

## COMMUNICATING THE WORK PROGRAMME

Consider a contracting organization which has received a prized order for a new project. Possibly over one hundred of the contractor's staff are going to be working on the new project for a prolonged period. All good news. But how do they know when to start and what to do?

### PROJECT AUTHORIZATION

The first official document used in many companies to start a new project is a works order or project authorization. This gives key information about the project in summary form. Apart from giving information about the project, the works order carries the signature of a director or senior manager which authorizes the start of work and other expenditure on the new project. The following items are among those likely to be included:

- Name and address of the customer or client
- Project site or delivery address (if different)
- Project title
- Project number (which should provide the root of the code of cost accounts and work breakdown structure)
- Name of the customer's project manager or key contact person
- Number and date of the customer's purchase order or contract
- Project description and scope of supply
- Serial and revision numbers of key documents, such as the project specification
- Pricing details and agreed terms of payment
- Key dates in the project life cycle
- Departmental budgets
- Name of project manager

## WORK-TO LISTS

While the works order or other project authorization document gives instructions across the organization in broad management outline, it does not carry enough detail from which to issue and control work down to the level of separate jobs in all the separate departments and groups. The most effective and convenient tool for that function is the work-to list, derived from the project network. This provides each manager with a list of all project tasks for which he or she is responsible, together with essential schedule information. Ideally, the computer should filter tasks so that reports can be relevant to each departmental manager. Departmental filtering can be facilitated by giving every activity a departmental code. The computer should then sort and print the list for each department in ascending order of the activities' scheduled start dates. The earliest possible start dates from time analysis will have to suffice if resources have not been scheduled. Other sort sequences may be more appropriate for some departments. The person responsible for expediting purchase orders might, for example, find it more convenient to have all the lead time activities for purchased goods listed in order of their planned completion (delivery) dates. Work-to lists provide managers or their delegates with valuable schedules and checklists from which to issue tasks and follow them up for monitoring and managing progress.

## STARTING UP

Project start-up is covered in Chapter 24. Key issues in implementation include the following.

## KICK-OFF MEETING

When the contract has been won and work authorized, the kick-off meeting is a good way to get things started. The project manager, having first been thoroughly briefed on all known aspects of the project, must call together the principal participants and brief them in turn. This is the time and place to explain the project's general technical and procedural requirements, warn of specific risks, quantify deliverables, obtain everyone's agreement and commitment, and generally encourage all concerned to get their forces mobilized and motivated.

## STARTING EARLY

One of the biggest risks in managing progress is failure to start a project on time. A project which starts late is likely to finish late. It can be difficult for an organization to activate a new project at the time and rate of working envisaged in the schedule. Delay in signing the project contract can be one reason for delay, perhaps while a few final details are negotiated or for the more mundane reason that one of the authorized signatories is temporarily unavailable.

No work should be allowed to start on a commercial or industrial project until a firm contract exists between contractor and client. This is an inviolate rule that should be ground into every self-respecting manager from birth. However, as with most rules, there is an exception.

In most projects, the rates of working and expenditure follow a well-known pattern. If the work or costs are plotted cumulatively against time, a characteristic *S* curve results (see Figure 18.3, p. 311). The rate rises slowly at first, while preparations are made and the resources are mobilized. Expenditure is at its highest rate near the middle of the project. Work and expenditure then tail off as the project ends, and the curve converges on the final cost. In an engineering project, for example, the first weeks of active project life cycle might be used for planning, investigating standards, resolving queries with the client, establishing procedures, etc. Some companies use checklists for controlling this preliminary work, and put the checklist in the form of a standard preliminary network diagram. All these early activities are likely to need no more than one or two people. It can be seen from Figure 18.3 that this early work is unlikely to account for a significant part of the total expenditure. Yet this work must be done before the main project activities can start and many of these early tasks will lie on the project critical path. If the time available for the project is tight, or if the company wants the project finished quickly for other reasons, it might be advantageous to commit commercial heresy and allow some or all of these preliminary activities to go ahead, and to incur some costs, before the contract with the client has been signed. There are risks. In the event that the contract is not awarded, the preliminary expenditure will have to be written off. There is a danger that the contractor's price bargaining position will be weakened if the client discovers that work has already begun. Caution is obviously necessary. The contractor can limit the risk by issuing a preliminary internal works order that releases only a very restricted budget, specifies the work allowed and names the individuals authorized to carry out that work. The risk has to be evaluated and weighed against the benefit of bringing the project completion date forward by one, two or even more months.

## MANAGING PROGRESS IN THE VARIOUS PROJECT FUNCTIONS

A simple control cycle can be described for accomplishing each activity. The steps are as follows:

1. Prompted by the work-to list, the manager responsible allocates the work to the appropriate person, group or other resource as near as possible to the scheduled time.
2. The manager ensures that all necessary facilities and information are provided and that the task requirements are fully explained and understood.
3. Work is monitored against the schedule so any problem or possible delay is identified.
4. If any potential problem is identified, corrective action is taken. The severity of such action will be in inverse proportion to the amount of float remaining for the activity.
5. At set intervals, and on completion of the task, progress information is fed to the project manager and to the computer so that the project schedule can be updated and kept valid.

### PROGRESS CHASING

In the ideal modern system, it should be possible for all progress information to be reported and entered into the computer control system by the responsible managers or their delegates, using the local area network. Project managers, being ultimately responsible, may not rely entirely on other managers for progress monitoring and control. Partly for this reason and to ease the administrative load on all managers, routine progress monitoring can be delegated to one or more specially assigned people, who may have job titles such as progress clerk or progress chaser. These people should cooperate with the various departmental managers to gather information against work-to lists and report as necessary to the project manager and the relevant computer system. (The role of the project office is described in Chapter 8.)

## ASSESSING TASK PROGRESS

In addition to controlling progress, each manager is expected to assess the progress achieved and report this to the project manager or the planner so the schedule can be updated and kept valid. If a computer schedule is used which is updated and re-issued at intervals, all new data and progress information must be related to the next 'time-now' date. This is the date (decided by the planner) which the project management software uses as the start date from which to calculate the next revised schedule. Most computer programs allow the progress of an activity to be assessed in a number of different ways. Here are some of the possibilities:

1. Report that the activity has started, or will be started, by time-now. This information should prevent the computer from rescheduling activities which are already in progress.
2. An assessment of progress achieved. This might be expressed as:
   - estimated duration remaining to completion after time-now;
   - estimated percentage completion achieved at time-now; or
   - an estimated completion date for the activity.
3. Report that the activity has been completed, or will have been completed at time-now.

## ENGINEERING DESIGN

Estimates of activity durations usually tend to be optimistic. The project manager finds that when the work actually takes place, some activities take longer to finish than the time allowed in the plan. It is common practice to measure engineering and drawing progress in terms of percentage completion. Thus, if a particular design job were to be estimated as taking four weeks, the progress might be reported as (say) 75 per cent complete, from which the project manager and any other interested person would conclude that one week's work remained. It is, unfortunately, true that most people tend to be optimists when making assessments of their achievements. Thus, the project manager with several years' experience should not be surprised when this particular job is finished not one week later, but after three weeks, and then with questions still to be answered on some finer engineering point or other.

Optimistic estimates can be highlighted using a milestone tracker diagram

(Figure 26.1). The milestone in this example, for a gearbox design, was estimated to be delivered in week 20. These are often called milestone slip diagrams, because milestones are expected to slip. However, that is a bad attitude (Chapter 16), so milestone tracker diagrams is a better name. Often all the project milestones are put on a single chart to give a view of progress as a whole.

### Tracker diagram: preparation

The tracker diagram requires the following series of steps in preparation:

1. Draw two axes at right angles to each other and scale these axes in weeks. The total period allowed should be at least as long as that which the milestone could take under the worst possible conditions. The axes should be equal in

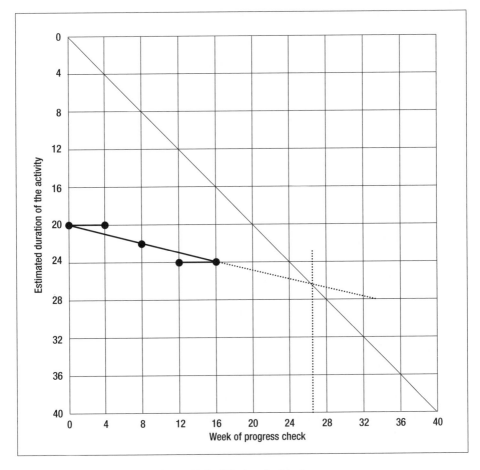

**Figure 26.1   Milestone tracker diagram**

value. Note that the scaling of the y (vertical) axis is in the reverse direction from that expected in a normal graph. Zero is at the top instead of at the origin. (The diagram is sometimes drawn rotated about the diagonal, that is the planned date along the top and the actual date down the vertical axis).

2. Draw a diagonal line from the top of the y axis (zero) to the maximum duration point on the x axis (which is 40 weeks in this example).

3. Plot the estimated delivery date of the milestone (week 20) at week zero on the time-now axis.

### Tracker diagram: application

After the gearbox designer has been at work for four weeks, her supervisor asks how things are going. She replies that all is going well and she expects to finish in the 20 weeks originally estimated. This is plotted on the diagram, as shown. After a further four weeks, at week eight, a further progress check shows the designer to be less confident. She thinks she will need a further 14 weeks before she finishes. This is equivalent to a revised total duration of 22 weeks, and this result is plotted on the diagram at week eight. During further checks at weeks 12 and 16 the designer has revised her estimates again and now expects the total duration to be 24 weeks. Again, these results are plotted on the diagram. At any time during these progress checks the project manager can draw the best possible straight line to connect these revised estimates. If that straight line is projected to the right, it will intersect the diagonal line at a point which can be taken to predict the delivery date of the milestone.

### Almost finished

Another problem facing the manager trying to get a project designed on time is the frequency with which engineers and designers report their work as 90 or 95 per cent complete, leaving that last tantalizing 10 or 5 per cent just out of reach. The shrewd manager will quickly learn to apply a few simple rules that should get progress back on course. The first requirement is to identify a set of milestones or key events in the plan that allow no compromise in interpreting whether or not they have been achieved. These events, which should appear on the project network (and will therefore have the benefit of scheduled dates) must be chosen at intervals that are not too far apart. A good general rule when planning targets is to choose events where jobs pass from person to person, or from department to department. Thus the handover of a drawing from designer to checker or the release of a particular set of fully checked and approved drawings might be real indicators of progress.

### Design information from external sources

Engineering design activities very often depend on information from outside sources. In the case of a large construction project, this information can include considerable correspondence from the client and many suppliers. Engineering can be also be held up while waiting for the client to approve various documents, which might include certain drawings, specifications and purchase documents. The project manager must ensure close monitoring of these information exchanges and see to it that no external organization is allowed to put the success of the project at risk by avoidable delays.

On larger projects it will probably be necessary to impose office procedures on all correspondence and document transmissions, whether these are by mail or electronic means. All important communications need to be monitored to make certain that every message needing an answer gets that answer promptly. These transmissions may need to be given serial numbers and subject codes so that they can be filed for future reference.

## SUBCONTRACTED ENGINEERING DESIGN SERVICES

Engineering companies sometimes offload work to external design offices, either at times of overload or as a more permanent policy to maintain staffing flexibility. It is not unknown for a company to operate with a small core of permanently employed professional engineers, and to have a substantial amount of detailed design work being performed in several external offices. The two most apparent risks to project deliverables introduced by this practice are:

- dilution of company standards or quality;
- loose control of progress.

The quality aspect can be covered to some extent by ensuring that the external offices are certificated to relevant quality standards, such as ISO 9000 (Chapter 16). A more positive step is to arrange for one or more supervising engineers from each regularly used external office to be trained in the company's own offices so they absorb the host company's standards and culture. When they return to their own offices, they become an effective extension of the company's own engineering management. A useful arrangement for controlling progress in external offices is to appoint a qualified and experienced person as a subcontract liaison engineer. This person can visit each external office at frequent, regular intervals to deliver and collect work, monitor progress and give on-the-spot answers to most technical queries.

## PURCHASING ACTIVITIES

Purchased materials and equipment often take a long time to obtain and are likely to be critical. Particular attention must therefore be given to progressing the purchasing function. It will be assumed that an efficient purchasing organization exists and that appropriate supplier selection procedures are followed (Chapter 35). The first requirement is to ensure that critical items are ordered as early as possible. This might mean arranging for the engineering design department to release purchasing information early. It may not be good enough to wait for the official issue of the parts list, bill of materials or purchase schedules to get such goods on order. Even in cases where final design details cannot be given with confidence for bought-out components, it can be possible for outline information to be provided that will enable external manufacturers to reserve capacity.

Expediting is important. For the straightforward supply of catalogue items this might simply mean making checks with a supplier during the period between placing the order and expected delivery, so that the supplier is kept reminded of the contract obligation and to reveal any difficulty as soon as possible. For major equipment purchases visits to the manufacturer's premises might be necessary, sometimes combined with physical inspection and the witnessing of tests.

## MANUFACTURING ACTIVITIES

All good manufacturing establishments will have their own methods for production control and these are outside the scope of this handbook. The project schedule should give the required start and finish times of each manufactured assembly or subassembly and the manufacturing managers should be relied upon to work within those limits. Progress chasers see that work is moved from each work station to the next without undue delay. The whole process can be speeded by the use of just-in-time methods, although these may not be appropriate for special project work. The timely physical movement of machined parts, subassemblies and other production jobs between work stations is particularly important for project progress. If a job requires, say, ten operations from raw material to completed part, and if it takes a day to move that job between each work station, then the part will spend two weeks in the factory sitting on racks or trolleys.

A project manager who has access to the manufacturing facilities employed on the project can spend profitable time walking through the factory regularly (perhaps once a day). Just ten minutes is often sufficient for the project manager to note whether any job is held up. A stack of steel piled in a corner for a few days might be an indication that the production management have downgraded the

490

priority on this project work to the advantage of some other project manager who is able to shout louder.

## CONSTRUCTION

At a construction site (which may be thousands of miles removed from the project manager and the home office) it is customary to establish a management team which controls work on the spot. The size and organization of this team can vary, from just two or three individuals on a small project to a substantial management and administration team for a larger job. Adequate communication facilities must be established between the project site and the contractor's head office. This used to be a serious problem with some international projects and remote sites before the days of communication satellites.

Procedures are well established in the construction industry for monitoring and measuring progress. This applies to activities carried out by the company's own staff and to the work of subcontractors. Quantity surveyors work with people from the site management team to ensure that work is progressing at the planned rate. Much of the work can be assessed in terms of simple physical quantities, such as tonnes of earth moved, amount of steelwork erected and so on.

Organizational arrangements can have a marked effect on the degree of day-to-day control that the site manager must exercise on the work of the various trades. A managing contractor who employs no direct labour but relies instead on subcontractors would need less day-to-day involvement than one who employed its own direct labour.

It is obviously essential that all materials are delivered to site at the right time and in good condition. Thus the project purchasing organization has a prime responsibility towards maintaining construction progress. The site manager will report any shortages, preferably when they are foreseen rather than waiting for them to happen, and the purchasing organization will be expected to take urgent action to get the goods to site.

No less important than the flow of materials and equipment to site is the supply of construction information. This takes the form of drawings, equipment suppliers' installation instructions, take-off lists, engineering standards, specifications and erection instructions. Construction often starts before engineering design is completely finished. Thus there is a danger of construction work outstripping the supply of drawings and other engineering information. Drawings sent to a construction site are usually stamped to show they have passed the necessary checking and approval stages. 'Released for construction' is a typical legend for this purpose. Design engineers are sometimes unable to release drawings fully for construction. They might be awaiting final details of

**491**

bought-out equipment before power supply requirements and fixings can be added to the drawings. In these circumstances the incomplete drawings may be released provisionally for construction, perhaps with a rubber-stamped legend reading 'Released for construction with holds'. A drawing released with holds can often allow some planning and limited work to take place on-site.

The use of network float is another point worthy of mention. It is easy to allow all float to be taken up in the engineering design phase, so that the construction site team are left with no remaining float and therefore find themselves squeezed for time. One way out of this difficulty is to add a special final activity to the project network which does not represent work, but which adds an artificial delay of, perhaps, four weeks to the end of the programme. This has the effect of driving float away from the front (engineering) end of the network, and provides a safety buffer for construction activities. This is not unfair to the engineers. Most project difficulties, at least most of the excusable ones, occur on-site. Engineers are not likely to be affected by ice, snow, floods, running sand, strikes, fights, thefts or any of the other unforeseen problems which the site manager faces.

## HIGHER LEVEL PROGRESS CHECKS

When attempting to manage progress at the level of individual activities it is easy to lose sight of the big picture. An example based on the engineering design function can be used to illustrate this point.

Consider a project on which the engineering design effort is expected to need 100 people during (say) the tenth week. The project manager should have access to this figure from the resource schedule (Chapter 20). Whether the detailed feedback on progress is good or bad, the project manager would be advised to ask, 'How many engineers are actually working on my project this week?' The answer might produce a shock: not 100 engineers, but only 60.

I remember carrying out a similar check myself once. An external, subcontracted, drawing office was supposed to be making numerous detail drawings, based on layouts and specifications produced by our in-house senior engineers. At the time of the check the schedule showed that 30 external staff should be busy on the project. Our check found only six. Yet engineering progress was confidently being reported by our internal managers as being in step with the plan. Urgent investigation found that the in-house senior engineers were reporting their layouts as completely finished, but were not releasing them to the external office for detailing. They were reluctant to let their work go, perhaps through some lack of confidence in their designs or so that they could give a few late tweaks to move their work nearer to absolute perfection. This problem was put right immediately by firm action from the engineering director, but the problem would not have been revealed in time without the independent, global check on the rate of working.

## SPECIAL PRIORITY CASES

It is generally not good management practice to attempt the allocation of priorities to work outside the normal scheduling sequence. Manufacturing, for example, is a function in which attempts to allocate priorities are fraught with risk of failure. Labelling work as priority A, B or C might seem a good idea, but eventually all work becomes priority A. However, there are occasions where special action is needed. The cost to a project of a failure which delays the production of one small item can be out of all proportion to the cost of obtaining that item. Particularly disastrous is the case of an assembly, possibly containing complex electronic or electromechanical gadgetry, which fails catastrophically on its final test. Possibly some single component has broken down, causing other components to be lost. Situations such as this are even more difficult to resolve when it transpires that the failures were caused by design errors, so that the whole cycle of design and manufacture has to be repeated.

There is a procedure which can cope well with such problems. It depends on the issue of an *immediate action order* (IAO). The usual documents seen in the factory or engineering offices are printed on ordinary plain paper, so one document looks much like another. The first thing which strikes one about an IAO is that it is anything but an ordinary piece of plain paper. These top priority documents are printed on paper with brilliantly coloured diagonal stripes (fluorescent if possible). They cannot fail to be seen on a desk or worktop. Another feature of IAOs is that, because they are so special, they have to be authorized at general manager or managing director level. They are so special that their use has to be restricted. They must not be allowed to proliferate or their impact will be lost. The rule, therefore, is that no more than one IAO may be sanctioned at any one time.

Once authorized, there is no limit placed on the expenditure allowed to get the job done. If the offices or factory must remain open all night, or over Christmas, then so be it. If materials are only available in Sweden and the factory is in Cornwall, then those materials must be obtained by the quickest route regardless of cost. An IAO commits all departments, so that in the case of a design fault the engineering department must correct the relevant drawings without delay. Normal quality standards must still be respected, but those responsible for carrying out inspection and testing will be bound by the urgency of the order. The

**493**

IAO is carried from department to department by a progress chaser, who date- and time-stamps its arrival and departure times at each departmental manager's desk. The progress chaser remains with the IAO until the job is done.

In companies where this system operates, managers learn to fear IAOs. They are a nuisance. They carry risk of criticism or rebuke from higher management if they are not properly obeyed. They command priority over all other work – even to the extent of stopping a machine in mid-cut, removing the workpiece and resetting the machine to take the immediate job. The logic is seen when by spending perhaps £15 000 to finish a job which should only have cost £1000, a project delay of several weeks is avoided. The cost of the immediate action is likely to be very small in relation to the savings in total costs and reputation.

Immediate action orders get dramatic results. A tiny prototype 5000 volt transformer for military equipment burned out on test. It had taken six weeks to manufacture and was difficult to make, being encased in an intricate electroplated copper gauze screen and then encapsulated in epoxy resin. Manufacturing operations were subject to numerous quality checks against a stringent military specification. The successful replacement took three days from the start of redesign to final test.

## PROGRESS MEASUREMENT

Progress measurement is not the same thing as progress management because, by itself, it does not imply the taking of action. Measurement is, however, necessary for several reasons, the two most important of which are as follows:

1. To provide an equitable and certifiable basis for interim claims for payment. Thus the work of subcontractors has to be measured to establish when and how much they can bill the main contractor (or the client) for work done. A main contractor's own work should be measured for similar reasons. The inclusion of key events or milestones in the plan is a good way of identifying the timing and amounts of interim payments.
2. It is necessary to measure at any stage in most projects the actual value of work finished or in progress. This information can be used in reports and to compare expenditure trends with cost estimates and budgets.

### EARNED VALUE ANALYSIS

Earned value analysis is a methodology for comparing the achieved value of work in progress against the project schedule and budget. It can be performed at the single activity level but its maximum benefit depends on looking at all activities and rolling the results up through the hierarchy of the work breakdown structure. As with any measurement technique, earned value analysis is not a progress control tool in itself. It can only highlight a need for corrective action by indicating trends. The method does, however, have the advantage of being able to show trends fairly early in the project life cycle.

Earned value analysis depends on the existence of a sound framework of planning and control, including:

- a detailed work breakdown structure;
- a correspondingly detailed cost coding system;
- hierarchical and complete tabulation of all project tasks with their approved budgets;
- inclusion of all authorized changes to the project at the appropriate times;
- timely and accurate collection and reporting of cost data;
- regular progress reviews;
- a method for quantifying the amount of work done at each review date;
- inclusion of work in progress in all reviews;
- a competent administrator.

The basic principles can be described using the milestone tracker diagram (Figure 26.1). The original estimate for this work was 20 weeks. Suppose that this work is costing £1000 per week, so that the corresponding total budget is £20 000. Assume, for simplicity, that the expenditure rate is linear. Consider a reporting date of week 16. At this time the activity should be 80 per cent complete, for which the budgeted cost would be 80 per cent of £20 000. In earned value analysis terms, this would be expressed as follows:

$$BCWS = £16\,000$$

where BCWS is the budgeted cost of work scheduled to be complete at the reporting date.

Here we are looking at just one activity, but BCWS would usually have to include all project work scheduled to be complete at the reporting date. BCWS must include not only all work actually finished, but also the completed portion of all work in progress. Returning to the single package of work in Figure 26.1, we know that this activity is running late and the latest estimate from the milestone tracker chart shows a likely total duration of 25 weeks. If the activity expenditure is at the expected level of £1000 per week, the likely cost will be £25 000 instead of £20 000. It could be said that, at week 16, the percentage of work achieved is not 80 per cent, but only 64 per cent. The earned value analysis expressions which describe this state of affairs are as follows:

ACWP = £16 000

where ACWP is the actual cost of work performed to date:

BCWP = £12 800

where BCWP is the budgeted cost of work performed (budget cost appropriate to the amount of work actually achieved). These results can be used to produce the following indices.

Cost performance index (CPI) $= \dfrac{BCWP}{ACWP}$

Schedule performance index (SPI) $= \dfrac{BCWP}{BCWS}$

For the single package of work in the tracker diagram, the index is 0.8 in each case. Values greater than unity point to performance better than plan. Values less than unity, as here, indicate negative variances and the need for action to correct the trend.

When the measurement takes into account all the project's work, these factors can be used to calculate the estimated costs remaining to completion or the predicted final project cost, as described in Chapter 18 and illustrated in Figure 18.1. It is neither usual nor necessary to use a tracker diagram to assess progress on every activity in progress. Many construction or manufacturing activities can be measured in terms of physical quantities. Progress assessment on most activities, however, is a matter for expert judgment. When comparing performance against budget for the whole project, it is important that the budget figures used include all increments relating to authorized changes. See Harrison (1992), Webb (1994) or Fleming and Koppleman (1996) for a fuller treatment of earned value analysis.

## CHANGES

Any change to an active project is likely to threaten progress and increase costs. It is true that there are companies which welcome their client's requests for changes, since these can provide reasons for levying additional charges and extending the timescale at the client's expense. Once the project is active, any change can be an increase in project scope which the contractor can sell at a price not restricted by external competition. Project managers, however, usually view all changes as nuisances.

## CHANGES WHICH NEED CONTROL PROCEDURES

Changes can occur at any stage in a project. Some are relatively insignificant, because they happen early, cause little wasted effort and do not affect the project as it was originally defined in the sales specification and contract. For example, a designer may have to make several attempts at a difficult design problem before a drawing can be produced which is suitable for release to the production or construction organization. It would not be reasonable or practicable to expect the designer to seek formal approval every time he or she wiped the computer screen and started again. There is a way to decide whether or not an action should be regarded as a change needing formal management approval. This is to ask whether or not the proposed change would alter any information on a document that has already been issued to authorize work. This definition means that a formal procedure should be applied whenever a proposed change would affect:

- the contract document or any of its attachments (in which case the controlling change document would probably be called a project variation order or contract variation);
- an issued purchase order (the change would probably be called a purchase order amendment);
- any drawing or specification which has previously been issued for manufacture, purchasing or construction.

These changes can be interactive, so that a contract variation originated by the client (for instance) might result in a series of engineering changes and purchase order amendments.

## CONTROL PROCEDURES FOR ENGINEERING CHANGES

Before a proposed engineering change is allowed to go ahead, it is usual to assess its risks, examining the possible effects carefully in all respects (technical, manufacturing or construction methods, commercial, safety, reliability, timescale and costs). Because no one person can usually be found in the organization who is capable of assessing all these factors, a committee of departmental managers or other experts, which might be called the change committee, is often formed for the purpose. A change committee might contain a senior representative of the key company functions. A typical composition could be as follows:

1. The chief engineer, acting as design authority
2. The quality manager, acting as the quality authority (or the inspecting authority)
3. The manufacturing manager, as the manufacturing authority

4. The commercial manager
5. The purchasing manager

All requests for engineering changes should be submitted to the change committee in a suitable standard format (a form was suggested in Chapter 15, Figure 15.4). The procedure should ensure that change requests are dealt with properly, without undue delay, and that the actions decided by the committee are followed up. Not least of these actions is the updating and re-issue of drawings and other affected documents.

The change control procedure should be centred on a technical clerk or project coordinator, who can serial number and register each request and then use the register to control its progress. Monitoring must continue until each change request is either rejected by the committee or fully implemented. The coordinator must keep those who are likely to be affected (including the request originators) informed of the committee decisions. In a typical arrangement, the change committee will meet at regular intervals (perhaps weekly or every two weeks) to consider change requests in batches. The committee will consider each change on its merits and potential risks.

In one multinational company the view was taken that all changes would initially be classified as either 'essential' or 'desirable'. Essential changes would include those necessary to guarantee safe and reliable operation of plant or to correct errors. These might be approved without comment, sent back to the originator for more information or an alternative proposal, given approval in a modified or limited form, or rejected altogether. Changes requested by the customer would also fall into the essential category, most of these resulting in additional revenue. Changes classed as desirable would always be rejected. The slogan was 'If it's essential we must do it, if it's only desirable we won't.'

## DESIGN FREEZE

Sometimes project organizations recognize that there is a point in the design and implementation of a project after which any engineering change would be either very inconvenient or unacceptably damaging to costs and progress. This leads the organization to announce a 'design freeze' for the project. In some companies this is called 'stable design'. The idea is to deter anyone from having the temerity to suggest any further change. The change committee will refuse approval for any change request once design has been frozen, unless the originator can show compelling reasons such as safety or a funded customer request. Ideally the customer should also be bound by the design freeze, or at least should be made to pay heavily for the privilege of breaching it.

### OTHER PROCEDURES RELATED TO ENGINEERING CHANGES

There are at least three procedural systems that are similar in many respects to engineering change procedures, especially in manufacturing companies:

1. Engineering queries: requests for advice from manufacturing departments where drawings and specifications are unclear or appear to contain errors.
2. Production permits and concessions: requests from the manufacturing departments for permission to depart from design or process instructions in one or more respects.
3. Inspection rejection reports, where the degree of rejection is marginal and the design authority must rule whether or not to allow a concession.

Change procedures and their related systems are described more fully in Lock (2000).

## PROGRESS MEETINGS

Progress meetings provide a forum in which progress difficulties and risks can be discussed and actions agreed. Each meeting should be managed efficiently by the chair, with the aid of a sensible agenda, so that it deals effectively with all matters related to keeping the project on schedule but is not side-tracked into technical and other issues that should more properly be dealt with elsewhere. Progress meetings should also be kept as short as possible, given that those attending are probably busy, short of spare time, highly paid and needed back in their own departments actually to do work rather than simply discuss it. It is not a bad plan to arrange that progress meetings, at least those which only involve in-house staff, are started at a fairly late hour in the working day. Then there is a real incentive to get on with the business. Of course, this argument would not apply to a project where the client had travelled thousands of miles to attend the meeting.

### FREQUENCY

The frequency of progress meetings depends on the duration and complexity of the project. For a highly intensive project carried out at feverish speed over just a few weeks or months, it might be deemed appropriate to hold short progress meetings every week. Monthly is a more usual interval for most projects.

One company in my experience managed to abolish regular progress meetings. All project departmental managers were issued with work schedules from a multiproject model and a project coordination group controlled progress against these schedules on a day-by-day basis. As soon as any activity seemed in danger of running beyond its latest permissible date action was taken to bring the work back on schedule. No specific action was taken to stop progress meetings: it was simply realized that they were no longer taking place.

However, a project manager has no alternative but to call progress meetings when the participants come from different departments or organizations, and either cannot agree their planned commitments or have to meet to agree the joint actions necessary to overcome genuine difficulties and get the programme back on course.

## COMMITMENTS

During progress meetings it is common for individuals to be asked to make estimates or to give promises of fresh dates by which late or additional jobs can be finished. The chairman will ensure that promises with vague wordings such as 'the end of the week' or 'sometime next month' or (worst of all) 'as soon as possible' are not allowed. The chairman must insist on firm, measurable commitments. If any member of the meeting feels that the promises being made by others are unrealistic, he or she should (politely) say so, in order that all possible consideration is given in advance to the likely problems. All promises and commitments must be as realistic as possible. How many of us have attended progress meetings where, from one meeting to the next, the same item keeps cropping up with the only result being that a new, later, promise is given each time?

## MINUTES

Progress meetings are a waste of time when the agreements reached are not followed up to ensure that promises are kept. The control document for this purpose is that containing the minutes of the meeting. The minutes should be:

- concise, giving short statements of actions agreed;
- annotated to show those persons required to perform or manage the agreed actions;
- issued promptly, as soon as possible after the meeting;
- distributed to all those present plus any other person to whom action had been assigned by the meeting.

# PROGRESS REPORTING

Progress reporting takes place at many levels, formally and informally, on any project of significant size. At the simplest level reporting is person to person when, for example, a supervisor performs the daily rounds and asks how individual jobs are progressing. Then follows an ascending hierarchical structure of reporting, involving other departments, subcontractors, purchasing and shipping organizations, finally reaching the level of regular, comprehensive cost and progress reports to the client. The lowest and most detailed level of reporting is concerned with collecting data from which to keep the schedule up to date. This was discussed earlier in this chapter.

## EXCEPTION REPORTING

Strictly speaking, the more senior a person is in the management structure of the project, the less detail he or she should be given about progress. Those managers responsible for taking action when things look like going wrong should not be given a long list of jobs which are on course with potential problems hidden among them. It is necessary to pick out the problem activities and highlight them. Then managers' time can be focused on resolving the problems. Every item in danger of running late or exceeding its cost constitutes an exception that should be reported. When a computer is used for scheduling, it is possible to edit lists so that only late or critical activities are shown. There are several techniques for reducing the number of activities in reports for individual managers still further, so that each only receives information on critical activities within his or her area of responsibility.

Material shortage lists are a good, if specialized, example of exception reports. They list all items of purchased materials and equipment which are urgently awaited to maintain or regain work momentum. The purchasing department is then able to concentrate the efforts of its expediting section on getting the goods delivered.

## PROGRESS REPORTS TO THE CLIENT

If the project is large in terms of time and cost, the client will want to know how the project is progressing at any time. This information is usually presented in the form of a progress report (typically issued monthly). It is usual to combine progress reports to the client with cost reports and statements showing how project funds are being used. The main contractor of a large international project might include the following items in regular reports to the client:

1. A written account of progress achieved to date, with special emphasis on progress achieved since the previous report.
2. Photographs showing physical progress.
3. Some form of quantified evidence to back up the progress claimed. This might include, for example, a table of drawing achievement showing:
   - total drawings required for the project;
   - number of drawings issued this reporting period;
   - total number of drawings issued to date;
   - number of drawings in progress and not started;
   - percentage of total engineering design and drawing finished.
4. A statement of the position regarding purchased equipment, possibly in the form of purchase and order schedules.
5. A cost report, showing in tabular and graphical form the expenditure to date on main areas of the project and the totals. The cost report should include the latest predictions of total final project expenditure and would also give the client up-to-date cash flow forecasts.
6. A short summary of the work planned for the next reporting period.
7. A list of problems caused by the client in holding up the supply of information, approvals or funds. That is, a schedule of actions which the contractor requires from the client.
8. A summary of project variations, separated into those which have been approved and those which are undergoing appraisal.
9. A summary of important documents and correspondence communicated during the reporting period, highlighting those which still have to be satisfactorily answered.

Project managers or their superiors should edit reports for clients carefully to ensure that the contents represent a true picture of the project's progress. It is not necessary, obviously, to tell the client of every silly mistake made during design or manufacturing, provided that such mistakes are correctable within the time and cost constraints of the contract. The client must, however, never be misled or intentionally misinformed. If a problem is foreseen which poses a real threat to the timescale, to the budget or to the technical performance of the finished project, then the client must be told. A client who is left to find out such problems by default will not feel that the project manager has acted to protect its best interests. The client should feel justified in asking how the contractor felt able to ask a fee for managing the project when, at best, there appears to have been no awareness of the problem and, at worst, deception.

## REFERENCES AND FURTHER READING

Fleming, Q. W. and Koppelman, J. M. (1996), *Earned Value Project Management*, Project Management Institute, Upper Darby, PA.

Harrison, F. L. (1992), *Advanced Project Management*, 3rd edition, Gower, Aldershot.

Lester, A. (1991), *Project Planning and Control*, 2nd edition, Butterworth-Heinemann, Oxford.

Lock, D. (2000), *Project Management*, 7th edition, Gower, Aldershot.

Rosenau, D. R. Jr. (1998), *Successful Project Management*, 3rd edition, Wiley, New York.

Webb, A. (1994), *Managing Innovative Projects*, Chapman & Hall, London.

## RELATED TOPICS

| | |
|---|---|
| Project office | Chapter 8 |
| Project definition | Chapters 14 and 25 |
| Configuration management and change control | Chapter 15 |
| Project quality and attitudes | Chapter 16 |
| Project organization | Chapters 17, 30 and 38 |
| Estimating cost | Chapter 18 |
| Project schedule | Chapter 19 |
| Managing resources | Chapter 20 |
| Procurement | Chapter 30 |
| Management support | Chapters 41 and 42 |
| Conflict management | Chapter 43 |
| Competence development | Chapter 39 |

# Part V
# Commercial

# INTRODUCTION TO PART V

In Part V we consider the commercial and financial issues. The project is undertaken to provide benefit to the owner and repay the investment in the project. We need to predict before the project starts that it will make a profit, to convince people to invest in it and to optimize the outcome. We therefore need methods of appraising the project, raising the finance and managing the financial risk.

### Chapter 27: Project appraisal

In Chapter 27 Dennis Lock describes investment appraisal techniques. Using examples, he explains the need to consider all the costs of the project and illustrates several techniques, including payback period, net present value and internal rate of return. He then links the techniques to feasibility and risk analysis and suggests how they can be used to compare strategies for a project.

### Chapter 28: Two-phase parametric discounting

In Chapter 28 Chris Chapman explains how to apply investment appraisal techniques to projects with long time horizons. In these cases the analysis can lead to the subtraction of two large numbers, where small changes in parameters can appear to swing decisions. He describes a two-phase parametric approach. In the first phase a model is created which nests the large numbers to balance their effect. The critical parameters are identified and the ranges that flip the decision determined. In the second phase probabilistic analysis is applied to key parameters to determine the expected and most likely values for the decisions.

## Chapter 29: Managing finance

Tony Merna discusses project finance in Chapter 29. He describes the features of project finance, the types of finance available and financial instruments used to raise those types of finance. He considers financial engineering, but devotes half the chapter to the management of financial risk. He shows how the nine-stage risk management process from Chapter 21 converts into a five-step process for managing financial risk.

# 27   Project appraisal

## *Dennis Lock*

This chapter examines some of the issues connected with financial investment decisions for new projects. Several techniques exist to help managers, investors and funding institutions to make 'go' or 'no-go' decisions or to choose between two or more strategic options according to the financial outlook. Financial appraisal techniques can, however, only be regarded as indicators that contribute to a wider decision-making process. There may be overriding ethical, safety, welfare, legal or environmental reasons for having to adopt a different course from the financial ideal. Furthermore, it is often the case that data or assumptions used in pre-project calculations (perhaps with limited information available about the embryonic project) can prove to be dangerously inaccurate when the project takes shape. The procedures described in this chapter, although important, are therefore not the only ingredient in the mix of data, judgement, intuition and courage needed by investors.

## THE NEED TO CONSIDER TOTAL COSTS

Here is an example, based on an actual case, to illustrate what can go disastrously wrong when all the parameters and data for a new project proposal have not been properly considered (in other words, when the definition and scope of the project have not been fully established). The lessons to be learned from this example apply generally to all project proposals and appraisal methods.

### MINI-COMPUTER PROJECT: PROPOSAL AND FINANCIAL APPRAISAL

A computing department manager in an engineering company had to rely on external bureaux computer facilities whenever a mainframe machine was needed. At that time the only computing facilities within the company were a few separate personal computers with modest capabilities. The computing manager wanted to expand his power and influence by installing a new computer, but the financial director was firmly opposed to the idea and the associated capital expenditure. The computing manager, like many of his peers, was competent not only in computing techniques but also in company politics. Choosing a time when the hostile director was thousands of miles away on an extended tour, he produced a proposal to buy a computer that could, among other things, act as a central word-processing station for all the firm's secretaries and typists. He put forward the financial argument shown in Figure 27.1 to support the proposal.

## MINI-COMPUTER PROJECT: THE REALITY

Faced with the promising figures, a meeting of the available directors authorized the plan and the office services manager was instructed to arrange accommodation and installation. In the event the costs were far higher than budget, because the project had not been properly thought through. The actual costs were as shown in Figure 27.2, and for the following reasons the predicted first-year productivity benefits were not achieved:

1. The word-processing software was peculiar to the equipment and unfamiliar to all the secretarial staff.
2. Secretarial efficiency was not increased immediately and staff cuts took longer to implement than forecast.

| Costs and savings | £ | £ |
| --- | --- | --- |
| Initial capital outlay | | |
| ● Computer, with word-processing software including six printers and ten visual display units | | 60 000 |
| Projected savings in first full year of operation | | |
| ● Saving of two secretaries' annual salaries and other costs owing to increased productivity (an implied staff reduction) | 30 000 | |
| ● Saving of professional engineers' time (by having certain standard format documents stored on disk, reducing the work need to write and check each new application of these documents) | 25 000 | |
| ● Saving in external bureaux costs for computing which could be carried out in-house in future | 10 000 | |
| Total annual savings | | 65 000 |

Figure 27.1    Budget proposal for a mini-computer investment

| Actual first year costs | £ |
|---|---:|
| Computing equipment, purchased as quoted | 60 000 |
| Allocation and redecoration of accommodation | 1 500 |
| Structural alterations (door widening) | 850 |
| Removal of radiators and water pipes | 300 |
| Installation of air conditioners and heaters | 2 500 |
| 'Clean' electrical supply and new wiring | 1 200 |
| Automatic fire extinguishers and alarm | 1 800 |
| Purchase and installation of raised floor | 2 550 |
| Underground cableducts between buildings | 1 500 |
| Cabling from computer room to users' offices | 3 500 |
| New telephones | 300 |
| Purchase of 6 additional printers | 6 000 |
| Additional visual display units | 5 000 |
| Purchase of 12 printer acoustic hoods | 4 200 |
| Insurance premiums | 300 |
| Training costs for 28 secretaries | 5 000 |
| Increase in annual electrical costs (24-hour operation including air conditioning) | 5 000 |
| Total first year costs | 101 500 |

Figure 27.2 Mini-computer investment, the reality

3. It was necessary to engage two extra people for the computer department, at salaries higher than those of the secretaries.
4. Computer crashes, shutdowns for maintenance, and slowness caused by overloading caused work loss and idle time among the secretaries and led to staff dissatisfaction.

The operating problems were eventually overcome and the system did become useful. However, the computing capacity had to be increased twice, needing yet more investment. Maintenance and repair costs, ignored in the original cost forecasts, soared from the second year of operation onwards.

Before ever allowing this investment to take place, the board of directors should have demanded to see a properly argued case for the project, with total costs, proposals from suppliers of alternative equipment and an assessment of the possible risks. Another essential point missed was that the end-users (secretaries with experience of word processing) were not asked for their views beforehand. This project was forecast to recover its initial investment after about one year. In fact, in spite of very hard work from the computing staff to overcome all the problems, this project never paid for itself.

## CASH FLOW SCHEDULING

A cash flow projection is a prerequisite in most financial project appraisal calculations. A few relevant definitions follow.

### CASH OUTFLOWS

A cash outflow is any item of expenditure for, or resulting from, the project. Cash outflows for a typical project could include:

- salaries, expenses, purchases, overheads, payments to contractors, suppliers and agents, professional fees, rental and hire charges, interest payable on loans and anything else which contributes to the total project cost;
- operating costs: the costs incurred by the end-user when operating the equipment, building or other outcome of the initial project;
- tax payments in respect of liabilities incurred through cash inflows generated by the project.

### CASH INFLOWS

Any item of revenue or cost saving resulting from the project is a cash inflow. Typical cash inflows include:

- sales revenues generated by the project;
- royalties or licensing fees earned;
- reductions in taxation through allowable expenses, incentives or concessions;
- proceeds from the sale of plant, buildings or materials released for disposal as a result of the project;
- proceeds expected from the disposal of the project itself when it reaches the end of its planned operational life.

### NET CASH FLOWS

Net cash flow is the difference between cash outflows and cash inflows, either during a specified period or for the whole project. Net flows can obviously be inflows or outflows.

### TIMING

In all except the very simplest case, the timing of outflows and inflows is crucial. It is important, therefore, that all the data are carefully tabulated, with each item shown in the period when it is expected to occur. Taking one example, cash flows resulting from tax liabilities or allowances to set against tax generally lag their causal events by at least one year.

A cash flow spreadsheet will always be divided into rows or columns corresponding to consecutive, equal periods in the timescale. The periods chosen will depend on the total period covered by the appraisal (which might extend beyond the initial project construction or manufacture to include several years of use or operation). Calendar months or quarters are often appropriate for short-term projects. Half or whole years are more likely to be chosen when assessing larger projects. It is usual and convenient to align the periods chosen with one of the following, depending on the commercial framework and the nature of the project:

- The organization's normal accounting periods
- The accounting periods of a client (especially for a project requiring large investments from the client)
- Fiscal periods (periods used for government finance or tax accounting)

### MATCHING TIMING TO THE PROJECT SCHEDULE

Information from both the project schedule and the cost estimates or budgets is needed before a cash flow schedule can be prepared. At the time of the initial financial appraisal such information may not be available in great detail, but there must at least be a good outline of the principal items of expenditure and of the significant events in the project life cycle. Figure 27.3 illustrates the essential ingredients in their logical sequence.

## APPRAISAL USING BREAK-EVEN ANALYSIS

Break-even analysis is a simple process of discovering how long it is expected to take, under a given set of circumstances, before the cash inflows generated by the project reach and start to exceed the total expenditure. The time forecast for this to happen is called the payback period. Payback analysis is another name for this process.

### TOLL ROAD PROJECT

Road users from a small town had suffered inconvenience for many years because of the need to make a detour of several kilometres round the large estate belonging to Lady Y. A proposal has been made to Lady Y by her estate manager

**513**

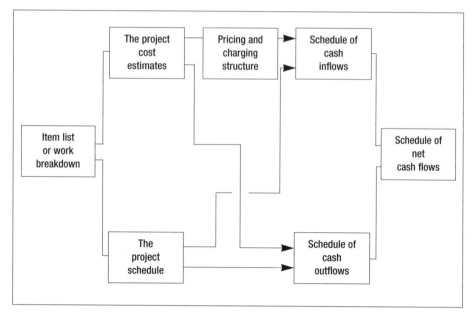

**Figure 27.3   Elements of net cash flow scheduling**

that she should, by improving an existing estate road, open a toll road that would provide a valuable saving in journey times for local residents and businesses. The scheme would be expected to produce significant additional income for the estate.

### Toll road project: cost and revenue data

The estate manager has obtained reliable estimates from a managing contractor, who would carry out all the design and construction work for a total fixed price of £400 000. The expected revenues would be based on 250 private car users and 100 commercial vehicle drivers using the road each day, for both outward and return trips (a total of 700 daily crossings). Each car driver would be asked to pay a toll of 35p per crossing, and commercial users would pay 50p. Any possible increase in usage for later years was not considered. The road would be open for 364 days each year, but would be closed on Christmas day with the objective of preventing the route from becoming a designated right of way. It would be necessary to deploy one or two existing farm workers as toll keepers, and there would be some maintenance costs after the first year of operation. These operating costs were expected to be £25 000 in the first full year of operation and £50 000 in subsequent years. In practice the effects of taxation and any loan charges on capital would also have to be considered, but these have been excluded for simplicity.

### Toll road project: break-even analysis

Lady Y's son was enthusiastic about the project and produced the calculation shown in Figure 27.4 as justification. Each year runs from 1 April to 31 March. A simple arithmetic exercise reveals that the initial outlay of £400 000 will be overtaken by net cash inflows at some time during the eighth year of full operation. Another way of expressing this is to say that the payback period is just over eight years from the start of the project. This result can also be produced using a graph, Figure 27.5.

## DISCOUNTING METHODS

Whenever a financial analysis extends over a period which exceeds two or three years, straightforward addition or subtraction of cash inflows and outflows (as in the simple break-even method) is likely to produce a misleading result. This is because the useful value of any given sum of money depends on the date when it is due to be received or paid out. The argument is that £1000 today is worth more than £1000 in the future because today's £1000 is available for immediate investment to increase its future value. Suppose a person receives £1000 now and has to pay it back in one year's time. That person can invest the £1000 immediately, perhaps at 7 per cent net annual rate. By the time £1000 is repaid, the amount received will be worth £1070, a profit of £70. Financial analysts would say that £1070 is the future value of £1000. Alternatively, they would say that

| | Outflows £ | Inflows £ | Net flows £ |
|---|---|---|---|
| **Year 1** | | | |
| ● Construction | 400 000 | None | |
| | | | (400 000) |
| **Year 2** | | | |
| ● Toll keepers | 25 000 | | |
| ● Car tolls | | 63 700 | |
| ● Commercial tolls | | | 75 100 |
| **Subsequent years** | | | |
| ● Toll keepers | 25 000 | | |
| ● Maintenance | 25 000 | | |
| ● Car tolls | | 63 700 | |
| ● Commercial tolls | | | 50 100 |

Figure 27.4   Cash inflows and outflows for the toll road project

515

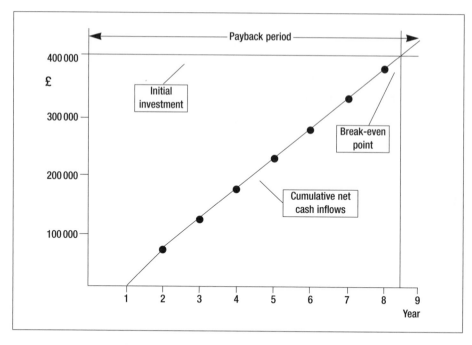

**Figure 27.5 Payback graph for the toll road project**

£1000 is today's net present value of the future £1070. In project financial appraisal, it is the combined net present value of all the future cash flows which is likely to be of most interest to the potential investor.

The process of converting future values back into net present values is known as discounting. Tables of discounting factors are available which cover a wide range of periods and different percentage discount rates. A short table is given in Figure 27.6. More extensive tables are widely published, but the use of PC-based spreadsheets to perform these calculations makes their use redundant now.

## NET PRESENT VALUE

The net present value of a proposed project is found from a calculation based on discounting all present and future cash flows. The results have several useful applications, as follows:

1. To evaluate the likely worth of a proposed investment in a new project. The total period considered would usually extend well beyond completion of the initial project to include all or a substantial part of the operating life of the facility created by the project.
2. The net present values of two or more different strategies for the same project

**516**

| Year | 1% | 2% | 3% | 4% | 5% | 6% | 7% | 8% | 9% | 10% | 11% | 12% | 13% | 14% | 15% | 16% | 17% | 18% | 19% | 20% |
|---|---|---|---|---|---|---|---|---|---|---|---|---|---|---|---|---|---|---|---|---|
| 0 | 1.000 | 1.000 | 1.000 | 1.000 | 1.000 | 1.000 | 1.000 | 1.000 | 1.000 | 1.000 | 1.000 | 1.000 | 1.000 | 1.000 | 1.000 | 1.000 | 1.000 | 1.000 | 1.000 | 1.000 |
| 1 | 0.990 | 0.980 | 0.971 | 0.962 | 0.952 | 0.943 | 0.935 | 0.926 | 0.917 | 0.909 | 0.901 | 0.893 | 0.885 | 0.877 | 0.870 | 0.862 | 0.855 | 0.848 | 0.840 | 0.833 |
| 2 | 0.980 | 0.961 | 0.943 | 0.925 | 0.907 | 0.890 | 0.873 | 0.857 | 0.842 | 0.826 | 0.812 | 0.797 | 0.783 | 0.770 | 0.756 | 0.743 | 0.731 | 0.718 | 0.706 | 0.694 |
| 3 | 0.971 | 0.942 | 0.915 | 0.889 | 0.864 | 0.840 | 0.816 | 0.794 | 0.772 | 0.751 | 0.731 | 0.712 | 0.693 | 0.675 | 0.658 | 0.641 | 0.624 | 0.609 | 0.593 | 0.579 |
| 4 | 0.961 | 0.924 | 0.889 | 0.855 | 0.823 | 0.792 | 0.763 | 0.735 | 0.708 | 0.683 | 0.659 | 0.636 | 0.613 | 0.592 | 0.572 | 0.552 | 0.534 | 0.516 | 0.499 | 0.482 |
| 5 | 0.952 | 0.906 | 0.863 | 0.822 | 0.784 | 0.747 | 0.713 | 0.681 | 0.650 | 0.621 | 0.594 | 0.567 | 0.543 | 0.519 | 0.497 | 0.476 | 0.456 | 0.437 | 0.419 | 0.402 |
| 6 | 0.942 | 0.888 | 0.838 | 0.790 | 0.746 | 0.705 | 0.666 | 0.630 | 0.596 | 0.565 | 0.535 | 0.507 | 0.480 | 0.456 | 0.432 | 0.410 | 0.390 | 0.370 | 0.352 | 0.335 |
| 7 | 0.933 | 0.871 | 0.813 | 0.760 | 0.711 | 0.665 | 0.623 | 0.584 | 0.547 | 0.513 | 0.482 | 0.452 | 0.425 | 0.400 | 0.376 | 0.354 | 0.333 | 0.314 | 0.296 | 0.279 |
| 8 | 0.923 | 0.854 | 0.789 | 0.731 | 0.677 | 0.627 | 0.582 | 0.540 | 0.502 | 0.467 | 0.434 | 0.404 | 0.376 | 0.351 | 0.327 | 0.305 | 0.284 | 0.266 | 0.249 | 0.233 |
| 9 | 0.914 | 0.837 | 0.766 | 0.703 | 0.645 | 0.592 | 0.544 | 0.500 | 0.460 | 0.424 | 0.391 | 0.361 | 0.333 | 0.308 | 0.284 | 0.263 | 0.243 | 0.226 | 0.209 | 0.194 |
| 10 | 0.905 | 0.820 | 0.744 | 0.676 | 0.614 | 0.558 | 0.508 | 0.463 | 0.422 | 0.386 | 0.352 | 0.322 | 0.295 | 0.270 | 0.247 | 0.227 | 0.208 | 0.191 | 0.176 | 0.162 |
| 11 | 0.896 | 0.804 | 0.722 | 0.650 | 0.585 | 0.527 | 0.475 | 0.429 | 0.388 | 0.351 | 0.317 | 0.288 | 0.261 | 0.237 | 0.215 | 0.195 | 0.178 | 0.162 | 0.148 | 0.135 |
| 12 | 0.887 | 0.789 | 0.701 | 0.625 | 0.557 | 0.497 | 0.444 | 0.397 | 0.356 | 0.319 | 0.286 | 0.257 | 0.231 | 0.208 | 0.187 | 0.169 | 0.152 | 0.137 | 0.124 | 0.112 |
| 13 | 0.879 | 0.773 | 0.681 | 0.601 | 0.530 | 0.469 | 0.415 | 0.368 | 0.326 | 0.290 | 0.258 | 0.229 | 0.204 | 0.182 | 0.163 | 0.145 | 0.130 | 0.116 | 0.104 | 0.094 |
| 14 | 0.870 | 0.758 | 0.661 | 0.578 | 0.505 | 0.442 | 0.388 | 0.341 | 0.299 | 0.263 | 0.232 | 0.205 | 0.181 | 0.160 | 0.141 | 0.124 | 0.111 | 0.099 | 0.088 | 0.078 |
| 15 | 0.861 | 0.743 | 0.642 | 0.555 | 0.481 | 0.417 | 0.362 | 0.315 | 0.275 | 0.239 | 0.209 | 0.183 | 0.160 | 0.140 | 0.123 | 0.108 | 0.095 | 0.084 | 0.074 | 0.065 |
| 16 | 0.853 | 0.728 | 0.623 | 0.534 | 0.458 | 0.394 | 0.339 | 0.292 | 0.252 | 0.218 | 0.188 | 0.163 | 0.142 | 0.123 | 0.107 | 0.093 | 0.082 | 0.071 | 0.062 | 0.054 |
| 17 | 0.844 | 0.714 | 0.605 | 0.513 | 0.436 | 0.371 | 0.317 | 0.270 | 0.231 | 0.198 | 0.170 | 0.146 | 0.125 | 0.108 | 0.093 | 0.080 | 0.069 | 0.060 | 0.052 | 0.045 |
| 18 | 0.836 | 0.700 | 0.587 | 0.494 | 0.412 | 0.350 | 0.296 | 0.250 | 0.212 | 0.180 | 0.153 | 0.130 | 0.111 | 0.095 | 0.081 | 0.069 | 0.059 | 0.051 | 0.044 | 0.038 |
| 19 | 0.828 | 0.686 | 0.570 | 0.475 | 0.396 | 0.331 | 0.277 | 0.232 | 0.195 | 0.164 | 0.138 | 0.116 | 0.098 | 0.083 | 0.070 | 0.060 | 0.051 | 0.043 | 0.037 | 0.031 |
| 20 | 0.820 | 0.673 | 0.554 | 0.456 | 0.377 | 0.312 | 0.258 | 0.215 | 0.178 | 0.149 | 0.124 | 0.104 | 0.087 | 0.073 | 0.061 | 0.051 | 0.043 | 0.037 | 0.030 | 0.026 |

**Figure 27.6   Discount factors for calculating net present values**

can be compared to indicate the most favourable option. The highest (or least negative) net present value points to the best financial choice. This application can be used to:

- help in the choice between two or more different technological processes;
- assist in the choice between different logistics or strategic approaches to a large and complex project;
- assist in deciding whether to buy, lease, lease-purchase or rent expensive items of plant and equipment.

3. To estimate the rate of return achieved on the capital invested (the internal percentage rate of return is equal to the discounting percentage rate that gives a net present value of zero).

Net present value calculations may also be required in project feasibility studies as part of the argument to obtain financing or for authorization to proceed.

### The effects of monetary inflation

Inflation is an obvious case where monetary values can change significantly with time. However, although the effects of inflation have to be allowed for when estimating the costs of a project for budgeting and tendering, inflation is often ignored when calculating net present values. This convention is probably based on the assumption that inflation affects both sides of the equation and therefore tends to cancel. An alternative is to consider whether the discount factor is gross return or return net of inflation. If the former, then all future costs and revenues should be increased by inflation; if the latter, they should be expressed at current values. The effect is very much the same, except where some costs and revenues have differential inflation rates, in which case the former approach should be used.

### TOLL ROAD PROJECT: NET PRESENT VALUE

The payback period for the toll road project was seen to be just over eight years, (Figures 27.4 and 27.5). With cash movements considered over such a long period, however, it is necessary to set aside the simple payback result and discount all the future cash flows. Once again the effects of taxation and any loan interest payable on capital have been ignored for simplicity.

Figure 27.7 shows the net present value calculation. A proforma has been used to ensure that all the entries are set out logically and clearly. The proforma need only be very simple, but confusion and errors will occur if one is not used. The use of a proforma greatly simplifies the whole calculation and is strongly recommended unless a suitable computer application is available instead. The

## Net present value calculation

| Project title | Toll road for Lady Y | Monetary units: Pounds | Date: December 2001 |
|---|---|---|---|
| This case: | 10 year operation | Periods used: Years | Discounts rate 8 % |

| Period | Item | Cash flows at present cost | | | Discount factor | Discounted cash flow |
|---|---|---|---|---|---|---|
| | | Outflows | Inflows | Net flows | | |
| 0 | Initial construction cost | 400 000 | | (400 000) | 1.000 | (400 000) |
| 1 | Toll keepers costs<br>Car toll revenue<br>Commercial vehicle tolls | 25 000 | 63 700<br>36 400 | 75 100 | 0.926 | 69 543 |
| 2 | Toll keepers costs<br>Maintenance costs<br>Car toll revenue<br>Commercial vehicle tolls | 25 000<br>25 000 | 63 700<br>36 400 | 50 100 | 0.857 | 42 936 |
| 3 | Toll keepers costs<br>Maintenance costs<br>Car toll revenue<br>Commercial vehicle tolls | 25 000<br>25 000 | 63 700<br>36 400 | 50 100 | 0.794 | 39 779 |
| 4 | Toll keepers costs<br>Maintenance costs<br>Car toll revenue<br>Commercial vehicle tolls | 25 000<br>25 000 | 63 700<br>36 400 | 50 100 | 0.735 | 36 824 |
| 5 | Toll keepers costs<br>Maintenance costs<br>Car toll revenue<br>Commercial vehicle tolls | 25 000<br>25 000 | 63 700<br>36 400 | 50 100 | 0.681 | 34 118 |
| 6 | Toll keepers costs<br>Maintenance costs<br>Car toll revenue<br>Commercial vehicle tolls | 25 000<br>25 000 | 63 700<br>36 400 | 50 100 | 0.630 | 31 563 |
| 7 | Toll keepers costs<br>Maintenance costs<br>Car toll revenue<br>Commercial vehicle tolls | 25 000<br>25 000 | 63 700<br>36 400 | 50 100 | 0.584 | 29 258 |
| 8 | Toll keepers costs<br>Maintenance costs<br>Car toll revenue<br>Commercial vehicle tolls | 25 000<br>25 000 | 63 700<br>36 400 | 50 100 | 0.540 | 27 054 |
| 9 | Toll keepers costs<br>Maintenance costs<br>Car toll revenue<br>Commercial vehicle tolls | 25 000<br>25 000 | 63 700<br>36 400 | 50 100 | 0.500 | 25 050 |
| 10 | Toll keepers costs<br>Maintenance costs<br>Car toll revenue<br>Commercial vehicle tolls | 25 000<br>25 000 | 63 700<br>36 400 | 50 100 | 0.463 | 23 196 |
| Project net present value forecast for this case ———▶ | | | | | | (40 679) |

Figure 27.7 Net present value calculation for the toll road project

519

proforma is now often created on a spreadsheet and the calculations can be done rapidly. This can include 'what-if?' analysis, with several alternative options compared. Notice that the case details are written at the top of the form in Figure 27.7. Some project appraisal calculations have to be repeated many times for different parameters or strategies and it is very important to be able to distinguish each of these from its fellows. Another point to notice is that discounted cash flow schedules always start from year zero and not from year one. Think of this as '0' for the year of origin. Figures in parentheses are negative quantities (losses or cash outflows).

A study of Figure 27.7 shows how the cash inflows and outflows have been set out in their respective years to show the net cash flow before discounting (fifth column from the left). A discount factor of 8 per cent was chosen for this project, this being approximately midway between the bank lending and investors' interest rates current at the time. It was decided to carry out the calculations for a project operating life of ten years. It was felt that this was a realistic time for the road to remain serviceable and able to cope with traffic flows before any significant extensions or improvements would become necessary. The discount factor of 8 per cent results in a net present value for the toll road project, rounded to three significant figures, of minus £40 700. Clearly this result would disappoint the potential investor.

## TOLL ROAD PROJECT: INTERNAL RATE OF RETURN ON INVESTMENT

Another use of net present value is to predict the annual percentage rate of return that the investment might earn over a given period. The method is to carry out a series of net present value calculations for different discounting rates, with the purpose of finding the discounting rate that will yield a net present value of zero. This process can be taken to its conclusion by reiterating the calculation with small changes in the discounting rate until the net present value is as near to zero as possible. A faster method is to plot a series of net present values as a graph and then read off the point at which the curve intersects the zero axis. This graphical method has been followed for the toll road project using the data in Figure 27.8. With modern computer-based spreadsheets, these calculations can be performed in seconds. These results have been plotted as a graph in Figure 27.9, where it can be seen that the forecast rate of return for the toll road project taken over ten years of operation is a little over 5.5 per cent.

## GENERAL

The examples in this chapter have been kept simple, but they illustrate the

| Discount rate (%) | Net present value (£) |
|---|---|
| 12 | (94 560) |
| 10 | (69 410) |
| 8 | (40 679) |
| 6 | (7 738) |
| 5 | 10 722 |

**Figure 27.8   Internal rate of return calculation for the toll road project**

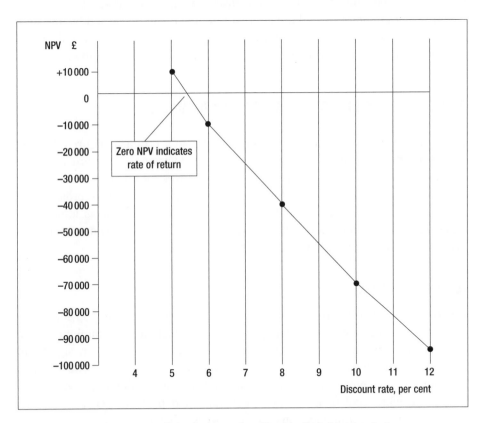

**Figure 27.9   Rate of return on investment for the toll road project**

principles of using discounted cash flow to indicate the net present value of a particular project strategy or its expected rate of return on investment. The techniques are applicable to any proposed investment, whether the project is for manufacturing, construction, petrochemical processing, mining, agriculture or any other purpose.

Discounting methods should always be considered for any comparisons of cash inflows and outflows where the period extends beyond two or three years. The calculations are straightforward provided that all the data are carefully tabulated.

One difficulty could be choosing an appropriate percentage discount rate. This applies particularly when calculating the net present values of alternative expenditure options (rent or buy decisions, for instance). If there is no company accountant or other suitably qualified person willing to offer advice, no great harm should be done by pitching the discount rate somewhere between the current bank lending rate and the interest rate that could be earned by investing in a suitable deposit account. Alternatively, by calculating the internal rate of return you can consider whether that is reasonable at current lending rates.

## PROJECT FEASIBILITY STUDIES AND RISK ANALYSIS

Financial appraisal is a comforting process because it produces figures that can be regarded as a way of justifying investment decisions. They are useful in helping to convince financial backers that their investments will be safe. They give the analyst or investor something to grasp, even in proposals for projects that are really so complex and full of risks that accurate prediction is impossible. Financial appraisal techniques must therefore be seen in the wider context of project feasibility study and risk analysis.

### FEASIBILITY STUDIES

Proposals for projects requiring significant investment should obviously be subjected to some form of feasibility study before significant commitments are made. Feasibility studies for projects on the grand scale are often significant projects in their own right, taking years to complete and consuming considerable expenditure. It is, however, painfully apparent, from the number of projects in the public eye which fail to meet their cost, time and performance targets, that feasibility study recommendations are not always reliable.

### EXAMPLE

Suppose that an independent consulting engineering company has been commissioned by an international financing organization (the World Bank for instance) to conduct a feasibility study for the huge investment needed to exploit a recently discovered deposit of copper ore in a third world country. The project, to build a mining and metallurgical complex on a virgin site, would take many years to design and build before any useful amounts of copper could be produced and sold.

Much data would need to be collected and the study would have to investigate and quantify various possible processing methods and logistic strategies in depth. For example, one project strategy might involve having a smelter and a refinery built specially at the new site, while another case could evaluate the alternative of building only a smelter, and shipping unrefined copper to an existing refinery elsewhere in the world. For each case considered the study report would forecast the expected return on investment, derived from a mix of estimated capital costs, output rates for the product, operating costs, all other expenses, revenue from copper sales and tax implications.

In practice many things can happen to ruin the predictions of the feasibility study, even where considerable care has been taken. Some of the technology used may be advanced and unproven. There may be flaws in the chosen contractor's performance or professional capability, or it may be financially unsound. All manner of climatic, geological or other environmental problems can arise. Political unrest might erupt. There are well-known cases of projects held up by the discovery of archaeological remains or because steps have had to be taken to avoid disturbing wildlife (hibernating bears held up one project for several winter months). Even if the copper mining project went ahead as planned, adopting the recommended strategy, with everything well built, on time and within budget, the market price of copper could fall disastrously during the ten years or so needed to bring the project to full production. On the other hand, there is always a chance the price of copper may rise.

Similar uncertainties can be cited for many large projects. An industry in which feasibility studies have a habit of proving wrong is property development, particularly where industrial and office property is built speculatively. A proposal to build a prestigious office tower might seem to be a very attractive investment at a time of high rents and fierce demand for office space but these factors might change during the period of construction so that the investors are left with a fine but empty building. This does not mean that the initial feasibility studies are unnecessary, or that the studies are necessarily flawed. It does demonstrate, however, that all the possible risks – technical, environmental, political and commercial – should be listed and, where possible, tested in mathematical models for their possible significance.

## SENSITIVITY ANALYSIS

Sensitivity analysis is a method for testing the possible effects of risk on the net present value of a proposed project. This is performed by varying data in one or more of the parameters, according to the analyst's perception of the possible risk. For example, if there is doubt about the timing or amount of revenue that a project is expected to produce, the analyst can repeat the initial discounted cash flow calculation several times, changing the revenue predictions in small percentage steps each time to test the resulting effect on net present value or rate of return. In the toll road project, it is possible that the amount of traffic using the road might be less than predicted: the analyst could test the effect on net present value of reducing the predicted toll revenues by (say) 5 and 10 per cent.

## SIMULATION

It is usually possible to estimate limiting upper and lower values for parameters thought to be at risk. Best and worst market prices, highest and least possible capital costs, longest and shortest project duration, and many other parameters can be considered in this way. Using a computer, it is possible to repeat a discounted cash flow calculation many times, with one of the parameters being varied within its specified worst-to-best range. The actual value used in each reiteration is chosen by the computer, by pure chance, governed by random number selection (known as the Monte Carlo method). Provided that enough reiterations are carried out, the use of random numbers should ensure that the spread of net present values follows a normal distribution. The analyst and potential investor are thus provided with a probability graph or statement, giving the mean and standard variation for net present value according to the perceived risk of the parameter tested. The next chapter provides a more structured approach to this problem for projects lasting decades.

## REFERENCES AND FURTHER READING

Aston, J. and Turner, J. R. (1995), 'Investment appraisal', in J. R. Turner (ed.), *The Commercial Project Manager*, McGraw-Hill, London.

## RELATED TOPICS

# 28 Two-phase parametric discounting

### Chris Chapman

The discounted cash flow (DCF) techniques of investment appraisal, described in the last chapter, require the adoption of a planning period (often of between five and ten years but perhaps as long as twenty) over which the calculations are done. The underlying assumption (at least in the private sector) is that beyond that planning period the profitability of the project will fall to the cost of capital as other companies enter the market and the sponsoring organization loses competitive advantage. However, many important investment appraisal/capital budgeting decisions (especially in the public sector) can involve both significant time horizons (up to fifty years) and significant uncertainty. DCF techniques as described in the last chapter reduce to the subtraction of two large numbers to produce a small number, especially where there are significant decommissioning costs or residual value after a 50-year period, and so decisions can be swung by small variations in key parameters. Techniques have been developed which nest large numbers, to make the calculation less dependent on them, and which investigate the variation of the investment decision over ranges of key parameters. This chapter describes those techniques.

Significant time horizons make a discounting framework essential, which in turn raises issues about the use of internal rate of return (IRR) versus net present value (NPV), and the value of a simple annualized cost or payback period calculation, in some cases. The argument in favour of NPV as a basic framework has been generally accepted (see Chapter 27), but adapting the NPV discounting framework to the presentational needs of a particular situation can be important, and how to do this is not so widely appreciated. Chapman and Cooper (1983) illustrated the value of a discounted payback period analysis when considering a decision where the planning horizon is a key source of uncertainty. That paper used as an example investing in insulation for the walls of a house in the UK when how long the investor/house owner will continue to own the house is a key issue. It also discussed the value of a discounted terminal value analysis when the

**527**

terminal value of the investment at the planning horizon is the key source of uncertainty. It used as an example a choice between hydroelectric power or coal-fired electric power faced by the State of Alaska, which was the decision that motivated the development of the approach described. Both these examples are considered in the context of a particular but quite general approach to 'parametric discounting'. This chapter is based on later work (Chapman and Howden 1997) which applies this flexible approach to selecting an appropriate presentation framework using an NPV basic framework in a case when IRR or annualized annual cost might be the appropriate choice, but the choice of discount factor is itself uncertain.

Chapman and Howden (1997) also introduced a second phase of the analysis, where not only ranges of the key parameters are considered, but probabilistic variations are used to calculate an expected value of the decision. Significant uncertainty can make the estimation of expected values of parameters using a direct single estimated value approach questionable. One response is simple direct sensitivity analysis, or a more formalized parametric analysis process, which relates sensitivity to plausible ranges for the parameters, and parameter changes which flip the decision, to order the parameters in terms of the importance of associated uncertainty. A second response is the use of probabilistic approaches, which define relative probability for parameter values over their plausible range, and then compute expected values and summary parameter ranges (NPV for example) via analytical or simulation procedures to control bias and measure uncertainty.

This chapter describes the use of a first phase parametric approach based on the work of Chapman and Cooper (1983), and then illustrates the advantages of adding a second phase probabilistic approach (Chapman and Howden 1997). This two-phase approach is a useful general approach. The form of analysis and the presentation of results can be highly dependent upon the circumstances of particular decision situations, and one or other of the two phases could effectively disappear, reducing the two-phase approach to a single-phase special case. However, this chapter argues that exclusive reliance on the methodology of either phase is defective relative to a combined approach in the proposed sequence.

The chapter starts by defining an example decision which is a simplified version of a decision considered in the Department of the Environment consultative document *Review of Radioactive Waste Management Policy Preliminary Conclusions* (DoE 1994) to defer or not defer disposal of UK nuclear waste. Key simplifications, some of which affect the later development of the methodology, are indicated. A parametric approach is considered in relation to the example decision. The case for a first phase parametric approach in such contexts is illustrated by way of the example. The case for second phase risk analysis is then developed, in five areas for five somewhat different reasons, using the example. Particular attention is paid to probabilistic treatment of the discount rate. A concluding section suggests that there is a case for widespread use of this two-phase approach in capital budget decision-making. The process described in this chapter can be embedded in the project risk management process described in Chapter 21, or vice versa, as appropriate.

## A SIMPLIFIED VERSION OF THE EXAMPLE DECISION

Assume that if the UK proceeds to deep repository disposal of medium level nuclear waste 'now', the 'capital' cost will be £2500 million. However, disposal can be deferred for 50 years, when the 'capital' cost will be £5000 million, with additional interim 'storage' costing £135 million per annum (all costs are in 1994 prices). Assume the standard test discount rate is 6 per cent real, with standard sensitivity tests at 4 per cent and 8 per cent. At 6 per cent deferral has a £100 million NPV advantage relative to proceeding now. This is a simplified version of the UK's decision as discussed by the Department of the Environment (1994). The more complex version also cites a proceed now 'capital' cost of £2500 million, with unspecified deferred 'capital' cost and interim 'storage' cost figures of comparable magnitude, and a £100 million NPV advantage for deferral using a 6 per cent real discount rate. Key simplifications, which are important in practice and relevant to some of the discussion later, include avoiding the following:

1. 'Capital' expenditure profiles over the construction periods.
2. Interim 'storage' costs which vary over the 50-year deferral period and include additional planning, management and permissions costs.
3. Expected 'capital' costs and additional interim 'storage' costs based on probabilistic treatment of a range of repository construction, interim storage and other issues.
4. High/low disposal volume bands to compute expected costs and provide separate scenarios for assessment purposes.
5. Modelling a chance (80 per cent or greater cited) that delay would lead to the loss of the Sellafield site, with complex knock-on consequences, including significantly increased transport costs, imbedded in our simplified example's deferral 'capital' cost.
6. Considering a possible 25-year delay intermediate case.

## PHASE ONE: PARAMETRIC APPROACH

Following the approach developed by Chapman and Cooper (1983), and the techniques of the last chapter, the NPV of repository delay (V) can be calculated as:

$$V = + C_0 - \Sigma \ (t = 1...n) \ S \ R_t^t - C_n \ R_n^n$$

where

$C_0$ = £2500m, initial capital cost,
$C_n$ = £5000m, deferral capital cost,
S = £135m, annual storage cost,
$R_t$ = $1/(1 + D/100)$, discount factor in year t,
D = 6 per cent, real discount rate,
n = 50, the number of periods (years) in the planning horizon.

We can simplify the definition of V by defining composite parameters in a nested structure:

$$V = N - SR$$

where

R = $\Sigma(t = 1...n) \ R_t^t$, a composite discount rate factor,
T = $C_n \ R_n^n$, the present value of deferral capital cost,
N = $C_0 - T$, the present value of the capital cost saving.

The decision criterion for preferring deferral is:

$$V > 0$$

In these terms the basic NPV approach treats V as a final level composite parameter, and uses expected values for all parameters and the criterion V > 0 directly. An IRR approach adopts the condition V > 0, and determines an upper limit on D given expected values for all other parameters. An annualized average cost approach rewrites the criterion in the form N/R > S (variants determining minimum values for N or S given expected values for other parameters). A discounted payback approach determines the minimum value for n given expected values for all other parameters.

Chapman and Cooper (1983) suggested a nine-step method to develop the above model. Although some steps may seem redundant in this case, it is useful to include them all.

### Step 1: Select an initial value for n, the planning horizon

The value of n should make sense as a nominal planning horizon. We used n = 50 because that was the base case. The base case also considers n = 25. Other values are possible, n = 25 and 50 being illustrations of 'significant deferral', as distinct from 'minor delay'. The illustrative nature of n = 50 is worth remembering. The choice n = 50 is not a parameter based on economic or policy considerations. This is an example of a step which may seem redundant, but addressing it explicitly is a useful reminder of the nature of the n = 50 assumption.

### Step 2: Estimate the composite discount factor, R

This step requires a value for n, the reason this step is second. It also requires values for D and hence $R_t$, policy variables from a Department of the Environment (Treasury) perspective. From an economic perspective, D is an expected value for a complex economic variable which reflects productivity growth and social preferences of present versus future benefit (see Chapters 10, 13, 14 and 27). Although it was assumed here that D, and hence $R_t$, are constant with time, many empirical studies have shown that the rate fluctuates over time. Coping with fluctuating values of D can require analysis by spreadsheet models or complex simulation involving Markov process modelling (Trigeorgis 1993) which are beyond the scope of this chapter. The point of the parametric method described here using the nested parameter structure is facilitation of some forms of such deep analysis with a clear indication of its role. The exact pattern of $R_t$ variations does not matter provided the cash flow structure is 'passive'. What matters is the composite rate R. If the cash flow structure is not 'passive', the two-stage approach described here is not robust. This occurs if a decision tree structure or a real options structure can be embedded in a way which has a significant impact, because branching into very different scenarios is feasible (see Trigeorgis 1993). In these cases, computer simulation will be necessary. Alternatively we suggest the use of a comprehensive project risk management process (see Chapter 21) in the estimation of the parameters for the DCF process, embedding the process described in Chapter 21 in the process described here.

### Step 3: Estimate N

N is the present value of the capital cost saving resulting from deferral. This step requires a value for $R_n{}^n$, to compute $T = C_n R_n^n$, the reason Step 3 is preceded by Step 2. It also requires a value for $C_0$ and $C_n$. The nested parameter structure is useful so that 'errors' associated with $C_n$ and $C_0$ cancel out apart from the $R_n^n$ factor effect on $C_n$. This could be important if there is uncertainty about $C_0$ which also applies to $C_n$ (positively correlated 'errors'), perhaps related to technical choices. It is equally important if technical alternatives require consideration in form of real choices as distinct from suitable assumptions. Such choices may be independent of S, n or $R_t$ other than the $R_n^n$ effect. This step helps to focus on the N aspect of the N/R versus S relationship which is at the core of the NPV criteria.

## Step 4: Estimate S

S is annual running cost, here the storage cost (additional cost per year for surface storage). This step may also involve uncertainty and technical choices which are independent of n, $R_t$, $C_0$ or $C_n$, and important dependencies which require explicit attention. Ensuring consistency is the key reason for putting this step after Steps 1 to 3. For example, if exploration of S suggested major expenditure would be required within 40 years to ensure surface storage was safe, n = 30 might be worth exploring, as a potentially more attractive deferral option. The purpose of the process as a whole is insight, not just numbers. The step structure and the associated nested parameter structure are designed to help the formation of insight.

## Step 5: Define a credible range for all key parameters

We need to define a 'credible range' for all key basic and composite parameters estimated in Steps 1 to 4: n, D (R), N ($C_0$ and $C_n$) and S. A comparable level of credibility for all ranges is essential, but a precise probabilistic interpretation (like a 90 per cent confidence band) is not. For present purposes assume that a credible range for D is 0 per cent to 8 per cent. The associated arguments are complex and beyond the bounds of the concern for methodology addressed here, but the asymmetry is important. The essence of the argument for 0 per cent is concerned with a moral view involving a need to ensure that future generations do not have to pay for the mistakes of their forebears, and a willingness to pay now for the costs of such an approach. History may eventually vindicate this view, but not necessarily. The essence of the argument for 8 per cent is a Treasury sensitivity analysis limit which might be argued to be no more plausible than 0 per cent. In brief, the long-term real interest rate on government stocks (over centuries) is about 3 per cent, arguments for 0 per cent or 8 per cent involving largely incompatible opposing perspectives which hit the limits of credibility even for their proponents around these figures. Chapman and Cooper (1983) give examples of decisions where the range of values of n, N and S are critical.

## Step 6: Tabulate and graph the impact of variations of key parameters

Use the results of earlier steps to produce tables like Figure 28.1 and related figures like Figure 28.2 for all parameters identified in Step 5. Use these tables or graphs to define parameter limits in relation to expected (or policy) parameter values used earlier. In the case of Figures 28.1 and 28.2, D = 5.7 per cent is the parameter limit; D must be greater than 5.7 per cent for the deferral option to be preferred

## Step 7: Use these results to identify key parameters

The parameter bounds in Figure 28.1 (0 and 8 per cent) and the parameter limit associated with a change in sign for V (visible by inspection on Figure 28.2 as D = 5.7) clearly indicate the sensitivity of D. The emboldened row in Figure 28.1 shows V = £100 million for D = 6 per cent, the example result cited earlier. Similar tables for all other parameters suggest some credible changes can flip the decision, but none so easily or profoundly.

| D | T | N | R | N/R | N/R – S | V |
|---|---|---|---|---|---|---|
| 0 | 5000 | −2500 | 50.00 | −50 | −185 | −9250 |
| 2 | 1860 | 640 | 31.42 | 20 | −115 | −3600 |
| 4 | 710 | 1790 | 21.48 | 83 | −52 | −1110 |
| **6** | **270** | **2230** | **15.76** | **141** | **6** | **100** |
| 8 | 110 | 2390 | 12.23 | 195 | 40 | 740 |

Figure 28.1   Summary parameters as a function of the real discount rate D

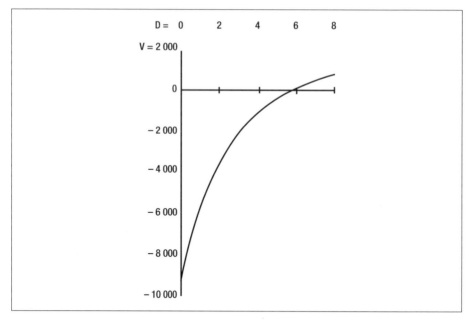

**Figure 28.2    Plotting V as a function of D from Figure 28.1**

### Step 8: Choose an appropriate form of assessment

This initial sensitivity analysis can be used to choose a form of assessment which suits the nature of the decision and the users' preference. Treasury preference for NPV is clear (Chapman and Howden 1997), but Figure 28.2 suggests IRR might be preferable. Because we are using a differential cash flow, and a parametric analysis framework, the usual concerns about an IRR approach do not apply. For reasons explored in relation to Step 9, Figure 28.1 also suggests the possible use of an annualized average cost approach.

### Step 9: Explore relationships between parameters

Finally we need to explore and illustrate relationships between key parameters in a manner appropriate for the users. Figures 28.1 and 28.2 (and their equivalents for other key parameters in other contexts) are a useful basis for this kind of exploration. Consider Figure 28.2 first. With $D = 0$ there is a massive NPV advantage in immediate disposal, because all the surface storage costs (S) and the doubling of the capital cost (from $C_0$ to $C_n$) are saved. This advantage declines as D increases, initially at a massive rate (because of the impact of the $R_n^n$ factor on $C_n$), but with a rate of change in V which declines as D increases. Now consider Figure 28.1, the intermediate columns in particular:

534

1. With $D = 0$, T (the present value of $C_n$) is the full 5000 and N (the present value of the capital cost saving resulting from deferral) is $2500 - 5000 = -2500$. R is simply 50, so the annualized capital cost saving associated with deferral (N/R) is –50. Given an annual storage cost (S) of 135, this implies a total annualized cost saving associate with deferral (N/R – S) of –185. Over the 50-year planning horizon this –185 per year equates to –9250.

2. With $D = 2$, T (the present value of $C_n$) is only 1860 and N (the present value of the capital cost saving resulting from deferral) is $2500 - 1860 = 640$, this 'saving' becoming positive in the $D = 1$ to 2 range. R has now reduced to 31.42, so N/R = 20 (the annualized cost saving associated with deferral). This in turn implies N/R – S = –115, V = –3600.

3. With $D = 4$, 6 and 8 these changes continue. By $D = 6$ the value of N/R – S has become positive (6), as has V (100).

The insights provided by Figure 28.1 might lead to a simple summary statement like:

> If 6 per cent is the 'correct' discount rate, we need to save about £6m/annum more than the currently assumed £135m in storage costs to make proceeding immediately worth while. If 8 per cent is 'correct', we need to save an extra 195 – 135= £60m/annum in storage costs. However, if 2 per cent is 'correct', which seems more plausible than 8 per cent, we are 135 – 20 = £115m/annum worse off if we defer disposal. The asymmetry of these results and the uncertainty about an appropriate discount rate suggests that proceeding immediately would be prudent, and deferral could prove to be a very high risk strategy future generations may not thank us for.

Some readers may wish to question the validity of this interpretation if they hold strong views on an appropriate value for D or the appropriateness of nuclear waste disposal. We do not defend a particular decision or recommendation here; we simply argue that this form of parametric analysis is useful as a first phase approach to understanding the issues, because it provides insights which other approaches do not, as illustrated by the simplified example.

## PHASE TWO: PROBABILISTIC APPROACH

The phase one parametric approach was initially adopted by UK Nirex Ltd to prepare figures for the DoE (1994). Four areas showed less sensitivity than D values, but suggested further probabilistic analysis for quite different reasons.

1. One area was the capital costs, $C_0$ and $C_n$. As risk assessment of these two costs clearly suggests positive correlation, the difference between the costs (adjusted by discounting) being the key, probabilistic analysis in this area

reduced concerns about capital cost uncertainty. That is, reasons for large values of $C_0$, $C_0$ risks, usually apply to $C_n$ too. In this context conventional probabilistic cost risk analysis of $C_o$ and $C_n$ was adopted (see Chapman *et al.* 1985).

2. A second area was the storage costs, S. The engineers involved found that a decision tree (Markov) approach let them model realistic decisions given realistically assessed alternative uncertain futures. This increased their confidence that they had an unbiased estimate of S, as well as giving them a feel for associated uncertainty and a feel for future operating policy. In this case, a somewhat different form of probabilistic analysis was involved (see Raiffa 1970). This kind of Markov process, linked to decisions about what to do with nuclear waste in surface storage, is rather different to the real option models noted earlier (Trigeorgis 1993), but it allows consideration of the same issues.

3. A third area was different scenarios for the amount of disposed volume. Confidence in the probabilities associated with high and low disposal volumes was not high, even at the end of the Nirex analysis. This was part of the reason for reporting scenarios to the DoE as well as associated expected values. It was essential for Nirex to work with specific values of this variable to pursue meaningful calculations. Nirex had to distinguish a risk which was clearly beyond the control of Nirex. Further, the DoE took advice from a range of other parties, including waste producers, so the use of separate scenarios allowed the DoE to form its own views of probabilities associated with these scenarios, drawing on a range of sources. In this case the model was conventional textbook decision analysis (Raiffa 1970), and the nature of the probabilities was the key issue.

4. A fourth area concerned the probability that the current Nirex site at Sellafield might be lost for repository purposes if disposal were delayed. This probability was thought to be very high by the DoE, 80 per cent or more, with very significant knock-on cost implications. Arguably the case against deferral would have been lost if recognition of this risk in probabilistic terms by the Treasury had not been a key concern for Nirex. In methodology terms, this was more conventional decision analysis, dominated by one key uncertainty. In the simplified context of the example used here, doubling the capital cost if deferral takes place has been used. Direct modelling of this uncertainty would reduce associated bias potential.

5. Review of the DoE report (1994) suggests a fifth reason why probabilistic analysis might be useful: probabilistic treatment of D. The relevant 'bottom line' is paragraph 21 of Annex C:

21: The conclusion was that allowance for data shortcomings, uncertainties and other factors did not significantly affect the balance of benefits and costs as summarised in Para. 11 above, with the impact of factors tending to increase the benefit of delay being broadly offset by those operating in the opposite direction. In particular, it was concluded that the outcome for 50 year delay, as reported in Para. 11, provided a reasonable indication of the economic case for repository delay at 6% discount rate.

A 6 per cent discount rate has been assumed (as a policy variable, not an expected value) in association with a tight symmetric sensitivity analysis (4 per cent and 8 per cent bounds). However, the discount rate should be treated as an estimate, in which case a probabilistic approach suggests itself. A simple first order probability model of DoE (1994) perceptions is 'the probability of D is 1/3 for each of three values D = 4%, 6% and 8%, with an expected value of 6%'. What are the implications of this model? Using Figure 28.2, it yields an expected NPV of

$$(- 1110 + 100 + 740)/3 = -90,$$

a negative benefit of about £90 million associated with deferral. This result is clearly not consistent with paragraph 21 cited above. To obtain an expected value of +£100 million using discrete alternatives at 4 per cent, 6 per cent and 8 per cent for D and attributing a 0.5 probability to D = 6 per cent ($P(D = 6$ per cent$) = 0.5$), we find we need $P(D = 4$ per cent$) = 0.17$ and $P(D = 0.8$ per cent$) = 0.33$. We calculate these figures by assigning $P(D = 4$ per cent$) = P$, and solving the equation:

$$(-1110 \times P) + (100 \times 0.5) + (740 \times (1 - 0.5 - P)) = 100$$

Both the high value (0.33) of $P(D = 8$ per cent$)$ and the asymmetry ($P(D = 4$ per cent$)$ half the size of $P(D = 8$ per cent$)$) do not seem very credible. Altering the assumed value of $P(D = 6$ per cent$)$ over a credible range does not significantly affect this argument. A first order probability model which seems much more credible is

$P(D = 0) = 0.2$
$P(D = 2) = 0.2$
$P(D = 4) = 0.2$
$P(D = 6) = 0.2$
$P(D = 8) = 0.2$

In this case the expected NPV is

$$(-9250 - 3600 - 1110 + 100 + 740) \times 0.2 = -2640,$$

a negative benefit of £2640 million associated with deferral. This illustrates how the probabilistic approach can lead to alarmingly different conclusions from the initial phase one approach, on which paragraph 21 (DoE 1994) cited above is based. The associated probability distribution is debatable, but the alarm is credible. We argue that a debate based on such first order probability models, recognizing that different perceptions of P(D) will exist, might be enlightening. In particular, the need to be explicit about the likelihood of different possible credible values eliminates the ability of people to avoid looking at the implications of values they do not wish to consider, for various possible reasons. This is comparable to a basic benefit associated with the introduction of PERT (programme evaluation and review technique) three-point estimates (optimistic, pessimistic and most likely) for activity durations for project planning purposes in the late 1950s and early 1960s (Moder and Philips 1970). People can deliberately bias single-value estimates on the high or low side, and put up a plausible case for their single-value estimates. Making a plausible case for a deliberately biased probability distribution is much more difficult. Probability distributions associated with D provide the model with transparency which is a key model attribute. It also avoids unconscious bias associated with the use of single-value estimates which are held to be either the most probable value or an appropriate policy value drawn from an asymmetric distribution (which means they are not expected values).

This example makes the case for five somewhat different reasons for a second phase probabilistic approach to some NPV calculations. There may be many more. This case does not contradict the case for a first phase which is non-probabilistic, adopting the parametric analysis outlined earlier. In the example context it should be clear that proceeding directly to a single style of probabilistic approach would not be helpful. More generally, a simple linear approach to estimating all the parameters needed for any analysis in a one-pass operation is highly inefficient. We need to use a first pass to identify where and how to refine estimates that need refining for subsequent passes, an idea developed at length by Chapman and Ward (1997) to the simple two-phase form of the approach suggested here.

## CONCLUSIONS

The example decision involves very large numbers, and it involves emotive issues of direct financial interest to all UK residents and the residents of other countries facing similar issues. This provides motivation for ensuring that a sensible approach is taken in practice, and that the rationale for the approach taken is understandable and defensible.

However, the approaches and rationales explored in this chapter are not limited to large-scale public decisions of this kind. Any choice between alternatives may involve some if not all the issues explored here, including, as a special case, choices when one alternative is 'do nothing'. The development of the parametric approach of this chapter was motivated by a choice by the State of Alaska between hydro or coal-fired electric power development. However, the approach was illustrated by an example about whether or not to insulate the walls of a UK domestic residence (Chapman and Cooper 1983). It follows that it might be useful to approach personal decisions like whether or not to insulate the walls of your home using the ideas explored in this paper, and it is relevant to any organization's either/or choices when discounting is relevant. The essence of the approach is as follows:

1. Start with a parametric analysis, to make transparent which parameters drive the decision, and how credible ranges for those parameters affect (or not) the preferred decision.
2. Use a nested structure for this parametric analysis, to clarify parameter variations that cancel each other out, and the role and impact of component decisions.
3. Use probabilistic analysis for some of these parameter ranges as part of a second phase for a variety of specific reasons, but not as a general rule, the test being 'Are there particular reasons why it would be useful to develop a probabilistic estimation approach for this parameter?'
4. If the discount rate is an important parameter, consider probabilistic treatment to clarify the asymmetric effects of variations in the discount rate in relation to credible bounds on the appropriate discount rate, despite the commonly held view that the discount rate is the parameter least suitable for probabilistic treatment.

A key limitation of this approach as described here is the assumed 'passive' NPV framework. If multi-stage decisions which involve important biases can be embedded in the cash flow model, more complex real option or decision tree approaches may be needed to consider relevant decision points and the value of alternative routes from those decision points. Our preference is for the explicit use of decision tree models via a comprehensive project risk management process approach to evaluation cost, revenue and other parameters used for investment evaluation purposes (see Chapter 21 and Chapman and Ward 1997).

## ACKNOWLEDGEMENT

The author would like to thank Elsevier Science Ltd for permission to draw extensively on Chapman and Howden (1997).

## REFERENCES AND FURTHER READING

Chapman, C. B. and Cooper, D. F. (1983), 'Parametric discounting', *Omega, The International Journal of Management Science*, **11**(3): 303–10.

Chapman, C. B., Cooper, D. F. and Page, M. J. (1987), *Management for Engineers*, Wiley, Chichester.

Chapman, C. B. and Howden, M. (1997), 'Two phase parametric and probabilistic NPV calculations, with possible deferral of disposal of UK Nuclear Waste as an example', *Omega, The International Journal of Management Science*, **25**(6): 707–14.

Chapman, C. B. and Ward, S. C. (1997), *Project Risk Management: Models, Techniques and Insights*, Wiley, Chichester.

Chapman, C. B., Phillips, E. D., Cooper, D. F. and Lightfoot, L. (1985), 'Selecting an approach to project time and cost planning', *International Journal of Project Management*, **3**(3): 141–9.

Department of the Environment (DoE) (1994), *Review of Radioactive Waste Management Policy Preliminary Conclusions: A Consultative Document* (Radioactive Substances Division, Department of the Environment, Room A523, Romney House, 43 Marsham Street, London SW1P 3P4).

Ingersoll, E. J. Jr. and Ross, S. A. (1992), 'Waiting to invest: investment and uncertainty', *Journal of Business*, **64**: 1–30.

Moder, J. J. and Philips, C. R. (1970), *Project Management with CPM and PERT*, 3rd edition, Van Nostrand, New York.

Raiffa, H. (1970), *Decision Analysis: Introductory Lectures on Choices Under Uncertainty*, Addison-Wesley, New York.

Trigeorgis, L. (1993), 'The nature of option interactions and the valuation of investments with multiple real options', *Journal of Financial and Quantitative Analysis*, **28**: 1–20.

Ward, S. C. (1989), 'Arguments for constructively simple models', *Journal of the Operational Research Society*, **40**(2): 141–53.

## RELATED TOPICS

540

# 29 Managing finance

## Tony Merna

Since the early 1980s there has been a growing realization about the limitations of public funding for infrastructure development, both in the industrialized and developing countries. Besides the problem of accountability often leading to high cost of provision for the consumers, public funding with its associated political considerations invariably leads to poor performance and uneconomical pricing which puts severe strain on government budgets. This realization has gradually led to the adoption of private funding for infrastructure projects. One of the ways in which this is being achieved is project financing.

Project financing is not a new tool, but it has gained importance, because the concept has gradually evolved to mean a very specific financing technique. In this new environment, the lenders of funds look only to the cash flows and earnings of the project as the source of funds to repay their investments and not at the creditworthiness of the sponsoring organization. This has opened a number of avenues for the funding of new ventures that have no track record. Because a project is a distinct entity, separate from that of the promoter, and does not substantially impact the balance sheet, the creditworthiness of the sponsors, it is also known as non-recourse or limited-recourse financing. The relationship among the various parties in project financing is established through a variety of contractual arrangements.

It is essential that the modern project manager is familiar not only with contractual relations and risks associated with the technical aspects of projects, but also with the financing of projects. The financial instruments and financial engineering utilized in procuring successful projects is often just as important as the technical elements of the project.

## PROJECT FINANCE

The term 'project finance' is used to refer to a wide range of financing structures. However, these structures have one feature in common – the financing is not primarily dependent on the credit support of the sponsors or the value of the physical assets involved. In project financing, those providing the senior debt place a substantial degree of reliance on the performance of the project itself. Project finance can be defined as:

> A financing of a particular economic unit in which a lender is satisfied to look initially to the cash flows and earnings of that economic unit as the source of funds from which a loan will be repaid and to the assets of the economic unit as collateral for the loan.

Merna and Owen (1998) have described the concept of project finance with specific reference to a BOOT (Build–Own–Operate–Transfer) project as follows:

> Each project is supported by its own financial package and secured solely on that project or facility. Projects are viewed as being their own discreet entities and legally separate from their founding sponsors. As each project exists in its own right, Special Project Vehicles (SPV) are formulated. Banks lend to SPVs on a non- or limited-recourse basis, which means that loans are fully dependent on the revenue streams generated by the SPV, and that the assets of the SPV are used as collateral. Hence, although there may be a number of sponsors forming the SPV, the lenders have no claim to any of the assets other than the project itself.

### BASIC FEATURES OF PROJECT FINANCE

From the above brief descriptions the following basic features of project finance may be identified:

1. Special project vehicle (SPV)
2. Non-recourse or limited-recourse funding
3. Off-balance-sheet transaction
4. Sound income stream of the project as the predominant basis for financing
5. A variety of financial instruments
6. A variety of participants
7. A variety of risks

#### Special project vehicle (SPV)

The first step in project financing is the setting up of an SPV as a separate company from the promoter's organization and operating under a concession, normally granted by government. The seed equity capital for the SPV is usually provided by the sponsors of the project company. An SPV is usually highly geared, that is it has a high debt–equity ratio.

### Non-recourse or limited-recourse funding

In non-recourse funding the lenders to the project, both debt as well as equity, have no recourse to the general funds or assets of the sponsors of the project. However, in limited recourse, access to the sponsor's general assets and funds is provided if the sponsors provide a guarantee of repayment, but only for certain risks. In the event of poor performance of the project the project management team may be removed by the lenders (under step-in clauses).

### Off-balance-sheet transaction

The non-recourse nature of project finance provides a unique tool to project sponsors to fund the project outside their balance sheet. This structure enables funding of a variety of projects which might not otherwise have been funded particularly when the sponsors either:

- are unwilling to expose their general assets to liabilities to be incurred in connection with the project or are seeking to limit their exposure in this regard; or
- do not enjoy sufficient financial standing to borrow funds on the basis of their general assets.

### Sound income stream of the project as the predominant basis for financing

The future income stream of the project is the most critical element in any project financing. The entire financing of the project is dependent on an assured income stream since lenders and investors have recourse to no funds other than the income streams generated, once it is completed. Further, assets of the project may or may not have residual value. The project sponsors, therefore, have to demonstrate evidence of future income through various means, for example a power sales contract for a power plant, a concession agreement for a toll road project allowing the collection of tolls or tenant leases for a commercial real estate project.

### A variety of financial instruments

A project finance operation may involve a variety of financial instruments.

**Debt**   The most important element in project finance is debt capital. The main attribute of debt capital is a specified return for the lender over a specified period

**543**

of time. In project financing the return on debt capital is linked to the income flows of the project entity and is protected only against the assets of the project. There are a variety of debt instruments such as pure loans, bonds and non-convertible debentures. Debt raised from external sources is known as *senior debt* and is repayable before equity and subordinate debt. Debt raised from equity holders is known as *subordinate debt* (see *mezzanine finance*).

**Equity**    The process of funding a project normally begins with the setting up of a particular project legal entity floated by the project sponsors, often an SPV. The project sponsors provide the seed equity capital for this project company. Later the project entity may also raise equity funds from the general public to part finance the construction and early operation phase. Equity is risk capital and is subordinate to debt in terms of charge over the assets of the company. It shares in the profits of the project and any appreciation in the value of the enterprise, without limitation. The return on the equity, however, is the first to be affected in case of financial difficulties being faced by the project entity.

**Mezzanine finance**    There are some kinds of financial instruments that are primarily in the form of debt but also share some qualities of equity capital. They are generally referred to as quasi-equity (or subordinate debt). This includes convertible debentures, preferred stocks and other instruments with attributes of both debt and equity. Subordinate debt is sometimes treated as equity in the calculation of debt–equity ratios.

**Contractors, suppliers and purchasers**    In the financing of many projects, the contractors provide funding in the form of equity contribution or by extending credits. Similarly, suppliers of equipment participate in project financing through supplier's credit which is often supported by the export credit guarantee organizations of the supplier's country. Most of the projects financed under project finance have specified purchasers. For example, a power project may sell its product to a power distribution agency via a transmission company. The power purchaser can participate in the project financing by extending advances against future purchases of power. It may also contribute to equity capital.

**Sureties**    These are the contingent funds allocated by the guarantors of the loans, suppliers' credits and advances to the project company to protect the interests of the lenders and investors against any financial losses.

**Insurance**   These are the resources allocated by the insurance companies to compensate for the losses of the project in case of casualties, such as fire and other insurable events.

### A variety of participants

A project finance operation involves a variety of participants. It has private participants who play the major role, government that provides necessary incentives and domestic as well as international investors and lenders (multilateral, bilateral and commercial).

**Private participants**   Private sector companies and other private participants (domestic as well as foreign) often play the central role in a project financed through project finance techniques. The involvement of the private sector is in almost every aspect of the project:

- As the primary sponsor of the project. This is normally in conjunction with a host government sponsor in the case of developing countries. The involvement of the host government in the project builds the necessary confidence among the lenders and investors of the project having full government support.
- As the main party responsible for the construction and operation of the project.
- As the principal financiers of the project through private financial institutions and commercial banks.
- As guarantors or other sureties for certain types of transactions.
- As insurers and as purchasers of the output.

**Government**   The role played by the host government is generally crucial to the success of projects financed through project finance techniques. Most of the developing countries suffer from relatively underdeveloped legal and financial systems. The project finance, however, depends on very elaborate legal contract systems. As against a public funded project where performance of all the agencies involved in the project is monitored through a bureaucratic system, in project finance the performance is ensured through contracts and penalties. The first and foremost task of the host government, therefore, is to ensure that requisite legislative and statutory reforms are put in place to make the project finance a viable alternative to public funding of projects. Besides this, the host government may also participate in the project in various ways:

- As co-sponsor of the project along with private sponsor.
- By contributing to the equity capital.
- By contributing to the loan capital.

- By providing certain types of guarantees, such as against political risk.
- By providing certain resources required by the project which may be still within government control, such as coal supplies for a thermal power plant.
- By purchasing the output produced by the project, such as electricity.
- By providing certain fiscal incentives, such as tax exemptions, tax holidays and subsidies.

**Foreign governments**   In many projects financed through project finance techniques the involvement of foreign governments is important. They participate in the project in various ways:

- By providing bilateral loans to the project.
- By supporting the loans provided by private lenders and suppliers' credits through National Export Credit Guarantee Agencies.
- By purchasing the product of the project company, like electricity.
- By providing raw material for the operation of the project.

**Multilateral agencies**   In many projects financed through project finance techniques multilateral financial agencies, such as the World Bank, International Finance Corporation, Asian Development Bank and African Development Bank, become involved. Their involvement is generally complementary to the private financing of the project and provides a catalytic role. The wide experience and involvement of expert teams of these agencies in financing infrastructure projects in developing countries provides confidence to other lenders and investors in the project. These agencies normally participate by providing loans and equity and through co-financing with other multilateral agencies.

### A variety of risks

In conventional financing methods, the lenders look not only at the prospect of the project becoming successful but also at the general creditworthiness of the project sponsors. The risks associated with a particular project are not critical because the lenders have access to the general assets of the project sponsors. In project financing the borrower is usually an SPV. The SPV will normally not have any past history since it is created just to implement and operate a specific project. Further the lenders and investors have no or limited recourse to the general assets of the sponsor company. The key to project finance development, investing and lending is diligence in understanding the risks associated with a project and careful attention to how they are allocated among project participants. It is much easier to put money into an ill-conceived project than to pull it out. Risks include the following:

546

**Project risk**    Careful reflection about how a proposed project is intended to work in good times and bad is just as appropriate for a power plant (power contract revenues) in the developing world as it is for an airport terminal serving a leading US city (rental income from airlines and concessions). The evaluation of the risks of diminution and interruption of the future revenue stream is the central question around which project finance revolves.

**Borrowers' credit risk**    As well as the project risk associated with the project itself there are risks associated with the creditworthiness of the SPV created for the implementation of the project. There is risk of default by the SPV on its liabilities due to bankruptcy or general deterioration in the financial condition of the company.

**Sponsors' credit risk**    In project financing the stakes of the sponsors are limited to the resources invested by the sponsor company in the project. The market credit rating of the SPV is different from the credit rating of the sponsor company. The involvement of known and renowned sponsors, however, gives strength to the project company and any change in the credit rating of the sponsor company is likely to affect the credit rating of the project company; more so if it is adverse. This can affect the cost of funds being raised by the company.

**Sovereign risk**    In much project financing, the host country government provides guarantees or counter guarantees for the capital raised by the project company. The credit rating of governments is known as the sovereign credit rating. Any change in the sovereign credit rating may also affect the viability of the project.

## FINANCIAL INSTRUMENTS

All projects require financing. No project progresses without financial resources. However, the nature and amount of financing required during different phases of the project vary widely. In most projects the rate of expenditure changes dramatically as the project moves from the appraisal stage, which consumes mainly human expertise and analytical skills, to the design stage, then to the manufacture and construction phase and finally the operational phase. Broadly speaking, a project may be said to pass through three main phases:

1. Project definition and appraisal (see Chapters 25 and 27)
2. Project implementation/construction (see Chapter 26)
3. Project operation (see reference to The Missing Chapter on p. 428).

The precise shape of the cash flow curve for a particular project depends on various factors such as the time taken in setting up the project objectives, obtaining statutory approvals, design finalization, finalization of the contracts and finalization of the financing arrangement, and the rate and amount of construction and operation speed. (Chapters 18, 19 and 20 describe the estimating and scheduling of the use of cash and resources.) The negative cash flow, until the project breaks even, clearly indicates that a typical project needs financing from outside the project until it does break even. The shape of the curve (see Figure 18.3) also reveals that in the initial phase of the project relatively less financing is required. As the project moves on to the implementation phase there is a sudden increase in the requirement for finance, which peaks at the completion stage. The rate of spending is also depicted by the steepness of the curve. The steeper the curve the greater the need for finance to be available. Once the project is commissioned and starts to yield revenues (see Figure 27.5), the requirement for financing from outside the project becomes less and less. Finally, the project starts to generate sufficient resources for the operation and maintenance and also a surplus. However, even after the break-even point, the project may require financing for short periods, to meet the mismatch between receipts and payments.

In project financing, it is this future cash flow that becomes the basis for raising resources for investing in the project. It is the job of the project finance team to package this cash flow in such a way that it meets the needs of the project and at the same time is attractive to the potential agencies and individuals willing to provide resources to the project for investment. To achieve this objective effectively a thorough knowledge of the financial instruments and the financial markets in which they trade is essential.

Projects have to raise cash to finance their investment activities. This is normally done by issuing or selling securities. These securities, known as financial instruments, are in the form of a claim on the future cash flow of the project. At the same time, these instruments have a contingent claim on the assets of the project, which acts as a security in the event of future cash flows not materializing as expected. The nature and seniority of the claim on the cash flow and assets of the project vary with the financial instrument used. Merna and Owen (1998) describe financial instruments as the tools used by the SPV to raise money to finance the project. Traditionally, financial instruments were in the form of either debt or equity. Developments in the financial markets and financial innovations have led to the development of various other kinds of financial instruments which share the characteristics of both debt and equity. These instruments are normally described as mezzanine finance. The various types of financial instruments are defined below:

- *Debt* Those securities issued by the project that make it liable to pay a specified amount at a particular time. Debt is senior to all other claims on the project cash flow and assets.
- *Ordinary equity* Ownership interest of common stockholders in the project. On the balance sheet, equity equals total assets less all liabilities. It has the lowest rank and therefore the last claim on the assets and cash flow of the project.
- *Mezzanine finance* This occupies an intermediate position between the senior debt and the common equity. Mezzanine finance typically takes the form of subordinated debt, junior subordinated debt and preferred stock, or some combination of each.

Besides debt, equity and mezzanine finance a project may also utilize certain other types of instruments such as leasing, venture capital and aid.

Since the financing requirement of a project depends on the future cash flow, which depends on time, another way of classifying financial instruments is temporal in nature, that is long-term financing instruments and short-term financing instruments:

1. *Long-term financing* Debt, equity and mezzanine finance that has a repayment obligation beyond one year.
2. *Short-term financing* Financial instruments that normally have a repayment obligation up to one year.

### LONG-TERM FINANCING INSTRUMENTS

A project raises long-term financing primarily for long term investment purposes. Long-term financing is needed because the asset created by the project has a gestation lag before it starts to yield revenues. Long-term financing helps the project by deferring, partly or fully, the servicing of the securities sold until the project starts to generate revenues. The main forms of debt, equity and mezzanine financial instruments are listed in Figure 29.1.

### SHORT-TERM FINANCING INSTRUMENTS

Projects require short-term debt of two kinds. First, for *working capital requirement*. These funds are required once the project has been commissioned to cover the time lag between payments to be made for the purchase of raw materials, components and equipment for the operation of the project and receipt from the sale of the product. Second, as *bridging finance* to meet temporary deficits in cash balance when there is a known source of funds which can be fully relied upon to

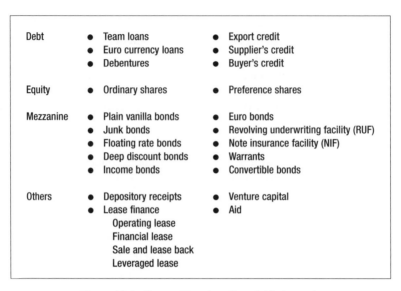

| Debt | | |
|------|------|------|
| | • Team loans | • Export credit |
| | • Euro currency loans | • Supplier's credit |
| | • Debentures | • Buyer's credit |
| Equity | • Ordinary shares | • Preference shares |
| Mezzanine | • Plain vanilla bonds | • Euro bonds |
| | • Junk bonds | • Revolving underwriting facility (RUF) |
| | • Floating rate bonds | • Note insurance facility (NIF) |
| | • Deep discount bonds | • Warrants |
| | • Income bonds | • Convertible bonds |
| Others | • Depository receipts | • Venture capital |
| | • Lease finance | • Aid |
| | Operating lease | |
| | Financial lease | |
| | Sale and lease back | |
| | Leveraged lease | |

**Figure 29.1   Forms of long-term financial instruments**

liquidate the bridging loan. The short-term financing options available to a project for working capital requirements during the operation phase, other than the internal resources, can be broadly classified in three categories:

1. Unsecured bank borrowing
2. Secured borrowing
3. Other sources such as commercial paper or banker's acceptance

## FINANCIAL ENGINEERING

Just as engineers use special tools and instruments to achieve engineering perfection, financial engineers use specialized financial instruments and tools to improve financial performance. The term 'financial engineering' can be defined as:

the development and creative application of financial technology to solve financial problems and exploit financial opportunities

or

the use of financial instruments to restructure an existing financial profile into one having more desirable properties.

Financial engineering techniques are used widely in modelling and forecasting financial markets, development of derivative instruments and securities, hedging and financial risk management, asset allocation and investment management and asset/liability management. The tools used by financial engineers are the new financial instruments created during the last two to three decades – forwards, futures, swaps and options. These basic tools are combined in different ways by financial engineers to build more complex systems to meet specific requirements for their clients. The basic instruments and some of their variants include:

- forward rate
- forward exchange rate
- forward interest rate
- forward rate agreement (FRA)
- financial futures
- swaps (interest rate swaps and cross-currency swaps)
- options
- caps
- floors
- collars
- swaptions
- compound options
- asset backed securities.

## FINANCIAL RISK MANAGEMENT

Many projects are considered high risk because of the amount of uncertainty involved in the method of financing them. The chance of a project succeeding can be increased by identifying the risk associated with the finance and taking the necessary actions. The risks associated with financing major projects, whether by public or private organizations, are numerous. All client organizations need to consider the risks typically associated with major projects – construction and operation risks, the risks associated with revenue generation and also the risks associated with how the project is to be financed. The risk associated with the methods of repayment is the uncertainty of cash inflows and outflows. Many projects need flexible repayment mechanisms to ensure success should changes in cash flows occur. Project cash flows should be assessed between the worst and best scenarios to ensure that repayments can be made should risks occur.

Sound financial risk management starts with a sound project case.

### APPRAISAL AND VALIDITY OF FINANCING PROJECTS

The financial viability of a project must be clearly demonstrable to potential investors and lending organizations. In assessing the attractiveness of a financial package project sponsors should examine the risks associated with the project. There are three basic financial criteria which need to be achieved in projects:

1. Finance must be cost-effective, so far as possible.
2. The skilled use of finance at fixed rates to minimize risks should be adopted.
3. Finance should be acquired over the long term thus eliminating refinancing risk.

The project must have clear and defined revenues that will be sufficient to service principal and interest payments on the project debt over the term of the loans, and to provide a return on equity which is commensurate with development and long-term project risk taken by equity investors. For example, the European Investment Bank (EIB) will normally fund infrastructure projects for a period of 25 years and industrial and process plants up to 14 years. Institutional investors such as insurance companies and pension funds consider projects with fixed rates of return up to 20 years to match the cash flow characteristics of their liabilities. Lenders often refer to a robust finance package as one which will allow repayment of loans under a worst case scenario.

When selecting the sources and forms of capital required, the strength of the security package, perception of the country risks and limits and the sophistication of local capital markets should be considered.

One of the most important elements to be satisfied in a project is how to provide security to non-recourse or limited-recourse lenders. If a promoter defaults under a project strategy utilizing a non-recourse finance package, the lender may be left with a partly completed facility which has no market value. Thus to protect lenders various security devices are often included:

● Revenues are collected in one or more escrow accounts maintained by an escrow agent independent of the promoter company.
● The benefits of various contracts entered into by the promoter, such as construction contract, performance bonds, supplier warranties and insurance proceeds, will normally be assigned to a trustee for the benefit of the lender.
● Lenders may insist upon the right to take over the project (step-in clauses) in case of financial or technical default prior to bankruptcy and bring in new contractors, suppliers or operators to complete the project.
● Lenders and export credit agencies may insist on measures of government support such as standby subordinated loan facilities which are functionally almost equivalent to sovereign guarantees.

The successful elements required in funding projects could include limited and non-recourse credit, debt financing entirely in local currency, equity finance in currencies considered relatively strong, major innovations in project financing, confident project creditors and governments prepared to accept some risks and provide limited resources. The contract between the client and lender can only be determined when the lender has sufficient information to assess the viability of a project. In most projects the lender will look to the project itself as a source of repayment rather than the assets of the project. The key parameters to be considered by lenders include:

- total size of the project: the size of the project determining the amount of money required and the effort needed to raise the capital, internal rate of return on the project and equity;
- break-even dates: critical dates when equity investors see a return on their investments;
- milestones: significant dates related to the financing of the project;
- loan summary: the true cost of each loan, the amount drawn and the year in which drawdowns reach their maximum.

A properly structured financial loan package should achieve the following basic objectives:

- Maximize long-term debt.
- Maximize fixed rate financing.
- Minimize refinancing risk.

It is important to realize that the financial plan may have a greater impact on the terms of a project than the physical design or construction costs.

### FINANCIAL RISK MANAGEMENT PROCESS

Both borrowers and lenders need to adopt a risk management programme (RMP, Chapter 21). Risk management should not be approached in an ad hoc manner but should be structured. In Chapter 21, a nine-step risk management process was suggested. The five steps of a financial RMP are as follows:

1. Identify the financial objectives of the project.
2. Identify the source of the risk exposure.
3. Quantify the exposure.
4. Assess the impact of the exposure on business and financial strategy.
5. Respond to the exposure.

### IDENTIFYING FINANCIAL OBJECTIVES

The first step is to develop a clear understanding of the project. Borrowers and lenders need to determine their objects regarding the financing of a project.

Many borrowers seek long term loans with repayments made from revenues. The risk of not meeting repayments is often reduced when the borrower has sufficient earnings at the start of operation to service the debt. Many projects, however, suffer commissioning delays which increase the borrowers' loans and repayments. In many cases borrowers will seek grace periods from lenders to cover such delays. Lenders seek positive cash flows and must ensure that their objectives are met by providing the best loan package. If a short-term loan is the lender's objective then the major risk will occur at the start of operation and should the project not generate sufficient revenues the lender may need to consider debt-for-equity swaps as was the case in the Channel Tunnel project.

Once the project objectives are defined the total costs, including construction and operation costs, are determined and a cumulative cash flow model is prepared. The model can be used to quickly estimate the NPV, IRR and payback period of a project (see Chapter 27). This model is initially prepared without considering potential risks. It is essential that the estimates and programmes are reflective of cost and time over the project's life cycle. The risk of inaccurate estimates based on fixed budgets often leads to optimistic cash flows which do not truly illustrate the effects of risk occurring during a project.

In many cases the cost of finance is not included in the cash flow at this stage. Many organizations prefer to use the return on investment (ROI) as the measure of profitability. I, however, recommend that the cost of finance along with all other projected costs and revenues should be incorporated in the cash flow as this provides a more accurate illustration of the project's finances. Working capital should also be considered in the cash flow as certain risks may occur and result in further borrowing over and above that estimated.

## IDENTIFYING, QUANTIFYING AND ASSESSING FINANCIAL RISK

The word 'risk' is normally associated with an unexpected and undesirable change, yet this is, not always true for financial transactions. In financial transactions there are always two parties who hold diametrically opposite perspectives. Consider the case in which a project SPV decides to fund its capital requirements partly through an issue of fixed rate coupon bonds. If after the issue has been made the market interest rate goes up, then the issuer of the bond will be well pleased because it will continue to pay a lower coupon rate to the investors. However, the investors in the bond will view it as undesirable because they will continue to receive the already fixed coupon rate. The same change (event) is desirable for one party and undesirable for another. On the other hand, had it been a floating rate bond issue the issuer of the bond would have regarded an increase in interest rate as undesirable and the investors in the bond would have seen it as desirable. Since in a financial transaction there are always two parties a particular change can affect the two parties in a diametrically opposite way. It is therefore more prudent to define risk as any variation in an outcome.

## Sources of financial risk

Financial risk may be defined as the impact on the financial performance of any entity exposed to risk. This definition makes it clear that any event or act which has impact on the financial performance of an entity is a financial risk. This is a very broad definition and it is difficult to prepare a foolproof list of all possible events or acts which might have an impact on the financial performance of an entity. However, broadly speaking the principal sources of financial risk may be classified under the following headings:

1. Currency risk
2. Interest rate risk
3. Equity risk
4. Commercial risk
5. Liquidity risk
6. Counterparty risk
7. Country risk

## RESPONDING TO FINANCIAL RISKS

Financial risk management can be defined as the design and implementation of systems or procedures for controlling financial risk. Complete protection against any movements in the factors causing financial risk implies hedging against both adverse and benign outcomes. This may not always be the best approach in a financial transaction. For example, a borrower of US dollars, based in the UK, would like to protect itself against the strengthening of the US dollar but might like to benefit from the weakening of the US dollar.

It should also not be forgotten that managing financial risk with the help of various financial engineering techniques does not come free. A cost has to be paid for the use of these instruments. An instrument of hedging against risk which gives complete protection but no benefits in case of favourable movements in the risk variable may be cheaper to procure than an instrument which provides protection against adverse movements but allows the benefits in case of favourable movement to flow to the hedger. Financial engineering tools such as FRAs, forwards, futures and swaps guarantee a particular outcome but no benefits in case of favourable movements. Options, on the other hand, guarantee a particular outcome but also allow the benefit of favourable movements. It is

555

therefore vital that, before a decision regarding the use of a particular tool of risk management is taken, the objective of the risk management should be clearly defined. The success or failure of the risk management strategy depends on the predetermined objective of the risk management.

### Responding to currency risk

There are various instruments available for managing currency risk. If a project SPV wants to eliminate the impact of fluctuation in exchange rates, it can use instruments like forward exchange contracts or can enter into a cross-currency swap or futures deal. For example, if a UK-based company has to repay a short-term US dollar loan maturing six months from now, it can enter into a six months forward contract and fix the rates for buying US dollars now. This transaction provides a complete hedge against any movement in the sterling/dollar exchange rate – adverse as well as favourable. The company will, therefore, not benefit if the US dollar weakens. If the company feels that the exchange rate may turn in its favour but still does not want to take any risk it may buy an option. This will fix the sterling/dollar rate now but will give the company the option to buy from the open market if the rates are favourable to the company. Similarly the company can use other option instruments such as a cap, a floor or a collar, or one of the exotic option tools such as the average rate and average strike options and compound options to manage its currency risk exposure. Depending upon the company's perception of the market it can choose one of the financial engineering instruments which best approximates to its requirement of hedging the currency risk exposure at the best price.

In developing countries the derivative market is either non-existent or at a developing stage. Public enterprises or the government have traditionally borne the exchange risk in these countries. With privatization the local private project sponsors are now facing serious problems in hedging the currency risk. The risk of currency depreciation, therefore, falls on the project sponsors and ultimately on the consumers of the services. To hedge the currency risk private sponsors in these countries try to link the price of the service to some international currency. There is therefore an urgent need to develop derivatives markets in these countries so that project investors can take advantage of the facilities and protect themselves against the currency risk.

### Responding to interest rate risk

There are also a host of financial engineering instruments available to manage interest rate risk. First and foremost is a forward rate agreement (FRA). For example, if a company wants to borrow after six months for a further six-month period, and expects the market interest rate to rise when it has to borrow, it may buy an FRA today. This will fix its interest obligation now for borrowing in the future, giving total risk cover.

Buying an interest rate futures can provide the same level of protection but a futures contract has to be done in the standardized format prescribed by the market regarding the unit of trading, interest rate and maturity. It cannot be tailored to meet the specific requirements of the client as in the case of an FRA. Both FRAs and futures are extensively used for managing interest rate risk.

Whereas FRAs and futures can provide protection against exposure in the short term, swaps can help manage long-term interest rate exposure. Just like FRAs they can be tailored to meet the specific requirements of the client. Some of the varied ways in which swaps can be used to manage interest rate risk are shown below.

**Floating-to-fixed swap**    is one of the most straightforward swap applications for converting a floating rate risk to a fixed rate thereby eliminating any further exposure to interest rate movements. For example, consider a borrower that has taken a five-year loan at LIBOR+50BP (London Interbank Overnight Rate + 50 base points; this is equal to 0.5 per cent) and fears that interest rates may go up. It may enter into a fixed rate interest swap with a bank or any other counterparty where it receives a floating rate of LIBOR+50BP from the counterparty and pays it a fixed rate depending on the prevailing swap rate for five years. This insulates the borrower from any movement in the LIBOR.

**Fixed-to-floating swap**    although less common can facilitate conversion of a fixed interest rate liability to a floating rate liability. For example, a company borrowed three years ago for five years at a fixed rate of interest in order to keep its liability fixed and also because it did not anticipate that the interest rate would fall. Now if the interest rate has declined and it is expected to maintain this level until the loan matures then the company may change its view and wish to convert its fixed rate liability to floating rate. It can then enter into a floating rate swap with a counterparty and benefit from the low floating rate. In this case, however, it is exposed to increase in interest rates.

**Fixed-to-floating-to-fixed swap**    can be used by a company to convert a fixed liability to floating, and if the interest rates become unfavourable in floating then the company can enter into a second swap from floating to fixed.

**Cross-currency fixed/floating-to-fixed/floating swap**    can be used by a company which is in a position to access capital markets in different countries and in different currencies simultaneously. Such a company can borrow from the

**557**

cheapest market in fixed/floating rate and thereafter swap the loan to the desired currency again in fixed/floating to make the borrowing the cheapest.

All the instruments of interest rate risk management just discussed above guarantee a fixed interest rate according to the company's objective, and thereby completely eliminate the risk. Options, on the other hand, can provide protection against the adverse movements of the interest rate and preserve the opportunity to benefit from the beneficial movements. For example, buying an FRA provides a specific interest rate for a nominated time period to the buyer. However, buying an option on FRA, also known as an *interest rate guarantee* (IRG), grants the holder the right to choose between a specific interest rate, or the interest rate prevailing in the market at the time of option exercise. A borrower can buy a call option on an FRA, giving right, not obligation, to the holder to strike at a particular interest rate. If the interest rate eventually turned out to be higher than the strike rate, the borrower can exercise the option and use the underlying FRA to cap the borrowing costs. If rates turned out to be lower, the borrower can allow the option to expire and borrow at the market rates. An investor can use a put option to guarantee a minimum return on the investment.

Caps, floors, collars, captions and swaptions can also be effectively used to manage interest rate risk. Caption and swaption are particularly relevant for contingent situations, a much cheaper rate protection, for handling embedded debt options, extending or curtailing swaps and for speculation.

### Responding to equity risk

Equity risk manifests in the variation in the value of individual shares. Any movement in the market price of the equity directly affects the owners of the equity. The tools of financial engineering, such as futures and options, can be effectively used by the owners of the equity to manage equity risk.

For the issuer of the equity, the risk of changes in the price of equity is not direct but indirect. The market price of the equity is a rough barometer of the health of the company. If the company has been performing well or has a good potential for better performance then the market price of the equity of such a company will be high. More and more investors will want to own the shares of such a company. It will provide good potential to raise additional funds either through the issue of more equities or through debt instruments. Whereas external investors can use the financial engineering instruments to manage their risk, the issuer of the equity is not permitted to deal in its own shares. It has internal information about the company which may tempt it to indulge in undue speculation at the cost of the owners of the equity, who do not have access to such information. However, sometimes companies in need of funds when their equity price is falling resort to issue of bonus shares to the existing equity owners at below market price to retain the interest of these investors in the company and to raise resources. In the long run the company must show good results if it wants its equity to perform well.

### Responding to commercial risk

Developments in contract law have enabled substantial progress in the management of commercial risk. Many types of commercial risks can be managed to a large extent with the help of contract law.

The concept of target cost contract can be of significant help in reducing the commercial risk relating to the completion of a project. Under target cost contract there is a bonus for the early commissioning of the project and a penalty for late completion. This carrot and stick provision normally puts substantial pressure as well as incentive on the contractor to complete the project at the earliest date or at least without any delay. For example, in a project to construct a power plant in India, the private sponsor will pay a penalty of US$30 000 every day beyond the agreed commissioning date for the first six months and a higher penalty thereafter. It is also possible to manage the capacity specification of the project by linking the capacity to a fixed payment. If the contractor is able to achieve the capacity, then it receives the payment, otherwise it loses it.

It is also quite common to transfer construction risk to specialized construction companies by using a turnkey contract. Turnkey contracts have been widely used as the basis of the construction contract(s) in the procurement of both publicly funded and BOOT projects. In some cases the turnkey contract has been awarded on the basis of a lump sum or index linked lump sum price. Many principal and promoter organizations see the turnkey contract as a means of allocating most of the risks associated with the design, construction, commissioning and early operation of a facility. The choice of a turnkey contract can often be determined by the funds made available by lenders, equity providers and through grants to a promoter. Export financing tended to favour the turnkey contract and many developing countries were eager to adopt a turnkey contract as a means of financing a project. The lump sum price offered in a turnkey contract is often considered an advantage by promoters who have a limited budget and are not in a position to incur additional costs.

Risk related to the operation of the project is managed through an operations contract. The contract may specify the operational obligations such as the maintenance or the availability of the capacity. For example, in a power project the maintenance contract may specify that the plant may be available in effective working order from a specified period of time.

The risks related to input and outputs can be managed using purchase and supply contracts. These include take-and-pay and take-or-pay contracts. Under a take-and-pay contract, the purchaser is obliged to pay for what the project produces and delivers. This guarantees that there will be a secure market for the produce. Under a take-or-pay contract, the purchaser is obliged to pay for the produce, whether or not the delivery is taken. In this case the obligation to pay often exists even if the output has not been produced. The obligation under take-or-pay is an obligation to pay by the take-or-pay obligor and is not limited by total destruction of facilities, acts of God, nuclear explosion, confiscation, condemnation, etc. Similarly, for input supplies the project may enter into long-term contracts for the supply of input with the input suppliers. If the purchaser of the output is a public sector undertaking, like a public sector power transmission and distribution agency, then the private sector power generating company can insist on a guarantee from the government for take-and-pay or take-or-pay contracts. If the project has to procure input from the open market then variants of almost all the tools of financial engineering are generally available to manage the input cost risk. In fact the first derivatives to be traded on the Chicago Board of Trade, established in 1848, were the commodity futures. Financial futures came much later in 1972. In developed financial and commodity markets use of commodity swaps, caps, collars and even options are quite common.

Another method of managing commercial risk is insurance. Although the private market for insurance against commercial risk is relatively small, there is great potential for its development. With the gradual withdrawal from infrastructure projects of governments who normally took all the risk, the development of private insurance for managing commercial risk is absolutely essential if the privatization process is to be successful. This will not only help in meeting the requirement of managing the commercial risk, but existence of such a market will also have a catalytic influence on privatization. Governments can help develop this market by encouraging the setting up of guarantee funds and by making some initial contribution to them. For example, a London insurance market is to provide insurance for traffic risk for a Mexican toll road.

### Responding to liquidity risk

Successful management of the liquidity risk hinges on successful cash management of the project. Delays in construction and commissioning, problems with the operation of the project and problems of input supplies and offtake of the produce may lead to unmatched cash inflows and cash outflows and hence liquidity risk. As discussed earlier in relation to commercial risk management, the adoption of proper contractual arrangements can help manage these risks to a great extent. The problem of liquidity due to cost overruns can be managed by arranging a standby loan. Although standby loan facilities are expensive compared with the normal type of loan they provide a safety net in the case of cost overruns.

Another method of managing liquidity risk is debt–equity swap. If the liquidity problem is for a short period and the project has a good potential for success then the providers of debt capital may agree to convert their debt into equity. This gives them an opportunity to share in the profits of the company in the future. Conversion of debt to shares totally changes the nature of liability of the company. With shares, the company pays the shareholders only when a dividend is declared. This helps manage the liquidity of the company but at the cost of reduced gearing. Debt-for-equity swaps were considered for the Channel Tunnel project.

### Responding to counterparty risk

The counterparty risk of the lender is much more than the counterparty risk of the borrower. The borrower can ensure the disbursal of the credit by tying up the credit with known and reputable lenders. The lenders, however, have been traditionally managing the default risk by the borrower through a guarantee from the project sponsors. In project financing, where the recourse to the project sponsors is either limited or nil, the lenders normally insist on a guarantee from the borrowers bank.

### Responding to country risk

Country risk is the risk which is under the control of the borrowing country. Host governments can provide guarantee against such events. If the purchaser of the produce of the project is a public sector monopoly, then government can provide guarantee for the take-and-pay or take-or-pay contracts. But such guarantees are not always acceptable to international lenders. They may, many times, look for guarantees from the creditor countries or from multilateral banks to ensure against country risk. Even if a multilateral agency agrees to provide the guarantee the role of the host government does not disappear because the multilateral agencies typically insist on a counter guarantee from the host government.

Guarantee against country risk is also provided by the export credit agencies in OECD countries. They offer guarantee against risk of non-repayment to their national exporters or banks that extend credit to overseas importers of goods and services. In their most limited form, export credit agency guarantees or insurance may be extended only against sovereign risk, with exporter or bankers responsible for the commercial risks. In most cases the guarantee covers both the

**561**

sovereign risk and the commercial risk. Since the primary motive behind setting up these agencies is promoting export the insurance premium charged by these agencies is highly subsidized. The maximum cover of these guarantees is often a small amount of the total project financing.

In order to promote flow of private capital to developing countries, several multilateral development banks, including the World Bank and the Asian Development Bank, have developed guarantee schemes. The World Bank guarantees, which are only for debt capital and not for equity capital, help developing countries access international capital markets and lengthen the maturity of the borrowing. The World Bank also issues guarantees for project financing under its Extended Cofinancing Facility, to cover sovereign risk associated with infrastructure projects. In the case of the Hub River Project in Pakistan, out of the US$680 million in international syndicated commercial loans, the World Bank provided guarantees to various commercial lenders covering US$240 million of debt. The Multilateral Investment Guarantee Agency (MIGA), an affiliate of the World Bank, has been specifically set up to specialize in the provision of country risk coverage. MIGA specializes in guaranteeing against currency transfer (inconvertibility), expropriation, war and civil disturbance and breach of contracts.

## CONCLUSIONS

One of the essential pillars of the global economic growth is the development of infrastructure facilities. Predominant public funding of the development of these facilities, until the early 1980s, has not been able to keep pace with the growing demand for these facilities. The method of public funding of infrastructure development has also been found to suffer from the problems of accountability, high cost and poor performance thereby constraining the ability of the public sector to accelerate investment in infrastructure.

The method of project financing through concession contracts provides a viable solution to this problem. Using this technique, project promoters have been able to structure and mobilize private capital for discreet infrastructure, industrial and other commercial projects. The beauty of project financing is that it helps structure financing for a project entirely on the basis of the future revenue streams of the project. Such a financing has no recourse to the general assets of the project promoter.

A project need not confine itself, for its financing needs to the conventional tools of the loan and equity. The revolution in financial engineering techniques has opened a wide range of financial products to meet the specific requirements of a project.

The revolution in corporate financing and the ingenuity of the financial engineers have led to the development of a wide range of financial products to meet the specific needs of corporate entities. The development in mezzanine financing instruments, such as bonds, convertibles and warrants, which have a lower charge on the assets of the company as compared with loans and a higher charge as compared with equity, are very effective because of their easy marketability. The concepts of forwards, swaps, futures and options are tools that may be used to change the financial profile of a company and also to meet the needs of effective risk management.

Financial risks are distinct from the risks of the other two basic constraints in a project – risk of specification of a project and risk of the schedule. It cannot be denied, however, that the specification risk and schedule risk invariably affect the financing of a project.

## REFERENCES AND FURTHER READING

Merna, A. and Dubey, R. (1998), *Financial Engineering in the Procurement of Projects*, Asia Law and Practice, Hong Kong. (This chapter is a summary of the major elements of this book.)

Merna, A. and Njiru (1998), *Financing and Managing Projects*, Asia Law and Practice, Hong Kong.

Merna, A. and Owen, G. (1998), *Understanding the Private Finance Initiative*, Asia Law and Practice, Hong Kong.

Merna, A. and Smith (1996), *Guide to the Preparation and Evaluation of Build–Own–Operate–Transfer (BOOT) Project Tenders*, 2nd edn, Asia Law and Practice, Hong Kong.

Merna, A. and Smith (1996), *Projects Procured by Privately Financed Concession Contracts*, **1**, 2nd edn, Asia Law and Practice, Hong Kong.

Merna, A. and Smith (1996), *Projects Procured by Privately Financed Concession Contracts*, **2**, 1st edn, Asia Law and Practice, Hong Kong.

## RELATED TOPICS

| | |
|---|---|
| Estimating and scheduling cash flow | Chapters 18, 19 and 20 |
| Project definition | Chapter 25 |
| Project appraisal | Chapter 27 |

# Part VI
# Contractual

# INTRODUCTION TO PART VI

In Part VI we consider contracts and contract management. No project sponsor has all the skills internally to do all the work of a project, except on the smallest of projects. Goods and services must be bought in, and this requires people to make contracts so that they know the basis on which they are working with each other and to deal with any disagreements that subsequently arise.

### Chapter 30: Roles and responsibilities in project procurement

In Chapter 30 Nigel Smith describes the roles various parties can fulfil on a project, especially the managerial roles. He then shows how different types of contracts attempt to define these roles and deal with the relationship that arises between the client, its contractors and subcontractors. He describes the traditional procurement route first, client–engineer–construction contractor, and uses this as a basis against which to compare others. He then discusses some of the other more modern, but now common, approaches. Finally, he considers some of the novel routes now being tried. He also sets out the terms and conditions for the employment of project managers.

### Chapter 31: Partnering, benchmarking and alliances

Denise Bower and Fotis Skoutzos consider partnerships and alliances in Chapter 31. These are becoming increasingly popular, especially in the relationship between client and contractor, in an attempt to remove the adversarial culture that has built up in the construction industry. The authors describe partnering and how alliance contracts can be benchmarked, and discuss how incentives can be built into partnering arrangements.

## Chapter 32: Contract law

In Chapter 32 Peter Marsh describes contract law. His coverage is primarily based on English law, but many of the elements of English contract law are common in other legal systems. He explains the elements of contract formation, including offer, acceptance and consideration, and describes conditions of invalidity, frustration and terms and warranties.

## Chapter 33: Contracts and payment structures

In Chapter 33 Peter Marsh considers different methods of pricing contracts, including fixed price, cost plus and remeasurement. He describes contract structures, how the contract price is set, and how progress is measured and payments made as the project progresses.

## Chapter 34: Standard forms of contract

Parties to a contract can draw up a bespoke contract document at the start of every project, but that is both inefficient and subject to error. It is better to use standard forms of contract, which are tried and tested, based on expert knowledge and readily available. Almost every industry has standard forms of contract, especially the three branches of the construction industry. In Chapter 34 Stephen Simister and Rodney Turner describe the use of standard forms and provide a list of some of those available.

## Chapter 35: Procurement

There are many contract types available to the client and other contracting parties. In Chapter 35 Peter Baily describes how the client organization goes about entering a contract. He describes how they choose the contract type and the contractors they will use, and examines several topics relating to project procurement for the purchasing of both services and goods.

## Chapter 36: Bidding

Contract management is often written from the client's perspective. In Chapter 36 Stephen Simister addresses that balance. He describes how a contracting organization should bid for work, considering in turn each of the three stages in the bid process: before receiving the invitation to tender, bid preparation and submission, and contract negotiation.

## Chapter 37: Managing variations, claims and disputes

The main purpose of the contract is to describe how the relationship will work. However, it would be dangerously complacent to assume it will work perfectly every time. It is therefore necessary to deal with situations where it will be less than perfect. Hopefully, in most cases the changes to the contract will be relatively small variations and they can be dealt with simply. It is even possible to deal with quite large changes within the structures of most contracts. However, in the worst cases there is disagreement about the extent of the change or who is responsible. This may lead to a more extensive claim, and if either party disagrees about the claim, that will lead to a dispute. In Chapter 37 Peter Marsh describes variations, claims and disputes.

# 30 Roles and responsibilities in project procurement

## Nigel Smith

No organization has all the skills required to do anything but the most simple of projects. Additional skills required for the completion of projects must be bought in from external sources. In this chapter, we consider the roles required throughout the project supply chain, particularly during the design and construction stages, and what contract types are available to provide the additional roles in different ways. The contract is the mechanism by which:

- project managers are employed;
- goods and services are procured;
- the commercial nature of the project process is defined.

It is important for project managers to be aware of how to operate effectively using the contractual procedures to optimal advantage. This chapter reviews the roles of different parties to a project and different contracting practices designed to provide the client organization with those services. It covers the traditional approach and some of the more recent but now common practices, as well as emerging ones. The chapter also describes standard terms for project managers and comments on future trends.

## PROJECT PROCUREMENT

Ideas for projects arise from many sources, including strategic planning, market forecasts, process re-engineering or suggestion by a speculative developer. A client considers the viability of these concepts to determine the extent to which it wishes to participate. This varies from client to client and project to project, from being a wholly internal, private project executed by direct labour to a public sector concession awarded to an external promoter. Whatever delivery structure is adopted, similar functions need to be undertaken, many of which must be sourced from outside the client's organization. The roles and responsibilities for the management of a project can be viewed as a hierarchical sequence of interlinked functions (Figure 30.1). These cascade down from the strategic, market and commercial drivers acting on the client and progress through the various parties in the entire supply chain. Due to the range of types of procurement strategies used in projects this generic diagram may use separate titles for groups which in practice might be a single organization or even a single individual. Further, the rationale for the linkages included in the diagram would have to be modified to remain compatible with the structure and numbers of parties involved in the project.

One of the most important decisions to be taken after the client is satisfied with the project concept and viability is the choice of procurement strategy. This has to identify the number of parties involved and their responsibilities. This is not always straightforward and it is important to remember there are always alternative procurement routes available for any project. A number of differing sources estimate that the selection of the most effective procurement strategy compared with possible strategies could produce cost savings of about 8 per cent. This is significant when it is remembered that profit margins in construction are frequently of the order of 1–2 per cent.

In this chapter we consider a number of different procurement strategies available to fulfil the roles illustrated in Figure 30.1. We start by considering the traditional approach, and then describe others as variants on this model. Ultimately it is the client who must determine the procurement strategy to its optimal advantage.

## ROLES AND RESPONSIBILITIES IN A TRADITIONAL PROCUREMENT STRATEGY

As a starting point for the consideration of the roles and responsibilities of parties to a project suitable for all types of business, engineering or industry, we consider the traditional structure used extensively in the UK construction industry. This involves three parties:

- A client who initiates and sanctions a project.
- A consultant who undertakes the feasibility and design.
- A contractor who is responsible for implementing the project.

Procurement strategies adopted by a project must recognize the prevailing culture and structure of the indigenous construction industry, as these will have a major influence on the effectiveness of any strategy adopted. In the UK

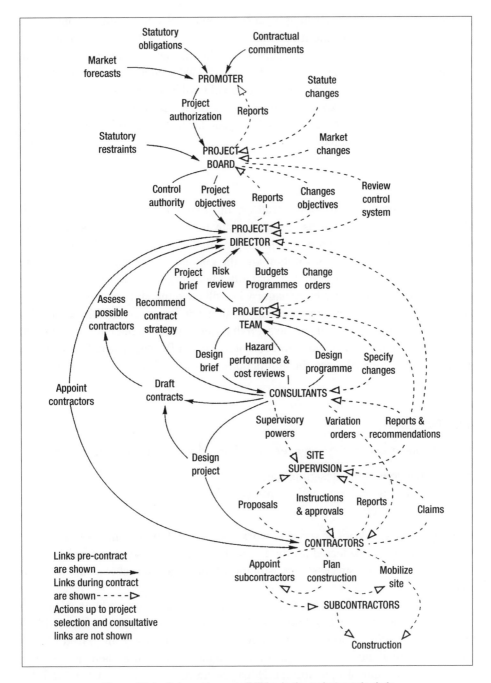

**Figure 30.1    Roles and responsibilities in the project supply chain**
*Source*: After Nunos and Wearne (1984)

construction industry, it has long been common practice to combine many of the roles in Figure 30.1 into the three fundamental roles listed above. Although not as popular as it was 20 years ago, this traditional procurement strategy still accounts for more than 50 per cent of all heavy civil engineering construction in the UK. It is also the basis for the Institution of Civil Engineers standard forms of contract, of which the seventh edition is the most recent version (1999). This strategy will therefore be outlined as a template against which other procurement strategies can be evaluated.

## THE CLIENT

In the traditional procurement strategy, the client is the organization which desires the project, often owns the site, usually funds the project and is frequently the end-user. (Often in property development the client is the developer, the eventual owner a financial institution and the end-user an organization that rents the building.) It is also assumed that the client organization will contain the project board and the project manager who will have the authority and expertise to commence the procurement of the design and construction phases of the project. From Figure 30.1, it can be seen that this equates to the internalization of the roles and links associated with Promoter, Project Board, Project Director and Project Team. Nevertheless these functions remain and have to be undertaken effectively.

## THE CONSULTANT

Consultants or consulting engineers are charged with three main functions:

- Management of the design process
- Assistance in tendering and contract administration
- Site supervision

Typically, a design brief or scope of works is prepared by the client organization and consultants are selected on the basis of the quality of service provision and fee competition. The successful consultant will then have direct contract with the client.

Changes are now occurring to improve the working of the traditional system. For some time, the ICE *Conditions of Contract* (1999) has been the most widely used model form of contract in the UK. This is despite its being based on the assumption that the consultant as well as being paid by the client is also the independent arbiter of the contract. However, more recently the ICE issued the *New Engineering Contract* (1995), which recognized for the first time the roles of 'designer', 'project manager' and 'site supervisor' as 'client agent' roles, with their duties and responsibilities defined accordingly. The role of independent arbiter is replaced by an external 'adjudicator', whose fees are paid equally by client and contractor (see Chapter 37). This was a major component of the Latham Report (1994). As we shall see, this new contract can apply to almost the complete range of procurement strategies and several clients are considering it as a direct replacement for contracts used in the traditional procurement strategy.

## THE MAIN CONTRACTOR

Traditionally, a single main contractor would be appointed, usually after the completion of the design, to undertake construction only. The contractor would have responsibilities for planning the works, mobilization, construction and opening or commissioning. However, the traditional procurement system contains some inherent characteristics that adversely affect and restrict the effective construction of the works. First, by precluding the contractor from the earliest stages of a project, the opportunity to incorporate construction expertise at an early and cost-effective stage is wasted and subsequent changes enforced by requirements of practicability are often costly. Second, the client and consultant may have been working on the project for many months or, on large projects, for a number of years. But at tender stage a contractor is given between eight and ten weeks to understand the project, to liaise with members of the supply chain, to assess the risk and to produce a tender price. This tender price has to be high enough to protect the contractor from the consequences of risks for which it has responsibility, but low enough to be successful in a competitive tendering system based on the lowest evaluated price being successful. Third, there is often pressure from the client for the contractor to commence work on site at the earliest possible opportunity. This is usually a false economy as a short period of pre-construction planning time can often result in substantial time and cost savings on site. These savings can often be shared in some way with the client.

## SUBCONTRACTORS

In the simplest form of contract, the main contractor may undertake the complete contract. However, it is common practice to make use of specialist subcontractors to undertake sections of the works. The subcontractor will have specific knowledge and expertise, with appropriately trained staff, which enables it to undertake specialist work more competitively than the main contractors. With or without subcontractors there will also be a supply chain of varying complexity consisting of vendors, suppliers and service providers.

## THE PROJECT MANAGER

So where in the traditional procurement system is the project management expertise? It is common for many organizations to 'manage by projects' and to employ key personnel as project managers. Indeed the client, the consultant, the contractor and the subcontractor may all have project managers. However, in terms of the complete project, it is the client's project manager that is considered to have responsibility for all the phases of a project and to execute the project management function. At some level inside the client organization, possibly the Board of Directors, a decision has to be made to authorize the project and to determine the terms of reference of the project manager. Terms are discussed in greater detail later in this chapter.

## THE PROCUREMENT PROCESS

One of the first actions of the project manager, after determining viability and degree of risk, is to determine the project objectives. In all projects the primary targets, time, cost and performance are important. However, it is likely that one will be dominant. There are a host of secondary and tertiary targets which need to be considered. Typically the degree of involvement of the client and/or the project manager, the innovation required, interfaces with external organizations, inclusion of international organizations and many other factors need to be considered to establish the clear aims of the project. Only if the project purpose and objectives can be clearly defined can the most appropriate procurement strategy be identified. However, events might occur that require modifications or changes to the project objectives, and constant monitoring is necessary. This cycle is illustrated in Figure 30.1 between the Project Board and Project Director.

The project manager then has to consider his or her own internal project team and the other main parties, the consultant and contractor. The project team conduct risk analyses and investment appraisal, undertake feasibility studies, develop the project brief and determine the procurement strategy. For each contract the project manager considers the project objectives in terms of the combined selection of an organizational structure, a contract type, a tendering strategy and a model form of contract. In the traditional procurement strategy the consultants are appointed on the basis of a project design brief and competitive tendering. The project team and the consultant will interact during the design process and in the preparation of construction contract documentation. After completion or substantial completion of the design, the contractor is appointed on the basis of a priced bill of quantities and competitive price. It is usual for the project team to have undertaken a prequalification exercise prior to tender. This is popular with both clients and contractors. Clients favour prequalification because it removes financially or technologically weak organizations and ensures a large competitive 'pool' of contractors, each of which is appointable. It is also popular with contractors because prequalification removes organizations without the necessary skills, experience and management expertise and allows them to compete with peer group members who will have similar costs and overheads. Interestingly enough the appointment of a subcontractor is more likely to be based on negotiation of the price with the organization identified as being the 'best partner' than on open competition.

As mentioned above, other parties involved in the project may have their own internal staff with the job title project manager. Their role is to act as the point of contact between the client's project manager and the organization's own staff and to manage their own component of the project to meet their predetermined targets and objectives. It is therefore an important part of the project team's brief to try to harmonize the goals of these other project managers with those of the client's project manager and of the project as far as is practicable.

For the rest of this chapter it is the role of the client's project manager, or the organization undertaking that role, which will form the basis for discussion, thereby providing a view through the whole project life cycle. The client's project manager has responsibilities, some of which are contractual and others non-contractual. Model forms of contract differ in their structure and in the allocation of risks and obligations. Consequently, the client's project manager could find most of the contractual roles imposed from a contract of engagement or employment and might not have a direct contractual role in the contract between client and contractor, as in the ICE seventh edition conditions of contract. Alternatively, the client's project manager could have a main contract role with specific obligations and duties, as discussed earlier in regard to the ICE new engineering document conditions of contract (1995).

## ROLES AND RESPONSIBILITIES IN ALTERNATIVE PROCUREMENT STRATEGIES

Other established procurement strategies exist in construction and in other sectors and disciplines, but all of these can be examined by comparison with the traditional system. For the purposes of this chapter two main types of procurement strategies will be discussed, integrated strategies and management strategies, but within each type there are a large number of variants.

## INTEGRATED STRATEGIES

As the name suggests the essence of this type of strategy is to integrate roles and responsibilities for phases of the project. In particular the design, engineering and construction phases are integrated, removing the interface which in practice is often a cause of dispute and conflict. Hence, the client, by giving a single organization responsibility for both phases, transfers the management of interface problems and any associated risks. However, this is offset by the client losing control over a major part of the project life cycle.

If the project life cycle, as shown in Figure 30.2, is studied, it is clear that the design and construction phases of the project coincide with the maximum capital investment and thus the roles and responsibilities of the parties at this stage are significant. Although there is a plethora of integrated procurement strategies they can be considered under three subcategories which reflect the extent of the project life cycle for which a single organization takes responsibility. From interrogation of Figure 30.2, we can identify subcategories, 'design and build', 'turnkey' and 'concession', with responsibilities ranging from part of design and construction phases to almost the whole project cycle.

### Design and build

The simplest of the three, the design and build strategy, requires the client, often with a consultant, to complete the usual front-end activities, but instead of appointing a contractor on the basis of a completed design, only an outline design or a design brief would have been prepared. The design and build contractor would then be responsible for the detailed design and the engineering or construction and the management of that interface. These contracts tend to be used for relatively straightforward work, where no significant risk or change is anticipated and when the client is able to specify precisely what is required. Usually but not always the contractor is paid on a fixed price, lump sum basis to provide an incentive for the contractor to be cost-effective and to limit the client's investment.

### Turnkey

Turnkey contracts as the name suggests are contracts where the client, on completion, turns a key in the door and everything is working to full operating standards. Consequently turnkey contractors have responsibility for the design, construction and commissioning phases of a project. Frequently this will also involve the procurement of all main items of plant and equipment. Under this strategy the client's project manager usually prepares a performance

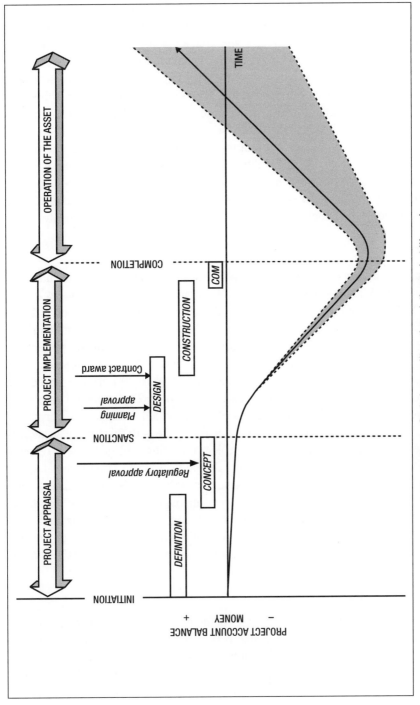

**Figure 30.2 Capital expenditure through the product life cycle**

The cumulative effect of several variable factors is to give a spectrum of uncertainty (shaded area) about the best prediction
*Source:* After Smith (1996)

579

specification and a scope document which determine the performance and the location and design constraints respectively. Due to the increased responsibility the cost of tendering is also increased and hence smaller numbers of bidders are invited. Typically selection is based on the evaluation of a two-package tender submission. Each bidder prepares a technical package containing process design, engineering design, procurement routes, erection and construction schedules and resources, certification and approval and commissioning procedures, and a financial package indicating the lump sum price and such breakdown as is required by the client. Once the contract has been placed the client role is severely limited and the client's ability to make any changes other than a formal contract variation is almost non-existent. The turnkey contractor's project manager has much greater multidisciplinary responsibilities and has to coordinate along the supply chain and across a series of project phase interfaces.

### Concession

The transfer of almost the entire project is the possibility considered under the concession or Finance–Build–Own–Operate–Transfer (FBOOT) strategy (Smith 1996). This approach was encouraged by the UK government in the early 1990s under the Private Finance Initiative and in the late 1990s under the Public Private Partnership Programme. This subcategory covers almost all of the project life cycle including operation and maintenance, and the functions, roles and responsibilities of most of the parties identified in Figure 30.1 are integrated into a single organization, usually known as the promoter. The promoter is often a single project joint venture of minimal asset value formed solely for the purpose of undertaking the project. The other principal difference with this type of strategy is that the promoter has to arrange the project financing and generate a revenue stream sufficient to service the debt, operate the facility and provide an adequate return. In this case the roles and responsibilities of the client's project manager are also transferred to the promoter's project manager but with the additional complexities caused by the promoter not being a single organization. The implications for the project manager are considerable and the effect of working within collaborative structures is investigated in greater detail later in the chapter.

### MANAGEMENT STRATEGIES

The key element in this group is the additional emphasis placed on management of the project. The underlying principle is that additional management expertise can be provided to the client and hence provide benefits in terms of fitness for purpose, buildability, performance and risk management that will more than offset the cost of the expertise. This additional management resource is provided to the client when it is required and removed on completion without affecting the number of permanent staff in the client's organization.

As shown in Figure 30.3, the parties operate in a different manner with the management contractor appearing as a separate entity and working closely with the client's staff and the client's project manager in particular. The management contractor would be appointed at a very early stage in the project. The type of organization operating in this role in the UK could be a consultant but is usually a contractor who would be experienced in the type of work and would otherwise be a likely tender bidder. In the of role of management contractor a small team drawn from the contracting organization's staff would be selected and engaged usually on the basis of fee reimbursement plus profit margin. Naturally, to avoid possible conflicts of interest, the organization is then excluded from tendering for any of the works contracts. The management contractor works extremely closely with the client's project manager, almost like additional client staff and it would therefore be counter-productive to place harsh or onerous performance terms on the management contractor.

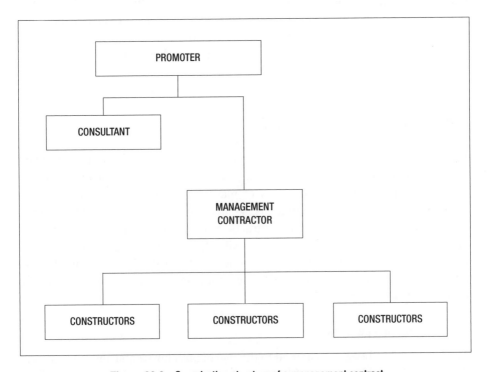

**Figure 30.3   Organization structure of a management contract**
*Source*: After Smith (1996)

**581**

The other parties have slightly modified roles also. The consultant is now engaged by the management contractor and will liaise on buildability and practical issues of design throughout the contract. The other different feature clearly shown in Figure 30.3 is that the use of a single main contractor has been replaced by a series of work package contracts. The management contractor selects and manages these contracts, and solves any interface problems which may arise between them. Each contract could vary, with some lump sum fixed price and some cost reimbursable, dependent upon risk and time constraints. By packaging the work into such small components, the contracts can be used to give greater client flexibility to overlap sections of the work and to assist with risk management. Hence to be effective the contract must produce benefits to the project manager in terms of access, flexibility to make change and effective management of construction which are less than the cost of engaging the management contractor team.

Each work package contract is managed by the management contractor in conjunction with the client's project manager on behalf of the client. Consequently the client has no privity of contract, that is no direct contractual relationship with the consultant or works contractors, which places much greater importance on the relationship between client's project manager and the management contractor. It is important that there is a degree of trust and common commitment if the contract is to be undertaken to reach its maximum potential benefit.

## EMERGING PROCUREMENT ROUTES

During the 1990s there was a clear trend away from adversarial contracting strategies towards collaborative working, which has direct implications for the role and responsibilities of the project manager. In any type of collaborative working, there is a need to align goals, so incentives are often used, and there is a need for new agreements and contracts and a greater requirement for good management practice. Chapter 31 deals with the different types of collaborative working in detail, so this chapter will concentrate on the implications of these different organizational and contractual combinations from the viewpoint of the project manager.

### Joint ventures and partnering

The industry has been accustomed to the use of both horizontal and vertical joint ventures (JVs) and consortia for many years. More recently other forms have become apparent, including the various forms of partnering, such as alliancing, term partnering, project specific partnering, and forms of collaborative ventures to form promoter groups for Private Finance Initiative (PFI) projects. To operate these forms of procurement requires a culture change within organizations and, more importantly, requires new project management skills to deal with a range of new roles and responsibilities.

## Public Private Partnership (PPP)

Public private partnerships (PPPs) are a separate class of organizations which operate in a variety of ways but share the obvious common feature of having both public and private sector funding. Many projects which are politically desirable, in other words that have a higher social cost–benefit analysis than their financial analysis, cannot be funded by private finance on commercial terms. Their viability is ensured by the public sector reducing project risk to an acceptable level. The use of direct public debt financing is used very much as a last resort and risk sharing, concessions for existing revenue generating facilities and the provision of indirect benefits like tax holidays are more likely to be adopted. Nevertheless, if there is public sector involvement the public sector will want to be included in the project management process. Working within these hybrid organizations, the project manager is confronted by the culture clash between the two types of organizations and yet still has to make effective project decisions.

## Dispute resolution

Disputes and more importantly dispute resolution are key issues in any collaborative agreement (see Chapter 37). Increasingly, the project manager is involved in finding equitable, speedy and cheap methods of resolving disputes and maintaining focus on the project. If disputes are left for any length of time they can affect trust and commitment to the project, and the long-term stability of the collaborative agreement could be at stake. At the most extreme levels, parties might leave and need to be replaced; an option which should have been foreseen and allowed for by the negotiation of an agreement which allows for equitable withdrawal as well as equitable entry. However, the vast majority of disputes do not fall into that category and are often suitable for alternative dispute resolution (ADR) procedures.

ADR has been adopted in most countries around the world. It can be simplified as a series of six steps (Figure 30.4). The lower two steps, 'prevention' and 'negotiation', are present in all model forms of contract and are a core part of the traditional roles and responsibilities. Similarly the final two steps, 'arbitration' and 'litigation', are also available to most contracts, although sometimes they can only

**583**

| Steps | Cost/Hostility | Name | Process |
|---|---|---|---|
| 1 | Low | Prevention | Risk allocation, Incentives for cooperation, Partnering |
| 2 | | Negotiation | Direct negotiations, Step negotiations |
| 3 | | Independent Expert | Dispute review board, Standing arbitrator or Independent expert |
| 4 | | Mediation | Non-binding resolution, Mini-trial, Advisory opinion, Advisory arbitration |
| 5 | | Arbitration | Binding resolution |
| 6 | High | Litigation | Civil Court, Judge, Jury |

**Figure 30.4   Dispute resolution steps**

*Source*: After Dispute Avoidance and Resolution Task Force (DART) Report

be used on completion of the contract and tend to be lengthy and expensive. It is the middle two steps which as compulsory procedures form the basis for ADR, namely 'independent expert' and 'mediation'. Any dispute which cannot be satisfactorily resolved by negotiation, goes to the independent expert. This person, agreed upon before the start of the contract, is provided with both sides of a dispute, usually within specific and fairly limited time periods. The expert then responds within another fixed period of time with an expert opinion of the issues. This is purely an expert view, it is not legally constituted, it is not binding and it need not be equitable, but it does give the parties to the dispute a view of how the matter is likely to be viewed by others. This is sufficient sometimes for one party to accept another view on a dispute. However, if the expert's view does not result in any resolution, then the next step is mediation. A trained mediator, who ideally is not a lawyer, is agreed by both parties and his or her fees are paid jointly by the parties. A mediator tries to establish a middle ground position which is less than either side really wants but hopefully is close enough to convince the parties to settle with no real winners or losers. Again this is not mandatory but the parties are aware that unless a settlement is reached at this stage the next stage will involve legal representation, will be time-consuming and will be expensive.

## The project manager

Although the role of project manager is similar in any collaborative venture, the longer the duration of the collaborative agreement the more difficult it becomes for the project manager to resolve the dichotomy of working with long-established but time-limited partners. In one sense the role is facilitated by increased knowledge, understanding, trust and commitment but complicated by the finite nature of relations and the commercial imperatives of possible future competitive strengths.

### Splitting the roles of the engineer

The Institution of Civil Engineers has produced a new model form of contract, *The New Engineering Contract* (NEC) (1995), which recognizes the trend towards collaborative working and highlights the need for good project management. One of the main features of this contract is the replacement of the previously pivotal role of the engineer with a set of client's agent roles, namely 'designer', 'supervisor' and 'project manager', and with the new role of adjudicator, an external role supported equally by payments from client and contractor. On small projects the three client's agent roles might be undertaken by a single person but normally this form of contract is giving clear cognizance to the three complementary roles which were formerly imposed on the engineer.

This contract is to be commended as a valuable attempt to clarify this difficult area of the roles and responsibilities of the project manager for construction contracts. The more traditional contract does not formally identify a project manager role and the precise nature of responsibilities is variable from organization to organization and from project to project. The NEC has provided a degree of certainty and common understanding for this complex problem.

## STANDARD TERMS FOR PROJECT MANAGERS

Despite the relative longevity of the role and function of the project manager, progress has been very slow on the development of model forms of engagement. To date project managers have been employed using standard contracts for service providers, consultants and others, modified for the purpose, or bespoke forms of contract. Naturally the terms recommend appointing only qualified project managers and it is expected that they will be appointed in the earliest stages of the project.

In the UK in 1998, the APM developed a set of standard terms for the appointment of a project manager (APM 1998). As with any model form, these terms are applicable to any project, in any location at any time and are drafted under English Law. Needless to say, there is a mechanism for incorporating relevant specific project data; in this case it is known as the schedule of particulars. Like all model forms, these terms will bring benefits in understanding, ease of use and common documentation if they become widely established.

The flexibility and applicability of the standard terms is further increased by having a permanent set of core terms and the choice of one from a number of sector specific schedules of services. One of the first tasks of the contract is to provide precise definitions of terms. In this document the 'client' is identified as the project manager's employer. The schedule of services will contain a listing and the client and the other stakeholders will decide what is to be added or deleted from the schedule to suit the particular project under consideration.

Payment is always a key issue. The terms contain a fee schedule for payment to the project manager on the basis of fixed prices, time-related charges and/or reimbursement of expenses. The issue of incentives is important, particularly as many projects are undertaken on an incentive basis. Should the project manager be paid at a professional rate with no variation or should a related incentive be linked to either the main contract or client satisfaction? Should even part of the fee be at risk if the project manager fails to perform? At present these options are not included in the standard terms but could be added if required.

## FUTURE TRENDS

In the UK, the construction industry has been relatively slow to innovate despite the advantages of improvements in other sectors and the general advances in establishing the discipline of project management. The introduction of the Construction Design and Management Regulations, the Latham Report (1994) and more recently the Egan Construction Task Force Report (1998) has indicated a move towards a more project-focused, collaborative system of working and sharing best practice and world class performance.

Managing by projects is now becoming accepted across all sectors of industry. Even service provider organizations are moving towards the mechanism of internal and external projects as the basis for strategic development, managing change and adopting best practice. The emphasis given to the 'front-end' activities by project management has enhanced its appeal to general business in addition to the more traditionally project-based sectors. This spread of project management is likely to continue. It is interesting to note that European bankers recently publicized the 'project' to introduce the Euro, a term which would not have been used a few years ago.

It is always difficult to predict the future but in essence this is what project management is about. Hence to foresee the future of project management itself is even more of a challenge. However, a number of issues stand out. Business in general is moving towards operating the concept of sustainability. This has implications for the wider contractual environment and the role of the public, or society, in projects. Equally people are increasingly concerned about environmental and community issues and the temporary and permanent effects caused by the implementation and subsequent operation of projects. The roles and responsibilities of project managers are likely to be widened to incorporate these additional demands. Indeed, until any project, in any location, at any date can be guaranteed to be completed on time, within budget and to the specified quality there will always be a need for project managers.

## REFERENCES AND FURTHER READING

Association for Project Management (1998), *Standard Terms for the Appointment of a Project Manager*, APM, High Wycombe.

Egan, J. (1998), *Rethinking Construction*, Construction Task Force Report, London.

Institution of Civil Engineers (1999), *Conditions of Contract and Forms of Tenders, Agreements and Bonds for Use in Connection with Works of Civil Engineering Construction*, 6th edition, Thomas Telford, London.

Institution of Civil Engineers (1995), *The New Engineering Contract*, 2nd edition, Thomas Telford, London.

Latham, Sir Michael (1994), *Constructing the Team: Final Report of the Government/Industry Review of Procurement and Contractual Arrangements in the UK Construction Industry*, The Stationery Office, London.

Nunos, G. E and Wearne, S. H. (1984) *Responsibilities for Project Control during Construction*, School of Technological Management, University of Bradford.

Smith, N. J. (ed.) (1996), *Engineering Project Management*, Blackwell Scientific, Oxford.

Turner, J. R. (1995), *The Commercial Project Manager*, McGraw-Hill, London.

## RELATED TOPICS

# 31 Partnering, benchmarking and alliances

## *Denise Bower and Fotis Skountzos*

The 1990s were characterized by a need to seek new strategies to lower costs and to gain competitive advantage. This chapter discusses how the construction industry uses partnering, benchmarking and incentive contracts to improve its efficiency and provide customer satisfaction. Partnering is an approach to conducting business in an environment where attitudes are changing rapidly. It is the affirmation by all in the construction process that they want to work together. It should not be seen as a cosy arrangement. Benchmarking can assist performance improvement in partnering arrangements and thereby deliver additional benefits. This chapter also identifies the importance of motivation through the application of incentive schemes as a tool to stretch the standards in the construction industry. Even though incentives are not unique in partnering arrangements, they are used to reinforce the behaviour expectations and promote a more proactive, cooperative relationship between the parties.

## BACKGROUND

Relationships in the construction industry have always tended to be adversarial, with the parties resorting to contractual claims and litigation, which lengthen timescales and increase costs. These adversarial relationships and the industry fragmentation were identified by the Latham Report (1994) as major barriers to improving quality and productivity. The modern competitive environment has lead to an increased need for enhanced productivity and reduced cost. Partnering as a construction method aims to remove the traditional barriers between client and contractor and provide the framework which will ensure that all who are involved in the project understand their objectives and are working towards the same end.

In the early twenty-first century, organizations must gain a competitive edge both domestically and internationally (see Chapter 2). The modern business environment and intense global competition have created the need for organizations to compare themselves with the best in the world, learn from them and try to overtake them. As a result of this, there have been many initiatives encouraging improvement in various sectors within the construction industry, which has practised benchmarking as a technique for continuous improvement to enhance achievements in areas such as cost reduction, timely delivery and safety. In a partnering arrangement benchmarking can assist performance improvements and establish a continuous improvement philosophy.

The acknowledgement of the important role of motivation and its influence on project success has led to the increased use of incentive schemes in contracts. Incentives are used as a tool to align the project objectives of the client and contractor and not just to motivate the contractor. It is of great importance that incentives for all participants link their performance to the project objectives. Incentives are a key element of achieving commonality in partnering.

## PARTNERING

Contracting in the construction industry is very competitive and highly risky. In many instances the perception of conflicting objectives among the parties involved in a construction project leads to adversarial, confrontational and unrewarding relationships (Associated General Contractors of America 1991). The application of the concept of partnering came into existence in the US construction industry in the early 1980s as an effort to improve the relationships between the different parties involved in the construction process. Partnering plays a key role in attaining continuous improvement in design and delivery of construction projects, with latest reports suggesting that cost savings of 40 per cent can be achieved. It has encouraged parties to the construction process to solve problems and eliminate waste, thus promising to change the adversarial culture of the industry. The partnering approach relies on the idea that the best conflict resolution strategy is one that prevents conflicts from occurring. Therefore the main objective of partnering is to encourage all parties to a contract to change their relationship from adversarial to cooperative. This change in relationships requires changes in attitudes to achieve mutual trust, respect and open communication among all parties involved (Abudayyeh 1994).

### THE BASICS OF PARTNERING

The Construction Industry Institute defines partnering as:

a long-term commitment between two or more organisations in achieving common project objectives by maximising resource effectiveness.

(CII 1991)

The key elements are trust, long-term commitment and shared vision. In partnering, trust develops confidence and encourages open communication, exchange of ideas and sharing of resources. Long-term commitment allows constant improvement of technology and methods, reinforces the mutuality of the parties, reduces the rivalry of the traditional contracting system, reduces the attractiveness of litigation and introduces feelings of camaraderie among the parties. Shared vision is the set of common project objectives, formed by consensus through open expectations and established within a candid environment (CII 1991; Crowley and Karim 1995). Partnering is primarily an attitude adjustment where the parties to the contract form a relationship of teamwork, cooperation and good faith performance. The parties are required to look beyond the strict bounds of the contract to develop this cooperative working relationship which promotes their common goals and objectives.

Partnering has been defined in many ways:

Partnering is a new word for being reasonable, conscientious, and professional. For those who have always kept their goals in sight it is not new, it is just effective project management

(Larson 1995)

Partnering is a synergy – a co-operative, collaborative management effort among contracting and related parties to complete a project in the most efficient, cost-effective method possible, by setting common goals, keeping lines of communication open, and solving problems together as they arise.

(American Arbitration Association 1993)

[Construction partnering means] developing a co-operative management team with key players from the organization involved in a construction contract. The team focuses on common goals and benefits to be achieved through contract execution and develops processes to keep the team working towards those goals. Partnering means exercising leadership for the entire engineering team.

(US Army Corps of Engineers 1991)

Partnering is a management approach used by two or more organisations to achieve specific business objectives by maximising the effectiveness of each participant's resources. The approach is based on mutual objectives, an agreed method of problem resolution and an active search for continuous measurable improvements.

(Bennet and Jayes 1995)

Partnering can therefore be simply defined as a relationship in which (Cook and Hancher 1990):

- all seek win-win solutions;
- value is placed in long-term relationships;
- trust and openness are norms;
- an environment for profit exists;
- all are encouraged to openly address any problem;
- all understand that neither benefits from exploitation of the other;
- innovation is encouraged;
- each party is aware of the other's needs, concerns and objectives, and is interested in helping their partner achieve them.

It is also important to be aware of what partnering is not (CIB 1997):

Partnering is not a new buzz word for marketers to bandy about to make the same old product more saleable. It also is not:

- A new form of construction contract – it is a procedure for making relationships work better
- An excuse for not working hard to get the best from suppliers and customers
- A soft option
- A quick fix for a weak business – strong players make each other stronger, weak ones destroy each other
- Only about systems and methods – it is about people, enabling them to operate more effectively and efficiently

## FORMS OF PARTNERING

Partnering can be based on a single project (project specific partnering) or on a long-term commitment (strategic partnering). Both project specific and strategic partnering can play a significant role in moving the construction industry away from the traditional adversarial approach.

Project specific partnering is defined as:

a method of applying project specific management in the planning, design and construction profession without the need for unnecessary, excessive, and/or debilitating external party involvement.

(Stephenson 1996)

Strategic partnering is defined as:

a formal partnering relationship that is designed to enhance the success of multiproject experiences on a long-term basis. Just as each individual project must be maintained, a strategic partnership must also be maintained by a periodic review of all projects currently being performed.

(Stephenson 1996)

Project specific partnering suggests a project is entered into with specific sets of objectives which may not be adaptable to a long-term commitment. The main concern for project specific partnering is the time available to set all the essential features in place, and still manage to maintain a successful project. One of the benefits of a project specific partnership is that it has greater long-term significance than strategic partnering for several reasons:

- It does not restrict market entry.
- Price features and improvements are easier to monitor in the relationship.
- Stimulation for competition still exists.

Dedication at the highest levels will have to embrace the project specific partnering philosophy sufficiently to make it work. The mechanisms of joint workshops and facilitators obviously have an influence on the partnering process and the cooperation of participants should allow partnering to generate its own momentum. The challenge of project specific partnering is to allow the benefits available from a strategic partnering arrangement to operate without adversarial relationships developing.

Strategic partnering provides increasing benefits from the lessons learnt on earlier partnered projects. It involves the development of a broader framework focusing on long-term issues, therefore the benefits and problems will be extended to another project to enhance success. Strategic partnering can be used to deal with a planned increase in construction activity that a client is unable to handle with existing staff. It is sensible to start a strategic partnering arrangement by identifying and ranking market sectors in terms of their suitability for partnering. In identifying a market that could provide a basis for partnering, it is important to consider the following recommendations (Hensey 1997):

- Establish a benchmark of performance in the market.
- Define criteria for acceptance or rejection of the potential partner's performance.
- Chart a clear plan for further performance improvements as the partnering arrangement develops.

## THE KEY ELEMENTS OF PARTNERING

It has been suggested that the essence of partnering is the recognition of common goals and the creation of an atmosphere of trust, teamwork and goodwill, which will facilitate the achievement of these goals. The European Construction Institute (ECI) classifies the key elements of successful partnering in two categories: the attitudinal factors and the techniques and procedures of partnering. The two elements of the latter category will be examined through the partnering process, as they represent well-tried and successful practices for achieving harmonious working relationships and can be applied advantageously,

**593**

with greater or lesser formality, to projects of all sizes. Together they constitute the structured management framework of partnering (ECI 1997). The attitudinal factors include commitment, trust, development of mutual goals and objectives, and a change of culture.

## Commitment

The most important element in establishing a partnering relationship is commitment. Commitment of all parties, as well as everyone with a stake in the relationship, to the shared vision and goals of the project begins with top management and is built into all levels of the project team. Much dedication and hard work by all management levels will be needed to change the traditional adversarial manner of the construction industry. Periodic meetings will ensure the continued commitment of stakeholders, introduce new participants to the partnering process and reinforce team goals. A long-term relationship creates an atmosphere in which companies can achieve a competitive advantage by addressing problems in areas that require constant improvement or extensive time to solve.

## Trust

Partnering is founded on trust. Teamwork is not possible if there is cynicism about others' motives. There is better understanding through the development of personal relationships and communication of the goals and the risks undertaken by each stakeholder. With understanding comes trust and with trust comes the possibility for a synergistic relationship. The partners must recognize that by sharing information, accepting diminished control of a part of its operations and tolerating contact with outsiders, each firm can obtain benefits that would exceed the firm's individual capability. Trust serves to combine the resources and knowledge of the partners in a fashion intended to eliminate adversarial relationships.

## Mutual goals and objectives

A fundamental requirement of partnering is to agree mutual goals and objectives. Their role is to ensure that everyone's best interest will be served by concentrating on the success of the project as a whole. Bennet and Jayes (1995) suggest that issues such as improved efficiency, cost reduction, guaranteed profits, fast construction, shared risks, reliable flow of design information and lower legal costs, to quote a few, may be included in the mutually agreed objectives. In finding common ground, the parties soon realize that 'they are in this together' and that success is dependent upon their commitment and ability to work as a team.

## Culture

A crucial issue in any partnering arrangement is the attitude of the various parties. Traditional adversarial attitudes do not work, and hence the need for a change in culture. At the outset of the relationship, the parties must have the fundamental belief that they are embarking on a project of mutual benefits, with common goals and objectives. A shift from the 'win-lose' strategy to a 'win-win' plan is imperative. Successful partnering is based on principle-centred working relationships among stakeholders and not on contractual, legal-based relationships.

The partnership cannot run itself, no matter how strong the commitment of management and the participants. It is widely supported that a partnering champion should be appointed at an early stage to promote the partnering concept and culture to the organization, and maintain them throughout the life of the project. The champion will provide the administrative and logistical support that is required to make the partnering agreement work. His or her activities will include scheduling and arranging follow-up meetings, distributing information to all parties and follow-up of procedures and plans developed in partnering meetings. Since partnering promotes success in achieving goals that are of paramount interest to the project manager – quality, cost management, safety and profit, to name a few – he or she would be the logical choice for champion. However, a vital point to remember is that it takes the entire team to make it work.

Partnering is not appropriate on all projects, nor is the size of the project the sole criterion for deciding to partner. The parties that consider embarking on a partnering relationship should identify the sources of risk associated with the project (see Chapter 21) and assess which party is most capable of managing them. It should be accepted that every party is entitled to make a profit and that risks and rewards must be shared fairly. The parties should also be prepared to commit themselves to the partnering principles. It should be kept in mind throughout the process that the focus of partnering is to build cooperative relationships, avoid or minimize disputes and actively pursue the attainment of common goals by the contracting parties.

Following the decision to try partnering on a particular project or contract, and having completed the process designed to provide an environment for developing the cooperative attitude and commitment, the next step is to select the partners. Although the basic principles may be the same, different procedures are applied

**595**

for the private and public sector clients. In its most effective form partnering will encompass the entire supply chain, including clients, contractors, subcontractors and suppliers in the relationship. The process of selection of partners applies equally to any of the relationships in this chain. The selection is based more on soft issues, such as the parties' understanding and views of partnering, the relevant experience, the resources to be allocated to the project, their management experience and the quality procedures. ECI's *Partnering in the Public Sector* (1997) introduces a five-step selection process:

1. Brief contractors on commitment to partner.
2. Advertise the intention of the client, including the intent to partner.
3. Pre-qualify potential tenderers.
4. Award contract to successful tenderers.
5. Debrief successful tenderers.

It is best to initiate the partnering process as quickly as possible and start aligning objectives, creating trust and establishing teamwork among all those concerned with the project. The workshop is a vital tool for any partnering project. (The workshop may involve the value management workshop process described in Chapter 14 or the start-up workshop process described in Chapter 24). The workshop should be run by an independent facilitator and held at a neutral location. The substance and successful outcome of the workshop are far more important than the mechanics of conducting it. Issues to be addressed during the workshop include the following (Harback, Basham and Buhts 1994):

1. Communication guidelines and ground rules
2. General partnering concepts
3. An understanding of conflict and conflict management
4. Choice of a partnership name
5. Improvement of team communications
6. Development of a mission statement
7. Team discussion and quality indicators
8. Development of partnership goals
9. Stages of team evolution
10. Follow-on task for the partnership
11. The partnering charter.

The initial workshop should be followed by regular reviews and follow-up workshops to assess the progress of the partnership, keep the parties focused and ensure that the actions taken are consistent with the charter objectives.

The partnering charter is the threshold document in which the parties set forth their mission statement, mutual goals and objectives, and commitment to the partnering relationship. There is no single approach to drafting a partnering charter. The charter should include a mission statement expressing the partners' commitment and agreement to communicate openly and to share information in order to avoid surprises. The partnering charter should also include specific, identifiable goals and objectives, such as:

- delivering the product or service ahead of schedule;
- identifying problems at the first opportunity;
- jointly resolving problems at the lowest possible level;
- seeking fair treatment for all participants;
- limiting cost growth;
- eliminating litigation through the use of alternative dispute resolution (ADR) procedures.

When the parties have established their goals and objectives, they must ensure that they are mutually agreed upon, so that everyone will be actively focused on achieving them. The charter is drawn up during the initial workshop by the participants with the assistance of the facilitator. It must be signed by all the participants in the workshop. Copies of the charter are to be displayed in head and site offices.

The facilitators are not members of the technical or managerial group. They are independent and objective individuals, skilled in team building and group dynamics. They manage the process of the meetings, and not what is decided. Their attention is focused on how decisions are made. Sometimes they may serve to gather information for all team members to support the decision-making process. Above all, the facilitators must remain neutral on the subject under discussion, and their goal is to assist the team in reaching consensus.

The aim of the monitoring process is to ensure that the objectives set out in the partnering charter remain on track. The monitoring criteria, established at the initial partnering workshop, relate both to relationships and to project performance. Performance evaluation reports are normally made monthly, by individual members of the client and contractor organization appointed either at or immediately after the initial workshop. In general, the performance evaluation procedures help to remedy problems that have occurred on the project because of delays in getting the process started.

Continuous improvement should be the prime concern of all parties involved in the project, since without a commitment to it the full range of benefits from partnering will not be realized. Continuous improvement is not possible without benchmarking. Any improvements made to a process should be developed and approved by both parties, and be beneficial to both parties. The continuous improvement process should start at the lowest level possible within the contract and should involve the people who are going to be directly affected by the area of improvement. Furthermore, it should operate in a similar way to quality circles. By continually reviewing the performance of all parties against set objectives it is possible to see an improvement in the project in terms of quality, productivity gains, increased efficiency and staff development.

If an atmosphere of 'trust, dedication to common goals and an understanding of each others expectations and values' is to be maintained, potential disputes must be addressed quickly, effectively and at the lowest possible level. A ladder of dispute resolution should be established with dispute identification and resolution being taken care of by the parties at an operational level where possible. Only where internal resolution has failed, or will do greater harm than good, should the parties look towards the external dispute resolution methods advocated by the Latham Report (1994). Resolving disputes at the lowest level reduces the number of escalated disputes that must be resolved by management and consequently reduces unwanted strain in the relationship. At the initial workshop a dispute escalation ladder is usually set up. The non-contractual dispute resolution procedure should be agreed post-contract at the initial workshop and incorporated into the partnering arrangement.

Julia Pokora and Colin Hastings (reported by Chartlett 1996) identified nine key building blocks for creating effective partnership performance:

1. *Effective screening for fit* There should be compatibility between organizations if they are to work together. There may be problems where the history, culture, values, management style and systems of the partners are not compatible.
2. *The right contractual foundation* A contractual base, which encourages joint problem-solving, information-sharing and risk-taking, should be sought. There should be a move away from an adversarial approach to working and a move towards joint incentives to minimize costs and maximize performance.
3. *Agreeing what the stakeholders want* Different stakeholders have different priorities and success criteria. Stakeholders should be encouraged to be explicit about what is important to them and ways should be devised for exploring and resolving differences in the spirit of problem-solving, rather than attempting to avoid or minimize potential areas of conflict.
4. *Team start-up and team building* Personal relationships and shared understanding can be developed through team start-up workshops.
5. *Making visible different capabilities* Partners should exchange knowledge and experience in a mutually advantageous way. It therefore needs to be established what knowledge and experience each organization has for exchange.

598

6. *Joint scoping*   The client and key parties must work together in defining the scope and specification of the project. There must be a determination to reach a commonly understood and agreed view of what is to be done and how it is to be done.

7. *Partnership information and communication systems*   Compatibility of information and communication systems of each participating organization needs to be ensured.

8. *Ground rules for cooperation*   There must be a charter or agreement which summarizes the expectations of each party and outlines their aspirations for how they want to work, the behaviours expected of people and the practical methodologies used to achieve this.

9. *Learning review and dissemination*   Where the relationship is to endure beyond the initial project, there will be a period of evolution in an innovative way. Attention needs to be paid to the learning process and systems established for reviewing this learning process. Where good practice is established it may be beneficial to disseminate it to others.

## BENEFITS OF PARTNERING

For all the stakeholders of a project, partnering is a high-leveraged effort. It may require increased staff and management time up front, but the benefits accrue in a more harmonious, less confrontational process, resulting in a successful project, without litigation and claims. The partnering process empowers the project personnel and all stakeholders with the freedom and authority to accept responsibility and do their jobs by encouraging decision-making and problem-solving at the lowest possible level of authority.

Substantial benefits can be gained by all members of a project who embrace the partnering concept. For the design professional these might include a reduced exposure to construction claims, a reduction in the shifting of risks inherent in design and construction, an enhanced role in providing design and construction phase services, and a restoration of the ability to provide interpretations of design intent and solutions to problems. Design professionals should expect decreased operational expenses because of the reduction in time and cost spent defending claims and meritless demands, and in preparing to participate in contractor and owner litigation. Finally, they should expect an increased opportunity for successful project completion because of the non-adversarial climate.

Although there is continued room for further refinement, the results so far have been very encouraging. There are many benefits of the partnering process (Baden Hellard 1995; Cook and Hancher 1990; Busch and Pinnell 1994;

**599**

Stephenson 1996; Larson 1995; Weston and Gibson 1993). This section briefly describes those most noticeable to all parties involved.

## Mutual benefits

- Lower risk of time and cost overruns as the contractor and client are working together to complete the project.
- Completion on time.
- Reduced exposure to litigation – efficient resolution of problems.
- Less confrontation through informal conflict management procedures. The sharing of information and the environment of trust contribute to the swift solving of problems, before they escalate to disputes.
- Avoidance of litigation through a jointly developed dispute resolution mechanism.
- Improved performance and project quality. There is a higher quality because energies are focused on the ultimate goal of construction and not misdirected to adversarial concerns.
- Early anticipation and resolution of problems. The partners proactively anticipate problems and design an action plan addressing how those problems will be jointly resolved or avoided. They recognize problems will occur during contract performance and that the existence of these problems does not mean that their relationship has failed.
- Reduced administration and oversight. With increased communication and empowerment by senior management, partners find a significant reduction in the need for layers of administration. Furthermore, a reduction in administration costs has been observed.
- Reduced time and cost of contract performance. By establishing open communication as a guiding principle, parties to partnering arrangements have found that issues are raised more expeditiously. This enables the partners to meet or exceed contractual schedule requirements and avoid costly mistakes or rework.
- Increased innovation through open communication and trust, especially in the development of value engineering, changes and constructability improvements.
- Increased opportunity for a financially successful project because of the non-adversarial, 'win-win' attitude.
- Buildable designs.
- Improved safety. Taking joint responsibility for ensuring a safe work environment for contractor and client employees reduces the risk of hazardous work conditions and avoids workplace accidents.

### Benefits to the client

- Reduced cost associated with contractor selection, contract administration, mobilization and the learning curve of beginning a project with a new contractor.
- Reduction in fixed overheads.
- Reduced involvement of senior management in handling adversarial claims.
- Effective utilization of personnel resources.
- Better opportunity for innovation and value engineering.

### Benefits to the contractor

- Secured profits and better cash flow, through more realistic pricing and regular payments.
- The long-term, non-adversarial aspects of partnering imply that revenues may be more stable.
- Opportunity to refine and develop new skills in a controlled and low risk environment.
- Optimum use of resources.
- Improved productivity and lower administrative costs, due to focus on the project rather than on case-building.
- Lower overhead costs.

Clients seem to be attracted to partnering due to the growing body of evidence that suggests that partnering can deliver the 30 per cent cost savings advocated by the Latham Report (Hosie 1997). On the other hand, it can be argued that the appeal of partnering to the contractors is that it can offer long-term relationships and more secure profits. However attractive partnering may be to both clients and contractors, there are barriers that may inhibit its successful application.

## BARRIERS TO SUCCESSFUL PARTNERING

Partnering represents a significant change in the way projects are managed in the construction industry. Such change is likely to meet resistance. A study by Larson and Drexler (1997) revealed that barriers to successful partnering might stem from five main themes. A summary of their findings is presented below.

### Mistrust and interpersonal barriers to cooperation

These barriers include failure to build a true relationship of trust, fear of the unknown and change, differing values and culture, and a lack of understanding of risks and how they are redistributed in a partnering environment. Many people have an instinctive suspicion of the other party due to their past experiences. They are concerned that information divulged could be used against them at a later day. They also cannot admit that there is another way. In summary, it can be said that some people simply cannot accept partnering as a long-term way of doing business.

### The nature and structure of projects that inhibit partnering

The main barrier here appears to be related to government and legal issues. Public projects require complete documents and a fixed price, precluding full partnering. The construction industry seems to be too reliant on legal protection. Furthermore, the low bid methods of awarding projects appear to lead to built-in conflict. Other project structure issues identified as barriers include the internal bureaucracy at many companies, difficulty in finding the appropriate partner and the fact that some projects are simply not appropriate for partnering.

### Perceptions of the partnering process that discourage partnering

A number of factors associated with the partnering process itself were identified as barriers. The first of these was the perceived lack of common goals among the parties involved in the construction industry. Real-time cost associated with trying to align both organizations with every undertaking was also identified as a barrier. Project planning was claimed to be often inadequate. Finally, partnering costs were seen as too costly in an industry that prides itself on operating 'lean and mean'. The importance of these perceptions increases if one considers that an expected consequence of partnering is cost reduction.

### Knowledge and skill barriers

Unfamiliarity with or misunderstanding of partnering concepts were identified as important barriers. Others were the inexperience in this type of approach to contracting, the lack of understanding of the partner companies' culture and 'old-fashioned management'.

### The lack of firm commitment to partnering

The level of commitment, or lack thereof, especially from top management, was identified as a barrier.

## BENCHMARKING

Benchmarking, in its current form, is derived from the work of Robert Camp in the late 1970s. Essentially it has a number of key characteristics. It is a management tool that has its roots in the business environment. It is used to identify changes needed in products and processes to achieve better company performance. From a comparison of the manufacture of photocopiers in the USA and Japan, Camp (1989, 1995) devised a model of benchmarking supported by a number of steps. It involves analysing an existing situation, identifying and measuring factors critical to the success of the product or process, comparing them with other businesses, analysing the results and implementing an action plan to achieve better performance. Since then a number of models and processes have been developed and applied across a broad range of subject areas (Pickrell and Garnett 1996).

Benchmarking definitions have mainly been derived from experiences in manufacturing. There are slight deviations in definitions, depending on the focus and scope of application. According to Camp (1989), 'Benchmarking is the search for industry best practices that lead to superior performance.' In this definition the author portrays a very generalized view of benchmarking. The focus is on adopting the best practices or methods to achieve superior performance. The definition implies that the best practices are to be pursued, regardless of where they exist.

### BENCHMARKING IN CONSTRUCTION

The focus of benchmarking in manufacturing is the ability to meet customer requirements and to adopt innovative practices regardless of their source. Over the years manufacturing organizations have developed measures to assess their performance. Construction, because of the diversity of its products and processes, is one of the last industries to embrace objective performance measurement. This does not diminish the potential benefits that can be derived. However, benchmarking attempts in construction are bound to face difficulties. The fact that a number of organizations get involved in designing and constructing a single project, and the temporary nature of the construction process, make the benchmarking task a complex one.

Benchmarking only works if consistent methods of measuring the performance of operations can be developed and introduced. Such methods do not exist in the construction industry. That adds to the difficulty in using benchmarking effectively as a basis for comparison. The majority of the relatively limited number of studies devoted to construction productivity and performance measurement is concerned with the identification of sources of delays, rather than with the analysis of measuring systems and techniques (Mohamed 1996).

Benchmarking needs to be tailored to the construction industry. However, there are a number of factors that may hinder its use. First, the nature of the construction industry itself, with its large number of variables makes a direct comparison difficult. Such variables are location, size and type of project and level of technology. The efficiency of the project team can be further hampered by the diversity in cultural backgrounds of the team. The real difficulty, however, lies in the way in which improvement of the process requires each individual company to change. This may not be reflected in the benefit accrued to that company, although it is possible that a company operating further downstream will reap the rewards from the improvement. There is, therefore, little incentive for resource outlay by one company if the benefit is assigned to another. To some extent all these problems have been addressed by the manufacturing and service industries. Benchmarking provides a rigorous and tested methodology to facilitate the change process, but it should first be tailored for use in a construction environment (Pickrell and Garnett 1996).

If the construction industry is to manage its affairs successfully, it must have a measurement system to monitor best practices and productivity. Benchmarking is therefore an essential and powerful tool for business improvement. Its adoption by the industry could result in measurable performance improvement, facilitating real cost reduction. Benchmarking is not simply about recording statistical data relevant to construction projects, but is a continuous process of comparing methodologies of the many processes of construction and their resultant effect – both within the industry and outside when possible. By encouraging the industry to share and then to strive to meet or exceed current 'best practice', benchmarking should provide a catalyst for change and improve performance (CIB Working Group 11 1996).

## BENCHMARKING AND PARTNERING

A particular strength of benchmarking is that it can be used alongside many other improvement techniques. A recent consideration has been the potential benefits to assist partnering. There are several ways in which benchmarking and partnering link, as in the need for performance measures. Benchmarking can assist performance improvement in partnering arrangements in many ways. Pickrell and Garnett (1996) suggest the following three levels as an example:

1. Within the general business, with benefits assisting partnering arrangements, for example improving data transfer.

2. On a project-to-project basis with partners, increasing the use of standardized products.
3. Between partnering arrangements (as in learning from the positive experiences of other arrangements). It can include different arrangements within the organization, partnering arrangements in different sectors of the same industry and partnering in other industries.

At the moment there are few ways of proving the benefits of partnering in the construction industry. This constitutes one of the main barriers for the use of partnering. Hence, metrics are used to establish an organization's position. Once business leaders have been identified, implementation of their reasons for being better can take place. A criticism of partnering is reduced competition. Benchmarking allows the companies to keep a view on the competition, which can then be fed back into the partnering arrangement (Pickrell and Garnett 1996).

Within the partnering environment, benchmarking becomes a generic and holistic approach to continuous improvement. Therefore it may not be necessary to make comparisons with a world-class and established organization, since it will take a long time to complete a full and incremental step procedure to the benchmarking exercise. Unless the size of the organization has the resources required, it may be impractical to fully implement the findings owing to the size of gap that may be involved. In spite of the criticisms directed against UK companies that do not benchmark against world leaders, the way forward for partnering arrangements is to set incremental steps on a continuous basis, with world-class performance as a long-range goal (NEDO 1993).

Benchmarking should be used to compare with other projects, with a wide range of comparators used to identify where improvements can be made. The achievement of continuous improvement requires individuals and teams who do not idly accept the status quo, but constantly seek opportunities for improvement. It is essential to measure performance in the areas agreed in the workshops at specified intervals and to feed back the results to the project team. Simple measures that could be developed and refined as the project proceeds can be used as a starting point (CIB Working Group 12 1997; CIB 1998). The principles of benchmarking *vis-à-vis* the effectiveness of the partnering charter being used should be addressed by the group at the workshops. This involves reference to the charter goals and the targets which the group consider necessary to achieve the objectives. These targets are a measure (indicator) of the level of success or failure for each of the goals (CIB Working Group 12 1997).

Benchmarking in partnering can be used as a tool for improvement. The achievement of continuous improvement is a prime motive for partnering.

**605**

Without a commitment to continuous improvement, the full benefits from partnering will not be realized. Continuous improvement is not possible without benchmarking. Benchmarking best practices is essential for survival at the beginning of the twenty-first century (CIB Working Group 12 1997; NEDO 1993).

# INCENTIVES AND PARTNERING

## THE ROLE OF INCENTIVES IN PARTNERING

What attracts contractors to partnering is the better and long-term relationships that the process engenders. Incentives in the form of target costs with shared savings between client and contractor are also an attractive aspect of partnering arrangements. Perhaps the simplest explanation for the growth in popularity of partnering is its ability to realize a basic truth; if the project is completed on time, to a high quality and within budget, then all participants are going to reap financial benefits. Long-term partnering offers its own incentives in the form of a stable workload over an extended period. Incentive payments linked to time, cost, quality or safety are usual. The important distinction between the partnering arrangement and the traditional target cost contract is the emphasis on quality and safety as target factors. What attracts clients to partnering is the growing body of evidence that, as a procurement method, it is better placed to deliver the cost saving of 30 per cent advocated by Latham (1994) (see Hosie 1997).

Clients and contractors are creating partnerships with the aim of achieving the objectives of both parties: higher profit to the contractor at lower cost to the client. The measurement of the performance of the partnership is an important feature of the concept. The main objective is to continually improve the processes and the products. The aim is to ensure that every year produces improved performance. Continuous improvement should be the concern of all the parties involved in the project, as it is only effective when all parties are motivated to its achievement. The end result is a measurable increase in value, whilst properly meeting the client's needs (CIB 1998; Bennet and Jayes 1995).

Incentives are not unique to partnering contracts and are not used universally in partnering relationships. When incentives are used in partnering, they serve to reinforce behaviour expectations, focusing attention on the traditional measures of costs and schedule, and on quality improvement, innovation and interface enhancement. The two categories of incentives are monetary and non-monetary. Monetary incentives include adjustable fee, cash awards if criteria are met, bonus/penalty as percentage of base fee, shared savings on cost-plus-guaranteed-maximum and safety/schedule incentives. Non-monetary incentives are designed to express appreciation for the employees' efforts, resulting in better employee performance (such as gifts, barbecues and partnering newsletters identifying high performers) (CII 1991).

Profit sharing schemes serve to concentrate everyone's efforts on minimizing the impact of high risk items that occur on a project. Rather than expecting some parties to carry risks, which may or may not occur, it is more efficient for the whole team to have a real incentive to work hard when problems arise to solve them at the lowest cost. Profit sharing is one way of achieving this change in attitude. The use of profit sharing often gives rise to questions about who provides the extra money that is shared out. Clients sometimes assume they will have to pay more to provide the incentives for everyone else. Bennet and Jayes (1995) suggest that partnering provides extra money from greater efficiency and avoiding wasted effort otherwise used in pursuit of adversarial approaches. In other words, they advocate that partnering, by improving the traditional inefficient approaches, delivers the extra money needed to fund real incentives for the whole project team, including the client. Financial incentives are usually provided through profit sharing. This is especially effective where the criteria used to determine each firm's share are carefully related to the agreed mutual objectives.

An incentive–disincentive payment system can be used as a prevention technique of issue resolution. It involves payment of a bonus, or incentive, to a contract party for performing its work in a superior manner, to the specified quality. The bonus may relate to cost, time, quality, safety or other such measurable components of the total job performance. If the standards set are not achieved by a measurable point of the project, the disincentive clause is triggered and the contract party is penalized for less-than-satisfactory performance on the project. Incentives–disincentives tend to affect the project staff in a manner that is considered by some as threatening and by others as a stimulant to do the work better within the contract specified quality. It is important though to understand that incentives and disincentives do not necessarily resolve issues. They simply encourage, by the promise of reward, prompt resolution of those problems (Stephenson 1996).

Bennet and Jayes (1995) report that partnering is most likely to be successful if the agreed mutual objectives provide a realistic chance that all the parties will earn a fair return. The mutual objectives may include many issues, but common subjects include improved efficiency, cost reduction, guaranteed profits, reliable product quality, certain completion on time, continuity of workload, shared risks, reliable flow of design information and lower legal costs. They suggest that it helps project teams to find good mutual objectives if they are reinforced by well thought out incentive schemes. The success of a partnering relationship will be enhanced by the use of incentive performance schemes (CII 1991).

## INCENTIVE SCHEMES AS A MEANS TO STRETCH TARGETS

CII's Partnering Task Force (1991) incorporated shared incentives, as part of the establishment of performance measurement systems and continuous improvement processes, into the partnering implementation process. This involves consideration of an incentive modification to the agreement through which the partners can share costs and rewards associated with improvements, the setting of incentives all the way down to individuals and documenting and communicating early accomplishments.

The incentive performance schemes are tools to measure risks and rewards of the partnership. Performance can be assessed against predefined benchmarks for various classifications of performance indicators. These indicators combine traditional elements such as productivity and man-hour ratios. However, future improvements can only come about by successfully creating a greater 'business focus' with the emphasis on the results, rather than the process. Performance categories may include productivity, performance, safety and environment, and management control. These performance factors are interrelated and interdependent.

It is essential to ensure continuous improvement in performance when partnering. Performance should be measured regularly and the results used to set tougher targets for the next period. The improvements achieved each year should be recorded in a report to the main boards of all firms involved in the partnering arrangement to ensure top management's continued commitment. It is important to agree at the outset the most appropriate tools to achieve an objective measurement of performance. Workshops should identify the distinctive improvements that the project intends to make and devise a clear measure of how success will be judged (CIB 1998; Bennet and Jayes 1995).

The benefits and rewards can be achieved through challenging established practice and the search for 'something different'. A tool deployed in this area is the creation of stretch targets on specific deliverables, creating the scenario where existing methods could not possibly yield the target result. Individuals or both teams, contractor and client, should share the benefits from inventiveness. By incentivizing the contract we stretch targets, looking at the standards, which have been identified through benchmarking, to achieve best value for money. Incentivization creates a more proactive, cooperative relationship between the partners.

# CONCLUSIONS

## PARTNERING

The construction industry has been heavily criticized for its low productivity and poor performance and is under increasing pressure to improve productivity, safety, the quality and value of the final product, and the efficiency and effectiveness of its processes. Partnering has been seen as a project management tool to overcome the traditional obstacles that can adversely impact a successful construction project. Implementing a partnering agreement requires the recognition of common goals by all parties, the creation of an atmosphere of trust and teamwork and commitment to a long-term relationship. We believe that the key elements of partnering highlighted here are crucial to the development of a successful partnering relationship. Despite the fact that partnering is a relatively new concept, it has been used successfully on a number of projects and there are substantial benefits to be gained by all parties from its use. However, barriers to the growth of partnering do exist and may inhibit its successful application. An active partnering process during the preparation of a project can result in significant cost improvement.

## BENCHMARKING

The aim of any benchmarking effort is to introduce improvements to better meet customer needs. Various authors have described benchmarking as an improvement process used to discover and incorporate best practices that will lead to superior performance. Benchmarking is based on the philosophy of continuous improvement. A number of factors that may hinder the use of benchmarking in construction have been identified, the main one being the nature of the construction industry itself with its large number of variables that makes direct comparison difficult. Therefore benchmarking should first be tailored for use in the construction environment. One of the main advantages of benchmarking is that it can be used alongside many other improvement techniques. Benchmarking in partnering can be used as a tool for continuous improvement to set targets for incremental steps with world-class performance as a long-range goal.

## INCENTIVES

The study of the relevant literature has revealed the important role incentives can play in construction contracts. The contractual relationship between the client and the contractor is a key to project success. Taking advantage of a contractor's general objective to maximize its profits by giving it the opportunity to earn a greater profit if it performs the contract efficiently lies at the core of incentive contracting. Incentivization can create a more cooperative relationship between parties, overcoming the traditional adversarial approach to contracting. It requires, though, time and a clear objective of what is to be achieved. Structuring an effective incentive programme could prove to be a complex undertaking. The purpose of the incentives is not just to motivate the contractor but to tie performance of all participants to the project's objectives. The proper use of an incentive contract aligns the priorities of project participants who would otherwise have diverse motives.

When incentives are used in a partnering setting they focus attention not only on the traditional measures of cost and schedule, but also on quality improvements, innovation and interface enhancement. It is of the utmost importance to ensure continuous improvement in performance when partnering. Incentive performance schemes have been used as tools to measure the risks and rewards of the partnership and set tougher targets to achieve for the next period of time.

## REFERENCES AND FURTHER READING

Adudayyeh, O. (1994), 'Partnering, a team building team approach to quality construction management', *Journal of Management in Engineering, ASCE*, **10**(6), November/December.

American Arbitration Association (1993), *Construction Industry Dispute Avoidance: The Partnering Process*, American Arbitration Association, NCDRC, New York.

Associated General Contractors of America (AGC) (1991), *Partnering: A Concept for Success*, Associated General Contractors of America, Washington, DC.

Baden-Hellard, R. (1995), *Project Partnering: Principle and Practice*, Thomas Telford, London.

Bennet, J. and Jayes, S. (1995), *Trusting the Team: The Best Practice Guide to Partnering in Construction*, Centre for Strategic Studies in Construction, The University of Reading.

Busch, J. S. and Pinnell, S. S. (1994), 'Dispute management programs: partnering, claims management and dispute resolution', in *Proceedings of the Project Management Institute 25th Annual Symposium, Vancouver*, Project Management Institute, Sylva, NC, October.

Camp, R. C. (1989), *Benchmarking: The Search for the Industry Best Practices that lead to Superior Performance*, ASQC Quality Press, Milwaukee, WI.

Camp, R. C. (1995), *Business Process Benchmarking*, ASQC Quality Press, Milwaukee, WI.

Charlett, A. J. (1996), 'A review of partnering arrangements within the construction industry and their influence on performance', in *Proceedings of the International Council for Building Research Studies and Documentation (CIB), W89 Beijing International Conference, Beijing, China*, October. http://www.bre.polyu.edu.hk/careis/rp/cibBeijing96/papers/130_139/138/p138.htm

Construction Industry Board (CIB) Working Group 11 (1996), *Towards a 30% Productivity Improvement in Construction*, Thomas Telford, London.

Construction Industry Board (CIB) Working Group 12 (1997), *Partnering in the Team*, Thomas Telford, London.

Construction Industry Board (CIB) (1998), 'Fact sheet on benchmarking', Construction Industry Board home page, http://www.ciboard.org.uk/factsht.htm, February.

Construction Industry Institute (CII) Partnering Task Force (1991), 'In search of partnering excellence', *Special Publication No. 17-1*, CII, Austin, TX.

Construction Industry Institute (CII) (1995), 'Use of incentives', *Implementation Status Report, 1995 CII Conference*, CII, Austin, TX.

Construction Industry Institute (CII) Partnering Task Force (1996), 'Model for partnering excellence', *Research Summary No. 102-1*, CII, Austin, TX.

Cook, L. and Hancher, E. (1990), 'Partnering: contracting for the future', *Journal of Management in Engineering, ASCE*, **6**(4), October.

Cook, S. (1995), *Practical Benchmarking*, Kogan Page, London.

Crowley, G. L. and Karim, A. (1995), 'Conceptual model of partnering', *Journal of Management in Engineering, ASCE*, **11**(5), September/October.

European Construction Institute (ECI) (1997), *Partnering in the Public Sector*, ECI, Lougnborough.

Harback, H. F., Basham, D. L. and Buhts, R. H. (1994), 'Partnering paradigm', *Journal of Management in Engineering, ASCE*, **10**(1), January/February.

Hensey, M. (1997), 'Strategic planning; development and improvements', *Journal of Management in Engineering, ASCE*, **13**(1).

Hosie, J. (1997), *Partnering – The Next Milestone in Construction Procurement?*, Construction Law Review, London.

Larson, E. (1995), 'Project partnering: results of study of 280 construction projects', *Journal of Management in Engineering, ASCE*, **11**(2), March/April.

Larson, E. and Drexler, J. A. Jr. (1997), 'Barriers to project partnering: report from the firing line', *Project Management Journal*, **28**(1), March.

Latham, Sir Michael (1994), *Constructing the Team: Final Report of the*

**611**

*Government/Industry Review of Procurement and Contractual Arrangements in the UK Construction Industry*, The Stationery Office, London, GB, 1994.

Mohamed, S. (1996), 'Benchmarking and improving construction productivity', *Benchmarking for Quality Management and Technology*, **3**(3).

National Economic Development Organisation (1993), *Partnering Without Conflict*, NEDO, London.

Pickrell, S. and Garnett, N. (1996), 'Generic benchmarking in construction', in *Proceedings of the International Council for Building Research Studies and Documentation (CIB), W89 Beijing International Conference, Beijing, China*, October.
http://www.bre.polyu.edu.hk/careis/rp/cibBeijing96/papers/130_139/138/p138.htm

Stephenson, R. J. (1996), *Project Partnering for the Design and Construction Industry*, Wiley, New York.

US Army Corps of Engineers (1991), *Construction Partnering: The Joint Pursuit of Common Goals to Enhance Engineering Quality*, US Army Corps of Engineers, Omaha, NB.

Weston, D. C. and Gibson, G. E. Jr. (1993), 'Partnering-project performance in U.S. Army Corps of Engineers', *Journal of Management in Engineering, ASCE*, **9**(4), July/August.

## RELATED TOPICS

# 32 Contract law

## Peter Marsh

This chapter provides a layman's guide to the main points of English contract law as it applies to commercial organizations. It in no way replaces the need for legal consultation in case of difficulty or dispute. If such cases do arise then it is essential to seek professional legal advice at the earliest opportunity, before action is taken which may damage your company's position. This chapter considers the essential elements of a contract, factors which make a contract invalid and the terms or conditions and warranties.

## CONTRACT FORMATION

There are four essential elements for a binding contract to be formed between two companies:

1. Offer
2. Acceptance
3. The intention to be legally bound
4. Consideration

### OFFER

An offer in law is both a statement of the terms upon which a party is willing to contract and an expression of willingness to do so if an acceptance is given of those terms. It must be distinguished from an 'invitation to treat' (of which the classic example is the display of goods in a shop window), which is an indication of the terms upon which the seller is willing to do business, but not that they would accept any offer that was made. The commercial significance of this distinction is that a price list issued generally by a seller does not constitute an offer unless it is clearly evident from the terms of the price list that the seller intends to be bound by any order which the buyer places. An offer can be withdrawn at any time before it is accepted unless there is a separate contract under which the seller undertakes to keep it open for a certain period. This is because any promise made by the seller in a quotation to keep the offer open for, say, 60 days would not be binding, because it would not be supported by consideration (see below). However, withdrawal of the offer (revocation as it is often termed) is only effective when it has actually been received by the person to whom the offer was made. Accordingly if an offer is accepted prior to the receipt of the notice of revocation, then a valid contract exists and the purported revocation is of no effect.

## ACCEPTANCE

An acceptance of an offer becomes effective when it has been communicated to the person who made the offer. Assuming the offer has been sent by post, the acceptance has been communicated when the return letter is addressed, properly stamped and posted. Where the acceptance is by telex or facsimile, then the timing of acceptance is when the message is received on the machine of the person making the offer during normal working hours for that business. If the message is received outside these hours, it becomes effective at the moment the office reopens. The principal difficulty with acceptance is that to be effective in creating a contract its terms must coincide with those of the offer. Very often this is not the case. The seller makes an offer on their terms of sale and the buyer purports to accept but on their terms of purchase. In law such an 'acceptance' is classified as a counter-offer which the seller is free to accept or reject. At that stage, no contract exists and there are three possibilities:

1. Nothing is done to resolve the matter but in due course the goods are delivered and accepted by the buyer. By delivering the goods the seller is regarded as having accepted the buyer's terms by conduct. This would not apply if the goods were accompanied by a delivery note referring to the seller's conditions which the buyer accepted.
2. The supplier returns a tear-off acceptance slip which was part of the buyer's order and which states that the supplier accepts the order on the buyer's conditions. The contract will then be on the buyer's conditions. This will be so even if the seller returns the slip with a letter which refers back to the seller's tender. This was interpreted by the court in *Butler Machine Tool Co Ltd* v. *Ex-Cell-O Corporation* as only being a reference to the price and identity of the goods.

3. The seller can only protect themselves by referring in the letter specifically to their acceptance being on their terms of sale. This would then amount to a counter-offer which the buyer could either accept or reject. If the buyer did nothing and there was no further discussion of the terms of contract then no contract would be formed until there was acceptance by conduct, for example by the buyer taking delivery of the goods.

## THE INTENTION TO BE LEGALLY BOUND

Normally this requirement is easily satisfied where the transaction is between two commercial organizations. The parties may, however, not wish their agreement to be legally binding and if they state so expressly then the court will give effect to this. This is rare but it has happened with so-called 'Letters of Comfort' issued by banks when they have not been willing to give a guarantee of financial support.

More common are instances where one of parties indicates that they have no intention to be legally bound by making their offer 'subject to contract'. There can then be no binding agreement until the parties have entered into a formal contract and, with sales of land, contracts have been exchanged.

Where the parties have left open important matters for future agreement, the court may also decide that the parties did not intend to be bound until such matters had been agreed. Similarly, an agreement to negotiate is not a contract because it is too uncertain to be enforced. To make the agreement binding, it would be necessary to establish in the contract a mechanism for settling the matters left to be agreed by reference to a third party whose decision the parties agree to accept as final and binding.

## CONSIDERATION

Consideration is a highly technical concept peculiar to common law. It requires that for a binding contract to arise, an act or promise of one party must have been given in exchange for an act or promise by the other. Note, the consideration must exist; it does not need to be adequate. It cannot be claimed that a contract did not exist because the consideration was not adequate recompense for the offer. Normally there is no problem about consideration in a commercial contract, since the seller undertakes to supply the goods or do the work in consideration of the promise of payment by the purchaser. However, there are four situations in which the doctrine can have commercial significance.

## Standing offers

Tenders are sometimes invited for an indefinite quantity of goods which the purchaser thinks they may require over a period of time. Unless the invitation states to the contrary, the purchaser by accepting such a tender does not bind themselves to order anything and is under no liability to the successful tenderer until they actually do place an order. Similarly unless they have given consideration for keeping their offer open, the supplier may withdraw their tender at any time, but is obliged to fulfil any order which is placed before they do withdraw.

## Promises to keep offers open

We saw above that a statement in a tender such as 'our offer is valid for 60 days' is not binding on the tenderer and they may withdraw it at any time before it is accepted. The reason is simply that the purchaser has given no consideration for the promise. It is possible for the purchaser to create consideration and in effect turn the offer into an option. Moreover, since the consideration need not be adequate, the amount could be largely nominal, say £5.

## Promise post-contract to pay bonuses

The rule has been that when A is bound by a contract to perform certain obligations for B, then A's performance of their obligations could not provide consideration for a promise by B to make additional payments. However, it has now been established that if B's promise to pay is not due to pressure brought by A amounting to economic duress, and B gains practical benefits from the promise, then the promise is enforceable. The practical benefits obtained by B from A's performance on the original contract provide the consideration. This was established in a case in which a subcontractor who was in financial difficulties and likely to complete the work late was promised a bonus if they completed on time. By obtaining completion of the subcontract work to time, the main contractor obtained practical benefits, in particular they avoided having to pay damages for delay (*Williams* v. *Roffey Bros & Nicholls (Contractor) Ltd* (1991)).

## Payment of lesser sum than a liquidated debt

If one party to a contract agrees to accept a lesser sum in settlement of a liquidated amount which is due to them, then that agreement will not be binding unless supported by some consideration other than the payment itself. Such consideration could be payment at an earlier date than required under the contract or the performance by the debtor of some other obligation of benefit to the creditor. In the absence of any consideration, the creditor can sue for the balance of the liquidated amount. In *D & C Builders* v. *Rees*, a firm of builders in severe financial difficulties accepted a payment of £300 in full settlement of the amount of £482 which they were owed. It was held by the Court of Appeal that they were entitled to recover the balance.

## LETTERS OF INTENT

Like many other expressions in common commercial use, letters of intent have no distinct legal meaning. In order to determine what the parties meant when issuing and acting upon a letter of intent it is necessary to examine objectively what the parties did and said. The following are therefore only guidelines:

1. Generally a letter of intent does not give rise to any legal obligation on the part of either party. It is simply an expression of present intentions.
2. However, in addition to expressing an intention to award the contract to the supplier, the letter of intent may go on to authorize the supplier pending conclusion of negotiations to do certain work or purchase materials. If the supplier does so, but the contract is never concluded because the parties never reach agreement, then the purchaser is bound to pay a reasonable sum for the work done or materials supplied. However, since there never was a contract between them the supplier is under no contractual liabilities as regards defects in the work or as to the time of its completion.

## INVALIDITY FACTORS AND FRUSTRATION

After its formation a contact may be upset by one of several factors. These may be conveniently grouped together as:

- mistake
- misrepresentation
- duress
- frustration.

### MISTAKE

Only very rarely will a contract be held to be void or non-voidable for mistake. The mistake must be something fundamental, such as the existence of the goods, or where there is such confusion between the parties that there cannot objectively be said to be any agreement between them. A mistake as to quality will only ever

**617**

upset the contract if it concerns some fundamental quality without which the goods would be essentially different from those which they were believed to be.

## MISREPRESENTATION

Although there are four classes of misrepresentation – fraudulent, innocent, negligent and under the Misrepresentation Act 1967 – it is only the last which is of commercial significance in the law of contract. Negligent misrepresentation belongs to the law of tort with which we are not concerned. It is a misrepresentation under the Act if the statement is false and the party making it cannot show that he or she had reasonable grounds for believing it to be true. The other party's remedy is to recover damages.

## DURESS

A contract is only valid if is entered into freely and voluntarily. Physical pressure to persuade someone to enter into a contract is fortunately very rare but there is now recognized a new category of duress, namely economic duress. This arises when the will of one party has been coerced by that of the other and the pressure exerted is illegitimate, such as a refusal by one party to carry out the contract unless a new contract is made under which they are paid more money. The effect of economic duress is to make the contract voidable and the innocent party can recover any payments made as a result of the duress. Mere commercial pressure will not be sufficient to constitute duress nor will the fact that the one party has had to agree to harsh terms because of the weakness of their bargaining position.

## FRUSTRATION

A contract will only be considered as frustrated, and therefore at an end, if it becomes impossible for it to be performed by reason of an event beyond the control of the parties. It is not sufficient that its performance for one party becomes more difficult or more expensive.

# CONDITIONS AND WARRANTY

English law draws a distinction between two types of terms of contract, conditions and warranty. Conditions are essential terms, the breach of which allows the injured party both to rescind the contract and to claim damages. A warranty is a lesser term for the breach of which the only remedy is in damages. However, the meaning of the terms in any given contract is a matter of construction. The court may well decide that looked at objectively a term described as a 'condition' can only have been meant as a lesser term so its breach gives rise to no right to rescind the contract. Equally the use of the term 'warrant' in a contract may be held to be equivalent to guarantee and its breach give rise to a right to rescind. However, all the provisions of the Sale of Goods Act 1979 relating to quality and fitness for purpose are described by the Act as conditions. In insurance law, the opposite meaning is given to the term 'warranty', which is used to describe an essential term of the insurance policy. More recently the courts have introduced the concept of intermediate or innominate terms, the breach of which when it occurs may be either so serious that it would justify rescission or only serious enough to justify a remedy in damages alone.

## THE CONTRACT PRICE

If a lump sum quotation is submitted and accepted, the contractor or supplier is obliged to complete the work or supply the goods without additional payment, even if doing so becomes more difficult or entails work beyond what they originally envisaged, unless the contract provides otherwise or there was misrepresentation on the part of the purchaser. In an old case involving a lump sum contract to build a house, flooring was omitted from the specification and it was held that the contractor must put it in without additional payment as it was clearly indispensably necessary to complete the house. Subject to the express terms of the contract, the entitlement of the contractor or supplier to payment of the contract price arises when they have performed the contract. However, there is a difference between contracts for work and materials such as building contracts and those for the supply of goods:

1. With a contract for work and materials, the contractor is normally entitled to payment when they have substantially completed the work, even if there are some minor defects or omissions for which the purchaser is entitled to make a reasonable deduction until the work is completed. Only if, as rarely happens today, the contract is construed as an entire contract, is the contractor not entitled to any payment until they have completed satisfactorily all the work which was required under the contract.
2. With a contract for the sale of goods, unless the contract expressly provides otherwise, the seller's obligations as to the quality of the goods and their compliance with the contract description are conditions of the contract. If that is breached, the purchaser is entitled to reject the goods (unless section 15A of the Sale of Goods Amendment Act 1994 applies). So normally there is no

obligation to make payment until goods complying wholly with the contract have been delivered, unless the purchaser is willing to accept them in their defective condition and offset or counterclaim for the reduction in value.

## PASSING OF PROPERTY

The general rules for the passing of property are laid down under the Sale of Goods Act 1979. The Act draws a distinction between specific goods and those which are unascertained. Specific goods are those which are identified and agreed upon at the time of the contract. Unascertained goods are those which are either generic, say 100 tons of cement, or still to be manufactured or part of an undivided bulk. Section 17 of the Act sets out the rules which are to apply to the two categories of goods unless the contract states otherwise. With specific goods which are in a deliverable state the property passes when the contract is made regardless of whether delivery or payment is postponed. The property in unascertained goods passes when they have been unconditionally appropriated to the contract. This means that the goods must be irrevocably attached to the contract so that it is those goods and no others which are the subject of the sale and the seller has completed all their contractual obligations and so notified the purchaser.

The fact that the property in the goods has passed to the purchaser, but they have not yet paid for them, leaves the seller in a vulnerable position if the purchaser were to go bankrupt or into liquidation. For that reason clauses which provide for the reservation of title until payment has been received in full are popular with sellers. The legal effect of any such clause depends on the way it is drafted and can raise complex problems. The following is therefore only a brief outline:

1.  Where the goods unaltered are still in the buyer's possession, the seller will be entitled to recover them. If the clause so provides, this right will enable the seller to recover not only those particular goods but all others which they have sold to the purchaser and for which payment has not been made; the so-called all sums clause. This is particularly important to the seller where they are making regular deliveries.
2.  If the goods have been used in the manufacture of other products, so that they no longer have a separate identity, then the seller loses their right to recover them.
3.  If, unusually, the clause provides that the purchaser holds the goods as bailee for the seller, and is under a fiduciary duty to account to the seller for the whole of the proceed of sale, the seller may have the right to recover such

proceeds, if they have been placed in a separate bank account and so can be identified.

## PASSING OF RISK

One reason for the importance of the clause relating to the passing of property is that, unless a contract provides otherwise, the risk in the goods passes to the purchaser at the same time as the property passes. Thus, if the seller introduces a clause into the contract under which the property in the goods does not pass until they have been paid, even once they have been delivered, then they should ensure that the risk in the goods passes to the purchaser on delivery. The purchaser is then responsible, say, to have them insured against theft or damage. Likewise a buyer who is going to make payments while the goods are still in the course of manufacture should provide for the property in the goods to pass to them on payment, but that the risk should remain with the seller until after delivery

## DELIVERY

The Sale of Goods Act 1979 provides, in §29(2), that the place of delivery of the goods is the seller's place of business unless the contract makes a contrary intention clear. In fact, in modern trading, there will frequently be a contrary intention since in most instances the purchaser will want the seller to deliver the goods. The obligation to deliver is discharged by the seller if they deliver the goods at the buyer's premises without negligence to a person apparently having authority to receive them.

It is also provided in the Act that delivery to a carrier is presumed to be delivery to the purchaser. However, this will be so only if the seller has made a reasonable contract of carriage with the carrier. In the case of *Thomas Young & Sons* v. *Hobson and Partners* (1949), electric engines were sent by rail insecurely fixed at the owner's risk. The purchaser was held entitled to reject the goods since they should have been sent at the carrier's risk.

## TIME FOR COMPLETION

In a contract for building or engineering works, time is not of the essence unless the contract so provides. In a contract for the sale of goods, time will generally be regarded as of the essence unless the contract provides to the contrary. The significance of time being of the essence is that even if the supplier is late by a single day, then the purchaser will be able to reject the goods and claim damages. If time is not of the essence then the purchaser's only remedy will be in damages.

It is normal to provide that the supplier or contractor is entitled to an extension of the time for completion if they were delayed by an act or default of the purchaser or by other mitigating circumstances. However, it is to the purchaser's advantage if these circumstances are restricted to ones which are genuinely totally beyond the control of the supplier or contractor. It is also suggested that the circumstances which would justify a claim for an extension should be identified specifically. The use of wide-ranging phrases such as 'any cause beyond the contractor's reasonable control' can lead to problems. In *Scott Lithgow* v. *Secretary of Defence* (1989) a clause reading 'any other cause beyond the contractor's control' was held to include delays due to manufacturing problems in a subcontractor's works. One phrase which should be avoided unless defined is *force majeure* which has no definite meaning in English law.

## DAMAGES

The object of an award in damages is to place the injured party in the same financial position as they would have been had the contract been performed properly, provided that the losses are not too remote.

Essentially the rule on remoteness is that the type of loss or damage which is recoverable is that which the parties could reasonably have contemplated at the time when the contract was concluded would be not unlikely to follow from the breach in question. A loss of a particular type could reasonably have been contemplated either because it would arise naturally in the ordinary course of events as a result of the breach or because it should have been contemplated from the particular facts known to the parties at the time of contracting. A supplier of machinery required for production would be taken to know that in the ordinary course of events, a purchaser would suffer a normal loss of profits if delivery were to be delayed. But they would only be liable for profits substantially above the normal level if at the time of entering into the contract the buyer had made that fact known.

Because of the difficulties and uncertainties surrounding the issue of what damages a purchaser will be entitled to if the works are completed late, the contract will often specify the damages which can be recovered per day or week of delay generally up to a maximum. In commercial practice such a clause is often referred to as a penalty clause, but in law there is a sharp distinction between liquidated damages and a penalty:

1. Liquidated damages are a genuine pre-estimate of the losses the purchaser reasonably foresees as likely to arise from the delay or, if they consider that amount to be excessive, some lesser sum. If there is a delay then the

purchaser is entitled to recover the amount included in the contract as liquidated damages regardless of whether they have actually suffered that loss or not. However, they cannot for that breach of contract recover more than the liquidated damages.

2. A penalty is a sum put into the contract which is excessive in relation to any loss which the purchaser could reasonably anticipate they would suffer as a result of the delay. It is there to frighten the contractor into completing on time. If the clause is classified as a penalty, then it is void and the amount is not recoverable in any action by the purchaser before the courts or an arbitrator. However, this does not alter the fact that the contractor is late and in breach of contract and the purchaser can still recover damages under the ordinary rules given above.

Reference is frequently made in a contract that the supplier or contractor is not liable for 'consequential damages'. It is not clear what that expression covers. Suppliers often think it refers to any loss of profit, but this is not true. In a recent case, it was decided that consequential damages were damages other than those resulting directly and naturally from the breach of the contract. What arises directly and naturally can obviously include a loss of profits. If a supplier or contractor wants to place a limit on their liability for damages, they must use much wider wording such as 'any loss of profit, loss of use, loss of production, loss of contract or any financial or economic loss or for any direct or consequential damage whatsoever'. The only problem then is whether or not such wording would pass the test of reasonableness under the Unfair Contract Terms Act 1977 (see page 626).

## QUALITY AND PERFORMANCE

Note that all these obligations are strict, they do not depend on proof of negligence, nor can the seller escape liability by showing that they took all proper steps to ensure goods were of the right quality or that they were not personally to blame.

1. *Description*   Under the Sale of Goods Act 1979 §13 in a sale by description there is an implied condition that the goods will correspond to the description. For a contract to be classified as a sale by description then it must have been within the reasonable contemplation of the parties that the purchaser was relying on the description in making the decision to purchase so that the description becomes an essential term of the contract.

2. *Satisfactory quality*   Where a seller sells goods in the course of business there is an implied condition under the Sale of Goods Act 1979 §14(2), as

amended by the Sale of Goods Act Amendment Act 1994, that the goods will be of satisfactory quality. This term replaces the old one of merchantable quality. This term does not apply to anything making the goods unsatisfactory which was specifically drawn to the buyer's attention before the contract was made or where the buyer examines the goods before contract and which such examination should have revealed. For the purpose of the Act goods are of satisfactory quality if they meet a standard which a reasonable person would find satisfactory taking into account any description of the goods, the price and other relevant circumstances. The following are stated to be aspects of the quality of the goods:

- Fitness for all purposes for which goods of the kind in question are commonly supplied
- Appearance and finish
- Freedom from minor defects
- Safety
- Durability

3. *Fitness for purpose*   While §14(2) is concerned with fitness for purpose for all purposes for which the goods in question are commonly sold, §14(3) deals with the position where the buyer has some particular purpose in mind which may not be a purpose for which the goods are commonly sold. It does provide that if the buyer makes it clear to the seller the particular purpose for which the goods are required, either expressly or by implication, then there is an implied condition that they are fit for that purpose. This subsection is narrower than §14(2), satisfactory quality, in that it requires the buyer to have relied on the seller's skill and judgement. On the other hand, it is wider in that the goods may in fact be of satisfactory quality but not fit for that particular and uncommon purpose which the buyer made known to the seller. So goods may be perfectly suitable for all destinations in the world to which they are commonly sent, but be unsuitable for some particular destination where there are very extreme weather conditions and the goods may be left exposed in the open. In those circumstances, a buyer would only be likely to succeed in an action against a supplier if they had made known in advance the conditions for which the goods were required, so the seller would have known to supply goods suitable for that purpose. In the case of *Aswan Engineering Industry* v. *Lupdine Ltd* (1987) pails were stacked in the open on the dockside in Kuwait in a temperature of up to 70 °C and no notice given to the supplier. It was held that there was no breach of merchantable quality and no breach of fitness for purpose under §14(3). Although the case was decided before the revision to the Sale of Goods Act it is considered that the decision would still be the same under the new definition of satisfactory quality.

## PAYMENT

Unless the parties otherwise agree, time of payment is not of the essence of a contract either for the sale of goods or for work and materials. Delays in interim payments by the buyer do not therefore give the seller or contractor the right to terminate or at common law to suspend performance of a contract. Nor was there any right of the seller to be paid interest, until the Late Payment of Commercial Debts (Interest) Act 1998 came into effect for contracts entered into after 1 November 1998. At present, the Late Payment Act only applies where the contract is between a small business, that is one employing less than 50 persons, and either a UK public authority or a large business employer, that is one employing over 50 persons. It is expected that the Act will be made applicable to contracts between two small business in two years from the end of 1998 and between all businesses two years later. The contracts covered by the Act are those for the supply of goods and services, and so include standard forms of contract for building and engineering projects. Broadly the effect of the Act is that where it applies there is a statutory right of interest of 8 per cent above bank rate if payment is delayed beyond the date for payment specified in the contract. If no date is specified, then the date used is 30 days from the date of performance of the obligation to which the debt relates. The right of statutory interest may only validly be excluded if there is a substantial contractual remedy for late payment.

With all but very major contracts for the supply of goods, payment is made by the buyer in full after the goods have been accepted. For contracts for construction work and for most contracts for services, it is the general practice that stage payments are made as the work proceeds. The Housing Grants, Construction and Regeneration Act (the Construction Act) now provides a statutory right to stage payments for all construction contracts to which the Act applies and which extend more than 45 days. A construction contract is basically any contract for building or civil engineering work or the provision of architectural or other similar professional services in connection with such contracts. There is no lower limit to the value of the contracts covered by the Act, but there are excluded contracts with a residential occupier for the house which he or she occupies or intends to occupy. Under the Act there must now be a right to stage payments, an adequate mechanism for determining what payments are due under the contract and a final date for payment. Only if a notice satisfying the provisions of the Act has been given can payment be withheld after the final date for payment. The Construction Act also for the first time gives a statutory right under certain circumstances to suspend performance. If a sum due is not paid in full by the due date and no effective notice to withhold payment has been given, then after seven days' notice the party to whom payment should have been made may suspend performance for so long as payment in full is not made.

Also outlawed under the Act are 'pay-when-paid' clauses, that is commonly used clauses under which the contractor only undertakes to pay their subcontractors when they themselves are paid by the client. Now such clauses will only be valid when the person who pays the person due to pay, in the above example the client, becomes insolvent.

The Act allows for the parties to formulate their own contracts complying at least with the Act but provides that if they fail to do so then the Scheme for Construction Contracts SI 1998 No. 649 will apply. There are even more important provisions in the Act relating to the use of adjudication to resolve disputes which are dealt with in Chapter 37.

## GUARANTEES AND EXCLUSION CLAUSES

For commercial reasons it has long been the practice of suppliers and contractors to limit their liability in damages for the supply of defective goods and the carrying out of defective work. Often such exclusion clauses are to be found in clauses headed 'Guarantee'. The supplier or contractor usually offers to repair defects arising within a limited period of time from delivery or completion. However, they exclude all liability for breach of any express contractual terms or those implied by law as to the quality or fitness for purpose of the work or for any other breach of their obligations. With contracts between businesses, such clauses fall under the Unfair Contract Terms Act 1977. Despite its title, the Act only deals with terms that seek to limit or exclude liability The Act is complex but broadly its main provisions provide for the following:

1. Liability for death or personal injury cannot be excluded or restricted by any contract term.
2. A contract term by reference to which a person seeks to exclude or restrict his or her liability for negligence giving rise to any other loss or damage is only valid to the extent to which it passes the test of reasonableness.
3. The implied statutory terms which relate to the description, quality or fitness for purpose of the goods/work in any contract for the supply of goods, hire or work and materials can only be validly excluded or restricted if the clause so doing satisfies the test of reasonableness.
4. Where the contract is on a party's standard terms of contract then he or she cannot:
   - when in breach of contract exclude or limit his or her liability for that breach of contract; or

- claim to render a contractual performance substantially different from that to be expected or in respect of the whole or any of contractual obligations render no performance at all, unless the contract term satisfied the test of reasonableness

## THE TEST OF REASONABLENESS

The onus or burden of proof is on the person seeking to rely on the clause to show that it is reasonable having regard to what was known or ought to have been known to the parties at the time of contract. The Act lays down certain guidelines to be taken into account in determining whether the test of reasonableness has been satisfied or not, of which the following are most important:

1. The strength of the bargaining position of the parties one to another.
2. Whether the purchaser received an inducement to agree to the term or could have contracted with someone else without such a term.
3. Whether the purchaser knew or ought reasonably to have known of the existence and extent of the term.

In addition, if the clause restricts the liability to a specified sum then two other guidelines become relevant:

- The resources available to the supplier to meet the liability.
- How far it was open to the supplier to cover himself by insurance.

It now seems clear that the resources available to the supplier will include those of the group to which they belong.

There have now been many cases under the Act but each is very much a decision on its own facts. It has generally been held that in a contract between two business organizations of similar bargaining power, the parties should be left free to apportion risks as they think fit, especially when the risk is insurable. However, it now seems clear that a clause will not satisfy the test of reasonableness if it deprives the purchaser of the implied conditions under the Sale of Goods Act to quality and fitness for purpose, unless the purchaser is given substantial rights to have defects made good. Also an exclusion clause which seeks to deprive the purchaser of the benefit of specific terms in the specification relating to the performance of the goods is also likely to fail the test of reasonableness (*Edmund Murray* v. *BSP International Foundations Ltd*). It may also be difficult for the seller to exclude the purchaser's rights to recover direct damages suffered as a result of the breach although the restriction of these damages to a limit commensurate with the supplier's insurance cover may be reasonable. Exclusion of consequential damages may also be reasonable but there is now the difficulty of knowing what this expression covers. Much importance would also seem to be attached to the extent to which the seller in the course of the negotiations for the contract showed themself by their conduct to be fair and reasonable.

## PROFESSIONAL SERVICES

The professional person rendering a service, such as a doctor, lawyer, engineer, architect or surveyor, is in a different position from a supplier or contractor. His or her duty is to exercise the reasonable skill and care to be expected of an ordinarily competent member of that profession. Unless the terms of the contract provide otherwise, and they only very rarely do, the professional person does not guarantee the achievement of a result. A term will not be implied into that person's contract to that effect as a matter of law but only may be so implied in a particular case as a matter of fact if it is justifiable to do so in all the circumstances.

## RELATED TOPIC

Adjudication        Chapter 37

# 33 Contracts and payment structures

*Peter Marsh*

The nature of the contract between the purchaser and the contractor can take one of a variety of forms. The nature of the contract depends on a range of issues, including the scope of the work, the responsibility of the contractor, the risk involved and the urgency. In this chapter we consider the types of contract structures adopted, different pricing regimes and the terms of payments. We also describe the issues to be considered when selecting the different options.

## CONTRACT STRUCTURES

When choosing to use contractors, the purchaser may follow one of several procurement routes, distinguished by the following features:

- Whether responsibility for the design, procurement, construction and commissioning is placed with one organization, or is to be divided between several, separate organizations.
- Whether the main contractor will both manage the project and undertake construction, or will be responsible for the management only with the construction work undertaken by others, working either as subcontractors to the main contractor or as separate contractors employed directly by the client.
- The basis upon which payment is to be made.

There are several procurement routes commonly in use:

1. *The traditional system* Used in building and civil engineering contracts where the design responsibility is primarily that of the architect or engineer employed by the client and the contractor or contractors are primarily responsible for construction only. Some design work may be undertaken by specialist subcontractors nominated by the client, but this can raise difficult

629

questions of design responsibility. The client through their architect or engineer retains control of design during construction and of the general management of the contract. When required, they will issue variation orders. A variant of this may be for the appointment by the client of a project manager to provide management services and for the architect or engineer's functions to be limited to design.

2. *The turnkey contract*  Where a single firm is employed by the client to undertake the design, procurement, construction and commissioning of the entire works, including managing the process. The client is only responsible for the preparation of their statement of requirements which becomes the strict responsibility of the contractor to deliver. This type of contract is used mainly for the design and construction of process plants and for projects financed using non-recourse financing such as one done under the Private Finance Initiative (PFI). The client does not retain an engineer in the traditional sense during construction and the client's functions are limited to those of inspection, payment and ensuring that the works meet their performance guarantees. This type of arrangement is sometimes called Engineering, Procurement and Construction (EPC).

3. *The design and build contract*  Equivalent to 2. above in the building and civil engineering industry. Here, the contractor is responsible for design as well as construction. The contractor's detailed design is often developed from a conceptual design prepared by the client's designers prior to tender and the client's design team are often seconded to work for the contractor after contract award. The client will, however, retain an engineer to protect their interests.

4. *Construction management and management contracting*  Similar to 3. above in that the contractor is responsible only for the management of the contract, with all construction work done by others. The distinction is that in construction management the subcontractors engaged to do the work are contractually responsible directly to the client while managed by the construction manager, whereas in management contracting they are employed by the management contractor as subcontractors. Design is often the responsibility of the client through the architect or engineer but the design process is managed by the contractor. Sometimes design is also made the responsibility of the contractor.

5. *Guaranteed maximum price*  Combines construction management with design and build. In outline this is typically as follows. The contractor is initially responsible for the management of the design phase of the contract including programming, coordinating the work of designers, including specialist firms, and tendering for the various packages of work. At a point

where a substantial portion of the contract has been tendered for, the contractor agrees a guaranteed maximum price with the client. The contract form for this second phase as well as the contractor's fee for overheads and profit will have been agreed at the time of the contractor's appointment for the first phase.

The appropriate method for a particular project depends on a number of factors including the following:

1. *The method of financing*  If the project is financed by non-recourse financing, that is the project itself provides the security for the loans (see Chapter 29), the banks are almost certain to insist on a turnkey route so the entire design is the responsibility of the contractor and the client's only responsibility is the preparation of their statement of requirements.
2. *The need to ensure the earliest feasible date of completion*  The quickest method is construction management with the contractor responsible at least for the management of design. This allows design and construction to proceed in parallel. It does not, however, provide the client at the outset with a firm price
3. *The need to ensure the lowest initial capital cost*  This is most likely to be achieved using the traditional method although there is a risk that the consultant's design may not be the most economic since it will not have been tendered in competition. On the other hand, a contractor's design might not take account of the lifetime costs. There is also the risk of variations and claims which can cause the out-turn cost substantially to exceed the initial estimate.
4. *Certainty of the out-turn costs*  This is most likely to be achieved through the use of the turnkey method which is why it is favoured by the banks. Of course, this will only be so if it is feasible for the contractor to provide a total lump sum for the contract, which means that they must be able to obtain the complete information necessary for a firm lump sum tender. Also all the information must be available at the required time. This may increase the time required for tendering. It also means that the client must not change their mind later.

## THE CONTRACT PRICE

There are three main ways in which the contract price may be expressed or calculated:

1. Lump sum
2. Remeasurement, schedule of rates or bill of quantities
3. Cost reimbursement

On a single contract the different ways may be combined. On a building contract, the above-ground element of a building may be on a lump sum basis while the foundations are done on an approximate bill of quantities subject to remeasurement. The supply portion of a chemical plant may be done on a lump sum, while the installation of the plant is on cost reimbursement, but with the contractor's overheads and profit compounded as a lump sum.

The work package approach is a variant of the lump sum method. It is suggested as one of the main options in the New Engineering Contract (ICE 1995) where it is called a priced contract with an activity schedule. The contractor prepares a list of all the activities which they expect to carry out in undertaking the work, and each activity is priced as a lump sum.

The choice of which way to price the work depends largely on the amount of information the purchaser can provide the contractor at the time of tendering, the conditions under which the work will be carried out, and thus the risk which it is sensible to expect the contractor to accept. A further factor will be the manner in which it is proposed to finance the project. If non-recourse financing is to be adopted, then almost certainly the banks will wish to see the project contracted for on a turnkey lump sum basis.

## LUMP SUM

From the purchaser's viewpoint, and that of any financier, the ideal is a firm lump sum with the minimum provisions for variations or claims. It establishes the amount of the commitment in advance, it provides the maximum incentive to the contractor to complete the work on time and it reduces to a minimum the amount of administration involved after the contract has been let. However, these benefits will be obtained only if it has been possible for the contractor to tender realistically. It follows from this that in addition to the general information required by a tenderer, they must be able to assess the following from information provided by the purchaser, their own engineering staff or prior experience of similar work:

1. The ground conditions on the site.
2. Material quantities and specifications. Labour hours and trades both for shop production and on site. This will mean that method statements must have been produced.
3. Descriptions and quantities of bought-out items. This requires decisions to have been taken, for example, on sizes and capacities.

4. Types of constructional plant which will be required and for what periods.

5. The time required by the various categories of design staff involved.

6. The site organization and facilities which will be required and for how long.

7. Factors which will affect site productivity.

8. Geographical and climatic factors as they affect site work.

9. Access to site.

10. Local availability of materials and labour.

For work which is to be subcontracted, the firm must provide similar information to all the subcontractors to enable them to make a similar assessment.

The above is a formidable list. It confirms the need for the purchaser to give complete and accurate information before a lump sum price can be produced. It also indicates that for a major project, considerable time and cost will be expended in the preparation of the tender for a lump sum contract. What must be remembered is that every time a tenderer guesses, it may guess wrong, and if the tenderer is successful in obtaining the contract every wrong guess costs someone money. Moreover, if the contractor is to remain in business in the long run, that someone can only be the purchaser whether on that contract or another.

Just as the contractor's problem on lump sum tendering is to assess the risks involved, so the purchaser's problem is the time it takes for the information to be gathered and processed to reduce those risks to reasonable proportions. Some element of risk will always remain; that is the very nature of contracting. The problem of obtaining information in time arises particularly on contracts which involve work below ground, such as foundations for a structure, tunnelling or sinking of shafts. The drilling of extensive boreholes and examining the results takes time which management is frequently not prepared to accept. Even then there is no certainty that the conditions encountered below ground will be as predicted.

### BILL OF QUANTITIES

A distinction must be drawn between two ways in which the term 'bill of quantities' is used.

In standard forms of building contract, where quantities form part of the contract, the contract price is a lump sum, not for the building as a whole, but for the stated quantities of work described in the bills of quantity. These quantities are an accurate estimation of the work to be performed by the contractor except where any quantity is stated to be approximate. If greater quantities of work are necessary to complete the works then the contractor is entitled to be paid extra under the variations clause in the contract. The value of work in addition to the stated sum, or for which only an approximate quantity was given in the bills, is determined by measurement and is priced at rates given in the bills. Thus, although the contract starts as a lump sum it is the client who essentially bears the risk that the quantities are not an accurate estimation of the work, although the contractor takes the risk of an error in pricing. However, under the JCT standard form of building contract (JCT 1980) there are also a number of provisions under which the contractor is entitled to be paid an additional loss and expense, which will be discussed further under claims (see Chapter 37).

In civil engineering contracts, by contrast, the bills of quantity are only an approximate estimate of the quantities of work to be performed and, unlike a building contract, do not define the work for which a lump sum price is quoted. In a civil engineering contract there is no lump sum price quoted in the standard form of tender and it is stated in the ICE conditions that the price is to be determined by measurement of the work done. The valuation of that work is then made in accordance with the rates given in the bill of quantities, unless, for any item, the difference between the actual quantity and the bill quantity is such that in the opinion of the engineer the bill rate is unreasonable or inapplicable. There is no necessity in this case for the change to have been the result of a variation. It is assumed that the contractor's rates and prices for the work as stated under the contract are correct and sufficient. Thus for a change of rate to be accepted, the change in quantity must be such as to require a change in the method of working requiring different plant or organization or be so excessive as to completely change the scope of work. An example was the case of *Mitsui v. A.G. of Hong Kong* where the billed quantity of the most expensive tunnel lining was 275 m and the actual 2448 m (*sic*). The billed quantity to be left unlined was 1885 m and the actual 547 m. The billed quantity of steel required for lining was 40 tonnes; the actual was 2943. Not surprisingly, the contractor claimed the engineer had the power to adjust the rates in the contract. More surprisingly the Hong Kong government claimed it had no such power. The Privy Council decided in favour of the contractor. As they pointed out, if the government were right there was a large element of wagering inherent in the contract.

In both building and civil engineering forms the contractor when pricing has to estimate the quantity and cost of the materials, labour, supervision and plant which will be required to execute the work. Since the largest elements are usually labour and plant, the assessment of productivity is a vital part of the estimating process. This in turn is closely related to:

- the physical conditions under which the work will be carried out, due, for example, to the time of year;
- the possibility of carrying out the work in a planned way with a reasonable

**634**

degree of continuity, due, for example, to drawings arriving on site well in advance of the scheduled commencement date of construction.

These points are referred to again when discussing variations and claims in Chapter 37.

## COST REIMBURSEMENT

On some projects, where the facility delivered will earn substantial revenue, finishing by the earliest possible date is regarded as more important than obtaining the lowest capital cost. Yet the extent of the lack of definition of the project or the anticipated risks are such that it is impractical to expect the contractor to assume the risks of even a measurement and value contract of the type just discussed. In these circumstances the only alternative is some form of cost reimbursement.

The obvious problem is that paying the contractor the actual costs of carrying out the work provides no incentive for the contractor to minimize the costs. Indeed many contractors do not like cost reimbursement because of the inefficiencies which it can breed within their own organizations. Therefore, various types of incentive or target cost contracts have been devised as a means of combining the flexibility and speed associated with cost reimbursement with a measure of financial discipline and an incentive to achieve economy and efficiency. All these forms of contract have certain features in common:

1. The principle of design and construction being conducted in parallel rather than in series.
2. The tendering by the contractor of a target cost either as a series of lump sums for the carrying out of defined packages of work or for a bill of quantities.
3. The tendering by the contractor of its fee inclusive of profit and overheads.
4. The recording of the actual costs incurred by the contractor which should exclude any costs associated with defective work or re-work to remedy defects.
5. At the end of the contract the making of a comparison between the target and the actual costs. For this purpose the target must be adjusted to reflect any variations or other events for which the contractor is allowed compensation under the terms of the contract.
6. The sharing between the purchaser and the contractor of the difference between the adjusted target and the actual costs in proportions set out in the contract

Where the forms of reimbursement contract differ is in their treatment of the contractor's management fee. The Engineering and Construction Management form provides for this to be a percentage of the actual cost and to be included within the comparison between target and actual cost. In other forms the contractor's fee is a lump sum and is not made part of the comparison. Where the management fee is to be a lump sum, the most careful definition is needed of the items to be included in the target cost and those to be included in the management fee. For example, it may be advantageous for the purchaser to include within the management fee if it is to be a lump sum elements such as the costs of the procurement of materials and of the site management staff and facilities. As to the percentage sharing arrangements between the contractor and the employer, various alternatives are available, but it is suggested that these arrangements should be kept as simple as possible and that it is recognized that there are two objectives:

- To provide the contractor with a genuine incentive to complete the work for a cost below the target.
- To protect the purchaser from the worst effects of a substantial cost overrun.

If time is particularly important, it is possible to build in an additional incentive by varying the share of the savings accruing to the contractor according to whether or not the contract is completed early or late. This may be done as shown in Figure 33.1.

There are many problems with target cost contracts:

1. There is the setting of the target itself. The intention must be that the target is realistic and is not to be either beaten or exceeded by significant amounts. It should not be far outside the normal limits of estimating accuracy. However, the target cost form of contract has been chosen because the uncertainties and risks involved in the contract do not allow the tendering of a lump sum price.
2. Because of the risks and uncertainties, including those arising from the lack of design definition, there is a real chance of substantial variations being required during the course of the contract. The effect of variations on the actual cost will be picked up automatically in that the contractor is to be paid the actual costs of doing the work. However, it is also necessary for the target cost to be adjusted to take account of the variations. While this may be easier if the target costs are contained in comprehensive bills of quantity, the rates may well not be applicable to the change which has occurred especially if it is of a design nature. Nor is the use of bills of quantity applicable to all types of contracts.
3. The use of a target cost contract imposes a substantial administrative and

| Early/late completion (weeks) | Contractor's share of savings (%) |
|---|---|
| −6 | 90 |
| −4 | 75 |
| −2 | 60 |
| 0 | 50 |
| 2 | 35 |
| 4 | 20 |
| 6 | nil |

**Figure 33.1   Incentives in a cost reimbursable contract for early completion**

supervisory burden on the client in checking the contractor's actual costs, in identifying costs which should be disallowed and in negotiating variations to the target so it remains effective as an incentive. If all this is not done then the contract will simply slide into straightforward cost reimbursement. On the other hand, to do it all in a timely and appropriate manner will add cost for the employer, which is unlikely to have the resources to do the work involved and will have to engage outside professional assistance probably in the form of quantity surveyors or cost engineers experienced in the type of work in question.

## TERMS OF PAYMENT

Terms of payment are a matter on which the commercial, technical and financial sides of the employer's business may find themselves pulling in different directions. The employer may attain the best commercial and technical result if they offer the tenderers terms of payment which while providing the employer with reasonable contractual safeguards impose the minimum strain on the contractor's financial resources. There are a number of advantages to this approach:

1. The employer avoids having to restrict the tender list to large firms possessing the resources to finance the contract, whose overheads and prices are likely to be higher than those of smaller companies (this assumes, of course, that such smaller companies are otherwise technically and commercially competent to carry out the work).
2. It ensures that the tenderers do not have to inflate their tender prices by financing charges. In many instances the rate of interest which the contractor has to pay when borrowing will be higher than that paid by the employer.

637

3.  It gives encouragement to and allows the employer to take advantage of firms possessing technical initiative who would otherwise be held back from expanding by lack of liquid cash.
4.  The employer minimizes the risk of being saddled with a contractor who has insufficient cash with which to carry out the contract and of having therefore to either support the contractor financially or terminate the contract.

On the other hand, to offer such terms means that the purchaser has to finance the work in progress, tying up their own capital in advance of obtaining any return on the investment. It could therefore be argued that with a project such as a new factory or power plant it would impose the least financial strain on the employer if they could avoid paying anything at all until the project was earning money. There are also two other arguments which are often used to support the case for only paying at the end when the contract is complete:

1.  Payment on completion provides the contractor with the best possible incentive to finish the whole of the work by the date for completion. It is far more effective than imposing liquidated damages for delay.
2.  Paying monthly as the work proceeds, as is normal in building and civil engineering contracts, has encouraged the establishment of small contractors who do not possess the technical and managerial competence to undertake the work, tender low, uneconomic prices and lack the cash resources to fund the work when they run into difficulties. It is too easy to set up as a builder by hiring labour on a self-employed subcontract basis and the necessary plant, and buying materials on credit terms which mean that they are in fact paid for by the purchaser. Such firms do not last very long, but their presence while they are in business is one of the reasons why tender prices are uneconomic and too low to support the required level of investment, especially in training. They are also a prime cause of the adversarialism and claims culture prevalent in the industry.

There is some truth in both these arguments, but the practice in the construction industry is too well established. Even the Latham Report, *Constructing the Team* (1994), did not recommend the abolition of interim payments, although it did recommend that payments should be related to the completion of milestones or activities.

Merely financing the contractor by paying them monthly for the quantity of work performed, whether any item has been completed or not, is not considered to be to the purchaser's advantage.

Similarly, waiting to pay until completion of the whole of the works would lose purchasers the advantages identified at the beginning of this section and would be unlikely to be acceptable to the industry. In any event, under the Housing Grants Construction and Regeneration Act 1998 if the contract is a construction contract as defined by the Act and will last more than 45 days there must be provision for stage payments although an unscrupulous employer could find ways to defeat the intent of the Act. On balance and in conformity with the spirit of the Act and of the Latham Report the preferred solution is to pay against completion of defined activities as is provided for in Option A of the New Engineering Contract (ICE 1995), 'Priced Contract with an Activity Schedule'. The contractor when tendering prepares the activity schedule although the purchaser when inviting tenders can state any particular activities which they wish to have priced or any activities which they wish to be grouped together. Each activity or a group of activities is then priced as a lump sum. On each assessment date, say monthly, the project manager determines which activities or group of activities have been completed and the contractor is paid for the completed work. It is important to note that payment is only made for completed activities or, where they are grouped, against completion of the group. There is no payment for a percentage complete. This method is suitable for building, mechanical and electrical engineering and process plant contracts.

However, as noted earlier, not all contracts can be tendered for on a lump sum basis. If it is impracticable to do so because of the uncertainties involved in assessing the quantities, so that a bill of approximate quantities is needed, then it is traditional to pay on a monthly basis the value of work which has been completed. However, the possibility should always be considered of tying in payment with the completion of certain milestones which can be identified from the programme. The milestone could be, for example, the construction of a foundation for a particular item of mechanical plant. Payment would then be made only against completion of that item ready to receive the plant.

Two problems particularly associated with monthly payment of remeasurement contracts are the practice of contractors to over-measure during early months of the contract and to front-end load by artificially increasing the rates for items of work carried out early. The use of an activity or milestone method of payment would overcome the first of these. The second can be avoided by allowing the contractor to identify as an activity, say, the preparation of the site.

## DELAY IN PAYMENT

Where the contract provides for payment to be made against some clearly defined event, and for the payment to be within a specified period of that date, there is no excuse for delay in payment. The specified date may be either from the issue by the architect or engineer of a certificate of completion or from receipt by the purchaser of an invoice which the contractor was entitled to submit, depending on the contract. Late payment is quite simply a breach of contract although one of the commonest committed. Many contracts do in fact provide for the payment of interest on delayed payments. Further, if payment is delayed after notice from the contractor for more than a specified period, the contractor may be entitled to suspend work or even to terminate the contract, although these rights do not exist at common law. If the contract does not provide a substantial contractual remedy for late payment, then the Late Payment of Commercial Debt (Interest) Act provides that interest shall be payable at 8 per cent above base rate in respect of late payments. The Act is now in force on contracts for the sale of goods or engineering and building works which are between a small business (less then 50 employees and a large business (more than 50 employees) in respect of payments due from the large business. The Act does not specify a mandatory period for payment, although if no period is stated then the period is 30 days from delivery or performance of the service. In practice a period of 30 days from the certificate of the event having been achieved should be sufficient for any well-organized employer. There is also now a limited right for the contractor to suspend performance of a construction contract under the Construction Industry Act if payment is delayed beyond final date for payment and no effective notice to withhold payment has been given.

## ADVANCE PAYMENTS

The general rule is that payments made in advance of the contractor starting work or of delivery of equipment to site should be avoided so far as possible. If for commercial reasons such payments have to be made then they should always be secured by a bond which is on first demand.

## PROGRESS PAYMENTS DURING MANUFACTURE

On contracts which include the manufacture of plant, it is again suggested that progress payments in advance of the actual delivery of such plant to site should be avoided. The primary reason is the purchaser's lack of security for such payments and the difficulties of recovering them if the manufacturer gets into financial difficulties. If for commercial reasons it becomes necessary to make such payments then:

- plant to at least the value of the payment should be identified, marked as such, separately stored and the contract should state that on payment it becomes the property of the purchaser;

640

- such plant should, however, also be stated in the contract to remain at the risk of the manufacturer until at the earliest it has been delivered to site and may be depending upon the contract until the works as a whole have been accepted by the purchaser.

## RETENTION MONEY

With contracts for building and civil engineering works and large contracts for supply and installation of plant and equipment, it is usual for the purchaser to retain a proportion of the contract price until the work have been completed, passed its tests (if any) and accepted by the purchaser. This percentage varies but is usually between 10 per cent and 20 per cent. On acceptance, half of this money is normally released and the balance held during the defects liability period as security for the performance by the contractor under their obligations to make good any latent defects which appear in the work. It is released at the end of this period provided that all defects have been remedied to the purchaser's satisfaction. Contractors often ask for the second half of the retention money to be released to them on completion against a bank guarantee. There can be no real objection to this provided again that the bond is payable on first demand.

## REFERENCES AND FURTHER READING

Institution of Civil Engineers (1995), *The New Engineering Contract*, 2nd edition, Thomas Telford, London.
JCT80 (1980), *Joint Construction Tribunal Standard Forms of Contract*, 2nd edition, Royal Institute of British Architects, London.
Latham, Sir Michael (1994), *Constructing the Team: Final Report of the Government/Industry Review of Procurement and Contractual Arrangements in the UK Construction Industry*, The Stationery Office, London.

## RELATED TOPICS

# 34 Standard forms of contract

## Stephen Simister and Rodney Turner

We saw in Chapter 30 that the relationship between the client and the supplier of goods and services is generally controlled by means of a contract. The contract sets out the intentions of the two parties, so should any dispute arise the true meaning of the roles and responsibilities of both sides is clear. At least that is the intention. However, even when intentions are written down their meaning is often unclear and expensive court cases are brought to try and resolve disputes. Generally the parties to a contract do not want to end up in court and they will seek to establish a contract that is acceptable to both sides and makes their intentions clear. This is the role of the standard form of contract.

In this chapter, we compare bespoke and standard forms of contract, and then describe some of the standard forms available.

## BESPOKE VERSUS STANDARD FORMS OF CONTRACT

Bespoke contracts are written specifically to suit the circumstances of the relationship they are to control. For instance, if you wanted an extension built on your house you might draw up a bespoke contract with a local builder which sets out various facets of the relationship such as:

- when the builder is to start and finish the project;
- how much the builder will get paid and when; and
- what happens if the extension is not to the agreed quality standard.

The bespoke contract is tailored to suit the exact circumstances for which it was written. On a small undertaking such as a house extension the time and effort required to write such a document should not be too arduous. However, it is a legal document and advice should be sought from an appropriate expert, and this will obviously add cost to the task. For a more complex undertaking the drafting of a bespoke contract can be extremely arduous as well as expensive.

The alternative to bespoke contracts are standard forms of contract. Standard forms are produced within a range of industries typically by professional bodies serving those industries or by committees specifically set up for the purpose. The building and construction industry seems to be the best served by standard forms with a huge number available. Where a standard form of contract is available that suits your project it is generally considered best to use that instead of a bespoke contract. The rationale behind this is outlined below.

## WHY USE STANDARD FORMS?

Standard forms of contract are generally prepared by an organization or body which has a genuine interest in a particular industry. To produce a standard form of contract requires considerable effort and is something that is not undertaken lightly. For instance, in 1998 the UK's Association for Project Management published standard terms for the appointment of a project manager. These standard terms took some two years to draft. They consist of two parts, the first part is the agreement and the second is an industry specific schedule of service; its arrangement is shown in Figure 34.1. By splitting the terms into two parts the APM is able to cover all industries within which project managers may work. The terms were written in response to a request from industry. This brings the APM in line with just about all other professional bodies which produce their own standard terms of appointment for the appointment of architects, engineers, lawyers, surveyors, etc.

As previously mentioned, the building and construction industry has produced a wide range of standard forms of contract. In the UK the most widely known are the suite produced by the Joint Contracts Tribunal (JCT). This body is drawn up from a range of representative professional and trade bodies within the construction industry. JCT produces more than sixty forms of contract and subcontract together with guidance notes on their use. Figure 34.2 gives a range of standard forms for various branches of the construction industry and related industries in the UK.

Standard forms of contract purport to provide a representative viewpoint of the industry which they serve. Rather than favour one particular party to the contract, standard forms should represent both parties on an equal and fair basis by providing for an equitable distribution of risk. Of course, this nirvana does not suit everybody, and in the UK some clients produce their own standard forms. For instance, Defence Estates looks after all MOD property

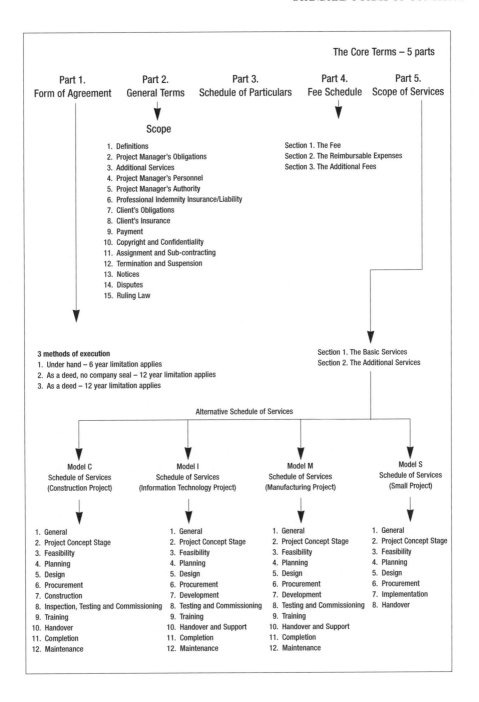

**Figure 34.1 APM standard terms for the appointment of a project manager**

645

| Industry | Institutions | Standard form | Type |
|---|---|---|---|
| Project management | APM | Project management | Professional services |
| Building | JCT | JCT SF 98 (6 versions) | Price |
| | JCT | JCT CD 98 | Price |
| | JCT | JCT IFC 98 | Price |
| | JCT | JCT MC 98 | Price |
| | JCT | JCT Prime Cost 98 | Prime cost |
| | JCT | JCT Measured Term 98 | Remeasurement |
| | RICS | Project Management | Professional services |
| Process | IChemE | Red Book | Price |
| | | Green Book | Cost |
| | | Yellow Book | Subcontract |
| Civil construction | ICE | ICE 6th | Remeasurement |
| | | ICE D&C | Price |
| | | NEC | Variable |
| Mechanical and Electrical | IMechE, IEE | MFI | Price |

**Figure 34.2 Standard forms of contract produced by the construction and engineering industries in the UK**

and its new form of contract called DEFCON 2000 favours the client to the extent that the contractor carries quite a high proportion of risk. The counter-argument is that contractors will not sign contracts they are not comfortable with. However, the balance of power lies fairly with the client and as the contract comes into use there will inevitably be acrimonious disputes which lead to court cases which perhaps a less adversarial approach may have prevented.

## SUMMARY

Standard forms of contract are available in the majority of industries and their use is to be preferred over a bespoke form. By using standard forms, clients are demonstrating that they wish to abide by industry standards and not impose unfair terms that shift the balance of power too much in their favour.

# REFERENCES AND FURTHER READING

Association for Project Management (1998), *Standard Terms for the Appointment of a Project Manager*, Association for Project Management, High Wycombe.

CIRIA 85 (1982), *Target and Cost Reimbursable Construction Contracts*, Construction Industry Research and Information Association, Report No 85.

CIRIA 100 (1983), *Management Contracting*, Construction Industry Research and Information Association, Report No 100.

Dingle, J., Topping, D. and Watkinson, M. (1995), 'Procurement and contract strategy', in J. R. Turner (ed.), *The Commercial Project Manager*, McGraw-Hill, London.

Institution of Chemical Engineers (1981), *Model Forms of Conditions of Contract for Process Plant, Lump Sum Contracts (Red Book)*, Institution of Chemical Engineers, Rugby.

Institution of Chemical Engineers (1992a), *Model Forms of Conditions of Contract for Process Plant, Reimbursable Contracts (Green Book)*, Institution of Chemical Engineers, Rugby.

Institution of Chemical Engineers (1992b), *Model Forms of Conditions of Contract for Process Plant, Subcontracts (Yellow Book)*, Institution of Chemical Engineers, Rugby.

Institution of Civil Engineers (1991), *Conditions of Contract and Forms of Tenders, Agreements and Bonds for Use in Connnection with Works of Civil Engineering Construction*, 6th Edition, Thomas Telford, London.

Institution of Civil Engineers (1995), *The New Engineering Contract*, 2nd edition, Thomas Telford, London.

Institution of Mechanical Engineers (1992), *MFI Model Forms of Contract*, MEP Ltd, Bury St Edmunds.

JCT 80 (1980), *Joint Construction Tribunal Standard Forms of Contract*, 2nd edition, Royal Institute of British Architects, London.

Royal Institute of Chartered Surveyors (1992), *Project Management Agreement and Conditions of Engagement*, 2nd edition, Royal Institute of Chartered Surveyors, London.

Wright, D. (1993), *Model Forms of Conditions of Contract for Process Plant, An Engineer's Guide*, Institution of Chemical Engineers, Rugby.

## RELATED TOPICS

# 35 Procurement

## Peter Baily

Purchasing has been defined as:

> the process by which organizations define their needs for goods and services, identify and compare the suppliers and supplies available to them, negotiate with sources of supply or in some way arrive at agreed terms of trading, make contracts and place orders, and finally receive the goods and services and pay for them.
>
> (Baily 1987)

It is in the details of this process that project purchasing differs from purchasing for batch production or continuous production, rather than in the aims and objectives. The aims and objectives at their most basic are to arrange for the supply of goods and services of the required quality at the time required from satisfactory suppliers at an appropriate price. But to achieve these basic aims, purchasing departments may need to engage in a variety of activities aimed at subsidiary objectives, including purchase research, supplier development and so on.

Project purchasing has two main subdivisions: buying parts and materials, and placing subcontracts. Closely associated with these buying activities are the related activities of expediting (or progressing), which is intended to ensure delivery on time, and inspection and quality control, which are intended to ensure delivery to specification, together with stores management and stock control.

## SOME SPECIAL CHARACTERISTICS OF PROJECT PURCHASING

Differences between project purchasing and purchasing for other operations are most noticeable on large projects. Small projects do not differ much in their purchasing requirements from jobbing production or (if they are undertaken on a regular and frequent basis) batch production. Batch production, with most batch sizes in the 6 to 6000 range, accounts for two-thirds of UK manufacturing output. As far as the printer and binder are concerned, this handbook is itself part of batch production, although for the editor and publisher it is more an example of project production. Differences exist in:

- the way specifications are arrived at (with a single client playing a dominant role);
- the way suppliers are identified and compared (with the client often involved and sometimes insisting on the use of particular sources of supply);
- the often complicated details of cash flow and payments in and out.

Project production is essentially discontinuous, in comparison with batch production and continuous production. Even though the company concerned may expect to undertake a series of projects of similar type, nevertheless each project stands on its own. It is therefore very important to devise and negotiate terms and conditions of contract which are appropriate for the individual project and which so far as possible cover all eventualities.

Differences also exist in the way the purchasing people, and those on associated activities, are slotted into the organization structure. For large projects, the project manager may have full-time staff, including a purchase manager, attached to the project for several years. Much has been written about matrix organizations, which do not comply with classical organization theories because senior people answer to at least two bosses. The project purchasing manager, for instance, would be responsible both to the project manager and to the purchasing director in the permanent organization structure. He or she would in principle have line responsibility to the senior project manager and functional responsibility to the purchasing director: one would be concerned with *what* is to be done and *when*, while the other would be concerned with *how* it should be done. In practice things are not always quite so clear-cut, which is why people in matrix organization structures have to be able to cope successfully with fluid situations, political pressures, uncertainty and conflicts of interest.

An important responsibility of such a project purchasing chief for a very large project would be manpower planning, which would, of course, be done in consultation with his or her immediate bosses. Some purchasing staff would be seconded to the project for the whole of its duration or at any rate the greater part of it. Others would be attached for a shorter period. It might be necessary to cope with peak workloads by hiring outside personnel on short contracts. At the other extreme, some of the purchasing work could be dealt with no doubt by permanent staff who had not been attached to the project full time, as part of their normal work.

# THE PROJECT PURCHASING MANAGER

A sample job description for a project purchasing manager on a very large project taking years to complete is given in Figure 35.1.

1. Reports directly to the project manager and liaises with other managers in the project team.
2. Provides a procurement service to the project manager. This includes subcontracting, ordering equipment and materials, expediting, inspection and shipping.
3. Represents the project manager in meetings with the client on all procurement matters.
4. Prepares procurement procedures for the project in agreement with the project manager, corporate procurement management and the client.
5. Ensures that the project procurement procedures are adhered to.
6. Directly supervises the chief subcontracts buyer, chief buyer, senior project expediter and the senior project purchasing inspector.
7. Reviews and agrees regularly with the project manager and with corporate procurement management the manpower needs of the project procurement department.
8. Maintains close liaison with corporate procurement management on all project procurement activities.
9. Supervises the preparation of:
   - conditions of contract and subcontract;
   - list of approved suppliers and subcontractors;
   - detailed inspection procedures;
   - shipping documentation; and
   - all other documentation required for project procurement.
10. Agrees the names of firms to be invited to tender in conjunction with the client.
11. Attends the opening of tenders when sealed tender procedures apply.
12. Monitors and reviews procurement progress on a continuous basis and prepares monthly status reports. Attends and reports to project progress meetings whenever the progress of purchases and subcontracts is being considered.
13. Signs bid summaries before their submission to the project manager and the client, after ensuring that the correct procedures have been followed.
14. Supervises the placement of all procurement commitments, whether these are by letter of intent, purchase order, contract or any other form.
15. Ensures that copies of purchase orders, correspondence and all relevant documents, including drawings, specifications, test certificates, operating and maintenance manuals, are correctly distributed to the client, the project manager or elsewhere as laid down in the project purchasing procedures.
16. Obtains from suppliers and subcontractors schedules of work compatible with the project programme.
17. Ensures that negotiations concerning orders and subcontracts are properly conducted and takes personal responsibility if they are critical.
18. Ensures that invoice queries from the invoice checking section are promptly dealt with by procurement staff.

Figure 35.1   Sample job description of a project purchasing manager on a very large project

## SUBCONTRACTING

Large projects are usually the subject of one main contract between the client (or customer, purchaser or employer if these terms are preferred) and the main contractor. The main contractor will then place a number of subcontracts, which themselves constitute contracts between it and the subcontractors (Chapter 33). The client is not legally a party to these subcontracts, but will usually take part in the process of awarding them, deciding on the subcontractors, approving the terms and conditions and so on. In effect the client is subcontracting part of its purchasing activity to the main contractor and will naturally want to keep an eye on things (except in turnkey contracts) and perhaps also to stipulate that certain preferred firms should be used as subcontractors. This can be seen from the points 3, 4, 10 and 15 in the project purchasing manager's job description example in Figure 35.1. Computerized databases are increasingly being used to assist in finding possible subcontractors and suppliers.

Suppliers have a long way to go between finding a possible customer and actually getting the business. Quality capability is important. Track record is very important. At the time the British offshore oil and gas industry was getting under way, the government set up the Offshore Supplies Office (OSO). This was established to ensure that available business was not pre-empted by overseas-based organizations which had built up track records in offshore work in South America, North America and other parts of the world to the exclusion of home-based organizations which were trying to break into new market opportunities. A voluntary agreement between the Offshore Supplies Office and the operators included, for example, the following clauses:

1. All potential suppliers selected to bid are given an equal and adequate period in which to tender, such period to take into account the need to meet demonstrably unavoidable critical construction or production schedules of the operator.
2. Any special conditions attached to the materials, the source of supply of components and materials, and the inspection of goods are stated in the specification or enquiry documents.
3. Stated delivery requirements are not more stringent than is necessary to meet the construction and/or production schedules of the operator.
4. Where the requirement includes the need to develop equipment or proposals in conjunction with the operator, all bidders are given equal information at the same time.
5. When the operator is unable to identify a reasonable number of suitably qualified UK suppliers for its invitation to tender, it will consult the OSO before issuing enquiries.

6. The enquiry documents require the potential bidders to estimate the value of the UK content of the goods and/or services to be supplied.

7. When the operator has determined its decision for the award of contract, in the case of non-UK award it will inform the OSO prior to notifying selected suppliers and will give the OSO a reasonable time, in the circumstances applying, for representation and clarification. This procedure will be followed in the case of subcontracts referred by main or subcontractors to the operator for approval. Where the operator does not intend to call for prior approval of subcontracts, the procedure for adherence to the Memorandum of Understanding and this Code of Practice will be agreed between the operator and the OSO. Where this gives the OSO access to the operator's contractors and subcontractors this procedure will not diminish the direct and normal contractual relationship between the operator and its suppliers. The principle will be adopted that following disclosure of prior information to the OSO on intended awards no subsequent representation to the operator by a potential supplier, other than at the request of the operator, will be entertained.

8. To satisfy the OSO that full and fair opportunity is being given to UK suppliers operators will, on request, make available to officers of the OSO such information as they may reasonably require about:
   - the programme of intended enquiries to industry necessary to implement the anticipated overall programme of exploration and/or development to the extent that this information has not already been made available to the Department of Energy. (The operators may supply this information in any format convenient to themselves provided it is sufficiently comprehensive to enable the OSO to assess the potential opportunity for UK industry.)

How long such agreements should last, and indeed whether or not there is still any justification for them, are matters outside the scope of this chapter.

## THE PURCHASING CYCLE

Conventional notions of the purchasing cycle which apply in batch production, mass production or in merchandising are less appropriate to the realm of the complex project. Large complex projects, such as the construction of complete factories, fully equipped hospitals and offshore oil rigs, are carried out all over the world. Purchase departments are involved on both sides of the contract: on the client's side, in obtaining and helping to analyse tenders and in contract negotiation; and on the contractor's side, in obtaining information from subcontractors and suppliers that is needed in preparing the bid or tender. Once the contract is settled, a large number of orders and subcontracts need to be placed by the contractor's purchase department, usually with the approval of the client.

It is often desirable to use the expert knowledge and experience of contractors in converting the preliminary functional specification into the final build specification. Two-stage tendering is sometimes used for this purpose. There are several versions of this. The World Bank, in its booklet *Guidelines for Procurement under World Bank Loans*, suggests that the first stage could be to invite unpriced technical bids. Based on these, a technical specification would be prepared and used for the second stage, in which complete priced bids are invited.

It is difficult to reconcile the public accountability requirement that all tenderers have equality of information and are bidding for the same specification with the common-sense purchasing principle that exceptional expertise on the part of a supplier should be used in preparing the specification. To expect a contractor with unique design and construction ability to tell the client the best way to do a job, without payment, and then in the second stage to lose the contract to a low bidder with less design capability, seems unlikely to work out. Such firms sometimes insist on some version of the cost-plus contract or on negotiated contracts.

Once the contract has been signed, purchasing work goes ahead on placing the subcontracts. Very often this has to be done in conjunction with the client, as shown in Figure 35.2. Specifications are prepared, possibly in consultation with vendors and incorporated in the Request for Quotation documents. Normal practice is to allow a month for quotations to be submitted, although on bigger subcontracts running into millions of pounds' worth of work more time may be necessary. Further discussion with suppliers may take place after receipt of tenders, to clarify matters, before the bid analysis is prepared for discussion with the client.

An example of a bid analysis form is shown in Figure 35.3. This provides columns in which to list the bids received, allowing comparisons with budget, freight and duty, escalation and other extras. The form also includes a questionnaire on the vendor selected, in which explicit reference must be made to its past record, experience, shop facilities, test equipment and other important aspects of vendor selection.

Whatever procedure is adopted, it is unusual for a bid for a major subcontract to be accepted exactly as made, despite the parity of tender principle. Several meetings between the buyer and the preferred bidder (or bidders) may be required to negotiate aspects of the specification and commercial terms and conditions. After all bids have been received and appraised, with perhaps only one bidder still in the running, detailed negotiations still continue to establish identity

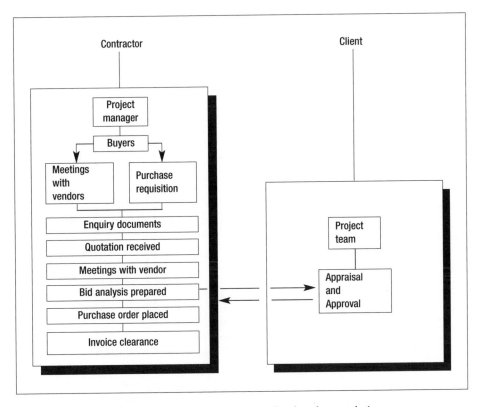

**Figure 35.2   Subcontracting procedure for a large project**
This diagram illustrates the respective roles of the project manager and client at the time of bidding.
*Source*: Adapted from Stallworthy and Kharbanda (1983)

of view between the parties. This should not be seen as an attempt by the buyer to squeeze more concessions out of a supplier who has already put in its final price. Given the timescale, bidders have to concentrate their effort on specification, price and completion date. Selection of a subcontractor can be made on this basis, but buyers will still want to hammer out the commercial terms and technical people may still want to tinker with the design.

Delay in finalizing contract terms or specification details leads to the use of letters of intent. These simply say 'we intend to place the contract with you' and in English law they are not binding on either party (see Chapter 32). Consequently they may not have the desired effect of enabling work to start unless the contractor is able to trust the purchaser. An unconditional letter of acceptance, on the other hand, sets up a binding contract between the parties. Somewhere between the two is the instruction to proceed which authorizes the contractor to start work on specified parts of the contract and possibly states an

**655**

| Vendors asked | (1) | (2) | (3) | (4) | (5) | (6) | Budget | | |
|---|---|---|---|---|---|---|---|---|---|
| | | | | | | | | Requisition no. | |
| | | | | | | | | All costs are tabulated in the currency indicated in the job procedure, namely | |
| Exchange rate used | | | | | | | | Selected vendor | |
| (Date) | | | | | | | | Reasons | |

**Questionnaire on selected vendor**

Is past record satisfactory?

If no past record has shop been surveyed or investigated?

Are shop facilities adequate?

Is experience adequate?

Is test equipment adequate?

Are subcontractors or subvendors involved?

If so is abnormal expediting/inspection effort required?

Are extra exped/inspection costs expected due to shop location performance or sub-contracting?

Do prices represent a good deal under present market conditions?

| Questionnaire on selected vendor | |
|---|---|
| Is past record satisfactory? | |
| If no past record has shop been surveyed or investigated? | |
| Are shop facilities adequate? | |
| Is experience adequate? | |
| Is test equipment adequate? | |
| Are subcontractors or subvendors involved? | |
| If so is abnormal expediting/ inspection effort required? | |
| Are extra exped/inspection costs expected due to shop location performance or sub-contracting? | |
| Do prices represent a good deal under present market conditions? | |

Escalation ⎫
Duties  ⎬ Percentage included in above price calculations
Taxes  ⎭

Total percentage applied to quoted prices

Freight, packing, handling etc. amount

Total price delivered site

Estimated extras

Above normal procurement cost

Total comparative cost for selection

Quoted delivery time — Schedule:

Estimated delivery on site (including shipping time & slippage)

| | Compiled by | Signature | Date |
|---|---|---|---|
| Procurement recommendation | | | |
| Technical review & recommendation | | | |
| Project approval | | | |
| Construction approval | | | |
| Management approval | | | |
| Client approval | | | |

**Figure 35.3  Example of a bid analysis form**
This form is designed to make sure that all the relevant aspects of vendor selection are reviewed and compares the bid and tender price with the cost in the budget or control estimate.
*Source*: Adapted from Stallworthy and Kharbanda (1983)

upper limit to the expenditure which the contractor can make on the authority of the letter. Purchasers usually follow up or accompany the letter of acceptance with an official order form, in order to get the contract into normal administrative and accounting procedures.

# PURCHASED MATERIALS AND EQUIPMENT

Projects vary enormously in size, complexity, duration and the nature of their location (a factory in Russia, a hospital in the Middle East, a bridge over the Bristol Channel, a tunnel joining two islands). Some are less innovative and more routine than others but most require the procurement of materials and equipment such as pipe, valves and cables, none of which was designed specially for the project and the acquisition of which falls more into line with routine purchasing. All must be available on time. All must meet specification. All must be suitably priced if the project costs are to stay within budget.

Even in large projects such purchases may be handled in the purchasing department by staff not attached to the project but who make such purchases as part of their normal work. (It may be better to second such staff to the project team if the work involved occupies them full time for significant periods.) Getting deliveries in on time, product guarantees and fixed prices, together with the legal, commercial and financial complications of operating on a world scale, can provide a variety of challenges to the purchasing staff affected.

## PRICE ANALYSIS AND COST ANALYSIS

In the consideration of quotations, some form of price analysis is always used. Sometimes a more specialized technique is brought into play to support, for example, negotiations about cost-based pricing. This technique is cost analysis.

Price analysis attempts, without delving into cost details, to determine if the price offered is appropriate. It may be compared with other price offers, with prices previously paid, with the going rate (if applicable) and with the prices charged for alternatives which could be substituted for what is offered. Expert buyers deal with prices daily and, like their opposite numbers on the other side of the counter, they acquire a ready knowledge of what is appropriate. When considering something like a building contract, which does not come up daily, they refer back to prices recently quoted for comparable buildings. When several quotations are received, some will be above the average and some below it. Any prices well below the norm should be examined with care. If a supplier is short of work, a price may be quoted which covers direct labour and materials cost without making the normal contribution to overheads and profit. Accepting such an offer can be beneficial to both supplier and purchaser, but it may be prudent to ask why the supplier is short of work. It can happen to anyone, of course, but in this instance have customers been 'voting with their feet' because the supplier's work is not satisfactory?

Low prices may be the result of a totally different position: a seller may have enough work on hand to cover overheads (that is expected sales revenue already exceeds break-even point) and is consequently able to make a profit on any price which is above direct cost. Such offers are not necessarily repeatable; next time round the price quoted may be higher to cover full costs.

Low prices may also be quoted as special introductory offers to attract new customers, giving them in effect a fair trial of the goods or services. This can be regarded as a form of compensation to the purchaser for the risk which it incurs in switching to an untried source. Some buyers do not like accepting such offers, regarding the arrangement as opportunism. Building long-term working relationships with proven suppliers matters, of course, more than a single purchase at a cheap price, but this does not exclude acceptance of special offers in all cases. Management may be pleased with the immediate cost reduction resulting from a one-off low price purchase, but there is a danger that they will expect the buyer to do even better next time. This problem can be overcome if it is made clear that special offers are, as their name implies, special to the particular occasion: they cannot be made the basis for standard price expectations.

Low prices can also be quoted simply through a mistake of the supplier or through its incompetence. Suppliers should be given the opportunity to correct such mistakes or withdraw their offers if the price appears to be suspiciously low (say more than 25 per cent below the price which would normally have been expected). Insistence on a contract at low quoted prices has led to bankrupt suppliers and unfinished contracts, and thus to additional costs for the purchaser, when this point has been ignored.

High prices may be quoted as a polite alternative to refusing to make any offer by sellers with full order books. Buyers should not write off such suppliers as too expensive since next time round they could well submit the lowest bid if conditions have changed. High prices may also be quoted because a better specification, more service, prompter delivery, etc. is offered. Obviously such offers should be considered with care. The best buy, not the cheapest price, is the buyer's objective.

Cost analysis examines prices in quite a different way from price analysis. It concentrates only on one aspect, namely how the quoted price relates to the cost of production. When large sums are involved, and a considerable amount of cost analysis needs to be done, full-time estimating staff or cost analysts may be employed for the purpose by the purchase department. These people are as well qualified to estimate a purchase price as their opposite numbers in suppliers' sales departments are to estimate a selling price: they have the same qualifications, engineering experience and costing knowledge plus specialist knowledge of sheet metal processing, light fabrication, electronics or whatever is relevant. Usually suppliers are asked to include detailed cost breakdowns with their price quotations. Some are reluctant to comply, but if one supplier does, others find it hard not to follow suit. Differences between a supplier's cost breakdown and the purchaser's cost analysis can then be examined one by one to arrive at a mutually agreed figure. Cost analysis is also used by purchasing management to set negotiating targets for buyers.

Cost analysis is a useful technique for keeping prices realistic in the absence of effective competition. It concentrates attention on what costs ought to be incurred before the work is done, instead of looking at what costs were actually incurred after the work is completed. This seems more likely to keep costs down (as well as less expensive to operate) than the alternative of wading through a supplier's accounting records after contract completion, probably employing professional auditors to do it.

## AMENDMENTS TO PURCHASE ORDERS

It is sometimes unfortunately necessary to amend or even cancel purchase orders. This should, of course, be avoided if possible. Good practice is for buyer and seller to agree on all details of specification, price, terms and delivery when the order is placed, and for both parties to comply with the agreement as it affects them. Buyers do not always seem to be aware that if their purchase order constitutes a contract, they have no legal right to amend or cancel it without the seller's consent, since a contract is equally binding on both parties. In the interests of goodwill, however, suppliers are usually willing to accept amendments. Changes to specification, programme changes, increases or reductions in the quantity required, and changes from the buyer's own customers are reasons why buyers may seek to amend purchase orders.

Any amendment incurs the risk of delay and confusion. To avoid confusion it is necessary to ensure that an amendment is notified not only to the seller, but also to each internal department that received copies of the original order. One way to do this is to give details of the amendment on the same form as is used for purchase orders. If the original purchase order was numbered 7300, for example, the amendment form could be numbered 7300A. Some firms prefer to use a specially printed form. This should have the same number of copies as the purchase order form and should be distributed in the same way. Even if these methods are not used and the amendment is notified to the supplier by letter, it is important to ensure that every person who received one or more copies of the original purchase order also receives copies of all subsequent amendment letters, and files these with the order copies.

## ELECTRONIC DATA INTERCHANGE (EDI)

Increasingly, routine communications between trading partners, such as orders, delivery schedules and invoices, go direct from computer to computer, rather than by typed documents sent by post which may then have to be typed yet again into a computer. EDI has been defined by the International Data Exchange Association as:

> the transfer of structured data, by agreed message standards, from one computer system to another, by electronic means.

A considerable saving in paperwork, postage and administrative time is claimed for EDI. Further savings may result from shorter lead times, making possible lower stocks. Against this, fees have to be charged for access to networks, annual subscriptions paid, and hardware and software bought and maintained. EDIFACT (Electronic data interchange for administration, commerce and transport) is being developed as a general message standard. Specialized standards include EDICON (electronic data interchange construction), devised by the construction industry to cover electronic trading in the industry from design, quotation and tendering through to invoicing.

Items such as request for quotation, the quotation itself, purchase order, acknowledgement. delivery instructions, dispatch note, invoice, statement and credit note are often sent electronically rather than through what is sometimes referred to as snail mail. Technical data such as specifications, CAD/CAM data and so on are also increasingly sent by e-mail with attachments, file transfer protocol, etc. Paperless trading systems of this kind are widely used in retailing and manufacturing and play an increasing part in project purchasing.

## REFERENCES AND FURTHER READING

Baily, P. (1987), *Purchasing and Supply Management*, 5th edition, Chapman & Hall, London.

Baily, P., Farmer, D. H., Jessop, D. and Jones, D. (1998), *Purchasing Principles and Management*, 8th edition, Financial Times/Pitman Publishing, London.

Stallworthy, E. A. and Kharbanda, O. P. (1983), *Total Project Management*, Gower, Aldershot.

## RELATED TOPICS

# 36 Bidding

## Stephen Simister

The previous chapters in this part of the handbook focus on the commercial issues more from the client's perspective. This chapter is concerned with the process suppliers of goods and services will typically go through when they are asked to submit a price for undertaking a piece of work. In order for a project to be undertaken goods and services must be procured by the client organization. Just as the client will have a strategy for procuring these goods and services, the supplier will have a similar strategy to win a particular contract.

Suppliers are not simply passive players waiting for clients to contact them. They are actively involved in creating opportunities and develop quite complex procedures to obtain the more lucrative contracts. In this chapter we will examine the entire bid process from when a supplier is first considered for a particular piece of work to when contracts are signed between the client and the supplier.

## MANAGING THE BID PROCESS

If companies are not successful in submitting winning bids their workload will soon dry up. Therefore considerable attention is required to manage the bid process. It is common for a proposal manager to oversee the entire process. The proposal manager is the project manager for the bid process. He or she should treat the bid process like a project and plan and manage it like any project. The proposal manager will require support from a number of people including account managers who may have particular knowledge of the client and technical managers with detailed knowledge of the tasks to be undertaken during the potential implementation of the project. In larger organizations there may be a business development manager who is often an experienced project manager in his or her own right and is now using that experience to win more work for the company. The people required to support the proposal manager can be identified in a responsibility chart.

The bid process is managed as a single entity within the bidding organization but the activities that take place are often delegated to very separate units within it. The reason for this is that the process, while seeming superficially quite simple, is actually complex. Bidding for a piece of work represents a considerable amount of investment for an organization and with a typical success rate of 1 in 5 there is constant pressure to improve this ratio and keep the costs of bidding as low as possible. As shown in the flow chart in Figure 36.1, the bid process has three stages which will now be considered in more detail.

## THE BID PROCESS

The bid process is the process that the supplier will undertake in order to arrive

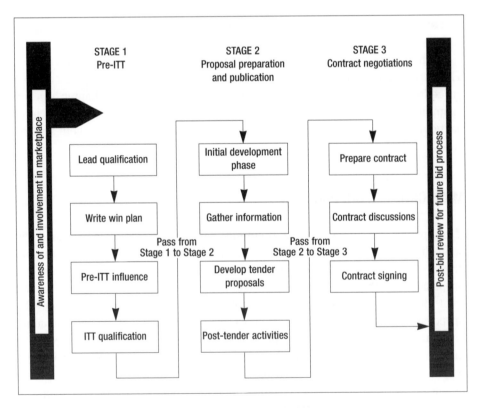

**Figure 36.1  Main activities in the bid process**

at a successful bid which secures a contract with the client. It contains activities which start as soon as a lead has been detected, continue with the response to the invitation to tender (ITT) and finish after winning or losing the opportunity. The process can be divided into three stages:

**Stage 1: Pre-ITT**    Suppliers try to influence the client or organization writing the ITT and to define their strategy after reception of the ITT. The goal in this stage is to establish yourself as the proactive bidder in the client's mind and where possible influence the writing of the ITT so it fits your company's profile the most appropriately. This could be where your company has access to a particular technology or skill that is not widely available elsewhere.

**Stage 2: Proposal preparation and publication**    The supplier creates a proposal which is 100 per cent compliant with the ITT, develops a proposal presentation and executes the post-tender submission strategy defined in the win plan. The goal of these activities is to become the preferred supplier.

**Stage 3: Contract negotiations**    An implementation agreement is reached with the most favourable terms and conditions for the supplier. The ultimate goal of this phase is a contract for the implementation of the client's requirements.

Some of the activities that need to take place within these three stages are shown in the flow chart in Figure 36.1 and are discussed below.

## MAIN ACTIVITIES IN THE BID PROCESS

### STAGE 1: PRE-ITT

This stage is concerned with actually getting on the bidding list that a client is putting together. Clients will typically select only a few firms, perhaps three to five, to submit bids for their project. One of the initial difficulties clients face is how to pick the suppliers that will be invited to bid.

#### Lead qualification

To be invited to submit a pre-qualification ITT the supplier must be active in the marketplace. This will typically involve not only undertaking work in a particular business activity but also ensuring that personnel are involved in business development with current and potential future clients. Whilst most organizations will have about two-thirds of their business as repeat work they are constantly losing clients for a variety of reasons and have to seek out new opportunities. It is during this phase that a decision must be made as to whether a bid will be submitted. It may happen that whilst a bid sounded attractive in its outline form, the pre-qualification documentation may show that the project is not suited to the supplier. Typical areas that suppliers will need to consider in this respect are shown in Figure 36.2.

Once a decision has been made to submit a pre-qualification bid a strategy will need to be developed to submit a winning bid.

## Write win plan

The areas that need consideration to decide if the supplier should bid or not are essentially the ones that also need considering in writing a bid plan. The supplier needs to put itself in the client's position and ask why it should be given the work. A lot of suppliers use a SWOT (Strengths, Weaknesses, Opportunities, Threats) analysis in this respect. The supplier has made a positive decision to bid for the work and will commit resources to this bid. If unsuccessful the supplier should be able to identify some benefit of having undertaken the bid and this also needs to form part of the win plan.

---

**For our organization:**

- Do we have the resources available to prepare the tender?
- Do we have the resources available to undertake the project if we win the work?
- How strong is the competition?
- Do we have a solution to offer the client?
- Does the project offer us the business opportunity in which we are interested?
- What standards do we have to comply with?
- Are we strong in this area or is it an area we wish to develop?
- What are our potential contractual obligations and can we fulfil them?

**For our subcontractor suppliers:**

- What is their position in relation to this project?
- Do they have a solution?
- Are they known to be favoured by the client?

**For the client:**

- Does the client have a budget and do we know what it is?
- Has the client clearly articulated what it wants?
- In the client organization who is for and against us and what is their relationship with the project?
- Has the client undertake a similar venture before and who with?

---

Figure 36.2 Typical questions considered in decision to tender at the pre-qualification stage

### Pre-ITT influence

While developing the pre-qualification bid the supplier is normally allowed direct contact with the client organization. This opportunity should be used to maximum effect. The supplier should be asking pertinent questions that demonstrate its expertise in the area of interest. In some instances it may be possible to suggest to the client that a supplier's technology is the only one to use and try to gain an advantage over other technology.

During the client meetings it should also be possible to determine who are the key decision-makers in the organization and which of these are for or against the supplier. Effort can then be directed towards trying to win over the latter people whilst supporting those who favour the supplier.

### ITT qualification

The pre-qualification bid has been submitted and the supplier has been successful in going forward to the next stage. The supplier needs to reflect on its performance for further bid opportunities as well as prepare itself for moving into the next stage.

If a supplier is unsuccessful at pre-qualifying, most clients are willing to provide a debriefing session which allows the supplier the opportunity to find out what went wrong, which areas it needs to work on and, for future market intelligence, who won through to the next stage.

### STAGE 2: PROPOSAL PREPARATION AND PUBLICATION

This stage is concerned with putting together tender documents which not only comply with the client's requirements but also demonstrate the supplier's competence in the tendering process. The tendering process is quite an investment in resource typically adding some 5 per cent to the cost of most contracts.

### Initial development phase

The pre-qualification document will form the basis of the tender and act as a structure on which to build. The first task is to check that all the tender documentation has been received and that the supplier understands what needs to be delivered. It may be that the scope of work has been changed since the qualification stage and this needs to be studied to ensure that the supplier is still interested in submitting a bid.

**667**

## Gather information

Once the requirement is understood an appropriate solution can be developed. Information to develop the solution needs to be gathered and, if required, expertise outside the organization sought. The information gathering exercise is crucial as it generally takes some time and whilst it is still ongoing people have to make decisions based on what is currently available.

## Develop proposal

This is where the bulk of the work lies. The supplier has to develop its proposals to a stage where it is confident that they meet the client requirements and in such detail that accurate cost and programme estimates can be made. The amount of detail involved is generally not far short of what is required to actually execute the project. Once again the supplier will generally be liaising with the client, trying to find out if there are any preferred solutions and obtaining feedback on suggestions being put forward.

## Post-proposal activities

After the tender has been submitted the supplier will generally be invited to discuss its proposals with the client, once the client has had time to analysis them. Normally the client will wish to clarify various aspects of the tender and investigate if there is any room for negotiation over aspects of the proposal.

## STAGE 3: CONTRACT NEGOTIATIONS

Once the tender has been accepted, a formal contract needs to be drawn up which sets out the obligations of the supplier and client in the execution of the project. While the outline of the contract will have formed part of the tender documentation, the exact details are often subject to negotiation after the tender has been awarded. For instance, the exact starting date of the project will need to be set.

## Prepare contract

A contract that reflects the type of relationship the two parties want to enter into needs to be drafted. Some industries, such as construction and building, have a wide range of standard forms of contract (see Chapter 34). Alternatively clients may have their own standard forms. In all circumstances a contract has to be drawn up which states the intentions of the parties and accurately reflects both the client's requirements and the supplier's tender. During this phase the supplier

668

also needs to think about what its stance will be during the contract discussions. There may be a particular point which is important to the supplier and to get agreement on this it will be willing to sacrifice some other detail. These items need thinking about so that the personnel undertaking the negotiations know what approach to take on crucial issues.

### Contract discussions

This is where the finite detail of the client–supplier relationship is dealt with. Both sides have invested considerable resources to reach this negotiation stage. However, both sides also want to try and negotiate the most favourable conditions for themselves. In construction it is not uncommon for contractors to commence building on-site whilst still negotiating the details of the contract. This is obviously not a desirable situation and the contract should be signed prior to any work commencing on the project. Ultimately both parties have to sign the document and so there must be agreement on the terms and conditions set out in the contract.

### Contract signing

The actual act of signing can in some circumstances be rather a show-piece with the press invited to a ceremonial signing of the contract. In most circumstances, the signing of the contract is undertaken by management, typically at board level. These people will normally have not been involved in the negotiation of the contract so will be trusting that their negotiating staff have done an appropriate job.

## POST-BID REVIEW

Once the contract has been signed the supplier then concentrates on actually delivering the goods and services that the client requires. As part of the bidding process a review of the bid should be undertaken to identify lessons learned for use in the next exercise. Topics to be addressed might include the following:

1. Why did the client choose our company?
2. Was the client completely satisfied with our presentation and proposals?
3. Was our approach the right one or just the best of a bad bunch?
4. Was the offered solution correct or did protracted negotiations have to take place to hone the requirements?
5. Were our cost and programme appropriate to meet the client's needs?

While the bid process should be evaluated immediately after the successful signing of the contract it may also be useful to hold a review once the project is complete. A post-project review can provide an insight as to the accuracy of the tender put forward measured against the executed costs. This can provide input into future tenders and adjustments made to future bids accordingly.

## CONCLUSIONS

For suppliers the bidding process consists of three stages:

1. Pre-ITT
2. Proposal preparation and publication
3. Contract negotiations

While the supplier's aim is to win the contact, it does not want to do so at any price. The supplier has to be able to influence the client to the extent that the client wants the supplier to win the contract as well. In these circumstances the supplier will be able to negotiate quite favourable terms for itself.

Bidding is concerned with predicting the future since the supplier has to commit to a price and time framework before the work is undertaken. Because of this the supplier has to build up an accurate database of information drawn from previous contracts and evaluated against the bids for those contracts. The post-bid review is vital in assisting this feedback.

Suppliers have to become experts in preparing and submitting winning bids if they are to survive and grow in an increasingly competitive market.

## REFERENCES AND FURTHER READING

Bartholomew, S. H. (1999), *Estimating and Bidding for Heavy Construction*, Prentice-Hall, San Francisco, CA.

Bernink, B. (1995), 'Winning contracts', in J. R. Turner (ed.), *The Commercial Project Manager*, McGraw-Hill, London.

Miles, M. (1992), *Stronger Competitive Bidding*, Lawrence & Leong Publishing, New York.

## RELATED TOPICS

# 37 Managing variations, claims and disputes

## *Peter Marsh*

Like all good relationships, contracts can go wrong. Often we would like to pretend otherwise, to stick our heads in the sand and assume all is and will remain rosy. Usually it will be so, but we must make plans for things going wrong. Most contracts have written into them clauses to deal with the unusual, and that is right and proper. If variations and other disputes are planned for, then their impact and cost will be reduced.

In this chapter we consider how to deal with unplanned or unusual events. We start with variations. Variations are inevitable; we cannot predict the future and plan for every eventuality. Hopefully they can be kept to a minimum, and variations arising from poor quality of design and decision-making avoided; variations will be essential rather than nice-to-have changes or plain mistakes. Many variations will result in a claim for additional payment. Some claims will be accepted, some challenged. If the parties cannot agree a claim, they will go into dispute, and that then needs to be resolved. We consider the impact of the Construction Act 1998 and the Arbitration Act 1996, both of which arose partially out of the Latham Report (1994), and we consider the response of contracting practice to them. Finally, we describe adjudication procedures.

## VARIATIONS

Variations may be described not unfairly as the cancer of contracting. Their cumulative effect can combine to destroy the best of contracts; the habit of ordering them is in itself a disease. What causes this disease? The causes are many but the principal ones are as follows:

1. *Inadequate allowance for thinking time*  It is distressing but true that many managers are not convinced that progress is being made unless holes are

being dug, equipment is being manufactured or code written, and so start work before the project is properly planned. Morris and Hough (1987) describe how the project manager on the computerization of PAYE resisted starting before he was ready, and the project had a successful outcome; whereas Hougham (1996) describes how, ten years later, the team working on the computerization of London Ambulance started work before they were ready, leading to a national disaster.

2. *Inadequate specifications*   One finds a great reluctance amongst people to be completely specific as to what they require, as to the services to be provided by the purchaser and as to the actual conditions under which the work will be carried out

3. *Insufficient attention as to whether what the tenderer is offering is exactly what the purchaser wants to buy*   The tendency is to say 'It seems generally all right; we can sort out the detail later.'

4. *Lack of discipline*   In the matter of variations it is often far easier to say 'Yes, while we are about it we might as well have that done', than to say firmly 'No, it's not necessary.'

5. *Improvements to avoid obsolescence*   With the rapid rate of technical change taking place today, any major plant or system is likely to be out of date in some respects long before it is completed. This applies particularly to information technology and telecommunications systems. It may well be that some upgrading is essential now but it is often far better to have the system built and installed as it was originally designed and ensure that the facilities exist for later developments. The later the stage in the project, the more it costs to make changes (Turner 1999), and so you reach a point where changes must be avoided unless they are absolute show-stoppers.

6. *Genuinely unforeseeable circumstances*   It would be idle to pretend that no variation is ever justified. There are times when it is essential to vary the works or system. Variations must be allowed for in the original thinking and procedures set in place for their control. Anyone who thinks they can avoid variations completely is a fool or a liar, or both. Therefore variations must be accepted and planned for.

It is often not appreciated that even a quite simple change of specification can have a dramatic impact on a contractor, especially if that contractor also has a design responsibility. The change may involve the contractor in:

- design work which because of the change is now not needed;
- additional design work including studying the consequential effect of the variation on a number of drawings;
- cancellation of, or modification to, orders already placed on their own works or outside suppliers;

674

- the placing of new orders;
- delay and/or re-phasing of the design and manufacturing programme to accommodate the variation;
- delay in delivery of material due to re-phasing of work or concentration of work into a shorter period with consequential overtime costs and loss of productivity;
- extending the period of the contract.

Figure 37.1 illustrates how these items contribute to the cost of a variation. It follows from this data that the cost effect of the variation will be reduced the earlier it is ordered. The figure takes no account of the effect of the variation on the programme as a whole. If it is small, a single variation will have little impact on the programme (though the New Engineering Contract says that all variations must be assumed to have a time and cost impact). The figure also takes no account of the double administrative cost effect on the contractor of having to go through the same operation twice. Again, if it is only one item few contractors would seriously quarrel with accepting it as one of the hazards of contracting.

The trouble starts when not one variation but a whole series of variations causes a disruption to the regular progress of the work, loss of productivity and a substantial extension to the contract programme. The time spent by the

| Additions | Deductions |
|---|---|
| 1. Works or bought-out cost of the new item | 1. Works or bought-out cost of the item to be replaced |
| 2. Percentage for overheads and profit related to works or bought-out cost | 2. Percentage for overheads and profit related to works or bought-out cost |
| 3. Man-hours cost for the installation of the new item | 3. Man-hours cost for the installation of the item to be replaced |
| 4. Percentage for overheads and profit on installation costs | 4. Percentage for overheads and profit on installation costs |
| 5. Charge for additional design including overheads and profit necessary to incorporate the new item | 5. Charge for any design work including overheads and profit which will no longer be required |
| 6. Design, labour and material costs, related overheads and profit and consequential modification to the remainder of the plant system including study of the drawings to see if any are necessary | |
| 7. Cancellation charges payable to outside suppliers | |

**Figure 37.1  Factors affecting the cost of a variation**

In this example one or more items of equipment are to be deleted from the specification and replaced by others.

contractor's head office staff will then become totally disproportionate to that anticipated at tender, and coupled with the extension to the programme may affect the contractor's ability to undertake other work. Under these circumstances the purchaser must expect that the contractor will seek to recover these additional costs and also seek recompense for the impact on its ability to obtain other business.

Claims for delay and disruption are never easy although those for site work where the facts can often be established from contemporary site records are easier than those for overheads. However, it is important to distinguish between the two bases of claim which the contractor may make for head office overheads and profit. First, there is a claim for overheads only which is based on the additional managerial time and expense required to deal with the problems created by the excessive number of variations. To establish such a claim the contractor must provide evidence of the additional managerial time expended and not simply add on an arbitrary percentage (see the case of *Tate and Lyle* v. *GLC* (1982)).

The claim for overheads and profit is for the allegation that by reason of the extended contract period and involvement of their staff, the contractor has been deprived of the opportunity to earn a contribution to its fixed overheads and profit. In the building industry, it is common for the contractor to calculate such a claim by the use of a formula. However, in principle that must be wrong. The formula is only a means of quantification. Before it can be used, the contractor must prove that as a result of the delay, they suffered some loss by showing that the delayed contract deprived them of the opportunity to obtain other work on which a margin for overheads and profit could have been earned. This means that the contractor must prove:

- there was other work available which would have been profitable;
- that they did not obtain this work; and
- that the failure to obtain the work was the direct result of the delayed contract.

It is only when these facts have been proved that the use of a formula as a method of quantification of loss has any validity. The difficulties of proving those facts are recognized. However, the basic principle of English law is that it is for the contractor to prove it has suffered a loss arising directly from the purchaser's actions, and the automatic substitution of a formula which takes no account of actual loss suffered cannot be justified.

## PRICING OF VARIATIONS

There are often difficulties in negotiating variations, especially on lump sum contracts where there may be no mechanism for doing so established in the contract itself. The purchaser will think the contractor is taking them for a ride, but may genuinely be unappreciative of what trouble and cost their simple instruction has caused. The purchaser will also be acutely aware that it is impractical for them to get competitive quotations. The contractor may be anxious to recover any ground lost in post-tender negotiations. Neither side is likely to be in a mood for making concessions but the purchaser is likely to be in the weaker negotiating position.

For contracts priced on a bill of quantities or schedule of rates (see Chapter 33), the problem is not as great provided that the quantities in the bill are not grossly exceeded or diminished as a result of the variation and the work is being executed under the same conditions. Different conditions may, for instance, be work conducted at a different time of the year than it was anticipated that the original work would be executed.

With lump sum contracts for which there are no rates quoted for individual items of work the problem is more difficult. In the New Engineering Contract (ICE 1995), a valiant effort has been made to solve this problem by requiring the contractor to quote as part of their tender a schedule of cost components. For the purpose of tender comparison quantities are assumed by the employer and included in the invitation to tender.

This schedule gives the cost components in terms of various categories of labour for design, manufacturing and site work together with related overhead percentages, the costs of materials and plant and other overhead costs. The variation is then priced by making a comparison between the forecast actual cost for the work originally included in the tender and the forecast actual cost arising as a result of the variation together with the contractor's fee. The comparison is specifically not made by deleting the original contract price for the work and substituting the forecast actual cost. It is also made clear that the variation is not to be priced by using any of the rates and prices included in the contract, say in the bill of quantities.

There are several difficulties with this method apart from its obvious administrative cost and complexity. One is that while one can compare staff and labour rates, and indeed overheads on their own, they mean very little without knowledge of the contractor's productivity. One firm's rates may be higher than another's but this may well be offset by higher efficiency.

## TIMING OF PRICE NEGOTIATIONS

A vital factor in the successful control of variation is the timing of price negotiations. Too often because of the pressure for the achievement of physical progress of the work and the complexities in the price change, instructions are given to the contractor to make the change, with the alteration in price to be negotiated later. Ideally the sequence of events should be as follows:

1. The purchaser decides that a particular variation would be desirable.
2. The contractor is instructed to assess the effect of the proposed variation in terms of:
   - price
   - time
   - performance.
3. The contractor submits their proposals under these headings.
4. If the purchaser decides to proceed with the variation then they negotiate with the contractor on the amendments to the price, time for completion and performance requirements.
5. Once agreement has been reached the purchaser issues a formal variation order in standard form serially numbered.
6. The contractor proceeds with work.

The New Engineering Contract uses a similar series of steps. It seems a long series and the temptation is to go straight ahead and tell the contractor to start work. Indeed there will be genuine emergencies when it is necessary to do just that and tidy up the paperwork afterwards. But in so doing, not only any possible negotiating advantage is lost but also any enthusiasm on the part of the purchaser's staff to make variations is removed and financial control of the contract is lost. Except in the case of a real emergency it should be difficult to order variations.

## CLAIMS

Claims can be considered under three headings:

- Ex gratia
- From excessive ordering of variations
- Default by the client in their obligations under the contract.

### EX-GRATIA CLAIMS

These are claims made when the contractor can find no contractual basis for the claim but considers that because of some unexpected event there is a moral or commercial obligation on the client to pay compensation. An example would be a fixed price contract entered into before the huge and unexpected rise in oil prices in the 1970s which could not have been foreseen by the contractor and for which therefore no allowance was made in its price. The difficulty for the contractor is that while it may be true that they suffered losses, there is ordinarily no reason why the client should pay compensation. Payment can only possibly be justified if, in the face of serious and unforeseeable difficulties in the performance of the contract, for which the contract provides no right for additional payment, the contractor made extraordinary efforts to overcome these and completed the work to specification and by the time for completion. Then the contractor may rely on the client's goodwill but on nothing else. Faced with a contractor going bankrupt or completing, it may be cheaper for a client to make an ex-gratia payment.

## CLAIMS ARISING OUT OF EXCESSIVE VARIATIONS

These have been discussed above under the heading Variations.

## CLAIMS ARISING OUT OF THE CLIENT'S DEFAULT

Under all contracts there are some obligations for the client to perform, for instance in making the site available and supplying information and facilities which if they are not provided on time and to specification will result in the contractor incurring additional costs. A claim for the recovery of those costs is often linked with one relating to the number of variations. The great difficulty for the contractor is that although it may be obvious that work has been disrupted and delayed, it may also be very difficult to itemize each cause to a specific effect and therefore to additional cost

It may be possible today for the contractor by the use of an appropriate computer program to use the technique of impact analysis. This establishes the impact of individual causes on a series of logically connected events within the network for the contract. However, the practical application technique requires the knowledge of how the work was programmed, how it progressed, when the delaying events occurred and the interaction between one delay and another. This emphasizes the need for contemporary data and for the work on the analysis to start at the time and not at the end of the contract.

Because of the difficulties of determining the effect of individual events contractors often try to present their claim on a 'total loss', 'global' or 'rolled up' basis. This has the obvious advantage that the contractor does not have to prove the individual loss arising from each event but only make a broad-brush calculation based on the total cost overrun. From the employer's point of view, the disadvantage is that they do not have particulars of the sums being claimed. Nor do they have the basis on which it is alleged in each instance that they, rather than the contractor, or some external cause, is responsible for the loss in question. The employer's ability to challenge the contractor's claim is therefore much reduced.

From the decisions in English law on the validity of 'rolled up claims', the position is that the contractor must demonstrate that they have made every effort practicable to itemize the causes of delay or disruption and their individual effects. Only where the contractor can show that the complexity of the interrelationship between a number of causes is such that it is impractical to do this is it likely that a court or arbitrator would accept a 'rolled up claim'.

## CLAIMS PRESENTATION AND MANAGEMENT

There are a few basic rules to be followed in preparing for and presenting claims:

1. Consider the possible areas of claim from the start of the contract and plan accordingly. Don't wait until they happen.
2. Make sure that all involved know any particular areas of risk which have been accepted under the contract which might normally entitle a claim to be made but would not on this contract.
3. Keep accurate and contemporary records from the start of the contract. A good factual site diary prepared at the time is essential on a construction contract. (The problem is that this does lead to the impression that the first file opened by a contractor on a construction site is the claims file. Unfortunately it is necessary. However, ensure that it is understood that the purpose of the file is to resolve problems, not make claims.)
4. Where it is considered that a claim may arise in respect of design work, ensure that the records are sufficiently detailed to identify the number of man-hours spent and by whom on the revisions to each drawing or the preparation of new revised drawings, and the reasons for the revisions.
5. Make a record of the requirements for the giving of notice of claims under the contract and ensure that these are followed through in practice.
6. Ensure that all correspondence with and from the client which could have an impact on claims is reviewed as are all minutes of meetings.
7. In presenting the claim make sure that it contains:
   - a short executive summary;
   - clear references to the terms of contract on which the claim is based;
   - all essential data which is required to understand the claim, such as critical dates, extensions of time applied for and granted, variation orders issued, etc.;

- copies of the programme, minutes and other documents supportive of the claim

## DISPUTES

In the late 1990s major changes occurred in the ways in which disputes under a contract can be resolved, especially if the contract falls within the definition of a construction contract under the Housing Grants Construction and Regeneration Act 1998 (the Construction Act). First, was the Arbitration Act 1996 and, second, the mandatory provisions of the Construction Act relating to the determination of disputes by adjudication.

### THE ARBITRATION ACT 1996

Arbitration had gained a bad reputation for being too slow, too expensive and too involved with technical issues having no substantive merit. The primary reasons for this are listed below:

- In practice arbitration procedures had closely followed those of the courts although not required to do so by law. Arbitration had been referred to as 'wigless' litigation and borrowings from court procedures included such elements as discovery of documents and the rules of evidence.
- There had been in many instances no power to exclude in advance of the arbitration proceedings through the commercial contract itself the right to appeal to the High Court on a point of law.
- Clauses were invalid that allowed an arbitrator to decide with the agreement of the parties on the grounds of equity and fairness *ex aequo et bono*.
- English arbitration law was difficult to discover being contained in the judgements of the courts and the two principal statutes, the Arbitration Acts of 1950 and 1979.

For all these and other reasons it was decided that a new Act was required to set out in a form which was comprehensive and easy to read the English law relating to arbitration. The following changes were introduced by the Act:

1. The introduction of an objectives clause which states:
   - the object of arbitration is to obtain the fair resolution of disputes by an impartial tribunal without unnecessary expense and delay; and
   - the parties should be free to agree how their disputes should be resolved subject only to such safeguards as are necessary in the public interest.

2.  The tribunal has the power to decide on all procedural and evidential matters subject only to the right of the parties to decide such matters for themselves. These include:
    - whether any and if so which documents or classes of documents should be disclosed;
    - whether any and if so what questions should be put and answered by the parties and when and in what form this should be done;
    - whether to apply strict rules of evidence or any other rules as to admissibility, relevance or weight of any material;
    - whether and to what extent the tribunal should itself take the initiative in ascertaining the facts and the law;
    - whether and to what extent there should be written or oral evidence or submissions.

Hence the conduct of the arbitration proceedings provided that the parties agree, or in the absence of their agreement the tribunal decides, can be tailored in such a way as to achieve the objectives of the Act.

On the subject of appeals, it is now open to the parties to agree in their commercial contract to exclude the right of appeal entirely. In any event, an appeal can only be made if:

- the parties agree; or
- the court decides that the decision of the tribunal was obviously wrong; or
- the question is one of general public importance and the decision of the tribunal is at least open to serious doubt and that it is just and proper in all the circumstances that the court should determine the question.

Unless the court decides that the decision of the tribunal was obviously wrong, it is likely that in practice it will only allow an appeal if the point of law concerns the interpretation of a standard contract in general use, and which is of significant importance to the industry concerned with that form of contract. The court is given wide powers to support the arbitration tribunal especially in relation to complying with the tribunal's orders regarding procedural matters, such as the production of documents, exchanging witness statements and so on, which have in the past been the cause of substantial delays.

There is one significant problem with the Act which has caused some to recommend that arbitration should not be included within a construction contract although all standard forms in general such as those issued by the ICE and the JCT do retain arbitration. In the past where an application was made to the court for summary judgement under Order 14 because it was considered there was no arguable defence to the plaintiff's claim, then even if the contract contained a clause that all disputes were to be referred to arbitration, the court had a discretion to hear the application instead of staying it to arbitration.

Under section 9 of the new Act the discretion of the court has now been removed and it appears that if the contract does contain an arbitration clause then the court must stay the matter to arbitration. This has been confirmed in the case of *Halki Shipping Corporation* v. *Sopex Oils* (1997) where there was no real defence to the claim by the plaintiff, but as there was an arbitration clause in the contract the dispute had to be stayed to arbitration.

Applications for summary judgement are relatively common in the construction industry usually for payment for work done for which a certificate of the architect or engineer has been issued but payment has not been made. Now it appears that assuming there is an arbitration clause in the contract the court would not be able to hear the application if it was disputed by the other party, however flimsy the defence.

Leaving that point aside what are the perceived advantages of arbitration as opposed to recourse to the courts?

- Confidentiality: the proceedings are in private
- Informality
- Speed
- Use by the arbitrator of his or her technical knowledge

However, apart from the first, these advantages are all dependent upon the parties agreeing as to how the proceedings should be handled or the arbitrator taking a very firm line and using to the full his or her powers under the Act. The likelihood of either party agreeing to anything except something to their own advantage, which means that it will almost certainly be to the disadvantage of the other, seems remote.

That brings out the essential point that arbitration will only ever be as good as the arbitrator, and highlights the importance of his or her selection. Good arbitrators are usually expensive and it is, of course, one of the disadvantages of arbitration that the costs of the arbitrator have to be paid for by the parties. Also, even though the courts can be slow, they are available to the parties. In arbitration, the parties' choice of the person to act as arbitrator can be affected by his or her availability to act, since good arbitrators do tend to get booked up well in advance. With the reforms currently taking place in civil procedure the advantages of arbitration over the courts, except for the issue of privacy, do not appear to be significant.

## ADJUDICATION

One of the key reforms proposed by the Latham Report (1994) was that there should be in all construction contracts a procedure for the rapid resolution of disputes. This procedure would operate while the contract was being performed with either party having the right to challenge the decision at arbitration once the contract was completed. In the event, after a long gestation period, the Construction Act provides that:

> a party to a construction contract as defined by the Act has the right to refer a dispute arising under the contract for adjudication under a procedure complying with the Act.

The Act then goes on to provide that:

> the contract shall:

(a) enable a party to give notice at any time of their intention to refer a dispute to adjudication

(b) provide a timetable with the object of securing the appointment of the adjudicator and referral of the dispute to him within 7 days of such notice

(c) require the adjudicator to reach a decision within 28 days of referral or such longer period as is agreed by the parties after the dispute has been referred

(d) allow the adjudicator to extend the period of 28 days by up to 14 days, with the consent of the party by whom the dispute was referred

(e) impose upon the adjudicator to act impartially

(f) enable the adjudicator to take the initiative in ascertaining the facts and the law

The Act goes on to provide that:

- the contract shall provide that the decision of the adjudicator is binding until the dispute is finally determined by legal proceedings, arbitration or agreement between the parties. The parties could accept the decision of the adjudicator was final
- the adjudicator is immune from being sued for anything done or not done by him in deciding the dispute unless the act or omission is in bad faith
- if the contract does not contain a procedure complying with these requirements then the Scheme for Construction Contracts shall apply

At the time there was significant antagonism towards these provisions particularly from leading construction lawyers. This was based on their views that adjudication was not needed, it was not workable and would increase rather than decrease antagonism in the industry. After over a year's operation of the Act it is clear that it is workable and it has provided quick answers to resolving disputes which would have previously dragged on for months. Much of the credit for this must be given to the judges of the Technology and Construction Court for their robust upholding of the adjudicator's decisions when challenged on legal technicalities. However, it does not seem to have reduced adversarialism which remains a chronic construction industry problem. It is clear that the JCT amendments do comply with the Act and therefore the Statutory Scheme will not apply to contracts let under any of its standard forms. With the ICE amendments it is not so certain that they comply since the ICE has sought to retain the decision-making powers of the engineer. Its amendments state that there is no dispute between the parties until either the engineer has given his or her decision and one party objects to it or the engineer has failed to give a decision within the time allowed. Only then can a dispute be referred to adjudication. Whether this trick will work or not remains to be seen. It clearly does not comply with the spirit of the Act.

Many construction contracts are not let on these standard forms and unless they are drafted to include provisions relating to the adjudication which comply with the Act then the Statutory Scheme will be deemed to be substituted. In summary the Scheme provides for:

- the method of appointing the adjudicator;
- the adjudicator being a natural person not in the employ of either party;
- powers for the adjudicator but only with the consent of the parties to deal with related disputes under different contracts;
- the right of the adjudicator to open, review and revise any certificate except one which under the contract is final and conclusive;
- the adjudicator to act impartially and in accordance with the terms of the contract and its applicable law;
- the adjudicator to take the initiative in ascertaining the facts and the law necessary to determine the dispute and to decide on the procedure to be followed in the adjudication.

The weakest area in the Act is the lack of any clear means of enforcement of the adjudicator's decision. It appears that the only way in which enforcement is possible is by an application to the courts for summary judgement. However, there is the obvious risk that any such application might be opposed by the other party. Further, assuming that the contract contained an arbitration clause, the case would have to be stayed by the court to arbitration under the 1996 Arbitration Act and the decision in Halki Shipping Corporation to which reference was made earlier. It is for this reason that the JCT and the ICE in their amendments to their standard forms of contract have provided that the arbitration clause does not apply to any action to enforce the decision of an adjudicator.

## REFERENCES AND FURTHER READING

Hougham, M (1996) 'London Ambulance Service computer aided dispatch system', *International Journal of Project Management*, **14**(2).

Institution of Civil Engineers (1995), *The New Engineering Contract*, 2nd edition, Thomas Telford, London.

Latham, Sir Michael (1994), *Constructing the Team, Final Report of the Government/Industry Review of Procurement and Contractual Arrangements in the UK Construction Industry*, The Stationery Office, London.

Morris, P. W. G., and Hough, G. (1987), *The Anatomy of Major Projects: The Reality of Project Management*, Wiley, Chichester.

Turner, J. R. (1999), *The Handbook of Project-based Management*, 2nd edition, McGraw-Hill, London.

## RELATED TOPICS

# Part VII
# People

# INTRODUCTION TO PART VII

In Part VII we examine the soft skills of project management, that is the management of the people. We consider human resource management in the project-based organization and competence development. We discuss many issues associated with the management of the people on the project team, and other stakeholders. We describe how to make effective teams and examine the role of the manager as leader. We consider the stakeholders, and the management of the conflict that can arise, and also assess the impact of different cultures and ethical standards of project managers.

### Chapter 38: Managing human resources in the project-based organization

In Chapter 38 Anne Keegan and Rodney Turner describe how the management of human resources differs in a project-based organization from that in the old functional, hierarchical, line management organization. In particular they consider personnel selection, career development and the skills development of both individuals and the organization.

### Chapter 39: Project management competence in the project-based organization

Martina Huemann and Roland Gareis continue the theme of competence development in the project-oriented company in Chapter 39. They describe the competence development of both individuals and the organization as a whole. They introduce a project management competence model and show how it can be used to benchmark the competence of both individuals and the organization.

## Chapter 40: Managing teams: the reality of life

In Chapter 40 Tony Reid describes the management of project teams. He gives practical guidelines on the development of high performing teams and describes several techniques for improving their performance.

## Chapter 41: Managing and leading

In Chapter 41 David Partington considers the leadership role of the project manager, whether there is a difference between managing and leading, and whether leadership is something that can be learnt. Certainly good leaders can make themselves better by improving on the behaviours that work, and to that end David sets out some of the theories of leadership. He describes trait and behavioural theories (two 'one-size-fits-all' theories), and contingency and visionary theories (two situational approaches.)

## Chapter 42: Managing stakeholders

Stakeholders are all the people who have an interest in the outcome of the project. Some can be for you, some against. In Chapter 42 Bill McElroy and Chris Mills discuss how to manage the project's stakeholders. They describe a stakeholder management process and give hints and tips on successful stakeholder management.

## Chapter 43: Managing conflict, persuasion and negotiation

Sometimes the stakeholders will be just plain difficult or they may have a truly different opinion of the project from other members of the team. That can lead to conflict. In Chapter 43 Bob Graham describes the management of conflict. He shows how to avoid conflict and resolve it if it occurs. He also describes the power of information in avoiding conflict and sets out a strategy for using a project information system as a tool to avoid conflict.

## Chapter 44: Managing culture

Parties to a project can come from a range of backgrounds, from different professions or different countries. Their different backgrounds can lead to different cultural traditions. In Chapter 44 David Rees describes the impact of culture on business and how it can be managed.

## Chapter 45: Managing ethics

Finally, in Chapter 45, Alistair Godbold describes business ethics, particularly as they relate to projects. Evidence shows that in the long run, it is better to behave ethically, because in the long run it leads to better performance of your business. Alistair describes different ethical approaches, how they differ around the world, and offers some practical tips.

# 38 Managing human resources in the project-based organization

## Anne Keegan and Rodney Turner

This handbook is based on the premise that we live in a world in which projects and multidisciplinary working are key vehicles for delivering corporate strategy (see Chapter 2; Kanter 1983; Handy 1995). The increasing use of projects over the last forty years reflects rapid change in the nature of markets and technologies. Projects are spreading from the traditional strongholds of construction, aerospace and shipbuilding to all kinds of industries including the software industry, insurance, banking and education. It would seem that all industries can benefit from project-based working (Hastings 1993). The widespread use of projects as a way of organizing work has managerial implications for organizations in areas such as governance, operational control and the management of knowledge and learning (Turner and Keegan 1999). It also impacts directly on the human resource practices of organizations. Every time a new project is developed, the human configuration of the organization must change, demanding adaptability and flexibility from employees and managers.

Human resource management (hereafter called HRM) has a long and distinguished history stretching back more than eighty years to the pioneering work of the earliest practitioners (see Niven 1967; Megginson 1985; Paauwe 1991). HRM aspects of project-based working are among the key issues of strategic importance for project-based firms. In recent years, progress has been made in developing new concepts in human resource management applicable to different branches of industry and in different types of organizations (see Bacon *et al.* (1996) on small firms, Garrahan and Stewart (1992) on the international automotive industry). This represents a promising advance on the general prescriptive model of HRM evident in the early part of the 1980s which was largely dominated by ideas developed in the post-Second World War era. In this chapter we describe HRM practices and processes we have observed used for managing people in project-based organizations in strategically important sectors of industry.

## FROM OPERATIONS TO PROJECTS

From the mid-nineteenth century to the immediate post-Second World War period the industrial scene was characterized largely by manufacturing firms organized along bureaucratic lines and managed through functional hierarchies carrying out operations which were stable and routine by design. In the decades after the Second World War the introduction of new technologies and materials led to a huge increase in innovation in industry. The scope of activities undertaken by firms widened considerably as firms sought to respond to changing consumer preferences. Innovation became a normal part of business activity, a prerequisite to survival instead of a fancy addition. Projects were frequently established to carry on this novel work. In the beginning these projects were isolated from operations and designed to produce something outside the normal stream of work (Burns and Stalker 1961).

Projects were a new undertaking for most firms and differed from operations as a method of organizing and harnessing human, technological and financial resources. Unlike operations, projects are transient. Unlike operations, projects are always novel and therefore, to varying degrees, unpredictable in their outcomes (Turner 1999). Operations set the status quo and rely on its being maintained for their survival while projects upset the status quo because they are unique, novel and transient. And unlike many operations that are capital intensive and rely on standardized skills, projects are heavily dependent on specific human inputs in the form of project team members who bring skills together in unpredictable ways. A cursory reading of recent management literature reveals that projects are no longer the isolated entities they once were. They are no longer the skunk works placed discreetly in the parking lot or the odd group of researchers working alone in an office far from normal workers and normal activities (Burns and Stalker 1961). Projects now pervade most organizations and have become accepted as a regular feature of doing business. In many cases, projects are the core activity of organizations and the centre of value added activity.

In observing HRM practices in the project-based firm, we have identified three core issues in successfully managing people in such organizations (Keegan and Turner 1999):

- Selection in the project-based firm
- Career development for a changing environment
- Knowledge management and learning.

694

## SELECTION IN THE PROJECT-BASED FIRM

The selection of people is an important issue for project-based firms. Variations in selection practices are evident according to whether the skills and knowledge of potential employees are core to the firm and not easily substituted or peripheral and easily found on the labour market. In many areas of project-based work, particularly traditional areas such as engineering and construction, employees are substitutable due to standard skills acquired through relatively short training periods. For example, several categories of construction worker as well as administrative, security and catering personnel can be considered here. Project-based firms often utilize these workers on a contract-by-contract basis or outsource this work to specialist service providers. In these industries, project management is the key core competence, and project managers have the longest tenure with organizations. In other areas, particularly high technology industries, employees are far less substitutable and constitute the core competence of project-based firms. Programmers in proprietary technologies, project managers and client liaison personnel are just three of the categories of organization members less easily substitutable in the short or even medium term and represent the centre of value added for some of our case companies. Where employees are potentially core members of the firm, more time is taken to ensure that they are going to 'fit in' with the turbulent nature of project-based work. Selection of core staff – including technical experts and particularly project managers, leaders and supervisors – is conducted in a highly organic manner, meaning that emphasis is placed on informal methods of assessing people for employment.

The main practices used for selecting people to work for a project-based organization differ quite markedly from the functional, hierarchical organization and include:

- the use of headhunting both directly and through agencies;
- the use of personal contacts and 'the grapevine' in finding prospective employees;
- the hiring of personnel on project trials and work experiences;
- liaison with personnel at universities and technical schools, often over many years.

### THE GOAL OF SELECTION: THE RIGHT PEOPLE AT THE RIGHT TIME?

In project-based firms, we observed selection practices which Bacon *et al.* (1996) refer to as 'informally formal' practices. That is, companies have informal practices for managing selection, as shown in the list above. For most of the firms we have observed, finding the right people at the right time is not the most important goal when it comes to selecting personnel. People we have spoken to are on the whole cautious about the precision that can be attained in a transient client-led environment with respect to what it means to find 'the right people' and how sustainable such a definition might be. They indicate a more open attitude towards finding suitable candidates for their organizations and lay emphasis on the importance of supporting those people to grow with the organization and change as it changes. They tend to avoid go/no-go decisions in selection and emphasize selection by project, trial and work experience. Specific skills and knowledge sets are not as important as the adaptability of people to the changing environment within project-based firms and the willingness of organizational members to adapt as projects change and clients demand new approaches. Most of the firms we have observed avoid the use of selection tests in hiring decisions. They argue that decisions based on observing people at work, over time and in interaction with colleagues and clients is far more valuable than a go/no-go decision strategy based on one-off selection and assessment exercises.

## PROJECT-BASED FIRMS AS FLEXIBLE FIRMS

In addition to hiring people 'gradually' through projects and trials, most of the firms we have observed use contracting as a way to cope with qualitative and quantitative uncertainties in their business. This is a type of selection for the short term. In a leading engineering and construction contractor in the oil, gas and petrochemical industry, estimates of temporary employees range from 25 per cent to 40 per cent depending on the workload. Respondents at a supplier of bespoke systems to the telecommunications industry estimate that at least one-third of personnel, including project personnel, are employed on temporary contracts to work on projects. Similar estimates were given for the other organizations we have visited. This mirrors the ideas of freelances and core peripheral workers popularized by Handy (1988) and others. In both these models, the use of contract labour is a central feature. An important area of future research is to ascertain more precisely the amount of contract labour used by project-based firms and the delineation of strategies surrounding contract labour. Numerical flexibility can also be attained by the increased use of part time labour. As a twist on this theme, we have observed evidence of 'more than full-time' labour usage as distinct from 'part-time' labour usage as a strategy to cope with uneven workloads of projects. In one company we visited, project managers report work weeks of 60–80 hours. The potential for stress and burnout, particularly as projects often end up overlapping with no rest period in between, was reported by our respondents as an obvious tension within the workplace.

696

One implication of the use of high levels of contract labour in project-based firms is the importance of melding disparate groups of temporary and permanent employees into effective project teams. The successful achievement of this depends largely on how successful employees and managers are at coping with the disintegrative tendencies of project work and whether they display an emotional adaptability to new faces, new leaders, new colleagues and new conditions. Many firms use this as a strong indication of whether a new member will contribute to their organization or whether the relationship should be terminated early. In many companies, there is a pattern of newcomers leaving early in their probationary periods, whereas those with whom the company forges a stronger connection tend to stay for a long time. Although flexibility can be attained by surrounding a core of workers with a more flexible and dispensable periphery, the benefits may be illusory given the disenchantment of those in the periphery and attendant costs of training, selection and specialization required to maintain such an arrangement. However, project workers, especially those in the construction and oil, gas and petrochemical industries, have always worked in a transient environment. Project-based firms are transient firms because projects have a finite life span.

The potential difficulties of project-based ways of working are more relevant for those sectors experiencing a greater demand for innovation and higher levels of complexity. Resolving the tension of project-based work in terms of transience of employment is already a focal point for firms we have interviewed in the government and financial services sectors. In particular, the question of how to combine the machine bureaucracy with project based ways of working remains a taxing issue. For those firms where this is relevant, there is an emphasis on instituting culture change, training and socialization programmes to make the transition to a transient environment of project work easier for all.

## CAREER DEVELOPMENT FOR A CHANGING ENVIRONMENT

One of the clearest results from our work in project-based firms is the rapidly changing nature of career development and career profiles. Project-based firms in established industries such as engineering and construction are accustomed to shorter-term careers and the mobility of personnel. Organizations that have more recently adopted projects as an important form of operational control are faced with the reality that lifetime and long-term employment patterns are increasingly a thing of the past. Bastions of long-term employment such as universities and the civil service, as well as specific organizations like Phillips, Shell and Hewlett Packard, have all in recent years shifted towards shorter-term contracts and an emphasis on 'employability of staff' rather than employment guarantees.

## THE SPIRAL STAIRCASE CAREER

The spiral staircase is the image that best describes the career patterns in project-based firms. Spiral staircases sweep upwards rather than ascend in a narrow ladder-like manner. The sweeping element of the spiral staircase represents the breadth of expertise and knowledge required in a multidisciplinary project environment that people must gather through a range of appointments as their career develops. This differs markedly from climbing the ladder up the functional silo, where people are developed in a narrow specialism. In six years with ICI, Rodney Turner had six jobs, covering the complete life cycle of process plant from feasibility to design, construction and maintenance. This is illustrative of the competence development required for the project-based firm, in contrast to the narrow specialization of the functional silo.

In conceptualizing careers in project-oriented firms, we are also inspired by the Dutch artist Escher and his representation of the monk's staircase that is constantly ascending and descending at the same time. Escher's staircase captures for us the challenge in the modern versatile firm that people must always learn and unlearn, both ascending the staircase of knowledge, as they master one set of skills and knowledge, and then descending to the lower level of a new learning challenge only to ascend once again. Career development in the project-based firm is also clearly dependent on the initiative of employees and their willingness to master new skills, often at short notice. In this environment, employees must take responsibility for managing their own careers and use their own knowledge and initiative to advance. Our work with project-based firms suggests that the reframing of career expectations is a vital aspect of the support firms can offer their employees in coping with the reality of customized problem-solving and project-based work.

## REVISITING THE REWARDS ISSUE

Project-based firms are coping with a tension in their reward systems. This tension arises in the shift from traditional rewards, especially promotion 'upwards', to new forms of reward and recognition. It is becoming harder to reward people with promotion 'upwards' (and the prestige it affords) because hierarchies are flattening under cost pressures and under evidence that more organic forms of managing are appropriate in innovative, project-based firms. Project-based firms are placing emphasis on different types of rewards and encouraging employees to see development, and the prestige that normally went with promotions to a 'higher rank', in a new way.

ABB Lummus Global, a Dutch firm of engineering designers and constructors in the oil and gas industry, is a good example of this career reframing. It has developed a culture in which career development is couched in terms of projects of increasingly greater responsibility, complexity and challenge as opposed to taking a step up the clearly defined career ladder from junior to more senior roles. ABB Lummus Global has broken the long-established link between number of subordinates and the value placed on a member of the organization. Instead of number of subordinates, the amount of risk a person manages and the strategic importance of the projects on which people are working are given emphasis. The company stresses the importance of people moving across projects, to different areas within functions. It rewards people who take on new roles in order to expand their skills even if it is not an upward move in a traditional sense.

In several organizations from the engineering, electronic and financial services industries, we have met people who moved from senior positions within departments to new roles which provide development of their skills and knowledge, and more responsibility for adding value for the organization and for clients, but which are not a move 'upwards' in the traditional sense of more subordinates or a 'higher' rank. The Dutch consultancy firm Pink Elephant is also committed to the broad-based development of people and to the elimination of barriers to development including the shortening of hierarchies and the creation of a culture in which greater responsibility is taken as a hallmark of career development. In these firms, the spiral staircase career is widely evident.

## DEVELOPING NEW MANAGERS FOR THE NEW ENVIRONMENT

Many companies point to the strongly held beliefs of managers as a barrier to changing career expectations. The Dutch subsidiary of Ericsson offers training to help managers deal with a new environment with flattened hierarchies where managers need to secure the cooperation and consent of project team members in order to operate effectively. There is a shift from viewing careers in terms of promotion and subordinates to viewing careers as continuous processes of learning and successful completion of projects. The company concentrates on training and development practices to meet the new needs that arise in a changing world. For that reason, team building and coaching are an integral part of training employees to manage new career demands. Project managers are learning that the goal is not to manage subordinates, but to lead experts and technical specialists in knowledge work.

## DUAL OR MULTIPLE CAREER STRATEGIES

Von Glinow (1988) provides a description of technical career ladders in high-tech firms that is strongly mirrored in our experience. Dual career strategies have long been used by professional firms as a way to overcome the dysfunction of promoting technical experts to senior managerial and administrative roles (the Peter Principle, Peter and Hull 1969). Many firms have career paths for line and functional managers as well as technical experts and team managers. Ericsson propounds a 'Competence Model' where the competence of staff is seen as a triangle. Each of the three sides of the triangle represents a specific type of competence: human competence, technical/professional competence and business competence.

Not all of the firms in our study have tackled the Peter Principle problem with equal success. In one electronics firm technical people cannot advance as far as traditional line managers and this is a challenge the firm recognizes must be addressed if it is to continue carrying out effective projects utilizing highly knowledge-intensive personnel. Respondents report losing valuable personnel as a consequence of their being forced into line and departmental managerial roles as part of their progression. This loss has promoted a reorganization, only recently commenced, with the solution of this problem one of its major goals.

We have also found a strong tendency towards the creation of more diverse career ladders, breaking away somewhat from dual ladders emphasizing technical versus line management careers. We have recorded the addition of career ladders in sales and marketing, and in the management of human resources. However, an unresolved issue which emerges from our research is the tendency for the uppermost layers of governance still to be drawn from one stream, generally that of line managers, as opposed to the other streams of career development. This may act as a barrier to the development and retention of experts in non-traditional management roles.

## LEARNING FOR THE INDIVIDUAL AND FOR THE ORGANIZATION

The traditional functionally organized firm has a strong benefit for people: they have well defined functional homes to which they belong and through which they develop careers. In the project-oriented firm, those functional homes are less important to the way people work because projects provide the main source of operational control. In some companies, the project orientation has gone so far that the functional structure has all but been eradicated.

Take the example of Unisys in Vienna, a company providing bespoke computer and information technology systems. Unisys employs approximately 200 people in Vienna and serves the needs of mainly Austrian clients. It has abandoned the functional departments in the largest and most strategically important area of its activities, the ISG (Information Systems Group), and adopted a fully project-based way of organizing. Employees within the ISG are allocated to projects, which when completed are disbanded. The employee is immediately allocated to another project. There are no functional departments to which people belong and around which they form an identity. At the end of projects, there are no functional homes.

The elimination of functions and the creation of the project-based firm have advantages for firms like Unisys. One benefit is the reduction of costly overhead structures in the form of functional departments in which people physically have desks and a place to return to between projects. Indeed, there is no real 'between projects' with this approach to organization. Highly educated and skilled personnel are constantly moved between one project and another. As if to reinforce the 'movement' inherent in this approach to organization, Unisys in Vienna also has a policy of hot-desking in which people yield their traditional workstation and share desks with others on an as needs basis. Other companies in the IT sector, such as the Baan Company, also utilize hot-desking. One reason is that IT firms and other knowledge-intensive firms work so closely with clients that many workers spend much of their time in the client organization and not in the employing organization.

Having eradicated functions, the goal is to keep people utilized and so have a stream of new projects coming online. The emphasis on utilization is illustrated at Unisys by the recent introduction of rate realization as the key performance measure in the company. For knowledge-based firms like Unisys, keeping highly educated and expensively trained professionals working on projects is a key issue. Many companies experience this pressure. However, Unisys is one of a few firms where we find the elimination of the functional structure. In Ericsson, members are organized according to clients and also according to traditional areas such as operations, marketing and sales. In the Dutch company ABB Lummus Global, functions are retained as centres of expertise and efforts are made to encourage cooperative and non-segmentalist approaches to projects. In Raytheon Engineers and Contractors, there are no plans to eliminate functions which are seen as vital to the organization and which are regarded as providing crucial services to the value-adding heart of the firm, the projects. Most of our firms allude to the tension between projects and functions. Some respondents, especially from ABB Lummus Global, see the tension as helpful and regard the maintenance of project and functional elements as essential to the development of knowledge and expertise as well as the effective carrying out of projects. Project-based firms have lived with tension between project and function for a long time. However, although the project orientation is a strong feature of these firms in general, there are disadvantages to be considered when functions are de-emphasized or entirely eliminated. People may feel somewhat lost, lacking a 'place' to hang their hat or constancy in terms of the people with whom they work. We call this 'no home syndrome'. This is a general drawback of the temporary organization and also of the much vaunted virtual organization (Handy 1995).

## NO HOME SYNDROME AND THE ISSUE OF LEARNING

The no home syndrome has another serious drawback in that when functions are eliminated so too are repositories of organizational knowledge. There are only projects and project groupings which, because transitory, are not the best vehicle for capturing and sharing, let alone disseminating, knowledge. Although there is no doubt that a fluid project-based environment can speed up the response to client needs, the potential loss of knowledge, or transfer of learning from project to project, must be overcome for the benefits to be realized. The challenge for project-based firms is to try and nurture a learning environment in the absence of secure employment. Some lessons emerge as to how project-based firms are managing the challenge of learning and knowledge management.

By way of illustration, given that Unisys has adopted a highly project-focused way of working in Vienna, how does it cope with the drawback of the loss of a functional structure in its ISG? Unisys management, both locally and internationally, acknowledges that the loss of functional repositories of knowledge is a serious concern. It has practices in place to try and ameliorate these disadvantages in order to maximize the benefits, including trying (where possible) to ensure that there are additional people on a project so that two people are available to do the same job (two systems administrators/two programmers). The rationale here is to allow people to work together on similar tasks, especially new ones, so that each person can learn alongside another and the knowledge can be captured through the communication of the two people. In a supplier of business and financial data products, we have uncovered a pattern of innovation that relies heavily on the simultaneous and unplanned creativity of employees. As in the case of Unisys, this pattern of innovation and learning is shaped by the complex and unpredictable nature of the firm's markets for which there are few standards and even fewer guidelines. Both companies also use a variety of 'memory carriers' (Van der Bent et al. 1998) such as the intranet, project review procedures and formal and informal meetings to capture learning independently of individuals.

## IN THE ABSENCE OF 'NELLIES'

The practice of pairing people on projects that we found in Unisys reflects another

702

feature of the industry within which Unisys works. While 'sitting next to Nellie' has been a classic training and learning practice for decades, there are very few Nellies in Unisys. So rapidly changing are the technologies and solutions that Unisys offers to clients, that there are very few people experienced enough in the organization with whom newcomers can be paired in an effort to provide mentoring and coaching opportunities. 'Nellies' are created by sitting next to each other people who learn from one another through experimentation, rather than through the transfer of learning from an experienced individual to an apprentice. Although there may be some redundancy, there is a greater chance that the knowledge will be captured more effectively than if a person works alone. This system also ensures that knowledge is developed and learning captured continuously over the timescale of the project instead of simply at the end. The widespread use of mentoring as a form of training in recent years reflects the importance of ongoing learning and development in a changing environment.

## GOOD INTENTIONS

Many firms try to use project standards, reviews and the project close-out phase as opportunities to capture learning. The idea is that people home in on what they have learned during a project, and at the end of the project, and share this with others. On project standards and project reviews, there is overwhelming evidence that project members, in general, neglect this responsibility. This means that improvements made during the project are often lost. Time pressures at the end of projects often preclude the effective writing up of lessons learned or even face-to-face review between project team members and their colleagues. This is rendered even more difficult because at the end of projects, the energy of project team members is at its lowest level. Some respondents call into question the usefulness of project end review processes because of the argument that technical knowledge changes so much that an end project wrap-up is often not adequate.

Despite all this, respondents are also adamant that operating amidst a largely project environment requires special attention to be paid to capturing the advances made by people on projects and ensuring that the knowledge is less transient than the projects from which it emerged. To overcome these difficulties, some firms place formal processes for capturing learning on a corporate basis and hand responsibility for that to groups not directly involved with projects on an operational basis. Unisys, for example, has centres of excellence working to develop best practices across Unisys internationally. This helps to explain why local offices like Vienna have been able to move towards a fully project-based way of working. The loss of functions as repositories of knowledge is ameliorated by corporate-wide efforts to nurture learning and develop excellence in strategic areas. We encounter 'programmes' at Unisys for coping with issues of common concern, for example the Internet and the Millennium Bug, as well as areas of expertise such as 'practice management Europe' which offers services in managing the bid procedure to all Unisys offices. Ericsson, Reuters and ABB Global Lummus are other organizations that have 'programmes' in place which transcend national offices and offer the development of expertise and knowledge on an international basis. These programmes have at their heart the goal of developing best practice and knowledge for dissemination throughout the global network. These programmes offer an opportunity for the transience of projects to be ameliorated by a concentration of effort on learning from projects. In his study of 'new organizations' adopting a project-based focus, Hastings (1993) found that programmes of this nature were an important practice for developing and capturing learning on a corporate basis. All of these initiatives develop organizational memory, regarded as an important prerequisite for organizational learning.

Learning and knowledge sharing, although vital for the success of project-based firms, is one of the thorniest issues managers and employees deal with. Practical suggestions include the following:

1. The continued use of practices which capture and share knowledge, including project review procedures and project standards used as broad but flexible guidelines.
2. The strengthening of informal networks and opportunities for 'talk' within the company.
3. Greater attention paid to giving personnel the basic resource they need to capture and record their own learning for the purposes of externalization and socialization – people given time within the life span, and at the close-down, of projects (Nonaka and Takeuchi 1995).
4. And, finally, the maintenance of functions as centres of excellence, or the creation of corporate-wide resources to ensure that learning is developed within and between parts of the organization on strategic issues.

## CONTINUITY AND CHANGE IN PEOPLE MANAGEMENT

Project-based firms face specific challenges in people management for three reasons. First, the customized nature of problem-solving places a premium on success in attracting and developing people. Project workers often have a high level of customer contact, as customers are often involved in the design and delivery of outputs, from buildings to software systems, from banking solutions to wireless communications. Second, project-based firms are temporary organizations. Because projects are always 'unique, novel and transient', the combination of knowledge, skills and abilities required to meet client needs is continuously changing. Third, project-based firms are insecure places. The gain or loss of projects can have an immediate and dramatic impact on the sustainability of employment, and the numbers of people needed. Project-based firms, because of customized problem-solving, transience in skill and knowledge requirements, and the fluctuating nature of workload, represent an interesting site for the study of people management.

These three features impact on career development and reflect broader trends in employment in society in general. The pattern of career development emerging from our study comes close to Handy's (1995) vision of working life for all of us in the near future. According to Handy, permanent careers are fast disappearing in all areas of working life. In their place, firms offer opportunities. These include opportunities to train, retrain, be outplaced or developed in new directions. Handy (1995) cites the case of Dutch oil giant Shell who announced its intention to cease offering employees stable careers. On March 29 1995 Shell announced its decision to become a federation of project-focused businesses and an ending of 'guaranteed' careers for those working as expatriates. This major restructuring of Shell's personnel policy mirrors the broader changes we are finding, indicating that new patterns of career development are rapidly becoming an integral part of the landscape. As such, those concerns being addressed possibly reflect broader developments to which more attention should be paid.

Our observations might also be interesting in terms of broader developments in HRM from a theoretical perspective. Secure employment is not a strong feature of project-based firms. This runs counter to two of the core ideas in HRM theory and practice.

The policy of hiring large numbers of employees on projects and contracts is at odds with the centrality of employment security which is a cornerstone of HRM theory and practice. This idea has a long history within the HRM tradition and emerged partly because of the difficulties faced by early mass manufacturers. The ideal of lifetime and secure employment was subsequently reinforced by Human Relations theorists in the 1930s who emphasized the importance of social aspects of work and the power of informal groups and their influence on firm performance. Maslow (1943) suggested that security was important in efforts to meet basic human needs and to act as a prerequisite to the development of worker commitment and dedication. The power of these ideas is still evident many decades later. Influential HRM theorists even argue that employment security is a universally 'best' HRM practice (Pfeffer 1998). They further maintain that it is necessary for the creation of high performance work systems. However, this may not be the whole picture. Notwithstanding the long tradition of adhering to the ideal of lifetime and secure employment, such an ideal may not be suitable in the context of the project-based firm. In any event, it is not practised.

The second HRM orthodoxy that may not be valid in the context of the project-based firm is that of the importance of employment testing and systematic selection techniques. Employment testing is regarded as another HRM 'universal best practice'. It is taken to indicate that organizations value human resources and manage them effectively (Pfeffer 1998). Once again, we can trace this to the origins of HRM in the mass manufacturing paradigm, dominated as it was by ideas on scientific management and the attainment of effective 'person–job' fit. In every single firm in which we visited, selection takes place on the basis of projects, trials and work experiences. Headhunting is widespread and interviews are used to ascertain whether a potential candidate might be suitable for project-based work. All of this corresponds to recent calls by management theorists for managers to move away from the traditional emphasis in selection methods on the objective and the verifiable. Drucker, for example, has argued that managers must 'leap right over the search for objective criteria into the subjective' (Hams 1993). Sveiby (1997) also found evidence in his studies of knowledge-based, project-based and professional firms that intuitive assessment dominated all other methods of selecting candidates. Finally, referring again to a recent in-depth study of HRM practices in small firms in the UK, Bacon *et al.* (1996) found that managers prefer to manage in a way that protects the benefits of an informal and organic management system, and avoid the use of employment tests in every single case. Informality and intuition are an important part of selection techniques in project-based firms. Those firms in our study that have formalized their selection procedures tend to do so on a limited basis, formalizing, for example, the use of questioning on biographical or critical incidents, but still retaining intuitive assessment of candidates as the primary technique.

Our experience indicates that notwithstanding widespread theorizing on knowledge management, individual and organizational learning, this is still an area in which firms face great challenges. The practical difficulties of encouraging learning and promoting practices for developing organizational memory lag behind theoretical advances in this area. If our experience is representative of the picture in project-based firms in general, then the issue of learning must be a top priority for management as it is a strategic issue, but one for which there is much yet to be done.

## CONCLUSIONS

The project-based firm has been with us for some time and it exhibits key differences when compared with functional hierarchies that dominated the industrial landscape for over a hundred and fifty years. Project-based firms are heavily dependent on individuals, many of whom are not easily substitutable because of their knowledge, skills, customer contacts and ability to operate effectively in a transient environment. Project-based firms have a variety of practices in the areas of selection, careers and learning that reflect the challenges and opportunities of project-based work, and face difficult issues in managing people. In particular, patterns of practice which exhibit an 'informal formality' may provide a key to resolving the tension between the need for systematic practices and consistency, on the one hand, and intuitive organic practices that nurture innovation and flexibility, on the other. In a world where continuous learning has become a prerequisite for survival, people management practices in these project-based firms might provide valuable insights for other firms who are increasingly project based. We hope the issues we have identified and the propositions we have developed in three main areas of HRM in project-based firms might serve as a basis for developing deeper research and a better understanding of these firms, and people management practices in them.

## REFERENCES AND FURTHER READING

Bacon, N., Ackers, P., Storey, J. and Coates, D. (1996), 'It's a small world: managing human resources in small businesses', *The International Journal of Human Resource Management*, **7**(1), February.

Burns, T. and Stalker, G. (1961), *The Management of Innovation*, Tavistock, London.

Garrahan, P. and Stewart, P. (1992), *The Nissan Enigma*, Mansell, London.

Hams, G. T. (1993), 'The post-capitalist executive: an interview with P. F. Drucker', *Harvard Business Review*, May–June.

Handy, C. B. (1988), *The Future of Work, A Guide to Changing Society*, Blackwell, Oxford.

Handy, C. B. (1995), *The Age of Unreason*, Arrow Business Books, London.

Hastings, C. (1993), *New Organizational Forms*, Heinemann, London.

Kanter, R. M. (1983), *The Change Masters*, Allen & Unwin, New York.

Keegan, A. and Turner, J. R. (1999), 'The people side of project based organisations', *RIBES Working Paper 9921*, Rotterdam Institute of Business Economic Studies, Erasmus University, Rotterdam.

Maslow, A. (1943), 'A theory of human motivation', *Psychological Review*, **50**.

Megginson, L. C. (1985), *Personnel Management: A Human Resources Approach*, Irwin, Chicago IL.

Niven, M. (1967), *Personnel Management 1913–1963*, Institute of Personnel Management, London.

Nonaka, I. and Takeuchi, H. (1995), *The Knowledge Creating Company*, Oxford University Press, New York.

Paauwe, J. (1991), 'Limitations to freedom: is there a choice for human resource management?', *British Journal of Management*, **2**.

Peter, L. and Hull, R. (1969), *The Peter Principle*, William & Morrow, Toronto.

Pfeffer, J. (1998), *The Human Equation: Building Profits by Putting People First*, Harvard Business School Press, Boston, MA.

Sveiby, K. (1997), *The New Organizational Wealth*, Berret-Koehler, San Francisco, CA.

Turner, J. R. (1999), *The Handbook of Project-based Management*, 2nd edition, McGraw-Hill, London.

Turner, J. R. and Keegan, A. (1999), 'The versatile project based organization: governance and operational control', *European Management Journal*, **17**(3), June.

Van der Bent, J., Paauwe, J. and Williams, A. R. T. (1998), 'Organizational learning: an exploration of organizational memory and its role in organizational change processes', *RIBES Paper 9855*, Rotterdam Institute of Business Economic Studies, Erasmus University, Rotterdam.

Von Glinow, M. (1988), *The New Professionals: Managing Today's High-Tech Employees*, Ballinger, Cambridge, MA.

## RELATED TOPICS

# 39 Project management competences in the project-oriented organization

*Roland Gareis and Martina Huemann*

In the project-based organization, project management (pm) competences are not just required by individuals, but also by project teams and by organizations. These competences have to correlate. The pm competences of individuals performing project roles, such as project owner, project manager or project team member, have to be in accordance with the pm competences of the organization as a whole as documented in its procedures. The pm competences of individuals, project teams and organizations can be described, measured and further developed. As project management has to be considered as a core competence of the project-based organization (called in this chapter the project-oriented organization, POO), this competence has to be explicitly developed by the organization.

## STRATEGY, STRUCTURE, AND CULTURE OF THE PROJECT-ORIENTED ORGANIZATION

A POO is one which:

- defines management by projects as an organizational strategy;
- adopts temporary organizations for the performance of complex processes;
- manages a project portfolio of different project types;
- has specific permanent organizations to provide integrative functions;
- applies a 'new management paradigm';
- has an explicit project management culture; and
- perceives itself to be project-oriented.

The POO considers projects not only as tools to perform complex processes, but as strategic options for organizational design (Figure 39.1). Management by projects is the organizational strategy of companies dealing with an increasingly

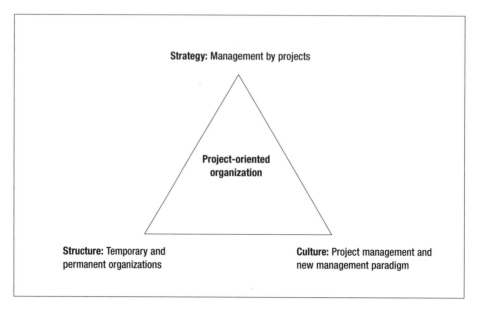

**Figure 39.1    Strategy, structure and culture of the project-oriented organization**

complex business environment. By applying management by projects the following organizational objectives are pursued:

- Organizational differentiation and decentralization of management responsibility
- Quality assurance by project team work and holistic project definitions
- Goal orientation and personnel development
- Organization of organizational learning by projects

POOs perceive projects and programmes as temporary organizations for the performance of complex processes, such as contracts for external clients, as well as product development, marketing campaigns or re-engineering activities for internal clients. The more projects of different types a company holds in its project portfolio, the more differentiated it becomes and the higher becomes its management complexity. To support the successful delivery of individual projects, and to ensure the compliance of the objectives of the different projects with company strategy, the POO must adopt specific integrative structures such as a strategic centre, expert pools, a pm centre of competence and a project portfolio steering committee. Some of these permanent organizations might be virtual.

The POO is characterized by the existence of an explicit pm culture, such as a set of pm-related values, norms and procedures. Further, in order to manage a

POO successfully, the application of a new management paradigm is required. Traditional management approaches emphasize detailed planning methods, focusing on the assignment of clearly defined work packages to individuals, relying on contractual agreements with clients and suppliers and using the hierarchy as a central integration instrument. Compared with this traditional approach, the new management paradigm can be perceived as comprising the core concepts of lean management, total quality management, business process re-engineering and the learning organization, which are:

- organization as competitive advantage;
- empowerment of employees;
- process-orientation;
- teamwork in flat organizations;
- continuous organizational change;
- customer-orientation; and
- networking with clients and suppliers.

## PROJECT MANAGEMENT AS A BUSINESS PROCESS OF THE POO

By perceiving project management as a business process of the POO, the methods of process management can be applied to design the pm process. By describing the pm process, by defining its objectives and by defining its deliverables, it is possible to measure the quality of the pm process. The pm process consists of the following subprocesses:

1. Project start
2. Project controlling
3. Project coordination
4. Management of project discontinuities
5. Project close-down

Objects of consideration in the pm process are the project objectives, the scope of work, the project schedule and the project costs, as well as the project organization, the project culture and the project context. The achievable deliverables of each pm subprocess, such as the different project plans, the project culture, the defined strategies to manage project environment relationships, project progress reports, minutes of project meetings, etc., can be compared with the resource requirements for the performance of the pm subprocess.

# PROJECT MANAGEMENT COMPETENCES OF INDIVIDUALS AND PROJECT TEAMS

Project management competence can be defined as the ability to perform the project management process efficiently. The pm competence relates to specific project management tasks to be fulfilled, and it exists if there is pm knowledge as well as pm experience. In the POO, pm competences can be differentiated for individuals, for project teams and for the organization.

The pm competences required by individuals differ according to the different project roles they fulfil. The following project roles can be performed by individuals:

1. Project owner
2. Project manager
3. Project management assistant
4. Project team member
5. Project contributor

The specific project management tasks to be performed, such as by the project manager, can be described in a role description. Figure 39.2 is a role description for a project manager.

The pm competence of a project manager is the ability to fulfil all responsibilities specified in the role description. Besides the pm knowledge and the appropriate pm experience depending on the project type, a project manager needs product, company and industry knowledge. In international projects cultural awareness and language knowledge are prerequisites too. The pm knowledge and experience required by the project manager depends on the pm approach applied by the POO. According to a process-oriented project management approach, the project manager requires knowledge and experience not just to apply pm methods but to design the pm process creatively. The ability to design the pm process relates to:

- the selection of the pm methods appropriate for a given project;
- the selection of the appropriate communication structures;
- the facilitation of the different workshops and meetings;
- the selection of the participants for the different workshops and meetings;
- the decision to involve a project coach;
- the definition of the appropriate form for the pm documentations (project handbook, project progress reports, project close-down report); and
- the definition of a project marketing strategy.

To perform successfully, a project team requires a specific team competence in

**Objectives**
- Representation of the project interests
- Assurance of the realization of project objectives
- Coordination of project team and of project contributors
- Representation of the project to the relevant environments

**Organizational position**
- Reports to the project owner
- Is a member of the project team

**Responsibilities in the project assignment process**
- Formulation of the project assignment with the project owner
- Definition of the core team members with the project owner

**Responsibilities in the project start process**
- Organization of the project start process (with the core team members)
- Know-how transfer from the pre-project phase into the project with the project team members
- Agreement on project objectives with the project team members
- Development of adequate project plans with the project team members
- Design of an adequate project organization with the project team members
- Development of a project culture, establishment of the project as a social system with project team members
- Performance of risk management and discontinuity management with the project team members
- Design of project context relations with project team members
- Implementation of project marketing with project team members

**Responsibilities in the project coordination process**
- Disposition of resources for the performance of work packages
- Controlling the results of work packages, ensuring the quality of work packages
- Approval of work package results
- Communication with members of the project organization
- Communication with representatives of relevant environments
- Project marketing

**Responsibilities in the project controlling process**
- Organization of the project controlling process (with the core team members)
- Determination of project status with project team members
- Agreement on or planning of corrective actions with project team members
- Further development of project organization and project culture with project team members
- Redefinition of project objectives with project team members
- Redesign of project context relations with project team members
- Project marketing with project team members
- Preparation of progress reports with project team members

**Responsibilities in the management of a project discontinuity process**
- Organization of discontinuity management process (crisis or change management) with project owner
- Contributions to the contents of the crisis or change management with project team members

**Responsibilities in the project close-down process**
- Organization of project close-down process with project core team
- Emotional close-down of the project and regarding the content with project team members
- Transfer of know-how into the line organization with project team members and representatives of line organization
- Final project marketing with project team members

**Figure 39.2   Role description 'Project Manager'**

713

addition to the pm competences of the single project team members. The pm competence of a project team is the ability to commonly create the 'Big Project Picture', to solve conflicts in the team and to agree on common project objectives. A project team needs the ability to cooperate in workshops and meetings. The common development and the application of project plans, such as a work breakdown structure, a schedule, a project environment analysis, etc., have to be understood as tools to support communication in the project team.

## PROJECT MANAGEMENT COMPETENCES OF ORGANIZATIONS

Not just individuals but also organizations have the capability to gather knowledge and experience and to store them in a 'collective mind' (Senge 1994; Weik and Roberts 1993). Willke (1998) describes organizational knowledge as hidden in the systems of organizational principles, which are anonymous and autonomous and define the way organizations work. It is hard to imagine that organizations possess a 'collective brain', but one could find the organization's knowledge and experience, for instance, in standing operational procedures, description of work processes, role descriptions, recipes, routines and databases of product and project knowledge.

To describe and measure organizational competence, models of organizational maturity can be applied. The first model relating to the measurement of the quality of the software development process, the SEI Capability Maturity Model, was developed by the Software Engineering Institute (SEI) (Humphrey 1989; Paulk *et al.* 1991). During the late 1990s several specific maturity models to describe and measure the organizational pm competence were developed (Fincher and Levin 1997; Goldsmith 1997; Ibbs and Kwark 1997; Hartman 1998). Most of them are based on the PMI's *Guide to the Project Management Body of Knowledge* (Duncan 1996). Traditional maturity models use four to five steps to describe and measure the competence to perform a specific in an organization. The scale usually used is initial, repeatable, defined, managed and optimized according to the SEI Capability Maturity Model (Paulk *et al.* 1991) (see Figure 39.3).

## THE PM COMPETENCE MODEL

The Projektmanagement Group of the University of Business Administration and Economics in Vienna developed a model of pm competence for self-assessing and for benchmarking the pm competence of organizations (Gareis and Huemann

| Maturity level | Description |
|---|---|
| 5 = optimized | ● Continual improvement of process |
| | ● Continual collection of data to identify |
| | ● Analysis of defects for prevention |
| 4 = managed | ● Process is quantitatively measured |
| | ● Minimum of metrics for quality and productivity exist |
| | ● Collection of process experiences |
| 3 = defined | ● Process defined and institutionalized |
| | ● Process groups defined |
| 2 = repeatable | ● Process depends on individuals |
| | ● Minimum of process controlling/guidance exists |
| | ● Highly risky in case of new challenges |
| 1 = initial | ● Ad hoc process, not formalized |
| | ● No adequate guidance |
| | ● No consistency in product delivery |

**Figure 39.3    Maturity levels of the SEI Capability Maturity Model**

1998). The basis for pm competence is the pm process model described above, with its sub processes. For the description and measurement of the pm competence, we suggest not the steps of the traditional maturity models but a spider's web, with six axes (Figure 39.4):

1. Project start
2. Project controlling
3. Project coordination
4. Management of project discontinuities
5. Project close-down
6. Design of pm process

The spider's web has the advantage that it is a multidimensional representation of the pm competence, allowing the maturities of different pm subprocesses to be visualized. The pm competence of a company or a business unit is presented by the shaded area, which results from connecting points of pm competence on the scale of the spider's web axes. For the pm subprocesses on the spider's web scale, four levels of competence are defined:

0. Not defined
1. Partly defined
2. Defined
3. Standardized

These are described further in Figure 39.5. In traditional maturity models, the maturity level 'optimized' is usually considered too. Our pm competence model

**715**

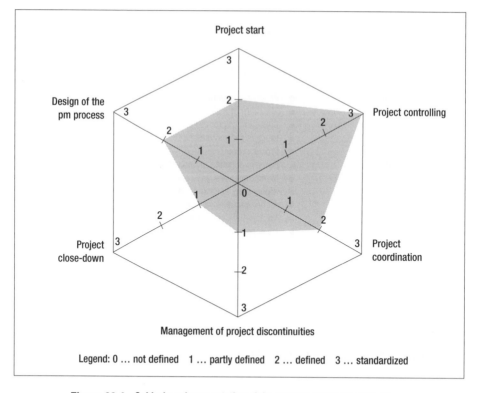

**Figure 39.4   Spider's web presentation of the organizational pm competence**

does not consider optimization, because it cannot be observed at the level of the single project and it does not apply to the pm subprocesses, but to the pm process as a whole. So the further development and optimization of project management is not part of the pm process but has to be considered as a separate business process.

Figure 39.4 represents the pm competence of a POO that has a lot of competence in project controlling, as it has a standardized controlling process, where it applies all required pm methods for all project types. The project coordination, the project start and the design of the pm process are scored 'defined'. Further improvement is primarily necessary regarding the project-close down and the management of discontinuities, where the pm competence is 'partly defined', that is only a few methods are applied for only a few project types.

The assessment of the pm competence of an organization is based on an IT-supported questionnaire with about 80 questions. As an example, the questions relating to the project start process are grouped into questions regarding project objectives, project risk, project context relationships, project organization and

| Scale | Description |
|---|---|
| 3 = standardized | All required pm methods applied for all defined project types |
| 2 = defined | Many pm methods applied for all defined project types |
| 1 = partly defined | Few pm methods applied for many projects |
| 0 = not defined | Few pm methods applied for a few projects |

**Figure 39.5  Maturity scale for the pm subprocesses**

project culture (Figure 39.6). For the single questions the current pm practice is assessed according to the answering possibilities:

1. Always
2. Sometimes
3. Seldom or never

To relate the answers to the questions to the competence points on the scales of the spider's web a weighting system is used. As the single pm subprocesses have different impacts on the project performance, different weights are assigned to the pm subprocesses. As the results for the project start process are the basis for all other subprocesses, it is perceived as the most important one.

B4.1: Which documents of project organization result from the project start process?

| Question | 1 | 2 | 3 |
|---|---|---|---|
| Internal project assignment | | | |
| Project organization chart | | | |
| Project role descriptions | | | |
| Project responsibility matrix | | | |
| Project communication structures | | | |
| Project specific organizational rules | | | |
| Project related incentive systems | | | |
| Others (please state: ..................) | | | |

**Figure 39.6  Sample question of the pm competence questionnaire**

# BENCHMARKING THE ORGANIZATIONAL PM COMPETENCE

In a pm benchmarking research project with companies from different industries pm competence was applied (Gareis and Huemann 1998). Figure 39.7 shows the practice of nine companies regarding documentation in the project start process. Partners 1, 2 and 3 are from the engineering industry, partners 4, 5 and 6 are from the IT industry, while partners 7, 8 and 9 are from the service industry. The engineering and IT companies perform primarily external projects, while the companies of the service industry mainly perform internal projects.

Generally, we can observe differences in pm competences for the performance of internal and external projects and of different industries. A comparison for internal and external projects showed that in internal projects 'softer pm methods', such as the project scenario analysis and the project environment analysis, are applied more frequently than in external projects. In a comparison of different industries, engineering companies seem very methods-oriented, while IT companies emphazise the design of the project organization too. Some IT companies apply, for instance, integrated project organizations, involving representatives of the client and of subcontractors in the project team and in the project steering committee. Project-related incentive systems are used in

B 4.1: Which documents of project organization result from the project start process?

| always | sometimes | seldom or never |
| --- | --- | --- |

| | Partner 1 | Partner 2 | Partner 3 | Partner 4 | Partner 5 | Partner 6 | Partner 7 | Partner 8 | Partner 9 | | Best Theory |
| --- | --- | --- | --- | --- | --- | --- | --- | --- | --- | --- | --- |
| Internal project assignment | | | | | | | | | | | |
| Project organization chart | | | | | | | | | | | |
| Project role descriptions | | | | | | | | | | | |
| Project responsibility matrix | | | | | | | | | | | |
| Project communication structures | | | | | | | | | | | |
| Project organization rules | | | | | | | | | | | |
| Project-related incentive systems | | | | | | | | | | | |

Figure 39.7  PM benchmarking results regarding the design of project organizations

engineering companies only. Further the following commonalities and differences could be observed:

- Internal project assignments are almost always a result of the project start process.
- Organizational charts are more frequently prepared by companies performing external projects.
- Project organization charts, description of project roles and responsibility matrices partly do not result from the start process.

The column 'Best Theory' shows the pm competence thought to be required by the Projektmanagement Group.

## FURTHER DEVELOPMENT OF PM COMPETENCES IN THE POO

Core competences as defined by Prahalad and Hamel (Prahalad and Hamel 1990; Hamel 1994) are an organization's fundamental capabilities, an integration of skills that are competitively unique. This means that these capabilities are difficult to imitate. The core competences enable the company to deliver a fundamental customer benefit and therefore contribute to the long-term survival of the company.

Project management can be perceived as a core competence of a POO, as it creates a competitive advantage. If a company has pm knowledge and experience, projects can be performed more efficiently than in companies without pm competence. Project management adds value to the customer. To ensure this competitiveness permanent further development of the pm competence is necessary. Pm competences have to be described, assessed and further developed for organizations, teams and individuals. The pm competence model described above can be applied to assess the status of the organizational pm competence of a POO and to identify potential for the further development of this competence in an organizational learning process. Similarly, individual and team learning have to be organized. Instruments for the further development of the pm competences have to be differentiated for individuals, teams and the organization as a whole (Figure 39.8). Instruments to develop the pm competence of individuals include self-assessments and training (classroom, on the job). Instruments to develop the pm competences of teams include workshops, reflections and supervisions. Instruments to develop the pm competences of the project-oriented company at an organizational level include pm benchmarking and organizational development projects.

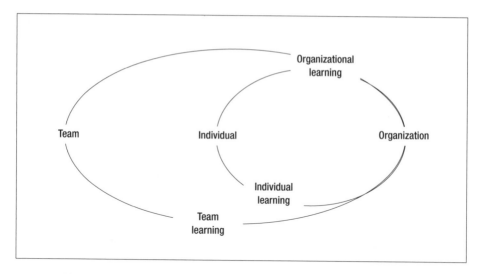

**Figure 39.8  Relationships between individual, team and organizational learning**

## SPECIFIC MANAGEMENT COMPETENCES IN THE POO

Even if project management is established as a core competence of a POO, additional competences to manage further specific processes of the POO are required, such as:

- programme management
- project assignment and project evaluation
- project and programme auditing and coaching
- project portfolio management.

These competences must be described, assessed and further developed.

## REFERENCES AND FURTHER READING

Duncan, W. R. (ed.) (1996), *The Guide to the Project Management Body of Knowledge*, Project Management Institute, Sylva, NC.

Fincher, A. and Levin, G. (1997), 'Project management maturity model', *Proceedings of the Project Management Institute 28th Annual Seminar/Symposium, Chicago*, Project Management Institute, Sylva, NC.

Gareis, R. and Huemann, M. (1998), 'A process-oriented pm-approach', *Proceedings of IRNOP III, the International Research Network on Organizing by Projects*, University of Calgary, Alberta.

Goldsmith, L. (1997), 'Approaches towards effective project management, project management maturity model', *Proceedings of the Project Management Institute 28th Annual Seminar/Symposium, Chicago*, Project Management Institute, Sylva, NC.

Hamel, G. (1994), 'The concept of core competence', in G. Hamel and A. Heene (eds), *Competence-based Competition*, Wiley, New York.

Hartman, F. (1998), 'Project management competence', *Proceedings of IRNOP III, the International Research Network on Organizing by Projects*, University of Calgary, Alberta.

Humphrey, W. (1989), *Managing the Software Process*, Addison-Wesley, New York.

Ibbs, W. and Kwak, Y. H. (1997), *The Benefits of Project Management: Financial and Organizational Rewards*, Project Management Institute, Sylva, NC.

Paulk, M. C., Curtis, B. and Chrissis, M. B. (1991), *Capability Maturity Models for Software*, Carnegie Mellon University, Pittsburg, PA.

Prahalad, C. K. and Hamel, G. (1990), 'The core competence of the corporation', *Harvard Business Review*, May/June.

Senge, P. (1994), *The Fifth Discipline Field Book: Strategies and Tools for Building a Learning Organization*, Doubleday, New York.

Weik, A. and Roberts, K. (1993), 'Collective mind in organizations: heedful interrelating on flight decks', *Administrative Quarterly*, **38**.

Willke, H. (1998), *Systemisches Wissensmanagement (Systemic knowledge management)*, Lucius & Lucius, Stuttgart.

## RELATED TOPICS

# 40 Managing teams: the reality of life

## Tony Reid

Everyone agrees that project teams are a good idea: true or false? Most teams start out full of energy, with good intentions and often offers of support. Unfortunately, fairly quickly things begin to look less certain. The consequence is that, instead of a surge of energy, there is a feeling of being alone, neglected, attacked even. The goals that were once clear now seem conditional on all sorts of other factors, while the sources of authority are joined by more shadowy influencers in the background who appear to be the ones who really call the shots. The next move is that team members are re-assigned back to their home base or to higher priority projects, often halfway through the assignment. Deadlines become immovable and unachievable, overtime and exhaustion set in. Management re-organizes the project team in exasperation, and demotivated people begin to fulfil every prophecy. At this moment you may be nodding your head as you recognize this as a familiar experience. The key question is why, and what can be done to avoid it happening?

It is with this scenario in mind that this chapter sets out to provide some basic, proven guidelines to help you create a capable project team. The guidelines do not require you to be a team development specialist: many organizations have halted their efforts in going in this direction because they were too costly, didn't provide quick enough results or were poorly understood by management. A warning for you: management has good intentions but poor follow-through due to pressures to produce quick results.

In reality many organizations are poor at project management and project leaders equally poor at team building. In the former instance, it is because there is insufficient discipline at pre-commencement, and in the latter it is because in creating a project the project leader does not see the team as a priority. Responding to the client, leaping into action, often with no apparent direction, is more likely to be the norm.

# RESULTS THROUGH TEAMWORKING

The evidence of high performing teams is around us all the time. Here are three examples:

1. Formula 1 racing teams are a clear example, with at least three key roles:
   - A star place for the individual driver;
   - An operational team performing the changes as the vehicle comes in for service; and
   - Behind the scenes a support team to provide the race strategy
2. Soccer teams are often made up of outstanding individual performers but work together towards a common goal on the day of the match.
3. Organizations that realize their business objectives, business improvement and rapid growth, for example Powergen using project teams to manage change since privatization.

Already perhaps there is a lesson to learn from the two sporting examples: what do they do that makes them different from other project teams? They spend 90 per cent of their time practising, rehearsing and developing their strategies and processes before they attempt the project. You may say that this is not possible to do in business, construction or IT, but there is a school of thought that says 'We don't know what we are capable of until we try!'

# PRACTICAL GUIDELINES

### PURPOSE

The amazing thing is that in the case of emergency we experience the ideal characteristics of teamwork – a willingness to get involved, to take any role, to work cooperatively together, all driven by a desire to rescue and to save others from pain or disaster. It is this power of purpose that seems to provide the direction, resource strategy and key roles of the team, often to great effect. So how can this principle be applied to every project? This is the first most important task for the project leader:

- To define the purpose of the project, clarify the definition with the client, and then share that purpose with the project team.

It sounds easy of course. Unfortunately, very often the client cannot articulate the purpose and this is the time when the project leader needs courage to explore and to challenge the client for measured definition. In addition, it is the time to involve other key team members in seeking additional clarification from their professional counterparts in the client's organization. This is the first collective team task.

Having sought clarity of definition and tested the interpretation with all of the key players now is the time to go public; it is the achievement of the purpose of the project that must become the dominant driver. It is the power of purpose that will drive the project forward and enable the project team to perform through all adversity:

● The purpose acquires real power when it is made visible.

This should become the project vision (a drawing of the intended building, a map of the intended system, a group of people sharing the new hospital resources). In addition, a similar but enlarged picture should be placed about the project site, in the project office and with the client, consultants, suppliers and other key stakeholders. In addition, this 'picture' could become the progress map gradually making the transformation from the existing circumstance to the final vision as it is duly updated as the project progresses. (This focuses the attention of the stakeholders on the success criteria (see Chapter 5).) It is the purpose that provides the 'meaning of life' for the period of the project and so enables project team members to identify a framework within which to determine their three most important needs:

1. What is expected of me?
2. Where do I fit in?
3. How am I getting on?

When these fundamental requirements of purpose and personal needs are satisfied you might ask yourself, 'Do I need to spend time at all on team building?' The answer may well be no!

## PROJECT TEAM SELECTION

If a group has cohesion, spirit and a sense of purpose, it can accomplish any project task, from installing a new IT system to raising money for the Red Cross. We believe that in order to achieve this magical balance you need to seriously consider the make-up of personalities in your prospective project team. Your reality may be that the team is composed of 'whoever is available at the time', hardly the way to select a team for the 'premier division', so fight this stance tooth and nail. One of the key merits of deciding to have a team is the possibility of a wide variety of talents and capabilities, so it is worth thinking about the nature of the project, the project needs and the characteristics of the other stakeholders who will need to be managed. The results of this examination will lead you to consider the best mix for the team; professional expertise is never enough. You might start by considering some of these key traits as essential requirements for your team:

- Those who seek to accomplish the task.
- Those who will be concerned with the quality of working relationships.
- Those who strive for closure and control.
- Those who seek the ideal solution.
- Those who want to leap into action immediately.
- Those who would prefer to ponder on the option and think things through.
- Those who excel at detail and those who love the concepts and the possibilities.

Using a rugby analogy, the project leader is the scrum half, who hands off an assignment to a package leader (back row), who uses support staff (forwards) to move a project ahead to a final goal (the try line). In practical terms you need to select a team to match the demands of the project. Many projects require extroverts to sell the project to the client and the support units in their own project organization. Equally there is a need for different more imaginative personalities who will generate alternative means for raising the money, plus a balance of others who will pound the pavements and follow through on commitment plans.

It's worth compiling key criteria for your project and drawing up a balance card to ensure that you select those team players that bring the skill, knowledge and experience with the personality to match the demands of the project (Figure 40.1). Take time to interview potential team members who have been chosen for their functional expertise to determine how they fit with the management style, culture and demands of the project. These are some questions you might ask:

1. Tell me about the best project leader you've worked for.
2. Why was he or she a good leader?
3. What was your least favourite leader like?
4. How did you handle things you didn't like about him or her?
5. Tell me about a disagreement between you and a previous boss. How did you resolve it?
6. What actions are necessary to make a high performance project team?

If you were responsible for selecting a professional sports team then the elements would be clearly defined roles for team members, an explicit purpose uniting the team, an agreed game plan and a coach. So, in addition to thinking about the team selection, consider whom you will choose as your personal or team coach or mentor.

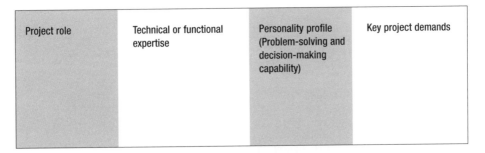

| Project role | Technical or functional expertise | Personality profile (Problem-solving and decision-making capability) | Key project demands |
|---|---|---|---|
| | | | |

**Figure 40.1    Balance card for project team selection**

## CONDITIONS FOR TEAMWORKING

Perhaps the most basic conditions for good teamworking would seem to be too obvious but frequently they are not truly considered. They are size, purpose, goals, skills, approach and accountability. Paying rigorous attention to these is what creates the conditions necessary for team performance. Listening to successful teams you will find that they are committed to their purpose, goals and approach. Alongside these thoughts you need to acknowledge that we do not easily take responsibility for the performance of others, nor lightly let them assume responsibility for us. By applying rigorous attention to these performance requirements and conditions for teamworking most groups can deliver the goods

## FOCUSING ON TEAM BASICS

Katzenbach and Smith (1993) suggest that managers should focus on team performance and team basics issues (Figure 40.2). It is through disciplined action, much the same as following a diet, that true teams are born. They shape a common purpose, agree on performance goals, define a common working approach, develop high levels of complementary skills and hold themselves mutually accountable for results. Integrated with this basic approach real teams always find ways for each individual to contribute and gain distinction.

## TEAM CHARTER

Team commitment might take the form of a team charter that sets out the common approach the team have adopted for themselves. The elements of such a charter could constitute the following:

- Purpose of the project
- Key performance goals
- Project team values

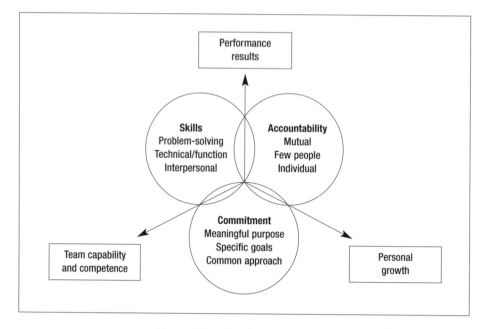

**Figure 40.2   Focusing on team basics**

- Roles and responsibilities
- Managing issues and conflict resolution
- Assessment and team effectiveness

### The purpose

We have already mentioned that purpose will have the most significant influence on the progress of the project and therefore the team, the key word being *visibility*.

### The key performance goals

The goals must be aligned with the project purpose and the organization-wide goals. The goals serve as benchmarks for which the project sponsor and each stakeholder group, those parties that have a vested interest in the team's success, will hold the team accountable. Some necessary groundwork will be required here to develop a clear understanding of the sponsor and stakeholder needs and expectations. The goals should be aligned to:

- organizational measures for return on investment and profits (see Chapter 13);
- team qualitative and quantitative goals that measure the project outputs  (see Chapter 14);

- individual goals that measure the results of team members (assigned through the responsibility matrix, Chapter 17).

The goals are likely to reflect the critical success factors that have been agreed with the client. For a re-engineering project team the critical success factors might be cycle time, costs and customer service. Others might be revenue enhancement, market share gain and employee satisfaction. A matrix that identifies accountability for goals should be created (Figure 40.3 and Chapter 17). The goal leader must ensure that the goals, when translated into workable objectives, are SMART, maybe even SMARTIES (Figure 40.4).

| Goals | Goal leader | Team members who will provide support | Key project demands |
|---|---|---|---|
| | | | |

Figure 40.3   Goal matrix

| S | Specific |
|---|---|
| M | Measurable |
| A | Achievable |
| R | Realistic |
| T | Time bound |
| I | Involve the appropriate team members |
| E | Environmentally safe and acceptable |
| S | Success-oriented |

Figure 40.4   SMART(IES) goals

## Project team values

Goals define what we seek to achieve; our values indicate how we will 'behave' to achieve them. Establishing these ground rules of agreed team behaviour is vital

**729**

to success. Often we discover what works by learning what does not work. Behaviour is so crucial to team success or failure that a willingness to abide by agreed values and norms should be a qualification for membership. Making that expectation non-negotiable sends a strong message. When people refuse to abide by expectations they are, in effect, deciding not to be on the team. Typically, values and norms evolve over time and often remain unspoken and unwritten unless they are violated. In practice there are some basic ground rules that can be defined at the outset:

- Share all relevant information.
- Focus on interest and not position.
- Be specific and use examples to illustrate the point.
- Disagree openly with other members of the team.
- Invite questions and comment.
- Expect all team members to participate.
- Make decisions by consensus.
- Explain the reasons behind the words.
- Respect and value each other's time.
- Conduct self-critique.

A significant influence will be the level of trust within the project team and this seems an appropriate place to suggest some ways of building it:

- Convey consistent principles.
- Give team members plausible explanations for actions.
- Offer status reports and forecasts.
- Make realistic commitments.
- Showcase what you know.
- Protect the interest of people who aren't present.
- Show compassion.
- Verify understanding.

## Roles and responsibilities

The functional roles and responsibilities for the project should be clearly defined within the team with a balanced load spread between the players on an equal basis. In addition to the conventional expert functions there are a number of other key duties that will need to be fulfilled. Here are some examples:

1. *Customer/client service contact*   Who monitors the client's expectations?
2. *Liaison with head office*   Who builds collaboration?
3. *Mr or Ms Integrity*   Who provides the role model of behaviour?

4. *Community and interface developer*  Who monitors how the project will impact on the community?
5. *Team motivator*  Who provides that extra burst of enthusiasm when all are down?
6. *Challenger and supporter of the workforce*  Who ensures that all views are taken into account?
7. *On-the-job educational developer*  Who seeks out novel ways of keeping people informed and up to date?
8. *Crazy idea and innovation challenger*  Who challenges conventional behaviour?
9. *Fun generator and celebration king/queen*  Who generates celebration and makes sure that the team honour individual and group accomplishments?

### Managing issues and conflict resolution

Managing project team issues should constitute a regular feature in the weekly review programme. One process that works effectively has five stages:

1. Ask team members to identify, without comment, the issues the team need to address. List these issues on a flip chart without any attempt to order or prioritize. Typically they will relate to team issues to do with procedures, practices, project strategy or roles and responsibilities, and sometimes morale and commitment.
2. Agree with the team the issues that should be challenged. There may be some that can be resolved very quickly, for example when information is needed. Prioritize the remainder and decide how many can be adequately examined in the permitted time.
3. The individual team member who raised the issue is then given the opportunity to present it in more detail and the other members are given the opportunity to ask questions for clarity. This part of the process often requires strong direction to ensure that the focus remains on clarification and not solution generation.
4. The issue presenter is then asked to affirm the definition of the issue; sometimes it might have changed out of all recognition from the original statement.
5. The other team members are then asked, in turn, to present their idea of a solution to the revised issue. The project leader will then have the task of deciding if further discussion and consensus agreement is necessary if the issue has wider implications.

With teams of independent, diverse thinkers, it is inevitable that differences will

731

arise (see Chapter 43). Establishing the ground rules as we have indicated will help. In addition it pays to agree on a process for managing conflict and identifying trained facilitators who can support positive conflict resolution:

1. Establish ground rules on how to manage one-on-one and team conflict.
2. Adopt a step-by-step model for conflict resolution based on:
   - questioning the situation;
   - identifying the problem;
   - determining the implications of the problem;
   - identifying the needs;
   - developing alternative forms of resolution to meet the needs;
   - evaluating the alternatives against the needs to determine the best choice;
   - generating appropriate action plans.

On occasions you might deliberately encourage dispute or productive conflict – it can lead to magic when team members express their opinions, no matter how disagreeable they may seem. More ideas are put on the table, which can lead to more discovery, which can lead to quantum leaps in improvement and innovation. Agree on an internal or external third party facilitator whom the team will use to assist them with more complex conflict.

### Assessment and team effectiveness

An important feature of team development is team effectiveness, and measuring the 'well-being' of a team is one way of determining team progress. Figure 40.5 gives a structure which works well and is recommended for use from the start of a project and conducted on a regular basis during the initial months. The model identifies seven key measures of team success and asks individual team members to make their own judgement against each measure before then sharing their results with the other members of the team. It is then up to the team to discuss any differences and to seek to find understanding and ways to resolve them.

## FURTHER OPPORTUNITIES FOR GROWTH

### THE THIRD COMPETENCE

Why is it that some project teams have succeeded where others have not? The answer could lie in another aspect of individual difference, that is the basic assumptions that we bring with us to every project problem and decision (see Chapters 44 and 45).

- One way of avoiding this trap is to think of yourself as an immigrant. Then you

| Item | 1 | 2 | 3 | 4 | 5 | 6 |
|------|---|---|---|---|---|---|
| Purpose – the team members understand the purpose and commit their energy to achieving it. | | | | | | |
| Role – all the team members have a common understanding of the team's role | | | | | | |
| Strategy – the team members understand the team's strategy and use it to guide their day-to-day activities | | | | | | |
| Processes – the team's processes are optimal for its role and purpose | | | | | | |
| People – the team members feel well utilized and valued | | | | | | |
| Feedback – the team constructively uses the feedback it receives | | | | | | |
| Interfaces – the team's key relationships with others are productive | | | | | | |

**Figure 40.5   Audit of team effectiveness**

are not hung up with what you believe the rules to be and you make no assumptions as to what is possible or not.

Perhaps these are some of your assumptions:

- I can't speak directly to the client.
- The suppliers are looking for ways to rip us off.
- The project team members are not willing to give it what it takes.
- Doing it the way I've always done it is the best way.
- People are not willing to change.
- You know your boss's goals.

The truth is that very often people have not been asked to contribute, they would be willing to change if you showed them how to and the suppliers are looking for continuity and would be happy to join your 'think tank' if you asked them. You do it your way because it's comfortable not because it's the best.

## COMMUNICATION

'Guys, we're in this together!' How often do you hear this? A plea when the walls seem to be finally caving in or a rallying cry to keep the team focused? To quote experience on a large engineering contract:

**733**

There was always a lot of disagreement, different ideas, different areas of emphasis. But there was always self-respect and respect for others.

So what constitutes enough sharing and communication? Here's one example:

- Meetings as a team every morning from 08.00 to 08.20.
- A meeting each week to review the progress, performance and process of relationships on the project – for a *maximum* of two hours
- A shared lunch break on Wednesdays in the project leader's office, simple buffet lunch, open house meeting to which all are invited, including key suppliers and support staff from the parent organization; no minutes taken, but mountains of information exchanged.
- When issues cannot be resolved at the weekly meetings, the full team gathers at the project leader's home on Sunday. They demand candour and objectivity.

The outcome of these practices was a fanatical belief in what the team were trying to achieve, which had a significant impact on each individual as well as the parent organization. They really believed they would make a difference. Some other ideas that come to mind:

- Humour board for jokes and stories
- Regular 'snapshots' of the team at work and play
- Go to the cinema, theatre, sports game together
- Continue to seek novel ways of sharing and developing understanding

### CREATING YOUR OWN REALITY

Every project offers the project team members the opportunity to create their own new reality. An example of this is Russian Olympian Vasily Alexeev. He was trying to break a weight-lifting record of 500 pounds. He had lifted 499 but couldn't, for the life of him, lift 500. Finally his trainers put 501.5 pounds on the bar and rigged it so it looked like 499 pounds. Of course, you can guess the result: he lifted it easily. Once he had created this new reality, other lifters went on to break his record. Why? Because they now knew it was possible to lift 500 pounds. The British athlete who broke a similar barrier was Roger Bannister when he became the first man to run the mile in under 4 minutes and as a consequence many others followed. The limits we set ourselves exist in our mind. Sometimes if we let our hearts do the talking and believe in our ability to overcome perceptions, we can create another reality. Just imagine the possibilities when the project team truly believe in the purpose.

## TEAM DECISION-MAKING

Team members bring unique experience, knowledge and skill to a team and very often cultural and language differences, an international construction team for example, and sometimes in these circumstances of multi-nationality, decision-making can become extremely onerous. One approach to this is the Delphi technique. It consists of collecting successive (usually two or three) rounds of inputs from team members, submitted without consultation between them. As each round is completed, individual inputs are consolidated and circulated back to the members for review before they provide the next input. Thus individuals see consensus developing, but without knowing who is adopting a given position, and without the potential biasing effect of face-to-face interaction. The resulting decision should reflect a position everyone can live with. This approach is particular useful when contentious issues have to be resolved, or when you need to minimize the likelihood that, because of their style or personality, certain individuals will have an undue influence on the team's decision.

## TEAM GROWTH AND DEVELOPMENT

This classic model for the journey that teams experience together seems to hold good:

- Forming – competent individuals
- Storming – competitive individuals
- Norming – competent team
- Performing – achieving team
- Mourning – appreciating team

This model provides a frame of reference for judging the growth and strength of the teamworking process and warrants periodic evaluation on the agenda at the project review meetings. The questions to ask might include the following:

1. At what stage of the model are we at the moment?
2. How does that fit with the project life cycle?
3. What actions are being taken to move the team to the next stage?
4. What are we learning from our collective experience?
5. How are we sharing that knowledge with other project teams?

If you were in the theatre you would find all of the elements of project team building, plus more. There would be the common goals, defined roles, interdependence, firm deadlines, coaching and feedback. The uniqueness in this list is coaching, a responsibility of every leader. In the theatre you would experience the greatest degree of coaching during rehearsal, perhaps the secret weapon of the most astute project leader. Consider when rehearsal could truly add value:

- Pre-commencement period
- Testing understanding of goals
- Potential problem analysis
- Risk analysis
- Presentation and meeting the media
- Project completion

And working and learning together to develop the team and personal skills in:

- process improvement techniques
- problem-solving
- group-conflict management
- interactive skills
- consensus and compromise
- process methodologies.

The team must learn to find their own solutions, they must realize that they are in control and that no one else is going to tell them what to do or how to do it. The team shares authority, and decision-making; ideally there should be no team bosses – only leaders and facilitators.

## PERSONAL DEVELOPMENT

A starting point is to introduce individual self-assessment as a process to identify personal attributes to be developed through the project. This process can be further reinforced in the following ways:

1. Ask each team member to assess privately his/her own contributions to the team.
2. Discuss how to encourage/support increased contributions from all members.
3. Brainstorm how to make members feel more included, confident or engaged.

To learn by experience, one has to experience, then reflect on that experience to extract the learning. Learning Boards can be located adjacent to or within the project environment to encourage project team members to share their learning experiences: perhaps a database can be introduced to build a knowledge base related to the project. Personal development is primarily the responsibility of the individual. In this age of rapid change, skills can become obsolete overnight. You have to keep pushing the envelope of your own experience and competence if you

736

hope to keep up with the evolving needs of your job and profession. Perhaps these few practical tips can help your capacity to stay ahead of change:

1. Learn to be a better listener – 'You don't learn when you're talking.'
2. Read professional journals and business magazines from different industries – once a week take time out to find two new things that relate to your project.
3. Let your children tutor you – they know more than you about a lot of subjects.
4. Volunteer – in most voluntary activities everyone is the same. It changes your perspective on hierarchy and authority.
5. Read what has stood the test of time – Aristotle, Shakespeare, Adam Smith.

## QUICK WINS

Developing high quality project teams is as much about public profile as it is about output and performance. Acknowledging the team members at an early stage can establish a commitment that will have endurance. What are some of the possibilities?

- Establish a project team base with its own identity on the door.
- Develop a challenging identity, logo or name to add character to the team.
- Select an identity that in some way characterizes the nature of the project. For example is it about speed of completion, high image or quality, innovative or original?
- Turn the logo into a lapel badge, a car sticker or attach it to documentation to share with other project partners.
- Involve people at the pre-commencement stage so they can contribute to project strategy.
- Meet other stakeholders such as the client, in-house support teams, suppliers, investors, local community influencers, statutory services that have some assessment function.
- Involve in-house or outside press agents as part of the project marketing machinery.
- Ensure that basic resources are quickly on board so that individuals can make an immediate contribution on their arrival.
- Start a cartoon board.
- Create an information board giving three vital pieces of information (Figure 40.6). There may be several boards located about the site, of a size to ensure the best visibility.

| New members | Project purpose | Member achievements |
|---|---|---|
| A welcome to new members of the team (individuals or other companies), with a definition of how they will be contributing, some personal history and a photograph. | A picture of how the project will be when completed.<br><br>Or a before progress framework (bar chart) and expected result. | An acknowledgement<br><br>As the project progresses this panel might be a grateful 'thank you' to the departing member.<br><br>Or it could be an opportunity to feature the contribution and performance of a member. |

**Figure 40.6    Project information board**

## TEAM LEADERSHIP

The project team leader today carries many roles; those of team facilitator, coach, mentor, as well as leader are the most apparent (see Chapter 41). Experience says that many project leaders survive by accident rather than design, perhaps the case for many organizations. Surviving by design means starting by taking stock of all stakeholders who have an interest in your project and determining who has influence and how they will benefit from the project, and don't forget the hidden stakeholders – people who may have personal reasons for not wanting this initiative of yours. Your analysis will reveal a surprising number of players: rate them as positive (supportive) or negative (resistant) and ask yourself these key questions about each of them:

1.  What do you want of them as a stakeholder: to provide funding, lend their name to the project?
2.  Consider the stakeholder's goals, values and needs.
3.  Consider what concerns he or she might have that would cause resistance.
4.  Determine what actions could address these concerns.
5.  Consider the stakeholder's possible objections. How will you respond?
6.  Determine the approach that is likely to work the best with this person – fact-based, value-based, participative or collaborative?

Again, the role is similar to that of an orchestral conductor, allowing each talented individual to have his or her moment of distinction, to cultivate the team spirit of each group in the orchestra and similarly allowing them their moment while maintaining a direction and symbiosis that presents a complete and whole picture.

## REFERENCES AND FURTHER READING

Briner, W., Hastings, C. and Geddes, M. (1993), *Project Leadership*, 2nd edition, Gower, Aldershot.

Katzenbach, J. R. and Smith, D. K. (1993), *The Wisdom of Teams*, Harvard Business School Press, Cambridge, MA.

## RELATED TOPICS

| | |
|---|---|
| Success criteria and stakeholders | Chapter 5 |
| Business value and profitability | Chapter 13 |
| Project value and goals | Chapter 14 |
| Configuration management | Chapter 15 |
| Responsibility matrix | Chapter 17 |
| Leading and managing | Chapter 41 |
| Managing stakeholders | Chapter 42 |
| Conflict resolution | Chapter 43 |
| Cultural difference | Chapter 44 |
| Ethics | Chapter 45 |

# 41 Managing and leading

## David Partington

What makes an effective leader? Are leaders born or can they be taught? To what extent does the effectiveness of a leader depend on the specific situation? How does leading differ from managing? What do effective managers and leaders do? Attempts to answer questions such as these have made the subject of leadership of central interest to managers and social scientists since the beginning of the formal study of management. The reason for this is the obvious link, in theory and in practice, between leadership effectiveness and business success.

In addition to its general importance to the business world, leadership has a special significance for project managers. One reason for this is that notions of leadership are central to that most fundamental project management principle – the project manager as single, integrative source of responsibility. Very small project groups – those with fewer than seven or eight members – can sometimes function without a leader, either one who is formally designated or one who emerges naturally. In all but the smallest groups, however, the operation of some sort of formal or informal leadership hierarchy is inevitable, and is necessary for the group to achieve its goals.

For some, the titles 'project leader' and 'project manager' are synonymous. Indeed, from the viewpoint of many people in organizations, leadership and management are indistinguishable. But another reason why leadership is taking on a new importance for many project managers lies in an emerging key difference between leadership and management, especially in the context of the implementation of planned change in organizations. (Rodney Turner addresses this point (Turner *et al.* 1996, Chapter 6) and concludes, by comparison with well known politicians, that management and leadership are different.) A comparison of traditional definitions of leadership with more recent ideas illustrates this difference. Defining for managerial purposes a word that is in common everyday usage is never straightforward. In common with words like power, control and politics, leadership is a potent word which has different meanings for different people. However, most traditional meanings combine three common elements, emphasized in the following definition:

> Leadership is the ability to *influence* the activities of a *group* of followers in their efforts to set and achieve *goals*.

This defines *transactional* leadership: the influence of a group of followers in the pursuit of defined, rational goals. This influence is normally achieved through the explicit or implicit offer of some form of reward, which may not always be wholly, or even partly, financial.

Theories of transactional leadership focus on the job of the leader as clarifier of role and task requirements, and as monitor and rewarder of task-related activity. Using definitions of transactional leadership like the one above, there is little to distinguish leadership from management, since most traditional and widely cited attempts to define management have tended to emphasize similar transactional roles. Fayol (1950), for example, defined the five roles of the manager as commanding, organizing, planning, controlling and implementing. Although some of Fayol's terms today sound unfashionably bureaucratic and militaristic they nevertheless present a strong parallel to the essential elements of transactional leadership. Mintzberg also emphasized the rational side of leadership, although in less belligerent fashion, defining the role in terms of eight skills: communication skills, information skills, people management skills, disturbance-handling skills, decision-making skills, resource allocation skills, entrepreneurial skills and reflecting (i.e. planning) skills.

In contrast with these traditional ideas of leadership and management, more recent perspectives of leadership tend to emphasize the *transformational* role of the leader in bringing about change. Transformational leaders 'change the way people think about what is desirable, possible and necessary' (Zaleznik 1977). Transformational leadership has a distinctive orientation towards identity, purpose and change. This subtle alteration in meaning not only sets leadership apart from the relatively ordinary concerns of day-to-day management, but also underlines why the concept of leadership is of special importance to project managers. Increasingly project managers are concerned not only with setting and pursuing goals, but also with managing meaning and changing the way people think as part of the complex influencing process inherent in project leadership.

This chapter examines the main strands of transactional and transformational leadership theory and discusses their implications for project management professionals.

# THEORIES OF LEADERSHIP

In pursuit of the holy grail of managerial performance there have been many attempts to distil the essence of effective leadership and to communicate that essence as information. The underlying idea is that this information can be absorbed and applied by anyone who is interested in becoming a leader or in appointing people to positions of leadership. Things are never that simple. Like all fundamental human issues, leadership reveals itself to be complex and multi-faceted. Attempts to pin it down have proved difficult and have led to conflicting answers. Indeed, few management concepts have incited as much controversy. Consider this quotation, attributed to Confucius:

> Of bad leaders, the followers say, 'They were bad leaders.'
> Of good leaders, the followers say, 'They were good leaders.'
> Of the best leaders, the followers say, 'We did it ourselves.'

This presents the view, currently popular in management thinking, that effective leadership comes from the involvement, participation and empowerment of followers. The notion of employee empowerment is associated with many positive modern ideas of management and leadership, including the flattening of hierarchies, the project team approach, employee productivity and satisfaction, and the harnessing of individual creativity to the pursuit of organizational goals. However, experience shows that attempts at employee empowerment can have negative outcomes, including lack of direction, alienation, overwork and stress.

This reveals the other side of the leadership coin to that suggested by the quote. On the one hand, few would disagree that leadership is participation. On the other hand, one may argue equally credibly and forcefully that leadership is accountability and creating structured responsibility within a body of rules. Further, one may argue that leadership is *doing*.

So how can managers and leaders create appropriately structured conditions in which they and their followers can perform to the best of their abilities? There are four main schools of thought, or approaches, to the study of leadership:

1. The trait approach
2. The behavioural approach
3. The contingency approach
4. The visionary approach

Each of the four has its own research tradition, its own underlying assumptions and its own purposes. An overview of the four approaches follows, with a discussion of some of their principal ideas in relation to project management.

## THE TRAIT APPROACH

The idea behind the trait approach to leadership research and theory is that effective leaders share the same inherent personal qualities and characteristics. The trait approach thus assumes that leaders are born, not made. The purpose of trait theories is the *selection* of leaders, by matching supposedly desirable generic traits to the traits of individuals. Attempts to identify and isolate leader traits have focused on three main areas:

1. Abilities, for example communication skills and technical know-how.
2. Personality variables such as self-confidence and introversion/extroversion;
3. Physical traits, including size and appearance.

The trait approach was prominent until the late 1940s. Although it has been challenged and supplemented by later ideas, it still attracts significant attention and is currently enjoying revival in the study of new approaches to leadership (see the *visionary* approach).

Researchers, mostly psychologists, have been concerned with identifying the common traits of leaders who have proved to be effective, by comparison with non-leaders. This is a tall order, since a cursory examination of the traits of a selection of well-known contemporary leaders such as Tony Blair, the Pope and Bill Gates shows that they are individuals with very different characteristics. Nevertheless, trait research has produced some valid findings. For example, one relatively recent study of the characteristics of real-life successful leaders found six consistent leadership traits (Kirkpatrick and Locke, 1991). These six traits and their implications for project managers are discussed below.

### 1. DRIVE AND AMBITION

Effective leaders are ambitious in their work and careers. The possession of drive is clearly an important attribute for project managers, since the success of many projects depends on the relentless, energetic and focused pursuit of difficult goals, in highly uncertain and volatile circumstances. Personal ambition is a significant characteristic of project managers. Turner and Keegan (1999) report that when they asked a senior project director how his firm identified those 25 year olds who would make good project managers and directors in twenty years time, he said: 'Those who are vocal with their ambitions.'

Most people who move into project management take a bold step away from the relative security of a line or technical function. Unlike some jobs where it is relatively easy, in the short term at least, to rest on one's laurels, project managers' ambition must be sustained. Establishing and maintaining career success in project management hinges on the highly visible outcomes of a manager's recent project assignments.

## 2. THE DESIRE TO LEAD AND INFLUENCE OTHERS

Effective leaders have a strong desire to lead and influence others. For project managers, such a desire is essential, since a key, defining role of a project manager is exerting influence in many ways, at many levels and in many directions. Good project managers have a strong ability to lead and motivate their team. They must also be skilled at building a winning relationship with their clients, ensuring the right level of senior management and external support for the project and getting the best from technical managers and specialist experts. To be able to lead and influence others, good leaders must be good communicators. Turner and Keegan (1999) report a project director who said that the essence of good leadership was to be able to 'Communicate the goal; communicate the process.'

## 3. HONESTY AND INTEGRITY

Effective leaders exhibit above average levels of honesty and integrity. Unlike some other important leadership traits, these are widely perceived as desirable and valued personal attributes in their own right. Their opposites, dishonesty and lack of integrity, oppose society's norms of acceptable behaviour. Because of the pioneering, multi-agency nature of many projects, there are frequent opportunities for the project manager purposefully to mislead factions who are associated less centrally with the project and its information processes, or to manipulate situations for personal advantage. Good project managers know that they are under the spotlight and that any benefits of less than total honesty and integrity will be short-lived at best.

## 4. SELF-CONFIDENCE

Effective leaders have a belief in their own abilities that goes with feeling in control of change. As a result, they are more likely to actively seek information, to act confidently and decisively on the basis of information which may necessarily be incomplete and to have the courage to change course if necessary. All of these behavioural attributes find strong resonance with the project manager's role.

## 5. INTELLIGENCE

Effective leaders tend to have above average intelligence and problem-solving ability. Project managers are faced with a constant need to find creative solutions to unprecedented problems, both managerial and technical. Their superior intelligence is often revealed by their unusual ability for breadth and depth of thinking.

## 6. TECHNICAL KNOWLEDGE

Effective leaders usually have in-depth technical knowledge of their area of responsibility. Some observers have claimed that project management is a generic ability, and that good project managers are able to apply their skills to any project, regardless of technology. To a limited extent this is true, since the unique quality of many projects will embody at least some element of technical novelty which must be learned or discovered. Indeed, there is some evidence of transferability of successful project managers from one industrial context to another. Nevertheless, few successful project managers would argue against the obvious benefits of possessing adequate technical knowledge relating to their project.

The shortcomings of the trait approach lie in its search for a common set of traits possessed by all leaders, regardless of what they are leading. The personal qualities needed to lead a nation, a religious order or a multinational corporation are clearly different. In the field of project management it is easy to argue that different project leadership characteristics are required at different phases in a single project, let alone from one project to another.

## THE BEHAVIOURAL APPROACH

The second school of thought about what makes an effective leader, the behavioural approach, signalled a move away from the trait approach. For a period of twenty years, starting in the late 1940s, the focus of attention turned towards the preferred behavioural styles of effective leaders.

The basic premise underlying the behavioural approach is that effective leaders behave in the same ways. Research has been aimed at identifying the behavioural styles of effective leaders. Do they tend to use a more democratic style or are they more autocratic? A number of studies of behavioural styles were carried out between the late 1940s and the late 1960s. Using subordinates' descriptions of the behaviour of leaders, including both successful and unsuccessful leaders, the studies attempted to identify the principal dimensions of leadership behaviour and to relate these to measures of performance. The broad finding was that much of leadership behaviour could be distilled and expressed on two dimensions, broadly relating to *task* and *people*. The dimensions are given variety of different labels; typical are the two axes of the Blake and Mouton (1964) 'managerial grid'. Blake and Mouton's two dimensions, scored on the grid from 1 to 9, are:

1. *Concern for production* Leaders with a strong concern for production emphasize technical and task aspects of work, including the organizing of work, work relationships and goals.
2. *Concern for people* Leaders who are strong on this dimension emphasize interpersonal relationships and consideration for subordinates' needs.

Using the grid, managers are rated according to the concerns which dominate their particular style in their pursuit of results. Their combined rating on the two dimensions expresses their behavioural style. The extreme styles are labelled and described by Blake and Mouton as follows:

- 1,1 Impoverished management (low concern for production; low concern for people): Exertion of minimum effort to get required work done is appropriate to sustain organization membership.
- 9,1 Authority-obedience (high concern for production; low concern for people): Efficiency in operations results from arranging conditions of work in such a way that human elements interfere to a minimum degree.
- 1,9 Country club management (low concern for production; high concern for people): Thoughtful attention to needs of people for satisfying relationships leads to a comfortable, friendly organization atmosphere and work tempo.
- 9,9 Team management (high concern for production; high concern for people): Work accomplishment is from committed people; interdependence through a 'common stake' in organization purpose leads to relationships of trust and respect.

Unlike the trait approach, which assumes leaders are born not made, the underlying rationale of the behavioural approach is that leadership behaviour can be learned. The purpose of behavioural theories is teaching people how to change the assumptions that control their behaviour in order to become more effective leaders. Blake and Mouton concluded the best performance was obtained by managers who scored high on both dimensions (a 9,9 style).

The clear implication of behavioural leadership theories for project managers is that they must possess both 'hard' and 'soft' project management skills, since

**747**

neglecting either will result in sub-optimal project performance. This hard versus soft dichotomy is well known to experienced project managers. Although the majority of basic project management textbooks concentrate on the 'hard' tools and techniques for planning and controlling cost, schedule and quality, the writers are usually at pains to point out the need for attention to the more elusive, 'soft' side of managing projects.

Like the pure trait approach, the simple behavioural approach suffers from problems of over-simplification, and the one-size-fits-all approach. We all know that different styles are often appropriate in different circumstances. These shortcomings were addressed in the next stage in the story of the study of leadership effectiveness, the contingency approach, which dominated the leadership research arena from the late 1960s to the early 1980s.

## THE CONTINGENCY APPROACH

Towards the end of the 1960s there was a growing tendency for management theorists in general to move away from universal theories which would apply in every situation towards 'contingency' theories, based on the idea that 'it depends'. In the area of leadership effectiveness, as it became apparent that neither trait theories nor behavioural theories would work in every set of circumstances, the search was on for situational variables which moderated the effectiveness of different leader characteristics or behaviours. The contingency approach focuses on isolating critical situational influences on leadership success, for example the clarity of the task, the degree of conflict in the group or the culture of the organization. Several important contingency theories of leadership effectiveness have been developed, some more complex than others. Although the various theories differ in their underlying assumptions regarding what is important about leaders' characteristics and situational variables, the way in which these contingency approaches are applied tends to follow the same pattern:

1. Assess the characteristics of the leader.
2. Evaluate the situation in terms of key contingency variables.
3. Seek a match between the leader and the situation.

One contingency theory of leadership which is currently the subject of a lot of interest, and which has important implications for the project environment, is the path-goal theory (House 1971). The theory is based on the idea that the role of the leader is to provide support and/or direction in providing a *path* which will help the followers to achieve their *goals*, at the same time ensuring that these match the goals of the group's task. Following the three steps listed above, the path-goal theory works as follows.

### Assess the characteristics of the leader

Path-goal theory identifies four leadership behaviours which contribute to the satisfaction and motivation of subordinates. Any combination of these may be exhibited, depending on the situation.

- Directive leaders define tasks, schedules and processes.
- Supportive leaders are friendly and concerned for followers' needs.
- Participative leaders involve followers in decisions.
- Achievement-oriented leaders set challenging goals and expect high performance.

### Evaluate the situation in terms of key contingency variables

Path-goal theory has two classes of contingency factors which affect the relationship between leader behaviour and performance:

1. Environmental contingency factors
   - Task structure
   - Formal authority system
   - Work group
2. Subordinate contingency factors
   - Locus of control (the extent to which people feel that they control their own destiny)
   - Experience
   - Perceived ability

### Seek a match between the leader and the situation

In path-goal theory, leader behaviour should be congruent with both environmental and subordinate contingency variables. Robbins (1997) lists eight ways in which path-goal theory works, which have tended to be supported by empirical evidence. These are described below, with examples of their implications for project managers.

1. Directive leadership leads to greater satisfaction when tasks are ambiguous or stressful than when they are highly structured and well laid out. When a project has the combined characteristics of high uncertainty and high importance, for example in the early stages of a key development initiative, more direction and guidance will be welcomed by subordinates.

2. Supportive leadership results in high employee performance and satisfaction when subordinates are performing structured tasks. On projects which involve the routine application of established processes, for example in the later, detail stages of engineering projects, subordinates will appreciate and be motivated by a friendly, caring leader.

3. Directive leadership is likely to be redundant among subordinates with high ability or with considerable experience. Project managers who over-emphasize cost, schedule and quality objectives to self-believing experts will be wasting their time.

4. The clearer and more bureaucratic the formal authority relationships, the more leaders should exhibit supportive behaviour and de-emphasize directive behaviour. Effective project managers with a high degree of formal authority acting within a highly proceduralized environment, for example on longer-term public sector projects, should have less need to emphasize a style of direction and guidance and more need to counter the possible alienating effects of bureaucracy by adopting a sympathetic approach.

5. Directive leadership will lead to higher employee satisfaction when there is substantive conflict within a work group. Conflict is often unavoidable, and under certain conditions may be beneficial to the project by avoiding apathy and keeping the team alive and creative. Whether conflict is functional or dysfunctional to the project, however, it will be less a source of dissatisfaction to individuals if the project manager exhibits directive behaviour.

6. Subordinates with an internal locus of control (those who believe they control their own destiny) will be most satisfied with a participative style. People who naturally feel in control of their world will find project managers who seek appropriate involvement in project decisions more agreeable as leaders.

7. Subordinates with an external locus of control (those who believe they have little control over their own destiny) will be most satisfied with a directive style. People who generally feel powerless over their environment will have a tendency to resign their futures to fate, and to avoid seeking out information for improved decision-making. They will derive satisfaction from project managers who let them know what is expected of them.

8. Achievement-oriented leadership will increase subordinates' expectations that effort leads to high performance when tasks are ambiguously structured. The motivational effect of setting challenging goals will be heightened on projects which are executed in organizations with a dual power channel, such as the project/functional matrix in a project engineering firm or the management/clinician structure of a hospital.

One of the features of path-goal theory which makes it especially relevant to the project environment is its simultaneous focus on the needs of (i) the task, (ii) the team and (iii) the individual. There can be a tendency for inexperienced project managers to over-emphasize the first one or two of these and to make false assumptions about the alignment between the motivation and satisfaction of individuals and the project's objectives.

## LEADER GENDER

Recently, much attention has been directed towards issues of gender in management and leadership, mostly in the form of debates and research on women in management. What is known about gender as a contingency factor in relation to leadership effectiveness? Studies show that the leadership styles of men have much in common with those of women. This is not surprising, given that those who occupy positions of formal leadership are both self-selected and selected by organizations on the basis of their self-confidence, intelligence, desire to lead and so on. But apart from the conclusion that similarities outweigh differences, it is apparent that women tend to employ a more participative leadership style, relying more on interpersonal skills such as negotiation and information-sharing to influence subordinates. Men tend to favour a more directive, command-and-control style, depending more on their formal authority. As the requisite styles of organizations and projects increasingly emphasize values of teamwork, participation, trust and cooperation, one may conclude that conditions for project leaders in many sectors are changing in favour of women.

## THE VISIONARY APPROACH

We have seen how the ideas which influenced the study of leadership until the 1980s moved through three overlapping stages, represented here as the trait, behavioural and contingency approaches. The successive influence of each of these approaches has been one of emphasis rather than exclusivity, and today all three traditions live on in various forms, forever building on their origins and adapting to the changing conditions of society.

In the 1980s a new focus and approach to the study of leadership emerged. It became apparent that many successful organizations had been subject to the influence of a 'visionary' or 'charismatic' leader. Therefore, attention turned towards the identification of the personal abilities and characteristics of leaders who were clearly capable of a form of leadership which went beyond traditional ideas about the transactional role of the manager.

Transactional leadership, which emphasizes tasks, goals and performance, is limited by the explicit and implicit contracts between leader and followers. Visionary, 'transformational' leaders, on the other hand, are able to unite leader and followers in the pursuit of a higher purpose which transcends individuals' self-interest. Bryman (1996) illustrates the differences between these two conceptualizations of leadership, listing their components as follows:

1. Components of transactional leadership
   - Contingent rewards: rewarding followers for meeting performance targets.
   - Management by exception: taking action mainly when task-related activity is not going to plan.
2. Components of transformational leadership
   - Charisma: developing a vision, engendering pride, respect and trust.
   - Inspiration: motivating by creating high expectations, modelling appropriate behaviour, and using symbols to focus efforts.
   - Individual consideration: giving personal attention to followers, giving them respect and responsibility.
   - Intellectual stimulation: continually challenging followers with new ideas and approaches.

Most studies of visionary business leaders have been concerned with people in the highest positions of seniority, especially chief executives. However, experience shows that many attempts at bold organizational change which go beyond normal rational goals, and which depend on the articulation of an extraordinary vision of the future, are originated by leaders in less senior positions of formal authority. Many examples of visionary change arise from managers of important technology-related business improvement projects, where visions of the future are more immediate and problems with existing business processes are more apparent. Others occur in subsidiaries of multinationals or other dispersed organizations, when finding imaginative ways of surviving and dealing with present and expected future local conditions is more pressing than implementing the latest head office fad.

These kinds of change initiatives are usually dependent for their success on a high degree of senior management or head office support, or at least non-interference. However, when senior managers have little to gain personally from the success of a transformational change project, and often a lot to lose, this can be too much to expect. For these reasons successful attempts at radical change which are driven from the middle of organizations are likely to be difficult to sustain.

Despite these problems, efforts at initiating and leading organizational innovation from lower down the management ranks are becoming more common.

This is partly due to the increasing exposure to unsatisfactory aspects of the status quo which is experienced by managers of more routine internal projects of change. A common example of this phenomenon is the widespread perception at non-senior levels in many organizations of the need to establish a stronger culture of project management. Moving towards a project culture for dealing with change has become a pressing need for many organizations. It is often driven by project managers who have experienced frustration with barriers to change, which were caused by departmental hierarchies and perpetuated by senior management.

## STAGES OF VISIONARY LEADERSHIP

There are four stages of visionary leadership. They represent clearly the distinctive life cycle of the kind of project or programme of change which, for an increasing number of people, has become a necessary feature of organizational life, and the new challenge for transformational project leaders.

1. The leader identifies the opportunity and the need for change, and formulates a vision of a future state that relates to those needs.
2. The leader communicates the vision, often by pointing out the unacceptability of the status quo.
3. The leader builds trust in the vision. The achievement of trust may be helped by building links with other powerful individuals and institutions with similar values or by showing followers what has been achieved by other organizations with related aims.
4. The leader leads by example and by empowering followers. Sometimes disempowering non-followers is also effective.

Some visionary leaders are better at forming and articulating visions than they are at implementing them, and some prominent visionaries have proved incapable of leading change successfully through the four stages. The following factors are those which commonly lead to failure in implementing transformational change:

1. *Moving at the wrong pace*   Problems can arise either from trying to achieve too much too quickly, resulting in change overload and intolerable employee stress, or from missing opportunities by not taking swift enough advantage of instability and dissatisfaction with the status quo.
2. *Inappropriate use of management consultants*   The right consultants can add value to a radical change initiative, especially in the early stages when the leader may need help and outside expertise in selling the need for change to those with the power to block it, and in formulating the detail. However, if the prolonged or excessive use of consultants makes them seem too central or

**753**

crucial to the change, the vision's underlying values can become distorted and followers may become disillusioned.

3. *Failure to put enough effort into communicating the opportunity and the need for change*   It is apparently too easy for leaders to forget or become distracted from the need for tireless efforts to communicate the vision of a better future. This is especially true in difficult times when general enthusiasm for the change is flagging.

4. *Inadequate scheduling*   Excessive formality and detail in planning and communicating change can be demotivating for followers who must own and implement the plans. On the other hand, leaders sometimes cause unnecessary confusion by avoiding scheduling the stages of the change. Sometimes this happens because leaders fear that formal plans may set them up for failure if the plans are not met. Another scheduling problem is tackling the easiest parts of the change first, whilst allowing the more intractable aspects to become even more entrenched.

5. *Inappropriate participation*   There is a trade-off between seeking too much involvement of followers in difficult decisions, especially when their advice is not used, and not allowing an appropriate level of involvement. The latter problem is especially likely to arise when one of the objects of the change is to establish a culture of increased participation.

## CONCLUSIONS

This chapter has traced the evolution of ideas about business leadership effectiveness through four stages, labelled the trait approach, the behavioural approach, the contingency approach and the visionary approach. We have seen that all four approaches have important implications for project management. In particular, the growing emphasis on transformational leadership means that exerting influence by changing the way people think has become a valuable project leadership skill.

As for the future, it is possible to foresee that, more than ever, project managers will need to understand how to manage relationships in which they are not formally in command. Just as traditional views about the transactional role of the manager are becoming increasingly out of date, leading-edge ideas about project management are aligning with newer conceptions of leadership. The basis of the world economy is moving towards finite alliances, partnerships and contracts. The need to lead such relationships through their life cycle places effective project leadership skills at a premium.

# REFERENCES AND FURTHER READING

Blake, R. R. and Mouton, J. S. (1964), *The Managerial Grid*, Gulf, Houston, TX.

Bryman, A. (1996), 'Leadership in organizations', in S. R. Clegg, C. Hardey and W. R. Nord (eds), *Handbook of Organization Studies*, Sage, London.

Fayol, H. (1950 [1916]), *Administration Industrielle et Générale*, Dunod, Paris.

House, R. J. (1971), 'A path-goal theory of leader effectiveness', *Administrative Science Quarterly*, September: 321–38.

Kirkpatrick, S. A. and Locke, E. A. (1991), 'Leadership: do traits matter?', *Academy of Management Executive*, May: 44–60.

Mintzberg, H. (1973), *The Nature of Managerial Work*, Prentice-Hall, Englewood Cliffs, NJ.

Robbins, S. P. (1997), *Essentials of Organizational Behaviour*, Prentice-Hall, Englewood Cliffs, NJ.

Turner, J. R. and Keegan, A. (1999), 'Governance and operational control in the versatile project-based organization', *European Management Journal*, **17**(2).

Turner, J. R., Grude, K. V. and Thurloway, L. (eds) (1996), *The Project Manager as Change Agent: Leadership, Influence and Negotiation*, McGraw-Hill, London.

Zaleznik, A. (1977), 'Managers and leaders: are they different?', *Harvard Business Review*, **55**: 67–78.

REFERENCES AND FURTHER Reading

# 42 Managing stakeholders

## Bill McElroy and Chris Mills

Regardless of how well you define and achieve the tangible deliverables of your project, failure to manage the project stakeholders adequately may cause your project to fail. This is not to say that project managers should disregard the need to satisfy the time, cost and performance objectives defined for their projects. Rather they should strive to achieve these objectives while also ensuring stakeholder satisfaction with the project and its outcome. This requires the project manager to view stakeholder satisfaction as a key project deliverable. As such, the project manager needs to be able to:

- identify stakeholders, and in particular key stakeholders;
- define what will constitute satisfaction for each;
- plan appropriate actions to ensure satisfaction;
- monitor the effect of these actions; and
- be prepared to implement corrective actions if the desired outcome isn't being achieved.

To help the project manager achieve the above, this chapter attempts to explain why stakeholder management is important. It defines stakeholders, provides a framework for identifying key stakeholders and outlines how to 'manage' stakeholders.

## DEFINITIONS

### WHY IS STAKEHOLDER MANAGEMENT IMPORTANT?

Many of the factors which influence a project are not only external to it, but also often lie outside the sponsor organization. For example:

- change of government
- change of public opinion
- regulatory requirements
- economic performance – both within the sponsor organization and nationally
- change of business environment
- change of business direction
- competitor performance.

Because such factors are external to the project it could be argued that the project manager should simply ignore them as they will be a 'distraction'. But these distractions can have a major influence on whether a project will be a success. For example, based on recent experience, the cost of dealing with pressure groups protesting against a new bypass can add up to 15 per cent to the cost of the project. So effective project managers need to adopt a proactive approach. The key element of this is the identification of those who embody the external influences on the project (the project *stakeholders*), and managing the influence that they will bring to the benefit of the project (*stakeholder management*). This influence need not be detrimental to project success. Many stakeholders can assist the project manager by using contacts, trust and knowledge not available to the project team.

Stakeholder management is particularly important when dealing with 'soft' business critical projects. In such projects the success criteria defined by the sponsor are often subjective, and any subversive efforts of the stakeholders will be less blatant than on projects with a high profile capital spend. An example of such criteria would be a desire to increase sales through a more 'proactive' response to customer enquiries. The achievement of such a goal would rely heavily on effective management of the project's stakeholders.

It was stated in the introduction to this chapter that the project manager should view stakeholder satisfaction as a key project deliverable. It should certainly be used as one of the measures of project success. However, as shown in Figure 42.1, whatever outcome is desired by individual stakeholders it will always be essential to safeguard support for future projects. The key point to remember is don't jeopardize future projects through poor relations now – effectively manage the project stakeholders not only to ensure success of the current project but also future ones as well!

## WHO IS A STAKEHOLDER?

The term 'stakeholder' is a relatively recent introduction to the project management vocabulary. As such it is difficult to identify a definition which is widely used and accepted. In preparing this chapter reference was made to BS6079:1996 *Guide to Project Management* which contains the following definition:

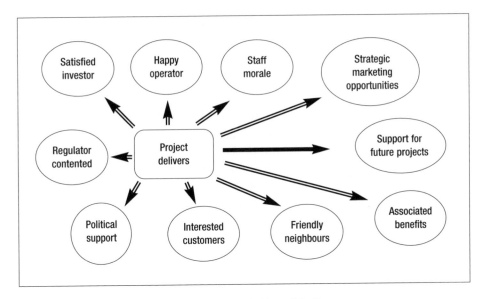

**Figure 42.1** **Stakeholder satisfaction**

A stakeholder is a person or group of people who have a vested interest in the success of an organisation and the environment within which the organisation operates.

In our view this definition, although robust, deals with stakeholders at too high a level. That is, it addresses organizational stakeholders rather than project stakeholders. It is therefore proposed that the BS6079 definition be slightly modified, as follows, to help identify stakeholders at a project level:

A project stakeholder is a person or group of people who have a vested interest in the success of a project and the environment within which the project operates.

There is, however, a further problem with this definition. Potentially there will be lots of people and groups with a *vested interest* in your project and the environment within which it will operate. Stakeholders are everywhere! Stakeholders may have a vested interest because they are:

- investing in the project;
- competitors;
- competing for resources;
- regulators;
- affected by the project implementation;
- affected by the project deliverables;
- and so on.

Project managers therefore have to focus on those stakeholders who really matter for their project. That is, they need to identify the key stakeholders. To clarify this, it is proposed that the definition above is expanded as follows:

> A key project stakeholder is a person or group of people who have a vested interest in the success of project and the environment within which the project operates *and* who have an influence over its successful outcome.

Expanding on this definition, project managers have to focus on those individuals or groups who are interested and able to actually prevent or help them (influence) deliver a successful outcome for the project. This also reflects the fact that the vested interest of certain stakeholders may not always be a positive one – they could be interested in seeing the project fail rather than succeed. Key project stakeholders feature in the right-hand half of Figure 42.2.

## WHAT IS STAKEHOLDER MANAGEMENT?

As with the term 'stakeholder' it is difficult to identify a common and widely used

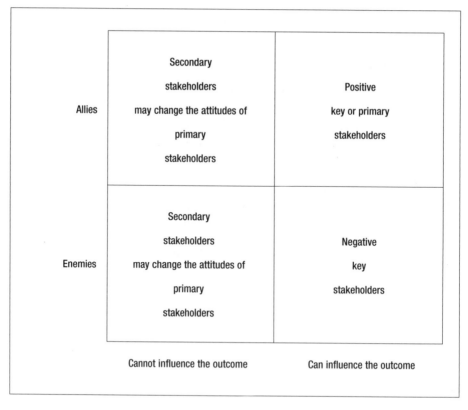

**Figure 42.2   Stakeholder identification grid**

definition for 'stakeholder management'. Again, when preparing this section reference was made to BS6079 and it was found that there was no definition given for stakeholder management. In the absence of this the following definition is proposed:

> Stakeholder management is the continuing development of relationships with stakeholders for the purpose of achieving a successful project outcome.

There are three key features of this definition. First, this is not a 'one-off' exercise (it continues throughout the project life cycle). Second, it is a two-way process (a relationship), not just telling stakeholders what you are going to do – you have to listen and negotiate as well. Third, stakeholders will make subjective assessments of project success. It is these assessments which will be remembered, long after compliance with the more objective success criteria of time, cost and performance have been forgotten.

## THE STAKEHOLDER MANAGEMENT PROCESS

The stakeholder management process is illustrated in Figure 42.3. The key steps in this process are as follows.

### IDENTIFY PROJECT SUCCESS CRITERIA

The project definition process should define the sponsor's success criteria in terms of time, cost and performance. Think beyond these, although they may be influenced by stakeholders. Consider those issues which are likely to affect or concern stakeholders directly. These are likely to be the softer issues surrounding the project, such as marketing, training or changes to working practices. Also, the environmental impact of construction projects, and associated project objectives to mitigate these, are increasingly attracting the interest of stakeholders.

### IDENTIFY RESOURCE REQUIREMENTS

A project manager needs access to many resources to execute a project effectively. As shown in Figure 42.4 'resources' are not confined to tangible items such as materials and finance. They include intangible items such as support and emotion. The majority of these resources will not be under the direct control of the project manager, but are supplied by a stakeholder. As such, access to resources will be at the discretion of the stakeholder. This is relatively obvious

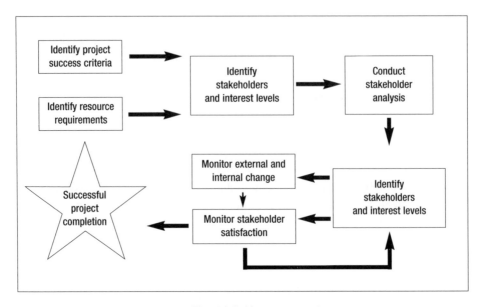

Figure 42.3   The stakeholder management process

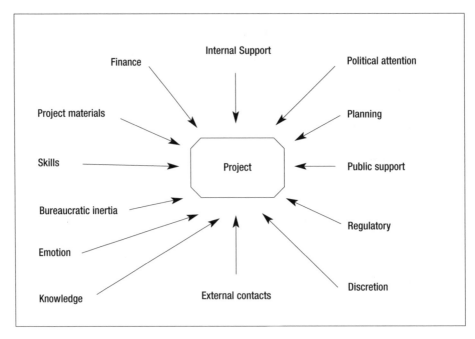

Figure 42.4   Stakeholder resources

when considering a stakeholder external to the organization undertaking the project. Some of these stakeholders can be bound by contract, although those supplying 'permissions' will be bound by statute and their decisions can be influenced by political expediency.

The availability of resources supplied by internal stakeholders should never be taken for granted, particularly in a matrix organization – the sponsor may well be committed to the project, but line managers might still be able to refuse to release key staff from operational responsibilities. For example, operator training may require the Operations Manager to identify trainees and make them available at the right time, but the Operations Manager might be always able to find more pressing issues to address in current operations.

This last example illustrates the importance of 'support' (internal and external) as a key resource provided by stakeholders. This relates both to their direct support (or opposition) for the project and to the support (or opposition) they can generate amongst other individuals and groups. As illustrated in Figure 42.5, stakeholders have a vital role to play as *change agents* – positively changing the way others view the project. As a general rule, the role of key stakeholders as change agents will be more crucial on soft projects. However, as indicated in Figure 42.5, the need for stakeholders to be incorporated as change agents is appropriate for both hard and soft projects. Examples of hard projects include:

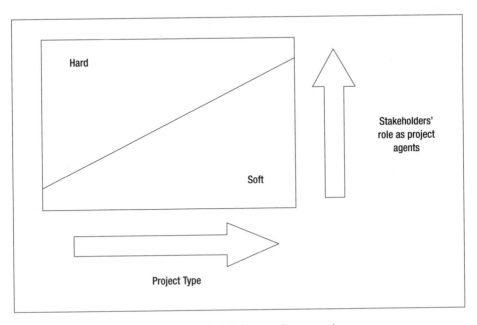

**Figure 42.5 Stakeholders as change agents**

- marketing a new road;
- explaining how to get the best results from new plant;
- getting users to think differently about software.

And examples of soft projects include:

- persuading people to change working practices;
- getting staff to think differently about profit;
- asking customers to purchase in new ways.

As has been said, and will be seen further below, it is naive to think that all stakeholders want to promote the change being delivered by the project. Also, there is a need to be clear on how the key project stakeholders will influence others and who will influence the key stakeholders.

## IDENTIFY STAKEHOLDER GROUPS AND INTEREST LEVELS

Brainstorm a key stakeholder list from the following classes:

- Employees
- Senior management
- Customers (internal and external)
- Suppliers (internal and external)
- Neighbours (physical and within the supply chain)
- Resource providers (people, time, finance, consents)
- Government (local, UK, EU)
- Opinion formers (media, commentators, industry pundits, unions, internal departments)

Record these stakeholders on a register. An example of a stakeholder register is given in Figure 42.6. For each one, identify what, to them, constitutes a successful project. Their idea of project success may be totally different from yours or your sponsor's. For example, a landowner may have no interest in the benefits a pipeline across his land will bring to a community several miles away. His idea of project success will be to attract maximum compensation for the use of his land. Stakeholders' objectives may not always be obvious to the project manager or those close to delivery of the project and may need further research. When developing the key stakeholder list be certain to include 'secondary' stakeholders. These are stakeholders who do *not* have direct influence over the project, but who are able to change the attitudes of the key stakeholders ('primary' stakeholders).

| Scheme: Rural sewerage scheme | | Review date: 24 Feb | | | | Reviewers |
|---|---|---|---|---|---|---|
| Stakeholder name / group | Objectives | Awareness H/L | Support H/L | Influence H/L | Strategy | |
| Project Manager | Meeting project success criteria of time, cost, performance | H | H | H | Ensure company and line manager support | |
| Sponsor | Remove problem of failures and customer complaints Minimize disruption and compensation payments | H | H | H | Obtain active support. Keep informed of progress proactively | |
| Local residents | Minimal noise and mess As quick as possible No more flooding | H | L | H | Face-to-face contact, agree local contact, provision for compensation | |
| Local authority | Be informed | L | L | L | Involve from start, keep informed | |
| Environment Agency | Stop incidents, environmental improvements, close communication | H | H | H | Maintain close communication | |
| Woodland Trust (environmental pressure group) | No environmental detriment Early input to planning process | H | L | H | Early communication and involvement. Encourage relationship with Environment Agency | |
| Landowners | Maximum compensation for land take | H | L | H | Isolate by negotiating compensation and access details early. Document before and after positions very carefully | |

**Figure 42.6   An example of a stakeholder register**

## CONDUCT STAKEHOLDER ANALYSIS

Stakeholders' attitudes to the project will vary. They will range from:

- complete opposition (roads protesters, redundant internal employees) to
- complete support (landscaping industrial waste, new office building for staff).

The stakeholders' attitudes may also vary over time, particularly if the stakeholders are being exposed to effective management by the project team. The actions associated with this effective management need to be focused on the key stakeholders. But knowing who these are is not enough. The project team need to base their actions on the following:

1. A refined assessment of the stakeholders' current attitude towards project success.
2. An awareness of the knowledge base on which the stakeholders' current attitude is based.
3. An understanding of the stakeholders' own objectives and how these can, if possible, be aligned with those of the project.

Guidance on mapping and analysis techniques to support the first two elements listed above are considered here. Steps taken to deal with the third element are outlined below.

The first step in the analysis is to assess the current level of support (or commitment) for the project amongst key stakeholders. But in order to provide information to guide effective stakeholder management this needs to be assessed against the commitment levels required to achieve success. This analysis can be produced as a matrix (Figure 42.7). The characteristics and behaviours of each level of commitment are:

- *Active opposition*  Will not accept change as proposed by project. Will expend time and energy telling others the project is 'wrong', and will try to turn supporters against the project. Will withhold resources from the project, either overtly or covertly.
- *Passive opposition*  Not happy with change as proposed by project, but will reluctantly accept it. When asked will voice opposition, but will not seek out opportunities to raise opposition to the project. Will provide resources to the project but may require coercing.
- *No commitment*  Will accept change. Not opposed to or supportive of the project. Happy to see it proceed but not concerned if it succeeds or fails. Will provide resources, but only if it does not impact on their own operations.
- *Passive support*  Wants change as proposed by project. When asked will voice

| Stakeholders | Active opposition | Passive opposition | Not committed | Passive support | Active support |
|---|---|---|---|---|---|
| Suppliers | | | XO | | |
| Executive directors | | | | X | 0 |
| Staff | X | | 0 | | |
| National politicians | | | | XO | |
| Finance Director | | | | 0 | X |
| Local politicians | | XO | | | |

X = current position    0 = required position

**Figure 42.7   Stakeholder commitment matrix**

support, but will not seek out opportunities to gather support for the project. Will provide resources to project when asked, but may require prompting.

● *Active support*   Eager for change proposed by project. Will expend time and energy telling others the project is 'right' and will try to change opposers' views – without prompting from the project team. Will ensure that resources are available to the project as and when required.

There are a number of features to note from the figure:

1. Changing a stakeholder's commitment level will require effort by the project team. This will have to be balanced with all of the other activities the project team will need to carry out. Therefore the team should not be over ambitious about how far they can move stakeholders, particularly, as in the case of 'staff', if they are currently actively opposed. The team should focus on the key stakeholders, those with the most influence to affect the success of the project, and aim to achieve the minimum commitment level needed to ensure project success.

2. Where the stakeholders' current commitment matches their required commitment level (as in the case of 'suppliers') they must not be ignored. It is all too easy for ignored stakeholders to misinterpret the lack of communication from the project team as disinterest in their objectives. They may respond in a like fashion when required to deliver resources or support. Worse, they may be swayed by active opposers and change their attitude to the project as a result.

3. As in the case of the 'Finance Director' there can be stakeholders whose active support may actually have a disruptive effect on the project. This is often due to their active support raising or reinforcing negative attitudes in other key stakeholders.

4. The impact of stakeholder commitment on provision of resources to the project needs to be carefully considered by the project team when developing project plans. Where the analysis indicates resources may not be readily available, have contingency plans ready.

This commitment analysis will help to focus development of an appropriate strategy for managing each key stakeholder. A summary strategy can be entered on the Stakeholder Register, as shown in Figure 42.6. In developing these strategies it is worth remembering the definition of stakeholder management and, in particular, 'the need for the continuing development of relationships'. Therefore the strategies developed need to incorporate actions which will continue throughout the project life cycle and involve two-way communications.

These communications will be most effective if they are based on an awareness of the stakeholder's knowledge base. Stakeholders' commitment levels will, to a large extent, be based on their level of knowledge of the project. And based on this knowledge, stakeholders will make judgements of how the project will help, or hinder, them in meeting their own objectives. It is these judgements which will determine the stakeholders' satisfaction referred to in the introduction to this chapter. The stakeholders' level of knowledge will range from:

- *full awareness* They have gained knowledge of the project by detailed research, focusing on those aspects of the project which will help them meet their own objectives to
- *total ignorance* They have gained knowledge of the project by hearsay not fact, and are therefore basing their attitudes towards the project on assumptions. Their decision on whether to increase their knowledge will depend on whether they believe they can use the project to further their own objectives.

These two attributes of stakeholders, commitment and knowledge, can be mapped on to a chart, such as that in Figure 42.8, to illustrate the knowledge base across the key stakeholders. To populate this chart plot each of the key stakeholders listed in Figure 42.6. Initially you will have to make certain assumptions regarding the knowledge base of each stakeholder. Be prepared to test these assumptions and revisit this chart throughout the project. There are a number of important points to note regarding where stakeholders lie on this chart:

1. *Quadrant 1 – Support/Aware*  These supporters must not be taken for granted. In order to retain their support they need to be assured that the project will indeed help them meet their own objectives.
2. *Quadrant 2 – Support/Ignorant*  This support is vulnerable and could easily be lost, particularly if the gaps in the stakeholder's knowledge base are filled by the views of opposers. The project team will therefore need to ensure that this support is protected and reinforced.
3. *Quadrant 3 – Oppose/Ignorant*  This is a key target area for the project team, especially if the commitment mapping (Figure 42.7) indicates that there are stakeholders in this quadrant whose commitment needs to be increased. This chart suggests that it may be possible to achieve greater commitment by filling the gap in the stakeholder's knowledge base with positive messages regarding the project.
4. *Quadrant 4 – Oppose/Aware*  These will be the most difficult stakeholders to

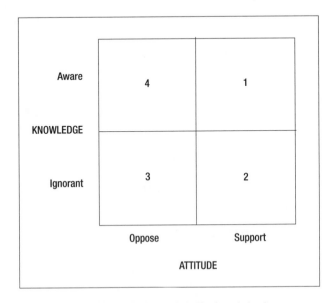

**Figure 42.8  Plotting stakeholder knowledge base**

manage. Indeed, as they are already aware, and are basing their opposition on this, it may never be possible to move them to support the project.

## DEVELOP STRATEGY FOR EACH STAKEHOLDER

The analysis outlined in the previous section focused on determining current and required stakeholder commitment levels, and the knowledge base giving rise to these attitudes. Building on this analysis stakeholder management strategies should be developed which focus on achieving the required future commitment levels by influencing the knowledge base. The respective movement in commitment level will therefore be driven by communications between the project team and the key stakeholders. As can be seen from Figure 42.7, gaining stakeholders' commitment to change is often vital to achieving project success. Unfortunately project managers rarely appreciate the scale and complexity of the communication tasks involved in gaining commitment, as shown in Figure 42.9.

Project managers must avoid merely focusing on the preparation and circulation of newsletters and briefing papers (i.e. raising awareness). As can be seen from Figure 42.9, they have to follow this up with more direct action if they are to gain widespread commitment to the change proposed by the project. If they do not check the stakeholders' understanding they can find opposers use this raised awareness as a basis to attack the project.

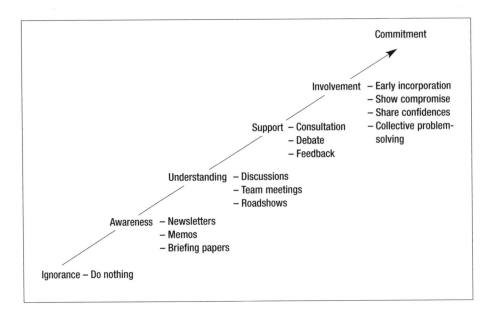

**Figure 42.9   Tasks involved in gaining commitment**

For ease of reference, the principle features of the various strategies that may need to be adopted have been outlined below in relation to the current knowledge base (Figure 42.8) and commitment levels (Figure 42.7).

### Quadrant 1 – Support/Aware

There are three key communication strategies to this group.

**Raising commitment**   This can generally be achieved by highlighting the role of stakeholders in achieving project success, particularly through ready access to resources and influencing the attitudes of other stakeholders. Prepare for these discussions by developing scenarios showing the effect of, say, late access to resources. Also, if seeking to increase commitment to active support you need to build on the stakeholders' awareness, and their desire to see the project succeed, in preparing them for discussions with other (opposing) stakeholders.

**Maintaining commitment**   Reinforce their positive view of the project. This is best achieved by repeatedly stressing the alignment between the project and their objectives. Obviously to do this the initial step is to find out what their objectives are.

**Lowering commitment**   This can be a particularly sensitive situation to deal with. After all these stakeholders want you to succeed, indeed they want to actively help you. So how do you tell them that their active support may actually help the project to fail! A possible way out of this tricky situation is to stress the need for the project team to coordinate the actions of stakeholders in order to ensure maximum benefit for the project. This can then be expanded to include the project team directing the stakeholders' actions. Even where this strategy is well implemented there is always a risk that the stakeholder concerned will see an opportunity to help the project and do, or say, its own thing – with perhaps unforeseen and negative results. This risk can never be fully removed and as such needs constant monitoring.

### Quadrant 2 – Support/Ignorant

As noted earlier this support is vulnerable and could easily be lost, even if these stakeholders are initially actively supportive of the project. Support could be lost by opposers raising doubts about whether the project will indeed help these stakeholders achieve their objectives. The project team must discover why these stakeholders are supporting the project. What is in it for them? Remember these stakeholders are ignorant of the details of the project. They are therefore basing their support on assumptions they have made regarding the project. These assumptions need to be checked.

Let's first look at where the stakeholders' assumptions are found to be valid. The project team need to reinforce the stakeholders' support by showing them that the project is indeed what they have assumed. Such confirmation can in itself often result in an increase in the stakeholders' commitment level – from passive to active support.

Now let's look at where the stakeholders' assumptions are not valid. Here we have a potential problem. If active opposers discover this they could use it to change these stakeholders' attitudes. However, this change in attitude could just as easily happen if the project team's communications with the stakeholders merely highlight that the project is not what they thought. So should the project team avoid this problem by trying to keep these stakeholders ignorant? There are two main weaknesses in such a passive strategy:

1. You cannot guarantee that the opposers will not fill the resulting communications void with negative messages.
2. You cannot increase commitment level (e.g. from passive to active support) if you don't communicate with the stakeholders (Figure 42.9).

We therefore recommend that a proactive strategy is adopted. This must itself be based on an assumption. That is that once the stakeholders are made aware of the project's details their support will turn to opposition. This opposition must then be quickly addressed through the strategy proposed below for Quadrant 3 – Oppose/Ignorant.

### Quadrant 3 – Oppose/Ignorant

As noted earlier, this is a key target area for the project team. If the project team do not take the time and effort to communicate with these stakeholders they will be targeted by the active opposers. This could result in a strengthening of their attitudes (from passive to active opposition). You therefore need to discover why they are opposed and be prepared to negotiate to move them to, as a minimum, passive opposition – they may not like the change but will reluctantly accept it. To achieve acceptance of change it is helpful to understand what influences such acceptance. Figure 42.10 provides an outline of factors which need to be considered and addressed in order to influence someone's acceptance of change:

1. *New benefits* Relative advantage – how much better does the new arrangement appear?
   - Will the new IS set-up really help?
   - Will the bypass really save much time?

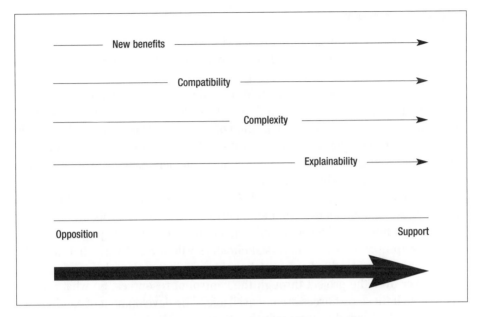

**Figure 42.10 What affects the stakeholders' position?**

2. *Compatibility*   How much will the stakeholder have to change?
   ● Does the office move mean I'll have to relocate?
3. *Complexity*   How easy is it to adopt the new system?
   ● Can I get it in one go or do I have to go through a dozen different processes?
   ● How many times will you be digging up my road?
4. *Explainability*   How simple is it to explain it all?
   ● Exactly how loud is a decibel?
   ● How smelly is a sewage farm?

Therefore the key elements of this strategy are:

● discovery of what is influencing the stakeholder's view of the project;
● discovery of what changes would be required to influence the stakeholder's acceptance of the project;
● framing propositions to the stakeholder in respect of the factors outlined above;
● negotiating with the stakeholder to achieve acceptance while minimizing the changes required.

**773**

## Quadrant 4 - Oppose/Aware

This is the most difficult situation to deal with. You are starting with stakeholders who, on the analysis carried out, have knowledge of your project and based on this are opposed to what you are trying to achieve.

Initially the same strategy should be adopted as for Oppose/Ignorant. However, there needs to be recognition that there may be little or no possibility of moving these stakeholders to a position of support for the project. This should not stop you from trying. A visible, positive change in attitude of one of these stakeholders will greatly enhance your chances of increasing or maintaining the commitment levels of other stakeholders.

A note of caution needs to be raised. A lot of energy could be wasted trying to change these stakeholders' attitudes, energy which would probably be better used on stakeholders in one of the other quadrants. Therefore be prepared for the possibility (probability) that these stakeholders will never change their attitude. As they have been identified as key stakeholders they therefore, by our definition, have power over the project through the control of resources. So what are you going to do if these resources are not available? The development of contingency measures to deal with this eventuality has to be a priority task for the project team and is indeed a key feature of the management strategy for these stakeholders.

### MONITOR AND REVIEW

The position and level of commitment of various stakeholders with regards to the analysis carried out above will constantly change as their knowledge base about the project changes. Also, new stakeholders may appear. Therefore the various steps shown in Figure 42.3 and outlined above need to be revisited at regular intervals. A question to ask in these regular reviews is 'Are the various stakeholders where you want them to be at this point in time?' Remember that you can't win them all. Focus on gaining the support of those who control key resources and those with the highest influence on project success or failure.

## HINTS AND TIPS

Here are some key points in a stakeholder management strategy:

1. Avoid helping to build opposing coalitions.
2. Become known as the monopoly supplier of information.
3. Respond quickly and appropriately to negative impressions.
4. Encourage supporters to meet and reinforce each other.

5. Don't abdicate responsibility for dealing with objectors outside the project team.
6. Use supporters to convert waverers. People are often less suspicious of an intermediary than the company or organization promoting the project.
7. Stress benefits not features.
8. Be prepared to change.
9. Plan ahead.
10. Be sensitive to changes in the business or political environment.

and remember the following:

1. Stakeholders must be identified.
2. Important stakeholders have power *and* an interest.
3. Stakeholder analysis and management is vital for project success.
4. Stakeholders' attitudes change throughout the project life cycle.
5. Dealing with stakeholders is often an intuitive process.

## ACKNOWLEDGEMENT

The authors would like to highlight the support and insights provided by Liam Fitzpatrick of CGI Corporate Consulting.

## REFERENCE AND FURTHER READING

BS6079 (1996), *Guide to Project Management*, British Standards Institute, London.

## RELATED TOPICS

| | |
|---|---|
| Project success criteria | Chapter 5 |
| Resource management | Chapter 20 |
| Project definition | Chapter 25 |
| Managing conflict | Chapter 43 |

# 43 Managing conflict, persuasion and negotiation

*Bob Graham*

Managing a project is almost by definition managing conflict, because the success of a project is often measured by the conflicting goals of producing a quality product at a low cost and to a quick deadline. These very goals are in conflict because a quality product often requires a higher cost and a longer deadline. A project can be done faster, but that often requires an increase in budget or a decrease in quality. You can save money on the budget, but that usually results in a decrease in product quality or an increase in project duration. In addition, the project stakeholders are often in conflict. The project represents something new and thus upsets the status quo. The departmental directors who supply the project team members might well want those people working on departmental rather than project work. In fact, the department directors may be fighting each other for headcount and so do not want to send anyone over to a project that may be associated with another department. Thus it seems that project management is conflict management as projects are built on conflicting goals and priorities. Managing all these conflicts often becomes the chief job of the project manager.

Managing this conflict requires the ability to persuade others in the organization to act in ways that will benefit the project. The concept of persuasion and negotiation is used in project management because the project leader typically does not have the command relationship of authority that is present in most departmental organizations. I do not know how many times I have heard statements like 'The problem in this organization is that the project leaders have all of the responsibility, but none of the authority.' To this comment I usually respond 'Welcome to project work'. In the process of project leadership, the lack of direct authority over project team members and other project stakeholders is considered the normal state of affairs. Successful project leaders realize that they must develop their powers of persuasion and negotiation in order to get the project completed.

This chapter will discuss some of the strategies the project manager can use to avoid and resolve conflict. We begin by examining the sources of conflict for if these sources can be eliminated much potential conflict can be avoided. This is followed by discussion of some techniques for resolving those conflicts that cannot be avoided. Finally, the importance of information in the conflict process is explored.

## AVOIDING CONFLICT

### UNDERSTANDING SOURCES OF CONFLICT

Prevention of conflict is the first step in managing conflict. It is therefore important first to understand the sources of conflict and work to eliminate those sources so they do not affect the project team. Most conflicts on projects arise from differences about the project goals, the utilization of resources on project teams or are a result of departmental differences or grudges. They arise because a person or a group of people feel frustrated in their ability to achieve their goals. Additional conflict can arise due to interpersonal differences or opposing points of view. The conflict develops out of a basic lack of or unwillingness to understand the other party's position (Pinto 1996). Thus to prevent conflict we begin by examining the sources of conflict, the various people involved in conflict and their points of view.

There are a variety of people in the organization who need to be influenced in favour of the project. One important group is the members of the project team. As these people typically do not report to the project leader, they must be influenced and motivated to devote their best work to the project effort. However, these people come from different departments and may have different work styles and values. In addition, people from one department may have stereotypes of people from other departments and may treat team members as the stereotype rather than the person. Also, it is natural to see one's own departmental aspect as most important for the success of the project, and thus feel that most resources should be allocated to that aspect. For example, people from Production who come to meetings on time may be irritated by people from Marketing who are late. All team members may see those from Accounting as just bean counters to be ignored, and those from Engineering may feel that theirs is the most important aspect of the project and should get most of the resource allocation. The potential for conflict is high.

Another important group of stakeholders is the departmental directors; those people who supply the resources to complete the project. Your project is only one of many projects that they must consider, so they too must be influenced to supply good people for the project. Indeed, conflict can occur in the allocation of people. In addition, departmental directors may be fighting among themselves over organizational priorities, and this will be reflected in your project. An important department is Finance, which supplies the monetary resources for the project. Project managers and team members usually feel that not enough financial resources are allocated, and this is a continuing source of conflict.

The group of senior managers must also be influenced to support this project, as projects are seldom successful without top management support (Pinto and Slevin 1987). Often one or more government agencies must also be included on the stakeholder list. The goals of both these groups could be quite opposed to those of the project team.

Finally, there are the end-users of the project, the people who will benefit most from the project completion, but who often give only lukewarm support as the project progresses. The needs of this group are often hard to pin down and change as the project progresses. The moving target of 'satisfying end-user expectations' often frustrates team members who may be used to more static job specifications. The pool of potential conflict is wide and deep here.

## MOTIVATING CONFLICTING PARTIES

The second step in managing conflict is to ensure that all parties to any conflict or potential conflict are motivated to find a solution or prevent the conflict from occurring. This occurs when people see it as being in their best interest to solve or prevent conflict. People can change their opinion and even see another's point of view if they feel it is advantageous to them. People do not usually continue behaving in a way that is detrimental to their achieving their own interests. The same is true for other project stakeholders such as your peers and superiors, as well as functional managers (department directors) who will be supplying the members of your team. The successful project manager will develop an influence strategy for these stakeholder groups as well as for team members to show them that conflict is not in their best interest.

## DEVELOPING AN INFLUENCE STRATEGY

The first step in developing an influence strategy is to produce a list of potential stakeholder groups. The next step is to develop a list of key people in these stakeholder groups. For example, within the project team, the core team members are probably the most important. Within the senior management group, the top manager who proposed this project and those that are ultimately supplying the manpower are probably most important. There may also be one customer that is more important than the others.

The next step is to ask yourself why these individuals should support your project. That is, what benefit will they derive from a successful project? If you are unsure of the benefit that key individuals might derive, you might want to discuss it with them. From understanding who benefits from this project you can develop a list of potential allies, along with the knowledge of the benefits you need to deliver to develop and maintain their support. These benefits are an important element in resolving conflict. A valuable complement to the list of 'allies' is a list of 'enemies', that is a list of key individuals who do not initially support the project. Although these people are not really 'enemies', they may not see the benefit of the project or may see it as detrimental to their success or that of the organization. It is important to understand why people do not support the project and then work to overcome their objections as the project progresses. Remember that all enemies are potential allies, if they can see the project as being in their best interest. Chapter 42 gives advice on identifying stakeholders. Figure 42.2 shows a way of viewing enemies and allies:

- Those who are in favour of the project and those who are against it.
- From these two groups, those who can influence the outcome and those who cannot.

## THE REWARD/RISK FACTOR IN MINIMIZING CONFLICT

The key factor in influencing anyone to do anything, including resolving a conflict, is to ensure that the rewards for doing it are greater than the risks involved. The assumption is if people understand and value the rewards for being on your project, and if you have taken the steps to minimize the risks involved in gaining the reward, they will see project work as being in their best interest. This way you can influence them to work on or otherwise support the project and minimize any potential conflict because it will be in their best interest to do so.

### Reward – perception of value

Most projects will have value to the organization, as well as value to the individual. The project manager must think clearly through the questions of 'Why are we doing this project?' and 'What are the potential benefits for the people who work on or support this project?' The project manager must then ensure that the potential team members and other stakeholders fully understand the nature of these benefits.

### Risk – perception of loss

Most projects will also have potential risks to the organization and potential project participants. The nature of these risks is subjective, and the evaluation of these risks is often a function of the individuals' risk preference profile. To begin to understand these risks, the project manager must ask the question 'What will the organization or the individuals potentially lose if they participate in this project?' Once this list is developed, the project manager must work to ensure that the potential losses are minimized. This information must then be passed on to potential project participants and stakeholders.

Thus the key to developing influence is to maximize the value while minimizing the risks. If the perception of value exceeds the perception of risk, the individuals will be motivated to work on or support the project. If the perception of risk exceeds the perception of value, the individuals will not be so motivated and may work against the completion of the project.

## INFLUENCING TEAM MEMBERS

When some managers think of value for team members, they think of money. Many project leaders then lament that they have little control over the salaries of the project team members. However, experience indicates that money is only one part of motivation. Indeed, there are many aspects of projects that people find inherently rewarding and of value. The project leader must use these non-monetary aspects to maximum benefit. Some of these values are discussed below.

### Satisfying customer requirements

This is the *raison d'être* of any project. It is also one of the principal benefits to all project stakeholders, and one of the most useful levers to use for managing conflict. Whenever two parties are in conflict over product features it is useful to focus on customer requirements and move away from focusing on which party is 'right'.

### Doing something new/learning a new skill

By definition, a project is something new in the organization. People generally enjoy variety in their work, and thus find value in doing something new and different. Most projects involve developing new technology or developing a new application for old technology. Either way the team members often learn some new skill. This aspect enhances people's self-worth, and also their future marketability. Learning and applying the latest methods or technology is

781

rewarding for many people. In addition, learning a new skill often helps people to add value to the organization, enhancing the organizational skill set.

### Networking and travel

Most projects cut across departmental lines, and this gives people exposure to other departments. These contacts can increase individuals' organization networks, as well as general knowledge about what they do in other parts of the organization.

### Developing a unique product

Most work in organizations involves repetition. Being on a team doing something new and unique can be rewarding. People also find much satisfaction in being able to point to a finished product and say 'I was on the team that made that product.'

### Positive visibility with senior management

This is an important reward for many people. In fact this may be one of the most important rewards held by project team members. People often feel it is to their advantage to be viewed positively by upper management. A conflict can often be managed by reminding conflicting parties that their conflict will not look good to upper management and that they should resolve it quickly.

However, there are also many risks associated with something as uncertain as a project.

### Negative visibility with senior management

The project leader must remember that there are two sides to the visibility coin. In some organizations, being associated with a failed project is another step closer to the exit door. Thus a good track record helps to recruit project team members. However, if the project leader is new at the job, he or she must display a lot of enthusiasm at the beginning of the project. If the project leader is very enthusiastic about the potential success of the project, potential team members feel there is a higher chance of success (which, of course, helps lead to success, thus becoming a self-fulfilling prophecy). If the project leader is not enthusiastic, then potential team members will feel there is little chance for success and will thus not be motivated to join the project team.

## No reward for project work

Lack of reward for project work is a typical problem in organizations that are new to project management. Reward systems and performance appraisals are typically departmentally based, as they should be. This means that organization members typically see their future, promotions, salary and the like tied to their performance in departments. The project leader, however, is attempting to get these people to join project teams, and there will be little motivation to do so unless the work on the project is also appraised and is counted as a part of the performance appraisal and review. The project leader must work to ensure that the project work will be used in performance appraisal and complete said appraisals for all member of the core team.

## Out of sight, out of mind

This is an associated risk. Potential team members may feel that if they are not working at all times on department work, then the department managers will 'forget' them and perhaps overlook them if a promotion is available. Thus the project leader must have a system for continually informing departmental managers about the work of their department members.

## A more exciting project may come along

There is not much the project leader can do about this fear, except be certain that the potential team members are fully aware of just how exciting this project is going to be.

The project leader must take steps to maximize the perceived benefits and to minimize perceived risk. In addition, team members must be made aware of the potential risks and rewards. This is an important part of the conflict resolution process.

## INFLUENCING OTHER STAKEHOLDERS

Numerous studies of successful projects point to the need for top management support, as well as the support of other project stakeholders (Wateridge 1995). Thus a part of the task of project leadership is influencing others to support your project. Influencing upper management and other stakeholders is very similar to influencing team members.

To begin with, the project leader must realize that influencing project stakeholders is a process, not an event. That is, some project leaders will hold stakeholder influencing events, such as a project start-up workshop, and feel that the influence has been set for the project. They often feel that their project will maintain a constant, high priority. However, priorities change, and stakeholders' feelings about and attention to a given project also change over time. So while a project start-up workshop is an excellent event for gaining support for a project, it is to be seen as only one event in a long and continuous process of developing and maintaining project support.

The process of developing project support begins by identifying the major project stakeholders, as was done above. For the next step the project leader must determine what value these various groups will obtain from a successful project. And for those that are not initially supportive of the project, what loss they feel the project will bring them. Common values received from projects are shown for the stakeholder groups as follows.

### Senior management

The common value for upper management is that the project will help to support a corporate strategy, such as entering a new market. If the strategy is successful, then the project will ultimately help to lead to higher profitability and other corporate goals. It is important that the project leader realizes just what strategy it is that the project is supporting. As projects unfold they are often scrutinized as to their expense, and are often felt to be expendable at budget review time. It is important that the project leader reminds upper management what strategy will suffer if the project does not receive continued support.

### Customers/end-users

The customers and end-users are the people who will gain benefit from the use of the end product. To satisfy the customers the project leader must be continually in touch with what the customers want from the product, as well as what they really expect from it. Experienced project leaders understand that what customers say they want, and what they really expect, are often two very different things. It is thus a task of the project leader continually to probe to discover what it is that the customers and end-users really expect from the end product.

There are two parts to discovering customer expectations. One is to develop a mindset of continuous exploration. This means the project team expects and welcomes a sequence of constant changes and suggestions from the customers and end-users. In the past, these changes were seen as irritants that delayed project progress. Now they should be seen as additional information that helps to ensure project success. The second part is using a series of prototypes to evoke responses. It is a fact of life that most people cannot really tell you what they expect from a product until they have experience of it. Developing prototypes allows customers to have this experience and to ask the classic question 'Well, how come it doesn't do this or that?' Of course, the customer never asked for it to do this or that, but the experience of the prototype will uncover that it expected it to do this or that. Obtaining customer reaction early and often can eliminate potential conflict at the end of a project.

## Department directors

This is the group of stakeholders that will be supplying the people to complete the project work. It is assumed that all of the people working on a project will be 'on loan' from various departments in the organization. It is thus important that the project leader consider the needs and desires of the managers of those departments.

Department managers are also trying to implement corporate strategy, so a knowledge of how the project supports corporate strategy is also important to gaining their support. However, department managers are also occupied with the more immediate task of scheduling people to perform the tasks of the department, as well as supporting other projects. Thus the more immediate questions run along the lines of 'What people do you want, for how much of their time, and when will they be finished?' It is thus important that the project leader reviews project plans, schedules and progress with department managers on a regular basis. The more complete and accurate information they have from you, the better they will be able to schedule people to meet the other demands that are placed on their departments. This will help to develop and maintain their support for your project.

## Other stakeholders

There may be some groups or individuals, even among those mentioned above, who will not initially support the project. With these people it is important that the project leader determines what they have at risk or what they feel they have to lose from successful completion of the project. Many times this feeling of risk and/or loss is due to misinformation or false assumptions about the project. Thus to gain the support of these groups or individuals, the project leader must discover what their assumptions are and work to inform. In fact, the project leader must do more than inform, as talk is cheap. He or she must demonstrate that the results of the project will not result in the loss the others expect. This is a long process and it often takes place over the life of the project. But it has many rewards.

For example, when I became a project manager it was at a college that did not have a computer when I walked in the door. Part of my job was to computerize the registration, billing and housing function. At that time it was assumed by most employees that when things went onto the computer everyone would lose their jobs. Gaining cooperation was difficult as everyone treated me like the grim reaper. I seemed to be in conflict with everyone until I understood the source of their perception of risk. When I was able to convince them they would not lose their jobs, and also demonstrated the value of the computer, much of the conflict evaporated.

## RESOLVING CONFLICT

Despite our best efforts, conflict happens and must be resolved. Pinto (1996) suggests three methods of resolving conflict which he classifies as confrontation, diffusion and avoidance.

### Confrontation

Confrontation methods seek the sources of the conflict so that conflicting parties can discuss the sources and work to resolve the conflict. A typical technique is a problem-solving meeting where the conflicting parties and the project manager meet and discuss conflict causes and possible resolution. This is a long process, frequently accompanied by high emotions from the parties concerned. If the meeting is not handled well, it can solidify conflict and ill-will, making possible resolution much more difficult. As many project mangers do not have the skill or the time to do this, obtaining outside help is recommended for this method.

### Diffusion

Diffusion methods try to diffuse the conflict for enough time for conflicting parties to work it out. One diffusion technique is to appeal to the common goal of the project, emphasizing that 'we are all in this together'. Another is compromise, the classic 'give and take' in which parties cease conflict because they get something they want while they give something the other party wants. While diffusion techniques address the conflict directly they do not require the discovery of the root causes of that conflict.

### Avoidance

Avoidance methods avoid directly addressing the conflict source while seeking to resolve it. One technique is for the project manager to send signals that the conflict is not a good idea. This is an attempt to show people it is not in their best interest to continue the conflict. Another technique is forced separation, that is hopefuly the conflict will go away if the parties are physically separated. However, this is not good for project management, which relies on close interaction of team members. A third technique is forced togetherness where the project manager gives two conflicting parties a task where they must work harmoniously together to be successful. In this way both parties see conflict resolution as being in their best interest.

## AN EXAMPLE OF FORCED TOGETHERNESS

In a large telephone company there were two groups, among others, who were responsible for installation of PBX switches for corporations. Two particular groups were in conflict and had been in conflict for quite some time. One group had a marketing orientation; the other was old line telephone engineers. The first group was responsible for determining customer requirements. The second group was responsible for designing and installing the equipment to solve the customer problems. This meant that the second group got its instructions from the first group. The marketing function, and many of the members of that group, was new to the corporation. The engineering function and most of the engineers had been a part of the company since the dawn of time. Both departments were very suspicious of the other and had various derogatory terms to describe one another. They did not like to work together.

A recent switch installation had gone badly. The telephone users claimed the switch did not meet their needs. They were furious and threatened to change companies for the next switch. Senior management of the telephone company demanded that this important customer be satisfied with the next installation. Marketing blamed Engineering for not correctly designing a switch that met customer needs, while Engineering blamed Marketing for not correctly determining user requirements. Both sides pointed to the other and said, 'We would not have this problem if those guys would just do their job correctly!' Obviously the level of conflict was getting in the way of understanding the true source of user dissatisfaction.

A project team with members from both departments was formed for the next switch installation. We began conflict management with departmental managers, convincing them that since senior management was interested in this customer, it was in their best interest to help resolve this conflict. As above so below. We also convinced all team members it was in their best interest to work together. At project team meetings we focused on understanding the end-user requirements. We initiated a process of forced interaction where two team members from each department went together to interview users, so they could understand together what the requirements were. While doing this they discovered the source of the problem was simple communications errors. By focusing on eliminating these errors and truly understanding customer and end user requirements, the conflict was resolved for that project.

## THE POWER AND VALUE OF INFORMATION

One of the final sources of conflict is lack of reliable information. Project leaders need to see themselves as the ultimate disseminators of information. Because of the uncertainty that surrounds most projects, they tend to generate much anxiety among the stakeholders and this can be a potential source of conflict. This anxiety is usually concerning the outcome, cost, final schedule and resource requirements of the project. Information is the only tool that the project leader has to relieve this anxiety. The project leader will find that he or she can have a large influence on the members of the organization by providing timely and complete information regarding the salient aspects of the project.

The first step in developing a project management information system is to determine what information it is that the stakeholders need to help them achieve their objectives. Some texts would advise the project leader to begin with a list of stakeholders and proceed to ask each of them what information they need about the project. However, experience has shown that the response to such a question does not reveal all that is needed. Many people find it difficult to answer a question about what data they need. They will give you an answer, but when the data is presented, they typically answer that it is not what they wanted. This often leaves the project leader puzzled and frustrated. The fact is that most people do not think in terms of data, but rather in terms of questions. Therefore, instead of asking 'What data do you need?' it is better to ask 'What questions do you have about this project?' Then the project leader and the stakeholder can work together to develop a set of information that answers those questions. Good information is that which answers stakeholders' questions, is easy for them to understand and is there when they need it. This requires that the project leader understands the questions and associated information from the stakeholders' points of view. The project management information system should then be developed to satisfy their needs, in much the same way that the entire project is developed to satisfy the needs of the customer/end-users.

### QUESTIONS ON OUTCOME

The questions about outcome are normally of three types.

## Functionality

The first is about what the final product will do when it is completed. This is a question for the project leader as well as the project stakeholders as the specifications will be changing as the project proceeds. The project leader must guard against the problem of suggesting a certain function will be available before it is certain that it will indeed be in the final product. So answers to questions about outcome should be in two parts. The first contains features that have definitely been decided. The second contains a list of features that are being considered. This list should be updated regularly and be distributed automatically to all stakeholders.

## Success

The second question about outcome is the 'Will it be successful?' type. Stakeholders want to know how this product compares with the competition, and its probability of market acceptance. The best way to answer these questions is to summarize the information gleaned from the customer or end-user representatives, show how the product is being designed to address those expectations and pass this to the stakeholders. If this cannot be done for competitive reasons (secrecy), then the stakeholders should be assured that it is indeed taking place.

## Market

A third outcome question is of the 'market segment' type. Stakeholders often want to know what market the product is aimed to satisfy. Thus the project leader needs to be continually aware of and searching for potential applications and markets for the product, and passing this information on to the stakeholders.

## QUESTIONS ABOUT THE SCHEDULE

Of course, the classic schedule question is 'When will it be ready?' Associated questions concern availability of prototypes and milestone reviews. This means that an updated schedule should be always available to stakeholders to answer these questions.

## QUESTIONS ABOUT RESOURCE REQUIREMENTS

Projects have a way of using up countless hours of resources, much of which is usually said to be unexpected. This often frustrates the department directors who are supplying that resource and is a continuing source of conflict. Their questions normally revolve around how much of the resource you are going to need, and when the resource will be again available to the department. Project leaders are understandably hesitant to answer such questions, as projections for requirements are difficult to make when you are doing something for the first time. In addition, initial estimates have a quality of being 'cast in stone', so that future changes in requirements cause friction with the department directors. Thus the requirements should be presented with a 'here is what we know so far' quality. The project leader should not just produce estimates and send them to the department directors. Rather he or she should personally explain all of the assumptions that contributed to that estimate, and indicate all of the factors that could cause that estimate to change.

Department directors, as are all of us, are much more amenable to change if they understand the reason for the change. It is up to the project leader to ensure that they know the reasons for all changes. Often just knowing the reasons for a change can eliminate a potential conflict. In addition to providing information that answers their questions, good information should also be there when it is most needed. Having the information available to stakeholders is often not enough. The project leader should attempt to determine when it is that the information will most likely be needed. Some simple questions to stakeholders like 'When do you usually discuss this project?' or 'What meetings do you go to where questions about this project come up?' can often reveal the best time to provide the information. For example, if there is a regular meeting where the project is discussed, it would be good to provide the information the day before that meeting. In that way the stakeholder could arrive at the meeting with the latest information. Timely information is current information that arrives just before the person needs it.

As a final note, it is important to remember that timely, accurate information is useless unless the person who is using the information understands what is being presented. Many people are not comfortable with information presented on Gantt charts and network diagrams. Thus the first few times that information is supplied, the project leader may need to personally review the format with the stakeholders to ensure that they fully understand what they are being presented with. If they cannot work with network diagrams and the like, then a different format should be developed with which they are comfortable.

Always remember that the information is being produced to relieve anxiety and avoid or resolve conflict. If the people cannot understand the information, it will actually increase the very anxiety it was designed to reduce. So the information should conform to the person, rather then expecting the person to conform to the information. In summary, good information answers their questions, is there when they need it and is easy to understand.

## CONCLUSIONS

It has been shown in this chapter that the task of running a successful project requires conflict avoidance and resolution. This requires leading by influence rather than authority. The keys to developing this influence lie in understanding individuals' risk/reward relationship, as well as the power of information. It was argued that the project leader can manage conflict and influence individuals to do their best on a project if team members perceive that it is in their best interest, and that the benefits outweigh the risks. The project leader must use information to show people the potential rewards, as well as the way risks are being addressed.

Developing influence is a process, not an event. In everyday terms, this means that the project leader can never really order team members to complete a task, but must persuade them, over and over again. The approach is for the project leader to ask him- or herself 'What is the benefit in doing this task?' and then approach the team members by first stressing the benefit. The project leader should then listen carefully to their responses, as their perceived risks are often contained in these responses. If the project leader can give information that shows how he or she is addressing those perceived risks, while continuing to show benefit, then the project leader will be leading by influence.

Such influence is normally much more effective than authority. However, it takes more time. The project leader will often feel the urge to just say 'Do it' in order to get things done. This may often be seen as a short-run necessity, but it leads to a long-run disaster. Use it sparingly.

## REFERENCES AND FURTHER READING

Pinto, J. K. (1996), *Power & Politics in Project Management*, Project Management institute, Sylva, NC.

Pinto, J. K. and Slevin, D. P. (1987), 'Critical success factors in effective project implementation', in D. I. Cleland and W. R. King (eds), *Project Management Handbook*, 2nd edition, Van Nostrand Reinhold, New York.

Wateridge, J. F. (1995), 'IT projects: a basis for success', *International Journal of Project Management*, **13**(3).

## RELATED TOPICS

# 44 Managing culture

## *David Rees*

You are looking forward to a new project challenge as you wave goodbye to Johnny and the kids at London Heathrow. You've done well these past few years, moving through the hierarchy of a large UK multinational telecommunications corporation to your present job of International Project Manager. Certainly your career path has taken a number of twists and turns since those days 15 years ago when you started out as a young graduate electronics engineer in what was then a public sector monopoly. How things have changed during that time. Moving through the ranks of technical specialist to supervisor, middle manager and now, since privatization, to the world of project management – and a senior one at that! And still only 37 years old, one of a handful of women in a work environment dominated by men. The organization itself has been through dramatic transformation:

- From non-profit-making public ownership to a commercial enterprise driven by a doctrine of maximizing shareholder value.
- From over 300,000 employees to just half that number now.
- From a mechanistic bureaucracy to a fleet-footed matrix structure.

You're rewarded on achievement – not just for turning up to work each day. On top of this, the business now operates across national boundaries. Global customers have to be served (and delighted), strategic alliances managed and international joint ventures pursued. Yes, Bangkok beckons. But this is a journey that has put a number of questions in your mind – the answers to which cannot exclusively be found in your company training room. You've been briefed by experts, both technical and behavioural, but you know that Project Poppit will be different from anything you've experienced before. Well, that's the nature of projects!

Reflecting upon this situation we can identify a number of elements that will be important determinants of project success. The focus of our interest for this chapter is the cultural factors. It may be useful at this point to consider what we mean by 'culture'.

## DEFINITIONS OF CULTURE

A starting point is to go back to the original meaning of the word *kultura* as the ancient Greeks interpreted it meaning 'to act upon nature'. Or the Latin form *cultura* – 'cultivating or tilling (the land)'. The general concept here is one of status and growth and can be applied in both a physical sense (agriculture) and a development mode (enlightenment, refinement).

Some interesting definitions of culture have been offered by two key researchers in this field:

> Culture is the collective programming of the mind, which distinguishes the member of one group or society from those of another.
>
> (Hofstede 1994)

> A fish only discovers its need for water when it is no longer in it. Our own culture is like water to a fish. It sustains us. We live and breathe through it.
>
> (Trompenaars 1993)

Further, there are varying contexts in which the term and its derivatives are used. We talk of personal tastes, manners and social etiquette as being 'culture-related'. Groups whose focus is on intellectual and artistic activities are often classified as 'cults'. Organizations and their subsets may take on identifiable 'corporate cultures'. A project management culture is an example of such a subset.

As Paula sets off for Thailand we can think of a range of culture-bound factors that may affect her success as a project manager:

- Her own status in terms of technical qualifications, age and gender.
- The organizational climate and management style under which she will operate.
- The whole concept of project management as a business philosophy.
- The local and cross-border environments in which she works.

Additionally, in her role she will have to manage a number of cultural issues related to the project stakeholders:

1. Does the customer understand the approach to service delivery?
2. Do project team members view time management in the same way?
3. Is project planning seen as a valuable tool for effective performance?

## CULTURE IN BUSINESS

Why should we be interested in business culture? To understand 'business culture' we need to consider three segments of what Garrison (1998) has referred to as the 'cultural iceberg'. A brief background to this conceptualization will make the 'iceberg' model (Figure 44.1) meaningful. Since 'culture' has been earmarked as a discipline of study in its own right we have seen many branches of the social sciences stake their claim for leading the theoretical development of the subject.

1. Anthropologists have been interested in the physiological development of the human species and the associated rituals, myths and beliefs that parallel these growth stages.
2. Sociologists tend to focus on the study of man as a social creature in their attempts to explain how communities and societies evolve.

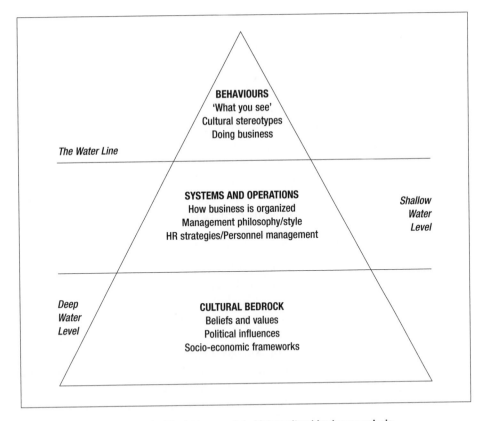

**Figure 44.1   The iceberg model of inter-cultural business analysis**
*Source*: Adapted from Garrison (1998)

795

3. Psychologists concentrate on mental processes and behaviours within the individual and their impact on others.
4. Political scientists examine power, authority and control structures within geographic, territorial and societal boundaries.
5. Economists attempt to understand the systems of exchange that enable resources to be developed and utilized in a range of human groupings.

Two conclusions can be drawn from the studies that emerge from these differing disciplines. First, these approaches help us to understand human behaviour and, in particular, management behaviour. Second, the understanding of culture gained from these disciplines can impact upon the performance of business organizations – including the management of projects. The implications of such conclusions are profound. Business success becomes a function of the degree to which we understand the effects of human behaviour and are able to act on such knowledge. This is the reason why organizations are keen to improve their management of business culture – they see this as an opportunity to gain competitive advantage.

Until quite recently an interlocking model bringing together these disciplines to help us understand business culture had been missing. The 'cultural iceberg' helps to rectify this and, in turn, provides an opportunity to manage our business methodologies such as project management, more effectively (Figure 44.1). If we imagine the iceberg at sea we can only physically see about 10 per cent of its mass. We are not immediately aware of what supports and shapes it beneath the waves. The 'iceberg' tip is a straightforward way of depicting the 'touchables' of a society. What we do not see are the 'untouchable' (or hidden) elements. Yet these elements are the very building blocks upon which our societies and organizations are based. They provide the superstructure and cultural 'fabric' from which behaviours will surface. The base of the iceberg represents the cultural 'bedrock' upon which the superstructure is constructed.

Trompenaars and Hampden-Turner (1997) likened culture to layers of an onion, each layer revealing another layer until the core is reached. The core represents *implicit culture* which are the basic assumptions on which a society is built. The middle layers suggest the underlying norms and values that have grown out of the core whilst the outer layers depict visible manifestations or *explicit culture* (Figure 44.2). Other writers have used the analogy of the lily being drawn from its structure beneath the surface of the pond – we see the flower but we don't see the substantive mass which gives it life. Similarly we can think of a tree with its roots in the ground as the 'bedrock', the trunk and branches as the 'superstructure' and the leaves, buds or flowers as the tangible outcomes of its existence.

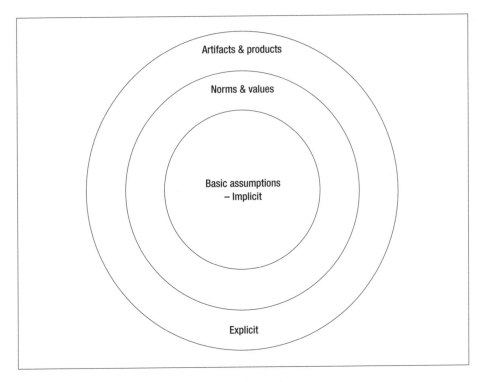

**Figure 44.2  The cultural onion**
*Source*: Trompenaars and Hampden-Turner (1997)

Let us take another look at the iceberg model to help us acquire a better understanding of how business culture develops.

At its base we have the cultural bedrock, foundations of the culture that are reflected in the evolution of the political and economic systems that pertain to that cultural environment. Garrison calls these *policonomy* factors. The way in which these systems themselves have evolved are sometimes extremely hard to trace. Often the very source of the bedrock has disappeared. Liken this to the discovery of the source of the River Nile – very difficult to find! To penetrate the policonomy of a particular societal culture we may need to go back a long way in history to discover the storyline. Some of it gets lost in the mists of time. Sometimes we arrive at a stage of investigation where seeking further evidence or proof becomes pointless – we are trapped in time. What becomes more important and relevant is how we can then work forward to the present day culture that we wish to understand better. Historical policonomy gives us some great clues. Social frameworks are created reflecting the key value and belief sets born out of the bedrock. These form the superstructure features from which our management and work systems emerge. So, for example, if we have a society which is based upon unquestioning obedience to rulers endowed with 'divine rights', we can expect rigid structures of management control and a management culture which will not tolerate dissent.

At the top of the iceberg we are at the behavioural 'output' level. This is our experiential level where we physically and mentally interact with cultural artefacts. We touch, taste, feel, smell and see culture. Our intuitive sense – the 'sixth' sense – could be likened to raising the state of 'cultural subconsciousness' to a level of consciousness – emotions, attitudes and beliefs that are there but can't always be rationalized. We move from the systems level of culture to the individual level – the personal experience. And this is where managers really feel the impact of culture on their day-to-day activities.

Managers are, of course, in a unique pivotal position. They themselves are products of the cultural bedrock and the resulting organizational systems. In turn, their task is to manage operations within the prevailing cultural norms of the enterprise. In other words they have a responsibility to administer the activities of the company according to prescribed sets of rules, regulations, processes, procedures and systems. But they also have an opportunity to influence and implement change depending on a variety of factors including their ability to challenge the prevailing corporate culture. This brings us to the heart of our topic – the management of cultures and the particular challenges for project managers. As a summary so far we can see that this methodology of analysing cultures can be applied to varying levels and situations – societal, industry, corporate, cross-cultural and so forth.

## IMPACT OF CULTURE ON PERFORMANCE

Is there any evidence that the management of culture in business can improve organizational performance? The answer is an unqualified 'yes'. Writers and management theorists have been hinting for decades at correlations between organizational culture and performance. Precise measurement of the impact of culture on company and project success will always be difficult. Most of us sense that there must be a strong link but it is difficult to establish the culture/performance tie-up. However, recent research efforts have started to produce more tangible data that builds an increasingly coherent picture of cultural impact on business.

Of outstanding note has been a study published by the Institute of Personnel and Development (1998). Researchers from Sheffield University and the London School of Economics were keen to determine whether organizational culture significantly predicts variation between companies in their performance and, if so, which aspects of culture appear most important. They interpreted organizational culture as 'the aggregate of employees' perceptions of aspects of the organisation' and developed an Organizational Culture Indicator which identified the cultural dimensions most frequently evaluated in organizations. The results of their investigations enabled them to explain that 29 per cent of the variation in productivity of the companies studied could be attributed to human relations dimensions, confirming their hypothesis in terms of the importance of culture in relation to company performance.

Now let us see how cultural factors impact on project performance.

## MANAGING CULTURE IN PROJECTS

Some writers are keen to emphasize that project management is a relatively new, American-initiated approach to achieving business success. It is true that many specific techniques used in managing projects today have been borne out of recent western management experience. These are, of course, discussed in detail elsewhere in this publication.

However, it is well to remember that the construction of the Egyptian Pyramids, the building of the Great Wall of China and the Roman Invasion of Britain were all fine examples of successful large-scale projects. If these projects were being run today, would performance be any better as a result of using contemporary project management techniques? (Forget technological advancements for the moment.) The answer to this is debatable and reminds us of the historical perspectives alluded to above. We should be careful in assuming that technique alone is responsible for 'better' project management. Once again, 'culture' stakes its claim. Consider those examples again. Would a project kick-off meeting with key stakeholders fit the highly autocratic style of the Pharaoh? Would Gantt charts be helpful in Chinese society where time may not be seen as a simple linear progression? And would PERT (program evaluation and review technique) appeal to Caesar's military leadership?

In fact, we do not have to dwell in the depths of history to identify the impact of culture on projects. Project management itself is a culture-bound concept. Some businesses embrace projects as 'a way of doing things' because it sits comfortably with the values and norms of the organization. This approach 'to getting things done' suits one industry better than another. Or maybe the principles of project management are more readily assimilated in a particular society. This discussion is not intended to question the wisdom of managing through a project approach but rather to remind ourselves again that one of the key challenges for project managers is to manage the cultural environment in which the activities are conducted.

In our quest to manage culture effectively let us remind ourselves of the nature of projects. Handy (1985) would describe project-oriented businesses (such as matrix organizations) as forms of a task culture. Projects are originated to achieve specific goals and tend to be objectives-driven. The culture brings together appropriate resources and enables the project manager and the team to deliver as best they know how. The key deliverables are usually measured against specific objectives pertaining to time, cost and quality – the classic project management performance triangle. Handy argues that influence is based more on expert power than on position or personal power. The view on expert power needs to be reconsidered. Plenty of large projects have been managed by non-experts. An example of this is the development of British Airways' Waterside Headquarters at London's Heathrow Airport where human resource specialists were involved as project managers.

Task cultures also breed team cultures which work powerfully to overcome divergent and disparate individual preferences. These draw upon group dynamics to get things done. Consequently, this culture can take on highly adaptable and flexible characteristics. Project teams can be formed at short notice, terminated rapidly and reformed. Individuals can be dedicated members of one team or hold membership of several project groups, each project having potentially different objectives, scale and technical content. Further, team members may play different roles in different project teams. An outstanding example of this form of total project culture is Oticon, the Danish hearing aid company that underwent a radical business transformation during the early 1990s (Morsing 1998). After the enterprise experienced severe difficulties in the 1980s which threatened its very survival, Oticon's new President, Lars Kolind, unveiled a vision, a strategy and a plan to provide the company with strong long-term competitive advantage. His whole approach was driven by establishing a project management culture. The strategic change required was formulated as a business transformation programme consisting of a number of interrelated projects all held together by a unifying vision. The vision was to transform the company from a technology-based culture to a market-focused culture and to change ways of working to achieve the desired goals.

The strategy to manage the cultural change required was to use project management approaches. The whole change programme became known as 'Project 330' with the overall aim of becoming 30 per cent more efficient within three years. Perhaps the most innovative change at Oticon involved a new organizational form and structure. Out went the old hierarchical management system where people were organized into specific functions and in came a new 'spaghetti' way of organizing. The 'spaghetti organization' embraced novel methods of working including multi-tasking, multidisciplinary project teams and self-management. Figure 44.3 captures some of these essential features. In this teamworking model individuals may play a 'normal' role according to their profession and training, but also switch into other roles in different teams. This represents a highly fluid and flexible work environment which can deliver competitive advantage.

Oticon has become a classic case study in how to manage culture. Imagine for a moment how dramatic the effect of transformation was for employees and managers working in the old culture. Suddenly, a revolution in the workplace was taking place. Kolind became the 'project manager as change agent' – big-time! First he created an overarching vision of what the organization needed to achieve and how this could be done. Next he set about project planning – creating objectives, identifying resources and developing a team. Then came implementation – ensuring that the old culture was honoured, bridges burned and the new culture welcomed in.

One lesson to be learned from this experience is how important symbolism can be. Kolind recognized this and ensured that the new culture was consolidated – closing elevators to encourage the use of stairs; refreshment points with flip charts; glass tubes through the building taking away waste paper. These examples remind us not only that culture has to be managed within projects but also that projects themselves often influence cultural change in organizations.

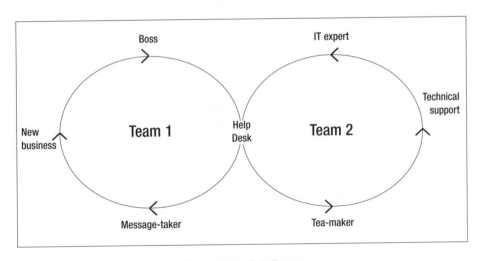

**Figure 44.3  Role fluency**
© Cultural Fluency Training and Development Ltd 1999

# MANAGING CULTURAL INTEGRATION

## STRATEGIC LEVEL

Events such as mergers, takeovers and acquisitions have become the subject of much attention from business analysts, corporate financiers and company lawyers in their search for competitive advantage. This has placed the 'hard' elements of the enterprise as the priority considerations when doing deals of this type. Far less attention has been paid to the cultural aspects of the deal. Similarly, organizations have experienced serious problems when forming new business entities such as joint ventures, strategic alliances and partnerships. The business strategy seems logical, the numbers work out and the technological advantages are clear. But when it comes to achieving the right 'cultural fit' a disappointing picture emerges (Figure 44.4). A quick tour of some recent research bears this out.

In their book *Smart Alliances*, Harbison and Pekar (1998) have identified cultural differences as one of the key implementation issues that needs to be carefully evaluated and managed during alliance formation. Successful alliance builders, they say, have knowledge of a potential partner's management culture prior to a deal. There is a growing list of alliances where performance has ranged from total failure to non-fulfilment of potential as a result of not achieving effective cultural integration between the alliance members.

Clearly there is a need to conduct due diligence in such situations across a broader range of factors – including cultural factors. So, as a first step to managing the cultural issues of organizational integration, 'cultural due diligence' is a process worth considering. For large deals, business transformation programmes and alliance formation, cultural due diligence should be thought of as a prerequisite before decision-making.

| Date | Institution/report | Finding |
|------|-------------------|---------|
| 1987 | London Business School | Highlighted lack of personnel and management audit, pre-acquisition, as a key weakness |
|      | People in Business survey | Deals too focused on financial issues |
|      |                    | M&A led by corporate financiers; other professions are needed in M&A teams |
| 1995 | Imperial College | Euro cross-border deals found that differences in management style bore a strong correlation to chance of failure |
| 1996 | Economist Intelligence Unit | Confirmation of above |

Figure 44.4   International mergers, acquisitions and alliances: the failure factor

Cultural due diligence is a new concept and there are various approaches to conducting the activity involving the measurement of the elements of corporate culture. Many instruments are available to conduct such assessments. Various behavioural aspects can be probed creating profiles of individuals, teams and organizations. Essentially this becomes an audit process where data are collected and analysed, 'culture gaps' identified and a 'culture profile' is drawn up. Figure 44.5 shows such an audit process. Garrison's (1998) Triangle Test is a highly useful audit and diagnostic tool that can be used in a variety of strategic situations: alliance/partnership/joint venture formation; mergers and acquisitions; strategic projects. The test investigates the three cultural segments of the iceberg – behaviours, work systems and bedrock – and can reveal useful profiles of, for example, potential international partners prior to a deal. The scores that can be obtained are depicted in Figure 44.6. The questions contained in the test have inevitably to do with the extent to which business cultures follow a range of patterns from:

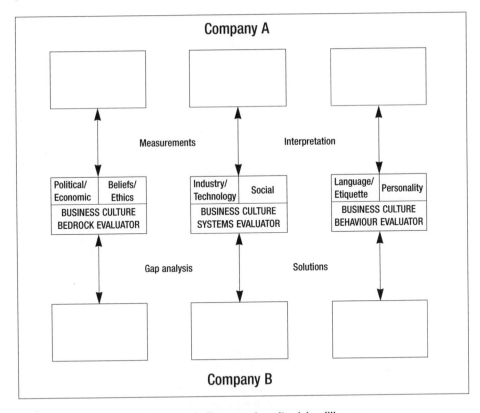

**Figure 44.5   Audit process for cultural due diligence**
© Cultural Fluency Training and Development Ltd 1999

- individualistic to corporatist bedrock;
- materialistic to communitarian work systems;
- open to closed behaviours.

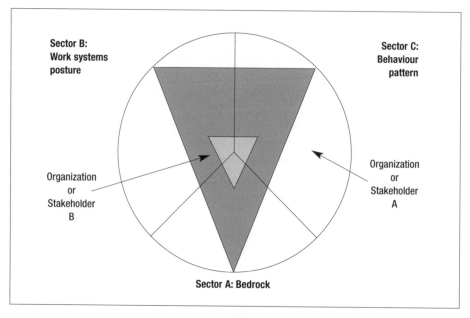

**Figure 44.6   The cultural triangle test**
*Source*: Garrison (1998)

Results can alert senior executives to potential difficulties arising from national cultural differences. They can indicate whether the project will be significantly impaired by cultural differences and in extreme cases they can significantly influence whether the deal should be done at all. In all cases the test can provide useful information about cultural gaps, how wide they are and what action may be required for a smooth integration plan. Integration planning can be seen as bringing two cultures together as the example of global alliances in Figure 44.7 demonstrates.

## PROJECT LEVEL

It can be seen that cultural audit and measurement can be applied to stakeholder management with projects. A list of stakeholders is compiled and a weighting can be applied based on the project manager's expertise and knowledge or other suitable criteria. Then the results of the measurement process can be tabled and a map constructed. This provides the project manager with valuable information

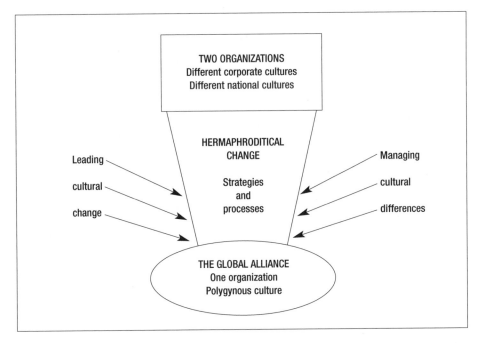

**Figure 44.7  Global alliances: managing cultural integration**
© Cultural Fluency Training and Development Ltd 1999

which can help him or her manage the cultural aspects of each stakeholder (Figure 44.8). Trompenaars and Hampden-Turner (1997) use the concept of culture mapping to illustrate dilemmas between cultural dimensions at an international level but the 'mapping' idea can be used to plot positions on a range of cultural issues in a mono-domestic environment, such as projects. Another example of culture mapping was provided by John Mole (1995) with the Mole Map, plotting cultural attitudes towards leadership and organization. His map produces a configuration of organic/systematic organizational structures and group/individual leadership styles.

## MANAGING INTERNATIONAL CULTURES

It is appropriate at this point to explore the particular challenges of the international project environment. A favoured approach by many researchers in the field of cross-cultural understanding is to establish 'cultural dimensions' (as mentioned earlier) to contrast different attitudes, values and behaviours. Although most writers would suggest a heavy note of caution against cultural

| Stakeholder | Type of relationship (strategic/ tactical) | Scale of importance (1–10) | Countries/ cultures | Cultural dimension A (e.g. cooperation) | Cultural dimension B (e.g. risk aversion) | Etc. |
|---|---|---|---|---|---|---|
| Customers | | | | | | |
| Shareholders | | | | | | |
| Trade unions | | | | | | |
| Community | | | | | | |
| Political authorities | | | | | | |
| Financial institutions | | | | | | |
| Suppliers | | | | | | |
| Partners/joint ventures | | | | | | |
| Parent/ subsidiary | | | | | | |
| Associate | | | | | | |

**Figure 44.8   Stakeholder mapping for projects**
© Cultural Fluency Training and Development Ltd 1999

stereotyping, the dimensions approach to cultural analysis does offer a pragmatic way of unpicking the cultural onion. Hofstede (1994) and Trompenaars (1993) have produced credible research and provided us with a reliable grouping of dimensions. These are indicated in Figure 44.9.

Using the cultural dimensions developed through Hofstede's famous research on national cultures, Turner (1999) has consolidated fieldwork undertaken by Jessen and arrived at a 'fitness for project management' country ranking table. The scores captured attitudes throughout the project life cycle towards initiation, planning, execution and termination. The country ranking is given in Figure 44.10. The results confirm that project management sits most comfortably as a management philosophy in western cultures. This type of information prior to project start-up can be helpful in managing behaviours across national cultures.

For example, at an operational level conflict will have to be managed at various

| Dimension | Refers to |
|---|---|
| Power distance | Autocracy v. democracy, distribution of influence |
| Individualism v. collectivism | Focus on individual or group |
| Universalist v. particularist | Principles of right and wrong; personal relationships |
| Specific v. diffuse | Legal processes and personal trust |
| Neutral v. emotional | Objective interactions v. emotional expressions |
| Uncertainty avoidance | Attitude to risk, uncertainty, ambiguity |
| Short term v. long term | Perspective on investment returns and results |
| Achievement v. ascription | Status, performance |
| Attitudes to time | Emphasis on past, present or future |
| Internal v. external | Motivation for self or outside world |

**Figure 44.9    The Hofstede and Trompenaars cultural dimensions**
*Source*: Hofstede (1994) and Trompenaars (1993)

| | | | |
|---|---|---|---|
| 1 | Germany | 10 | Sweden |
| 2 | Italy | 11 | Denmark |
| 3 | France | 12 | Japan |
| 4 | USA | 13 | Thailand |
| 5 | Netherlands | 14 | West Africa |
| 6 | Norway | 15 | Philippines |
| 7 | Great Britain | 16 | Yugoslavia |
| 8 | Arab countries | 17 | Malaysia |
| 9 | East Africa | | |

**Figure 44.10    Country ranking for project management**
*Source*: Turner (1999)

points during the project. Thomas, Killman and Swierczek (Swierczek 1994) have developed models of conflict-handling styles which can provide insights into differing national styles. Various studies have shown significant contrasts in conflict management on projects, particularly between managers from western cultures and those from the east. In one such study Law (1998) has overlaid the Hofstede dimensions against the Thomas/Killman/Swierczek model enabling us to see once again how culture impacts on key project behaviours such as conflict handling (Figure 44.11).

## MULTICULTURAL PROJECT MANAGEMENT

It has become apparent that project managers will need to manage projects differently according to the degree of multiculturism within the project. The key issue here is the manager's choice of performance measures for the project. The

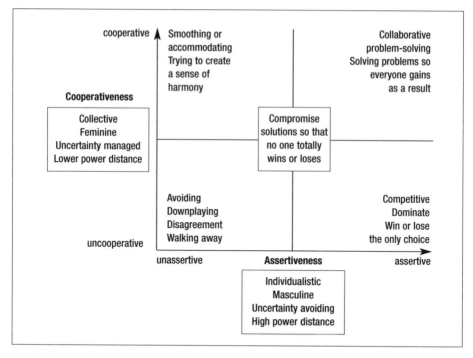

**Figure 44.11   Conflict handling on international projects**
*Source*: Law (1998)

classic measurements of time, cost and quality will, of course, prevail. But the project manager also needs to consider behavioural factors which will impact on the hard 'output' measures.

From her study on a Malaysian project, Law (1998) drew up a framework for managing multicultural projects based upon the relationship between the degree of multiculturalism and project complexity. She suggests that the project management focus must shift its emphasis according to the level of multiculturalism among team members and stakeholders, and needs to take into account the complexity of the project (Figure 44.12). Multiculturalism means the numbers and types of different nationalities. Complexity refers to size, technical factors and scope. According to these variables the project management focus will change.

## PARADIGM SHIFT

Increasingly, corporations that are striving to exploit the opportunities of world markets are reconfiguring their structures and changing the mental mindset of

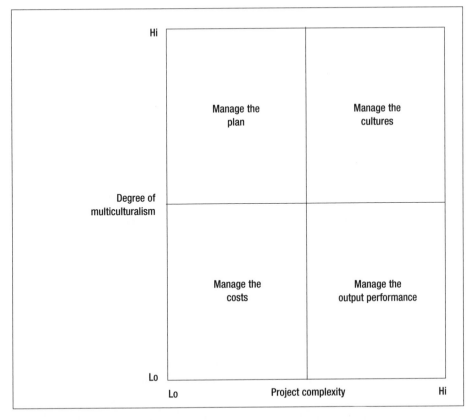

**Figure 44.12  Managing multicultural projects**
*Source*: Adapted from Law (1998)

the enterprise to help them deliver benefits of cultural diversity. Bartlett and Ghoshal (1989) proposed the Transnational Organizational Model as one which international corporations will aspire to achieve. Their conclusions suggest that global efficiencies have to be accompanied by local responsiveness and organizations should see diverse resources and diverse capabilities as strengths rather than obstacles to achieving success. Mechanisms for sharing information and sharing learning have to be put in place so that the potential advantages of diversity are realized.

For domestic-focused businesses the attainment of such an organizational model requires a paradigm shift, which for many will be revolutionary. Some profoundly held attitudes and behaviours will need to change. The belief cycle example in Figure 44.13 suggests commonly held beliefs in many UK organizations that will be under severe pressure to change. These types of beliefs may be built on hundreds – even thousands – of years of 'doing things a certain

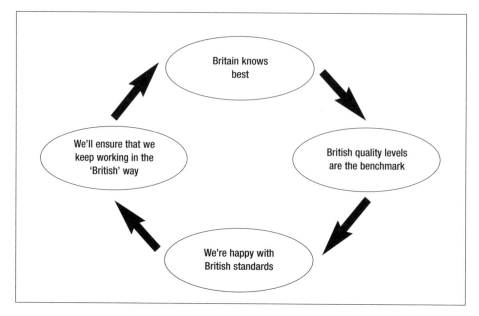

**Figure 44.13    Mono-cultural belief cycle**
© Cultural Fluency Training and Development Ltd

way'. For neutral observers the resultant behaviours may be described as potentially arrogant, possibly based upon technical superiority which disappeared a long time ago. One of the tasks for senior executives driving their businesses towards the idea of 'transnationalism' is to break into these cycles to leverage the advantages of cultural diversity. As a first step, an understanding of the links between beliefs, values, attitudes and behaviours is needed. If we align the beliefs with the bedrock elements of culture we can then see how emergent value and attitude sets will influence the development of work and management systems. Finally, the behaviours that physically and mentally touch us break the surface. Figure 44.14 models the links between beliefs, values, attitudes and behaviours as a cross-cultural comparison.

Some organizations have woken up to advantages of transnationalism but the majority have not yet climbed onto the starting blocks. Organization development efforts are increasingly likely to be ever more aligned with the need to manage transcultural change – change across national cultures. This represents a huge challenge for which most corporations are ill-prepared. Evidence from the field suggests this will be a long process, probably far longer than standard change management programmes in mono/domestic cultural environments. In fact, players in many industries worldwide have little choice but to climb aboard. The smart companies are starting to make that journey now.

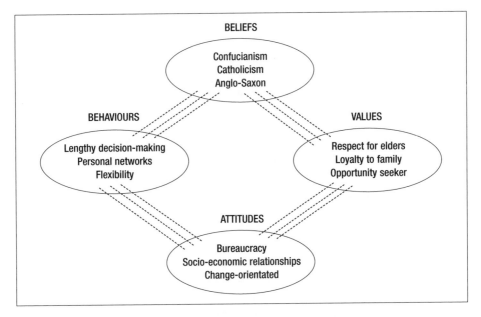

**Figure 44.14  Cross-cultural behaviour/belief cycle**
© Cultural Fluency Training and Development Ltd

What are some of the outcomes of such developments? There are several:

1. The national identity of the corporation may become quite diluted, heavily and deliberately so in some instances as organizations see marketing benefits from these developments. Telecommunications, power-generation and airlines are good examples of industries where this has started to happen.
2. Human resource strategies will need to be rethought. What type of people will organizations operating in transnational marketplaces be looking for? What key skills and competencies will be sought? Where should companies pitch their recruitment initiatives? And, of course, how should projects be resourced and managed?
3. Product innovation can be significantly improved through cultural 'recontextualization', enabling more effective differentiation to be achieved.
4. Challenging the way things are done in a particular culture can lead to process improvement, creativity and innovation in project working.

## CULTURAL FLUENCY

One of the key features to emerge from these developments is the concept of the culturally fluent organization. The ability of companies to achieve transcultural success is increasingly dependent upon a genuine understanding of how people do business around the world. This capability is known as cultural fluency and is achieved through:

- gaining an awareness of cultural norms;
- acquiring specific knowledge of cultural environments;
- developing relevant skills for transcultural working.

Cultural fluency may be defined as:

> The repertoire of cross-cultural awareness, knowledge and skills needed by people to perform effectively across international territories.

## CULTURAL TRAINING AND DEVELOPMENT

Clearly, this implies that specific training and development programmes need to be initiated to help people achieve appropriate levels of competency. The aggregate of these skills and competencies across the organization, the transformation of structures, processes and procedures, and the change of mindset from mono-culturalism to multiculturalism identifies the culturally fluent organization. Traditionally, businesses have seen the performance of their people in foreign markets linked to their ability to communicate in different languages. Languages are important, but language fluency is no longer the sole criteria for success in these environments. Global marketplaces have intensified, each diverse customer base having its own language. This drives the need for a lingua franca such as English. People are moving between cultures with greater frequency as they work on global assignments. It is unrealistic to expect language fluency in a short time. As global environments change so too must training and development responses. Solutions should be built on a clear identification of needs. When these are fully understood, appropriate programmes can be targeted for the right audience. Language fluency is one potential training solution but now a range of cost-effective approaches and programmes are available to organizations. Figure 44.15 shows the process for the formulation of appropriate training and development responses.

1. *Strategic cultural fluency* These roles involve strategic relationships across cultures – international business development, alliances and partnerships. Effective management of these relationships calls for special awareness of cultural behaviour at a senior level.
2. *Workgroup cultural fluency* Leading multicultural teams and international projects requires a repertoire of skills and techniques. The life span of global teams may be short, demanding excellence in team formation, development and close-out. Project managers need to acquire dexterity in managing multicultural stakeholders.

812

3. *Personal cultural fluency* Individual performance in handling working relationships and social etiquette can be enhanced through the acquisition of specific skills and knowledge. Interpersonal behaviour can be improved through foreign language learning, international English training and non-verbal communication skills.

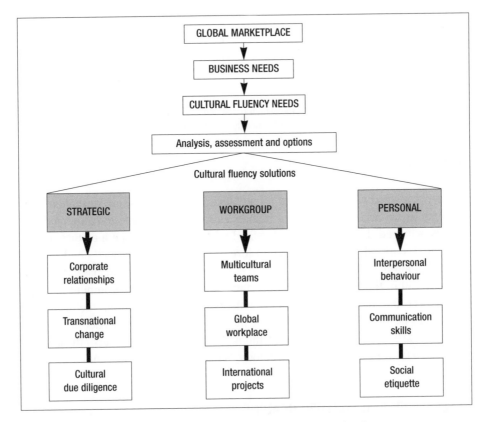

**Figure 44.15  Cultural training and development planning**
© Cultural Fluency Training and Development Ltd

For large projects, training programmes may be required to help manage cultural diversity between stakeholders. The model in Figure 44.16 can be applied to any cultural situation.

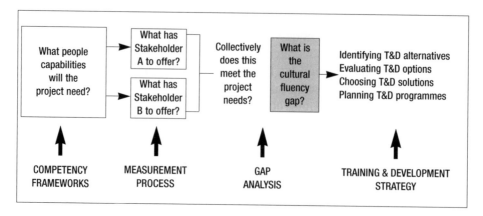

**Figure 44.16  Transcultural projects – training and development strategy formulation**
© Cultural Fluency Training and Development Ltd

## SOME CONCLUSIONS

Culture is a word which produces a complexity of meanings, interpretations and concepts. If we accept that culture influences how projects are implemented and what is achieved then we must understand what elements shape a culture and its associated cultural behaviours. Therefore, project mangers will need to pay increasing attention to managing culture effectively. This means managing cultural diversity within the project itself, understanding the cultural environment in which the project operates and striking a balance between cultural, technical and operational factors. Particularly when the international and cross-border dimensions of projects are considered, the management of culture is perhaps one of the greatest challenges facing project managers in today's global business environment.

## REFERENCES AND FURTHER READING

Bartlett, C. and Ghoshal, S. (1989), *Managing Across Borders: The Transnational Solution*, HBR Press, Boston, MA.

Garrison, T. (1998), *International Culture*, 2nd edition, Elm Publications, Huntingdon.

Handy, C. (1985), *Understanding Organisations*, 3rd edition, Penguin, London.

Harbison, J. and Pekar, P. (1998), *Smart Alliances*, Jossey-Bass, San Francisco.

Hofstede, G. (1994), *Cultures and Organisations*, Harper Collins, London.

IPD (1998), *Issues in People Management No 22*, Institute of Personnel and Development, London.

Law, J. (1998), 'An investigation of national cultural factors impacting the management of an international project in South East Asia', unpublished MBA dissertation, Henley Management College.

Mole, J. (1995), *Mind Your Manners*, Nicholas Brealey, London.

Morsing, M. (ed.) (1998), *Managing the Unmanageable for a Decade*, Oticon, Copenhagen.

Swierczek, F. W. (1994), 'Culture and conflict in joint ventures in Asia', *International Journal of Project Management*, **12**(1).

Trompenaars, F. (1993), *Riding the Waves of Culture*, Economist Books, London.

Trompenaars, F. and Hampden-Turner, C. (1997), *Riding the Waves of Culture*, 2nd Edition, Nicholas Brealey, London.

Turner, J. R. (1999), *The Handbook of Project-based Management*, 2nd edition, McGraw-Hill, London.

# 45 Managing ethics

## Alistair Godbold

Interest in business ethics has grown in reaction to the well-publicized scandals of the 1990s, including the fraud-related collapse of former 'blue chip' companies such as Polly Peck, Ferranti and Maxwell Communications, the dirty tricks campaign by British Airways against Virgin Atlantic, and the allegations of insider dealing in Blue Arrow by County NatWest. In America Sears Roebuck & Co. came under fire for its dubious car repair services. The list continues with companies such as General Dynamics, Daniels-Midland Co., NYNEX Columbia/HCA Healthcare Corp., Guinness and BCCI. All of these companies lost money as a result of their unethical actions and in some cases went out of business altogether. The above are the infamous and the large scale, there are many more that impact on a local scale or have yet to come to public notoriety. On the other hand, it is important when considering ethics in business, and more specifically in project management, not to become puritanical, and to remember that you are in business. The aims of the business, or a project, are not somehow rendered more profound or acceptable by attaching to them a spurious social or philosophical dimension. All that achieves is to remove the clarity that ensures that people do what is right in business and projects. Business and projects must be seen and managed in the wider context of all of the stakeholders, not just the narrow pursuit of a commercial aim, cost and timescale.

The ethical content of an organization's actions is only significant when there is a transaction with a stakeholder. Where there is no such transaction, there is no basis to judge the ethical content of an action. Business today is becoming more complex and more interrelated with other social phenomena. It is also international, operating in a world of complex social and economic interdependencies. Pressure groups are becoming more powerful, exercising legitimate power and representing the views of large sections of society. This was the case when Greenpeace mounted a campaign against Shell's plans to sink the Brent Spar oil platform in the North Atlantic. The actions of the company came under public scrutiny through the interests of the pressure groups, the media, the general public and Parliament.

In the opening paragraph I recalled some of the more obvious ethical issues, those that 'the man on the Clapham omnibus' would recognize as being an ethical decision. However, there are many more decisions in our everyday management careers that individually may be considered a matter of style, but when taken together project an image of how we behave, ethically or unethically.

The ethical dilemmas are those everyone can recognize, insider share dealing, accepting or offering bribes, etc. However, today's business and projects are composed of relationships with stakeholders, employees, members of the project team, customers, suppliers, users and people affected by the secondary impact of any change process. These are not one-time relationships; we may have to continue doing business with these people as customers, suppliers or partners in the future. In the short term it can pay to be unethical, you may win the contract by spotting a loophole in the specification, and choose to exploit it, you may improve your cash flow by paying your suppliers late or gain prestige by taking credit for the actions of a subordinate. These are all short-term advantages paid for by loss of long-term gains. The company's, or individual's, reputation in the marketplace precedes it and there are a finite number of players in any market. If we do not have a successful relationship with any of them, it may affect the competitive position of the company and the flexibility that any stakeholder is prepared to accept in this relationship. Business is about people, the relationships that people in business have with each other and the way in which they interact. Projects are a micro-environment of these relationships: project manager to team, project to customer, to user, etc. The management of these relationships is vital to the continuing success of the project or the parties taking part in them.

For the majority of people, working under pressure of deadlines and budgets, these relationship issues need to be actively managed. However, this chance of short-term gain through unethical behaviour is likely to occur frequently. The ability to recognize it, and resist its attractiveness, is that much more difficult. The principles for managing this kind of issue are similar to those needed to manage 'ethical dilemmas'. The application of these principles needs to be considered on a smaller scale than that described here.

## ETHICS AND PROJECT MANAGEMENT

In Chapter 4 a project was shown to be an activity different from the steady state of an organization. Projects may be undertaken by companies with temporary teams to achieve a set task, by groups who will work on one project, then move on to work on the next, or companies that specialize in projects for clients. All of these temporary teams have to work with each other and with other companies whom they may not have dealt with before. To establish a relationship quickly and start to work together it is important that there is a cultural fit between the two companies, that they can do business together.

The traditional view of the role of the manager is, as Milton Friedman (1970) put it, 'to make as much money as possible while conforming to the basic rules of society'. This principle can be applied to project managers as their role is to get the project completed on time and to budget, legally. This narrow definition is dysfunctional as it denies acknowledgement of the role other people play in fulfilling the objective of the project. A project cannot succeed without the help of senior management, the project team, suppliers, users and the customer. The above definition of project management implies a style of 'I win you lose', whereas projects are a non-zero sum game, both parties have to gain. Recognizing this interdependence under the pressure of deadlines and budgets requires a developed skill or judgement of the manager, except under the most obvious circumstances, and the pursuit of the long-term goal.

Projects are agents of change, they upset the status quo, and as such they can expect to meet resistance. Not only do projects create change in the organization as their principal product, they create change by the process in which they go about it. They are unique and as no norms have been established for them, this in itself may create uncertainty within their own structure. Projects use a variety of resources to achieve their objectives and these need to be integrated. They also produce change not only for the end-users of the change (building, computer system, business process, office move, etc.) but also for those people involved in getting to this end state. During these times of change people may feel insecure or threatened by the alteration of the status quo. These people will need to be able to trust the honour and openness of the project in order to contribute to its success. If they feel that the project has some hidden threatening agenda, this will add one more reason to resist the change brought about by the project. This is not to say that the outcome of the project must be of benefit to all, but that they must be clear and sensitively handled. If the outcome of the project is to reduce staff numbers, then this must be clearly articulated and people kept informed at every stage of the process. In order to reduce the risk to a project, it must be seen as ethical and trustworthy. For the project manager, discrete moral leadership rather than a public relations exercise is the key to reaping the benefits of ethics for temporary projects, individual project managers and the organizations for the long term.

This constant change and instability is one of the factors that differentiate the management of projects from the management of operations. Projects do not have a stable background against which to build up norms of behaviour and procedures. Instead, these norms and procedures have to be built up in a very short time in a very dynamic environment. A side effect of this is that there is no time to adapt and evolve these procedures as by the time they have been tried the environment has moved on. As a consequence project managers have a high degree of control over the health, welfare and well-being of all their stakeholders including team members. Another problem for project managers is that the members of their teams, customers and users will have their own different sense of morality, coming as they do from different backgrounds. This means project managers must clarify the values of the whole group to prevent any adverse clash of values in their relationships.

One of the duties of a project manager is to balance competing objectives of quality, cost, time and scope. Each of the project stakeholders – co-contractors, the project director, team members, the functional organization, subcontractors, users and society – has expectations of how these objectives will be balanced in accordance with its own perspectives. The relative weights applied to each of these stakeholders and the choices between the generic project goals will vary depending on the type and stage of the project (Mantel and Kloppenborg 1990). In most projects, cost is the most important goal once the specifications are set, and time becomes the most important as the project nears completion. It is this myopic concern with one or two variables that may put the project manager under ethical pressure to disregard the holistic needs of the other stakeholders. In this situation the project manager may manipulate the figures and compromise certain aspects of the project in order to satisfy this small number of variables. The figures may be manipulated or have a different spin put on them to make the project manager look good in this period, in the hope that everything will be all right in the next. Many managers see this practice as not too unethical due to the intense pressure they are under to perform (Bruns and Merchant 1990).

Project managers are leaders, they have views and beliefs shaped by their background, education and experiences. They, as managers, must pervade all operations throughout the project. They therefore have a key responsibility to manage the values of the project to ensure that they are effective in every action and that the agendas of the many stakeholder groups are balanced and 'ethical'. The project manager must manage the project with a set of values congruent with those of society and the stakeholders, and it is his or her responsibility to ensure that a common set of values are communicated throughout the life of the project. This is not only the responsibility of the project manager; project team members have a duty to themselves to ensure that their own work matches these values. Unless the project manager is aware of all of these relationships and responsibilities he or she will not be providing the optimum base for the project.

There are many aspects of the project manager's role that influence how ethically the manager performs the job, and how responsible he or she feels for the actions of the team. A major problem is the amount of information generated about progress, finance, decisions, views of stakeholders, etc. If this information is all passed to the project manager then he or she will suffer from 'information overload' and a large amount of the information passed to the project manager may be lost, degrading the manager's performance. Therefore it is important that the project manager receives only relevant information. However, this relies on a hierarchy of team leaders and work package managers deciding what is relevant and filtering the information. This filtering can introduce a bias of successive levels of management removing information that shows them in a bad light or is in their opinion not relevant, leading to 'negative information blockage'. This bias, or blockage, may not allow the project manager to manage because he or she does not have all the relevant information. Perhaps more importantly, the blockage will allow the middle levels of management to cover up bad or unethical practice. This might occur because they are trying to make themselves look good, but a more common problem is the emotional attachment they feel to a project. As people work on a project they become more committed to it and begin to feel any obstacle can be overcome and this may prevent them from recognizing real problems. It is the leader's role to ensure that channels of communication are open to allow all team members access to the project manager to report any issues that give them cause for concern, so that the manager does not have to rely totally on the information filtering through the hierarchy.

The most serious problem in terms of the pressure put upon the project manager lies perhaps in the role's most basic function: the interface between management and the professional discipline. Normally a project manager is expected to have a high level of skill in the field in which the project is conducted; in most engineering projects this will involve the project manager being an engineer. An engineer deals with the facts of the profession, designs, calculations and the more abstract notion of engineering judgement. The engineer's role is to assemble data and perform calculations to determine the course of action. A manager coordinates resources and takes decisions based on the recommendations of the team. However, the project manager is at the interface of these two roles; he or she must not only take decisions, but take them based on 'professional judgement'. In normal circumstances the distinction between the two roles can be maintained. However, when under pressure this distinction, with its associated moral and ethical consequences, can break down.

In this section it has been shown what pressures and complications are brought together in the role of project manager. The project manager has a great responsibility to the team, the public, the company and all other stakeholder groups. As a result of this the scope and nature of the job make it a very demanding but rewarding role.

## ETHICS AS A DIFFERENTIATOR

Much has been written in the press, the media and in everyday business dealings about the detrimental effect of ethics on business. However, ethics can be used as a positive differentiator. By differentiating itself from the competition, a company may be able to gain advantage. Ethics and competition are not mutually exclusive; competition is an essential part of business. Once equality in cost of production is achieved in a market, or cost of execution of a project, then the only way to stay in business is to become more efficient or differentiate. Many companies are already competing on these grounds, for example ethical investment funds, producers of green products and firms that trade on their ethical image.

In any business or project a company can possess three competitive weapons (Garvind 1992): productivity, quality and new products. Ethics can be added as a fourth weapon. To realize this edge, leadership, innovation and communication are needed. All of these are qualities of the good manager, and essential qualities of the project manager. In managing the ethics of a group, there are many parallels between ethics and quality. Both embody the long-term perspective, are customer-led, and involve doing things right and doing the right things. Where organizations have adopted and internalized a strong ethical culture that they can sustain, they are able to exploit this as a competitive advantage. The organization's reputation with its customers, employees and even suppliers of some high value added products can build strong relationships and lasting confidence. This can act as a barrier to entry to new firms entering the market. This tactic must be used with care as stakeholders and observers will look for lapses from this policy which may be harmful to the project. These lapses may be exploited by competitors or those who have some other agenda for the project and do not wish to see it achieve some of its outcomes.

## ETHICAL THEORY

To discuss the role that ethics play in project management it is necessary to present ethical points in terms of the underlying ethical theory. This section illustrates why it is important to understand this theory not only for use in this discussion, but for managers to think about and present their ethical arguments.

To argue the case of a moral viewpoint, managers need to be able to articulate these arguments in a form that is intellectually and theoretically valid. Some authors argue that in addition to the skills of ethical analysis and reasoning, ethical enquiry often requires an understanding of the nature of basic ethical principles, the status of knowledge in ethics and the relationships among ethics, law and religion (Benjamin and Curtis 1981). In many cases the moral values of managers, project managers and executives may often conflict with their role duties. What, according to Gandz and Hayes (1988), managers and executives are deficient in, are the skills of ethical analysis which allow them to reconcile their roles as managers and as socially integrated individuals. Not only must the managers be able to argue an ethical position in coherent terms, but they must be able to articulate this view to their peers and the various stakeholders in the company, or in the case of a project manager, the project. As Solomon (1985) puts it:

> No competent executive would think of taking the company to the bargaining table without a clear sense of objectives, limits and tactics. And yet some of the same executives lead their companies into the forum of public opinion with nothing but a grab bag of ethical platitudes.

The traditional way of reducing the variety of values, whether ethical or not, is to seek general principles. The principles or theory try to avoid the arbitrary treatment of individuals and cases and allow for consistency in policy and judgements. To be able to reason, articulate and discuss ethical issues, it is important to understand some basic philosophical theories in the field of ethics. The following paragraphs give an overview of the main ethical theories. There are two approaches to ethical theory: the rule-based approach and the utilitarian approach. The first says that there are a set of rules you must obey, the second suggests that you should do that which will produce most good.

The central thesis of deontological ethics (rule-based) is that the consequences of actions are not the primary consideration in deciding what ought to be done (Bowie and Duska 1990); it is the consideration of fairness and justice that takes precedence over the consequences of actions. These rule-based theories can be broken down into two types: absolute and conditional theories. The absolute theories, the main one of which is Kant's categorical imperative, say that people must do certain things if they are to be morally right. The conditional theories, such as prima-facie duties, also advocate a set of rules but suggest how and when it is appropriate to modify these duties.

The categorical imperative form of ethics was developed by Immanuel Kant (1724–1804). He attempted to show that there are certain moral rights and duties that all humans must follow, regardless of the benefits or otherwise that the exercising of these rights will accrue to the individual or to others (Velasquez 1992). This theory assumes that everyone should be treated as a free person equal to everyone else. Everyone has a right to such treatment and everyone must treat others in this way. The essence of the categorical imperative lies in the three criteria for moral correctness:

1. *Universality* The individual's reasons for acting must be reasons that everyone could act on, at least in principle.
2. *Transitivity* The person's reasons for acting must be reasons that he or she would be willing to have all others use as a basis of how they treat him or her.
3. *Individuality* The person 'should treat each human being as a person whose existence as a free rational person should be promoted' (Gandz and Hayes 1988).

The conditional rule-based ethics from the utilitarian aspect can be summarized in these two principles (Velasquez 1992):

1. An action is right from an ethical point of view if, and only if, the action would be required by those moral rules that are correct.
2. A moral rule is correct if, and only if, the sum total of the utilities produced if everyone were to follow that rule is greater than the sum total utilities produced if everyone were to follow some alternative rule.

In the rule-utilitarian approach, the fact that a certain action would maximize utility does not make it moral. In this approach you must first find the correct rule and then apply the utility criterion. The most common form of conditional rule-based approach from the adaptation of rule-based ethics is prima-facie duties. A prima-facie rule takes the form that other things being equal, one should tell the truth, obey the law and so on. The theory states that there are prima-facie (at first sight) duties that are morally binding and that ethical decisions constitute deciding which is the more obligatory, if and when there is a conflict. The six prima-facie duties are (Gandz and Hayes 1988):

- fidelity
- gratitude
- justice
- beneficence (the act of doing good)
- self improvement and
- non-maleficence.

The main problem with this theory is determining which is the appropriate rule, causing the user to focus too narrowly on the means, rather than the ends. Another problem is when duties conflict, deciding what weight and merit should be applied to each. Some argue this form can degenerate into traditional utilitarianism, by allowing the rules that give beneficial expectations more utility than those that do not allow such expectations (Velasquez 1992).

There are a number of ethical theories that explicitly designate some intrinsic aspect of the human act as the criterion for moral goodness or badness. Hedonism is an example of one of these forms of ethics. Its roots can be traced back to ancient Greece. The theory holds that as long as an act is capable of producing some pleasure (*Hedone* in Greek), it is good. This form of ethics has evolved to emphasize more rational pleasures and the promotion of peace of mind. Utilitarian ethics is a development of this theory. The theory is variously known as best result ethics, egoism or end point ethics (Gandz and Hayes 1988). The main exponents of this theory were Jeremy Bentham (1748–1832), and John Stuart Mill (1806–73). The essence of the theory can be stated as:

> An action is right from an ethical point of view if and only if the sum total of the utilities produced by the act is greater than the sum total of the utilities produced by any other act.
>
> (Velasquez 1992)

This form of ethics, it is argued, will naturally lead to a division of labour that will produce the best outcome for society (Bowie and Duska 1990). Thus, if people take responsibility for their own roles, society will flourish. However, there are many problems with this approach to ethics. For example, how does one estimate the plurality of values, happiness, pleasure, health, knowledge, friendship, comfort, pain, harm, etc. to evaluate the consequences of a proposed course of action? Even if one can estimate the utility of an action, you cannot simply add and subtract the various positive and negative consequences of the alternative courses of action. Further problems arise with this theory, mainly due to the concept of justice.

The relativist theory is perhaps the most contentious theory of all those discussed so far. It has become most fashionable since the Second World War. In its clearest form it is based on the existentialist philosophy of Jean-Paul Sartre. The essence of this argument is that ethics are merely a matter of taste (Donaldson 1992), and if one culture or country prefers one set of rules there is little that can be said or done about it. Sartre argued that there is a basic human nature given to us by a great designer, God, and so nothing to bind us by a certain way of action (Varga 1980). In this form of ethics, what people make of themselves stems from their own free actions, they create their values depending on their own situations and circumstances. These sentiments can be summarized by the expression, 'When in Rome it's all right to do as the (good) Romans do.'

Relativism avoids any attempt at paternalism and does not impose universal moral standards. This can be used to justify bribing foreign officials in order to gain a contract. If this is the accepted practice in the host country but not in the home country of the competing firm, it is still ethical to indulge in this practice. This form of action can be extended to environmental contamination and low levels of safety for workers which are acceptable in the society in which the projects are undertaken. There are many arguments against this form of ethics. Bernard Williams in his book *Morality* (1972) describes relativism as 'the anthropologist's heresy, possibly the most absurd view to have been advanced in moral philosophy'. Others have argued that if this theory were accepted without any restrictions, no order could be maintained in society and no state could function (Varga 1980). These objections forced even Sartre to modify the theory to a more acceptable form.

## ETHICS ABROAD

Many project companies now compete nationally and internationally. Many are global, with infrastructures or centres of expertise shared across national boundaries. When companies and their staff operate in this environment, problems can, and do, occur. They lose the backdrop of shared attitudes, familiar laws, judicial procedures and standards of ethical conduct. Practices that worked in the home country may not work in the host country. There may be different ethical conduct or cultural norms. This is not to say that one set of standards is better than another or that companies must abide by the higher standard in both of the moral codes. Some ethical theories, such as relativism, suggest that there is no absolute measure of ethical standard, just statements of the fashion of society at the time. I have heard of examples of companies that have sent engineers to work on projects abroad but have had to recall them due to their inability to reconcile their own ethical standards, congruent with their home country, with those of the country in which they find themselves working. This causes problems not only for the individuals and their perception of their career, but for the company in how to manage and resource the project. A way of resolving this is to use cultural relativism.

Problems involved when projects are conducted in multicultural environments with no reference points are many and not easy to resolve. However, the rest of this section provides some guidance on how practices that are just different may be distinguished from those that are wrong. Some cultures place different emphasis on equally valid ethical codes which may cause confusion. Americans place greater emphasis on liberty than loyalty, whilst the Japanese place emphasis on loyalty to their company and business networks. These issues may be addressed explicitly up front, before staff are exposed to these dilemmas. By giving staff a framework in which to think about these issues, they will be better equipped to deal with the issues for the benefit of themselves, the company and the project on which they are employed. When shaping the ethical behaviour of staff, or a company based in a foreign culture, you must be guided by three principles (Donaldson 1996):

- Respect for core human values, which determine the absolute threshold for all business activities.
- Respect for local traditions.
- The belief that context matters when deciding what is right and what is wrong.

In Japan the giving and receiving of gifts is an integral part of business life. Many western cultures may consider this custom as not just different, but wrong, as it could be seen as trying to unduly influence someone (bribery). Many companies have come to respect this tradition and have different limits for the giving and receiving of gifts in Japan than they do in the rest of the world. Respecting local traditions also means recognizing the strengths and weaknesses of different ethical norms. In the Far East, stealing credit from a subordinate is nearly an unpardonable sin.

The phenomenon of globalization in business suggests that for the world to be ethical and just there must be some global ethic. There are international regulatory frameworks and laws, and courts are emerging to deal with the technical issues of globalization, but the global business ethic is not yet here to help the project manager. But there have been many events contributing towards the creation of a global ethic (Kung 1997). The basic principles of the emerging global ethic are as follows:

1. Justice: just fair conduct, fairness, exercise of authority in maintenance of right.
2. Mutual Respect: love and respect for others.
3. Stewardship: human beings are only the stewards of natural resources.
4. Honesty: truthfulness and reliability in all human relationships (integrity).

These principles are more abstract than those contained in a company or professional institution ethics statement, but they do provide a mental framework in which to address these issues at a macro level.

## PRACTICAL HELP

Throughout this chapter I have discussed the role of ethics in management and more specifically project management, the role of ethics in the long-term view, the background to ethical theory and the specifics of managing ethics in a global business or at least a project in a foreign country. However, there are times when the manager does not have the luxury to think about the philosophical dimensions of an ethical dilemma and this is where a more prescriptive checklist or rule of thumb can be of use. The rules of thumb for ethical decision-making (in the domestic setting) come in varying degrees of complexity, some more useful than others. A more comprehensive rule that provides a mental framework in which to draw out many of the issues in a decision is described below (Dreilinger 1994):

1. Which *goals* or *priorities* does this solution support or work against?
2. Does the solution reflect the *values* of the organization and the decision-makers?
3. What are the *consequences* (in terms of benefit or harm) and ramifications (effect of time and outside influences) for each of the stakeholders in the following three areas: cost-to-benefit, rights-to-equity and duties-to-obligation? Are there any other consequences?
4. What qualms would the decision-maker have about the *disclosure* of a favourable decision to this solution to the CEO, board of directors, family, the public?
5. What is the positive or negative *symbolic potential* of this solution if understood – or misunderstood – by others? Will it contribute to building and maintaining an ethical environment?

Whenever making a decision that has some ethical dimension, it is important to keep monitoring the outcomes of the decision at every stage. This ensures that the decision is still the best and that any corrective action can be identified early.


## CONCLUSIONS

In this chapter I have discussed how ethics play an increasingly important role in business. This is due to many factors, including the heightened awareness of workers and the general public, and as a reaction against the greed and avarice of the 1980s. All managers, especially project managers, are under pressure to take short cuts, improve the figures and get immediate results. This puts them under ethical pressure. The decisions that the project manager takes are much less restricted than those in line management. The result of this is that project managers operate in a relatively unbounded, dynamic, often international environment, giving them greater freedom and scope, and their decisions wider effect. A more serious characteristic of project management, putting project managers under more ethical pressure, is the weak distinction between their professional and managerial roles. The international nature of many projects brings with it its own special set of ethical problems that must be handled for both the team members involved in the project and the project manager executing the project. To help the project manager deal with these ethical pressures there needs to be a more structured framework in which to take decisions.

A point made in this chapter is that much of today's management and especially project management is conducted in a complex interrelated environment with a finite number of players. If project managers are to succeed in this environment, they must be aware of these interrelationships and the impact they can have on the success of the project, or their next project and their career.

Ethics in projects and business need not be a threat but an opportunity, a way of differentiating yourself from the competition and exploiting some form of competitive advantage. This differentiation is best handled subtly and not as a public relations exercise. It can bring lasting benefits which may not only attract new business, but also ease the path to the completion of projects.

In this chapter several methods have been outlined that will assist project managers in their duties. These include an understanding of the background of ethical theory, an understanding of the issues that may face project managers, the way in which ethics play a vital role in the success of a project, both from the ethical dilemma and from the relationship maintenance perspective. A rule of thumb has been provided to act as a first check to help project managers consider the issues involved. Where projects are conducted in an international environment a further framework has been included to help the manager also assess and resolve these issues.

## REFERENCES AND FURTHER READING

Benjamin, M. and Curtis, J. (1981), *Ethics in Nursing*, Oxford University Press, Oxford.

Bowie, N. E., and Duska, R. F. (1990), *Business Ethics*, 2nd edition, Prentice-Hall International, Englewood Cliffs, NJ.

Bruns, W. J. Jr. and Merchant, K. A. (1990), 'The dangerous morality of managing earnings', *Management Accounting*, August.

Donaldson, J. (1992), *Business Ethics: A European Case Book*, Academic Press, London.

Donaldson, T. (1996), 'Values in tension: ethics away from home', *Harvard Business Review*, September–October.

Dreilinger, C. (1994), 'Ethics, what about thou shalt?', *Journal of Business Strategy*, July–August.

Friedman, M. (1970), 'The social responsibility of business is to increase profits', *New York Times Magazine*, 13 September.

Gandz, J. and Hayes, N. (1988), 'Teaching business ethics', *Journal of Business Ethics*, **7**.

Garvind, D. A. (1992), *Operations Strategy*, Prentice-Hall, Englewood Cliffs, NJ.

Kung, H. (1997), 'A global ethic in an age of globalisation', *Business Ethics Quarterly*, **7**(3).

Mantel, S. J. and Kloppenborg, T. (1990), 'Trade-offs on projects: they may not be what you think', *Project Management Journal*, **21**(1), March.

Soloman, R. C. and Hanson, K. (1985), *It's Good Business*, Atheneum, New York.

Velasquez, M. G. (1992), *Business Ethics: Concepts and Cases*, 3rd edition, Prentice-Hall International, Englewood Cliffs, NJ.

Varga, A. C. (1980), *The Main Issues in Bioethics*, Paulst Press, New York.

Williams, B. (1972), *Morality: An Introduction to Ethics*, Cambridge University Press, Cambridge.

# Index